1,296 ACT®

Practice Questions
Second Edition

Melissa Hendrix and
The Staff of The Princeton Review

PrincetonReview.com

Random House, Inc. New York

The Princeton Review, Inc.
111 Speen Street, Suite 550
Framingham, MA 01701
E-mail: editorialsupport@review.com

ISBN: 978-0-375-42970-5
ISSN: 1943-4847

Editor: Heather Brady
Production Editor: Kathy G. Carter
Production Coordinator: Deborah A. Silvestrini

Printed in the United States of America on partially
recycled paper.

10 9 8 7 6 5 4 3 2 1

Second Edition

Editorial
Rob Franek, VP Test Prep Books, Publisher
Seamus Mullarkey, Associate Publisher
Laura Braswell, Senior Editor
Heather Brady, Editor
Selena Coppock, Editor

Random House Publishing Team
Tom Russell, Publisher
Nicole Benhabib, Publishing Manager
Ellen L. Reed, Production Manager
Alison Stoltzfus, Associate Managing Editor

Acknowledgments

The following people deserve thanks for their contributions to this edition: Melissa Hendrix, Brian Becker, Rob Hennen, Mindy Myers, David Stoll, Danny Chun, Steve Voight, Calvin Cato, Kathy Carter, and Deborah Silvestrini.

Contents

Introduction

So you think you need more practice? Well, we have tons of practice right here for you. We have accumulated the equivalent of six full ACTs to help you get your best possible score on this beastly test! After all, the harder you practice, the better you'll be on test day.

Since you probably know the basics of how the test is conducted, we'll spare you that information. What we will give you here is a breakdown of the "tests" on the ACT.

1. English Test (45 minutes—75 questions)

In this section, you will see five essays on the left side of the page. Some words or phrases will be underlined. On the right side of the if page, you will be asked whether the underlined portion is correct as written or one of the three alternatives listed would be better. The English test covers topics in grammar, punctuation, sentence structure, and rhetorical skills.

2. Math Test (60 minutes—60 questions)

These are the regular, multiple-choice math questions you've been doing all your life. The easier questions tend to come in the beginning and the difficult ones in the end, but the folks at the ACT try to mix in easy, medium, and difficult problems throughout the Math test. A good third of the test covers pre-algebra and elementary algebra. Slightly less than a third covers intermediate algebra and coordinate geometry (graphing). Regular geometry accounts for less than a quarter of the questions, and there are four questions that cover trigonometry.

3. Reading Test (35 minutes—40 questions)

In this section, there will be four reading passages of about 800 words each—the average length of a *People* magazine article but maybe not as interesting. There is always one prose fiction passage, one social science passage, one humanities passage, and one natural science passage, and they are always in that order. After reading each passage, you have to answer 10 questions.

4. Science Reasoning Test (35 minutes—40 questions)

No specific scientific knowledge is necessary for the Science Reasoning test. You won't need to know the chemical makeup of hydrochloric acid or any formulas. Instead, you will be asked to understand six sets of scientific information presented in graphs, charts, tables, and research summaries. In addition, you will have to make sense of one disagreement between two or three scientists. (Occasionally, there are more than three scientists).

5. Optional Writing Test (30 minutes)

The ACT contains an "optional" Writing test featuring a single essay. We recommend you take the "ACT Plus Writing" version of the test because most schools require it. The essay consists of a prompt "relevant" to high school students on which you will be asked to write an essay stating your position on the prompt. Two people will then grade your essay on a scale of 1 to 6 for a total score of 2 to 12.

If you are unsure about any of the sections or if you want more strategies or conquering these kinds of questions, you can find more information at PrincetonReview.com or you can review our *Cracking the ACT* book.

What you should also know is that the key to raising your ACT score does not lie in memorizing dozens of math theorems, the periodic table of elements, or obscure rules of English grammar. There's more to mastering this test than just improving math, verbal, and science skills. At its root, the ACT measures academic achievement. It doesn't pretend to measure your analytic ability or your intelligence. The people at ACT admit that you can increase your score by preparing for the test, and by spending just a little extra time preparing for the ACT, you can substantially change your score on the ACT (and the way colleges look at your applications). After all, out of all the elements in your application "package," your ACT score is the easiest to change.

That being said, we have included in this book three complete practice ACT exams and the equivalent of three exams' worth of drill questions. Rest assured that these tests and questions are modeled closely on actual ACT exams and questions, with the proper balance of questions reflective of what the ACT actually tests.

At the beginning of this book, you'll find one complete ACT practice test. After you've taken that test, score it to learn your strengths and weaknesses. Next in the book, you will see three full-length drills for each subject type. The questions are compiled in the same arrangement as you would see on a real test, so you can keep track of your timing and your progress. These drills can help you get outstanding scores on the subjects you already do well in and better scores on the subjects you might be struggling with. After the drills, you'll find two more complete ACT practice tests. We suggest you use these to gauge your full testing capacity by taking them in an environment as close to the real conditions as possible. After the drills, you shouldn't be worried about your scores, and these two final practice exams will not only give you more practice, but they will also give you some assurance that all that practice will pay off in the end.

A final thought before you begin: The ACT does not predict your ultimate success or failure as a human being. No matter how high or how low you score on this test initially, and no matter how much you may increase your score through preparation, you should never consider the score you receive on this or any other test a final judgment of your abilities. When it's all said and done, we know you'll get into a great school and that you'll have an incredible experience there.

We wish you the best of luck, even though you won't need it after all this practicing!

The Princeton Review

Test 1

ACT ENGLISH TEST
45 Minutes—75 Questions

DIRECTIONS: In the five passages that follow, certain words and phrases are underlined and numbered. In the right-hand column, you will find alternatives for each underlined part. In most cases, you are to choose the one that best expresses the idea, makes the statement appropriate for standard written English, or is worded most consistently with the style and tone of the passage as a whole. If you think the original version is best, choose "NO CHANGE." In some cases, you will find in the right-hand column a question about the underlined part. You are to choose the best answer to the question.

You will also find questions about a section of the passage or the passage as a whole. These questions do not refer to an underlined portion of the passage but rather are identified by a number or numbers in a box.

For each question, choose the alternative you consider best and blacken the corresponding oval on your answer document. Read each passage through once before you begin to answer the questions that accompany it. For many of the questions, you must read several sentences beyond the question to determine the answer. Be sure that you have read far enough ahead each time you choose an alternative.

PASSAGE I

The Record

The moment I had been anticipating finally came on a seemingly routine Monday. I arrived home to find a flat package; left by the delivery man casually leaning against the front screen door. Reading the words *Caution! Do not bend!*

scrawled on the top of the box, I immediately recognized my uncle's sloppy handwriting. I quickly ushered the box

inside, and my heart skipping a beat (or two). I knew what the box contained but still felt as anxious as a child on Christmas morning. Could this *really* be the old vinyl record?

My hands trembled as I opened the box, of which I was thrilled to see that it did indeed contain the record I had been seeking for years. To an outsider, this dusty disc with its faded hand-written label would seem inconsequential. To others,

on the other hand, it was worth something far greater. The record was a compilation from the greatest musician I had ever known—my grandfather.

1. A. NO CHANGE
   B. package, left by the delivery man
   C. package; left by the delivery man,
   D. package, left by the delivery man,

2. F. NO CHANGE
   G. were scrawled on
   H. scrawl on
   J. scrawled

3. A. NO CHANGE
   B. inside,
   C. inside and
   D. inside, when

4. F. NO CHANGE
   G. box that
   H. box, and
   J. box

5. Given that all the choices are true, which one would most effectively illustrate the difference between outsiders' perception of the record and its actual significance to the writer's family?
   A. NO CHANGE
   B. In fact, the recording was not heard by many people outside my family.
   C. To my family, however, it was a precious heirloom.
   D. The disc would be in better condition had my uncle stored it in a sleeve.

GO ON TO THE NEXT PAGE.

Several years before he married my grandmother, Papa would make his living as a folk singer in a

band. Performing in music halls and local festivals. He recorded

a single album produced by Great Sounds Records before giving up his professional music career to pursue business. This

record was all that remained of his life's passion—in fact, there

had been only one surviving copy since Papa's death 10 years

earlier. It took many years of begging and pleading to convince my uncle to pass the record down to me.

I brought out my old record player from the attic and gently placed the disc on the turntable. As soft, twanging notes filled the room, I was transported to my grandfather's cabin, located at the foot the mountains. My cousins and I would gather around the campfire every night to roast marshmallows, cook hotdogs, and listen to my grandfather's old stories.

Of the many familiar favorites, Papa would pick up his guitar and play all of our familiar tunes.

When the record started playing one of my favorite songs, I struggled to hold back my tears. It was a bittersweet reminder of

6. F. NO CHANGE
   G. would have made
   H. would have been making
   J. had made

7. A. NO CHANGE
   B. band; performing
   C. band, which he had performed
   D. band, performing

8. F. NO CHANGE
   G. album, produced by Great Sounds Records,
   H. Great Sounds Records album
   J. album

9. A. NO CHANGE
   B. even so,
   C. since,
   D. for example,

10. F. NO CHANGE
   G. had been about
   H. is
   J. was to be

11. A. NO CHANGE
   B. begging
   C. pleadingly begging
   D. begging the plea

12. At this point in the essay, the writer wants to suggest the significance of his grandfather's cabin to the writer's upbringing. Given that all the choices are true, which one would best accomplish that purpose?
   F. NO CHANGE
   G. where I had spent many childhood summers.
   H. which I still remembered well.
   J. a family property for many generations.

13. A. NO CHANGE
   B. Playing all of our favorite songs, the many familiar tunes and guitar would be picked up by Papa.
   C. Papa would also pick up his guitar and strum familiar tunes, playing all of our favorite songs, of which there were many.
   D. Picking up his guitar, Papa would also play strumming familiar tunes all of our favorite, of which there were many, songs.

GO ON TO THE NEXT PAGE.

the man I loved and <u>missed,</u> Papa's gentle voice on the record,
₁₄

however, assured <u>me,</u> that he was still with me, both in spirit
₁₅
and in song.

14. F. NO CHANGE
    G. missed for
    H. missed.
    J. missed

15. A. NO CHANGE
    B. me
    C. me—
    D. me;

Passage II

Road Trips Back Home

During my junior year of college, it became a kind of ritual
for a group of us to hop in a car and "discover" a new suburb
every month. At first, we all agreed, we had come to college in
this major city to escape what we thought were our boring lives
in our various places of origin, but after a time, we realized that
it would be impossible for us to turn our backs on our old <u>lives</u>
₁₆

completely. <u>I grew up in Pennsylvania, many parts of which</u>
₁₇
<u>look like the ones we drove to.</u>
₁₇

The first stop was typically some old diner, which
reminded each of us of one from our various hometowns. There

we'd usually sit, chat with the restaurant's <u>owners</u> drink a cup
₁₈
of coffee, and figure out which new and exciting place we'd
be driving to next. Even now I can remember one diner in
Maryland, whose sign we could see flickering from the highway
as we turned off <u>looking forward to it in anticipation.</u> Although
₁₉
we had all agreed that it had to be a new town each time, we

16. F. NO CHANGE
    G. lives,
    H. live's
    J. lives'

17. Given that all the choices are true, which one best supports
    the point that the narrator and his friends all shared a com-
    mon background?

    A. NO CHANGE
    B. Many suburbs have become as populous as the cities
       they surround.
    C. The first major migration of families from the city to
       the suburbs occurred in the late 1940s and early 1950s.
    D. Our hometowns were all over the map, but they all
       shared a palpable likeness.

18. F. NO CHANGE
    G. owners;
    H. owners'
    J. owners,

19. A. NO CHANGE
    B. in anticipation.
    C. excited and looking forward to it.
    D. in anticipation and expectation.

GO ON TO THE NEXT PAGE.

tacitly agreed a few times to break the rules and come back to

this place. [20]

After we had taken nourishment (usually a grilled cheese

sandwich, a patty melt, or something similarly nutritious

that could be ordered from the menu) for our "big night out,"
21

we would then drive on. We got to know the lay of the land

so well that we could usually just follow our noses to the

kinds of places we liked to visit in these towns, typically

stopping by the biggest retailer we could find. There we'd

buy industrial-sized packs from childhood of instant noodles,
22

huge packs of soda, and other types of foods we all remembered

but which we were either too embarrassed to buy in front

of other people at the University market, or which were too

expensive in the city, where there is a lot more variety.
23

Going to as many places like this as we could, we were always
24

sure to happen upon something strangely familiar to us. The

place—whether it was one of a million grocery stores, movie

theaters, or fast-food restaurants—were unimportant; it seemed
25

that everywhere had something special for at least one of us,

20. At this point, the writer is considering adding the following true statement:

> Many diners have been forced to shut down to make way for larger, national chain restaurants.

Should the writer make the addition here?

- **F.** Yes, because it provides important contextual information relevant to the passage.
- **G.** Yes, because it helps readers to see why the narrator was drawn to this particular diner.
- **H.** No, because it interrupts the flow of the paragraph, which is primarily a personal reflection.
- **J.** No, because it alters the focus of the paragraph from a discussion of driving to a discussion of specific places.

21. **A.** NO CHANGE
B. whom could be ordered from
C. whom could order
D. that were ordering

22. The best placement for the underlined phrase would be:
- **F.** where it is now
- **G.** after the word *noodles.*
- **H.** after the word *soda.*
- **J.** after the word *remembered*

23. Which choice most effectively supports and elaborates on the description in an earlier part of this sentence?
- **A.** NO CHANGE
- **B.** where prices for such basic foods were steep.
- **C.** where we didn't like to drive the car.
- **D.** where most of us had only small refrigerators.

24. Which of the following alternatives to the underlined portion would NOT be acceptable?
- **F.** As we went
- **G.** While going
- **H.** While we went
- **J.** We went

25. **A.** NO CHANGE
B. was
C. have been
D. are

GO ON TO THE NEXT PAGE.

and even now, many years on, I still think of these trips fondly.
                                                          26

    Looking back, I'm still not sure why we took these trips.

Nevertheless, I have been living in an urban environment
       27
now for almost eight years, and should I ever have to move

back to the suburbs, I will certainly go reluctantly. Sometimes,

though, even now that I live in a different city, I'll still sneak

out to those kinds of places once in a while and just drive

about the town. I guess, in a way, many of those early memories
       28
are like that diner sign we could see from the highway; most

people would never notice that old sign, but to those of us who

cherish it in our hearts and what it represents, we all harbored
       29
a great hope that it would still be burning the same as we

remembered every time we drove by or came back.
                                          30

26. Given that all the choices are true, which one most effectively signals the shift in focus that occurs when moving from this paragraph to the next?

    F. NO CHANGE
    G. we all remained friends until we graduated.
    H. I regret not having spent more time in the city when I had the chance.
    J. I haven't been back to any of those places since I graduated.

27. A. NO CHANGE
      B. Therefore,
      C. Nonetheless,
      D. DELETE the underlined portion.

28. Which of the following alternatives to the underlined portion would NOT be acceptable?

    F. among the town.
    G. about.
    H. around.
    J. around the town.

29. A. NO CHANGE
      B. have a great fondness for it
      C. have strong feelings of adoration for it
      D. cherish it

30. F. NO CHANGE
      G. we were coming back.
      H. were returning.
      J. there was a return by us.

GO ON TO THE NEXT PAGE.

Passage III

> The following paragraphs may or may not be in the most logical order. Each paragraph is numbered in brackets, and question 45 will ask you to choose where Paragraph 3 should most logically be placed.

The Palio of Siena

[1]

Siena is an old, picturesque city located in the hills of Tuscany. Even though its inhabitants live modern lives, many historical markers from as far back as medieval Italy still remain throughout the city. ▢32 Another remnant from Siena's rich history that still plays a very prominent role today is the tradition of *Il Palio*.

[2]

Il Palio di Siena is a biannual horse race that is held twice a year, once in July and once in August. A field of ten bareback horses races three laps around a dangerously steep track circling the city's central plaza, the *Piazza del Campo*, each with two dreaded right-angle turns. Even though *Il Palio*

31. Which of the following alternatives to the underlined portion would be LEAST acceptable?

A. Although
B. While
C. Though
D. When

32. Which of the following true statements, if inserted here, would best connect the first part of Paragraph 1 with the last part while illustrating the main idea of this paragraph?

F. Like most Italian cities, Siena is very serious about soccer, a modern sport codified in England in the 1800s.
G. Cobblestone streets and Gothic architecture are blended with modern sidewalk cafes and trendy designer stores.
H. The city of Siena is certainly a mixture of ancient and contemporary practices.
J. Siena is a major cultural center that offers numerous examples of art and architecture by Renaissance masters.

33. A. NO CHANGE
B. a biannual race that is held two times a year,
C. a horse race that is held twice a year,
D. a biannual horse race, held

34. Assuming that a period will always be placed at the end of the sentence, the best placement for the underlined phrase would be:

F. where it is now.
G. after the words *horses race* (setting the phrase off with commas).
H. after the word *laps* (setting the phrase off with commas).
J. after the word *plaza* (setting the phrase off with commas).

GO ON TO THE NEXT PAGE.

lasted only about 90 seconds, its importance in Siena goes far
<u>35</u>
beyond the race itself.

[3]

Members are fiercely committed emotionally, socially,

and financially to their own *contrada*. <u>Because the members</u>
<u>36</u>
voluntarily tax themselves to support their own *contrada* and to

invest in a good horse and jockey for the biannual race. Jockey

salaries for a single race often exceed 250,000 euros! This

is, <u>however,</u> a small price to pay to achieve victory at *Il Palio*.
<u>37</u>
Seeing the colors and arms of their *contrada* in the winner's

circle is the most glorious event—even more so than getting

<u>married for</u> many Sienese citizens. Old men weep openly out of
<u>38</u>

sheer joy, and elated adults and children <u>parade. Throughout</u> the
<u>39</u>
city with their newly won silk banner, also called the *palio*.

[4]

The brief race is a spectacular culmination of an entire way

of life in Siena. Every citizen belongs to one of seventeen city

districts, collectively known as the <u>*Contrade*. *Contrada*</u> is the
<u>40</u>
term for a single district that has its own color and arms, such

as the *Aquila* (the eagle) or *Bruco* (the caterpillar). A *contrada*

is the source of so much local patriotism that every important

<u>event; from</u> baptisms to food festivals, is celebrated only within
<u>41</u>

one's own *contrada* and fellow members, <u>who</u> become more
<u>42</u>
like family.

[5]

After the actual race day, the *Palio* festivities continue for a

minimum of two weeks. Thousands of visitors from around the

35. **A.** NO CHANGE
    B. will last
    C. lasts
    D. had lasted

36. **F.** NO CHANGE
    G. Though this
    H. In addition, they
    J. They

37. **A.** NO CHANGE
    B. moreover,
    C. for instance,
    D. therefore,

38. **F.** NO CHANGE
    G. married—for
    H. married, for
    J. married; for

39. **A.** NO CHANGE
    B. parade; throughout
    C. parade throughout
    D. parade throughout,

40. **F.** NO CHANGE
    G. *Contrade*
    H. *Contrade*,
    J. *Contrade* yet

41. **A.** NO CHANGE
    B. event, from
    C. event: from
    D. event—from

42. **F.** NO CHANGE
    G. for whose
    H. whose
    J. whom

GO ON TO THE NEXT PAGE.

world travel to Siena during the <u>summer; not</u> only to witness
₄₃

the exciting race but also to attend the after-parties <u>were thrown</u>
₄₄
by the locals. While the *Palio* is not as important to outsiders
who do not live in Siena as it is to the Sienese, the race and the
festivities that follow are a spectacular experience.

43. A. NO CHANGE
    B. summer. Not
    C. summer not
    D. summer, not

44. F. NO CHANGE
    G. thrown
    H. were threw
    J. threw

Question 45 asks about the preceding passage as a whole.

---

45. For the sake of the logic and coherence of this essay, the
    best placement for Paragraph 3 would be:

    A. where it is now.
    B. before Paragraph 1.
    C. before Paragraph 2.
    D. before Paragraph 5.

PASSAGE IV

The following paragraphs may or may not be in the most
logical order. Each paragraph is numbered in brackets,
and question 59 will ask you to choose where Paragraph 2
should most logically be placed.

Sherwood Anderson the Pioneer

[1]

Sherwood Anderson saw his first novel, *Windy
McPherson's Son*, published in 1916, but it was not until
1919 with the publication of his masterpiece *Winesburg, Ohio*
that Anderson was pushed to the forefront of <u>it</u> in American
₄₆
literature. The latter book, something between a short-story

46. F. NO CHANGE
    G. this
    H. a new movement
    J. a thing

collection and a novel, <u>helping</u> to inaugurate an age of a truly
₄₇
homespun American Modernism.

47. A. NO CHANGE
    B. which helped
    C. helped
    D. was helped

GO ON TO THE NEXT PAGE.

[2]

As other writers began to supplant him in the popular imagination, Anderson <u>tireless</u> continued his literary experimentation until his death in 1941. In the contemporary
₄₈

popular imagination, Anderson's influence often <u>appears to be</u> diminishing. But it takes only a few pages of *Winesburg, Ohio*
₄₉
or many of his other short stories, articles, and novels to see that Anderson is still very much with us today and that much of what we understand about ourselves as Americans was made clear to us only by the pen of the advertising man from Ohio.

[3]

Sherwood Anderson would be seen by a new generation of American writers as the first author to take a real step <u>until</u>
₅₀
creating a type of literature that was in tune with something previously only associated with Europe. Anderson was able to

<u>fuse</u> his sense of the passing of the Industrial Age in America
₅₁
with a type of uniquely American expression that sought to replace previous literary conventions with more local expressions of fragmentation and alienation.

[4]

With *Winesburg, Ohio*, Anderson <u>inspired</u> a younger group
₅₂
of writers, among whose ranks were Ernest Hemingway and William Faulkner, to embrace their American experiences and to express them in ways separate from those being expressed by

European writers or American <u>expatriates, as American writers living abroad were known.</u> When *Winesburg, Ohio* finally
₅₃

48. The best placement for the underlined word would be:

  F. where it is now.
  G. before the word *death.*
  H. after the word *experimentation.*
  J. before the word *literary.*

49. Which of the following alternatives to the underlined portion would NOT be acceptable?

  A. can seem to be
  B. appeared to be
  C. seems to be
  D. can appear to be

50. **F.** NO CHANGE
  G. at
  H. toward
  J. DELETE the underlined portion.

51. **A.** NO CHANGE
  B. fuse;
  C. fuse:
  D. fuse,

52. Which of the following alternatives to the underlined portion would be LEAST acceptable?

  F. encouraged
  G. motivated
  H. forced
  J. emboldened

53. **A.** NO CHANGE
  B. expatriates, as American writers living abroad, were known.
  C. expatriates as American writers living abroad were known.
  D. expatriates as American writers living abroad, were known.

GO ON TO THE NEXT PAGE.

appeared in 1919, its general reception was <u>positive, but limited</u>
                                                        54

to those who were able to find copies of the book. <u>Anderson's</u>
                                                              55
<u>later books, such as *Dark Laughter*, would go on to sell many</u>
                                     55
<u>more copies.</u>
      55

[5]

In the 1920s, Anderson wrote some direct responses to the

more explicit examples of literary Modernism in Europe. In

the 1930s, Anderson wrote *Beyond Desire*. ⌐56⌐ But Anderson's

most important contributions in the 1920s and 1930s are best

felt indirectly through the works <u>of the various writers</u> he
                                           57
inspired. Anderson was among the first to explore the troubled

relationship between the city and the rural town, the direct

style to which we so often apply the <u>name, "American,"</u> and
                                             58
the idea that deeply intellectual concerns can be relevant to

everyday people as much as they can to academics. Even

today, Anderson's initial treatment of these themes remains

an important starting point for anyone interested in

American culture.

---

54. F. NO CHANGE
    G. positive but limited,
    H. positive; but limited
    J. positive but limited

55. Given that all the choices are true, which one best supports
the point that although Anderson's book was difficult to
find, those who read it were very impressed?

    A. NO CHANGE
    B. Many critics still preferred the older European models
of writing.
    C. *Winesburg, Ohio* remains one of Anderson's best-loved
books.
    D. Those who did secure a copy of *Winesburg, Ohio* felt
that it inaugurated a new age in American literature.

56. Given that all the following are true, which one, if added
here, would provide the clearest and most effective indication that Anderson was doing things that had not been
done before in American literature?

    F. , which addressed social questions that only social
scientists and propagandists dared touch.
    G. , which was heavily influenced by the literature of the
Southern Populist movement.
    H. , which has been named by many literary critics as a
highlight from Anderson's later work.
    J. , which was not as highly revered as *Winesburg, Ohio*.

57. The best placement for the underlined phrase would be:

    A. where it is now.
    B. after the word *contributions*.
    C. after the word *1930s*.
    D. after the word *inspired* (ending the sentence with a
period).

58. F. NO CHANGE
    G. name "American,"
    H. name "American"
    J. name, "American

GO ON TO THE NEXT PAGE.

Questions 59 and 60 ask about the preceding passage as a whole.

59. For the sake of the logic and coherence of this essay, Paragraph 2 should be placed:

   A. where it is now.
   B. after Paragraph 3.
   C. after Paragraph 4.
   D. after Paragraph 5.

60. Suppose the writer's goal was to draft an essay that would show the influence of one American author on the work of future authors. Does this essay successfully accomplish this goal?

   F. Yes, because it describes an interesting group of authors and focuses on the literature of a particular country.
   G. Yes, because it gives a brief description of Sherwood Anderson's writing career and discusses his influence on writers whom his work inspired.
   H. No, because it limits the focus to the contrasts between American writing and European writing.
   J. No, because it refers only to events that took place in the twenties and thirties.

PASSAGE V

Women at Work

World War II offered numerous employment opportunities for women in the United States. As the men headed to the war front, the work force retracted and diminished on the [61]

home front, and women begun to take over responsibilities [62]

traditionally assigned to men. These responsibilities included [63] work previously deemed inappropriate for women.

The government realized that participation in the war but [64] required the use of all national resources. American industrial facilities were turned into war production factories, and the government targeted the female population as an essential source of labor. Women worked in factories and shipyards

61. **A.** NO CHANGE
   B. retracted diminishingly
   C. diminished
   D. DELETE the underlined portion.

62. **F.** NO CHANGE
   G. has began
   H. would of begun
   J. began

63. **A.** NO CHANGE
   B. The traditionally male
   C. Which
   D. That

64. **F.** NO CHANGE
   G. and it
   H. although it
   J. DELETE the underlined portion.

GO ON TO THE NEXT PAGE.

as riveters, welders, and <u>machinists making</u> everything from
₆₅
uniforms to munitions to airplanes, they directly contributed

to the war effort. The number of women in the <u>workforce</u>
₆₆
increased from 12 million in 1940 to 18 million in 1944. By
1945, 36% of the laborers were women.

Women's increased presence in wartime workforces <u>were</u>
₆₇

not limited to factories and shipyards. ☐68 Thousands moved
to Washington D.C. to fill government jobs exclusively held by
men before the war. Some women engaged in farm labor, and
others joined the military as field nurses. The shortage of men

also led to openings in non-traditional fields, <u>such as day-care.</u>
₆₉
Since many players had been drafted into the armed services,
Major League Baseball parks around the country were on the
verge of collapse when a group of Midwestern businessmen
devised a brilliant solution to the player shortage.

The All-American Girls Professional Baseball League was
created in 1943 and offered a unique blend of baseball and
softball suitable for female players. <u>Founder, Philip K. Wrigley</u>
₇₀
<u>and League president,</u> Ken Sells promoted the new league with
₇₀
aggressive advertising campaigns that promoted the physical
attractiveness of female athletes. Photographs displayed women

65. A. NO CHANGE
B. machinists, making
C. machinists. Making
D. machinists, who made

66. F. NO CHANGE
G. workforce, for example in factories and shipyards,
H. workforce, such as factories and shipyards,
J. factory and shipyard workforce

67. A. NO CHANGE
B. are
C. was
D. have been

68. At this point, the writer is considering adding the following true statement:

> The marriage rate increased significantly during
> the war, as did the rate of babies born to unmarried
> women.

Should the writer add this sentence here?

F. No, because it does not echo the style and tone that has
already been established in the essay.
G. No, because it is not relevant to the essay's focus on
the changing roles of women during World War II.
H. Yes, because it contributes to the essay's focus on
women's roles in the home during World War II.
J. Yes, because it provides a contrast between women in
the home and women in the workplace.

69. Given that all the choices are true, which one provides the
most logical transition to the information presented in the
rest of this essay?

A. NO CHANGE
B. the most notable of which was baseball.
C. which many women had to give up after the war.
D. shaking American society to the core.

70. F. NO CHANGE
G. Founder Philip K. Wrigley and League president
H. Founder Philip K. Wrigley, and, League president
J. Founder, Philip K. Wrigley, and League president,

GO ON TO THE NEXT PAGE.

players with pretty smiles on their faces and baseball mitts
in their hands. Their silk shorts, fashionable knee-high socks,
71

red lipstick, having flowing hair directly contrasted with the
72
competitive, masculine nature of the game. These
photographs are indicative of the delicate balance between
feminine appeal and masculine labor that was expected
of all women throughout World War II. 73 Although

its' success lasted only a decade, the All American Girls
74
Professional Baseball League's role in expanding opportunities
for women during World War II and thereafter is everlasting. 75

71. Given that all the choices are true, which one most effectively helps the writer's purpose of helping readers visualize the players in the photographs?

   A. NO CHANGE
   B. at the plate during a live game.
   C. clearly focused on playing well.
   D. showing close camaraderie.

72. F. NO CHANGE
   G. their
   H. with
   J. and

73. If the writer were to delete the words *silk*, *fashionable*, and *red* from the preceding sentence, it would primarily lose:

   A. details that have already been presented in the vivid imagery of the previous sentence.
   B. a digression from the focus of this paragraph on the athletic talent of the players.
   C. description of what was written in the captions accompanying the photographs.
   D. details that highlight the femininity of the players in contrast to the masculinity of the game.

74. F. NO CHANGE
   G. it's
   H. their
   J. its

Question 75 asks about the preceding passage as a whole.

75. Suppose the writer's goals were to write an essay that would illustrate the range of non-traditional activities women pursued during wartime. Does this essay achieve that goal?

   A. Yes, because it explains the impact of the All American Girls Professional Baseball Team on public perception of women.
   B. Yes, because it gives several examples of women performing jobs during World War II that were typically filled by men.
   C. No, because it limits its focus to the type of work women engaged in during World War II.
   D. No, because it explains that women's importance in the workforce, especially in baseball, lasted only several years.

END OF TEST 1
STOP! DO NOT TURN THE PAGE UNTIL TOLD TO DO SO.

NO TEST MATERIAL ON THIS PAGE.

MATHEMATICS TEST

60 Minutes—60 Questions

DIRECTIONS: Solve each problem, choose the correct answer, and then darken the corresponding oval on your answer document.

Do not linger over problems that take too much time. Solve as many as you can; then return to the others in the time you have left for this test.

You are permitted to use a calculator on this test. You may use your calculator for any problems you choose, but some of the problems may best be done without using a calculator.

Note: Unless otherwise stated, all of the following should be assumed:

1. Illustrative figures are NOT necessarily drawn to scale.
2. Geometric figures lie in a plane.
3. The word *line* indicates a straight line.
4. The word *average* indicates arithmetic mean.

---

1. In the hiking trail shown below, X marks the trail's halfway point. If $\overline{YZ}$ measures 24 kilometers and is $\dfrac{1}{3}$ the length of $\overline{XZ}$, what is the total length, in kilometers, of the trail?

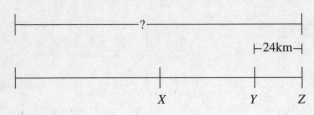

A. 144
B. 104
C. 96
D. 72
E. 48

2. What is the value of x when $\dfrac{4x}{5} + 7 = 6$?

F. $\dfrac{5}{4}$

G. $-\dfrac{4}{5}$

H. -1

J. $-\dfrac{5}{4}$

K. -5

DO YOUR FIGURING HERE.

GO ON TO THE NEXT PAGE.

3. Cyclist *A* averages 80 pedal revolutions per minute, and Cyclist *B* averages 61 pedal revolutions per minute. At these rates, how many more minutes does Cyclist *B* need than Cyclist *A* to make 9,760 pedal revolutions?

   A.   19
   B.   38
   C.   122
   D.   141
   E.   160

DO YOUR FIGURING HERE.

4. The perimeter of a square is 36 inches. What is the area of the square, in square inches?

   F.   6
   G.   9
   H.   18
   J.   36
   K.   81

5. For the rectangle shown in the standard (x,y) coordinate plane below, what are the coordinates of the unlabeled vertex?

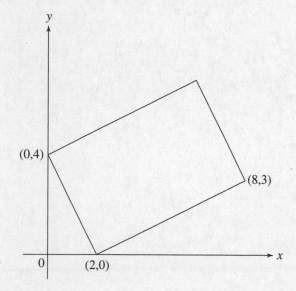

   A. $(4,5)$

   B. $(4,7)$

   C. $\left(5,\dfrac{7}{2}\right)$

   D. $(6,7)$

   E. $(10,4)$

GO ON TO THE NEXT PAGE.

DO YOUR FIGURING HERE.

6. Carla has 5 times as many notebooks as her brother does. If they have 42 notebooks between them, how many notebooks does Carla have?

   F. 30
   G. 33
   H. 35
   J. 37
   K. 47

7. If G is in the interior of right angle $\angle DEF$, then which of the following could be the measure of $\angle GEF$?

   A. 85°
   B. 95°
   C. 105°
   D. 115°
   E. 125°

8. Susie has three T-shirts: one red, one blue, and one black. She also has three pairs of shorts: one red, one blue, and one black. How many different combinations are there for Susie to wear exactly one T-shirt and one pair of shorts?

   F. 3
   G. 6
   H. 8
   J. 9
   K. 27

9. 20% of 20 is equal to 50% of what number?

   A. 2
   B. 4
   C. 8
   D. 10
   E. 200

10. There are 45 musicians in an orchestra, and all play two instruments. Of these musicians, 36 play the piano, and 22 play the violin. What is the maximum possible orchestra members who play both the piano and the violin?

    F. 9
    G. 13
    H. 22
    J. 23
    K. 36

GO ON TO THE NEXT PAGE.

11. What is the largest value of m for which there exists a real value of n such that $m^2 = 196 - n^2$?

A. 14
B. 98
C. 182
D. 196
E. 392

DO YOUR FIGURING HERE.

12. Phil earned $800 at his summer job and saved all of his earnings. He wants to buy a deluxe drum kit that is regularly priced at $925 but is on sale for $\frac{1}{5}$ off. The drum kit is subject to 5% sales tax after all discounts are applied. If Phil buys the kit on sale and gives the sales clerk his entire summer earnings, how much change should he receive?

F. $23
G. $37
H. $40
J. $77
K. None; Phil still owes $171.25.

13. Which of the following numbers is an imaginary number?

A. $\sqrt{64}$

B. $\sqrt{11}$

C. $-\dfrac{4}{\sqrt{3}}$

D. $-\sqrt{-64}$

E. $-\sqrt{64}$

14. Which of the following correctly factors the expression $25x^4 - 16y^8$?

F. $(25 - 16)(x^2 - y^4)(x^2 + y^4)$
G. $(5x^2 - 4y^4)(5x^2 + 4y^4)$
H. $(25x^2 - y^4)(x^2 + 16y^4)$
J. $(5x^4 - 4y^8)(5x^4 + 4y^8)$
K. $(5x^4 - 8y^8)(5x^4 + 2y^8)$

GO ON TO THE NEXT PAGE.

15. The figure below shows a portion of a tile floor from which the shaded polygon will be cut in order to make a repair. Each square tile has sides that measure 1 foot. Every vertex of the shaded polygon is at the intersection of 2 tiles. What is the area, in square feet, of the shaded polygon?

DO YOUR FIGURING HERE.

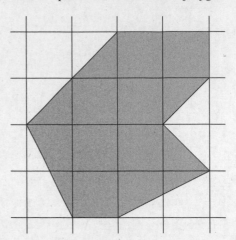

- **A.** 9.5
- **B.** 10.0
- **C.** 10.5
- **D.** 11.0
- **E.** 11.5

16. The percent P of a population that has completed 4 years of college is given by the function $P(t) = 0.001t^2 + 0.4t$ where t represents time, in years. What percent of the population have completed four years of college after 20 years, to the nearest tenth?

- **F.** 0.1
- **G.** 7.6
- **H.** 8.0
- **J.** 8.4
- **K.** 160.0

17. At Fatima's Fruits, a bag of eight grapefruits costs $4.40. At Ernie's Edibles, a bag of three grapefruits costs $1.86. How much cheaper, per grapefruit, is the cost at Fatima's Fruits than at Ernie's Edibles?

- **A.** $0.07
- **B.** $0.35
- **C.** $0.59
- **D.** $1.17
- **E.** $2.54

GO ON TO THE NEXT PAGE.

18. Which of the following is equivalent to $(x^4 - 4)(x^4 + 4)$?

    F. $2x^4$
    G. $x^8 - 16$
    H. $x^8 + 16$
    J. $x^{16} - 16$
    K. $x^8 - 8x^4 - 16$

DO YOUR FIGURING HERE.

19. Wade is making a tile mosaic. He begins the project by laying tile at a speed of 50 pieces per hour for 3.5 hours. He is then interrupted from his work for 60 minutes. He resumes working and lays tile at a speed of 35 pieces per hour, until he has laid 280 pieces of tile total. How many hours did Wade spend working on the mosaic after he was interrupted?

    A. 2.5
    B. 3
    C. 3.5
    D. 4
    E. 4.5

20. Point C (1,2) and point D (7,−10) lie in the standard coordinate plane. What are the coordinates of the midpoint of $\overline{CD}$?

    F. (1,8)
    G. (3,−6)
    H. (4,−4)
    J. (4,−6)
    K. (7,−4)

21. Michael is planning to put fencing along the edge of his rectangular backyard, which is 22 yards by 16 yards. One long side of the backyard is along his house, so he will need to fence only 3 sides. How many yards of fencing will Michael need?

    A. 38
    B. 54
    C. 60
    D. 76
    E. 352

GO ON TO THE NEXT PAGE.

22. What is the *y*-intercept of the line given by the equation
$7x - 3y = 21$?

    F.   −7

    G. $-\dfrac{7}{3}$

    H. $\dfrac{7}{3}$

    J.   7

    K.   21

DO YOUR FIGURING HERE.

23. On April 8th, a flower at Blooming Acres Florist was 15.0 centimeters tall. On April 16th, the flower was 17.4 centimeters tall. If the flower grew at a constant rate, on what day was the flower 16.5 centimeters tall?

    A.   April 11th
    B.   April 12th
    C.   April 13th
    D.   April 14th
    E.   April 15th

24. Which of the following expressions is equivalent to the expression given below?

$$(2x^3 - x - 1) - 3(x^4 + 2x^3 - 2x^2 - x + 3)$$

    F. $x^{14} - 3$
    G. $-3x^{14}$
    H. $-3x^4 + 8x^3 - 6x^2 - 4x + 8$
    J. $-3x^4 + 4x^3 - 2x^2 - 2x - 3$
    K. $-3x^4 - 4x^3 + 6x^2 + 2x - 10$

GO ON TO THE NEXT PAGE.

25. The playground equipment shown below has a ladder that is 6 feet tall and a diagonal slide that is 7 feet long. If the ladder makes a right angle with the ground, approximately how many feet is the base of the slide from the base of the ladder?

DO YOUR FIGURING HERE.

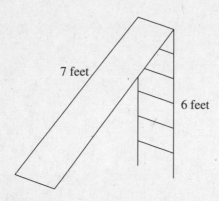

7 feet

6 feet

- **A.** 2
- **B.** 4
- **C.** 6
- **D.** 8
- **E.** 10

26. In a data set of 5 points, the mean, median, and mode are each equal to 8. Which of the following could be the data set?

- **F.** {5, 7, 8, 8, 12}
- **G.** {7, 7, 8, 8, 12}
- **H.** {7, 8, 8, 8, 12}
- **J.** {7, 8, 8, 10, 12}
- **K.** {7, 8, 8, 12, 12}

27. In a certain sequence of numbers, each term after the 1st term is the result of adding 2 to the previous term and multiplying that sum by 3. If the 4th term in the sequence is 186, what is the 2nd term?

- **A.** 2
- **B.** 4
- **C.** 18
- **D.** 60
- **E.** 174

28. Which of the following values of x does NOT satisfy the inequality $|x - 3| \geq 12$?

- **F.** −15
- **G.** −12
- **H.** −9
- **J.** 9
- **K.** 15

GO ON TO THE NEXT PAGE.

29. For all real numbers s, t, u, and v, such that $s + t + u = 29$ and $s < v$, which of the following statements is true?

A. $s + t + v < 29$
B. $t + u + v > 29$
C. $s + t + v = 29$
D. $s + u + v = 29$
E. $s + t + v > 29$

DO YOUR FIGURING HERE.

30. In the figure below, rectangle $ABCD$ shares $\overline{CD}$ with $\triangle CDE$, diagonal $\overline{BD}$ of the rectangle extends in a straight line beyond D to E to create $\overline{DE}$, and the measure of $\angle CDE$ is 155°. What is the measure of $\angle CBD$?

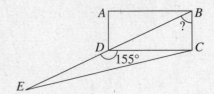

F. 25
G. 55
H. 65
J. 90
K. 155

31. If a, b, and c are positive prime numbers, in the equation $a - b = c$, either b or c must represent which number?

A. 13
B. 11
C. 7
D. 5
E. 2

GO ON TO THE NEXT PAGE.

32. Pierre competes in a triathlon, along a course as shown in the figure below. He begins swimming at starting point S and swims straight across the lake, gets on his bicycle at station A, bikes to station B, and then runs to finishing line F. The judges use a stopwatch to record his elapsed times of t_A, t_B, and t_F hours from point S to points A, B, and F, respectively. If the distance, in miles, between points S and A along the racecourse is denoted by SA, then what is Pierre's average speed for this race, in miles per hour?

DO YOUR FIGURING HERE.

F. $\dfrac{SA}{t_A}$

G. $\dfrac{SB}{t_B}$

H. $\dfrac{SF}{t_F}$

J. $\dfrac{SA}{t_F}$

K. $\dfrac{SF}{t_A}$

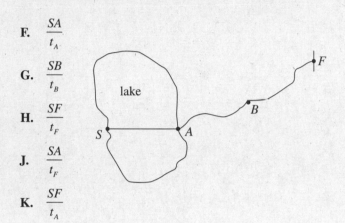

33. The triangle shown below has a hypotenuse with a length of 13 feet. The measure of $\angle A$ is 20° and the measure of $\angle B$ is 70°. Which of the following is closest to the length, in feet, of $\overline{BC}$?

(Note: sin 70° ≈ 0.9397
cos 70° ≈ 0.3420
tan 70° ≈ 2.747)

A. 4.4
B. 5.0
C. 12.0
D. 12.2
E. 35.7

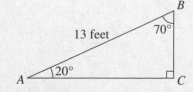

GO ON TO THE NEXT PAGE.

34. What is the value of $\dfrac{8}{y^2} - \dfrac{x^2}{y}$ when $x = -3$ and $y = -4$?

F. $-\dfrac{11}{4}$

G. $-\dfrac{7}{4}$

H. $\dfrac{7}{4}$

J. $\dfrac{11}{4}$

K. $\dfrac{56}{9}$

35. As shown in the figure below, with angles as marked, a ramp is being designed that will have a vertical height of 4 feet. Which of the following is closest to the horizontal length of the ramp, in feet?

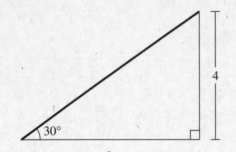

A. 5
B. 6
C. 7
D. 8
E. 9

36. In the diagram below, $\triangle ABC$ is isosceles and $\triangle BCD$ is equilateral. $\overline{AB} = \overline{BC}$ and the measure of $\angle ABC$ is half the measure of $\angle BAC$. What is the measure of $\angle ABD$?

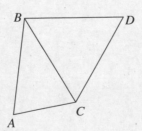

F. 36°
G. 60°
H. 72°
J. 96°
K. 150°

GO ON TO THE NEXT PAGE.

Use the following information to answer questions 37–39.

The coordinates of the vertices of $\triangle MON$ are shown in the standard (x,y) coordinate plane below. Rectangle $MPQR$ is shown shaded. Point P lies on $\overline{MO}$, point Q lies on $\overline{ON}$, and point R lies on $\overline{MN}$.

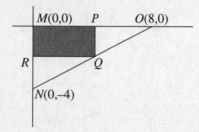

37. What is the slope of $\overline{ON}$?

A. -2

B. $-\dfrac{1}{2}$

C. 0

D. $\dfrac{1}{2}$

E. 2

38. Which of the following is closest to the perimeter, in coordinate units, of $\triangle MON$?

F. 12.0

G. 16.9

H. 18.0

J. 20.9

K. 92.0

39. What is the value of $\cos(\angle MNO)$?

A. $\dfrac{8}{\sqrt{80}}$

B. $\dfrac{4}{\sqrt{80}}$

C. 2

D. $\dfrac{1}{2}$

E. $\dfrac{\sqrt{80}}{8}$

GO ON TO THE NEXT PAGE.

40. In a Spanish class there are m students, of which n did NOT pass the last exam. Which of the following is a general expression for the fraction of the class that did receive a passing grade?

DO YOUR FIGURING HERE.

F. $\dfrac{m-n}{m}$

G. $\dfrac{m}{n}$

H. $\dfrac{m-n}{n}$

J. $\dfrac{n-m}{n}$

K. $\dfrac{n-m}{m}$

41. The solution set of $5x + 9 \geq 2(3x + 4) + 7$ is shown by which of the following number line graphs?

A.
B.
C.
D.
E.

42. An artist wants to cover the entire outside of a rectangular box with mosaic tiles. The dimensions of the box shown below are given in centimeters. If each tile is exactly one square centimeter, and the artist lays the tiles with no space between them, how many tiles will he need?

F. 75
G. 96
H. 108
J. 126
K. 150

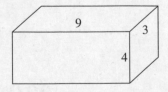

GO ON TO THE NEXT PAGE.

DO YOUR FIGURING HERE.

43. In the figure shown below, $\overline{BC}$ and $\overline{EF}$ are parallel and $\overline{AE} = \overline{FD}$. If $\angle ABC$ is 130° and $\angle BAE$ is 22°, what is the measure of $\angle AEF$?

- **A.** 50°
- **B.** 118°
- **C.** 152°
- **D.** 158°
- **E.** 164°

44. Given the figure below, what is the area of the trapezoid, in square inches?

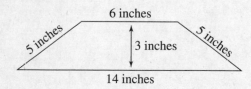

- **F.** 18
- **G.** 30
- **H.** 42
- **J.** 50
- **K.** 52

45. What is the solution set of $\sqrt[5]{x^2 + 4x} = 2$?

- **A.** {4}
- **B.** {8}
- **C.** {−4, 8}
- **D.** {−8, 4}
- **E.** {−2, ±2√2}

GO ON TO THE NEXT PAGE.

46. As shown in the figure below, a skateboard ramp leading from the top of a boulder is 10 feet long and forms a 32° angle with the level ground. Which of the following expressions represents the height, in feet, of the boulder?

DO YOUR FIGURING HERE.

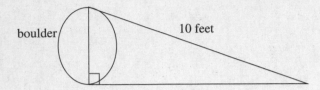

F. $10 \tan 32°$

G. $\dfrac{\sin 32°}{10}$

H. $\dfrac{10}{\cos 32°}$

J. $10 \sin 32°$

K. $10 \cos 32°$

47. The 4 integers j, j, k, and n have an average of 0. Which of the following equations *must* be true?

A. $k = n$
B. $k = -j$
C. $k + n = -2j$
D. $k + n = 0$
E. $k + n = j$

48. If $f(x) = \sqrt{x}$ and the composite function
$f(g(x)) = \sqrt{4x^2 - 5}$, which of the following could be $g(x)$?

F. $\sqrt{4x^4 - 5}$

G. $\sqrt{16x^4 - 25}$

H. $2x^2 - 25$

J. $4x^2 - 5$

K. $16x^4 - 5$

GO ON TO THE NEXT PAGE.

Use the following information to answer questions 49–51.

In the qualifying rounds for a race, Rusty and Dale drive their cars around a 6000-foot oval track. Rusty and Dale each drive 8 laps in the qualifying rounds in lanes of identical length.

49. On day one of the qualifying rounds, Rusty and Dale started from the same point, but their cars are reversed and each drives opposite ways. Rusty drove at a constant speed that was 8 feet per second faster than Dale's constant speed. Rusty passed Dale for the first time in 150 seconds. Rusty drove at a constant rate of how many feet per second?

   A. 16
   B. 20
   C. 24
   D. 32
   E. 40

50. This morning in the qualifying rounds, Rusty averaged 180 seconds per lap until he began the last lap. He then went into a lower gear. He averaged 190 seconds per lap for this qualifying round. How many seconds did Rusty take to drive the final lap?

   F. 155
   G. 160
   H. 185
   J. 200
   K. 260

51. Dale drove 6 laps in 90 minutes. At what average rate, in feet per hour, did Dale drive these 6 laps?

   A.   400
   B.   5400
   C.   10,000
   D.   24,000
   E.   48,000

52. Circle A has its center at point $(-5,2)$ with a radius of 2, and circle B is represented by the equation $(x + 4)^2 + (y - 2)^2 = 9$. Where is point $(-2,2)$ located?

   F. Inside circle A only
   G. Inside circle B only
   H. Inside both circle A and circle B
   J. Outside both circle A and circle B
   K. Cannot be determined from given information

GO ON TO THE NEXT PAGE.

DO YOUR FIGURING HERE.

53. A heart-shaped ornament is made from a square and two semicircles, each of whose diameter is a side of the square. The ornament is shown in the standard (x,y) coordinate plane below, where 1 coordinate unit represents 1 inch. The coordinates of six points on the border of the ornament are given. What is the perimeter, in inches, of the ornament?

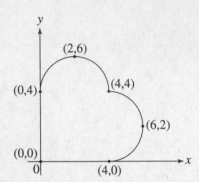

A. $4 + 2\pi$
B. $8 + 4\pi$
C. $8 + 8\pi$
D. $16 + 4\pi$
E. $16 + 8\pi$

54. A function $f(x)$ is defined as even if and only if $f(x) = f(-x)$ for all real values of x. Which one of the following graphs represents an even function $f(x)$?

F.

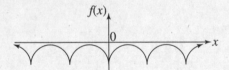

G.

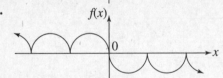

H.

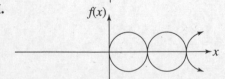

J.

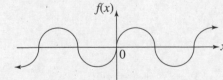

K.

GO ON TO THE NEXT PAGE.

55. In the standard (x,y) coordinate plane, point A is located at $(w, w + 5)$ and point B is located at $(4w, w - 5)$. In coordinate units, what is the distance between A and B ?

DO YOUR FIGURING HERE.

A. $\sqrt{9w^2 + 2w + 10}$

B. $\sqrt{9w^2 + 100}$

C. $9w^2 + 100$

D. $|w|\sqrt{11}$

E. $|w|$

56. $\triangle RST$ is a right triangle with side lengths of r, s, and t, as shown below. What is the value of $\cos^2 S + \cos^2 R$?

F. 1

G. $\sqrt{2}$

H. $\sqrt{3}$

J. $\dfrac{\sqrt{2}}{2}$

K. $\dfrac{1 + \sqrt{2}}{3}$

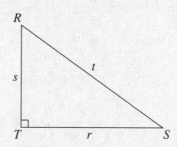

57. In isosceles triangle ABC below, the measures of $\angle BAC$ and $\angle BCA$ are equal and $\overline{DE} \parallel \overline{AC}$. The diagonals of trapezoid $DECA$ intersect at F. The lengths of $\overline{DF}$ and $\overline{EF}$ are 6 centimeters, the length of $\overline{DE}$ is 9 centimeters, and the length of $\overline{AC}$ is 27 centimeters. What is the length, in centimeters, of $\overline{FC}$?

A. 12
B. 15
C. 18
D. 33
E. 36

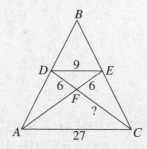

GO ON TO THE NEXT PAGE.

58. Which of the following represents the product of the matrices below?

DO YOUR FIGURING HERE.

$$\begin{bmatrix} 4 & -2 \\ 3 & -6 \end{bmatrix} \times \begin{bmatrix} 0 \\ 2 \end{bmatrix}$$

F. $\begin{bmatrix} -4 \\ -12 \end{bmatrix}$

G. $\begin{bmatrix} -12 \\ 0 \end{bmatrix}$

H. $\begin{bmatrix} -6 \end{bmatrix}$

J. $\begin{bmatrix} 6 & -12 \end{bmatrix}$

K. $\begin{bmatrix} -4 & -12 \end{bmatrix}$

59. If $\dfrac{(n+1)!}{(n-1)!} = 20$, then $n! = ?$

    A.   6
    B.   10
    C.   12
    D.   24
    E. 120

60. What is the ratio of a circle's radius to its circumference?

    F. $2\pi : 1$
    G. $2 : 1$
    H. $\pi : 1$
    J. $1 : \pi$
    K. $1 : 2\pi$

END OF TEST 2
STOP! DO NOT TURN THE PAGE UNTIL TOLD TO DO SO.
DO NOT RETURN TO THE PREVIOUS TEST.

NO TEST MATERIAL ON THIS PAGE.

READING TEST
35 Minutes—40 Questions

DIRECTIONS: There are four passages in this test. Each passage is followed by several questions. After reading each passage, choose the best answer to each question and blacken the corresponding oval on your answer document. You may refer to the passages as often as necessary.

Passage I

PROSE FICTION: This passage is adapted from the short story "Ruby" by Tristan Ivory (©2007 by Tristan Ivory).

Ruby's Downhome Diner was an institution. If you only spent one night in Franklin, Texas, someone would inevitably direct you right off Highway 79 and Pink Oak Road to Ruby's Downhome Diner, Ruby's, or The Downhome; whatever
5 name the locals gave you, there was always something there that you would enjoy.

Ruby's was named after Ruby Sanders, my grandmother. She had opened the diner with money she saved from cleaning houses and with personal loans from friends. By the time
10 I was born, Ruby's did enough business to pay off all debts and obligations. It didn't take long before my grandmother was a person of considerable stature in and around Robertson County, just like the restaurant that bore her name.

Ever since I was knee-high, I spent each sweltering
15 summer with my grandmother. This, truth be told, meant that for all practical purposes I lived at Ruby's Downhome. Time familiarized me with all nuances within the diner: there were five steps and four ingredients that separated peach preserves from peach cobbler filling; Deputy Sheriff Walter Mayes
20 preferred his eggs, always cooked over-easy, to finish cooking on the top of his ham before it was transferred to his plate; Mr. Arnold delivered the milk and the buttermilk on Mondays, Thursdays, and Saturdays; and there were days when I would need to go to the general store to pick up whatever was in
25 short supply. By the time I entered high school, I could have run the diner from open to close if my Grandmother were absent, but she never was.

Perhaps the single greatest contributing factor to the success of Ruby's Diner was the omnipresent personality of
30 its namesake. Even the most hopelessly spun-around visitor who happened inside those doors would know who Ms. Ruby was. There were no sick days, vacations, or holidays. Between 5 a.m. and 9 p.m., you knew where Ruby Sanders could be found. If the diner were a sort of cell, then my grandmother was
35 its nucleus; without the nucleus, the cell would surely perish.

The people who worked at Ruby's were as dedicated as Ruby herself. There were the regulars: Del (short for Delmont) did double duty as a short-order cook and janitor,

while Marlene and Deborah waited tables. Extra help would
40 be hired from time to time depending on the season and individual need. No matter how long those extra helpers stayed, they and everyone else who worked at the Downhome were family, and no one ever fell out of touch.

Ruby's did the things you'd expect a diner to do, as
45 well as the things you wouldn't. You could stop in and get yourself a nice cool drink for the road. Or you could pull up a stool at the counter and grab a steaming hot bowl of red pepper chili with a slice of corn pone or a dish of chilled and creamy homemade ice cream. Or better still, you could
50 grab a booth and try any number of full-plate entrees made to order. But you could also order a wedding cake a week in advance, take a weekend course in food preparation, or, when the time came, have your wake catered with dignity and grace.

When I was very young, I would spend most of my time
55 exploring every inch of Ruby's until the entire layout was printed indelibly in my mind. I could walk blindfolded from the basement where the dry goods were kept, up to the kitchen with the walk-in refrigerator chocked full of perishables, over to the main restaurant with row after row of booths and counter and stools,
60 well-worn but always cleaned after each patron had finished, and finally to the front porch, with its old wooden swing. I can see my grandmother moving from her station near the door to the kitchen, over to the counter and tables, and then back to the front again. Even now, I can see Del speedily making a double
65 order of hash, Deborah picking up a generous tip, and Marlene topping off a customer's sweet tea. Every summer sunset from that porch seemed to be more magnificent than the last.

As I got older, I took on more responsibility. There were fewer sunsets to watch and more work to be done. It was hard
70 but never dull work. The company kept me coming back despite the increasing allure of summer football leagues and idle moments with friends or girls. After all, the woman who built Ruby's was strong enough to make me forget those things, if only for the summer. I didn't know that I would never return
75 after my sophomore year of college, and for that, I am glad—I could not have asked for a better end to my long history at Ruby's. It warms my heart when I think of the last memory of Ruby Sanders: tying her silver hair into a tight bun, hands vigorously wiping down tables with a rag, enjoying a story
80 and a laugh as we closed for the night.

GO ON TO THE NEXT PAGE.

1. The narrator's point of view can most correctly be described as that of an adult:

   A. remembering the events that brought a particular place into existence.
   B. analyzing how different his current life is from how things were when he was younger.
   C. thinking about the qualities of his grandmother and her restaurant that made her well-respected in the community.
   D. curious as to how many people's lives were positively impacted by his grandmother and her diner.

2. One of the main purposes of the first part of the passage (lines 1–27) is to:

   F. explain how Ruby got the money to pay for the diner and her eventual success in paying off her debts.
   G. state that the diner had taken its name from the narrator's grandmother although many of the locals called it by different names.
   H. explain how Ruby was able to become the most important person in Franklin and that her restaurant was the best place for visitors to the city.
   J. introduce the primary setting of the story and to describe a central character.

3. Based on the narrator's characterization, Ruby Sanders would best be described as:

   A. always at the diner, though she often preferred to be absent.
   B. the main force holding the diner and its employees together.
   C. carefree, particularly when it came to hearing humorous stories.
   D. the only woman the narrator had ever respected.

4. Information in the last paragraph most strongly suggests that the narrator felt his last summer at the diner to be:

   F. disappointing because he didn't know it would be his last.
   G. something he was forced to do when he would rather have been playing football.
   H. pleasant although he did not know it would be his last.
   J. exhausting because of all his new responsibilities.

5. According to the narrator, working at Ruby's Diner was:

   A. easy but tedious.
   B. difficult but enjoyable.
   C. hard and monotonous.
   D. unpredictable and overwhelming.

6. According to the narrator, his grandmother was like the diner in that she had:

   F. a position of high standing within the community at large.
   G. a desire to make all people feel comfortable no matter who they were.
   H. an ability to make money within the community.
   J. a refusal to settle for anything but the best.

7. The statement in lines 44–45 most strongly suggests that the Downhome Diner:

   A. served the community in ways beyond simple dining.
   B. was the most significant place within Robertson County.
   C. gave the people who worked there great importance in Robertson County.
   D. was a place where the waiting times were often unpredictable.

8. The narrator describes Ruby's Downhome Diner as providing all of the following EXCEPT:

   F. cooking classes.
   G. football leagues.
   H. wedding cakes.
   J. corn pone.

9. The passage indicates that one of the ways in which the narrator was familiar with Ruby's Downhome Diner was shown by his:

   A. ability to teach the cooking classes held on the premises.
   B. awareness of the habits of visitors to Robertson County.
   C. detailed memory of the layout of the kitchen and the restaurant.
   D. unwillingness to leave at the end of each summer before his return to school.

10. According to the narrator, which of the following most accurately represents the reason he was able to forget the summer activities outside while working at his grandmother's restaurant?

    F. His tips and wages helped to contribute to his college tuition.
    G. His grandmother's restaurant was chronically understaffed.
    H. It helped him to gain stature in and around the community.
    J. He admired his grandmother's strength.

GO ON TO THE NEXT PAGE.

Passage II

SOCIAL SCIENCE: This passage is adapted from the entry "Happiness" from *The Psychologist's Scientific Encyclopedia* (© 2004 by The Scientific Press of Illinois).

Lee D. Ross, a psychologist at Stanford University, has a friend who lost both her parents in the Holocaust. According to the woman, the awful events of the Holocaust taught her that it was inappropriate to be upset about trivial things in
5 life and important to enjoy human relationships. Even though the circumstances of her life were tragic, the woman was extremely happy, perhaps due to an innate sense of well-being.

According to psychologists, most of our self-reported level of happiness, a measure researchers call "subjective
10 well-being," seems to be genetically predetermined, rather than caused by experience. A study carried out by Auke Tellegen and David Lykken of the University of Minnesota compared the subjective well-being scores of both fraternal and identical twins, some who were raised together and some who were
15 separated and raised in different families. By comparing the scores of the twins, Tellegen and Lykken determined that most of the differences in people's levels of happiness are determined by differences in genetic makeup.

A genetic predisposition toward a certain level of hap-
20 piness means that regardless of what happens in a person's life, he or she will eventually adjust to the new circumstances and report the same level of subjective well-being as before. The tendency for people to maintain a consistent level of happiness despite their circumstances, known as "hedonic
25 adaptation," benefits those whose life-experiences are beset by adverse conditions, such as permanent disability or sudden loss of income. Because they return to a "genetic set point," they eventually feel just as happy as they did before the unfortunate event.

30 However, hedonic adaptation also affects the happiness of people who experience positive changes in their lives. For example, in one study conducted in the 1970s among lottery winners, it was found that a year after the winners received their money, they were no happier than non-winners.

35 Despite the quantity of research that supports hedonic adaptation, there is still some debate within the scientific community over how much people can change their baseline happiness. Kennon M. Sheldon, a psychologist at the University of Missouri-Columbia, explains that many research
40 psychologists hypothesized that certain behaviors, such as choosing particular goals in life, could affect long-term happiness. However, scientific literature suggests that these behaviors provide only a temporary increase in subjective well-being.

45 Sheldon worked alongside Sonja Lyubomirsky of the University of California at Riverside and David A. Schkade of the University of California at San Diego to determine exactly what is known about the science of happiness. They compiled the findings of existing scientific studies in the field
50 of happiness and determined that 50 percent of subjective well-being is predetermined by the genetic set point, while only about 10 percent is influenced by circumstances.

However, people are not completely at the mercy of their genes. Lyubomirsky notes that 40 percent of what contributes
55 to people's happiness is still unexplained, and she believes that much of this may be attributable to what she calls "intentional activity," which includes mental attitudes and behaviors that people can modify and improve. Conscious choices such as demonstrating kindness, fostering optimism, and expressing
60 gratitude may work to influence subjective well-being in much the same way that diet and exercise can affect a person's inherited predisposition toward heart disease. Lyubomirsky hopes to learn the specific mechanisms by which these conscious strategies counteract genetic forces. She and Sheldon are cur-
65 rently expanding their study of subjective well-being to large groups of subjects to be observed over extended periods of time. Using these longitudinal studies, the researchers hope to discover the inner workings of the correlations between behaviors and mood.

70 Lyubomirsky and Sheldon's studies have found that simply choosing "happy" activities may not be the most effective way to increase happiness. Lyubomirsky says that other factors, such as variation and timing of intentional activities, are crucial in influencing happiness. For example, one study
75 has shown that subjects who varied their acts of kindness from one day to the next experienced greater happiness than those who repeated the same kind act many times. Another study demonstrated that writing a list of things to be grateful for only once a week was more effective in improving levels of
80 happiness than keeping a gratitude journal every day.

The study of happiness is still a relatively new area of psychological research. Traditionally, much more psychological research focused on depression and other disorders associated with destructive mental health, leading some psychologists
85 to suspect that overall levels of subjective well-being are low. But now that more studies are focused on positive psychology, there is evidence to the contrary. Researchers have discovered not only that personal choices improve subjective well-being from a genetic set point, but also that this level is higher than
90 traditionally expected. According to surveys conducted by the University of Chicago, only about one in ten people claim to be "not too happy." Most Americans describe themselves as "pretty happy," and 30 percent as "very happy," even without using intentional activities specifically to improve
95 their well-being.

GO ON TO THE NEXT PAGE.

11. The passage's focus is primarily on the:

A. search for the specific genes known to cause hedonic adaptation.
B. scientific studies investigating various influences on happiness.
C. attempts by experimental psychologists to develop cures for depression.
D. conflicting opinions of psychologists regarding the influence of genes on happiness.

12. Based on the passage, the subjects in the studies by Tellegen and Lykken and the subjects in studies by Lyubomirsky and Sheldon were similar in that both groups were:

F. part of large groups studied over an extended time.
G. intentionally engaged in acts of kindness.
H. asked to describe their own subjective well-being.
J. either identical or fraternal twins.

13. Which of the following questions is NOT answered by the passage?

A. To what extent is a person's level of happiness determined by his or her circumstances?
B. According to Lyubomirsky and Sheldon's studies, what are some specific things people can do to improve their subjective well-being?
C. Does the choice of specific life goals affect happiness over a lifetime?
D. According to Tellegen and Lykken, were twins who were raised together happier than twins who were raised apart?

14. The passage most strongly suggests that the primary goal of Lyubomirsky and Sheldon's research is to:

F. discover the specific mechanisms that may help people overcome the level of happiness determined by their genetic set point.
G. contradict Tellegen and Lykken's findings that genes are the primary determinant in a person's overall level of happiness.
H. find out whether keeping a gratitude journal or engaging in kind acts is more effective at improving happiness.
J. determine which behaviors most completely eliminate hedonic adaptation.

15. Which of the following statements best summarizes the findings of the University of Chicago surveys on happiness?

A. Earlier psychologists were mistaken to believe people are generally depressed and experience low levels of happiness.
B. Depression and other destructive mood disorders are uncommon in America.
C. People are happier if they do not try to improve their subjective well-being by writing in a gratitude journal.
D. Most people report a level of happiness higher than was traditionally expected by psychologists and researchers.

16. The passage indicates that all of the following people are likely to return to a genetically predetermined level of subjective well-being EXCEPT those who:

F. experience severe tragedy.
G. exercise regularly and eat a healthy diet.
H. practice intentional kindness.
J. win the lottery.

17. According to the passage, "hedonic adaptation" (lines 24–25) is a useful trait because it can help people to:

A. restore levels of happiness that have been interrupted or altered by tragic events.
B. forget that they have suffered a permanent disability or loss of income.
C. adjust quickly to positive circumstances like winning the lottery and become happier.
D. identify with immediate family members who share their genes and choose those who are more inclined to be happy.

18. If the author were to delete the first paragraph, the passage would primarily lose:

F. the idea that events people experience are not the least important factor influencing their subjective well-being.
G. a useful illustration of the idea that there may be little relationship between a person's circumstances and his or her level of happiness.
H. a clear and complete articulation of the essay's main point regarding hedonic adaptation.
J. all examples of adverse conditions people may overcome because of their genetic predisposition to happiness.

19. The main purpose of the final paragraph is to:

A. conclude that psychological researchers make many errors and tend to focus on the negative.
B. disprove the idea suggested by Ross's anecdote by showing that Americans are also happy.
C. cite a specific study that gives a positive view of people's overall levels of happiness.
D. undermine Lyubomirsky and Sheldon's studies indicating that people need to apply effort in order to become happier.

20. According to the passage, which of the following researchers have an ongoing collaboration?

F. Tellegen and Lykken
G. Sheldon and Schkade
H. Sheldon and Lyubomirsky
J. Schkade and Lykken

GO ON TO THE NEXT PAGE.

Passage III

HUMANITIES: This passage is adapted from the memoir *Literary Tourism* by Krista Prouty (© 2002 by Krista Prouty).

Just recently, I visited the House of the Seven Gables, in Salem, Massachusetts. Up until the moment I looked through my travel guide, I hadn't even known that there was an actual house, much less that it was in Salem. We had intended only
5 to visit the Salem Witch Memorials, but since I've been a Nathaniel Hawthorne fan since junior high, a side trip to the building that had inspired one of his greatest works seemed to be in order.

Let me back up a bit to explain. Ever since I was a
10 little girl, I've loved to read. Classics, in particular, thrilled me, taking me back in time to worlds that hadn't existed for hundreds of years. I knew, of course, that real people wrote these books, but somehow the authors didn't interest me very much. The whole point of reading was to explore other reali-
15 ties, and while I had a great deal of respect for anyone who could create those worlds, their life stories didn't hold much appeal. In college, I opted to major in literature, assuming that this would involve reading scores of wonderful books, which it did. It also meant, however, spending hours, days,
20 and weeks studying the people behind the books. Completing my professors' assignments, I felt more like a detective than a reader, scouring personal letters for hints of relationship problems, familial tragedies, or even fond memories that seemed reminiscent of storylines. I would analyze how authors'
25 childhood traumas might have influenced their writing, and I would try to discover any hidden secrets and vices. In inspired moments, I felt the advantage of this depth of knowledge—a piece that had been opaque to me would suddenly open up, as I grasped the personal truth the author was trying to convey.
30 More often, though, I found myself losing sight of the books in the forest of biographical details.

By the time I graduated, I was heartily sick of the whole business. Casting aside all previous plans of continued study, I gave away or sold all of my textbooks, keeping only a few
35 of my favorite books for pleasure reading. Over the years, I regressed to my natural habits—when I read, I did so with blinders on. My focus was solely on the book itself, and I gave no thought to the writer, aside from admiration for his or her skill. Reading this way was more enjoyable, and with
40 no professors watching, I was free to do as I pleased.

It was in this frame of mind that I learned of the existence of the actual House of the Seven Gables, so my enthusiasm had more to do with visiting a site featured in one of my favorite books than with visiting the former home of a famous
45 author. We found the house, parked the car, and walked in. The woman staffing the entrance desk informed us that visitors were allowed only as part of a tour. Although my plans had not included being herded through a rambling old house, I acceded and the tickets were duly purchased. As we waited
50 for the tour to begin, we wandered through the gardens, which were desolate during the winter months. Several buildings were clustered around the central garden area, and each structure had a sign explaining its historical relevance. The main building had been the original inspiration for <u>The House of the Seven</u>
55 <u>Gables</u>, another a counting house, and another the home of Nathaniel Hawthorne's family. As I gazed at the signs, a bit confused, having assumed that Hawthorne had lived in the main house, our guide arrived and ushered us all indoors.

For the next hour, we were inundated with facts about
60 Nathaniel Hawthorne's life. We learned that he had not, in fact, lived in the famous house. His family had struggled financially, and even the small house that bore his name on a plaque had ultimately proven too expensive. The guide told us about Hawthorne's troubled youth, the untimely death of
65 his father, his psychological battles, and his ultimate redemption through marriage with a woman he loved deeply. As I listened, for the first time I began to see Nathaniel Hawthorne not just as a talented writer but as a real person with a life as rich and complicated as my own. Maybe it was visiting his
70 home, maybe it was hearing the right words at the right moment, but whatever the cause, something clicked. The writer's personal dossier and his literary work no longer seemed to get in the way of each other, but instead blended seamlessly into a varicolored, complex, and beautiful tapestry. The work itself
75 is indeed the frame, but when we weave the threads of the author's life around that base, we are able to see the interactions between text and author, as they join to create a pattern more complete than either would be on its own.

GO ON TO THE NEXT PAGE.

21. The author of the passage indicates that she has learned that the personal details of an author's life:

A. get in the way of the literary work.
B. are always discussed in the author's works.
C. contribute to a reader's appreciation of the author's works.
D. help a reader understand his or her own familial tragedies and childhood traumas.

22. As it is used in line 22, the word *scouring* most nearly means:

F. purifying.
G. obliterating.
H. scrutinizing.
J. cleansing.

23. It can reasonably be inferred that the author of the passage visited the House of the Seven Gables because she wanted to:

A. explore in person a location she had read about in a novel.
B. take advantage of all the tourist attractions in Salem.
C. gain a deeper understanding of how the details of Hawthorne's past influenced his writing.
D. learn what Hawthorne endured during the Salem Witch Trials.

24. According to the author of the passage, the college professors referred to in line 21 most likely believe that:

F. the interactions between an author's life and work provide the reader with a more complete understanding than does the text alone.
G. learning about an author's life is more important than reading his books.
H. knowledge of the background of an author interferes with enjoyment of the text.
J. reading for pleasure is less useful than is reading for cultural analysis.

25. According to the second paragraph (lines 9–31), the author of the passage chose to study literature in college in order to:

A. scour personal letters for an author's secret vices.
B. read a great number of literary works.
C. demonstrate the falsity of the scholars' approach.
D. better grasp the connection between an author and his work.

26. According to the author of the passage, the likely result of following her professors' assignments was:

F. "to explore other realities" (lines 14–15).
G. grasping "the personal truth the author was trying to convey" (line 29).
H. "losing sight of the books in the forest of biographical details" (lines 30–31).
J. "to see the interactions between text and author" (lines 76–77).

27. It can reasonably be inferred from the passage that "the building that had inspired one of his greatest works" (lines 6–7) refers to:

A. the home inhabited by relatives of Nathaniel Hawthorne.
B. a popular attraction for tourists in Salem.
C. the site of historically important events.
D. a site that has fallen into a state of disrepair.

28. As it is used in line 75, the word *frame* most nearly means the:

F. isolated goal.
G. ultimate purpose.
H. auxiliary data.
J. focal point.

29. Following her visit to Salem, the author's attitude toward studying the lives of writers could best be described as:

A. incredulous disdain.
B. healthy timidity.
C. keen acceptance.
D. resigned frustration.

30. If the third paragraph (lines 32–40) were omitted from the passage, how would the structure of the passage be affected?

F. The transition from the author's past to the present would be less explicit.
G. The reasons for the author's trip would not be clear.
H. The introduction to the discussion of literature in the final paragraph would be lost.
J. There would no longer be definite evidence supporting the author's conclusion.

GO ON TO THE NEXT PAGE.

Passage IV

NATURAL SCIENCE: This passage is adapted from the article "A Tree Frog Grows Up in Hawaii" by Ashley C. Tulliver (© 2005 by Ashley Tulliver).

As night falls on Hawaii's Big Island, a low, jarring sound begins. It is a faint murmur at first, but as the darkness deepens, the sound grows louder, rending the stillness of the evening. These deep cries, from male *E. coqui* frogs, are met with
5 lower, guttural croaks from their prospective mates; during this time, the sound for which the coqui is named (ko-KEE) fills the air. This sound has become the theme song of a growing environmental problem: invasive species' threat to ecological biodiversity.

10   Native to Puerto Rico, the small tree frogs—measuring about five millimeters long—probably arrived in Hawaii as passengers aboard potted plants imported from the Caribbean. Once coquis explored their new environment, they found an abundance of food, including insects, tiny spiders, and mites.
15 In addition, they faced little ecological competition, as there are no other amphibians native to the islands, nor are there the snakes, tarantulas, or other Caribbean hunters that usually serve to keep the coqui population in check.

The way the coqui hatch also gives the coqui an advan-
20 tage in Hawaii's ecosystem. Frogs usually hatch into tadpoles, which require a consistent and substantial amount of water to survive. By contrast, the coqui emerges from the egg as a tiny but fully formed frog, which allows it to thrive in saturated moss, the dampened plastic that importers wrap around plants,
25 or even a drop of water on a plant leaf. Moreover, young coquis don't begin to emit their signature calls until they are about a year old; consequently, avian predators are unable to locate the tiny frogs by sound.

Perhaps the coqui's most noteworthy feature is its ex-
30 tremely loud calling song. To a listener one to two feet away, a single coqui can produce a mating call up to 100 decibels. The unusual volume of the frog's call is compounded by two other factors. First, coquis congregate closely on relatively small parcels of land; one recent survey found 400 adult frogs
35 in one 20-by-20-meter plot. This degree of concentration amplifies the sound the frogs make. Second, coquis tend to overlap their calls, with a single coqui seeking to fill gaps in other frogs' songs with its own effort to attract a mate. As a result, coquis create a "wall of sound" that is even more
40 pronounced because Hawaii boasts few other night-calling species. For these reasons, human residents of Hawaii tend to regard coquis as nuisances, polluting the air with their incessant noise.

Conservationists worry about other ramifications of the
45 coqui's invasion of the Hawaiian ecosystem. One problem is that while the coqui receives the bulk of residents' attention because of its nocturnal serenades, another, quieter genus of the frog—the greenhouse frog—represents an equal threat to the biodiversity of the island. As voracious insectivores,
50 coquis and greenhouse frogs are threatening the survival of arthropods (invertebrate animals with jointed legs, including insects, scorpions, crustaceans, and spiders), whose populations are already close to extirpation due to other foreign predators. Ornithologists fear that depleting the insect population
55 could result in serious consequences for Hawaii's food web, especially considering that the birds native to the islands are also insectivores.

Symbiotic interactions between the coqui and other invasive species pose another ecological threat. The presence
60 of coquis could permit the flourishing of other so-called "dissonant" species, such as non-native snakes that prey upon the frogs. Herpetologists have speculated that nematodes and other types of vertebrate parasites can be transported with coquis and can infect indigenous fauna. Furthermore, many
65 ecologists believe the proliferation of these frogs will further homogenize the island's biota.

Debate persists about how best to reduce or even eradicate the population of coquis and their cousins in Hawaii. Hand-capturing the tiny frogs is probably the most environmentally
70 sensitive way to remove them from their habitat, but their sheer number renders this approach inefficient. The maximum concentration of pesticides that would not damage fauna or flora has not been potent enough to kill the frogs. Seeking a more creative solution, scientists have had some success treating the
75 frogs with caffeine citrate, a drug typically prescribed to treat breathing and metabolic abnormalities in humans. Caffeine citrate can penetrate the coqui's moist skin, and the drug's high acidity essentially poisons the animal and inactivates its nervous systems. From a biodiversity standpoint, this
80 technique has the added benefit of posing almost no danger to plants, which lack a nervous system, or to insects, which have an impenetrable, hard exoskeleton.

Even if new techniques finally exterminate the coqui, experts are skeptical that the invader's current effects on the
85 1,000 acres of Hawaii's ecosystem can be reversed. This patch of land is not expansive in comparison to Hawaii's total 4.1 million acres, yet it is an indication of potential widespread disaster: since the habitat and its native residents have thus far been able to adjust to the presence of coquis, eliminating the
90 frogs could yield unintended and far-reaching consequences to the biodiversity of the habitat beyond arthropods. For now, scientists are likely to continue the delicate balancing act of limiting the coqui's population growth while preventing further damage to Hawaii's ecosystem.

GO ON TO THE NEXT PAGE.

31. Which of the following questions is NOT answered by this passage?

   A. On an annual basis, how often do coqui frogs mate and produce offspring?

   B. Which predators native to Puerto Rico are absent in the Hawaiian islands?

   C. What behavorial factors influence the volume of the coqui's calls?

   D. How could the coqui potentially disrupt the food chain on the islands it inhabits?

32. It is most reasonable to infer from the passage that the lack of amphibian life in Hawaii:

   F. benefits coquis, which don't have to compete for food and space.

   G. provides little opportunity for coquis to form symbiotic relationships.

   H. forces coquis to build their own nests in order to mate and breed.

   J. is a result of invasive species' attacks on the biodiversity of the islands.

33. Which of the following statements about the noise levels produced by the coqui is supported by the passage?

   A. The coqui males have lower, guttural croaks than do females of the species.

   B. Calls are louder when coquis are defending their territory than when they are mating.

   C. The calls of coqui sound particularly loud because there are no gaps of silence.

   D. Coqui are noisier at dawn and dusk than at other times of day.

34. The primary purpose of the third paragraph (lines 19–28) is to:

   F. describe wet weather conditions in Hawaii necessary for the coqui to breed.

   G. provide a physical description of the coqui's habitat in Hawaii compared to that in Puerto Rico.

   H. explain the ecological and behavioral advantages that permit the coqui to thrive in Hawaii.

   J. give an overview of the amphibian life cycle, from the tadpole to frog stage.

35. Compared to the language of the first paragraph, the language of the sixth paragraph (lines 58–66) is more:

   A. opinionated.

   B. scientific.

   C. optimistic.

   D. casual.

36. As it is used in line 53, the word *extirpation* most nearly means:

   F. competition.

   G. extinction.

   H. overpopulation.

   J. pursuit.

37. Which of the following ideas is presented in the passage as theory and not fact?

   A. Coqui frogs cluster together in high concentrations, hampering efforts to regulate their population.

   B. Store-bought poisons, in permissible doses, are not strong enough to kill the frogs.

   C. The exoskeleton of insects is a better defense against citric acid than the skin of amphibians.

   D. A decrease in Hawaii's insect population causes a decrease in bird populations.

38. The passage states that coquis often carry parasites called:

   F. nematodes.

   G. arthropods.

   H. scorpions.

   J. arachnids.

39. Which of the following statements best reflects the information provided in the passage about the relevance of the greenhouse frog to the discussion of the coqui?

   A. The greenhouse frog lives primarily indoors, whereas the coqui lives primarily in island rain forests.

   B. The greenhouse frog is less prominent than the coqui but can be equally damaging to the Hawaiian ecosystem.

   C. The greenhouse frog does not pose as dangerous a threat to the Hawaiian ecosystem as the coqui does.

   D. It is easier to locate and eliminate the coqui because the greenhouse frog does not produce loud mating calls.

40. The phrase "1,000 acres" (line 85) refers to which type of land in Hawaii?

   F. Caribbean ecosystem

   G. Bird sanctuary

   H. Rain forest

   J. Coqui habitat

END OF TEST 3.
STOP! DO NOT TURN THE PAGE UNTIL TOLD TO DO SO.
DO NOT RETURN TO A PREVIOUS TEST

SCIENCE REASONING TEST

35 Minutes—40 Questions

DIRECTIONS: There are seven passages in the following section. Each passage is followed by several questions. After reading a passage, choose the best answer to each question and blacken the corresponding oval on your answer sheet. You may refer to the passages as often as necessary.

You are NOT permitted to use a calculator on this test.

Passage I

A group of students studied the frictional forces involved on stationary objects.

In a series of experiments, the students used rectangular shaped objects of various materials that all had identical masses. One end of a plastic board coated with a polymer film was fastened to a table surface by a hinge so the angle θ between the board and table could be changed, as shown in Figure 1.

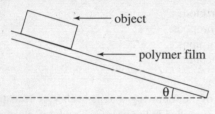

Figure 1

Objects were placed on the opposite end of the board, and the angle θ at which the object started to slide was recorded. The tangent of this angle represents the coefficient of static friction between the object and the polymer surface. This coefficient is proportional to the force required to move a stationary object. Higher coefficients mean that greater forces of friction must be overcome to initiate movement.

The dimensions of the objects gave them 3 distinct *faces* of unequal area as shown in Figure 2. Unless otherwise stated, the objects were placed on the ramp with Face A down.

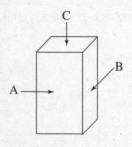

Figure 2

Experiment 1

Four objects made of different materials were placed on the ramp at a temperature of 25°C. The ramp was gradually raised and as soon as the object started to move, the angle θ of the ramp was recorded in Table 1.

Table 1	
Object material	θ (degrees)
Granite	12.1
Copper	16.8
Wood	22.0
Brick	31.1

Experiment 2

The procedure for Experiment 1 was repeated with the wooden object, varying which face was placed down on the ramp. Results were recorded in Table 2.

Table 2	
Face	θ (degrees)
A	22.0
B	22.0
C	22.0

GO ON TO THE NEXT PAGE.

Experiment 3

The procedure for Experiment 1 was repeated with the wooden object, varying the temperature of the polymer ramp. Results for 5 temperatures were recorded in Table 3.

Table 3	
Temperature (°C)	θ (degrees)
0	18.5
25	22.0
50	25.4
75	29.0
100	32.5

Experiment 4

The procedure for Experiment 1 was repeated with multiple wooden objects. For each trial, the objects were stacked on top of each other before raising the ramp. The angle θ where the stack started to slide was recorded in Table 4.

Table 4	
Number of objects	θ (degrees)
2	22.0
3	22.0
4	22.0

1. If the procedure used in Experiment 3 had been repeated at a temperature of 62.5°C, the angle required for the object to start moving down the ramp most likely would have been closest to which of the following?

   A. 27.2 degrees
   B. 29.2 degrees
   C. 30.3 degrees
   D. 31.4 degrees

2. Suppose the students had placed the 4 objects used in Experiment 1 on the ramp when it was flat and pushed each of the objects, such that the amount of force applied to each object gradually increased until it moved. Based on the results of Experiment 1, the object made of which material would most likely have taken the *greatest* amount of force to start moving?

   F. Brick
   G. Wood
   H. Copper
   J. Granite

3. Based on the results of Experiments 1 and 4, what was the effect, if any, of the weight of the object on the coefficient of static friction?

   A. The coefficient of static friction always increased as the object's weight increased.
   B. The coefficient of static friction always decreased as the object's weight increased.
   C. The coefficient of static friction increased and then decreased as the object's weight increased.
   D. The coefficient of static friction was not affected by the weight of the object.

4. In Experiment 1, the reason the students used objects made of different materials was most likely to vary the amount of frictional force between the:

   F. plastic board and the polymer surface.
   G. various objects and the polymer surface.
   H. objects made of different materials when brought into contact with each other.
   J. stacked objects, so that the objects would not fall over when the angle of the ramp was raised high enough to cause motion.

5. Which of the following ranks the different types of objects used, in order, from the material that presented the greatest resistance to movement to the material that presented the least resistance to movement?

   A. Granite, copper, wood, brick
   B. Copper, wood, granite, brick
   C. Granite, wood, brick, copper
   D. Brick, wood, copper, granite

6. The main purpose of Experiment 3 was to determine the effects of temperature on which of the following variables?

   F. Coefficient of static friction between wood and wood
   G. Coefficient of static friction between wood and polymer
   H. Mass of the wooden object
   J. Total frictional force of the polymer on all objects placed on the ramp

GO ON TO THE NEXT PAGE.

Passage II

Despite a global campaign since 1988 to eradicate *polio-myelitis* (polio), the virus that causes this disease continues to be endemic in four countries. This polio virus, which can exist as Type 1, Type 2, or Type 3, is most often transmitted through water that is contaminated by human waste. People can be immunized from this virus with a highly effective vaccine, which can be administered orally or by injection. Recent analyses of polio virus transmission have focused on the four polio-endemic countries India, Pakistan, Afghanistan, and Nigeria.

Study 1

In 2004, a temporary ban on polio vaccines was instituted in Nigeria in response to concerns that they were contaminated. Researchers reviewed World Health Organization (WHO) records to determine the number of Type 1 polio virus infections that were reported in Nigeria in 2004 and tallied their findings by month (see Figure 1). The World Health Organization has noted that in polio-endemic countries, official records underestimate the number of people actually infected, because numerous infected individuals do not report their symptoms to clinics or rely on local therapists who are not surveyed. In a polio-endemic country, for every person who has reported an infection, as many as ten people may actually be infected in the local population.

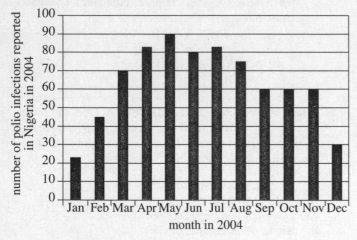

Figure 1

Study 2

Although polio eradication efforts have been most consistent in the urban areas of polio-endemic countries, these areas also have a high risk for a reemergence of polio, especially when the large urban populations are exposed to water contaminated with wastes that harbor the polio virus. In 2007, researchers analyzed the number of people who reported infections with Type 3 polio virus in the five largest cities in India. These cities were Mumbai in western India, New Delhi and Kolkata in northern India, and Chennai and Hyderabad in southern India. The analysis was undertaken in the months of June and August. June 2007 was chosen as a representative month for the dry summer season in India, during which there was minimal rainfall. August 2007 was chosen as a representative month for the wet monsoon season in India, during which there was daily rainfall. The results of the findings are shown in Figure 2.

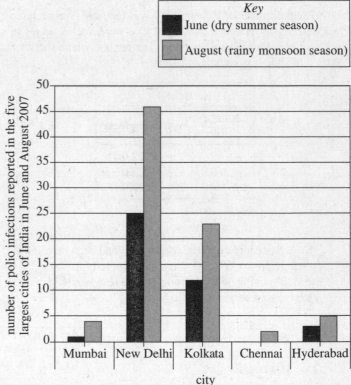

Figure 2

GO ON TO THE NEXT PAGE.

7. According to Figure 1, the greatest increase in the number of reported polio infections in Nigeria occurred between which two months?

   A. January and February
   B. February and March
   C. April and May
   D. November and December

8. It is estimated that for every person infected with the polio virus in an endemic country, there are 200 people at risk for contracting the virus. Given the results of Study 1, how many people would have been at risk for becoming infected with the polio virus in Nigeria in June 2004 ?

   F.   80
   G.   200
   H.   800
   J.   16,000

9. Given the information in Figure 2, which of the following might explain the difference in reported cases of polio in major Indian cities between June and August of 2007 ?

   A. Water is more likely to become contaminated with polio-infected human waste in periods of high rainfall.
   B. Water is less likely to become contaminated with polio-infected human waste in periods of high rainfall.
   C. The polio virus infects more people in India during the summer and monsoon seasons than during the autumn and winter seasons.
   D. Those diagnosed with the polio virus in June are able to recover by August.

10. Which of the following hypotheses was most likely tested in Study 2 ?

    F. The number of reported cases of polio infections varies significantly between Nigeria and India.
    G. Most cases of polio infections are not reported to medical authorities in India.
    H. Poliomyelitis infections affect more people in certain regions in India than in other regions.
    J. The number of reported cases of polio infections in India is greatest during the summer and least during the winter.

11. Polio-endemic countries are located in warm climates that harbor many mosquitoes. Would the presence of mosquitoes directly affect the transmission of the polio virus?

    A. Yes, because the polio virus is primarily transmitted through mosquitoes.
    B. Yes, because the polio virus is primarily transmitted through human waste.
    C. No, because the polio virus is primarily transmitted through mosquitoes.
    D. No, because the polio virus is primarily transmitted through human waste.

12. The comparison of reported polio infections in India in 2007, as shown in Figure 2, indicates that relative to the number of people in Kolkata infected with polio in June, the number of people infected with polio in Kolkata in August was approximately:

    F. half as much.
    G. the same.
    H. twice as much.
    J. ten times as much.

GO ON TO THE NEXT PAGE.

Passage III

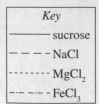

Osmotic pressure (Π) is the amount of pressure, in atm, required to maintain equilibrium of a solvent across a semipermeable membrane. At a constant temperature, osmotic pressure is dependent only on a solute's ability to dissociate or ionize in the solvent (*van 't Hoff factor*, *i*) and the concentration of solute particles. The osmotic pressure is determined by the equation:

$$\Pi = iMRT$$

M represents the concentration (in molarity, *M*), *R* is the ideal gas constant (0.0821 L atm mol^{-1} K^{-1}), and *T* (300 K) is the temperature in Kelvin (K). The value of *R* is assumed to be a constant for all osmotic pressure calculations.

The dissociation of a solute depends on its unique chemical properties. The van 't Hoff factors for some common substances are displayed in Table 1. Higher van 't Hoff factors correlate with greater dissociation or ionization. The effect of the van 't Hoff factor on the osmotic pressure may be seen in Figure 1.

Table 1	
Substance	van 't Hoff factor *
sucrose	1.0
NaCl	1.9
MgCl$_2$	2.7
FeCl$_3$	3.4
*Values at 300 K	

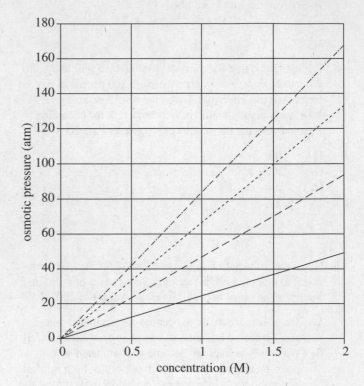

Figure 1

GO ON TO THE NEXT PAGE.

13. According to Figure 1, which of the following solutions would exhibit the *least* osmotic pressure?

    A. 1.0 M $FeCl_3$ solution
    B. 1.0 M $MgCl_2$ solution
    C. 2.0 M NaCl solution
    D. 2.0 M sucrose solution

14. If 1.0 M solutions of various solutes were prepared, which of the following solutions would have the highest level of ionization?

    F. Sucrose
    G. NaCl
    H. $MgCl_2$
    J. $FeCl_3$

15. Which of the following solutions would exhibit the closest osmotic pressure to that of a 1.5 M NaCl solution at 300 K, if the gas constant is 0.0821 L atm/ mol^{-1} K^{-1} ?

    A. 1.0 M NaBr solution ($i = 1.9$)
    B. 2.0 M NaBr solution ($i = 1.9$)
    C. 2.9 M Glucose solution ($i = 1.0$)
    D. 3.5 M Glucose solution ($i = 1.0$)

16. Based on Figure 1, as the concentration of solute decreases, the pressure required to hold solvent concentration across a membrane at equilibrium will:

    F. increase only.
    G. decrease only.
    H. remain constant.
    J. increase, then remain constant.

17. A scientist recently discovered a compound that ionizes readily in solution ($i = 3.8$) and results in low osmotic pressures. Are the findings of this scientist consistent with Figure 1 ?

    A. Yes, because $FeCl_3$ causes higher osmotic pressure than sucrose.
    B. No, because sucrose causes higher osmotic pressure than $FeCl_3$.
    C. Yes, because $FeCl_3$ causes lower osmotic pressure than sucrose.
    D. No, because sucrose causes lower osmotic pressure than $FeCl_3$.

GO ON TO THE NEXT PAGE.

Passage IV

Soil salinity is the concentration of potentially harmful salts dissolved in the groundwater that fills soil pores. Salinity is determined by measuring a soil's *electrical conductivity (EC)* and *exchangeable sodium percentage (ESP)*. High EC indicates a high concentration of dissolved salt particles; ESP indicates the proportion of electrical conductivity that is due to dissolved sodium ions.

Soil samples were collected from five different distances west of a particular river. Figure 1 shows the electrical conductivity of the soil samples at four different depth ranges measured in milli-Siemens per centimeter (mS/cm).

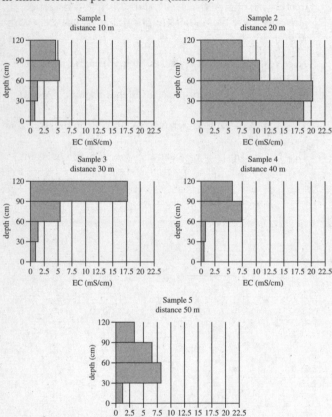

Figure 1

Figure 2 shows the exchangeable sodium percentage of the five sites at different depths.

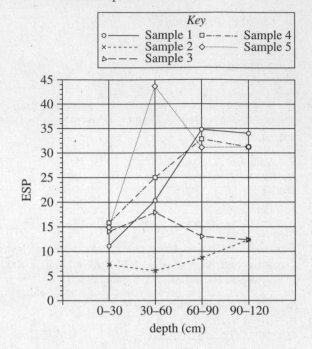

Figure 2

18. Figure 2 indicates that, compared with the soil tested in Sample 1, the soil tested in Sample 4 contains:

    F. a higher percentage of sodium ions throughout.
    G. a lower percentage of sodium ions throughout.
    H. a higher percentage of sodium ions at shallower depths only.
    J. a lower percentage of sodium ions at shallower depths only.

19. According to Figure 2, in the soil collected in Sample 3 at a depth of 30–60 cm, approximately what percent of the soil conductivity is due to sodium ions?

    A. 14%
    B. 17%
    C. 24%
    D. 44%

20. Based on Figures 1 and 2, the electrical conductivity due to sodium ions in the sample collected 40 m west of the river was:

    F. greatest at a depth of 90–120 cm.
    G. greatest at a depth of 0–30 cm.
    H. least at a depth of 30–60 cm.
    J. least at a depth of 0–30 cm.

GO ON TO THE NEXT PAGE.

21. Based on Figure 2, which of the following figures best represents the exchangeable sodium percentage for the five soil samples collected at a depth of 90–120 cm?

A.

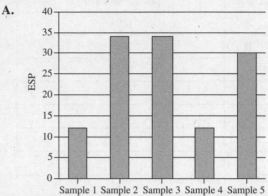

B.

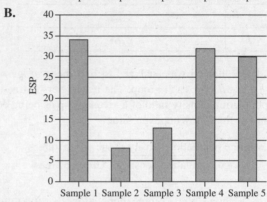

C.

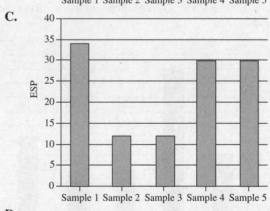

D.

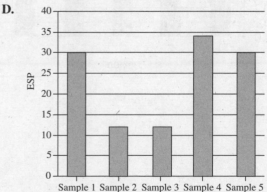

22. A student claimed that as soil moves away from a major water source, such as a river, the salinity of the soil increases. Is this claim supported by Figures 1 and 2 ?

F. No; the electrical conductivity and exchangeable sodium percentage both decreased from Sample 1 to Sample 5.

G. No; there was no consistent trend for electrical conductivity and exchangeable sodium percentage.

H. Yes; the electrical conductivity and exchangeable sodium percentage both increased from Sample 1 to Sample 5.

J. Yes; the electrical conductivity increased and exchangeable sodium percentage decreased from Sample 1 to Sample 5.

GO ON TO THE NEXT PAGE.

Passage V

A group of researchers performed the following study in order to investigate declines in primarily carnivorous polar bear populations in the Arctic over a 10-year period.

Study

The researchers obtained previously collected data from several areas previously identified as polar bear habitats. From this data, the researchers selected sixty 5 km × 5 km blocks that do not overlap with one another. The blocks were selected to fall into six groups, each with a different set of conditions selected in order to conform to criteria for listing animals as threatened species. Previous research has indicated that Arctic sea ice and available food are among the factors which may affect polar bear populations.

Table 1 identifies each of the groups utilized in the study. Conditions other than the ones listed were considered to be normal.

Table 1	
Group	Conditions
1	These areas had significantly decreased populations of marine mammals consumed by polar bears.
2	These areas had significantly increased populations of seaweed commonly consumed by marine mammals.
3	These areas had been subject to excess thawing of Arctic sea ice.
4	These areas were subject to the same conditions as Groups 1 and 3.
5	These areas were subject to the same conditions as Groups 2 and 3.
6	Unaffected polar bear habitat.

Data for each of the plots was collected, and the population density of polar bears was calculated in terms of adult polar bears/km^2. Table 2 shows the population density of the blocks in Group 6.

Table 2	
Area Label	Population density of Group 6 areas (polar bears/km^2)
A	0.93
B	2.10
C	0.21
D	0.72
E	0.88
F	0.72
G	0.91
H	0.53
I	1.12
J	0.74

The data collected was analyzed to find the *average population density ratio* for each group. The researchers defined the average population density ratio of a given group as being equal to the result of the following expression:

$$\frac{\text{average population density of the group's areas}}{\text{average population density of Group 6 areas}}$$

Figure 1 shows the average population density ratio of Groups 1–5.

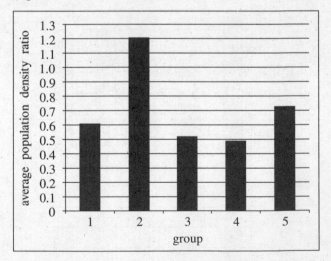

Figure 1

23. Which of the following statements provides the best explanation for why the researchers collected data for Group 6 in their study?

A. Group 6 provided data indicating the types of predators which most threaten polar bears in their natural habitat.
B. Group 6 provided a standard by which the other groups could be compared in order to determine how each set of conditions affected polar bear populations.
C. Group 6 provided a means by which the researchers could carefully identify and select the conditions for the remaining five groups.
D. Group 6 provided a means of determining the greatest number of polar bears that would be likely to survive in an area of 25 km².

24. Which one of the following is a question that most likely explains why Group 2 areas were included in the study?

F. Does an increase in the food source of their prey affect the population density of polar bears?
G. If additional masses of seaweed were to be introduced to the Arctic, would polar bears be increasingly omnivorous?
H. If additional masses of seaweed were to be introduced to the Arctic, would prey population density increase?
J. Does an increase in the number of prey animals living in the same area as polar bears affect the amount of Arctic ice?

25. Which of the following correctly ranks Groups 1–5 from the group where the conditions are *most* conducive to polar bear population density in the study to the group where the conditions are *least* conducive?

A. Group 1, Group 2, Group 3, Group 4, Group 5
B. Group 4, Group 3, Group 1, Group 5, Group 2
C. Group 2, Group 5, Group 1, Group 3, Group 4
D. Group 2, Group 1, Group 5, Group 3, Group 4

26. Which of the following is most likely an organism that the researchers identified as exhibiting a significantly decreased population when defining Group 1 ?

F. Snowy owl
G. Seal
H. Salmon
J. Polar bear

27. *Synergy* between two effects is said to exist when their combined effect is greater than the sum of each effect considered separately. The study appears to be designed such that the researchers can investigate possible synergy in which of the following two groups?

A. Groups 1 and 2
B. Groups 1 and 4
C. Groups 4 and 5
D. Groups 1 and 3

28. Before performing their analysis of the data, the researchers developed four different hypotheses. Each one of the four hypotheses below is supported by the results of the study EXCEPT:

F. Declining prey populations have had some effect on polar bear populations.
G. The melting of Arctic sea ice has a greater effect on polar bear populations than declining prey populations.
H. Declining prey populations have a greater effect on polar bear populations than the melting of Arctic sea ice.
J. The melting of Arctic sea ice has had some effect on polar bear populations.

GO ON TO THE NEXT PAGE.

Passage VI

Methane (CH_4) is an important energy source and a powerful greenhouse gas. CH_4 levels in the atmosphere are increasing, largely as a result of increasing livestock populations and energy emissions. Two scientists debate possible consequences of rising levels of atmospheric methane.

Scientist 1

Increasing CH_4 levels are a serious concern because, in the atmosphere, CH_4 can be converted into *formaldehyde* (H_2CO). H_2CO is a dangerous chemical, banned in some countries and used as an embalming fluid in others.

When *ozone* (O_3) is struck by solar radiation (light) in the presence of water, *hydroxyl radicals* ($\cdot OH$) are created (Reaction 1):

$$light + O_3 + H_2O \rightarrow 2 \cdot OH + O_2$$

When OH comes into contact with CH_4, another radical, $\cdot CH_3$, is formed (Reaction 2):

$$OH + CH_4 \rightarrow \cdot CH_3 + H_2O$$

In the presence of oxygen (O_2) and nitric oxide (NO), the highly reactive $\cdot CH_3$ is converted into H_2CO (Reaction 3):

$$\cdot CH_3 + NO + 2O_2 \rightarrow H_2CO + NO_2 + HO_2$$

The product HO_2 is unstable and reacts with NO, yielding more $\cdot OH$ (Reaction 4):

$$HO_2 + NO \rightarrow NO_2 + \cdot OH$$

Together, Reactions 2–4 are called a *chain reaction* because the OH formed in Reaction 4 can react with another CH_4 molecule in Reaction 2:

$$\cdot OH + CH_4 \rightarrow \cdot CH_3 + H_2O$$

$$\cdot CH_3 + NO + 2O_2 \rightarrow H_2CO + NO_2 + HO_2$$

$$HO_2 + NO \rightarrow NO_2 + \cdot OH$$

As a result, one $\cdot OH$ can convert a great deal of CH_4. At current CH_4 levels, this chain reaction is the primary fate of atmospheric $\cdot OH$, making the formation of H_2CO an urgent concern.

Scientist 2

H_2CO is a dangerous chemical, but atmospheric formaldehyde levels will not increase dramatically due to methane emissions. *Carbon monoxide* (CO) generation may be the greater concern. Hydroxyl radicals can break down methane, leading to the formation of H_2CO and nitric oxide, as in Reactions 1–4; in the presence of light, however, H_2CO quickly decomposes to CO and *hydrogen,* H_2 (Reaction 5):

$$H_2CO \rightarrow H_2 + CO$$

Furthermore, the OH generated by Reactions 1 and 4 will react rapidly with any H_2CO in the atmosphere to produce CO and water: (Reaction 6)

$$H_2CO + 2 \cdot OH \rightarrow CO + 2H_2O$$

In addition to reducing the amount of H_2CO by breaking down the H_2CO molecule, this reaction removes OH from the atmosphere, inhibiting the chain reaction of Reactions 2–4.

29. Which of the following substances do the two scientists agree must be present in order for $\cdot CH_3$ to be generated by atmospheric methane?

   A. H_3O^+
   B. NO_2
   C. HNO_3
   D. O_3

GO ON TO THE NEXT PAGE.

30. Which of the following graphs reflects Scientist 1's hypothesis of how levels of H_2CO in the atmosphere will change as more CH_4 is released into the atmosphere?

F.

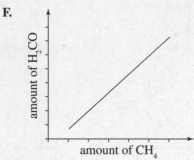

G.

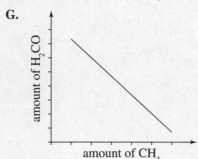

H.

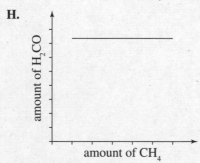

J.

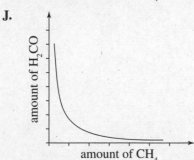

31. A student suggested that the molecular mass of either product in Reaction 5 would be greater than the molecular mass of the reactant in Reaction 5. Is he correct?

A. No; H_2CO is composed not of molecules, but of atoms.
B. Yes; the mass of a molecule of H_2CO is greater than the mass of either reactant.
C. No; the mass of a molecule of H_2CO is greater than the mass of either product.
D. Yes; the mass of a molecule of CO is greater than the mass of a molecule of H_2.

32. In certain parts of the atmosphere, the amount of O_3 is decreasing. As O_3 levels decrease, which of the following would Scientist 1 *most strongly agree with* regarding the levels of $\cdot CH_3$ and H_2CO in the atmosphere?

F. The amount of $\cdot CH_3$ would increase and the amount of H_2CO would decrease.
G. The amount of $\cdot CH_3$ would decrease and the level of H_2CO would remain constant.
H. The amounts of $\cdot CH_3$ and H_2CO would both decrease.
J. The amounts of $\cdot CH_3$ and H_2CO would both increase.

33. Of the following statements, with which would Scientist 2 *most strongly disagree*?

A. O_3 is involved in the generation of H_2CO in the atmosphere.
B. $\cdot OH$ is contributing to the formation of carbon monoxide in the atmosphere.
C. Solar radiation contributes to the break down of CH_4.
D. As CH_4 emissions increase, levels of H_2CO will rise dramatically.

34. After examining Scientist 1's hypothesis, Scientist 2 claimed that Reaction 3 would lead to increased levels of carbon monoxide. By which of the following explanations would Scientist 2 most likely support this argument?

F. Reaction 3 reduces the amount of NO present, inhibiting Reaction 4.
G. Reaction 3 produces H_2CO, which can react in Reaction 5 and Reaction 6.
H. Reaction 3 produces HO_2, which can react with H_2CO to produce CO.
J. Reaction 3 reduces the amount of O_2 present, making it more difficult for CO to form.

35. Further investigation has shown that Reaction 6 occurs on a large scale. Which of the following statements explains how the new evidence *most* weakens the argument of Scientist 1 ?

A. The OH produced in Reaction 4 reacts with CH_4.
B. The OH produced in Reaction 4 reacts with H_2CO.
C. The H_2O produced in Reaction 6 reacts with light and O_3.
D. The OH produced in Reaction 6 reacts with H_2CO.

GO ON TO THE NEXT PAGE.

Passage VII

A *Carnot heat engine* is an engine which runs by compressing and expanding a gas and transferring heat.

Figures 1 and 2 show the changes in pressure, P, and volume, V, that occur as two Carnot heat engines, A and B, run. For every gas, $PV = \Omega T$, where Ω is a constant and T represents the time.

The cycle begins as the gas is at its highest temperature and pressure. First, the gas expands, so volume increases while pressure decreases. As the gas expands, it can do work, such as pushing a piston. After the gas has run out of thermal energy and can no longer do work it is at its lowest temperature and pressure and the gas begins to be compressed, for instance a piston falling back down on the gas. As the gas is compressed, pressure increases while volume decreases and temperature begins to rise. In every Carnot heat engine, the gas ends at the same pressure, temperature, and volume as it began, thus completing a cycle.

Carnot Heat Engine B

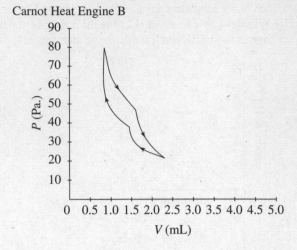

Figure 2

Carnot Heat Engine A

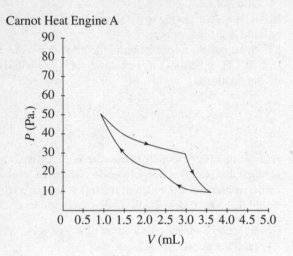

Figure 1

36. According to Figure 2, for Carnot heat engine B, when V was decreasing from its largest value and had a value of 1.5 mL, P had a value closest to:

F. 10 Pa.
G. 30 Pa.
H. 50 Pa.
J. 70 Pa.

GO ON TO THE NEXT PAGE.

37. For a new Carnot heat engine, F, a partial graph of V versus P is obtained.

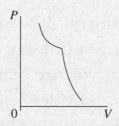

If Carnot heat engine F behaves like Carnot heat engines A and B, the remainder of the graph of V versus P for Carnot heat engine F will look most like which of the following?

A.

C.
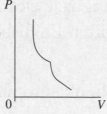

B.
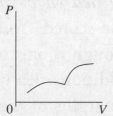

D.
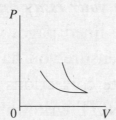

38. For Carnot heat engine A, the minimum value of P was obtained at a V closest to:

F. 0.5 mL.
G. 2.0 mL.
H. 3.5 mL.
J. 5.0 mL.

39. Consider the largest value of V and the smallest value of V on the graph in Figure 2. How are these values related?

A. The smallest value of V is –1 times the largest value of V.

B. The smallest value of V is 1/3 times the largest value of V.

C. The smallest value of V is 1 times the largest value of V.

D. The smallest value of V is 2 times the largest value of V.

40. The *reversible isothermal expansion* step of a Carnot heat engine cycle takes place when P is decreased from its highest value and V is increased from its lowest value. According to Figure 1, the *reversible isothermal expansion* step for Carnot heat engine A begins when V is closest to:

F. 1.0 mL.
G. 2.25 mL.
H. 3.0 mL.
J. 3.5 mL.

END OF TEST 4
STOP! DO NOT RETURN TO ANY OTHER TEST.

Directions

This is a test of your writing skills. You will have thirty (30) minutes to write an essay. Before you begin planning and writing your essay, read the writing prompt carefully to understand exactly what you are being asked to do. Your essay will be evaluated on the evidence it provides of your ability to express judgments by taking a position on the issue in the writing prompt; to maintain a focus on the topic throughout your essay; to develop a position by using logical reasoning and by supporting your ideas; to organize ideas in a logical way; and to use language clearly and effectively according to the conventions of standard written English.

You may use the unlined pages in this test booklet to plan your essay. These pages will not be scored. *You must write your essay on the lined pages in the answer folder.* Your writing on those lined pages will be scored. You may not need all the lined pages, but to ensure you have enough room to finish, do NOT skip lines. You may write corrections or additions neatly between the lines of your essay, but do NOT write in the margins of the lined pages. *Illegible essays cannot be scored, so you must write (or print) clearly.*

If you finish before time is called, you may review your work. Lay your pencil down immediately when time is called.

DO NOT OPEN THIS BOOK UNTIL YOU ARE TOLD TO DO SO.

ACT Assessment Writing Test Prompt

A number of health organizations are lobbying the Motion Picture Association of America (MPAA) to incorporate cigarette smoking into the criteria for a restricted, or R, rating for films. Since the R rating requires anyone under the age of 17 to be accompanied by a parent or guardian, supporters of this policy believe it would reduce the exposure youths may have to smoking as a glamorous habit and make these teens less likely to smoke as a result. Opponents of the policy believe it would curtail the creative freedom of the filmmakers. In your opinion, should movies be rated R if they contain cigarette smoking?

In your essay, take a position on this question. You may write about either one of the two points of view given, or you may present a different point of view on this question. Use specific reasons and examples to support your position.

ACT Diagnostic Test Form

1. **YOUR NAME:** _____
   (Print)   Last   First   M.I.

SIGNATURE: _____   **DATE:** _____ / _____ / _____

HOME ADDRESS: _____
(Print)   Number and Street

_____
City   State   Zip

E-MAIL: _____

PHONE NO.: _____
(Print)

SCHOOL: _____

CLASS OF: _____

> **IMPORTANT:** Please fill in these boxes exactly as shown on the back cover of your tests book.

2. TEST FORM

_____

3. TEST CODE

⓪	⓪	⓪	⓪
①	①	①	①
②	②	②	②
③	③	③	③
④	④	④	④
⑤	⑤	⑤	⑤
⑥	⑥	⑥	⑥
⑦	⑦	⑦	⑦
⑧	⑧	⑧	⑧
⑨	⑨	⑨	⑨

4. PHONE NUMBER

⓪	⓪	⓪	⓪	⓪	⓪	⓪
①	①	①	①	①	①	①
②	②	②	②	②	②	②
③	③	③	③	③	③	③
④	④	④	④	④	④	④
⑤	⑤	⑤	⑤	⑤	⑤	⑤
⑥	⑥	⑥	⑥	⑥	⑥	⑥
⑦	⑦	⑦	⑦	⑦	⑦	⑦
⑧	⑧	⑧	⑧	⑧	⑧	⑧
⑨	⑨	⑨	⑨	⑨	⑨	⑨

5. YOUR NAME

First 4 letters of last name				FIRST INIT	MID INIT
Ⓐ	Ⓐ	Ⓐ	Ⓐ	Ⓐ	Ⓐ
Ⓑ	Ⓑ	Ⓑ	Ⓑ	Ⓑ	Ⓑ
Ⓒ	Ⓒ	Ⓒ	Ⓒ	Ⓒ	Ⓒ
Ⓓ	Ⓓ	Ⓓ	Ⓓ	Ⓓ	Ⓓ
Ⓔ	Ⓔ	Ⓔ	Ⓔ	Ⓔ	Ⓔ
Ⓕ	Ⓕ	Ⓕ	Ⓕ	Ⓕ	Ⓕ
Ⓖ	Ⓖ	Ⓖ	Ⓖ	Ⓖ	Ⓖ
Ⓗ	Ⓗ	Ⓗ	Ⓗ	Ⓗ	Ⓗ
Ⓘ	Ⓘ	Ⓘ	Ⓘ	Ⓘ	Ⓘ
Ⓙ	Ⓙ	Ⓙ	Ⓙ	Ⓙ	Ⓙ
Ⓚ	Ⓚ	Ⓚ	Ⓚ	Ⓚ	Ⓚ
Ⓛ	Ⓛ	Ⓛ	Ⓛ	Ⓛ	Ⓛ
Ⓜ	Ⓜ	Ⓜ	Ⓜ	Ⓜ	Ⓜ
Ⓝ	Ⓝ	Ⓝ	Ⓝ	Ⓝ	Ⓝ
Ⓞ	Ⓞ	Ⓞ	Ⓞ	Ⓞ	Ⓞ
Ⓟ	Ⓟ	Ⓟ	Ⓟ	Ⓟ	Ⓟ
Ⓠ	Ⓠ	Ⓠ	Ⓠ	Ⓠ	Ⓠ
Ⓡ	Ⓡ	Ⓡ	Ⓡ	Ⓡ	Ⓡ
Ⓢ	Ⓢ	Ⓢ	Ⓢ	Ⓢ	Ⓢ
Ⓣ	Ⓣ	Ⓣ	Ⓣ	Ⓣ	Ⓣ
Ⓤ	Ⓤ	Ⓤ	Ⓤ	Ⓤ	Ⓤ
Ⓥ	Ⓥ	Ⓥ	Ⓥ	Ⓥ	Ⓥ
Ⓦ	Ⓦ	Ⓦ	Ⓦ	Ⓦ	Ⓦ
Ⓧ	Ⓧ	Ⓧ	Ⓧ	Ⓧ	Ⓧ
Ⓨ	Ⓨ	Ⓨ	Ⓨ	Ⓨ	Ⓨ
Ⓩ	Ⓩ	Ⓩ	Ⓩ	Ⓩ	Ⓩ

6. DATE OF BIRTH

MONTH	DAY		YEAR	
○ JAN				
○ FEB				
○ MAR	⓪	⓪	⓪	⓪
○ APR	①	①	①	①
○ MAY	②	②	②	②
○ JUN	③	③	③	③
○ JUL		④	④	④
○ AUG		⑤	⑤	⑤
○ SEP		⑥	⑥	⑥
○ OCT		⑦	⑦	⑦
○ NOV		⑧	⑧	⑧
○ DEC		⑨	⑨	⑨

7. SEX

○ MALE
○ FEMALE

8. OTHER

1 Ⓐ Ⓑ Ⓒ Ⓓ Ⓔ
2 Ⓐ Ⓑ Ⓒ Ⓓ Ⓔ
3 Ⓐ Ⓑ Ⓒ Ⓓ Ⓔ

OpScan iNSIGHT™ forms by Pearson NCS EM-255315-1:654321   Printed in U.S.A.

THIS PAGE INTENTIONALLY LEFT BLANK

The Princeton Review
Diagnostic ACT Form

ENGLISH

1 Ⓐ Ⓑ Ⓒ Ⓓ	21 Ⓐ Ⓑ Ⓒ Ⓓ	41 Ⓐ Ⓑ Ⓒ Ⓓ	61 Ⓐ Ⓑ Ⓒ Ⓓ
2 Ⓕ Ⓖ Ⓗ Ⓙ	22 Ⓕ Ⓖ Ⓗ Ⓙ	42 Ⓕ Ⓖ Ⓗ Ⓙ	62 Ⓕ Ⓖ Ⓗ Ⓙ
3 Ⓐ Ⓑ Ⓒ Ⓓ	23 Ⓐ Ⓑ Ⓒ Ⓓ	43 Ⓐ Ⓑ Ⓒ Ⓓ	63 Ⓐ Ⓑ Ⓒ Ⓓ
4 Ⓕ Ⓖ Ⓗ Ⓙ	24 Ⓕ Ⓖ Ⓗ Ⓙ	44 Ⓕ Ⓖ Ⓗ Ⓙ	64 Ⓕ Ⓖ Ⓗ Ⓙ
5 Ⓐ Ⓑ Ⓒ Ⓓ	25 Ⓐ Ⓑ Ⓒ Ⓓ	45 Ⓐ Ⓑ Ⓒ Ⓓ	65 Ⓐ Ⓑ Ⓒ Ⓓ
6 Ⓕ Ⓖ Ⓗ Ⓙ	26 Ⓕ Ⓖ Ⓗ Ⓙ	46 Ⓕ Ⓖ Ⓗ Ⓙ	66 Ⓕ Ⓖ Ⓗ Ⓙ
7 Ⓐ Ⓑ Ⓒ Ⓓ	27 Ⓐ Ⓑ Ⓒ Ⓓ	47 Ⓐ Ⓑ Ⓒ Ⓓ	67 Ⓐ Ⓑ Ⓒ Ⓓ
8 Ⓕ Ⓖ Ⓗ Ⓙ	28 Ⓕ Ⓖ Ⓗ Ⓙ	48 Ⓕ Ⓖ Ⓗ Ⓙ	68 Ⓕ Ⓖ Ⓗ Ⓙ
9 Ⓐ Ⓑ Ⓒ Ⓓ	29 Ⓐ Ⓑ Ⓒ Ⓓ	49 Ⓐ Ⓑ Ⓒ Ⓓ	69 Ⓐ Ⓑ Ⓒ Ⓓ
10 Ⓕ Ⓖ Ⓗ Ⓙ	30 Ⓕ Ⓖ Ⓗ Ⓙ	50 Ⓕ Ⓖ Ⓗ Ⓙ	70 Ⓕ Ⓖ Ⓗ Ⓙ
11 Ⓐ Ⓑ Ⓒ Ⓓ	31 Ⓐ Ⓑ Ⓒ Ⓓ	51 Ⓐ Ⓑ Ⓒ Ⓓ	71 Ⓐ Ⓑ Ⓒ Ⓓ
12 Ⓕ Ⓖ Ⓗ Ⓙ	32 Ⓕ Ⓖ Ⓗ Ⓙ	52 Ⓕ Ⓖ Ⓗ Ⓙ	72 Ⓕ Ⓖ Ⓗ Ⓙ
13 Ⓐ Ⓑ Ⓒ Ⓓ	33 Ⓐ Ⓑ Ⓒ Ⓓ	53 Ⓐ Ⓑ Ⓒ Ⓓ	73 Ⓐ Ⓑ Ⓒ Ⓓ
14 Ⓕ Ⓖ Ⓗ Ⓙ	34 Ⓕ Ⓖ Ⓗ Ⓙ	54 Ⓕ Ⓖ Ⓗ Ⓙ	74 Ⓕ Ⓖ Ⓗ Ⓙ
15 Ⓐ Ⓑ Ⓒ Ⓓ	35 Ⓐ Ⓑ Ⓒ Ⓓ	55 Ⓐ Ⓑ Ⓒ Ⓓ	75 Ⓐ Ⓑ Ⓒ Ⓓ
16 Ⓕ Ⓖ Ⓗ Ⓙ	36 Ⓕ Ⓖ Ⓗ Ⓙ	56 Ⓕ Ⓖ Ⓗ Ⓙ	
17 Ⓐ Ⓑ Ⓒ Ⓓ	37 Ⓐ Ⓑ Ⓒ Ⓓ	57 Ⓐ Ⓑ Ⓒ Ⓓ	
18 Ⓕ Ⓖ Ⓗ Ⓙ	38 Ⓕ Ⓖ Ⓗ Ⓙ	58 Ⓕ Ⓖ Ⓗ Ⓙ	
19 Ⓐ Ⓑ Ⓒ Ⓓ	39 Ⓐ Ⓑ Ⓒ Ⓓ	59 Ⓐ Ⓑ Ⓒ Ⓓ	
20 Ⓕ Ⓖ Ⓗ Ⓙ	40 Ⓕ Ⓖ Ⓗ Ⓙ	60 Ⓕ Ⓖ Ⓗ Ⓙ	

MATHEMATICS

1 Ⓐ Ⓑ Ⓒ Ⓓ Ⓔ	16 Ⓕ Ⓖ Ⓗ Ⓙ Ⓚ	31 Ⓐ Ⓑ Ⓒ Ⓓ Ⓔ	46 Ⓕ Ⓖ Ⓗ Ⓙ Ⓚ
2 Ⓕ Ⓖ Ⓗ Ⓙ Ⓚ	17 Ⓐ Ⓑ Ⓒ Ⓓ Ⓔ	32 Ⓕ Ⓖ Ⓗ Ⓙ Ⓚ	47 Ⓐ Ⓑ Ⓒ Ⓓ Ⓔ
3 Ⓐ Ⓑ Ⓒ Ⓓ Ⓔ	18 Ⓕ Ⓖ Ⓗ Ⓙ Ⓚ	33 Ⓐ Ⓑ Ⓒ Ⓓ Ⓔ	48 Ⓕ Ⓖ Ⓗ Ⓙ Ⓚ
4 Ⓕ Ⓖ Ⓗ Ⓙ Ⓚ	19 Ⓐ Ⓑ Ⓒ Ⓓ Ⓔ	34 Ⓕ Ⓖ Ⓗ Ⓙ Ⓚ	49 Ⓐ Ⓑ Ⓒ Ⓓ Ⓔ
5 Ⓐ Ⓑ Ⓒ Ⓓ Ⓔ	20 Ⓕ Ⓖ Ⓗ Ⓙ Ⓚ	35 Ⓐ Ⓑ Ⓒ Ⓓ Ⓔ	50 Ⓕ Ⓖ Ⓗ Ⓙ Ⓚ
6 Ⓕ Ⓖ Ⓗ Ⓙ Ⓚ	21 Ⓐ Ⓑ Ⓒ Ⓓ Ⓔ	36 Ⓕ Ⓖ Ⓗ Ⓙ Ⓚ	51 Ⓐ Ⓑ Ⓒ Ⓓ Ⓔ
7 Ⓐ Ⓑ Ⓒ Ⓓ Ⓔ	22 Ⓕ Ⓖ Ⓗ Ⓙ Ⓚ	37 Ⓐ Ⓑ Ⓒ Ⓓ Ⓔ	52 Ⓕ Ⓖ Ⓗ Ⓙ Ⓚ
8 Ⓕ Ⓖ Ⓗ Ⓙ Ⓚ	23 Ⓐ Ⓑ Ⓒ Ⓓ Ⓔ	38 Ⓕ Ⓖ Ⓗ Ⓙ Ⓚ	53 Ⓐ Ⓑ Ⓒ Ⓓ Ⓔ
9 Ⓐ Ⓑ Ⓒ Ⓓ Ⓔ	24 Ⓕ Ⓖ Ⓗ Ⓙ Ⓚ	39 Ⓐ Ⓑ Ⓒ Ⓓ Ⓔ	54 Ⓕ Ⓖ Ⓗ Ⓙ Ⓚ
10 Ⓕ Ⓖ Ⓗ Ⓙ Ⓚ	25 Ⓐ Ⓑ Ⓒ Ⓓ Ⓔ	40 Ⓕ Ⓖ Ⓗ Ⓙ Ⓚ	55 Ⓐ Ⓑ Ⓒ Ⓓ Ⓔ
11 Ⓐ Ⓑ Ⓒ Ⓓ Ⓔ	26 Ⓕ Ⓖ Ⓗ Ⓙ Ⓚ	41 Ⓐ Ⓑ Ⓒ Ⓓ Ⓔ	56 Ⓕ Ⓖ Ⓗ Ⓙ Ⓚ
12 Ⓕ Ⓖ Ⓗ Ⓙ Ⓚ	27 Ⓐ Ⓑ Ⓒ Ⓓ Ⓔ	42 Ⓕ Ⓖ Ⓗ Ⓙ Ⓚ	57 Ⓐ Ⓑ Ⓒ Ⓓ Ⓔ
13 Ⓐ Ⓑ Ⓒ Ⓓ Ⓔ	28 Ⓕ Ⓖ Ⓗ Ⓙ Ⓚ	43 Ⓐ Ⓑ Ⓒ Ⓓ Ⓔ	58 Ⓕ Ⓖ Ⓗ Ⓙ Ⓚ
14 Ⓕ Ⓖ Ⓗ Ⓙ Ⓚ	29 Ⓐ Ⓑ Ⓒ Ⓓ Ⓔ	44 Ⓕ Ⓖ Ⓗ Ⓙ Ⓚ	59 Ⓐ Ⓑ Ⓒ Ⓓ Ⓔ
15 Ⓐ Ⓑ Ⓒ Ⓓ Ⓔ	30 Ⓕ Ⓖ Ⓗ Ⓙ Ⓚ	45 Ⓐ Ⓑ Ⓒ Ⓓ Ⓔ	60 Ⓕ Ⓖ Ⓗ Ⓙ Ⓚ

The Princeton Review
Diagnostic ACT Form

READING

1 Ⓐ Ⓑ Ⓒ Ⓓ				11 Ⓐ Ⓑ Ⓒ Ⓓ				21 Ⓐ Ⓑ Ⓒ Ⓓ				31 Ⓐ Ⓑ Ⓒ Ⓓ		
2 Ⓕ Ⓖ Ⓗ Ⓙ				12 Ⓕ Ⓖ Ⓗ Ⓙ				22 Ⓕ Ⓖ Ⓗ Ⓙ				32 Ⓕ Ⓖ Ⓗ Ⓙ		
3 Ⓐ Ⓑ Ⓒ Ⓓ				13 Ⓐ Ⓑ Ⓒ Ⓓ				23 Ⓐ Ⓑ Ⓒ Ⓓ				33 Ⓐ Ⓑ Ⓒ Ⓓ		
4 Ⓕ Ⓖ Ⓗ Ⓙ				14 Ⓕ Ⓖ Ⓗ Ⓙ				24 Ⓕ Ⓖ Ⓗ Ⓙ				34 Ⓕ Ⓖ Ⓗ Ⓙ		
5 Ⓐ Ⓑ Ⓒ Ⓓ				15 Ⓐ Ⓑ Ⓒ Ⓓ				25 Ⓐ Ⓑ Ⓒ Ⓓ				35 Ⓐ Ⓑ Ⓒ Ⓓ		
6 Ⓕ Ⓖ Ⓗ Ⓙ				16 Ⓕ Ⓖ Ⓗ Ⓙ				26 Ⓕ Ⓖ Ⓗ Ⓙ				36 Ⓕ Ⓖ Ⓗ Ⓙ		
7 Ⓐ Ⓑ Ⓒ Ⓓ				17 Ⓐ Ⓑ Ⓒ Ⓓ				27 Ⓐ Ⓑ Ⓒ Ⓓ				37 Ⓐ Ⓑ Ⓒ Ⓓ		
8 Ⓕ Ⓖ Ⓗ Ⓙ				18 Ⓕ Ⓖ Ⓗ Ⓙ				28 Ⓕ Ⓖ Ⓗ Ⓙ				38 Ⓕ Ⓖ Ⓗ Ⓙ		
9 Ⓐ Ⓑ Ⓒ Ⓓ				19 Ⓐ Ⓑ Ⓒ Ⓓ				29 Ⓐ Ⓑ Ⓒ Ⓓ				39 Ⓐ Ⓑ Ⓒ Ⓓ		
10 Ⓕ Ⓖ Ⓗ Ⓙ				20 Ⓕ Ⓖ Ⓗ Ⓙ				30 Ⓕ Ⓖ Ⓗ Ⓙ				40 Ⓕ Ⓖ Ⓗ Ⓙ		

SCIENCE REASONING

1 Ⓐ Ⓑ Ⓒ Ⓓ				11 Ⓐ Ⓑ Ⓒ Ⓓ				21 Ⓐ Ⓑ Ⓒ Ⓓ				31 Ⓐ Ⓑ Ⓒ Ⓓ		
2 Ⓕ Ⓖ Ⓗ Ⓙ				12 Ⓕ Ⓖ Ⓗ Ⓙ				22 Ⓕ Ⓖ Ⓗ Ⓙ				32 Ⓕ Ⓖ Ⓗ Ⓙ		
3 Ⓐ Ⓑ Ⓒ Ⓓ				13 Ⓐ Ⓑ Ⓒ Ⓓ				23 Ⓐ Ⓑ Ⓒ Ⓓ				33 Ⓐ Ⓑ Ⓒ Ⓓ		
4 Ⓕ Ⓖ Ⓗ Ⓙ				14 Ⓕ Ⓖ Ⓗ Ⓙ				24 Ⓕ Ⓖ Ⓗ Ⓙ				34 Ⓕ Ⓖ Ⓗ Ⓙ		
5 Ⓐ Ⓑ Ⓒ Ⓓ				15 Ⓐ Ⓑ Ⓒ Ⓓ				25 Ⓐ Ⓑ Ⓒ Ⓓ				35 Ⓐ Ⓑ Ⓒ Ⓓ		
6 Ⓕ Ⓖ Ⓗ Ⓙ				16 Ⓕ Ⓖ Ⓗ Ⓙ				26 Ⓕ Ⓖ Ⓗ Ⓙ				36 Ⓕ Ⓖ Ⓗ Ⓙ		
7 Ⓐ Ⓑ Ⓒ Ⓓ				17 Ⓐ Ⓑ Ⓒ Ⓓ				27 Ⓐ Ⓑ Ⓒ Ⓓ				37 Ⓐ Ⓑ Ⓒ Ⓓ		
8 Ⓕ Ⓖ Ⓗ Ⓙ				18 Ⓕ Ⓖ Ⓗ Ⓙ				28 Ⓕ Ⓖ Ⓗ Ⓙ				38 Ⓕ Ⓖ Ⓗ Ⓙ		
9 Ⓐ Ⓑ Ⓒ Ⓓ				19 Ⓐ Ⓑ Ⓒ Ⓓ				29 Ⓐ Ⓑ Ⓒ Ⓓ				39 Ⓐ Ⓑ Ⓒ Ⓓ		
10 Ⓕ Ⓖ Ⓗ Ⓙ				20 Ⓕ Ⓖ Ⓗ Ⓙ				30 Ⓕ Ⓖ Ⓗ Ⓙ				40 Ⓕ Ⓖ Ⓗ Ⓙ		

I hereby certify that I have truthfully identified myself on this form. I accept the consequences of falsifying my identity.

_____

Your signature

_____

Today's date

The Princeton Review
Diagnostic ACT Form

ESSAY

Begin your essay on this side. If necessary, continue on the opposite side.

Continue on the opposite side if necessary.

The Princeton Review
Diagnostic ACT Form

Continued from previous page.

The Princeton Review
Diagnostic ACT Form

Continued from previous page.

The Princeton Review
Diagnostic ACT Form

Continued from previous page.

_____

_____

_____

_____

_____

_____

_____

_____

_____

_____

_____

_____

_____

_____

_____

_____

_____

_____

_____

_____

English Practice

DIRECTIONS: In the five passages that follow, certain words and phrases are underlined and numbered. In the right-hand column, you will find alternatives for each underlined part. In most cases, you are to choose the one that best expresses the idea, makes the statement appropriate for standard written English, or is worded most consistently with the style and tone of the passage as a whole. If you think the original version is best, choose "NO CHANGE." In some cases, you will find in the right-hand column a question about the underlined part. You are to choose the best answer to the question.

You will also find questions about a section of the passage or the passage as a whole. These questions do not refer to an underlined portion of the passage but rather are identified by a number or numbers in a box.

For each question, choose the alternative you consider best and blacken the corresponding oval on your answer document. Read each passage through once before you begin to answer the questions that accompany it. For many of the questions, you must read several sentences beyond the question to determine the answer. Be sure that you have read far enough ahead each time you choose an alternative.

PASSAGE I

Hats: On My Head, On My Mind

I do not remember how I came to like wearing a hat. Friends view it as an odd habit of mine, since so few people wear hats today. I think my fondness for hats comes down to the desire to <u>proclaim</u> what type of person I am. Telling the world
what kind of person resides directly below its brim is one of the principal jobs of any hat worth the name.

Even if we are not supposed to judge a book by its cover, we very often judge a person by his or her hat. [2] In a narrow sense, a top hat indicates to all that you are a magician, just as a mortarboard and tassel tells the world you just graduated.

<u>More generally,</u> a cowboy hat may say you are the strong, silent
type, while a beret <u>suggests, you are artistic and creative.</u> We even use hats as a kind of code for moral character, letting "white hats" and "black hats" serve as metaphors for "good

1. Which of the following alternatives to the underlined word would NOT be acceptable?

   A. announce
   B. declare
   C. compare
   D. advertise

2. The writer is considering deleting the preceding sentence from the essay. Should the sentence be kept or deleted?

   F. Kept, because it establishes the theme of this paragraph, the ways in which hats symbolize things about people and their actions.
   G. Kept, because it establishes the narrator's love of hats.
   H. Deleted, because the information it contains is contradicted in the previous sentence.
   J. Deleted, because the narrative is more interesting if readers are left to draw their own conclusions about the ways in which they personally interpret hats.

3. A. NO CHANGE
   B. (Do NOT begin new paragraph) Thus, as a general rule
   C. (Begin new paragraph) Generally,
   D. (Begin new paragraph) For example,

4. F. NO CHANGE
   G. suggests you are artistic, and creative.
   H. suggests, you are artistic, and creative.
   J. suggests you are artistic and creative.

guys" and "bad guys." Hats show <u>way up</u> in our figures of
5
speech as well. Home is where you hang your hat, while
declaring your desire to win a position is throwing your hat into

the ring. How could anyone not want to wear a hat, <u>especially</u>
6
<u>because it makes your hair messy?</u>
6

A hat can do even more things in everyday life. <u>Deserving</u>
7
congratulations, I say that my hat is off to them—and then I

can literally do exactly that. When someone has exciting news

for me, he can tell me to hold on to <u>my hat, if the news</u> has to
8
be kept secret, I can promise to keep it under my hat. He could

even tell me to remain calm and not be a mad hatter. [9]

Maybe the real reason I like wearing a hat, however, has

to do with getting away from everyday life. What I find so

interesting is the <u>possibility of using a hat,</u> to make myself more
10
like someone very different from my everyday self. A fedora

helps me to think of <u>me</u> as more of a street-smart tough-guy
11
private eye. Another hat, appropriately battered, helps me feel

5. **A.** NO CHANGE
   B. up
   C. features
   D. DELETE the underlined portion.

6. Given that all the choices are true, which one most strongly
   reinforces the author's attitude towards hats as it has been
   conveyed up to this point in the essay?
   F. NO CHANGE
   G. when it may cost a substantial amount?
   H. although you may forget one in a restaurant?
   J. when it can do so much?

7. **A.** NO CHANGE
   B. As they are deserving
   C. When people deserve
   D. To deserve

8. **F.** NO CHANGE
   G. my hat, although the event
   H. my hat. If the news
   J. my hat, especially when it

9. At this point, the writer is considering adding the following true statement:

   "Mad hatter" properly refers to the many nineteenth-
   century hat makers who suffered extensive neuro-
   logical damage after they were exposed to the toxic
   mercury fumes then utilized in hat construction.

   Should the writer make this addition here?

   A. Yes, because it helps support the idea that the author
   has affection for hats.
   B. Yes, because it provides a striking parallel between the
   author's interest in hats and Lewis Carroll's.
   C. No, because many individuals in the nineteenth century besides hat-makers were exposed to poisonous
   fumes.
   D. No, because its historical explanation of the scientific
   origins of the image of mad hatters does not fit with
   the essay to this point.

10. **F.** NO CHANGE
    G. possibility of using a hat
    H. possibility, of using a hat
    J. possibility, of using a hat,

11. **A.** NO CHANGE
    B. myself
    C. my own self
    D. I

like a daring adventurer <u>his</u> search for fabulous treasures will
₁₂
succeed against all odds.

On my last birthday, my family <u>that</u> gave me a Napoleon
₁₃

hat. I wonder, what are they trying to tell me? 14

12. F. NO CHANGE
    G. whose
    H. pursuing a
    J. making a

13. A. NO CHANGE
    B. are those who
    C. were among who
    D. DELETE the underlined portion.

14. The writer is considering concluding the essay with the following statement:

    > Ultimately, a hat on your head guarantees a song in your heart.

    Should the writer end the essay with this statement?

    F. Yes, because it restates the central idea of the essay in a memorable way.
    G. Yes, because hats have many uses.
    H. No, because the preceding sentence expressed the same idea using different words.
    J. No, because it does not have a meaningful connection to the central theme of this essay.

    Question 15 asks about the preceding passage as a whole.

    ---

15. Suppose one of the writer's goals had been to indicate that items of clothing can be used to communicate things, literally and figuratively, about their wearers. Would this essay have fulfilled that goal?

    A. Yes, because the essay reveals that the narrator uses hats to express his feelings and present himself as different kinds of people.
    B. Yes, because the essay reveals that hats have been symbols of royalty and power for centuries.
    C. No, because the essay indicates that the narrator prefers to wear hats from popular culture instead of history.
    D. No, because the essay establishes that the narrator's attitude towards hats may not be shared by his family and friends.

A Diamond in the Rough

Beginning around 1963, when people became able to buy cassette recorders with built-in microphones, amateur songwriters were able to record songs that had been formerly undocumented. One guitarist and saxophonist, Bruce Diamond, recorded nearly a hundred songs from his home in Lexington, Kentucky. Recently, hundreds of these rough recordings have been re-mastered. They have captured the attention of musicologists for a number of reasons.

First, it is seemingly apparent that Diamond's songs were influenced by many different popular artists of the day. One song sounds very similar to a complicated jazz song by Charlie

Parker. However, another song is the opposite of the song sounds like the straightforward rock of Buddy Holly. The

lyrics are very similar as well, and one is led to wonder what inspired them. One music critic observed that Diamond found

it completely effortless to switch back and forth between very different musical genres.

Diamond's recordings are noteworthy for their unique artistic voice—an interesting combination of jazz, bluegrass, and gospel styles. In one piece, Diamond starts with a long soulful intro leading into an upbeat verse. The verse's tempo and tone provide an interesting contrast to the mournful opening. The chorus combines elements of both in an unexpected but balanced way. Diamond seems to express in

16. **F.** NO CHANGE
    G. have been formerly
    H. are now being
    J. are formerly

17. Which of the following choices provides the most stylistically effective and concise wording here?

    A. NO CHANGE
    B. there is the impression given by Diamond's songs that he was
    C. Diamond's songs suggest that he was
    D. it is the impression Diamond's songs give that he was

18. **F.** NO CHANGE
    G. opposite of the song is sounding
    H. opposite; the song sounds
    J. opposite the song sounds

19. Given that all the choices are true, which of the following would best provide further detail about the lyrical subject matter?

    A. NO CHANGE
    B. dealing mostly with dating and automobiles.
    C. and he mostly uses rhymed couplets and alliteration.
    D. which are easy to understand because of Diamond's enunciation.

20. **F.** NO CHANGE
    G. without any strain or effort
    H. relatively simple and free of struggle
    J. totally free of complication

21. **A.** NO CHANGE
    B. verse,
    C. verses'
    D. verses

this song that he has overcome some emotional wounds but that

one remains conflicted. [23]
22

22. F. NO CHANGE
   G. he remains conflicted.
   H. they were conflicted.
   J. he is conflicting.

23. At this point, the writer is thinking of adding the following sentence:

> We have all experienced sad events and know very well what it is like to feel conflicted.

Should the writer make this addition here?

   A. Yes, because it shows the writer's compassionate feelings toward Diamond's difficult situation.
   B. Yes, because it adds extra emphasis to the subject matter of one of Diamond's most well known songs.
   C. No, because it strays from the paragraph's main focus on Diamond's unique songwriting voice.
   D. No, because it encourages readers to think about sad events in their own lives.

While sources of music from major music towns like
24
New Orleans, Detroit, and Nashville are abundant, little is

known about Lexington's music scene because the town

24. Which of the following choices would NOT be an acceptable alternative to the underlined portion?

   F. Despite the fact that
   G. Although
   H. Since
   J. Whereas

lacked a real recording studio. Therefore, since they
25
were recorded on two-inch tape, Diamond's songs
25

25. A. NO CHANGE
   B. because a built-in microphone recorded them,
   C. being that he played the songs into the recorder,
   D. DELETE the underlined portion.

in a city like Lexington offer music historians a rare
26
taste of the musical culture in the 1960s.

26. The best place for the underlined portion would be:

   F. where it is now.
   G. after the word *historians*.
   H. after the word *taste*.
   J. after the word *culture*.

No one knows how much Diamond was effected by other
27
musicians in Lexington, but he did perform regularly at a local

27. A. NO CHANGE
   B. affected by
   C. affected with
   D. effected with

blues bar and less frequently at a jazz dance hall. One thing,
28

28. F. NO CHANGE
   G. at a dance hall where jazz was played.
   H. as a musician at a jazz dance hall.
   J. playing jazz music at a dance hall.

though, is for sure: he <u>records</u> an interesting portfolio of songs,
₂₉

<u>and he may soon be a famous saxophonist.</u>
₃₀

29. A. NO CHANGE
    B. recorded
    C. is recording
    D. has recorded

30. Given that all the choices are true, which of the following would provide the best conclusion to this essay in relation to one of its main points?

    F. NO CHANGE
    G. and now they provide scholars with an example of Lexington music.
    H. and he probably never had to buy another cassette recorder.
    J. and he may have performed in other cities besides Lexington.

PASSAGE III

Going Underground

[1] When I left my home in rural Missouri to attend college in New York City, I didn't consider myself <u>a veteran subway rider.</u> [2] Luckily, I was able to overcome this
₃₁
fear by having my first trip by subway guided by a

<u>neighbor, named</u> Sasha. [3] He had grown up in Manhattan,
₃₂

so he was familiar with the <u>dense, intricacy</u> subway routes.
₃₃

[4] <u>During his childhood, he had taken</u> the subway almost
₃₄
every day as a child with his family, and so I was encouraged to set off with him to learn the ins and outs of the New York

31. A. NO CHANGE
    B. a person who knew the ins and outs of public underground trains.
    C. a master of all the skills necessary to travel by public transport.
    D. a veteran rider.

32. F. NO CHANGE
    G. neighbor; named
    H. neighbor named
    J. neighbor named,

33. A. NO CHANGE
    B. dense, intricate
    C. intricately, dense
    D. dense intricacy

34. F. NO CHANGE
    G. He had been starting to take
    H. His childhood was spent taking
    J. He had taken

subways. [5] Because of <u>my family's warnings,</u> I was afraid to
                              35

take the subway at first. [36]

Sasha showed me to the stop nearest our building and led
me down the steps from the busy street, steering me skillfully
through the fast-moving crowd. I couldn't decide whether to
buy my token from the imposing-looking woman on the left
or from the imposing-looking woman on the right, but Sasha
confidently tugged me right up to <u>them.</u> I managed to squeak
                                        37
out, "Canal Street, please," and the woman silently scooped up
my change and slipped a token through the slot in the window.

I couldn't tell to which platform to <u>descend, if</u> I had always
                                        38
used landmarks to find my way around my hometown. After

a little <u>searching, though,</u> I saw the sign that read "Canal St."
              39
suspended above the escalator, so Sasha and I climbed aboard
and rode down to our platform.

<u>I felt very conspicuous standing on the platform, waiting</u>
                                        40
<u>for our train to arrive.</u> Sasha distracted me by pointing out a
        40
performer across the tracks on the other platform. At first, I was

<u>confused like a whirlwind in my mind</u> about what the man was
                              41
doing. Then I saw that he was juggling all kinds of objects: milk
crates, thick books, and even bowling balls. I wondered if they

<u>would of been</u> there when we returned.
        42

35. **A.** NO CHANGE
    B. my familys' warnings,
    C. my families' warnings
    D. my families warnings,

36. For the sake of the logic and coherence of this paragraph,
    Sentence 5 should be placed:

    F. where it is now.
    G. after Sentence 1.
    H. before Sentence 3.
    J. before Sentence 4.

37. **A.** NO CHANGE
    B. the one on the left.
    C. her.
    D. the women.

38. **F.** NO CHANGE
    G. descend, which
    H. descend;
    J. descend, even though,

39. **A.** NO CHANGE
    B. searching though:
    C. searching, though
    D. searching, though:

40. Given that all of the choices are true, which one most ef-
    fectively introduces the action in this paragraph while sug-
    gesting the narrator's discomfort in her new surroundings?

    F. NO CHANGE
    G. Sasha's stylish boots clicked on the floor as he walked
        ahead of me.
    H. Although it wasn't rush hour yet, quite a few people
        stood waiting on the platform.
    J. Sasha explained that the first subway line in New York
        City opened in 1904.

41. **A.** NO CHANGE
    B. confused with uncertainty and curiosity
    C. confused by the initial lack of understanding
    D. confused

42. **F.** NO CHANGE
    G. would be
    H. should be
    J. could of been

When we were seated on the train, Sasha looked at me with a pleased expression, I suppose, he was proud of how well he had served as a guide. "You look like you belong here in the big city," he said, nudging me playfully in the side, which I shrugged and elbowed him back. I gazed at my reflection in the window and wondered if I had already changed.

We arrived at the Canal Street station, and we rode up the escalator toward the street, taking care to stand well to one side to let more impatient passengers by. I might just as well have been exploring an undiscovered continent and was emerging, with treasures and new wonders, from fantastic caverns. I'll always remember my first subway ride, when "going underground" took on an entirely new meaning.

43. **A.** NO CHANGE
    B. expression I suppose
    C. expression. I suppose
    D. expression, however, I suppose

44. **F.** NO CHANGE
    G. side, which he
    H. side. I
    J. side, where I

45. **A.** NO CHANGE
    B. I might just as well have been exploring fantastic caverns filled with the treasures and new wonders of an undiscovered continent.
    C. I might, filled with treasures and new wonders emerging from fantastic caverns, just as well have been exploring an undiscovered continent.
    D. Emerging from fantastic caverns, I might just as well, filled with treasures and new wonders, have been exploring a new continent.

PASSAGE IV

Black Holes—Astronomy's Great Mystery

Black holes are likely and possibly the most fascinating topic facing contemporary astronomy. The concept of a black hole—a region of space with such intense gravitational pull that nothing can escape—is truly the stuff of science fiction. That is what Albert Einstein believed, at least. His general theory of relativity predicted their existence, but he thought of his prediction as an error to be corrected, not a predictor of one of the strangest astronomical phenomena yet discovered.

Because Einstein didn't live to see it, the universe proved the accuracy of his calculations in 1970, when Cygnus X-1 was discovered about 7,000 light-years from Earth. It is about 8.7 times as massive as our Sun yet has a small diameter of only about 50 km. When you consider that the diameter of the Sun could accommodate over 100 Earths, it becomes clear that

46. **F.** NO CHANGE
    G. very probably to be
    H. possibly
    J. a possible likeness of being

47. **A.** NO CHANGE
    B. thinks
    C. have thought
    D. has thought

48. **F.** NO CHANGE
    G. Although
    H. Since
    J. DELETE the underlined portion.

49. **A.** NO CHANGE
    B. less
    C. fewer
    D. too little

fitting a mass almost nine times greater than that into a space of about 31 miles is truly remarkable. [50]

How do these singularities come into existence?
51

There are a number of theories to explain the process. The
52
most popular hypothesis suggests that black holes are fairly

common and involving the disintegration of a massive
53

star near the end of its lifecycle. At that stage, the star has
54

nearly exhausted its hydrogen supply, consequently losing its
55
ability to burn at a sufficiently high temperature to prevent

its collapse. The stars exterior, layers are blown away in a
56
supernova, while the interior layers collapse into a highly dense

core, which ultimately becomes the black hole.

Other theorists suggesting that black holes are the result of
57
a galactic game of bumper cars. The universe is teeming with

neutron stars. These are highly compact, very hot stars formed

50. If the writer were to delete the preceding sentence, the paragraph would primarily lose:

    F. a description that explains the purpose of studying black holes.

    G. information that helps the reader grasp the size of black holes by presenting it in understandable terms.

    H. a reference that explains how the black hole is compressed into such a small size.

    J. an unnecessary detail, because this information is repeated later in the passage.

51. Which choice provides the most effective transition from the previous paragraph to the new paragraph?

    A. NO CHANGE

    B. Why should we study black holes at all?

    C. Is the Sun going to collapse and become a black hole?

    D. What are the effects of such massive gravitational pull?

52. F. NO CHA\NGE

    G. Their are

    H. Their is

    J. They're are

53. A. NO CHANGE

    B. is involving

    C. will involve

    D. involve

54. Which of the following alternatives to the underlined portion would NOT be acceptable?

    F. close to

    G. close

    H. toward

    J. around

55. A. NO CHANGE

    B. supply; consequently

    C. supply, and consequently

    D. supply. Consequently

56. F. NO CHANGE

    G. stars exterior

    H. star's exterior

    J. star's exterior,

57. A. NO CHANGE

    B. has been suggesting

    C. will suggest

    D. suggest

during the supernova of smaller stars that are not sufficiently massive to create black holes. Likewise, on occasion these stars will actually collide with each other and together become massive enough to form a black hole.

Perhaps the most bizarre observation made about these phenomena involves the existence of "micro" or "mini" black holes. These peculiar items are very small, astronomically speaking. They have a mass far less than that of our Sun, and, frankly, the scientific community cannot explain and articulate fully how stars with so little mass could have formed black holes at all. That is a question for future generations of scientists to explore.

Question 60 asks about the preceding passage as a whole.

58. F. NO CHANGE
   G. Similarly,
   H. However,
   J. In addition,

59. A. NO CHANGE
   B. cannot explain or describe in any detail
   C. cannot explain
   D. not only cannot explain but also can't describe

60. Suppose the writer's goal had been to write a brief essay about how Einstein's skepticism stopped scientific inquiry into the existence of black holes. Would this essay successfully fulfill that goal?

   F. Yes, because black holes were not discovered until after Einstein's death.
   G. Yes, because no other scientists were mentioned by name as doing research into the subject.
   H. No, because Einstein later decided that black holes did exist and encouraged the scientific community to search for them.
   J. No, because no discussion is made of how Einstein's doubt affected the inquiries of other scientists.

PASSAGE V

An Argument for E-Waste Recycling

Drive through any suburb in the U.S. today, and it's hard to miss the bins, that have become companions to America's trashcans. Recycling has become commonplace, as people recognize the need to care for the environment. Yet most

61. A. NO CHANGE
   B. bins that have become companions,
   C. bins, which have become companions,
   D. bins that have become companions

62. F. NO CHANGE
   G. became
   H. becoming
   J. becomes

people's recycling consciousness is extending only as far
63

as paper, bottles, and cans. People seldom find themselves
64
confronted with the growing phenomenon of e-waste.
64

E-waste proliferates as the techno-fashionable constantly

upgrade to the most cutting-edge devices, which the majority
65

of them end up in landfills. Activists who track such waste
66
estimate that users discarded nearly 2 million tons of TVs,
VCRs, computers, cell phones, and other electronics in 2005.
Unless we can find a safe alternative, this e-waste may leak into
the ground and water dangerous toxins. [67] Burning the waste

also dangerous contaminates the air.
68

Consequently, e-waste often contains reusable silver, gold,
69
and other electrical conductors. Recycling these materials

63. **A.** NO CHANGE
    B. extended
    C. had extended
    D. extends

64. Which choice would most effectively begin this sentence so that it emphasizes a lack of awareness of this problem?

    F. NO CHANGE
    G. Many in our communities simply don't realize the dangers of
    H. A majority of local governments are assiduously studying
    J. Little attention is paid by the people in our neighborhoods to

65. **A.** NO CHANGE
    B. devices that
    C. devices, and
    D. devices after

66. **F** NO CHANGE
    G. Activists who track such waste,
    H. Activists which track such waste
    J. Activists, who track such waste,

67. At this point, the writer is considering adding the following phrase to the end of the preceding sentence:

    such as lead, mercury, and arsenic

    Should the writer add the phrase here?

    A. Yes, because it adds specific details clarifying which toxins are leaking.
    B. Yes, because it supports the idea that landfills have too much waste.
    C. No, because it doesn't specify how dangerous these toxins are.
    D. No, because it would be redundant in a paragraph that has already mentioned which toxins e-waste contains.

68. **F** NO CHANGE
    G. more dangerous
    H. most dangerous
    J. dangerously

69. **A.** NO CHANGE
    B. Particularly,
    C. Moreover,
    D. However,

reduces environmental <u>impact by</u> reducing both landfill
waste and the need to mine such metals, which can destroy
ecosystems.

     <u>A growing number of states have adopted</u> laws to prohibit
dumping e-waste. Still, less than a quarter of this refuse will

reach legitimate recycling programs. ☐72 Some companies
advertising safe disposal in fact merely ship the waste to third-

world countries, where it still ends up in landfills. ☐73

     Nevertheless, the small but growing number of cities and
corporations that do handle e-waste responsibly represent

70. **F.** NO CHANGE
    G. impact;
    H. impact so,
    J. impact of

71. **A.** NO CHANGE
    B. Adoptions are growing in state
    C. States have growingly adopted
    D. Growing states have adopted numbers

72. The writer is considering deleting the preceding sentence from this paragraph. Should the sentence be kept or deleted?

    F. Kept, because it provides a logical transition between the first and last sentences of the paragraph.
    G. Kept, because it provides meaningful statistics.
    H. Deleted, because it adds no new information to the paragraph.
    J. Deleted, because it would be redundant, given that the next sentence explains that some companies don't recycle.

73. At this point, the author is considering adding the following sentence:

    These organizations hamper progress by unsafely disposing of waste in an out-of-sight, out-of-mind location.

    Would this be a relevant addition to make here?

    A. Yes, because it completes the idea expressed in the preceding sentence.
    B. Yes, because it paints such organizations in a negative light.
    C. No, because it contradicts the following sentence.
    D. No, because it introduces a tangential point.

progress and a real step forward toward making the world a

74

cleaner, better place for us all. [75]

74. **F.** NO CHANGE
G. a real step forward in the progress moving
H. progress
J. real forward-stepping progress

75. At this point, the writer is considering adding the following sentence:

> Today, pollution is one of the most dangerous forces threatening our environment, and the government must work to regulate its effects.

Should the writer add this sentence here?

A. Yes, because it adds important details that suggest recycling is not the only concern of environmentalists.
B. Yes, because it provides additional information discussing the impact of recycling programs in urban areas.
C. No, because it digresses from the article's main point about e-waste and related recycling issues.
D. No, because government regulation is a complicated and controversial topic addressed elsewhere in the passage.

NO TEST MATERIAL ON THIS PAGE.

DIRECTIONS: In the five passages that follow, certain words and phrases are underlined and numbered. In the right-hand column, you will find alternatives for each underlined part. In most cases, you are to choose the one that best expresses the idea, makes the statement appropriate for standard written English, or is worded most consistently with the style and tone of the passage as a whole. If you think the original version is best, choose "NO CHANGE." In some cases, you will find in the right-hand column a question about the underlined part. You are to choose the best answer to the question.

You will also find questions about a section of the passage or the passage as a whole. These questions do not refer to an underlined portion of the passage but rather are identified by a number or numbers in a box.

For each question, choose the alternative you consider best and blacken the corresponding oval on your answer document. Read each passage through once before you begin to answer the questions that accompany it. For many of the questions, you must read several sentences beyond the question to determine the answer. Be sure that you have read far enough ahead each time you choose an alternative.

PASSAGE I

Building a Beauty Empire

In 1867, on an unassuming farm in tiny Delta, Louisiana, a daughter was born to former slaves Minerva and Owen Breedlove. Little did anyone realize that Sarah Breedlove,

orphaned at age six when her parents died, would grow up to become one of the most successful African-American

entrepreneurs in history. 3

At twenty, Sarah Breedlove found herself widowed with an infant daughter, A'Lelia. Sarah packed up her few belongings

1. **A.** NO CHANGE
   B. by
   C. under
   D. for

2. **F.** NO CHANGE
   G. who became an orphan as a child at the age of six years old when her parents died,
   H. whose parents died when she was just age six leaving her to be an orphan as a young child,
   J. tragically when her parents died becoming an orphan at the young age of six years old,

3. At this point, the writer is considering adding the following true statement:

   > Also born in Louisiana, Louis Armstrong went on to exert a similarly powerful influence on 1920s American culture as a jazz trumpeter.

   Should the writer add this sentence here?

   A. Yes, because it's important to know that other influential people were born in Louisiana besides the woman portrayed in this essay.
   B. Yes, because this reference shows that music was important during this period.
   C. No, because the role Louis Armstrong played in 1920s culture is irrelevant to the main topic of this essay.
   D. No, because the 1920s were not significant years in American history.

and moved to St. Louis, hoping to take advantage of its' more numerous opportunities.

She supported herself as a laundress there for the next eighteen years. In 1905, she came up with an idea that would revolutionize the cosmetics industry. By ten years, she would not only oversee a vast financial empire but also become one of the best-known women in the United States.

Sarah invented a scalp conditioning and healing formula, in part because she had suffered from a disease that resulted in hair loss. Sarah undertook countless journeys to sell her formula door-to-door. As well as in churches and lodges. She dubbed herself Madame C. J. Walker, taking the name of

her second husband, Charles J. Walker, who worked in the newspaper publishing business and who also lived in St. Louis. She claimed that the secret formula for Madame Walker's Wonderful Hair Grower had come to her in a dream.

At this time, there were relatively few beauty parlors, so many women received beauty treatments at home. Sarah taught her methods to other women, they focused on sales and became

known as the "Walker Agents." Below Sarah's supervision, these agents became familiar sights in their white shirts and black skirts. Sarah called them "scalp specialists" and hair

and beauty "culturists" using these terms to emphasize the professional nature of the treatments.

4. F. NO CHANGE
   G. it's
   H. their
   J. its

5. A. NO CHANGE
   B. Up to ten years,
   C. Within ten years,
   D. Before ten years,

6. F. NO CHANGE
   G. door-to-door; as well as
   H. door-to-door, as well as
   J. door-to-door: as well as

7. A. NO CHANGE
   B. a man who lived in St. Louis and who worked in newspaper publishing.
   C. a St. Louis newspaperman.
   D. a newspaper publishing businessman who was very well known in the St. Louis area.

8. F. NO CHANGE
   G. women, who
   H. women, with whom
   J. women those

9. A. NO CHANGE
   B. Above
   C. As
   D. Under

10. F. NO CHANGE
    G. "culturists"; using
    H. "culturists": using
    J. "culturists," using

[1] <u>In 1913, she traveled to the Caribbean and to Central America, but before that</u> Sarah concentrated on improving and developing the manufacture of her products. [2] One of the first of these charitable acts was her generous $1,000 donation to the city's YMCA. [3] In 1910, she established the Walker Company headquarters—which featured a factory in addition to salons

and a training school—in Indianapolis. [4] <u>Chosen</u> because it was then the largest inland manufacturing city in the country, Indianapolis became both Sarah's home and the first beneficiary

of her social activism and dedication to charitable causes. [13]

Social efforts dominated the latter years of Sarah's life. She contributed the largest donation to the effort to save Frederick

Douglass's <u>home, maintaining,</u> the building as a historical museum. In 1913, she organized her agent-operators into "Walker Clubs," promoting these groups' philanthropic work by offering cash prizes to those doing the most good in their communities. Upon her death in 1919, "Madame Walker"—now often regarded as the richest self-made woman in the United States during her lifetime—donated two-thirds of her company's net profit to charitable causes.

11. Given that all the choices are true, which one provides the most effective transition from the preceding paragraph to this new one?
   A. NO CHANGE
   B. After her daughter A'Lelia built a magnificent town-home in an exclusive Manhattan neighborhood,
   C. Aside from training a small "army" of agent-operators,
   D. When Sarah had designed a special Walker Method treatment for celebrated dancer Josephine Baker,

12. F. NO CHANGE
    G. chose
    H. choosed
    J. choosing

13. For the sake of the logic and coherence of this paragraph, Sentence 2 should be placed:
    A. where it is now.
    B. before Sentence 1.
    C. after Sentence 3.
    D. after Sentence 4.

14. F. NO CHANGE
    G. home, maintaining
    H. home; maintaining
    J. home maintaining,

15. Suppose the writer's goal had been to write a brief essay focusing on the development of the beauty industry in the early part of the twentieth century. Would this essay successfully accomplish this goal?

   A. Yes, because the essay focuses on the beauty industry of the 1920s, during which Madame C. J. Walker became wealthy.
   B. Yes, because the essay describes how Sarah invented a new formula to facilitate hair growth and treat scalp problems.
   C. No, because the essay focuses mainly on Sarah Breedlove Walker and her place in the history of American business and culture.
   D. No, because the essay describes other events taking place during this time that were more significant.

PASSAGE II

A Tale of Two Uncles

   [1] <u>As my uncle and I finished our dinners,</u> we were hardly
   saying a word. [2] For the most part, it was a very ordinary

   birthday <u>celebration.</u> [3] After we had my favorite meal, lamb
   chops, my uncle made me his famous banana split sundae for
   dessert. [4] Banana splits are best with two scoops of chocolate
   ice cream, in my opinion. [5] Normally, my uncle would get
   very excited watching me eat dessert and have me make wishes
   for the coming year. [6] However, as our spoons clinked around
   mounds of ice cream and banana, his mood turned sad and
   soft-spoken. [7] I knew the source of our tension: today was my
   eighteenth birthday and next month I'd be at boot camp. [18]

16. Which of the following alternatives to the underlined portion would NOT be acceptable?

   F. While my uncle and I finished dinner,
   G. My uncle and I were almost finished eating, but
   H. My uncle and I finished our dinners, however,
   J. As my uncle and I were finishing our dinners,

17. A. NO CHANGE
   B. celebration, just like always.
   C. celebration with nothing abnormal.
   D. celebration and traditional.

18. Which of the following sentences is LEAST relevant to the theme of the passage and could therefore be deleted?

   F. Sentence 2
   G. Sentence 3
   H. Sentence 4
   J. Sentence 6

He said that <u>joining the army</u> he had some strong
                    19
reservations about me rather than going to college. I told him
that I believed my father, who was killed serving in the Polish

army, would have been proud of my decision. [20] My uncle
responded that my father would have felt even better about me
staying out of harm's way. In fact, my uncle continued, the
reason that we moved to the United States was so that I would
be more protected than I was in Poland. I think my uncle also
found it surprising that I would want to join the U.S. army. He

often asked <u>me</u>—why I would risk my life for a country that
             21
was not my homeland. I told him that I considered America my
new homeland. He was shocked.

[1] He began reminding me of my Polish upbringing.
[2] My uncle has as many stories about my childhood <u>than</u>
                                                      22

I <u>do.</u> [3] He would take me to the local carnival in July. [23]
  22

[4] <u>One</u> would buy ourselves hotcakes and ride the ferris
    24
wheel. [5] When the strawberries came into bloom, we
would go hiking in the Tatras mountains. [6] He and I

19. The best place for the underlined portion would be:
    A. where it is now.
    B. after the word *reservations*.
    C. after the word *me*.
    D. after the word *than*.

20. If the writer were to delete the phrase "who was killed
    serving in the Polish army" (and the surrounding commas)
    from the preceding sentence, the paragraph would primarily lose:
    F. nothing, since this information is mentioned elsewhere
       in the paragraph.
    G. evidence that the narrator's father was considered a
       brave man.
    H. a necessary detail that supports the logical flow of
       ideas in the paragraph.
    J. an explanation of why the narrator is unwilling to join
       the Polish army.

21. A. NO CHANGE
    B. me,
    C. me
    D. me:

22. F. NO CHANGE
    G. as I do.
    H. then I do.
    J. DELETE the underlined portion.

23. At this point, the writer is thinking of adding the following
    sentence:

    > Different cities in Poland host carnivals during different months of the year.

    Should the writer make this addition here?
    A. Yes, because it relates to the essay's topic of celebration rituals in different cultures.
    B. Yes, because it gives the reader crucial background information about the narrator's cultural upbringing.
    C. No, because it offers information that does not help to preserve the focus of this paragraph.
    D. No, because it reiterates a detail that is mentioned elsewhere in the passage.

24. F. NO CHANGE
    G. You
    H. We
    J. They

would row canoes and have swimming races from our dock out to a big rock formation and back. [7] At night, we would lie on the porch in the sleeping bags, my

grandmother had bought, drink cocoa, and listen to the

chorus of crickets. [8] My uncle tells me ghost stories

under the starlit sky. [28]

When my uncle finished reminiscing, I assured him that

I still love Poland and will never lose sight of it's influence on who I am today. However, America gave my uncle an opportunity when an engineering firm in Pittsburgh offered

him a job seven years ago. After we immigrated to America, I became exposed to the cultural attitudes, social customs, and economic possibilities of growing up as an American child. My time in America has given me a deep love for it and loyalty to it. As we finished our dessert, I asked my uncle to make peace with my decision to defend Uncle Sam.

25. A. NO CHANGE
    B. bags
    C. bags;
    D. bags, that

26. F. NO CHANGE
    G. drank cocoa, and listen
    H. drank cocoa, and listened
    J. drink cocoa, and listening

27. A. NO CHANGE
    B. has told
    C. would tell
    D. was telling

28. Upon reviewing this paragraph and noticing that some information has been omitted, the author composes the following sentence, using that information:

    Sometimes, in the warm months of the fall, my uncle rented a rustic vacation home on Lake Drawsko.

    For the sake of the logic of this paragraph, this sentence should be placed after Sentence:
    F. 4.
    G. 5.
    H. 6.
    J. 7.

29. A. NO CHANGE
    B. its'
    C. its
    D. their

30. Given that all of the choices are accurate, which one provides the most effective and logical transition from the preceding sentence to this one?
    F. NO CHANGE
    G. Pittsburgh being the biggest city in Pennsylvania,
    H. He is a very well-respected engineer, and
    J. Although I have visited Philadelphia, Pittsburgh is where

Not the Same Old Song and Dance

After graduating from college, I decided to test my International Studies degree by living and working in China. I had studied only a year of Mandarin Chinese at university, so I struggled with adaptation early on. I poured myself into work at first, finding that enduring the same 12-hour workdays as

several of my Chinese coworkers was just as difficult as to adapt

to Chinese culture. All the while, at the same time, I slowly taught myself more Chinese with a language CD and forced myself to interact at local places like restaurants and markets. The easiest way to adapt, however, had been right under my nose the entire time.

 All I had to do was spend time with my coworkers outside

of work. My project team had already taken a quickly liking of me, and I had been invited to several functions. I hadn't accepted yet out of fear of being unable to communicate, but my feelings of guilt at having turned down so many kind invitations eventually outweighed that fear. When disappointed in myself, I acquiesced one night, knowing this would be an important step in learning the Chinese way of life. The ensuing

night would prove to be quite memorable and unforgettable.

 We began the evening with dinner. I proudly requested to order since I had learned quite a lot of food vocabulary. Everyone seemed surprised, and impressed by the variety of dishes I could order. Our post-dinner destination was a karaoke house (KTV), a very popular form of entertainment in

31. A. NO CHANGE
  B. study
  C. studying
  D. have studied

32. F. NO CHANGE
  G. when adapting
  H. as having adapted
  J. as adapting

33. A. NO CHANGE
  B. All the while,
  C. All while at the same time,
  D. While all the time was the same,

34. Which choice would most clearly and effectively express the obviousness of the best method of adaptation?

  F. NO CHANGE
  G. noticeable
  H. doubtful
  J. obscure

35. A. NO CHANGE
  B. quick liking of
  C. quick liking to
  D. quickly liking to

36. F. NO CHANGE
  G. (Do NOT being new paragraph) Disappointed in myself,
  H. (Begin new paragraph) When disappointed in myself,
  J. (Begin new paragraph) Disappointed in myself,

37. A. NO CHANGE
  B. memorable and hard to forget.
  C. as memorable as can be.
  D. memorable.

38. F. NO CHANGE
  G. seemed surprised
  H. seemed, surprised
  J. seemed; surprised

China. [39] The karaoke took place in a private room with just

our group. The experience was accompanied by embarrassment
as karaoke often is, but mine did not come from singing.
40

When one girl refused to sing a song I had chosen, I decided to playfully chant to her the songs number on the screen. The number was thirty-eight, but I chanted only three and eight, something which can be understood easily in English but is not common in Chinese. What I failed to realize was that the Chinese words for *three* and *eight*, when used as slang, can also mean *crazy*. Since my Chinese friends were not accustomed to number shortening, they could only assume I had just unreasonably insulted our female coworker. [42] After much confusion and a difficult explanation on my part, the matter was resolved, and everyone had a good laugh over it.

A valuable lesson was certainly learned by me about differences
43

in slang. [44] This experience was the first of many cultural

39. At this point, the writer is considering adding the following true statement:

> Karaoke did not originate in China.

Should the writer add this sentence here?

- **A.** Yes, because it supports that fact that karaoke is very popular despite being an import.
- **B.** Yes, because it adds to the international flavor of the essay.
- **C.** No, because it simply repeats a detail stated earlier in the essay.
- **D.** No, because it doesn't add to the focus of this paragraph.

40. F. NO CHANGE
G. embarrassment as,
H. embarrassment, as
J. embarrassment, as,

41. A. NO CHANGE
B. songs' number
C. song's number
D. songs's number

42. If the preceding sentence were deleted, the essay would primarily lose:

- **F.** a repetition of the main point of the essay.
- **G.** another example of slang errors between languages.
- **H.** a contrast with the paragraph's opening sentence.
- **J.** a detail of how the rest of the party reacted to the author's mistake.

43. A. NO CHANGE
B. I certainly learned a valuable lesson
C. A lesson learned was certainly valuable
D. Certainly learning a valuable lesson

44. If the writer wanted to emphasize that there are other differences in slang among languages besides the one discussed in the essay, which of the following true statements should be added at this point?

- **F.** Slang differences are difficult to understand.
- **G.** Slang is a popular way to communicate.
- **H.** Learning about other slang differences can help to avoid cultural misunderstandings.
- **J.** Daily conversation among peers often includes slang.

lessons I would learn by simply being social in a foreign
_____
                  45
environment.
_____
   45

45. Which choice would best summarize the main point of the essay as illustrated by the narrator's miscommunication experience?

   A. NO CHANGE
   B. intentionally insulting a local person in a foreign country.
   C. enjoying night life in a foreign country.
   D. studying a foreign language in an isolated environment.

PASSAGE IV

Life in the Bike Lane

[1]

When I was growing up, I used to ride my bike all the time. Even though I spent most of my childhood around the daunting, Pennsylvania, hills and mountains, I still loved to ride
_____
            46
wherever and whenever I could. I suppose for someone who was too young to drive, the bicycle provided a certain amount of freedom.

46. F. NO CHANGE
    G. daunting Pennsylvania hills
    H. daunting Pennsylvania hills,
    J. daunting, Pennsylvania, hills,

[2]

Along came my sixteenth year and a driver's license, and
_____
  47
that was it for the bike. When I finally got my driver's license, I

47. Which of the following alternatives to the underlined portion would NOT be acceptable?

    A. Then
    B. Next
    C. Subsequently
    D. In following

felt that I had turned a page in my life, and that its old bike was
                                                    ___
                                                    48
part of a previous chapter. There it sat for my last two years of high school and all four years of college while I gleefully drove back and forth even the distances smallest in length, through
                                    _____
                                                49
the worst traffic and weather conditions, and amid the mounting prices of gas.

48. F. NO CHANGE
    G. one's
    H. your
    J. my

49. A. NO CHANGE
    B. shortest and smallest distances,
    C. distances that were short, not long,
    D. shortest distances,

[3]

Then I moved out on my own and found that I had moved
             ___
             50
to a place where the car had a lot less allure. Fresh out of college, I didn't have bundles of money to throw around, and in

50. F. NO CHANGE
    G. myself out
    H. myself in
    J. in

my new environs, bundles of money <u>was exactly</u> what I needed
₅₁
to use the car with any regularity. Gas cost at least fifty cents
more per gallon than I was used to, and what would've been a
quick 30-minute drive where I grew up easily became a two-
hour drive because of all the traffic in this new place! 52

[4]

After I couldn't take any more, I <u>resolved and decided</u> that
₅₃
the next time I visited my parents, I would bring the bike out of
retirement. As if uncovering a lost volume of an ancient work, I

entered the attic with a flashlight, <u>even if I fought</u> off fear and
₅₄
cobwebs in equal measure. It seemed hopeless, I thought. Even
if I could find my bike in this above-house cavern, it wouldn't
be the same as it was before. I was so much older now, had
known the pleasures of the automobile, and was out of shape
from all the highway snacking and sitting. Then, there it was,
and I felt the surge that the <u>gold-rushers'</u> must have felt in Cali-
₅₅
fornia in the 1800s when they struck gold.

[5]

Needless to say, my joy at having rediscovered this long
lost friend was overwhelming, but it was amplified when I had
returned to my own place and began <u>by riding</u> the bike around
₅₆
town. I had been freed from four-dollar-a-gallon gas, traffic

jams, <u>and having been freed from the</u> interminable wait at the
₅₇
bus stop!

---

51. A. NO CHANGE
  B. weren't exacting
  C. was exact
  D. were exactly

52. If the writer were to delete the phrase "in this new place"
(placing an exclamation point after the word *traffic*), this
sentence would primarily lose:
  F. a contrast to the phrase "where I grew up" in the same
    sentence.
  G. factual information regarding the purpose of the au-
    thor's move.
  H. a contrast to the phrase "a quick 30-minute drive" in
    the same sentence.
  J. a logical connection to the place mentioned in Para-
    graph 1.

53. A. NO CHANGE
  B. resolution in my deciding
  C. resolved
  D. decidedly resolved

54. F. NO CHANGE
  G. fighting
  H. because I fought
  J. and had fought

55. A. NO CHANGE
  B. gold-rusher's
  C. gold-rushers
  D. gold-rushers,

56. F. NO CHANGE
  G. to riding
  H. to ride
  J. with riding

57. A. NO CHANGE
  B. and freed from the
  C. and the
  D. and from the freeing of the

[6]

I realized then that I had regained that freedom I had
enjoyed so much when I was <u>younger, in</u> my first apartment,
₅₈

this freedom had taken on a different character; [59]. Now it was
a freedom from the constraints that prevented me from doing
what I wanted to do in the city, that had me sitting in traffic or
spending all my hard-earned cash on gas. I had moved out of
the fast lane and into the bike lane, and I was finally able to get
the most out of my new life.

58. **F.** NO CHANGE
    G. younger, furthermore, in
    H. younger. In
    J. younger in

59. Given that all the following are true, which one, if added
    here at the end of this sentence, would provide the most
    effective transition to the following sentence?

    A. it wasn't just freedom of movement anymore
    B. not a character as in a play, but more in the sense of a
    "type"
    C. I had resolved to ride my bike any distance shorter
    than ten miles
    D. I had to get the brakes fixed before I could use it a lot

Question 60 asks about the preceding passage as a whole.

60. Suppose the writer had intended to write a brief essay
    detailing the transportation options for visitors to a major
    city. Would this essay successfully fulfill the writer's goal?

    F. Yes, because the writer discusses biking, driving, and
    taking the bus in detail.
    G. Yes, because this essay deals with the ways in which
    the city would have fewer traffic jams if more people
    rode bikes.
    H. No, because the essay focuses instead on the writer's
    personal feelings about biking and driving in the city.
    J. No, because the essay deals primarily with the conve-
    nience of driving and its superiority over other forms
    of transportation.

PASSAGE V

Man's Best Friend

[1]

More and more, people are treating their pets like royalty.
Where once it was considered extravagant to put a sweater or a
pair of shoes on a <u>dog that</u> it is almost to the point now where it
₆₁
is considered an abuse *not* to dress your dog for cold weather!

61. **A.** NO CHANGE
    B. dog, and
    C. dog and
    D. dog,

Large pet stores are not the only ones that benefit from people's
interest in dogs—raising pets has become an industry all its
own, with significant representation in the clothing, publishing,
and entertainment industries, to name a few. How did we ever
get this way?

[2]

Archaeologists have found cultural and skeletal evidence
of domesticated dogs as far back as 6500 BCE in Mesopotomia
and as far back as 8300 BCE in what is now North America. Put
simply, dogs have been around as domesticated animals for a
long time and in all different parts of the world. Some historians
suggest that dogs as a species evolved into something close
to their current form as many as 100,000 years ago, and many
historians estimate that dogs were first domesticated as many as
15,000 years ago. There are over 800 different breeds of dogs,
and many more that cannot be classified into a single breed.

[3]

Although dogs have been bred and domesticated for
many reasons throughout history, the primary reason for their
breeding in ancient times was their usefulness as hunting
companions. Dogs' agility and sense of smell still, to this day,
help hunters to capture their prey. Dogs were also often used
as protectors, whom primary responsibility was to sit in front
of a residence or place of gathering and scare away would-be
robbers and evildoers.

[4]

[1] Since the eighteenth century, by way of example, dogs
have been seen more as companions and family members than

62. Which of the following alternatives to the underlined portion would NOT be acceptable?

   F.   that are benefiting
   G.   that have benefited
   H.   benefiting
   J.   that having benefited

63. Given that all of the choices are true, which one would most effectively conclude this paragraph while leading into the main focus of the next paragraph?

   A.   NO CHANGE
   B.   Even since these early times, people have recognized the importance of keeping domesticated dogs.
   C.   Many argue that the dog has been as important to the unfolding of human history as has the horse.
   D.   The dog is a major subspecies of the wolf, and many features of its biological makeup are still similar to those of the wolf.

64. **F.**   NO CHANGE
   G.   Unless
   H.   Because
   J.   Whether

65. **A.**   NO CHANGE
   B.   who
   C.   whose
   D.   who's

66. **F.**   NO CHANGE
   G.   as a consequence,
   H.   by contrast,
   J.   moreover,

in such impersonal roles as hunters or guardsmen. [2] From
this point in time, the dog has increasingly filled the role of
domesticated pet, and according to the American Pet Products
Manufacturers Association, 39% of Americans currently own
at least one dog, and there are no fewer then 74 million
owned dogs in the United States. [3] Inspired by the ideas
of the Enlightenment, a social philosophy evolved that
began to treat all individuals as social equals, and people's

attitudes toward dogs begins to take on a more personal

character. ☐70 [4] Dogs came to be prized for their loyalty
and sacrifice, and as early as 1855, many have suggested, the
American English phrase "man's best friend" was already

commonplace in the language. ☐71

[5]

It should be no surprise, then, given this long and
progressive history of dog ownership, that people come to
think of their dogs more and more as near-human members
of their families. Think about all the indispensable, yet
underappreciated roles that dogs play in our lives—they are not
just our pets and "best friends"; they are also indispensable to
the practices of law enforcement, firefighting, and assistance to
the visually impaired, to name just a few. Although it may seem
at first that dogs are just lazy pets, on the one hand they are

67. A. NO CHANGE
B. roles,
C. roles:
D. roles;

68. F. NO CHANGE
G. less then
H. lesser than
J. fewer than

69. A. NO CHANGE
B. is beginning
C. began
D. had began

70. If the writer were to delete the phrase "take on a more personal character" from the preceding sentence, the essay would primarily lose:

F. an important description of a dog-breeding technique.
G. a detail that indicates how attitudes toward dogs have changed.
H. information that emphasizes the historical importance of dogs.
J. nothing, since this detail is the topic of the preceding paragraph.

71. For the sake of logic and coherence, Sentence 2 should be placed:

A. where it is now.
B. before Sentence 1.
C. after Sentence 3.
D. after Sentence 4.

72. F. NO CHANGE
G. indispensable yet underappreciated
H. indispensable; yet underappreciated
J. indispensable yet underappreciated,

73. A. NO CHANGE
B. for example
C. in actuality
D. more often than not

really much more than that. <u>Have a look</u> around and you'll find
₇₄
that dogs are an essential part of our modern society. So what if
they've got their own hotels and day spas these days—don't you
think they've earned them?

74. **F.** NO CHANGE
    G. Having a look
    H. To look
    J. Looking

Question 75 asks about the preceding passage as a whole.

---

75. Upon reviewing notes for this essay, the writer comes
    across some information and composes the following sen-
    tence, incorporating that information:

    > Furthermore, many ancient civilizations, Greek and
    > Egyptian among them, used trained war dogs to aid
    > them in battle.

    For the sake of the logic and coherence of the essay, this
    sentence should be:

    A. placed at the end of Paragraph 1.
    B. placed at the end of Paragraph 3.
    C. placed at the end of Paragraph 5.
    D. NOT added to the essay at all.

DIRECTIONS: In the five passages that follow, certain words and phrases are underlined and numbered. In the right-hand column, you will find alternatives for each underlined part. In most cases, you are to choose the one that best expresses the idea, makes the statement appropriate for standard written English, or is worded most consistently with the style and tone of the passage as a whole. If you think the original version is best, choose "NO CHANGE." In some cases, you will find in the right-hand column a question about the underlined part. You are to choose the best answer to the question.

You will also find questions about a section of the passage or the passage as a whole. These questions do not refer to an underlined portion of the passage but rather are identified by a number or numbers in a box.

For each question, choose the alternative you consider best and blacken the corresponding oval on your answer document. Read each passage through once before you begin to answer the questions that accompany it. For many of the questions, you must read several sentences beyond the question to determine the answer. Be sure that you have read far enough ahead each time you choose an alternative.

PASSAGE I

André Bazin's Nouvelle Vague

André Bazin died on November 11, 1958 after over 15 years of pioneering work in film criticism. His magazine, *Cahiers du Cinéma* (Cinema Notebooks), had been issued regularly since its founding 1951, and it had become the premier journal in French for the serious discussion of films. Bazin, working and living in Paris, had become one of the cities premier intellectuals. Despite all of the achievements
[1]
of Bazin's lifetime, the true fruit of his labor did not begin to become truly apparent until the year following Bazin's death.

It was in 1959 in Paris that the *nouvelle vague* (new wave) in
[2]

French cinema exploded onto the international film scene.
[3]

Bazin published his first piece of film criticism in 1943 and

pioneered a new way of writing about film, he championed the
[4]
idea that cinema was the "seventh art," every bit as deserving

1. **A.** NO CHANGE
   B. citys
   C. cities'
   D. city's

2. **F.** NO CHANGE
   G. in 1959 in Paris,
   H. in 1959, in Paris
   J. in, 1959 in Paris,

3. Which of the following alternatives to the underlined portion is LEAST acceptable?

   A. emerged
   B. released
   C. erupted
   D. burst

4. **F.** NO CHANGE
   G. film. He
   H. film he
   J. film. Although he

as the more respected arts of: architecture, poetry, dance, music,
painting, and sculpture. Many before Bazin's time thought of
the cinema as a simple extension of another art form: theatre.
In fact, in many early writings about film, it is not uncommon
to hear the authors speak of film. [6] Bazin, though, sought to
show that the cinema had every bit as much creative vitality
and craftsmanship as any of the other six arts. From this
fundamental belief came what was possibly Bazin's greatest

contribution to film criticism: *auteur* theory. [7]

    Auteur is the French word for *author*, and the suggestion
contained in both the word and Bazin's theory is that every
film is "authored" by a single mind just as a novel or poem is
the work of a single author. For Bazin, and the increasingly
influential group of critics working with him at the *Cahiers du
Cinéma*, the author of any film is its director, and to discern

a director's true style, perspective, or his sense of voice, the
critic has merely to watch a group of the director's films
with an eye to similarities between them. Accordingly, Bazin
and the *Cahiers* group were truly the first to discuss films
and the practice of cinema in general as the masterwork of
directors, rather than screenwriters or actors. With *auteur*
theory, nonetheless, Bazin created a new way of looking at

5. **A.** NO CHANGE
   B. of, architecture,
   C. of architecture,
   D. of, architecture

6. The writer is considering adding the following phrase to
   the end of the preceding sentence (deleting the period after
   the word *film*):

   > as a second-class substitute for the "legitimate theatre."

   Should the writer make this addition there?

   F. Yes, because it clarifies the sentence to show more
   specifically how critics talked about film.
   G. Yes, because it helps the reader to understand more
   clearly the subjects of Bazin's writing.
   H. No, because it fails to maintain this paragraph's focus
   on the *Cahiers du Cinéma*.
   J. No, because it speaks disparagingly about the practice
   of filmmaking.

7. At this point the writer is considering adding the following
   true statement:

   > Bazin's work is available in a text commonly read in
   > Film Studies classes, the collection *What Is Cinema?*

   Should the writer make this addition here?

   A. Yes, because it maintains the essay's focus on an important figure in French film criticism.
   B. Yes, because it gives a good sense of the type of reading students can expect in Film Studies classes.
   C. No, because it interrupts the discussion of a specific
   theory of Bazin's.
   D. No, because other information in the essay suggests
   that this statement is untrue.

8. **F.** NO CHANGE
   G. the director's voice,
   H. his voice,
   J. voice,

9. **A.** NO CHANGE
   B. meanwhile,
   C. still,
   D. DELETE the underlined portion.

films, and his early <u>works on</u> such influential directors as Orson
Welles, Vittorio de Sica, and Jean Renoir—remain, to this day,
pioneering works of film criticism that are studied and emulated

by film critics today. ☐11

Bazin's greatest achievement was the strong impression he
left on a young generation of French filmmakers and critics who

came on to the international scene <u>all over the world</u> just a year

after Bazin's death. In 1959, two films <u>changed the landscape
of international filmmaking:</u> François Truffaut's *The 400 Blows*
and Jean-Luc Godard's *Breathless*. In each film, the director has
taken Bazin's emphasis on *auteur* filmmaking to heart, and in
every frame, the viewer is reminded of the director's presence
by the overwhelming stylistic personality of shots and scenes.
Throughout the 1960s and 1970s, independent and avant-garde
filmmakers in places as disparate as France, the United States,
Italy, and Japan were beginning to exercise the new cinematic
freedom that Bazin had charted for them. <u>At that time,</u> whenever
a national film industry completely reinvents itself, it is carried
along by a group of *auteur* directors who refer to their films
as part of a *new wave*. Now there are legions of filmmakers,
Mohsen Makhmalbaf and Abbas Kiarostami in Iran or Alfonso
Cuaron and Guillermo del Toro in Mexico, for example, whose
inspiration can in some way be traced back to Bazin and his
humble work as editor of the *Cahiers du Cinéma* in France way
back in the 1950s.

10. **F.** NO CHANGE
    G. works, on
    H. works: on
    J. works—on

11. Which of the following sentences, if added here, would
    effectively conclude this paragraph and introduce the topic
    of the next?
    A. Bazin himself never made any films, but he always
    preferred the Italian Neorealist style.
    B. While Bazin's magazine was the place to read about
    classic films, Henri Langlois's *Cinematheque* was the
    place to see them.
    C. Despite these great written achievements in the *Ca-
    hiers du Cinéma*, Bazin's true and lasting influence lay
    elsewhere.
    D. Many film critics working in the later part of the
    twentieth century, such as Christian Metz and Gilles
    Deleuze, are clearly indebted to Bazin.

12. **F.** NO CHANGE
    G. in all parts of the world
    H. in every nation and country
    J. DELETE the underlined portion.

13. Which choice would most effectively guide readers to un-
    derstand the great importance of the two films discussed?
    A. NO CHANGE
    B. came out around the same time:
    C. joined the long list of films shot primarily in Paris:
    D. were created by directors who knew Bazin personally:

14. **F.** NO CHANGE
    G. Back then,
    H. Even now,
    J. In the end,

Question 15 asks about the preceding passage as a whole.

15. Suppose the author intended to write an essay that illustrates how the writings of one film critic have had an influence beyond the realm of film criticism. Would this essay successfully fulfill that goal?

   A. Yes, because the essay describes Bazin's influence on the six arts of architecture, poetry, dance, music, painting, and sculpture.

   B. Yes, because the essay describes Bazin's influence on both film criticism and filmmaking.

   C. No, because the essay discusses *auteur* theory and French films in general.

   D. No, because the essay states that Bazin's greatest achievements were as a filmmaker.

PASSAGE II

Preventing Biblioemergencies

Before I move next week, I will unwillingly return the books that I have checked out from the library. Sadly, I never even opened a couple of them, and the return of them will be
16

painfully abrupt. 17

16. F. NO CHANGE
   G. returning
   H. to have returned
   J. returned

17. If the writer were to delete the words *unwillingly, sadly,* and *painfully* from this paragraph, the paragraph would primarily lose:

   A. evidence undermining the author's later assertion that she loves to read.

   B. the sense that the author is unhappy about her move.

   C. an explanation of the motive behind the writer's intended actions.

   D. its emphasis on the writer's reluctance to lose any books.

I know that I have plenty of other books to read. There are
18
at least ten unread books of my own at home and ten more that I'm expecting in the mail. Still, whenever I return a book, I get that feeling of "*what if*": What if I run out of books?

Some friends of mine recently coined the phrase *biblioemergency* to describe just such a situation. A *biblioemergency* is when an avid reader, such as myself,

18. Which of the following alternatives to the underlined portion would NOT be acceptable?

   F. a lot
   G. a number
   H. numerous
   J. a bunch

discovers that she has nothing left to read, which I know that to

some people, that's no big deal, but to me, its a disaster.

Ever since childhood, I've made it a point to carry at least one sometimes two or more, books with me at all times. People ask me why I can't just make do with one book in my bag,

or none. But, I always point out, what if I finish them? What would I do then?

I think this all comes from a habit developed at an early age, due to my parents' use of books as pacifiers. Whenever my mother took me to a store or to an appointment, she

brought along books. As soon as I got fidgety, she'd supply me with a new book to keep me entertained, hopefully until

she had finished her business. [25] Now as an adult, I

nevertheless find it nearly impossible to wait patiently unless, of course, I have reading material.

19 A. NO CHANGE
    B. read.
    C. read that
    D. read,

20. F. NO CHANGE
    G. theirs
    H. they're
    J. it's

21. A. NO CHANGE
    B. at least one,
    C. at least one:
    D. at least one;

22. F. NO CHANGE
    G. the book I'm reading
    H. it
    J. those

23. A. NO CHANGE
    B. parents
    C. parents's
    D. parent

24. F. NO CHANGE
    G. I got fidgety
    H. After fidgeting,
    J. Getting fidgety,

25. At this point, the author is considering adding the following sentence.

    The best ones were the ones that had both pictures and words.

    If the information is taken to be true, should the author make this addition here?

    A. Yes, because it gives more information that is relevant to the previous comment.
    B. Yes, because it adds a detail that explains the main idea of the paragraph.
    C. No, because it contradicts information given in an earlier paragraph.
    D. No, because it is offensive and irrelevant to the passage as a whole.

26. F. NO CHANGE
    G. yet
    H. conversely
    J. consequently

[1] When I've run out of books in the past, <u>finding</u> myself
₂₇
reading the backs of cereal boxes or the labels on my clothes.
[2] Even though I will have to return my books to the library, I

plan to <u>packing</u> at least four or five in my carry-on luggage, as
₂₈
I do every time I travel. [3] That, my friend, is an experience I
never need to repeat. [4] If that sounds like a hassle, imagine
the alternative. 29

27. **A.** NO CHANGE
    B. being that I've found
    C. I've found
    D. having found

28. **F.** NO CHANGE
    G. have been packing
    H. pack
    J. be packing

29. Which of the following sequences of sentences makes this
    paragraph the most logical?

    A. NO CHANGE
    B. 2, 4, 1, 3
    C. 3, 1, 2, 4
    D. 4, 1, 2, 3

    | Question 30 asks about the preceding passage as a whole. |
    ---

30. Upon reviewing the essay, the writer is considering remov-
    ing the final paragraph. Should that paragraph be kept or
    deleted?

    F. Kept, because it returns to the opening idea and pro-
    vides a conclusion.
    G. Kept, because it reveals the writer's true motivation for
    refusing to return the books.
    H. Deleted, because it distracts from the focus of the
    passage.
    J. Deleted, because it repeats information already given
    without adding any new elements.

PASSAGE III

The Space Race

[1]

Writer and political commentator Robert <u>Heinlein, writing</u>
<u>about politics,</u> stated that mankind needs to venture out into
₃₁
space as a matter of necessity: "The Earth is just too small
and fragile a basket for the human race to keep all its eggs in."
In the 1960s, the political climate of the Cold War provided
the backdrop for the explosive race to the moon between the

31. **A.** NO CHANGE
    B. Heinlein
    C. Heinlein who was writing about politics
    D. Heinlein—writing about politics—

Russians and the Americans. [32] However, this was only the

first step from <u>our inner world</u> on Earth toward outer space. A
                      33
longer-lasting, and some say more important, achievement has

been the development of the *International Space Station*.

[2]

However, the *International Space Station* was

not created overnight. It can trace <u>it's</u> lineage back to
                                     34

Salyut 1, the very first space station launched in 1971 by the
         35
Russians. In most respects, *Salyut 1* was actually a failure. For

example, before <u>plummeting, to Earth, it orbited</u> the planet for
                                36
less than six months and was plagued by mechanical problems

that ultimately resulted in the deaths of three cosmonauts. [37]

Yet, the *Salyut* experiment proved that extraterrestrial habitation

was possible and allowed the Russians to develop other, more

32. The writer is considering adding the following phrase to the end of the preceding sentence (replacing the period after *Americans* with a comma):

> because both the Russians and the Americans wanted to reach the moon first.

Should the writer add this phrase here?

F. Yes, because it specifies that both groups were competing.
G. Yes, because it emphasizes to the reader the ultimate goal of the race.
H. No, because it is clear from earlier in the sentence that both groups were competing to reach the moon.
J. No, because it provides additional information that distracts the reader from the primary focus of the passage.

33. A. NO CHANGE
    B. inside the atmosphere
    C. within our planet
    D. the interior

34. F. NO CHANGE
    G. its'
    H. its
    J. their

35. A. NO CHANGE
    B. *Salyut 1* the
    C. *Salyut 1*; the
    D. *Salyut 1*. The

36. F. NO CHANGE
    G. plummeting to Earth, it orbited
    H. plummeting to Earth. It orbited
    J. plummeting to Earth; it orbited

37. The writer is considering adding the following clause to the end of the preceding sentence (replacing the period after the word *cosmonauts* with a comma):

> who were honored as heroes at their funerals.

Should the writer add this clause here?

A. Yes, because it was not the cosmonauts' fault that they were killed.
B. Yes, because it provides information that is not mentioned elsewhere in the passage.
C. No, because it distracts the reader from the main focus of the paragraph.
D. No, because no description of the funeral is provided.

technically successful space stations in the years that followed, the most famous of which was called *Mir*. [38]

[3]

Not to be outdone, the Americans looked to the mixed success the Russians enjoyed with *Salyut 1* and launched their own space station in 1973 called *Skylab*. Like the Russian space station, however, *Skylab* too had operational difficulties. Hit by debris, severe damage was suffered by it during the launch
₃₉
and was inoperable until astronauts repaired it during numerous spacewalks. Once it was repaired, however, astronauts focused on conducting mainly scientific experiments, and three
₄₀
separate crews successfully docked there throughout 1973 and 1974. Though additional missions were planned, none were
₄₁
ever launched, and *Skylab* fell back to Earth in 1979 after about six years in orbit.

[4]

[1] This space station was successful and launched in 2000
₄₂
and has hosted more than 17 crews from numerous countries since then. [2] The end of the Cold War in the 1990s meant that both nations could work together on the goal of achieving
₄₃
a sustainable habitat in outer space. [3] Ultimately, the Russian *Salyut* stations and *Mir* and the American *Skylab* laid the groundwork for the *International Space Station*. [44]

38. Which of the following true statements, if added here, would best point out how successful *Mir* was?

   F. *Mir*, in fact, orbited the Earth for 14 years and hosted more than two dozen long-duration crews.
   G. The name *Mir* actually means *peace* in Russian.
   H. Unfortunately, Russian cosmonauts would stay on *Mir* for so long that they were unable to walk when they returned to Earth.
   J. *Mir* fell to Earth in 2001 and ended in a way reminiscent of *Salyut* thirty years earlier.

39. A. NO CHANGE
   B. it suffered severe damage
   C. severely damaged it suffered
   D. it was suffering from severe damage

40. The best placement for the underlined portion would be:

   F. where it is now.
   G. after the word *Once*.
   H. after the word *focused*.
   J. after the word *three*.

41. A. NO CHANGE
   B. and 1974 though
   C. and 1974, though
   D. and 1974 though,

42. F. NO CHANGE
   G. successfully
   H. successfully and
   J. successful

43. Which of the following alternatives to the underlined portion would be LEAST acceptable?

   A. countries
   B. states
   C. lands
   D. cities

44. Which of the following sequences of sentences will make Paragraph 4 most logical?

   F. NO CHANGE
   G. 2, 1, 3
   H. 3, 1, 2
   J. 3, 2, 1

Question 45 asks about the preceding passage as a whole.

45. Suppose the writer had intended to write a brief essay about Robert Heinlein's contributions to space exploration. Would this essay fulfill that purpose?

    A. Yes, because the essay quotes Heinlein on the importance of space exploration.

    B. Yes, because the essay describes the development of space stations.

    C. No, because the essay is about *Mir*, which Heinlein did not explicitly discuss.

    D. No, because the essay offers a broader focus on the development of space stations.

PASSAGE IV

Inventions That Break Barriers

At the turn of the 20th century, Mary Anderson was a real-estate developer, rancher, and wine-maker. We don't know her name today for any of these reasons, however. Instead, Anderson made history <u>for</u> inventing automobile windshield wipers—a feat she accomplished in 1903, five years before Henry Ford even created the Model T. In 1902, while riding a trolley in New York City, she couldn't help noticing that the driver had to continually stop in order <u>to wipe</u> snow and ice from the windshield. Anderson thought <u>that there had to be a better way.</u>

46. F. NO CHANGE
    G. by
    H. to
    J. as

47. A. NO CHANGE
    B. to wiping
    C. for wiping
    D. and wiped

48. Which of the following alternatives to the underlined portion would NOT be acceptable?

    F. she could devise a better way.
    G. that there must be a better way.
    H. in which there had to be a better way.
    J. that a better way could be found.

<u>However she,</u> devised a swinging arm with a rubber blade that swung back and forth, swishing rain and snow from the windshield surface. Anderson's model was different from

49. A. NO CHANGE
    B. Instead she,
    C. On the contrary she,
    D. She

todays models, though, because it was hand-activated by a lever

from inside the car. Similar devices had been attempted and tried in the past, but Anderson's was the first to work and the first to be successfully patented. Interestingly, she could not sell the rights to her invention. A Canadian company told her that drivers would find the movement of the arm too distracting. So even though Anderson's windshield wipers became standard in

cars after 1915, her invention did not make her much money.

    Today, it is difficult for us to imagine driving without windshield wipers. In fact, women have been responsible for many practical inventions. Josephine Cochran, for example, declared, "If nobody else is going to invent a dishwashing machine, I will." She presented her working dishwasher at the

1886 World's Fair. At first not a huge success; the machine was used only by hotels and large restaurants. Household dishwashers did not become popular until the 1950s.

    Historically, women have held a minority of patents. In early U.S. history, social and legal barriers often discouraged women from patenting inventions. In Anderson and Cochran's time, women lacked the same legal rights as men, which

compelled many women patented their inventions under their husbands' or fathers' names. Although the true number of women inventors in history may not ever be known, it is evident

---

50. F. NO CHANGE
    G. today's models,
    H. todays' models
    J. today's models

51. A. NO CHANGE
    B. attempted
    C. attempted, and later, tried
    D. attempted, that is, tried

52. F. NO CHANGE
    G. would, find the movement of the arm
    H. would find the movement, of the arm,
    J. would find the movement of the arm,

53. A. NO CHANGE
    B. its
    C. it's
    D. their

54. Given that all the choices are true, which one would best introduce the new subject of this paragraph?
    F. NO CHANGE
    G. Today, we are the lucky recipients of Anderson's invention.
    H. Mary Anderson believed that driving could be made safer.
    J. Anderson was not the only female innovator of her time.

55. A. NO CHANGE
    B. success. The
    C. success, the
    D. success: the

56. Which of the following alternatives to the underlined portion would be LEAST acceptable?
    F. prevented
    G. disturbed
    H. dissuaded
    J. stopped

57. A. NO CHANGE
    B. to patent
    C. patenting
    D. patent

that women like Mary Anderson and Josephine Cochran saw

<u>problems</u> and devised simple and imaginative solutions. It is
58
unfortunate that the genius behind each of these innovations

<u>have not always been</u> rewarded or recognized, because these
59
women helped to create the efficient world we take for granted

today.

58. **F.** NO CHANGE
G. problems demanding solutions
H. dilemmas that could be solved
J. ways to fix problems

59. **A.** NO CHANGE
B. were not always
C. was not always
D. are not always

Question 60 asks about the preceding passage as a whole.

60. Suppose the writer's goal had been to write a brief essay
documenting key innovations in the automobile industry.
Would this essay successfully fulfill that goal?

F. Yes, because it highlights an important invention that
changed the way cars are driven.
G. Yes, because it tells readers how and when a key in-
novation in automobiles was introduced.
H. No, because it does not include information about
when the windshield wipers changed from hand-activated to automatic devices.
J. No, because it addresses only one automobile
invention.

Do Blue Bags Make a Green City?

In 1995, Chicago implemented its Blue Bag recycling

program. This program was different from virtually any other

throughout the world, particularly for a city of Chicago's size.

<u>Muncie, Indiana instituted a similar program, but it is a much</u>
61
<u>smaller city than Chicago.</u> Chicago's idea was that you could
61

61. Given that all the choices are true, which one provides the
most specific support for the statement in the preceding
sentence?

A. NO CHANGE
B. Almost all other major cities ask their residents to sort
recycling at centers or into specific receptacles.
C. Nearly every major city in the United States has
an aggressive plan for recycling, but they're not all
successful.
D. Chicago implemented many garbage collecting ad-
vances in the 1980s to cope with rodent problems.

throw your recycling away with your garbage as part of a
program that was new to the city. All you'd have to do is make
sure that when you threw your recycling into the dumpster or
put it out on the street, it was in a blue garbage bag rather than
a standard white or black bag. Many embraced the program
because they felt it wouldn't inconvenience residents and the
process would be similar to the normal garbage collection
residents were used to; collecting all the recyclable waste into a
bag, remembering the day for pickup, and then leaving the bag
on the curb or in a dumpster. These bags would be picked up
by the normal garbage collectors, and eventually, the blue bags
would be removed from the garbage and rerouted to various
recycling facilities.

This program hummed along, and was still going strong
when I moved to the city. The city's goal was to improve the
city's 13–19% recycling rate to the point where, of all the waste
collected, 25% of it would be recycled. In 2005, according
to a report by city officials, they had reached that goal, and
many believed that Chicago was becoming a truly "green" city.
Unfortunately, independent researchers told a much different
tale. According to their estimates, as little as 9% of the city's
waste was being recycled and the rates of recycling among
residents were still around levels they had been in the 1980s. In

other words, you could say that not much changes.

[1] So what was wrong for this program? [2] The Chicago
area is not overwhelmed by landfill issues as are some other
major cities, so many people who live in the city didn't think
recycling or diverting waste was all that important. [3] Then

62. Given that all choices are true, which description of Chicago's recycling process best supports the city's logic in its choice of program, as described in this paragraph?

   F. NO CHANGE

   G. which the garbage collectors would pick up every Wednesday.

   H. without the hassle of driving to a recycling center.

   J. instead of the old-fashioned way of throwing things away.

63. **A.** NO CHANGE
   B. to
   C. to,
   D. to:

64. **F.** NO CHANGE
   G. officials they
   H. officials. They
   J. officials; they

65. Which of the following alternatives to the underlined portion would NOT be acceptable?

   A. 1980s, so in
   B. 1980s; in
   C. 1980s: in
   D. 1980s, in

66. **F.** NO CHANGE
   G. not much had changed.
   H. not much would have changed.
   J. not much was to have changed.

67. **A.** NO CHANGE
   B. to
   C. with
   D. from

there were the actual mechanics of <u>running</u> the program.
68

[4] The biggest problem was probably the residents' lack of
interest. [5] These turned out to be much more complicated
than either the city or its various contractors ever expected.
[6] Imagine, for example, the magnitude of manpower and
financial investment <u>with such a requiring</u> to pull these select
69
bags out of the more than 5 million tons of garbage Chicagoans

dump every year! [7] What happens to all the bags <u>that</u> rip in
70
transit, with all those recyclables then mixed in with all the

other garbage? ☐71

In May 2008, the city decided to discontinue its Blue
Bag <u>program and replace</u> it with a new one. The cloud had a
72
silver lining, though; the controversy surrounding the Blue Bag
program, which was getting press alongside larger mounting
concerns about global warming and other environmental issues,
made the city's residents and business owners more aware of
the importance of recycling. Even during the Blue Bag program,
a trip to one of the city's public recycling centers <u>were</u> proof
73
that Chicagoans were interested in recycling. Many times I'd go

and, because the centers were so <u>lacking in</u> recyclables, I'd have
74
to take my recyclables to another center that was not so full.
Now, to replace the Blue Bag program, the city has begun to

68. Which of the following alternatives to the underlined portion would be LEAST acceptable?

   F. maintaining
   G. operating
   H. sustaining
   J. hiring

69. A. NO CHANGE
   B. of which much was required
   C. that were requiring much of
   D. that was required

70. F. NO CHANGE
   G. still that they
   H. as they
   J. seeing as they

71. For the sake of the logic and coherence of this paragraph,
Sentence 4 should be placed:

   A. where it is now.
   B. after Sentence 1.
   C. after Sentence 5.
   D. after Sentence 7.

72. Which of the following alternatives to the underlined portion would NOT be acceptable?

   F. program and to replace
   G. program they've replaced
   H. program, replacing
   J. program and decided to replace

73. A. NO CHANGE
   B. was
   C. is
   D. have been

74. Which choice presents this description in a way most
consistent with the writer's description of the recycling
centers?

   F. NO CHANGE
   G. undersupplied with
   H. neglected of
   J. overwhelmed by

institute the Blue *Bin* program, and there are many of us <u>whose</u>
hope that this program can right the wrongs of the last program
and make Chicago the truly green city we know it can be.

75. A. NO CHANGE
    B. whom
    C. who
    D. that

Math Practice

MATHEMATICS TEST

60 Minutes—60 Questions

DIRECTIONS: Solve each problem, choose the correct answer, and then darken the corresponding oval on your answer document.

Do not linger over problems that take too much time. Solve as many as you can; then return to the others in the time you have left for this test.

You are permitted to use a calculator on this test. You may use your calculator for any problems you choose, but some of the problems may best be done without using a calculator.

Note: Unless otherwise stated, all of the following should be assumed:

1. Illustrative figures are NOT necessarily drawn to scale.
2. Geometric figures lie in a plane.
3. The word *line* indicates a straight line.
4. The word *average* indicates arithmetic mean.

---

1. A magician performing at children's birthday parties charges $120.00 total for a one-hour performance with ten goodie bags for children at the party. She will provide additional goodie bags for $2.50 each. For an additional $25.00, she will also present a 15-minute laser light show. The magician is always paid on the day of the show, receives no tips or other additional payments, and never varies the length of the show. If the magician performs exactly four shows one weekend, presents the light show at three of those performances, and collects $635.00 total, how many additional goodie bags did she provide?

   A. 26
   B. 32
   C. 48
   D. 86
   E. 254

DO YOUR FIGURING HERE.

2. In an elite marathon runner's training, total mileage consists of miles run at or faster than marathon pace and miles run slower than marathon pace. The table below shows miles run at or below marathon pace and total mileage for an elite marathon runner for each of 3 consecutive years.

Running at or faster than marathon pace			
Year	# Runs	Total Miles	Miles/Month
2002	294	2,645	220.4
2003	179	1,614	134.5
2004	128	1,150	95.8
Total Mileage			
Year	Total Runs	Total Miles	Miles/Month
2002	414	3,725	310.4
2003	458	4,122	343.5
2004	554	4,982	415.2

In 2004, how many miles of the runner's total mileage were miles run slower than marathon pace?

F. 1,012
G. 2,972
H. 3,368
J. 3,832
K. 3,850

3. A 24-hour day is how many times as long as 60 seconds?

A. 12
B. 30
C. 365
D. 720
E. 1,440

4. A student reads a pages per day for d days and then reads b pages per day for $2d$ days. In terms of a, b, and d, how many pages did the student read?

F. $ad + 2b$
G. $ad + 2bd$
H. $2ad + 2bd$
J. $2abd$
K. $2abd^2$

5. A trapezoidal driveway has the dimensions, in yards, given in the figure below. What is the area, in square yards, of the driveway?

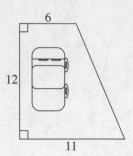

A. 42
B. 72
C. 102
D. 156
E. 204

6. The graph below shows the number of people visiting a museum during the first 5 months of the year. How many people need to visit the museum during June for the mean of the first 6 months to equal the mean of the first 5 months?

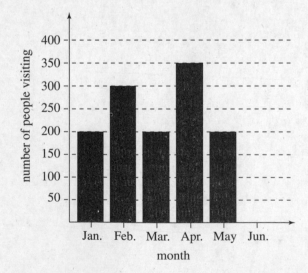

F. 0
G. 200
H. 250
J. 500
K. 1,250

7. A graduation cap is tossed upward. It is f feet above the ground s seconds after it has been thrown. The relationship between f and s is given by the equation $f = 60s - 17s^2$ where $0 \leq s \leq 3.5$. How many feet above the ground is the cap 3 seconds after it is thrown?

    A.   27
    B.   41
    C.   60
    D.   80
    E.   163

8. The highest and lowest test scores of five students in Mr. Canyon's science class are listed below. Which student had the greatest range of scores?

	High	Low
Alicia	93	76
Brandon	91	79
Cleo	99	81
David	74	56
Emily	89	70

    F.   Alicia
    G.   Brandon
    H.   Cleo
    J.   David
    K.   Emily

9. Nita, Craig, and Chris catch a total of 300 fish on their trip. If Chris catches 45% of the fish and Craig catches 25 fish, what fraction of the 300 fish does Nita catch?

    A. $\dfrac{23}{30}$

    B. $\dfrac{41}{60}$

    C. $\dfrac{1}{2}$

    D. $\dfrac{7}{15}$

    E. $\dfrac{1}{3}$

10. Given that $f(x) = 4x^2$ and $g(x) = 3 - \dfrac{x}{2}$, what is the value of $f(g(4))$?

    F.   1
    G.   4
    H.   8
    J.   16
    K.   64

11. In the grid shown below, each small square has a side length of 1 unit. In the shaded region, each vertex lies on a vertex of a small square. What is the area, in square units, of the shaded region?

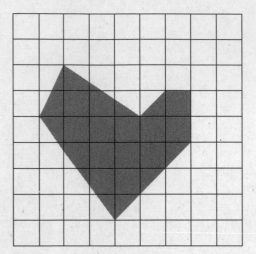

   A. 35
   B. 25
   C. 24
   D. 19
   E. 13

DO YOUR FIGURING HERE.

12. A ramp rises 6 inches for each 24 inches of horizontal run. This ramp rises how many inches for 62 inches of horizontal run?

   F. $15\dfrac{1}{2}$

   G. $20\dfrac{2}{3}$

   H.   44

   J.   80

   K.   248

13. What is the value of $y^x + (2x - 2y)$ when $x = 2$ and $y = -3$?

   A.   −10
   B.   1
   C.   7
   D.   16
   E.   19

14. In the figure below, the circle with center O is tangent to $\overline{AE}$, $\overline{BD}$, $\overline{CF}$, and $\overline{DE}$. The measure of angle $\angle BDE$ is 75° and the measure of $\angle DEA$ is 105°.

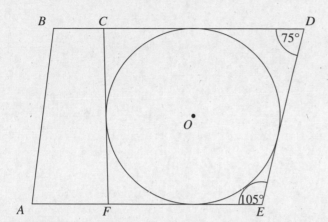

The lines in which of the following pairs of lines are necessarily parallel?

   I. $\overline{AB}$ and $\overline{DE}$

  II. $\overline{BD}$ and $\overline{AE}$

 III. $\overline{CF}$ and $\overline{DE}$

  F. I only
  G. II only
  H. III only
  J. I and II only
  K. I, II, and III

15. The day a clothing store puts out a batch of brand-name T-shirts it sells 95 shirts at $4.10 per shirt. However, each day the shirts are on the rack, the store reduces the price of the shirts by $0.02 and consequently sells 1 additional shirt with each price reduction. If x represents the number of $0.02 price reductions, which of the following expressions represents the amount of money, in dollars, that the store will take in daily in sales of these brand name T-shirts?

  A. $(4.10 + 2x)(95 + x)$
  B. $(4.10 - 2x)(95 + x)$
  C. $(4.10 + 0.02x)(95 + x)$
  D. $(4.10 - 0.02x)(95 + x)$
  E. $(4.10 - 0.02x)(95 + 0.02x)$

16. The expression $x^2 - 7x + 12$ is equivalent to:

  F. $(x - 12)(x + 1)$
  G. $(x - 4)(x - 3)$
  H. $(x - 4)(x + 3)$
  J. $(x - 6)(x - 2)$
  K. $(x - 6)(x + 2)$

17. When $x = 5$ and $y = 2$, the expression

$$\frac{xy}{70} + \frac{9}{5(x+y)} + \frac{1}{x+y} = ?$$

A. $\dfrac{19}{35}$

B. $\dfrac{58}{105}$

C. $\dfrac{1}{2}$

D. $\dfrac{4}{7}$

E. $\dfrac{5}{28}$

18. The minutes and seconds on a 60-minute digital timer are represented by 3 or 4 digits. What is the *largest* product that can be obtained by multiplying the digits in one of these representations?

(Note: When the timer displays 16:15, the product of the digits is $(1)(6)(1)(5) = 30$.)

F. 90
G. 2,025
H. 3,481
J. 3,600
K. 6,561

19. The difference of 2 integers is 6. The sum of the same 2 integers is 42. What is the lesser of the 2 integers?

A. 18
B. 19
C. 21
D. 23
E. 24

20. The area of the square in the figure below is 324 square centimeters, and the two small isosceles right triangles are congruent. What is the combined area, in square centimeters, of the 2 small triangles?

F. 108
G. 162
H. 216
J. 324
K. 648

324

21. Jasper wants to measure the altitude of his kite. He ties the kite string to a spike driven into the ground and measures the angle between the string and the ground. Then, he creates 2 similar triangles by adjusting the distance between an 8 foot pole and the spike until the angle created by a piece of string tied to the top of the pole and to the spike with the ground is the same as the angle he measured previously. The length of the string to the kite is 85 feet and the length of the string to the pole is 17 feet. Which of the following is closest to the height, in feet, that the kite is above the ground?

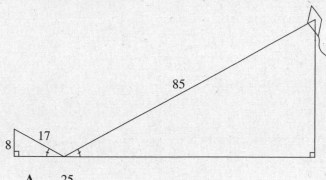

- **A.** 25
- **B.** 40
- **C.** 102
- **D.** 110
- **E.** 181

22. For what value of x, if any, is the equation
$(x-1)^2 = (x-7)^2$ true?

- **F.** −4
- **G.** −1
- **H.** 0
- **J.** 4
- **K.** There is no value of x for which the equation is true.

23. $\triangle ABC$, shown below in the standard (x,y) coordinate plane, is equilateral with vertex A at $(0,w)$ and vertex B on the x-axis as shown. What are the coordinates of vertex C?

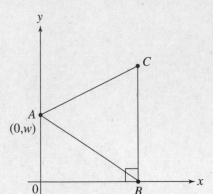

   A. $(w,0)$

   B. $(w,2w)$

   C. $(w\sqrt{3},w)$

   D. $(w\sqrt{3},2w)$

   E. $(2w,w\sqrt{3})$

24. The diagonal of a square quilt is $4\sqrt{2}$ feet long. What is the area of the quilt in square feet?

   F. $16\sqrt{2}$
   G. 16

   H. $4\sqrt{2}$
   J. 4

   K. $\sqrt{2}$

25. A painter needs to reach the top of a tall sign in the middle of a flat and level field. He uses a ladder of length x to reach a point on the sign 15 feet above the ground. The angle formed where the ladder meets the ground is noted in the figure below as θ. Which of the following relationships must be true?

   A. $\sin\theta = \dfrac{15}{x}$

   B. $\cos\theta = \dfrac{15}{x}$

   C. $\tan\theta = \dfrac{15}{x}$

   D. $\theta = \dfrac{15}{x}$

   E. $\dfrac{\sin\theta}{\cos\theta} = \dfrac{15}{x}$

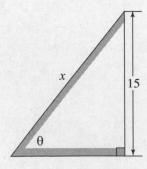

26. The equation $\sqrt{45+a} + \sqrt{a} = 15$ is true for what real value of a ?

F.   9
G. 16
H. 25
J.   36
K. 64

27. In rectangle $ABCD$ below, $\overline{BC}$ is 16 inches long and $\overline{CD}$ is 12 inches long. Points E, F, and G are the midpoints of $\overline{AD}$, $\overline{AB}$, and $\overline{BC}$, respectively. What is the perimeter, in inches, of pentagon $CDEFG$?

A.   48
B.   56
C.   96
D.   144
E.   192

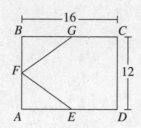

Use the following information to answer questions 28–30.

The table below details a recent census report about the commuting habits of U.S. workers age 16 or over for the years 2004, 2005, and 2006.

U.S. workers category	2004	2005	2006
Group*			
Total	130.9	133.1	138.3
Male	70.9	72.1	74.7
Female	60.0	61.0	63.6
Commute time†			
Under 10 minutes	14.9%	14.7%	14.8%
More than 25 minutes	40.4%	41.1%	40.8%
Means of transportation†			
Car	87.8%	87.6%	86.7%
Public transportation	7.8%	7.9%	8.4%
Bicycle	1.4%	1.4%	1.6%
Walked	3.0%	3.1%	3.3%
*in millions of people, rounded to the nearest tenth of a million †in percent, rounded to the nearest tenth of a percent Source: U.S. Census Bureau			

28. To the nearest percent, what percent of all U.S. workers age 16 or over in 2004 was female?

   F. 50%
   G. 48%
   H. 46%
   J. 44%
   K. 15%

DO YOUR FIGURING HERE.

29. The circle graph (pie chart) below represents the 2006 means of transportation for U.S. workers age 16 or over for the 4 transportation types listed. To the nearest degree, what is the measure of the central angle for the "Public" sector?

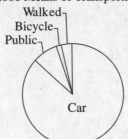

2006 Means of Transportation

   A. 8°
   B. 12°
   C. 20°
   D. 28°
   E. 30°

30. Expressed in millions of people, what was the average growth per year for female U.S. workers age 16 or over from 2004 to 2006, rounded to the nearest 0.1 million?

   F. 0.5
   G. 0.9
   H. 1.3
   J. 1.8
   K. 3.6

31. Two hoses attached to separate water sources are available to fill a cylindrical swimming pool. If both hoses are used, the time it will take to fill the pool can be represented by the following equation: $\dfrac{1}{T_1}+\dfrac{1}{T_2}=\dfrac{1}{T_c}$, where T_1 and T_2 represent the time needed for hoses 1 and 2, respectively, to fill the pool on their own, and T_c represents the time needed for hoses 1 and 2 to fill the pool working together. If hose 1 alone can fill the pool in exactly 20 minutes and hose 2 alone can fill the pool in exactly 60 minutes, how many minutes will it take to fill the pool if both hoses work simultaneously?

A. 3
B. 10
C. 15
D. 18
E. 40

DO YOUR FIGURING HERE.

32. A 5-sided die, which has sides 2, 3, 4, 5, and 6, is thrown. What is the probability that the die will NOT land on a prime-numbered face?

F. $\dfrac{4}{5}$

G. $\dfrac{3}{5}$

H. $\dfrac{2}{5}$

J. $\dfrac{1}{5}$

K. 0

33. For $f(x,y) = 7x + 9y$, what is the value of $f(x,y)$ when

$y = \left(\dfrac{5}{x}\right)^2$ and $x = 3$?

A. $\dfrac{68}{3}$

B. $\dfrac{214}{9}$

C. 36

D. 46

E. 96

4. What is the length, in coordinate units, of a diagonal of a square in the standard (x,y) coordinate plane with vertices at points $(0,0)$, $(4,0)$ and $(4, 4)$?

F. 3

G. 4

H. $4\sqrt{2}$

J. $4\sqrt{3}$

K. 8

35. What is the value of a if $\log_4 a = 3$?

A. 120

B. 64

C. 12

D. $\sqrt[4]{3}$

E. $4\sqrt{3}$

36. A certain 18-quart stockpot is filled completely with water and exposed to a heat source so that the water boils away at a constant rate. The water remaining in the stockpot can be approximated by the following equation: $y = 18 - 0.2x$, where x is the number of minutes that the pot has been heated for $0 \leq x \leq 90$, and y is the number of quarts remaining in the pot. According to this equation, which of the following statements is true about this stockpot?

F. After 0.2 minutes, 1 quart of water has boiled away.
G. After 1 minute, 0.2 quarts of water have boiled away.
H. After 18 minutes, 0.2 quarts of water have boiled away.
J. After 18 minutes, 1 quart of water has boiled away.
K. After 36 minutes, 18 quarts of water have boiled away.

DO YOUR FIGURING HERE.

37. The volume of a right circular cone with the bottom removed to create a flat base can be calculated from the following equation: $V = \frac{1}{3}\pi h(R^2 + r^2 + Rr)$, where h represents the height of the shape and R and r represent its radii as shown in the figure below:

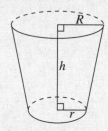

This formula can be used to determine the capacity of a large coffee mug. Approximately how many cubic inches of liquid can the cup shown below hold if it is filled to the brim and its handle holds no liquid?

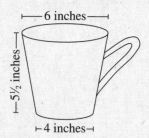

- **A.** 19
- **B.** 50
- **C.** 105
- **D.** 109
- **E.** 438

38. Which of the following is the set of real solutions for the equation $9x + 12 = 3(3x + 4)$?

- **F.** The set of all real numbers

- **G.** $\{0,1\}$

- **H.** $\{0\}$

- **J.** $\left\{-\dfrac{4}{3}\right\}$

- **K.** The empty set

39. The expression $\dfrac{\dfrac{\dfrac{3}{4}}{\dfrac{3}{4}-\dfrac{2}{3}}}{\dfrac{3}{4}-\dfrac{2}{3}+\dfrac{1}{2}}$ equals:

   A. $\dfrac{3}{28}$

   B. $\dfrac{4}{21}$

   C. $\dfrac{21}{4}$

   D. $\dfrac{28}{3}$

   E. $\dfrac{108}{7}$

40. A thin slice is cut from a bagel, creating the cross-section represented below. The diameter of the bagel is 144 mm and the width from the inner edge of the bagel to the outer edge is uniformly 56 mm. Which of the following is closest to the area, in square millimeters, of the shaded empty space inside the cross-section of the bagel?

   F.   100
   G.   450
   H.   800
   J.   3,200
   K.   16,000

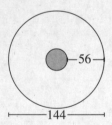

41. For all nonzero real numbers a, b, and c, what is the value of $a^0 + b^0 + c^0$?

   A. Undefined
   B. $a + b + c$
   C. 0
   D. 1
   E. 3

42. In the figure below, *ABCD* is a rectangle, *AB* = *AE*, and *E*, *F*, *G*, and *H* lie on *AD*. Of the angles ∠*BEA*, ∠*BFA*, ∠*BGA*, ∠*BHA*, and ∠*BDA*, which one has the greatest tangent?

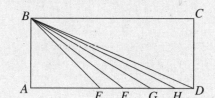

F. ∠*BEA*
G. ∠*BFA*
H. ∠*BGA*
J. ∠*BHA*
K. ∠*BDA*

Use the following information to answer questions 43–45.

The graph of *y* = *f*(*x*) is shown in the standard (*x*,*y*) coordinate plane below with points *V*, *W*, *X*, *Y*, and *Z* labeled.

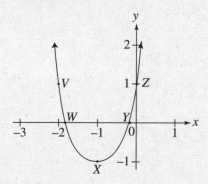

43. The *y*-intercept of the graph of *y* = *f*(*x*) is located at which of the following points?

A. *V*
B. *W*
C. *X*
D. *Y*
E. *Z*

44. The function *y* = *f*(*x*) can be classified as one of which of the following types of functions?

F. Trigonometric
G. Quadratic
H. Absolute value
J. Cubic
K. Linear

DO YOUR FIGURING HERE.

45. If $y = f(x)$ is to be reflected across the line $y = x$, which of the following graphs represents the result?

A.

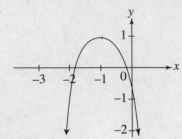

B.

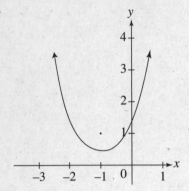

C.

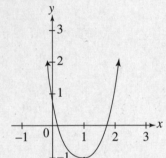

D.

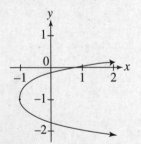

E.

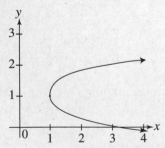

46. If a is a factor of 32 and b is a factor of 45, the product of a and b could NOT be which of the following?

F. 1,440
G. 288
H. 80
J. 54
K. 1

DO YOUR FIGURING HERE.

47. For each positive integer k, let k_o be the sum of all positive odd integers less than k. For example, $6_o = 5 + 3 + 1 = 9$ and $7_o = 5 + 3 + 1 = 9$. What is the value of $17_o \times 4_o$?

A. 16
B. 144
C. 256
D. 324
E. 816

48. If $(a, -3)$ is on the graph of the equation $x - 4y = 14$ in the standard (x,y) coordinate plane, then $a = $?

F. $-\dfrac{17}{4}$

G. -2

H. 2

J. 17

K. 26

49. For all $t > 0$, $f(t) = \dfrac{t^2 - 1}{t - 1} - t$. Which of the following is true about $f(t)$?

A. It increases in proportion to t.
B. It increases in proportion to t^2.
C. It decreases in proportion to t.
D. It decreases in proportion to t^2.
E. It remains constant.

50. In the figure below, X is on $\overline{WZ}$. If the angle measures are as shown, what is the degree measure of $\angle YXZ$?

F. $25°$

G. $37\dfrac{1}{2}°$

H. $65\dfrac{1}{2}°$

J. $112\dfrac{1}{2}°$

K. $114\dfrac{1}{2}°$

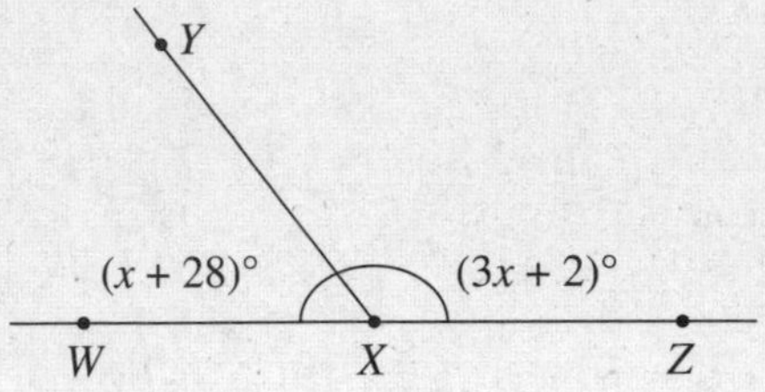

51. Points $(2,-2)$ and $(3,10)$ lie on the same line in the standard (x, y) coordinate plane. What is the slope of this line?

A. 12

B. 8

C. $\dfrac{1}{12}$

D. -8

E. -12

52. What is the degree measure of an angle that measures $\dfrac{7\pi}{15}$ radians?

F. $\left(\dfrac{360-7\pi}{15}\right)°$

G. $\left(180-\dfrac{7\pi}{15}\right)°$

H. $252°$

J. $84°$

K. $12°$

53. Which of the following gives the equation for the circle in the standard (x,y) coordinate plane with a center at $(4,-8)$ and a circumference of 10π square coordinate units?

A. $(x-4)^2 + (y+8)^2 = 25$
B. $(x-4)^2 + (y+8)^2 = 100$
C. $(x+8)^2 + (y-4)^2 = 25$
D. $(x+8)^2 - (y-4)^2 = 100$
E. $(x+8)^2 + (y-4)^2 = 100$

54. For some x and y that satisfy the equation $xy = -x^2$, which of the following is FALSE?

F. $x\left(\dfrac{1}{y}\right) = -1$

G. $x^2\left(\dfrac{1}{y^2}\right) = 1$

H. $x^2 + y^2 = -2xy$

J. $x^2 = y^2$

K. $x^3 - y^3 = 0$

55. Rectangle $ABCD$ lies in the standard (x,y) coordinate plane with corners at $A(4,2)$, $B(6,-1)$, $C(1,-4)$, and $D(-1,-1)$, and is represented by the 2×4 matrix $\begin{bmatrix} 4 & 6 & 1 & -1 \\ 2 & -1 & -4 & -1 \end{bmatrix}$. $ABCD$ is then translated, with the corners of the translated rectangle represented by the matrix $\begin{bmatrix} 1 & 3 & -2 & -4 \\ n & -3 & -6 & -3 \end{bmatrix}$. What is the value of n ?

A. 0
B. −1
C. −2
D. −3
E. −4

56. Three different functions are defined in the table below.

Symbol	Function	Description
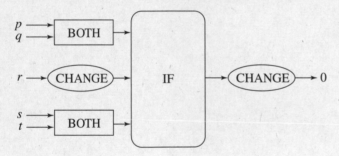 BOTH	BOTH	If both inputs are 1 the output will be 1. If both inputs are 0 the output will be 0. If both inputs are different the output will be 0.
1st → 2nd → 3rd → IF →	IF	If the first input is a 1, the output will be the second input. If the first input is a 0, the output will be the third input.
→ CHANGE →	CHANGE	If the input is 1, the output is 0. If the input is 0, the output is 1.

The diagram below uses three functions. The only values for p, q, r, s, and t are 1 and 0 . Which of the following inputs (p, q, r, s, t) will produce the output 0 ?

p → BOTH →
q →

r → CHANGE →   IF → CHANGE → 0

s → BOTH →
t →

F. (0,1,1,0,1)
G. (0,1,1,1,1)
H. (0,0,1,0,1)
J. (1,0,1,0,0)
K. (1,0,1,0,1)

57. Whenever $a > 0$, which of the following real number line graphs represents the solutions for x to the inequality $|x - a| \leq 3$?

A.
```
  ●───────────●───────────┤────→ x
 -a-3        a-3         a+3
```

B.
```
  ●───────────┤───────────●────→ x
 -a-3        a-3         a+3
```

C.
```
  ●───────────●───────────┤────→ x
 -a-3        a-3         a+3
```

D.
```
  ┤───────────●───────────●────→ x
 -a-3        a-3         a+3
```

E.
```
  ┤───────────●───────────●────→ x
 -a-3        a-3         a+3
```

58. Whenever x and y are both integers, what is $(6.0 \times 10^x)(5.0 \times 10^y)$ expressed in scientific notation?

   F. 30.0×100^{xy}
   G. $30.0 \times 10^{x^y}$
   H. 30.0×10^{xy}
   J. $3.0 \times 10^{x+y+1}$
   K. 3.0×10^{xy}

59. The points P, Q, R, and S lie in that order on a straight line. The midpoint of $\overline{QS}$ is R and the midpoint of $\overline{PS}$ is Q. The length of $\overline{QR}$ is x feet and the length of $\overline{PQ}$ is $4x - 16$ feet. What is the length, in feet, of $\overline{PS}$?

   A.   32
   B.   20
   C.   16
   D.   8
   E.   4

60. The circle below has an area of 64π cm^2. A central angle with measure 24° intercepts minor arc $\overset{\frown}{CD}$. What is the length of minor arc $\overset{\frown}{CD}$, in centimeters?

   F. $\dfrac{1}{8}\pi$

   G. $\dfrac{1}{4}\pi$

   H. $\dfrac{16}{15}\pi$

   J. $\dfrac{8}{3}\pi$

   K. 192π

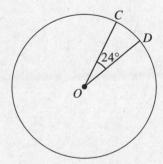

DIRECTIONS: Solve each problem, choose the correct answer, and then darken the corresponding oval on your answer document.

Do not linger over problems that take too much time. Solve as many as you can; then return to the others in the time you have left for this test.

You are permitted to use a calculator on this test. You may use your calculator for any problems you choose, but some of the problems may best be done without using a calculator.

Note: Unless otherwise stated, all of the following should be assumed:

1. Illustrative figures are NOT necessarily drawn to scale.
2. Geometric figures lie in a plane.
3. The word *line* indicates a straight line.
4. The word *average* indicates arithmetic mean.

---

1. Which of the following expressions is equivalent to $2a + 4b + 6c$?

   A. $8(a + b + c)$
   B. $2(a + 2b) + 3c$
   C. $2(a + 4b + 6c)$
   D. $2(a + 2b + 6c)$
   E. $2(a + 2b + 3c)$

2. When written in symbols, "The square of the product of a and b" is represented as:

   F. ab
   G. ab^2
   H. $(ab)^2$
   J. a^2b
   K. $(a^2b^2)^2$

3. Every week, Donald records the amount of mileage that has accumulated on his truck. On Monday, Donald recorded that he had driven 16,450 kilometers. After a week of deliveries, his new recording was 18,130 kilometers. He drove for thirty hours during that week. What was his average driving speed during that week to the nearest kilometer per hour?

   A. 38
   B. 41
   C. 48
   D. 56
   E. 59

4. The dimensions of a block of cheese are 12 inches by 3 inches by 3 inches. What is the volume, in cubic inches, of the block of cheese?

   F. 18
   G. 36
   H. 45
   J. 72
   K. 108

DO YOUR FIGURING HERE.

5. If x is a real number and $3^x = 81$, then $3 \times 2^x = ?$

   A.   3
   B. 16
   C. 24
   D. 48
   E. 81

6. For the songs on Charlie's mp3 player, the ratio of folk songs to rock songs is 3:11. Which of the following statements about the songs on his mp3 player is(are) true?

    I. There are fewer folk songs than rock songs.
   II. For every 11 rock songs, there are 3 folk songs.
  III. Folk songs comprise $\dfrac{3}{11}$ of the songs on Charlie's mp3 player.

   F. I only
   G. II only
   H. I and II only
   J. II and III only
   K. I, II, and III

7. Matt needs $5\dfrac{1}{9}$ gallons of hydrochloric acid for an experiment. He has $3\dfrac{1}{3}$ gallons already. How many more gallons of hydrochloric acid does Matt need?

   A. $2\dfrac{7}{9}$

   B. $2\dfrac{2}{3}$

   C. $2\dfrac{1}{8}$

   D. $1\dfrac{2}{3}$

   E. $1\dfrac{7}{9}$

8. As shown below, the diagonals of rectangle *EFGH* intersect at the point (–2,–4) in the standard (*x*,*y*) coordinate plane. Point *F* is at (–7,–2). Which of the following are the coordinates of *H* ?

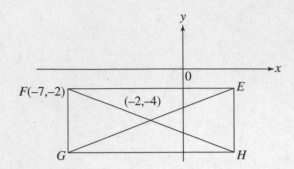

F. $\left(-4\frac{1}{2},-3\right)$

G. (–7,–6)

H. (3,–2)

J. (3,–6)

K. (–5,3)

9. Which of the following expressions is equivalent to
$$\frac{9x+45}{9}\ ?$$

A. 9*x* + 5

B. *x* + 45

C. *x* + 5

D. 6*x*

E. 45*x*

10. The expression 23*fg* – 6*f*(5*f* +3*g*) is equivalent to:

F. $5fg - 30f^2$

G. 25*fg*

H. 3*g* – 7*fg*

J. $41fg - 30f^2$

K. $30f^2 - 5fg$

11. A farmer sells strawberries at a market in both pint-sized containers and quart-sized containers. The farmer charges $3 for each pint, $5 for each quart, is always paid on the day of purchase, and sells no other goods. On a recent day, the farmer sold as many pint containers as quart containers and received $120 in sales. How many pints of strawberries did the farmer sell?

A. 12

B. 15

C. 24

D. 40

E. 50

12. A rectangular piece of cloth has a length of 6 feet and a width of 1.5 feet. Brad estimates that the area is 12 square feet. His estimate is approximately what percent *greater* than the actual area?

F. 75%
G. 66%
H. 33%
J. 25%
K. 17%

13. The *geometric mean* of 3 positive numbers is the cube root of the product of the 3 numbers. What is the geometric mean of 2, 4, and 27 ?

A.   6
B.   11
C.   21
D.   72
E. 216

14. A model for the number of questions on an assignment, when the assignment is worth p points, is $q = \dfrac{p^2}{50}$.

According to this model, what is the number of questions, q, for an assignment worth 80 points?

F. 128
G. 26
H. 80
J. 13
K.   3

15. The expression $x^2 + 2x - 15$ can be written as the product of 2 binomials with integer coefficients. One of the binomials is $(x + 5)$. Which of the following is the other binomial?

A. $(x^2 - 3)$
B. $(x^2 + 3)$
C. $(x - 3)$
D. $(x + 3)$
E. $(x - 5)$

16. The production cost of x computers for a company over one year is $175x + $150,000. To minimize production costs in a given year to $465,000, how many computers can the company make in that year?

F.   857
G. 1,725
H. 1,800
J. 2,657
K. 3,514

17. Given $g(x) = \dfrac{x^2 + \dfrac{7}{9}}{x^3 + \dfrac{11}{27}}$, what is $g(\dfrac{1}{3})$?

A. $\dfrac{216}{243}$

B. $\dfrac{21}{11}$

C. $\dfrac{96}{27}$

D. 2

E. $\dfrac{74}{33}$

18. Hannah is 5 years younger than Nora, who is x years old. Which of the following is an expression for Hannah's age in 2 years?

F. $x - 3$
G. $x + 3$
H. $x + 7$
J. $2x - 3$
K. 3

19. A rectangle is 5 times as wide as it is long. The area of the rectangle is 320 square feet. What is the perimeter of the rectangle, in feet?

A. 8
B. 40
C. 48
D. 64
E. 96

20. In the figure below, C and D are both on $\overline{BE}$, the measure of $\angle BAC$ is equal to the measure of $\angle DAE$ and the measure of $\angle ACD$ is equal to the measure of $\angle ADC$. Which of the following statements *must* be true?

(Note: The symbol $\cong$ means "is congruent to.")

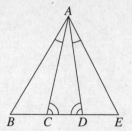

   F. $\triangle ABC$ is similar to $\triangle AED$.

   G.   The areas of triangles $\triangle ACD$ and $\triangle ADE$ are equal.

   H. $\overline{AB} \cong \overline{AD}$.

   J. $\angle CAD \cong \angle AED$.

   K. $\overline{AB}$ and $\overline{AE}$ are perpendicular.

21. Which of the following is equivalent to $8^{\frac{1}{4}}$?

   A. -1×8^5

   B. $\sqrt[4]{8}$

   C. $\sqrt{2}$

   D. $\dfrac{1}{8^4}$

   E. 2

22. Admission to the martial arts tournament is $30, but participants must purchase separate tickets for each event they wish to participate in once inside. Each event is the same price as any other event. The graph below shows the total cost for a person, for admission and events, as a function of the number of events paid for. One of the following is the price of a single event. Which one is it?

0	$30
1	$42
2	$54
3	$66
4	$78
5	$90

F. $11
G. $12
H. $13
J. $14
K. $15

23. A right triangle, shown below, has a longer leg measuring $16\sqrt{3}$ centimeters. How long is the hypotenuse of the triangle, in centimeters?

A. 8
B. $8\sqrt{2}$
C. 16
D. $16\sqrt{2}$
E. 32

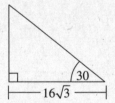

24. If you add up 5 consecutive odd integers that are each greater than 15, what is the smallest possible sum?

F. 75
G. 90
H. 95
J. 100
K. 105

25. A department store escalator is 25 feet long and forms an angle of 43° with the floor, which is horizontal. Which of the follow is an expression for the horizontal distance of the escalator from beginning to end?

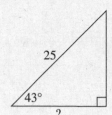

    A. 25 sin 43°
    B. 25 cos 43°
    C. 25 tan 43°
    D. 25 csc 43°
    E. 25 sec 43°

26. If $x - 15 = |-5|$, then $x = $?

    F.   −20

    G.   −10

    H. $\dfrac{2}{3}$

    J.   10

    K.   20

27. A grocery store is running a sale on seasonal berries. During the sale, the store sells packages of blueberries for $4 each and packages of strawberries for $6 each. Kate purchased nine packages of fruit for her mother's dinner party for $40. How many packages of blueberries did she purchase?

    A.   2
    B.   4
    C.   6
    D.   7
    E.   10

28. In $\triangle VWY$ below, X lies on $\overline{WY}$; Z lies on $\overline{VY}$; and a, b, c, and d are angle measures, in degrees. The measure of $\angle Y$ is 45°. What is $a + b + c + d$?

    F.   315
    G.   270
    H.   225
    J.   135
    K.   90

29. Triangle $\triangle ACE$, shown in the figure below, is isosceles with base $\overline{AE}$. B lies on $\overline{AC}$ and D lies on $\overline{CE}$. Segments $\overline{BE}$ and $\overline{AD}$ bisect $\angle AEC$ and $\angle CAE$ respectively. Which one of the following angle congruences is necessarily true?

DO YOUR FIGURING HERE.

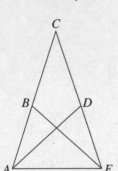

- **A.** $\angle CAE \cong \angle BEC$
- **B.** $\angle CAD \cong \angle AEC$
- **C.** $\angle CAE \cong \angle ACE$
- **D.** $\angle AEC \cong \angle ACE$
- **E.** $\angle BEC \cong \angle DAE$

30. A trapezoid has parallel bases that measure 3 inches and 9 inches and a height that measures 6 inches. What is the area, in square inches, of the trapezoid?

- **F.** 18
- **G.** 24
- **H.** 30
- **J.** 36
- **K.** 54

31. The table below lists the number (to the nearest 1,000) of book club members in the United States for 2001 through 2004. Of the following expressions with x representing the number of years after 2001, which best models the number of book club members (in thousands) in the United States?

Year	Number of members (in thousands)
2001	539
2002	542
2003	544
2004	547

- **A.** $539x + 2{,}001$

- **B.** $\dfrac{3}{8}x + 2{,}001$

- **C.** $\dfrac{8}{3}x + 539$

- **D.** $547x + 2{,}004$

- **E.** $2{,}001x + 539$

Use the following information to answer questions 32–34.

The table below shows the percents of U.S. citizens who had ever consumed a certain brand-name soda, out of all soda consumers, for each year from 1986 through 2006.

Year	Percent	Year	Percent	Year	Percent
1986	24.2	1993	53.2	2000	60.3
1987	26.3	1994	55.1	2001	61.5
1988	29.2	1995	56	2002	63.4
1989	32.4	1996	57	2003	65.9
1990	38.2	1997	57.8	2004	74.2
1991	45.3	1998	58.2	2005	78.7
1992	49.4	1999	59.1	2006	83.5

32. Which of the following years had the LEAST increase in the percent of U.S. citizens who had consumed the brand-name soda from the previous year?

   F. 1990
   G. 1998
   H. 2001
   J. 2004
   K. 2006

33. The figure below shows a scatterplot of the data in the table and solid lines that are possible models for the data. Which of the 5 lines appears to be the best representation of the data?

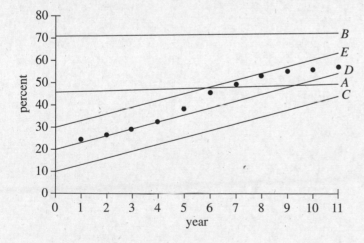

   A. *A*
   B. *B*
   C. *C*
   D. *D*
   E. *E*

34. By 2002 there were 74,672,120 U.S. citizens who had con-sumed the brand-name soda. According to this informa-tion, approximately how many people were soda consum-ers, of the brand-name soda or other sodas, in 2002 ?

F. 4,700,000,000
G. 150,000,000
H. 119,000,000
J. 47,000,000
K. 37,500,000

DO YOUR FIGURING HERE.

35. For all nonzero y and z, $\dfrac{(y \times 10^5)(z \times 0.0001)}{(y \times 100{,}000)(z \times 10^{-4})} = ?$

A. 10^9

B. 10

C. 1

D. $\dfrac{y}{z}$

E. $\dfrac{y^2}{z^2}$

36. The function $g(x) = x^4 - 2x^3 - 6x^2 - x + 5$ and line h are shown in the standard (x,y) coordinate plane below. Which of the following is an equation of line h, which passes through $(-1,3)$ and $(2,-21)$?

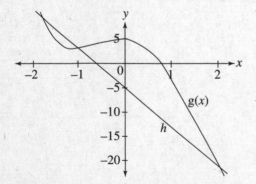

F. $-8x - 5$
G. $-8x + 5$
H. $-9x + 5$
J. $-9x - 5$
K. $-6x - 5$

37. Which of the following degree measures is equivalent to 2.25π radians?

   A. 101.25
   B. 202.5
   C. 405
   D. 810
   E. 1,620

DO YOUR FIGURING HERE.

Use the following information to answer questions 38–40.

Greg is making a triangular sail for a boat, shaped like a right triangle and shown below.

120 ft

50 ft

38. Sail material costs $8.99 for 150 square feet. If the material can be purchased in any quantity, which of the following is closest to the cost in dollars of the material needed to fill the area of the sail as shown?

   F. $360.00
   G. $280.00
   H. $200.00
   J. $180.00
   K. $25.00

39. To determine how much trim to buy for the sail, Greg calculated the sail's perimeter. What is the sail's perimeter, in feet?

   A. 275
   B. 300
   C. 290
   D. 220
   E. 170

40. The angle opposite the 120-foot side measures about 65.2°. Greg would like to make a second sail. This one will still be a right triangle with a 50-foot side as one leg, but the 120-foot side will be shortened until the angle opposite that side is about 10°. By about how many feet will Greg need to shorten the 120-foot side?

(Note: sin 10° ≈ .17, cos 10° ≈ .98, tan 10° ≈ .18)

F.   9
G.   49
H.   71
J.   111
K.   122

---

41. Rectangle *AKLD* consists of 5 congruent rectangles as shown in the figure below. Which of the following is the ratio of the length of $\overline{AK}$ to the length of $\overline{AD}$?

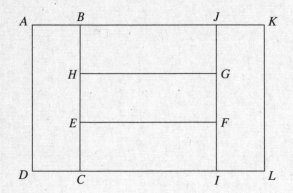

A.   1:1
B.   2:1
C.   5:3
D.   1:3
E.   2:3

42. Jackson High School's basketball team scored an average of 90 points in each of the first 10 games of the season. If it scored 102 points in each of the next 2 games, which of the following is closest to its average for all 12 games?

F.   102
G.   98
H.   96
J.   92
K.   90

43. A ferry boat travels from a dock on the mainland towards an island, stops to discharge and load passengers, then returns to the mainland dock. Among the following graphs, which one best represents the relationship between the distance, in kilometers, of the ferry from the island and the time, in minutes, from when the ferry leaves the mainland dock until it returns?

DO YOUR FIGURING HERE.

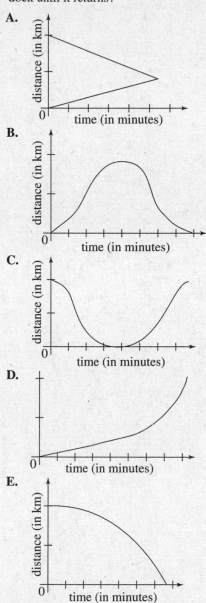

A.

B.

C.

D.

E.

44. A right triangle has sides measuring 12 inches, 35 inches, and 37 inches. What is the cosine of the angle that lies opposite the 35-inch side?

F. $\dfrac{12}{35}$

G. $\dfrac{35}{37}$

H. $\dfrac{35}{12}$

J. $\dfrac{12}{37}$

K. $\dfrac{37}{12}$

45. The noncommon rays of 2 adjacent angles form a straight angle. The measure of one angle is 4 times the measure of the other angle. What is the measure of the smaller angle?

A. 36°
B. 45°
C. 90°
D. 135°
E. 144°

46. A rectangular solid consisting of 18 smaller cubes that are identical is positioned in the standard (x,y,z) coordinate system, as shown below. Vertex M has coordinates of $(-1,3,0)$ and point O on the y-axis has coordinates of $(0,3,0)$. What are the coordinates of vertex N?

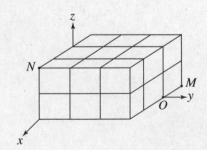

F. (3,0,2)
G. (2,2,0)
H. (3,0,–1)
J. (0,2,2)
K. (2,0, 2)

47. What is the median of the data given below?

$$18, 25, 19, 41, 23, 29, 35, 19$$

   A. 32
   B. 26
   C. 25
   D. 24
   E. 19

48. Let $a \otimes b = (-2a - b)^2$ for all integers a and b. Which of the following is the value of $-5 \otimes 3$?

   F. -15
   G. -2
   H. 49
   J. 91
   K. 109

49. For all negative even integers x, which of the following is a correct ordering of the terms x, x^x, $((-x)!)^x$, and $((-x)!)^{(-x)!}$?

   A. $((-x)!)^{(-x)!} \geq ((-x)!)^x \geq x \geq x^x$
   B. $((-x)!)^{(-x)!} \geq x^x \geq ((-x)!)^x \geq x$
   C. $x^x \geq x \geq ((-x)!)^{(-x)!} \geq ((-x)!)^x$
   D. $x^x \geq ((-x)!)^x \geq x \geq ((-x)!)^{(-x)!}$
   E. $x \geq ((-x)!)^x \geq x^x \geq ((-x)!)^{(-x)!}$

50. What is the perimeter of quadrilateral *STUR* if it has vertices with (x,y) coordinates $S(0,0)$, $T(2,-4)$, $U(6,-6)$, $R(4,-2)$?

   F. $2\sqrt{20}$
   G. $2\sqrt{5} + 2\sqrt{20}$
   H. $8\sqrt{5}$
   J. 80
   K. 400

51. The line with equation $5y - 4x = 20$ does NOT lie in which quadrant(s) of the standard (x, y) coordinate plane below?

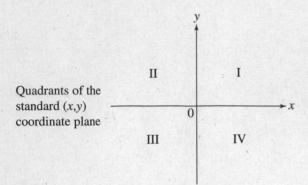

Quadrants of the standard (x,y) coordinate plane

- **A.** Quadrant I only
- **B.** Quadrant II only
- **C.** Quadrant III only
- **D.** Quadrant IV only
- **E.** Quadrants I and III only

52. The figure below shows representations of the first 4 triangular numbers, Δ_1 through Δ_4. What is the value of Δ_{24}?

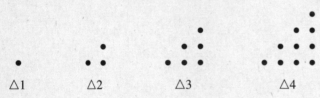

- **F.** 144
- **G.** 168
- **H.** 288
- **J.** 300
- **K.** 600

53. The four midpoints of the sides of a square represent four points on a circle. Line segments connect the opposing corners of the square. This circle and these line segments divide the square into how many individual, non-overlapping regions of nonzero area?

- **A.** 4
- **B.** 5
- **C.** 10
- **D.** 12
- **E.** 24

54. The circumference of a circle is 50 inches. How many inches long is its radius?

F. $\dfrac{25}{\pi}$

G. $\dfrac{50}{\pi}$

H. $\dfrac{100}{\pi}$

J. 50π

K. 100π

55. In the (x,y) coordinate plane, what is the diameter of the circle having its center at $(-6,1)$ and $(0,9)$ as one of the endpoints of a radius?

A. 10
B. 14
C. 20
D. 28
E. 100

56. The graph of the function $f(x) = \dfrac{x^2 - x - 3}{x - 1}$ is shown in the standard (x,y) coordinate plane below. Which of the following, if any, is a list of each of the *vertical* asymptotes of $f(x)$?

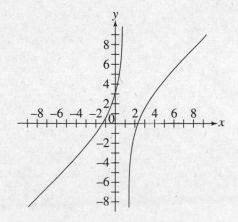

F. This function has no vertical asymptote.

G. $y = -\dfrac{1}{2}x + 1$

H. $y = 2x - 1$

J. $x = -1$ and $x = 2$

K. $x = 1$

57. The product of 2 distinct positive prime numbers is an even number, and one less than the product is a prime number. All of the following prime numbers could be one of the original prime numbers EXCEPT:

A. 2
B. 3
C. 5
D. 7
E. 19

58. Connecting the midpoints of opposite sides of any quadrilateral to the midpoints of the adjacent sides must always create which of the following?

F. Point
G. Line
H. Circle
J. Square
K. Parallelogram

59. If $a(x) = b(x) + c(x)$, where $b(x) = 3x^2 - 8x + 113$ and $c(x) = -3x^2 + 18x + 7$ and x is an integer, then $a(x)$ is always divisible by which of the following?

A. 6
B. 7
C. 10
D. 12
E. 15

60. Isosceles triangle T_1 has a base of 12 meters and a height of 20 meters. The vertices of a second triangle T_2 are the midpoints of the sides of T_1. The vertices of a third triangle, T_3, are the midpoints of the sides of T_2. Assume the process continues indefinitely, with the vertices of T_{k+1} being the midpoints of the sides of T_k for every positive integer k. What is the sum of the areas, in square meters, of $T_1, T_2, T_2, \ldots$?

F. 30
G. 40
H. 120
J. 144
K. 160

DO YOUR FIGURING HERE.

NO TEST MATERIAL ON THIS PAGE.

MATHEMATICS TEST
60 Minutes—60 Questions

DIRECTIONS: Solve each problem, choose the correct answer, and then darken the corresponding oval on your answer document.

Do not linger over problems that take too much time. Solve as many as you can; then return to the others in the time you have left for this test.

You are permitted to use a calculator on this test. You may use your calculator for any problems you choose, but some of the problems may best be done without using a calculator.

Note: Unless otherwise stated, all of the following should be assumed:

1. Illustrative figures are NOT necessarily drawn to scale.
2. Geometric figures lie in a plane.
3. The word *line* indicates a straight line.
4. The word *average* indicates arithmetic mean.

---

1. For each of 3 years, the table below gives the number of different routes a runner ran, the number of runs she ran, and the total number of miles she ran.

Year	Routes	Runs	Total Miles Run
2005	12	395	1,255
2006	12	396	1,014
2007	11	368	1,898

To the nearest tenth of a mile, what is the average number of miles the runner ran per run in 2005 ?

A. 2.5
B. 2.6
C. 3.2
D. 4.8
E. 5.0

DO YOUR FIGURING HERE.

2. The lengths of 2 sides are not given in the polygon below. If each angle between adjacent sides measures 90°, then, in meters, what is the perimeter of the polygon?

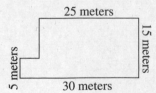

F.   75
G.   90
H.   95
J.   400
K.   450

3. Which of the following inequalities represents the graph shown below on the real number line?

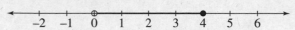

A. $0 < x < 5$
B. $0 < x \leq 4$
C. $-2 < x \leq 4$
D. $1 \leq x \leq 4$
E. $0 \leq x < 4$

4. What is the value of $4 + 3^{x-y}$ when $x = 3$ and $y = -1$?

F. 13
G. 16
H. 30
J. 85
K. 2,041

5. For integers x and y such that $xy = 14$, which of the following is NOT a possible value of x ?

A. 2
B. 1
C. -7
D. -8
E. -14

6. In cubic meters, what is the volume of a large cube whose edges each measure 6 meters in length?

F. 18
G. 36
H. 64
J. 108
K. 216

7. Pat's Pastries baked 80 apple pies and 50 loaves of apple bread to be sold at a 2-day Fall Festival. The pies were sold for $25 each and the loaves of bread were sold for $10 each. Which of the following expressions gives the total amount of money, in dollars, collected from selling all of the apple pies and B of the loaves of bread?

A. $35B$
B. $1,570B$
C. $B + 80$
D. $10B + 1,250$
E. $10B + 2,000$

8. In the figure below, W, X, and Z are collinear, the measure of $\angle WXY$ is $4a°$, and the measure of $\angle YXZ$ is $11a°$. What is the measure of $\angle WXY$?

F.   12°
G.   48°
H.   96°
J.   132°
K.   264°

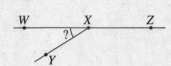

9. Each of the following values could represent a probability EXCEPT:

A.   0.00004

B.   0.7

C. $\dfrac{3}{10}$

D. $\dfrac{51}{60}$

E. $\dfrac{5}{4}$

10. For the first several weeks after hiring a private tutor, Teddy's score on a standardized test increased slowly. As Teddy began to understand the concepts more clearly, though, his standardized test scores improved more rapidly. After several more weeks, Teddy stopped working with his tutor and his scores did not improve any more. Which of the following graphs could represent all of Teddy's standardized test scores as a function of time, in weeks, after he hired a private tutor?

DO YOUR FIGURING HERE.

F.

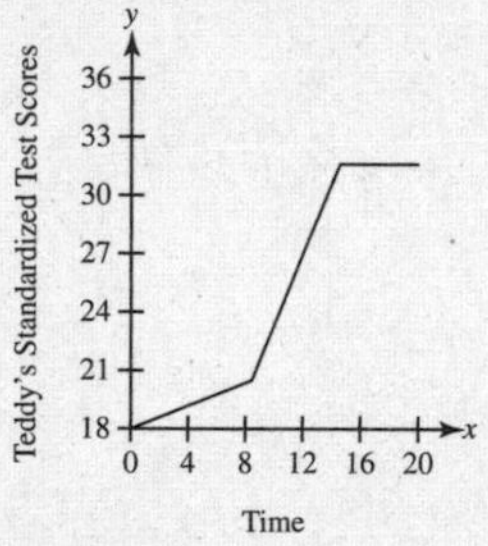

J.

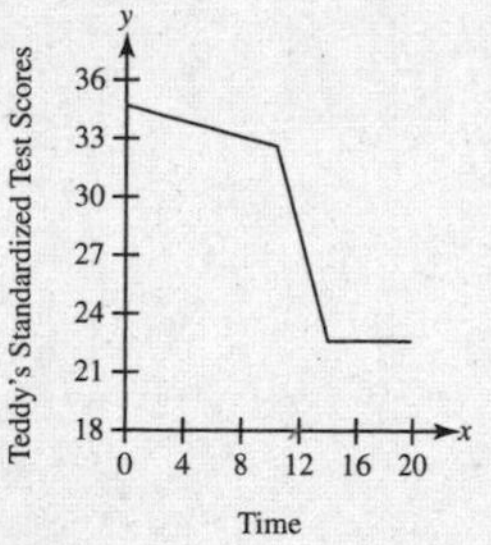

G.

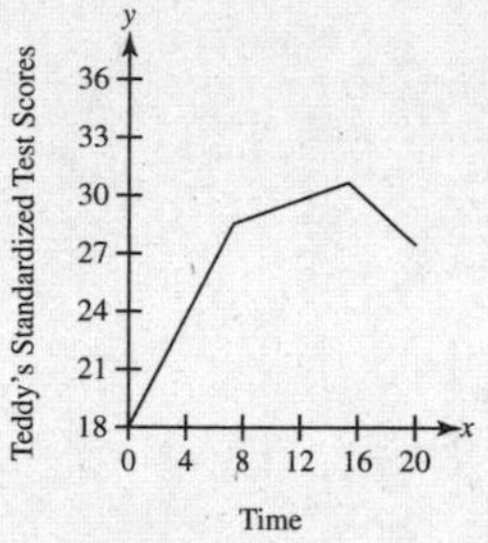

K.

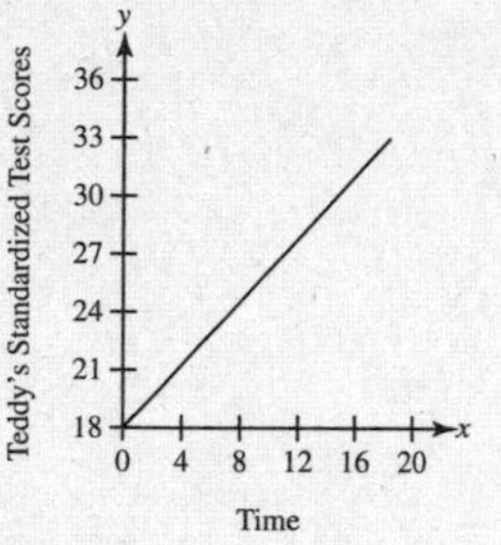

H.

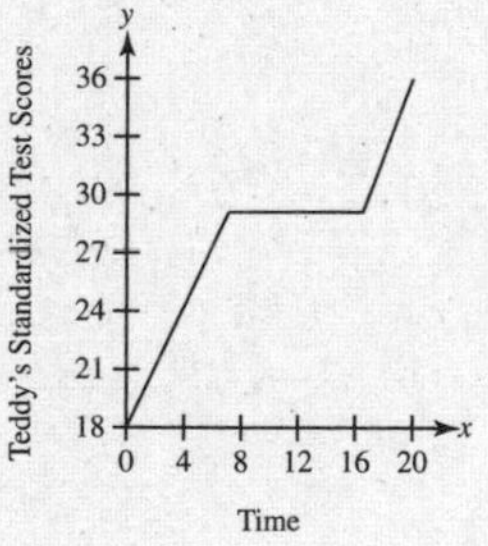

11. The Northampton Volunteer Association has built a rectangular sandbox for a local elementary school and is ready to fill it with sand. The sandbox is 60 inches wide, 72 inches long, and will be filled 18 inches deep. Under the assumption that 1 bag of sand can fill 3,600 cubic inches of the sandbox, what is the minimum number of bags of sand they will need in order to fill the sandbox?

A. 1
B. 7
C. 12
D. 21
E. 22

12. Salvador is trying to scale his rectangular self-portrait down to postcard size. The painting is 9 feet wide by 16 feet long. He is using a scale of $\frac{1}{3}$ inch = 1 foot for the postcard-sized self-portrait. What will be the dimensions, in inches, of Salvador's postcard-sized self-portrait?

F. $1\frac{1}{3}$ by 4

G. 3 by $5\frac{1}{3}$

H. 3 by 4

J. 27 by 48

K. 36 by 64

13. The Crestview High School student body is made up only of freshmen, sophomores, juniors, and seniors. 25% of the students are freshmen, 35% are sophomores, and 20% are juniors. If no student can be considered to be in two classes, and there are 150 seniors, how many students make up the Crestview High School student body?

A. 230
B. 500
C. 600
D. 750
E. 1,500

14. The circumference of a car tire is 75 inches. About how many revolutions does this car tire make traveling 225 feet (2,700 inches) without slipping?

F.   3
G.   14
H.   36
J.   225
K.   432

15. $(2 - 4t + 5t^2) - (3t^2 + 2t - 7)$ is equivalent to:

A. $2t^2 - 6t + 9$
B. $2t^2 - 2t + 9$
C. $2t^4 - 2t^2 - 5$
D. $8t^2 - 6t - 5$
E. $8t^4 - 6t^2 - 5$

16. At Blackstone Café, a regular entrée costs $18.00 while an entrée off the children's menu costs less. Cliff treats his niece to dinner at the café and spends $\frac{1}{3}$ of a gift certificate on her children's entrée and a drink. Afterwards, she orders a $6.00 dessert and he pays for that as well. When Cliff has paid for all of his niece's food, he has exactly enough money left on the gift certificate to pay for his regular entrée. How much money was the gift certificate worth?

F. $34.00
G. $35.00
H. $36.00
J. $37.00
K. $38.00

17. In June, Ms. Kunkel gave her English students 15 books to read over the summer. When classes resumed in September, she asked them what percentage of the books they had finished. Only one of the following values represents a possible percentage of books a student could have completed. Which one is it?

A. 65%
B. 68%
C. 70%
D. 80%
E. 85%

18. A geometric sequence has as its first 4 terms, –0.125, 1, –8, and 64. What is the 5$^\text{th}$ term of this sequence?

F. 512
G. 73
H. –55
J. –73
K. –512

19. Which of the following is equivalent to $(a - 5b)^2$?

A. $2a - 10b$
B. $a^2 - 25b^2$
C. $a^2 - 10ab + 25b^2$
D. $a^2 - 12ab + 25b^2$
E. $a^2 - 25ab + 25b^2$

20. As shown in the figure below, Tony has determined that he must ride his skateboard down a long ramp to be able to jump a shorter ramp with enough time to complete a new trick. First, he needs to determine the dimensions of both the shorter and longer ramps. Tony is on his skateboard at point K, 20 feet above the ground. He then notes that the vertical height $\overline{HJ}$ of the shorter ramp is 6 feet above the ground, and the length of the shorter ramp $\overline{GJ}$ is 9 feet. Approximately how many feet long is the longer ramp?

(Note: In $\triangle FKG$ and $\triangle HJG$, $\angle FGK$ is congruent to $\angle HGJ$.)

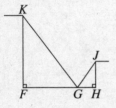

F. 3
G. 12
H. 15
J. 30
K. 35

21. What is the solution to the equation $9x - (3x - 1) = 3$?

A. -3

B. $-\dfrac{2}{3}$

C. $\dfrac{1}{3}$

D. $\dfrac{2}{3}$

E. 3

22. The area of $\triangle ABC$ below is 54 square meters. If altitude $\overline{BD}$ is 9 meters long, how long is $\overline{AC}$, in meters?

F. 3
G. 6
H. 9
J. 12
K. 15

23. Given $g(x) = 4x^2 - 8x + 2$, what is the value of $g(-5)$?

A. 442
B. 142
C. 67
D. -58
E. -138

24. A company will reimburse its employees' personal expenses on weekend business trips. It will reimburse $0.80 for every $1.00 an employee spends, up to $100.00. For the next $200 an employee spends, the company will reimburse $0.70 for every $1.00 spent. For each additional dollar spent, the company will reimburse $0.60. If an employee was reimbursed $400.00, approximately how many dollars must she have spent on a weekend business trip?

F. 667
G. 600
H. 500
J. 400
K. 367

25. The following table shows the ages of all the attendees of Camp Wannaboggin.

Age	9	10	11	12	13
Percent of campers	10%	24%	21%	37%	8%

What percent of the Wannaboggin campers are at least 11 years old?

A. 34%
B. 45%
C. 50%
D. 55%
E. 66%

26. What percent of $\frac{5}{8}$ is $\frac{1}{8}$?

F. 13%
G. 20%
H. 55%
J. 63%
K. 500%

27. The newspaper headline below tells about a power outage. If there are 63,000 residences in Springfield, how many residences were affected by the outage?

EXTRA! EXTRA!
Massive Local Power Outage
$\frac{2}{3}$ of Residences in Springfield Affected

A. 10,500
B. 21,000
C. 31,500
D. 42,000
E. 62,995

28. The ratio of a side of square X to the length of rectangle Z is 3:4. The ratio of a side of square X to the width of rectangle Z is 3:2. What is the ratio of the area of square X to the area of rectangle Z ?

F. 1:1
G. 2:1
H. 3:2
J. 9:4
K. 9:8

29. In her Algebra II class, Mrs. Pemdas writes the following statement on the board: "a varies inversely as the product of b^2 and c, and directly as d^3." She then asks her students to translate the statement into an equation. Which of the following equations, with k as the constant of proportionality, is a correct translation of Mrs. Pemdas's statement?

A. $a = \dfrac{kd^3}{b^2c}$

B. $a = \dfrac{kb^2c}{d^3}$

C. $a = \dfrac{b^2cd^3}{k}$

D. $a = \dfrac{b^2c}{kd^3}$

E. $a = kb^2cd^3$

30. In a certain isosceles triangle, the measure of the vertex angle is four times the measure of each of the base angles. What is the measure, in degrees, of the vertex angle?

F. 30°
G. 45°
H. 60°
J. 120°
K. 150°

31. A restaurant decides on the following production model, where N is the number of ounces of flour the restaurant purchases each month, based on the number of ounces, x, the restaurant uses during the preceding month. $N = x^2 - 600x - 160,000$. According to this model, what is the greatest quantity of flour, in number of ounces, that the restaurant can use during a month, without having to purchase any new flour the next month?

A. 800
B. 550
C. 400
D. 350
E. 200

Use the following information to answer questions 32–34.

A poor, frustrated artist named Fresco created a plan to make money. He collected trash, repurposed it into sculptures, then asked various celebrities to write and paint on these trash objects, which he then sold on his own as modern high art. The chart below separately shows the *cost* and *revenue* of his plan. The linear cost function, $C(x)$, represents the total money spent to make and market the art, while the linear revenue function, $R(x)$, shows the amount of money he has made in sculpture sales.

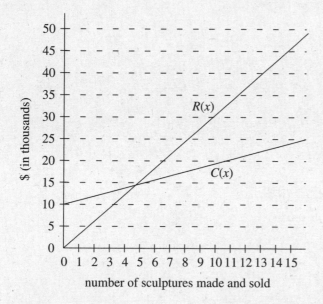

number of sculptures made and sold

32. Fresco initially spent money promoting the project in the media. He also had to pay the celebrities to participate. After 6 months, Fresco had created and sold x number of trash sculptures and finally broke even: he hadn't made or lost any money. How many sculptures did Fresco sell in his first 6 months of the project?

F.　3
G.　5
H.　7
J.　10
K.　15

33. The cost function in the chart is determined by a constant production cost per sculpture—in this case the amount Fresco pays each celebrity to participate—as well as a fixed cost, or the initial cost of promoting the project. What is the fixed cost of Fresco's trash sculpture project?

    A. $1,000
    B. $5,000
    C. $10,000
    D. $15,000
    E. $50,000

34. The selling price of each trash sculpture is an integer number of dollars. According to the revenue function, what is the selling price of one trash sculpture?

    F. $1,000
    G. $1,667
    H. $2,000
    J. $3,000
    K.   Cannot be determined from the chart

35. Which of the following is a *complete* factorization of the expression $12b^2c + 6bc + 3b$?

    A. $4bc + 2c + 1$
    B. $3b\,(9bc + 2c + 1)$
    C. $3b\,(4bc + 2c + 1)$
    D. $3b\,(4bc + 2c)$
    E. $6bc\,(2b + 6) + 3b$

36. Which of the following could be the equation of a line that passes through the points $(-2,-7)$ and $(2,17)$ in the standard (x,y) coordinate plane?

    F. $3x - 2y = 8$
    G. $6x - y = -5$
    H. $5x - 2y = 7$
    J. $9x - 2y = -16$
    K. $x + y = 6$

37. A circle has a radius that is the same length as the sides of a square. If the square has a perimeter of 64 square inches, what is the area, in square inches, of the circle?

    A.   16
    B. 16π
    C. 32π
    D. 64π
    E. 256π

DO YOUR FIGURING HERE.

38. What is the *y*-coordinate of the solution of the following system, presuming the system has a solution?

$$8x + y = 30$$
$$8x + 4y = 96$$

F. 1
G. 8
H. 19
J. 22
K. The system has no solution.

DO YOUR FIGURING HERE.

Use the following information to answer questions 39–41.

In the figure below, *M* is on $\overline{NL}$ and *Q* is on $\overline{PR}$. The measurements are given in feet. Both *NPQM* and *MQRL* are trapezoids. The area, *A*, of a trapezoid is given by $A = \frac{1}{2}h(b_1 + b_2)$, where *h* is the height and b_1 and b_2 are the lengths of the 2 parallel sides.

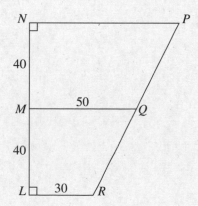

39. What is the area of *MQRL*, in square feet?

A. 3,200
B. 1,750
C. 1,600
D. 600
E. 500

40. What is the length of $\overline{QR}$, in feet?

F. $\sqrt{2,000}$
G. $\sqrt{1,640}$
H. $\sqrt{1,200}$
J. 50
K. 45

41. What is the diameter, in feet, of the largest circle that can be drawn inside *MNPQ* ?

A. 20
B. 40
C. 50
D. 60
E. 70

---

42. The figure below shows a ramp for skateboarders. The base of the ramp is 25 feet long, and it rises at a 10° angle.

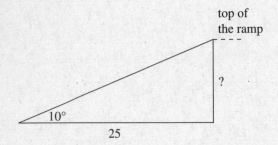

top of
the ramp

?

10°

25

Given the trigonometric calculations in the table below, how high off the ground will a skateboarder be at the top of the ramp, rounded to the nearest 0.1 foot?

cos 10°	0.985
sin 10°	0.174
tan 10°	0.176

F. 2.3
G. 2.5
H. 4.3
J. 4.4
K. 24.6

43. The 12 numbers on a circular clock are equally spaced around the edges of the clock. Belinda chooses an integer, *n*, that is greater than 1. Beginning at a randomly chosen number, Belinda goes around the circle counterclockwise and paints in every *n*th number. She continues going around and around the clock, painting in every *n*th number, until all twelve numbers on the clock are painted. Which of the following could have been Belinda's integer *n* ?

A. 2
B. 3
C. 6
D. 7
E. 9

44. Consider the exponential equation $y = \dfrac{p^{(x+1)}}{K}$, where K and p are positive real constants and x is a positive real number. The value of y decreases as the value of x increases if and only if which of the following statements about p is true?

F. $0 < p < 1$
G. $1 < p < 2$
H. $p > -1$
J. $p > 0$
K. $p > 1$

45. What is the distance, in coordinate units, between the points $M\,(1,-3)$ and $N\,(-5,5)$ in the standard (x,y) coordinate plane?

A. $\sqrt{14}$

B. $\sqrt{20}$

C. 8

D. 10

E. 20

46. During their daily training race, Carl has to stop to tie his shoes. Melissa, whose shoes are velcro, continues to run and gets 20 feet ahead of Carl. Melissa is running at a constant rate of 8 feet per second, and Carl starts running at a constant rate of 9.2 feet per second to catch up to Melissa. Which of the following equations, when solved for s, gives the number of seconds Carl will take to catch up to Melissa?

F. $8s + 20 = 9.2s$

G. $8s - 20 = 9.2s$

H. $\dfrac{20 + 9.2s}{9.2} = 8s$

J. $8s = 20$

K. $9.2s = 20$

47. Which of the following defines the solution set for the system of inequalities given below?

$$0 > 3x - 6$$
$$-4 < x$$

A. $x > -4$
B. $x < 2$
C. $-4 < x < 18$
D. $-4 < x < -2$
E. $-4 < x < 2$

48. At the company YouGroove, 35 employees work in the sales department and 50 employees work in the operations department. Of these employees, 15 work in both the sales and the operations departments. How many of the 110 employees at YouGroove do NOT work in either the sales or the operations departments?

F. 10
G. 15
H. 20
J. 35
K. 40

DO YOUR FIGURING HERE.

49. The slope of a line in the standard (x,y) coordinate plane is 4. What is the slope of a line perpendicular to that line?

A. 4

B. $\dfrac{1}{4}$

C. $-\dfrac{1}{4}$

D. -1

E. -4

50. The point $(24,3)$ on a standard (x,y) coordinate plane is halfway between points $(z,2z + 1)$ and $(15z,z - 4)$. What is the value of z ?

F. 1
G. 1.5
H. 3
J. 7
K. 24

51. How many 4-letter orderings, where no letters are repeated, can be made using the letters of the word BADGERS ?

A. 4
B. 7
C. 256
D. 840
E. 2,401

52. As shown in the (x,y,z) coordinate space below, the cube with vertices L through S has edges that are 2 coordinate units long. The coordinates of Q are $(0,0,0)$, and S is on the positive x-axis. What are the coordinates of O ?

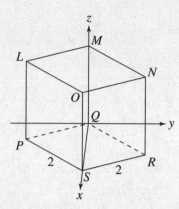

F. $(2,0,2)$

G. $(2,2,2)$

H $(2\sqrt{2},0,2)$

J. $(2\sqrt{2},0,2\sqrt{3})$

K. $(2\sqrt{2},2,0)$

53. Whenever a, b, and c are positive real numbers,

which of the following expressions is equivalent to

$\log_4 a - 2\log_8 b + \dfrac{1}{2}\log_4 c$?

A. $\log_4 a\sqrt{c} - \log_8 b^2$

B. $\log_4 \dfrac{ac}{2} - \log_8 2b$

C. $\log_4 \dfrac{a\sqrt{c}}{b}$

D. $\log_4 (a-c) - \log_8 2b$

E. $\log_4 (a-c) - \log_8 b^2$

54. If $-6 \le a \le -4$ and $3 \le b \le 7$, what is the maximum value of $|a-2b|$?

F. 10
G. 11
H. 18
J. 20
K. 42

55. The measure of the sum of the interior angles of a regular *n*-sided polygon is $(n - 2)180°$. A regular octagon is shown below. What is the measure of the designated angle?

    A.   135°
    B.   144°
    C.   200°
    D.   225°
    E.   315°

56. Which of the following trigonometric functions has an amplitude of 3 ?

(Note: the *amplitude* of a trigonometric function is $\frac{1}{2}$ the nonnegative difference between the maximum and minimum values of the function.)

    F. $f(x) = \frac{1}{3} \sin x$

    G. $f(x) = \cos 3x$

    H. $f(x) = \sin(\frac{1}{3} x)$

    J. $f(x) = 3 \tan x$

    K. $f(x) = 3 \cos x$

57. If A, x, and y are all distinct numbers, and $A = \frac{xy - 2}{x - y}$, which of the following represents x in terms of A and y ?

    A. $\frac{Ay - 2}{A - y}$

    B. $\frac{A - 2}{x - 1}$

    C. $\frac{A - y}{x - y}$

    D. $\frac{Ay - 2}{A + y}$

    E. $\frac{2}{y - A}$

58. In the figure below, lines p and q are parallel and angle measures are as marked. If it can be determined, what is the value of a ?

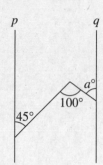

F. 35°
G. 45°
H. 55°
J. 100°
K. Cannot be determined from the information given

59. In the triangle below, the lengths of the two given sides are measured in centimeters. What is the value, in centimeters, of x ?

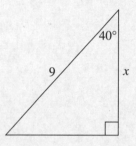

A. 9 sin 40°
B. 9 sin 50°
C. 9 cos 50°
D. 9 tan 40°
E. 9 tan 50°

60. An angle in the standard (x,y) coordinate plane has its vertex at the origin and its initial side on the positive x-axis. If the measure of an angle in standard position is (1,314°), it has the same terminal side as an angle of each of the following measures EXCEPT:

F. 594°
G. 314°
H. 234°
J. −126°
K. −486°

Reading Practice

READING TEST

35 Minutes—40 Questions

DIRECTIONS: There are four passages in this test. Each passage is followed by several questions. After reading each passage, choose the best answer to each question and blacken the corresponding oval on your answer document. You may refer to the passages as often as necessary.

Passage I

PROSE FICTION: This passage is adapted from the short story "Going Home" by Lucretia Prynne (© 2007 by Lucretia Prynne).

Summers in Alabama had always been hot. My childhood memories are filled with days spent floating in the pond, sitting on the porch swing, lying sprawled in front of any source of moving air, trying in vain to get, and stay, cool. But when
[5] I walked out of the airport, already tired from a three-hour flight that had been delayed by over half an hour, laden with suitcases and dressed for an overly air-conditioned office climate, the heat came over me like a blanket. An old, unwashed woolen blanket that had been soaked in water, allowed to dry
[10] crumpled on the floor, then resoaked and thrown at me in all of its mildewed glory. The short walk to the car-rental agency felt like a trek through the jungle; by the time I got to my rental, my shirt was soaked through in patches, my hair was limp and sticky, and my mood was foul.

[15] During the hour-long drive home, I had plenty of time to think. About why I had left, about all the things I had chosen to leave behind, about the life I had built for myself far away from this world of heat and poverty and depression. Lost in my thoughts, I found myself driving up the gravel road lead-
[20] ing to my childhood home before I realized where I was. The clapboard house looked the same as it had when I had left ten years earlier, save for a slight accumulation of the junk common to front yards in this part of the world. The old tire swing still hung askew from the hickory tree, half the ropes
[25] worn away from constant use. On the porch sat a rocker that had once been my grandmother's and a watering can that looked almost as old. Parking off to the side, I grabbed my bags anxiously, trying to calm my nerves, and braced myself.

No one ever used the front door to the house. I remembered
[30] that, of course, and walked instead to a side door that opened onto the kitchen. The door itself was propped open to allow for whatever breeze might meander by, the screen door shut to keep out the mosquitoes, giving me a view of the room. There was the kitchen table, covered in dents and scratches but
[35] polished to a high sheen; behind and to the right, the pantry, no doubt stocked full of the jars of preserves that my mother would have been making all summer; and straight ahead, my mother, standing at the sink. She had aged during the years of my absence. I could see it in the way she stood, slightly
[40] hunched over the sink, and in the color of her hair, pulled back

as always. She had to have heard me coming—gravel roads announce visitors from miles away—but she showed no sign that she knew I was standing there in the doorway, debating whether or not to knock.

[45] "Mother? It's me. I'm here."

Her back straightened as she replied, though she never turned or left the sink.

"Come on in, and be sure to close the screen door behind you. It's been a bad year for bugs."

[50] I opened the door and stepped back in time. When I had announced my plan to go away for school, she had asked me how I thought I was going to pay for it. When the holidays came around, and I told her I wasn't going to be able to come home, she didn't ask why, and when I stopped calling on a
[55] regular basis, she didn't then either. How many nights had I spent, hating her for making those decisions so hard for me? Already I could feel the anger rising, that she could act so unconcerned at my arrival, standing at the sink shelling peas. Her only daughter whom she hadn't seen for a decade.

[60] As I approached the sink, ready to demand an explanation, I saw that her hands were shaking, the peas falling into the sink as much as the bowl. She looked so much older, aged even more than I had thought, in the same faded dress she'd probably worn for five years. It suddenly hit me that all that
[65] time, she hadn't called not because she didn't care, but because she did. She had never been able to leave, but I had, and she understood that I needed to strike out on my own, far from here. Now here I was, in my fancy city clothes, with my college degree and impressive job, and she didn't know what to
[70] say. I bridged the gap the only way I knew how: I rolled up my sleeves, and started to help with the peas.

1. The primary purpose of the first paragraph is to:

   A. describe the narrator's transition from her everyday, working life in the city to the world of her rural childhood.
   B. explain why the narrator becomes so frustrated when she arrives at her mother's house in the countryside.
   C. give the reader enough background about the setting of the story to explain the events of the later parts of the passage.
   D. foreshadow the narrator's feelings of abandonment as described in the last paragraphs of the passage.

2. The narrator considers the weather in Alabama during the summer time to be:

   F. humid and extremely hot.
   G. unbearably hot and miserable.
   H. cool and breezy.
   J. pleasantly familiar.

3. It can reasonably be inferred from the second paragraph (lines 15–28) that the narrator's feelings upon seeing her childhood home are feelings of:

   A. surprise at the dilapidated state of the building.
   B. frustration and anger towards her mother.
   C. joy tinged with fatigue caused by her travels.
   D. familiar recognition combined with nervousness.

4. The best description of the point of view from which this passage is told is that of a:

   F. daughter describing her thoughts during an event in her adult life.
   G. daughter reminiscing about her distant childhood in Alabama.
   H. mother remembering her daughter's visit to the family home.
   J. mother who longs to visit her adult daughter but cannot.

5. As it is used in line 28, the word *braced* most nearly means:

   A. fastened.
   B. straightened.
   C. prepared.
   D. supported.

6. As revealed in the passage, the mother is best described as:

   F. harsh and uncompromising.
   G. uneducated yet wise.
   H. altruistic and warm.
   J. distant but caring.

7. The central concern presented in the passage is:

   A. the anger that a daughter feels towards her distant mother and her struggles to overcome this anger.
   B. the conflicting emotions experienced by the narrator upon her homecoming from her life in the city to the rural childhood of her youth.
   C. the narrator's realization that her mother has aged terribly during the four years the narrator spent in college.
   D. an older woman's cautious but willful acceptance of her daughter's foreign lifestyle as the older woman is forced to stay in her hometown.

8. The relationship between the narrator and her mother, as described in the last paragraph (lines 60–71) of the passage, could best be described as:

   F. extremely close, built on frank emotional openness and mutual respect of one another's independent decisions.
   G. based on unspoken thoughts, leading to occasional misunderstandings, but ultimately supportive and caring.
   H. antagonistic, largely due to the mother's unwillingness to support her daughter's independent decision to move away.
   J. a very distant relationship, largely nonexistent outside of rare visits on the part of the daughter.

9. The emotional states of the characters are primarily conveyed by the author's use of:

   A. metaphorical descriptions of the setting.
   B. subtle but emotionally charged dialogue.
   C. visual descriptions and narrative reflections.
   D. detailed psychological portraits by an objective narrator.

10. As revealed in the final paragraph, upon seeing her mother at the sink, the narrator, for the first time, realizes which of the following?

    F. She wants desperately for her mother to be more expressive of her emotions.
    G. Her mother has aged to such an extent that the daughter has trouble recognizing her and the house in which she lives.
    H. It is difficult to leave someone and not be able to visit them every year during the holidays.
    J. Her mother has been supportive of the narrator's decision to leave but has not expressed it in a way the narrator expects.

Passage II

SOCIAL SCIENCE: This passage is adapted from the article "From Kiva Han to Caribou Coffee" by Alan C. Thorwald in the collection *A Social History of Joe* (© 2008 by Grantalventi Books).

For some time, coffee has been the world's most popular beverage, with an estimated 400 billion cups consumed each year. The coffeehouse in society, however, has a rich history that goes beyond supplying you with your daily cup of double-
5 shot, half-decaf, skinny latte. Understanding how coffeehouses developed as social sites can permit a greater appreciation for the diverse ways that social communication occurs.

The social significance of the coffeehouse was not evident at first. The first documented coffee shop, *Kiva Han*, was
10 opened in 1475 in the Byzantine Empire's city of Constantinople (today known as Istanbul). Although one could purchase coffee at this establishment, the coffeehouse as a place for social gatherings did not emerge until 1554, when Constantinople saw two coffeehouses open almost simultaneously.
15 Subsequently, men in Middle Eastern countries considered the coffeehouse an ideal place to listen to music or poetry, play chess, read books, or hold conversations—with friends and strangers alike—on subjects ranging from politics to gossip. Even today, the coffeehouse is firmly entrenched in
20 many Arab nations as a gathering place for cultural dialogue and dissemination of ideas.

As with goods such as tea and tobacco, coffee came to Europe through trade routes and colonial expeditions, and the coffeehouse soon followed. In 1645, Europe's first cof-
25 feehouse opened in Venice, which through its proximity to the Middle East had become one of the primary gateways for goods imported from the Ottoman Empire. In 1652, an Armenian servant named Pasqua Rosee launched the first London coffeehouse with the help of his employer, a trader
30 who imported the coffee and established the business. Unlike many public spaces, coffeehouses were open to men of various social strata; consequently, these establishments became equated with egalitarianism and reform. Although not everyone lauded these social traits—Charles II famously deplored
35 the establishments as hotbeds of scandal-mongering and anti-royalist political scheming—by 1739, the phenomenon had become so popular that London contained no fewer than 551 coffeehouses. Coffeehouses were sometimes called "penny universities," because admission and a cup cost a penny and
40 because the atmosphere of learning was so pronounced. By the end of the eighteenth century, the clientele who populated these meeting places shaped the character of each coffeehouse. Certain coffeehouses became affiliated with political leanings, such as Tory or Whig, or with specific occupations, such as
45 merchant or lawyer.

The coffeehouse's cultural character had taken shape centuries before such establishments appeared in the United States, but they almost immediately began to take on a singularly American character. In fact, one of the coffeehouse's principal
50 influences was on architecture. Soldiers returning from World War II sought to replicate the coffeehouse experiences they had known in Europe; at the same time, the automobile was beginning to have a stronger influence on how Americans used public spaces. The result was the drive-in coffee shop,
55 which not only satisfied the increasingly on-the-go customer but also provided an outlet for architects who wanted to incorporate the postwar feelings of newness and hope that so many Americans embraced. These coffee shops inaugurated a new style of architecture, named "googie architecture" for
60 one prominent coffee haven, Googie's. Found primarily in the urban areas of Southern California and in the glittering new playground of Las Vegas, googie architecture eschewed many of the elegant trappings of the traditional coffeehouse, such as mahogany booths and brass railings. Instead, this style
65 employed many of the "futuristic" artificial surfaces of the era: Naugahyde seat covers, Formica tabletops, and linoleum floors. In addition, googie architecture replaced the sedately darkened rooms of the European coffeehouse with brightly lit, almost garishly colored décor. In all, the American version of
70 the coffeehouse concerned itself less with supplying a forum for communicative, social relationships than with offering a visual emblem of a nation's desire to shake off the past and plunge into the future.

Even today, when coffeehouses in the United States are so
75 ubiquitous that one may well expect them to soon outnumber residential homes, these institutions operate in more arenas than mere commerce. The now-familiar sight of the business-person poring over a laptop computer during ordinary office hours signals the degree to which coffeehouses reflect and
80 reinforce contemporary attitudes toward the world of work. For many, the coffeehouse offers an escape from the cubicle, from the unsatisfying, regimented life of the Big Company; that is, the coffeehouse can represent an office worker's quest for individual freedom, while the wireless service in many
85 coffee shops prevents a complete abdication of one's responsibilities. Critics may see the "wi-fi revolution" as another worrying trend toward the invasion of community space—and of *personal* time and space—by corporate concerns. But one thing is clear: The coffeehouse has proven to be remarkably
90 flexible in adapting to its cultural environs.

11. According to the passage, when did the United States begin to influence the character of coffeehouses?

   A. After World War II, when the automobile began to change the nature of public spaces.
   B. Prior to the rise of anti-royalist political scheming.
   C. When the number of coffeehouses began to exceed the number of residential homes.
   D. After the introduction of the wi-fi revolution.

12. The main idea of the passage is that:

    F. coffeehouses originated in the Middle East in the fifteenth century as coffee was increasingly imported by traders, but today, North American coffeehouses are increasingly seen as more authentic.

    G. coffee has been a very popular beverage throughout history, having been consumed by people from many continents over the course of many centuries.

    H. coffeehouses are useful indicators of the shifting nature of social communication and cultural norms.

    J. coffeehouses have always served to preserve traditional values and social and professional hierarchies.

13. Information in the second paragraph (lines 8–21) makes it clear that coffeehouses in sixteenth-century Constantinople:

    A. began to appear after the fall of the Ottoman Empire.

    B. were not commonly used for activities other than drinking coffee.

    C. were the first places where the local population could purchase coffee.

    D. were viewed by many local men as good places to listen to music or poetry.

14. The main idea of the third paragraph (lines 22–45) is that:

    F. in seventeenth-century England, many servants enjoyed the freedom and opportunity to work with their employers to open their own businesses.

    G. the growing popularity of coffeehouses in Europe by the eighteenth century was due in part to the accessibility the coffeehouses offered to men of different social strata.

    H. because it was extremely inexpensive to enter a coffeehouse and purchase a cup of coffee, the beverage became popular among university students.

    J. Venice's coffeehouses were more authentic than London's because Venice used its trade routes to the Middle East to import tea and spices as well as coffee.

15. The passage states that the original character of British coffeehouses changed in the late eighteenth century insofar as the coffeehouses:

    A. began as male-only institutions but later admitted women.

    B. started to serve coffees imported from parts of the world other than Turkey.

    C. began to cater to specific occupations and political groups.

    D. started to feature exotic imports such as Naugahyde.

16. As it is used in lines 68–69 to describe googie architecture, the phrase "brightly lit, almost garishly colored" most nearly means that the décor in American coffeehouses:

    F. allowed customers to be able to see each other better.

    G. offered a forum for social relationships.

    H. was deemed tacky by the clientele found in European coffeehouses.

    J. was a symbol of America's belief in a bright and hopeful future.

17. According to the passage, googie architecture in the United States:

    A. is famous for its brass railings and mahogany booths.

    B. was mainly inspired by the architecture of European coffeehouses.

    C. can be found in the urban areas of Southern California.

    D. is a popular architectural style for playgrounds in Las Vegas.

18. According to the passage, which development contributed to the creation of the drive-in coffee shop?

    F. The push to create new work spaces for business people

    G. New laws for operating European-style coffeehouses

    H. A lack of physical space in cities

    J. The rise of the automobile in American life

19. According to the passage, what is one criticism of the "wi-fi revolution" as it relates to coffeehouses?

    A. Unreliable technology makes coffeehouses poor substitutes for conventional offices.

    B. Conducting business in coffeehouses represents a problematic intrusion into other parts of personal life.

    C. Working on computers isolates customers from one another, betraying the original communicative ideals of the coffeehouse.

    D. Office workers stay so long in coffeehouses that getting a seat there is difficult.

20. The passage most strongly suggests that today:

    F. the coffeehouse is a unique institution in the way that it combines commerce and culture.

    G. contemporary coffeehouses reflect Americans' changing ideas of the workplace.

    H. coffee has become more influential across the world than has tea or tobacco.

    J. if not for coffeehouses, architects would not have been able to develop novel designs for public buildings.

Passage III

HUMANITIES: This passage is adapted from the memoir *Who I Was to Become* by Arnold C. Tiepolo (© 2008 by Arnold Tiepolo).

My economics professor was finally getting through to me. He was explaining the concepts of comparative advantage and opportunity cost, stating that individuals, companies, and countries choose their economic goals by comparing their ease
5 of attaining those goals to that of their competition as well as by considering what opportunities they would be forsaking in the process. For example, if it's easier to grow bananas in New Zealand than it is in Madagascar, then New Zealand has a comparative advantage in that industry. However, if the land
10 New Zealand would use to grow its bananas could otherwise be used to grow timber for the logging industry, then whichever commodity is sacrificed so that the other can be produced becomes the opportunity cost of that choice. As my professor continued applying these concepts to other global scenarios, I
15 started thinking that the same thought process takes place as each of us carves out his personality and ambitions.

No choice is made in a vacuum. An incoming freshman doesn't arbitrarily major in journalism any more than a country would haphazardly make bananas one of its chief exports.
20 The rational decision-making process we see in either case is a demonstration of self- and environmental analysis: what are my strengths, what are my priorities, and how good is my competition? As someone who teaches law school prep classes, I am often confronted by my students' quizzical
25 looks when I tell them I am not interested in pursuing law myself. Occasionally, I find myself quite tempted to venture down that arduous but rewarding path; however, I remind myself of how much I value my free time and how much of it would be sacrificed by my becoming a lawyer. On mornings
30 when I bike down to the beach with my guitar slung over my shoulder so that I can write songs in sandy tranquility, I am reminded of the immense trade-off between financial security and personal freedom.

In high school, my best (and practically only) friend and
35 I would routinely pull "all-nighters": filming music videos, playing hours of table tennis, and falling asleep trying to appreciate classic movies like *The Godfather*. For the most part, our peers at school recognized us as a single unit; maybe we were opposites, one "yin" and the other "yang," but we fused
40 together as one entity. My best friend was not viewed admirably by many, and several times I was entreated to ditch him so that I could be included in some other group. Although loyalty was a huge reason to remain his friend, I definitely weighed the opportunity costs of having one, unassailable friendship
45 versus having a multitude of more superficial friends.

When my older brother started playing piano at age eight, I idolized him and began taking piano lessons shortly thereafter. Within a few months, my piano abilities caught up with his. He decided, rather than sharing the instrument
50 with his brother, that he would abandon the piano in favor of the saxophone. Although his nine-year-old brain did not see it necessary to saddle me with guilt, he is quick to remind me today of how my encroachment upon his territory as the family's pianist led him to seek a new interest. My two broth-
55 ers and I are extremely similar, eerily clone-like versions of each other. While any one of us could have ended up being the filmmaker, the musician, or the novelist, we seem to have purposefully avoided each other's vocations so that we could have our own distinct identities.

60 The need to craft a personal identity is intrinsic to any-one's life. Americans' central ethos, especially if you listen to advertisers, is the expression of individuality. We conveniently forget that, in selecting our personalities, we are almost invariably making choices that thousands of others like us
65 are making, thereby negating any hope of true individuality. However, like economic ventures, our "gimmick" has to be unique only in our local context, whether that be our family, our circle of friends, our school, etc. Opening a barber shop is hardly treading on untouched entrepreneurial territory, but if
70 there is no barber shop in the neighborhood, such a business could be a welcome and prosperous presence. Similarly, I don't consider myself an innovator for pursuing a career in professional music, but within the context of my family that career choice has distinction.

75 While having an identifiable trait is a helpful way for people to categorize and remember you, our habitual gravitation towards labeling people according to their predominant features troubles me. When I consider every fork in the road my life has reached, I can envision any number of alternate
80 universes in which I am studying astrophysics, already raising a family, or backpacking across the Appalachian Trail. The potential energy to realize any of these scenarios was in me, but as soon as I chose one path, all the others seemingly imploded. I am reluctant to accept any rigidity to my person-
85 ality or occupation, knowing that there are untold numbers of concurrent directions my life could take. We are all that way: physicians who could be poets, dancers who could be real estate moguls, married people who could still be single. To oversimplify people by acknowledging only what we
90 currently see them doing is to ignore the deep reservoirs of possibility that brew just under the surfaces of their choices.

21. The word *vacuum* in line 17 refers to:

   A. thorough cleanliness.
   B. absence of environmental context.
   C. a person's subconscious.
   D. a large opportunity cost.

22. Which of the following best describes how the author uses the reference to *yin* and *yang* (line 39)?

   F. It provides an instance of the name-calling that the author and his best friend endured from peers who did not understand their close friendship.
   G. It demonstrates the author's friend's interest in Eastern mysticism as opposed to the author's primary interest in economics.
   H. It is analogous to the close bond between the narrator and his friend who are often seen as two parts that form a larger whole.
   J. It is analogous to the ways people waver between choices in their lives and will at times have one profession but wish they had chosen another.

23. The passage states that one of the author's brothers is currently a:

   A. novelist.
   B. pianist.
   C. real estate mogul.
   D. physician.

24. In the passage, the author refers to having considered becoming all of the following things in his adult life EXCEPT:

   F. a parent.
   G. a lawyer.
   H. a journalist.
   J. an astrophysicist.

25. As it is used in the passage, the term *gimmick* (line 66) represents:

   A. a means of defining one's individuality.
   B. the way advertisers trick people into wanting unnecessary products.
   C. what makes people living in the United States unique.
   D. an entrepreneurial venture chosen without sufficient forethought.

26. The author would most likely agree with which of the following statements about "opportunity cost" and "comparative advantage" mentioned in the first paragraph?

   F. They are the central claims of any modern economic theory and are the cornerstones of any class in the subject.
   G. They were instrumental in the author's various decisions in life, particularly his decision to open a barber shop.
   H. They are so useful because they can be applied without reference to any surrounding context.
   J. They are ideas from economics that may also be useful in considering topics other than economics.

27. The "we" in line 86 is most likely:

   A. the author and his brothers.
   B. the author and other Americans.
   C. the author and his best friend.
   D. the author and his alternate visions of himself.

28. Based on the passage, the author most likely began playing piano when he was:

   F. younger than eight years old.
   G. eight years old.
   H. nine years old.
   J. in high school.

29. Which one of the following would the author most likely see as an example of oversimplifying others by "acknowledging only what we currently see them doing" (lines 89–90)?

   A. Assuming a physician wants to be a writer or poet.
   B. Assuming a lawyer only pretends to like his or her job.
   C. Assuming a mathematician is good only at math.
   D. Assuming a politician no longer wants to be a politician.

30. Which of the following statements about the author and his siblings is supported by the passage?

   F. They would stay up all night filming and watching movies in an attempt to spend less time communicating with each other directly.
   G. Every hobby one of them chose was ruined by another encroaching upon it, and they soon abandoned most things they started.
   H. They drew straws to see who would pursue what career, allowing the career of each to be determined completely by chance.
   J. Although very similar, they sought to differentiate themselves from each other by choosing different careers.

NATURAL SCIENCE: This passage is adapted from the entry "Dr. Pete Vukusic, Exeter University" from *Thirty Contemporary Scientists* (© 2007 Beekman and The Rat Publishers).

In the future, we may be painting the walls of our houses or choosing the color of our cars by looking at the wings of a butterfly. Dr Pete Vukusic, a researcher at Exeter University in the United Kingdom, has been researching the source of
5 brilliant iridescent color on butterfly wings; he hopes natural design will improve manmade devices as scientists learn to replicate nature's photonic architecture. Vukusic's research focuses on animals that create brilliant color not through pigmentation, but through physical structure.

10 Instead of pigments—chemicals that color the skin of humans and many other animals—the butterfly wings' iridescent color is produced by tiny nanostructures that look similar to upside-down Christmas trees. When light strikes these structures, each wavelength is reflected at different
15 angles, striking different descending branches. Eventually, only one wavelength is reflected back in the direction of the viewer, producing the brilliant single wavelength of iridescent color, brighter and more luminous than any individual color produced by pigment. It is similar to looking into the
20 ocean and seeing not just the surface of the water, but also schools of fish and plant life below. This color-producing element of butterfly wings is the inspiration for a range of potential applications from paints, fabrics, and displays to anti-counterfeiting measures or the ultimate radar camouflage
25 for planes. One of the most immediate applications, however, may be in the use of cosmetics.

L'Oreal, a major cosmetics company, is using Dr. Vukusic's research to develop lip, eye, and nail color that the company claims will give customers surrealistic effects they
30 could never obtain with traditional makeup. While humans will use these effects primarily to enhance their appearance, creatures like winged insects and peacocks use chemistry to produce color for various reasons; for example, a bright blue morpho butterfly might use its intense color to be visible to
35 its peers from far away, while another creature might employ it as a type of camouflage.

To re-create the brilliant colors that appear in nature, scientists vary the thickness of nano-scale layers of material like mica, liquid crystals, or silica. When these techniques
40 are applied to cosmetics, the makeup appears white, but once applied and exposed to light, vibrant color will show and change depending on the angle from which it's viewed. Vukusic concedes that some may find more important or serious applications for this technology, including optical
45 computing, car paint, and anti-counterfeit measures for credit cards, but he contends that there's no way to say which applications are more or less useful or technologically more or less valuable.

As research continues, scientists may also find that their
50 best inventions inadvertently replicate the technology of nature. For example, in 2001, Alexei Erchak and colleagues at the Massachusetts Institute of Technology (MIT) demonstrated a method for building a more efficient light-emitting diode (LED). Most light emitted from standard LEDs cannot escape,
55 resulting in what scientists call a low extraction efficiency of light. The LED developed at MIT used a two-dimensional (2D) photonic crystal to enhance the extraction of light and layered structures called Bragg reflectors to control the emission direction.

60 Pete Vukusic and Ian Hooper at Exeter have now shown that swallowtail butterflies evolved an identical method for signaling to each other in the wild; they depend on their fluorescence to establish territory and communicate with other butterflies of the same species. Swallowtails have dark
65 wings with bright blue or blue-green patches; the wing scales on these swallowtails act as 2D photonic crystals, infused with pigment and structured in such a way that they produce intense fluorescence. Pigment on the butterflies' wings absorbs ultraviolet light that is then re-emitted, using fluorescence,
70 as brilliant blue-green light. Most of this light would be lost were it not for the pigment's location in a region of the wing which has evenly spaced micro-holes through it—essentially mother nature's version of a 2D photonic crystal. Like its counterpart in a high emission LED, it prevents the fluores-
75 cent color from being trapped inside the structure and from being emitted sideways. The scales also have a type of mirror underneath them to upwardly reflect fluorescent light emitted downward, working just like Bragg reflectors in high emission LEDs. Dr. Vukusic contends that the way light is extracted
80 from the butterfly's system is more than an analogy; it's all but identical in design to the LED.

Vukusic is quick to point out that the idea of substituting light for pigments in creating colors isn't new. At least since Isaac Newton's seventeenth-century book *Opticks:*
85 *or, A Treatise of the Reflexions, Refractions, Inflexions and Colours of Light*, which describes, among other things, how color is produced in peacock feathers, scientists have believed pigments aren't the only things that can produce colors. But it wasn't until recently that scientists began learning how to
90 re-create the same effect using nano-scale particles. Despite years of research in the field, there appears to be little danger that Dr. Vukusic and his colleagues will run out of avenues to explore. Taking into account the fact that tens of thousands of species employ iridescence—not just butterflies, but beetles,
95 birds, and fish as well—there's much work still to be done, and many discoveries yet to be made.

31. What comparison does the author make between pigment and structure?

A. Colors produced by pigment are more brilliant than those produced by structure.
B. Colors created by structure are more brilliant than those produced by pigment.
C. Pigment and structure work in much the same way to create brilliant colors.
D. Colors produced by structure are twenty times more brilliant than those produced by pigment.

32. As it is used in line 35, the word *employ* most nearly means:

F. hire.
G. pay.
H. retain.
J. use.

33. It is most reasonable to infer that if the innovations of the cosmetics company referred to in line 27 were successful, which of the following would occur?

A. Many other scientists would be hired to create similar products for competing cosmetic companies.
B. Dr. Vukusic's research would no longer be available for uses such as car paint or anti-counterfeit measures.
C. People would be able to create unique and previously unattainable visual effects with their appearance.
D. People would realize that such surrealistic effects are better confined to animals and insects in the natural world.

34. Which of the following best describes how the phrase "schools of fish and plant life below" (line 21) functions in the passage?

F. As an example of what iridescent light looks like to Dr. Vukusic
G. As a comparison that suggests iridescence provides more to see than the flat color on the surface of an object
H. As an illustration of how iridescence is also seen in fish and plant life
J. As a suggestion to encourage people to appreciate the beauty of nature

35. According to the passage, swallowtail butterflies are dependent on:

A. camouflage.
B. light.
C. photonic crystals.
D. fluorescence.

36. Which of the following questions is NOT answered by the passage?

F. Why can't most light emitted from standard LEDs escape?
G. Why might a bright blue morpho butterfly use brilliant color?
H. How do swallowtail butterflies emit brilliant blue-green light?
J. How is a butterfly's fluorescent color produced?

37. As it is used in line 70, the word *lost* most nearly means:

A. missing.
B. useless.
C. omitted.
D. withdrawn.

38. Which of the following statements best describes light in a butterfly's wing and its significance in relation to a photonic crystal, according to the passage?

F. Butterfly wings are made of hundreds of tiny photonic crystals, each emitting a ray of light.
G. If butterfly wings did not contain photonic crystals, butterflies would not be able to signal their peers from long distances.
H. Because the wing has tiny holes that work like a photonic crystal, brilliant color is able to escape from the wing.
J. The tiny scales of a butterfly's wing are able to reflect light much like a photonic crystal works in an LED.

39. According to the model for color-producing nanostructures as it is presented in the passage, what is the route that light travels to create iridescence?

A. Reflects at angles, reflects to viewer, hits the structure
B. Reflects to viewer, hits the structure, reflects at angles
C. Reflects at angles, hits the structure, reflects to viewer
D. Hits the structure, reflects at angles, reflects to viewer

40. The passage states that which of the following combinations of qualities rarely occurs in the same material?

F. Standard LEDs with fluorescent light
G. Standard LEDs with a high extraction of light
H. Standard LEDs with a low extraction of light
J. Standard LEDs with intense pigmentation

READING TEST

35 Minutes—40 Questions

DIRECTIONS: There are four passages in this test. Each passage is followed by several questions. After reading each passage, choose the best answer to each question and blacken the corresponding oval on your answer document. You may refer to the passages as often as necessary.

Passage I

PROSE FICTION: This passage is adapted from the novel *A Passage to America* by Aditi C. Thakur (© 2003 by Aditi Thakur).

I'm shivering in the air conditioning. I've never gotten used to the swirl of chilled air in the apartment. I'd like to open the window, to welcome in the hot bright yellow sun, but the superintendent has painted all the building's windows
5 shut for some unexplained reason.

Ramesh won't be home from the university for several hours, I know. The project he's working on is keeping him at the lab until later in the evenings these days. Still shivering, I mull the choices for our evening meal, scanning the vegetables,
10 herbs, and spices I collected at the specialty food market this morning. Even after five years in the United States, I find I still seek the patterns of our life in India, including my daily morning visits to the market to do the day's food shopping.

As I pore over the curled turmeric roots and the bright
15 orange and red mangoes—both of which appeared in the market's bins today for the first time—I remember the first time I went to an American-style supermarket. Intimidated by the unfamiliar streets and landmarks of our new city, Ramesh and I had spent the first month of our American life eating all
20 our meals at restaurants within walking distance of the flat. Ramesh had concocted his lunches from items purchased at the university's "convenience store"; he joked that convenience was really the only desirable thing the shop offered. Once we had exhausted the menus at each of the nearby restaurants,
25 I promised that I would brave the supermarket so we could both have a taste of the home we'd been aching for.

Naturally—or rather, unnaturally—the store was cold, and I was glad I had decided to bring along my *dupatta* to shield my otherwise bare shoulders.

30 At first, the enormous quantity of goods and the wildly varied colors everywhere I looked were impressive. But then I noticed that the produce section—it seemed surprisingly tucked away on the end farthest from the doors, as if the store were somehow ashamed of it—lacked items we considered
35 favorites or even staples: no dried lentils or chickpeas, no cherimoyas or pomegranates. I wandered up and down the aisles, wondering at the slabs of meat sealed within cocoons of plastic, and at the seemingly infinite rows of boxes, each of which somehow housed "dinner for the whole family." Un-
40 able after a time to focus on the boxes' labels, I turned to a gangly, uniformed teenager who was pretending to straighten the ginger-ale bottles on the bottom shelf.

"Excuse me, please, I am wondering whether you could help me find…" I began.

45 He glanced up at me, noting my *sari* with an eye that felt at once piercing and uncritical. "Aisle 7, on the right," he squeaked, with a wide, unexpectedly amiable grin.

My irritation at having been so easily categorized faded somewhat at discovering two shelves' worth of jars of chutneys
50 and mixes, including one imported tandoori paste that had been one of our favorites back in India. But as I unsteadily but successfully navigated the checkout lines and paid for my few, familiar products, I observed that the supermarket's fluorescent ceiling bulbs effectively bleached out the shelves'
55 contents. The bottles and boxes no longer seemed exotic or glamorous. It seemed to me that no matter how insistently the labels tried to draw attention to the wonders within their containers, the vividness of their colors would inevitably appear flat and lifeless under the homogenizing light.

60 I still go to the supermarket sometimes, but recently a colleague of Ramesh's recommended that we go to the outskirts of the city to shop at a new Indian market, where I went this morning. The old woman who manages the place moves quickly from stall to stall, urging customers to sample
65 pieces of fruit or explaining how adding one more ingredient will perfect the planned dish. She reminds me, almost painfully, of my grandmother, who was similarly convinced that she could make others' lives better through shared food or wisdom—my grandmother, to whose image I've often come
70 back whenever I've needed consolation or company.

I trace my finger along the beige granite countertop, as if conjuring up the rough wooden surface in my grandmother's kitchen. As a child, I'd believed the dark wood had retained every nick from every vegetable chopped, and every stain
75 from every fruit that had yielded its sticky sweetness to my grandmother's swift, sure knife. I think of the fourteen distinct spices, each with its own grainy texture and subtle but

memorable color, that she pounded into dust with her mortar
and pestle. Then I recall the grayish, unfriendly curry powder
80 I'd seen in the American supermarket, so unlike the familiar
result of my grandmother's efforts. I sigh.

I don't really need to begin to prepare our dinner yet. I've
learned to combine the specialty market's fresh produce with
the supermarket's "quick prep" sauces and pastes, so making
85 dinner isn't the all-day task it often was for my grandmother
and even my mother. Even so, I decide to ward off the cold
by shrugging on a sweatshirt embossed with the university's
logo, and I set myself to work.

1. It can most reasonably be inferred from the passage that
the narrator regards her grandmother as:

A. comforting.
B. frightening.
C. foolish.
D. out of touch.

2. The narrator makes clear that she shops for food in the
mornings because:

F. that's when the produce arrives at the specialty market.
G. her husband works late at his job in the university lab.
H. the outdoor market is cooler during the morning hours.
J. she used to shop in the mornings when she lived in India.

3. As presented in the passage, how does the narrator's attitude toward living in the U.S. change from when she was
a recent arrival until the present day?

A. At first, she was intimidated by unfamiliar surroundings, but she has since learned to blend Indian and
American ways.
B. At first, she was excited about the prospect of learning
new ways, but she has since become disillusioned by
the people she meets.
C. At first, she enjoyed eating out at restaurants with her
husband, but she has begun to miss him as he increasingly works late.
D. At first, she is thrilled by the supermarket displays, but
she now refuses to leave her apartment.

4. The third paragraph (lines 14–26) primarily emphasizes
that the narrator's visit to the supermarket is motivated by
the fact that:

F. the narrator and her husband are both suffering from
homesickness.
G. groceries are more inexpensive at the supermarket.
H. unlike the specialty market, the supermarket is within
walking distance.
J. the narrator can't find the items she needs at the Indian
specialty market.

5. When the narrator mentions the location of the produce
section of the supermarket (lines 32–33), she is implying
that:

A. the produce section has everything she needs to make
dinner.
B. she is surprised that the produce section is not centrally located.
C. produce sections in Indian supermarkets are always
out in the open.
D. she is surprised to find an imported Indian product
there.

6. How can the conversation between the narrator and the
supermarket clerk (lines 43–47) best be characterized?

F. The narrator is pleased that the clerk is friendly and
able to tell her where to find the items she's looking for.
G. The narrator is shocked and upset by the clerk's hostil-
ity toward her.
H. The narrator is annoyed that the clerk knew what she
wanted before she asked.
J. The narrator wishes the clerk had been more coopera-
tive instead of being distracted by her clothing.

7. The narrator refers to the supermarket's "fluorescent ceiling bulbs" (line 54) in order to:

A. draw a contrast between the supermarket and the outdoor markets she remembers from India.
B. explain how her perception of the store's offerings had
changed.
C. suggest one reason that the supermarket terrified her.
D. describe why she was able to see the fruits and vegetables more clearly.

8. As it is used in line 79, the word *unfriendly* most nearly
suggests that:

F. the narrator thinks that the clerk doesn't want her to
buy the curry powder.
G. the narrator considers this curry powder to be different
from the curry powder with which she is familiar.
H. the narrator doesn't like the ingredients in the curry
powder.
J. the curry powder has been imported from another
country.

9. The narrator apparently believes which of the following
qualities is shared by the old woman who runs the specialty market and the narrator's grandmother?

A. Frailty
B. Stinginess
C. Sociability
D. Nervousness

10. The narrator indicates that, unlike her grandmother and mother, she:

    F. doesn't always spend all day preparing the evening meal.
    G. doesn't wear Western-style clothing.
    H. mingles easily with people she doesn't know.
    J. doesn't like air conditioning.

Passage II

SOCIAL SCIENCE: This passage is excerpted from "Record Lows" by Clarence Tetley. The article comes from the book *Can Music Survive the Digital Revolution?* by Clarence Tetley and Lawrence Twinnings (© 2008 by Clarence Tetley).

Glenn Spelling's Northern Virginia record store is on the verge of closing. He has rare collectibles in 8-track, vinyl, tape, and cassette format, but the rarest commodity in his store is a customer. His landlord would not renew the store's lease
5 on the building but allows Spelling to remain open until new tenants arrive.

"It's pretty sad to be living on borrowed time," sighs Spelling, "knowing it's only a matter of days until you run out of inventory or the landlord kicks you out."

10   Spelling may not be the only record store owner whose days in the business are numbered. Over 900 independent record stores have perished since the rise of digital music sales in 2003. Current estimates suggest that fewer than 2,000 remain in the U.S. The ones that are hanging on are
15 seeing their customer bases slowly erode, particularly among younger crowds. This slump in business is not isolated to the mom-and-pop independents.

Nationwide chain Tower Records was forced to declare bankruptcy in 2004.

20   Whereas large record store chains used to be essential ingredients in the lucrative hype machine of record labels, radio stations, and artists, record stores nowadays are not required for the recipe. Two different but simultaneous economic trends have effectively rendered record stores as obsolete as some
25 of the bands they carry.

One giant threat to record stores is the rise of digital music downloads. Younger music consumers are increasingly willing and likely to buy their music one song at a time over the internet and listen to it on their portable MP3 players. Since
30 1999, digital downloads have reduced CD sales by twenty to thirty percent. Recent technology allows thousands of songs to be held by a device the size of a pack of gum. This makes the notion of buying a physical commodity like a CD, which is harder to put in one's pocket than an MP3 player and holds
35 less than 1% as much music, seem downright prehistoric.

The second factor contributing to record stores' demise is the emergence of the "Superstore," franchises such as Target and Wal-Mart, which have a range of inventory as wide as that of an entire shopping mall. As recently as ten years ago,
40 consumers expected to go to any number of different specialized stores to buy such disparate items as groceries, clothing, and music. Superstores hold the allure of allowing a shopper to make all those purchases at the same cash register.

Because superstores expect to sell a larger volume of
45 goods than that of a specialized store, superstores can slash their prices to razor-thin profit margins (or sometimes even sell items such as CDs at a small loss just to get customers in the door). This is an ambitious business model, developed by Sam Walton; it involves an incredible amount of initial capital
50 to build the titanic warehouses that encase superstores and to buy the immense cornucopia of goods that will fill them. Furthermore, to attract customers, the stores need to keep prices lower than those of their competition, which means it will be years before a superstore recovers the initial money
55 put into building it. However, once established, superstores have so much leverage in the marketplace and loyalty from their customer base that they can prosper indefinitely.

Record stores are economically powerless to match those prices. "Everyone's getting their CDs at the record label's
60 wholesale price," explains Eric Tasker, owner of Funktown Records in Cincinnati. "If we marked up our CDs as little as [superstores] do, we wouldn't have enough revenue to pay for labor and expenses, let alone turn a profit." Tasker says that giant stores like Best Buy and Wal-Mart are able to buy in
65 such bulk that they can often broker special deals with record labels that lower the wholesale price, further disadvantaging smaller chains and independent stores.

Some record store owners such as Spelling concede the greater affordability of superstore prices and struggle
70 to come up with a reason why record stores deserve to stick around. "If you already know what you want, then I can see buying a CD wherever it's cheapest, but if you want to be able to talk to people about music and discover new bands, you need a record store. I guess most people don't want to
75 do that anymore."

Some do, however, and it's about the only silver lining to the dark cloud hovering over the record store industry. Well, it's a *gray* lining actually. Older men, ages 40–60, comprise the largest segment of record store consumers, and they don't
80 seem to be lured away by the cheaper superstore prices or the more efficient digital downloads. For these shoppers, many of their formative musical memories from childhood revolve around hanging out at their local record store, absorbing the alternative culture transmitted through posters on the wall
85 and provocative album covers. They discovered many of their favorite bands by discussing music with the "experts" who work at record stores. Buying music is not merely shopping around for the cheapest price; it is an experience of immersion into the world of music, something that allows them to escape
90 from their grown-up, career-driven lives and reconnect with their youthful inspirations.

11. According to the passage, which of the following is an accurate statement regarding the number of record stores?

A. Since the rise of digital music sales in 2003, over nine hundred stores have gone out of business.

B. Twenty to thirty percent of record stores that specialize in 8-track, vinyl, tape, and cassette are expected to close in the next ten years.

C. Before the rise of digital music in 2003, there were fewer than 2,000 independent stores in business.

D. Over the next ten years, another 900 stores are expected to perish.

12. Which of the following best describes the *silver lining* described in the last paragraph (line 76)?

F. Older, more technologically savvy men are relieved that innovations in downloading allow them to no longer have to travel to record stores.

G. Record stores have been forced to become cheaper and more efficient in a desperate attempt to lure superstore customers back.

H. The improved marketing of posters and album covers has been found to discourage the practice of digital downloads.

J. Older men who savor the experience of shopping at record stores remain a loyal customer base for record store owners.

13. In the context of the passage the phrase "downright prehistoric" (line 35) is used to support the idea that:

A. older men cannot find music in 8-track, vinyl, tape, or cassette formats in most record stores.

B. downloading digital music to an MP3 player offers a size and capacity that the CD format cannot match.

C. the downloading speed of most computers is too sluggish to appeal to consumers.

D. young people would buy more CDs if the CDs were reduced in size.

14. It can reasonably be inferred from the passage that Spelling has which of the following attitudes toward consumers who have stopped using record stores?

F. They do not share any interests with the type of inquisitive shoppers who go to record stores not knowing what they want.

G. They will not find any sense of community in buying their music online since there will be no cashier to talk to while ringing up their sale.

H. They are correct in believing that record stores do not always have the best prices available for a given CD.

J. They are chiefly to blame for the hardships facing record stores, despite the fact that many people blame superstores instead.

15. In the context of the passage, the first paragraph is intended to:

A. criticize Spelling's record store for failing to keep up with the modern music market.

B. explain the lack of interest most music consumers have in collectibles.

C. demonstrate that even record stores with valuable and rare merchandise are struggling.

D. suggest that record store owners do not really understand real estate.

16. It can be reasonably inferred from the passage that before 1999, consumers purchasing their music over the internet led to digital downloads reducing CD sales by:

F. less than 20 percent.

G. between 20 and 25 percent.

H. between 25 and 30 percent.

J. more than 30 percent.

17. According to the passage, what enables superstores to be able to sell products at small or even non-existent profit margins is:

A. the significant amount of capital required to build such a superstore.

B. the expectation of selling higher quantities of merchandise than smaller stores.

C. the greater amounts of products they can carry due to their warehouse sizes.

D. the ambitiousness of the economic planners who crafted their business models.

18. According to the passage, what effect has Sam Walton had on the record store industry?

F. Record stores have based their business models on one he created.

G. He tried to change the record store industry's model of community.

H. He was one of the record store industry's most passionate critics.

J. He was involved in the evolution of the superstore, which is a competitor of record stores.

19. The passage offers all of the following as reasons modern consumers might not shop at record stores EXCEPT:

A. a higher price tag on goods available more cheaply elsewhere.

B. a fear of being unwelcome in a community of music "experts."

C. a preference for a different format of music than the CD.

D. the ability to buy music, groceries, and clothing all at once.

20. The author states that superstores will recover their initial building costs:

    F. once all their capital is invested.
    G. once all their goods are purchased.
    H. once the store finally opens.
    J. several years after the store has opened.

Passage III

HUMANITIES: This passage is excerpted from the article "The Road to Reconciliation" by Patsky Irktour (© 2006 by The Ames Iowan)."

Growing up, I was surrounded by art. Paintings, prints, pottery, even rugs and blankets—nearly everything in the house was decorated with some kind of design or image. My parents were both first generation immigrants, and they said
5 that the art reminded them of home. Anytime we went to visit the family still living in Mexico, my parents would stop at roadside bazaars, searching for new treasures, while I waited impatiently in the car, playing a video game or listening to music. Back in Los Angeles, they would proudly show their
10 new purchases to friends, and all of the adults would reminisce about their childhoods in Mexico.

In college, I found that this early exposure to art had affected me profoundly. I entered a fine arts program, with the eventual goal of working as a curator at some major mu-
15 seum, like the Getty. The more I learned about the European masters, the more enamored of them I became. Every visit home, I brought with me a print for my parents, something by Rembrandt or Titian, in order to expose them to what I considered "true art." In my eyes, these European artists were
20 the true masters of the form, and I saw my parents' collection as almost shameful. It seemed so primitive—the colors too bright, the figures too stylized. Whenever I tried to express this to my parents, they would smile and listen, then hang the print I had brought in my bedroom.

25 During my second year of college, a friend and I decided to go on a road trip during our spring break. We planned a route from Phoenix, where we attended school, down into Mexico, then on to Los Angeles. Spending a few days on each leg would allow us a couple of days to drive back to Phoenix
30 before school started with only one day to spare, so as soon as our midterms ended, we headed out.

The first few days were filled with the usual road trip misadventures—a flat tire, a long walk to the gas station after our car ran dry on the highway, and a late night spent
35 looking desperately for a motel. By the time we arrived in Santa Ana, Mexico, and found my grandmother's house, we were both exhausted, furious with each other, and ready to break down crying. My grandmother, seeing the state of affairs written across our faces, sent us off to bed almost as
40 soon as we arrived.

The next morning, we woke to the smell of fresh coffee, eggs, chorizo, and tortillas. As I ate, I thought of my parents and past breakfasts at their home. Maybe that's why, when we went for a walk in the downtown area, I wandered into
45 an artist's studio situated just off the central square. I had a vague idea of picking something out for them, to present upon our victorious arrival in California. As soon as I entered, though, I realized this wasn't a studio in the sense that I had expected. There was art for sale on display, but there was also
50 a man sitting at an easel, painting. Curious, I wandered over.

As I looked over his shoulder, my shadow fell across his canvas, but he paid me no mind. His body was slightly hunched over, to help him stay balanced on the small stool he used as a seat. His eyes were squinted almost shut and his
55 attention didn't appear to be on the canvas at all. He seemed, instead, to be seeing something else entirely, something that wouldn't quite come into focus. The half-finished picture on the canvas was of a girl, maybe eighteen years old, standing with her back to the viewer, looking over her shoulder. Her
60 hair was in a long braid that fell down the length of her back, with hairs coming loose, as if in the wind. The braid itself was painted as a solid, gleaming, black mass, but the stray hairs were each painted with an individual life, seeming about to blow out of the painting. Her face was still unfinished, along
65 with the backdrop. As I stood watching, the artist suddenly launched himself at the canvas, adding details to the face at a furious pace. Under my gaze, the girl's expression took shape. Her eyes looked straight at the viewer with a look, half wistful, half angry, as though reproaching the viewer
70 for something.

Once the eyes were done, the artist leaned back and sighed. I wanted to talk to him, ask him about this girl, whether he had known her, but the look on his face seemed to rule out any conversation. It wasn't that he looked unfriendly so much as
75 that he looked like he was otherwise occupied, his thoughts on some past time, approachable to a stranger only through this painting. I slowly, quietly, walked out of the studio, as anyone would when leaving the presence of a master.

21. Which of the following best characterizes the narrator's initial childhood feelings toward Mexican art?

A. It was familiar and thus lacking in interest.
B. It was primitive and used too many geometric designs.
C. It symbolized the only form of "true art."
D. Because it reminded her of home, it was beloved.

22. In the second paragraph (lines 12–24), the parents' response to their daughter's gifts of prints can best be described as:

F. grateful.
G. tolerant.
H. horrified.
J. perplexed.

23. The narrator's point of view in this passage could best be described as:

A. a grown woman reflecting on her past experience.
B. a child describing her first encounter with Mexican art.
C. an artist explaining the process of creation.
D. a parent fondly recalling a child's mistaken beliefs.

24. When the narrator states that she "saw [her] parents' collection as almost shameful" (lines 20–21), she most nearly means that she:

F. felt that her parents were unable to afford high quality art.
G. would feel uncomfortable inviting her college friends home to visit.
H. believed that her parents' art was inferior to the art she studied at school.
J. could not understand why her parents chose to display any art.

25. As it is used in line 47, the word *victorious* most nearly means:

A. conquering.
B. aggressive.
C. winning.
D. successful.

26. Which of the following is the most accurate description of the emotional transition experienced by the narrator in the passage?

F. A young artist moves away from the more familiar art of her heritage and comes to appreciate art produced by other groups.
G. A student moves from dismissing the art with which she grew up to eventually appreciating its merits.
H. The narrator recognizes the superiority of her cultural heritage and rejects the European tradition she had previously studied.
J. An art student decides to pursue her career as a traditional Mexican artist after she visits an art studio in Mexico.

27. The old man in the studio is portrayed as:

A. skilled yet uneducated.
B. focused and talented.
C. insightful but rude.
D. hesitant and forgetful.

28. As it is used in line 66, the phrase " launched himself at the canvas" most nearly means to:

F. attack the piece of artwork.
G. paint without skill.
H. paint more actively.
J. hesitate momentarily.

29. It can most reasonably be inferred that the narrator's decision not to speak to the painter (lines 72–74) is due to:

A. her fear that the painter will be unwilling to respond to her questions.
B. the painter's own silence during the time that he is painting.
C. a feeling of honor and respect for the painter's talent.
D. her pride that she is more familiar with "true art" than the painter.

30. The sixth and last paragraphs (lines 51–78) most nearly indicate that after her experience watching the painter, the narrator is:

F. condescending yet curious.
G. bored yet tolerant.
H. humbled and respectful.
J. annoyed and offended.

NATURAL SCIENCE: This passage is adapted from the entry "Migration" from *Wallace Wimpole's Bird Book* (© 1998 by Wallace Wimpole).

It has been well known among even casual observers of the natural world that many bird species make seasonal trips between cooler breeding grounds in the spring and summer, and warmer locations in the autumn and winter. Migration is
5 a part of the annual cycle of over 50 billion individual birds worldwide. (This is not to say all birds migrate; there are many species, particularly in the tropics, that maintain a single residence year round.) However, the biological mechanisms that prompt birds to choose a particular date to begin migra-
10 tion are complex and seem to be influenced by many factors.

The most obvious pressure on the timing of seasonal bird migration is the weather. As the weather cools and precipitation increases, birds living in temperate climates move in the direction of warmer weather. However, seasonal weather pat-
15 terns are notoriously unpredictable. Cloud cover can obscure even reliable measures of the seasons, such as the position of the sun and the stars. Therefore it is clear that birds must rely more heavily on an internal clock to time their seasonal movements. In fact, biologists have observed a phenomenon known
20 as "migratory restlessness" in caged birds at the same time the wild members of their species set off on seasonal migrations.

For most migratory birds, food supply is a major factor that contributes to the need to move from one location to another. Birds must have ample nutrition to reproduce, and
25 seasonal changes in weather affect the availability of berries, nuts, insects, rodents, and other sources of nourishment. Furthermore, birds must store a great deal of energy in the form of body fat to fuel their migration, so they have to leave while their reserves are high, before changes in weather cause
30 the food supply to dwindle. Many species seem to anticipate changes in weather and food sources, and adjust their migration schedules to accommodate significant variations in weather and food supply that occur from year to year, causing scientists to speculate that unknown internal stimuli may have a strong
35 effect on the timing of the migration decision.

In 1967, Russian ornithologists Viktor Dolnik and Tatiana Blyumental collected chaffinches as they migrated along the Baltic Coast. By examining the fat content and food in the gut of the carcasses of birds gathered at different stages of the
40 waves of migration, and then comparing these findings to the number of birds out of the total population yet to migrate, the scientists determined the social influence fat, healthy birds have on the remaining population that was not as physically fit for migration. Dolnik and Blyumental found that on the first
45 day of each wave of migration, only very fat birds flew. These birds left at sunrise, on days when weather conditions were favorable. They did not feed before beginning their migratory flight, instead relying on stored fat for energy.

On the second day, the chaffinch migration began again
50 in the morning with fat birds. By the afternoon the migration volume peaked, as more and more lean birds began to migrate, many with the morning's food still in their stomachs. By the third day, almost all the birds that began to migrate were very lean. These birds began their migration only after
55 feeding in the morning. Often these leaner birds began their migration despite inclement weather. Dolnik and Blyumental suggested that the social pressure exerted by the large volume of healthier birds in the flock that had already begun to migrate was an influence strong enough to override the lean birds'
60 poor physical readiness and the adverse conditions as factors in their decision to migrate. The scientists conducted their experiment on only one species, and though chaffinches are typical of diurnal migratory land birds, they do not accurately represent sea birds, raptors, or nocturnal species. Nonetheless,
65 Dolnik and Blyumental's work suggests that social pressure could explain why many different species of birds choose to migrate at apparently unfavorable times.

Some migratory birds travel much further than chaffinches. Most migrants spend a great deal of time storing energy to
70 make trips that take a matter of days or weeks to complete, and travel tens to hundreds of kilometers, spending most of their lives in residence at their breeding grounds and their winter habitats. A few species, however, can spend months of each year en route between residences continents apart, and
75 expend little more energy flying than sitting still. Wandering albatrosses spend almost all their time in the air, either migrating or foraging over oceans, moving up to 2000 kilometers on a single foraging expedition, and flying over 250,000 kilometers in a year (a distance equivalent to 4.6 times around
80 the earth's equator.) Such sea birds rely on their specialized wing structure to hold them aloft in air currents that transport them long distances, and some travel back and forth along the same paths on schedules dictated by the prevailing winds.

31. The main purpose of the passage is to:

    A. discuss the research techniques of scientists studying bird migration.

    B. provide data on the distances traveled seasonally by various migratory bird species.

    C. describe various factors that stimulate migratory behavior in birds.

    D. prove the effects of weather on bird migration.

32. The author uses the information in parentheses in lines 6–8 primarily to:

F. prevent readers from misunderstanding the statistic cited in the previous sentence.
G. debunk claims that the biological mechanism for migration is complex.
H. imply that ornithologists disagree about whether birds choose their migration schedule.
J. prove the assertion that the migration cycle is changing due to global warming.

33. The passage mentions which of the following as a limitation to Dolnik and Blyumental's research?

A. Their focus on only one species of diurnal migratory land birds with a relatively short migration path
B. Their selection of the Baltic Coast
C. Their destruction of healthy birds for research purposes
D. Their inaccurate counts of the total number of birds in each flock, because of the constant movement of individual birds

34. The main purpose of the third paragraph (lines 22–35) is to:

F. specify the many sources of food birds use as energy to fuel their migratory movements.
G. document the weather conditions that impact birds' ability to fly.
H. present a variety of reasons why the availability of nourishment is important in the timing of bird migration.
J. summarize several scientific principles discovered by observing migratory birds.

35. As presented in the passage, the statement in lines 44–45 is best described as:

A. an assumption based on a small sample of a few captured chaffinches.
B. a characterization based on the comparison of the fat content of the bodies of many individual chaffinches.
C. an observation based on the visual appearance of chaffinches as they flew over the Baltic Coast.
D. an opinion based on the personal preferences of Dolnik and Blyumental.

36. It can reasonably be inferred that researchers have measured the longest migration periods and distances for which of the following types of migratory birds?

F. Land birds
G. Sea birds
H. Tropical birds
J. Temperate birds

37. Based on the passage, scientists observe that compared to wild birds, caged birds may be:

A. less likely to use weather conditions to time their migrations.
B. more likely to amass stores of body fat.
C. unable to differentiate between day and night.
D. just as capable of sensing the changing of the seasons.

38. Suppose that a scientist were to replicate the exact conditions of Dolnik and Blyumental's experiments as described in the passage. At which of the following times would the scientist reasonably expect to find the greatest number of birds migrating?

F. On the first day of the migration wave in the morning
G. On the second day of the migration wave in the morning
H. On the second day of the migration wave in the afternoon
J. On the third day of the migration wave in the afternoon

39. Based on the passage, how should the statement that Dolnik and Blyumental "determined the social influence healthy birds have" (lines 42–43) most likely be understood?

A. Dolnik and Blyumental found a greater number of healthy than unhealthy chaffinches in flocks that migrated.
B. During waves of migration, lean chaffinches were found to emulate the feeding behavior of fat chaffinches.
C. Dolnik and Blyumental discovered that chaffinches became less healthy as the migration continued.
D. After fatter chaffinches flew, Dolnik and Blyumental observed greater and greater numbers of leaner chaffinches begin to migrate.

40. The author most nearly characterizes the migratory pattern made by wandering albatrosses as:

F. common for coastal birds.
G. typical of temperate migrants.
H. uncommon among migratory birds.
J. unusual for long-distance migrants such as sea birds.

READING TEST

35 Minutes—40 Questions

DIRECTIONS: There are four passages in this test. Each passage is followed by several questions. After reading each passage, choose the best answer to each question and blacken the corresponding oval on your answer document. You may refer to the passages as often as necessary.

Passage I

PROSE FICTION: This passage is adapted from the short story "Into the Past" by Amanda C. Thomas (© 2004 by Amanda C. Thomas).

Even at eight in the morning, the thermometer was heading up towards 80 degrees when my mother put me and my brother Kiran on the southbound bus heading from our home in New York City to our aunt and uncle's place in North
5 Carolina. Her new job on the third shift of the garment factory gave us the potential for a better life ahead, but she was wary about leaving us alone at home in the evenings and overnight. I had never been outside of New York City before, so I was nervous about moving, not to mention that I had never met
10 my aunt and uncle before.

"Now Essie, you be on your best behavior, mind your elders and watch out for your little brother, you hear me?" Her words were admonishments, but I saw the tear in the corner of her eye and knew that she'd miss us over the next
15 three months. She stood still, arm upraised in farewell, until her lemon-yellow dress became no more than a pinprick in the distance.

Kiran and I had promised each other that we would notice all the things that were different from New York while we were
20 on our trip. In the bus, the heat of the road was balanced to some degree by the breeze blowing in through the windows. We pressed our noses up to the glass, peering out as the dense thicket of buildings thinned, then disappeared altogether as we hit the unfamiliar farm country in the South. We chewed the
25 soggy pickle and butter sandwiches our mother had packed for us, sucking the juice out from between the slices of white, soft bread and watched the green fields rush by.

We were greeted at the bus station by Uncle Desmond, a quiet man whose skin shone dark from working out in the
30 sun. He said almost nothing as he took us back to his neat, white house with its red barn that looked just like my mother's descriptions of it and the pictures in books I'd seen when I was younger. At first glance, Aunt Millie seemed the polar opposite of my mother. Where my mother was all sharp lines
35 and tight angles, Aunt Millie was almost blurred, her hair looser and her hips more ample. Still, her kind face and shrewd glance at our city outfits showed the same deep intelligence.

"We're gonna have to see if some of your cousins' old overalls can be taken up for you. Don't want to get your nice
40 things scuffed up. Farm life's not easy on fancy dresses and patent leather shoes and you'll both be doing your share of the chores around here, that's for sure! Now your cousin Ike'll show you where to go to get washed up for dinner."

I had never seen so much food in my life before that
45 first meal at the farm. Collard greens, biscuits with red-eye gravy, fried chicken, macaroni and cheese—I'd eaten most of these dishes at home, but here they tasted different in a way that was hard to put a finger on at first. As though they were *from* somewhere, instead of appearing magically on our
50 kitchen table. They tasted the way the farm smelled—of the animals and the earth. I glanced over at Kiran, and he was digging in hungrily.

The next day, Kiran and I were roused early by Aunt Millie carrying two smaller versions of what, presumably,
55 had been Ike's old overalls. Ike and Desmond, who had both been awake hours earlier, came by carrying pails of warm milk, some of which would be put to household use while the main load was put by to be picked up by a cheese-making facility in Virginia.

60 Ike then taught us to gather eggs from the chickens in the henhouse. This quickly became my favorite task over that summer. I loved going out into the early dawn, the air still cool and damp and feeling my bare feet sink into grass wet with dew. I'd approach the coop with great care not to
65 disturb the slumbering ladies, as I thought of them, making sure not to betray my presence by any quick movement or careless noise. Then, with infinite gentleness, I'd reach out, my hands rustling under the soft feathers of the hens, sensing their respiration, their warmth, feeling for the smooth white
70 eggs and placing each one I found carefully into my basket.

At night I would take a bath and Aunt Millie would take time away from her evening chores to braid my hair. But instead of the intricate patterns my mother liked to make, Aunt Millie gave me looser plaits and even sometimes gathered them
75 into a single tail inching down my neck. Sometimes, when Aunt Millie seemed in an especially good mood, we would condition it with egg yolk and milk, which Aunt Millie would work into my hair gently massaging each strand, working the mixture deep into the roots. Afterwards I was pleased to see
80 how the brittle, frizzy ends softened.

My body became loose-limbed from the outdoor exercise and I noticed Kiran growing stronger and bolder as he ran through the fields with Ike. In the afternoons when it was too hot to do anything else, we'd lie in the shade of the huge oak
85 tree, chewing on grass stems, lost in the sweet, green taste and our own thoughts.

1. The narrator's imaginative way of viewing her surroundings is best demonstrated in her description of the:

   A. farmhouse.
   B. hens in the chicken coop.
   C. way Aunt Millie braids her hair.
   D. way the earth smelled.

2. It can most reasonably be inferred from the passage that the narrator:

   F. thinks New York City is superior to the farm.
   G. has never visited Uncle Desmond and Aunt Millie's farm before.
   H. sees the visit to the farm as the most important event in her life.
   J. loves her Aunt Millie more than her mother.

3. The narrator's use of sensory details, such as the feel of the hen's feathers and the taste of the grass stems, most strongly suggests that:

   A. trauma in her childhood made her unable to speak to anyone other than her brother Kiran.
   B. the unfamiliarity of life outside New York makes her more aware of her physical surroundings on the farm.
   C. because she is shy around her extended family, she is more perceptive than her brother Kiran is.
   D. her closeness with Aunt Millie shows her how to appreciate changes in her new environment.

4. In line 35 the narrator describes Aunt Millie as "blurred," which most nearly suggests that:

   F. unlike the narrator's mother, Aunt Millie doesn't have sharp features and sophisticated clothing.
   G. Aunt Millie is older than the narrator's mother, so she has a bad memory and forgets things.
   H. Essie doesn't see well because she often reads books under her bedcovers.
   J. Aunt Millie doesn't have as distinctive a personality as the narrator's mother does.

5. It can reasonably be inferred from the passage that the narrator views life on the farm as:

   A. requiring a great deal of hard work that is not appreciated by her aunt and uncle.
   B. an escape from the difficulties of living in impoverished, restrictive conditions in New York City.
   C. a place where daily chores, even those that require that the narrator wake up early, can be enjoyable and satisfying.
   D. a place where the physical nature of the local recreational activities are more suited to boys than to girls.

6. It can reasonably be inferred from the passage that which of the following events happened first in the narrator's life?

   F. She learned to collect eggs from the henhouse.
   G. She met her Aunt Millie and Uncle Desmond.
   H. She visited North Carolina for the first time.
   J. She lived in New York City.

7. As depicted in the ninth paragraph (lines 71–80), the relationship between the narrator and Aunt Millie is best described by which of the following statements?

   A. Aunt Millie feels close to the narrator, as shown in the way she puts aside other tasks to braid and condition Essie's hair.
   B. Aunt Millie feels emotionally cut off from the narrator because of the young girl's city manners.
   C. Aunt Millie loves the narrator in spite of their different ways of seeing the world.
   D. Aunt Millie is indifferent toward the narrator, seeing her as another part of her daily work.

8. Which of the following statements most nearly captures the sentiment behind the narrator's comment that the food at the farm house tastes like it is "*from* somewhere" (line 49)?

   F. "The food tasted just like the food I had in New York."
   G. "The food tasted fresh from the fields, instead of from a supermarket."
   H. "The food tasted like no other food that I had ever tasted."
   J. "The food tasted strongly of the rich soil that Uncle Desmond tilled."

9. Details in the second paragraph (lines 11–17) most strongly suggest that the narrator's mother:

A. hopes her children will have a good time on the farm, enjoying their summer vacation before school starts again.

B. feels saddened by the children's departure and will miss them while they're away.

C. believes that life on the farm will teach them the self-discipline they need to survive in the city.

D. is afraid for them during the long bus ride and hopes the children will not speak to strangers.

10. Which of the following statements about why the narrator and Kiran will spend the summer on the farm is supported by the passage?

F. The narrator is weak and sickly, needing the fresh air of the farm to recover her health.

G. Aunt Millie and Uncle Desmond will teach the children valuable work skills.

H. The narrator and Kiran wanted to develop a relationship with their cousins.

J. The children's mother worried about leaving them alone while she worked.

Passage II

SOCIAL SCIENCE: This passage is adapted from the article "Let Me Think About It: Plants and Consciousness" by Andres C. Tejada (© 2010 by Andres Tejada).

Sheila Jennings was making her rounds at the Boston Botanical Gardens gently humming songs to the lilies she was watering and speaking directly to a patch of ferns into which she was scooping fertilizer. To a casual observer, she
5 appeared to be entertaining herself during her morning routine, but Sheila's friendly behavior around the plants is actually called "social reinforcement" and is one of her job requirements. The idea that interacting with these plants will help them flourish has been common sense to gardeners for ages,
10 but it has attained some scientific credibility mainly since the work of Clive Buckner first came to light.

Forty years ago he conducted a series of experiments on his plants using "lie-detectors," polygraph galvanometer equipment. These experiments led him to conclude that plants
15 possess a means of perception that allows them to react to human thoughts.

The scientific community was shocked. It is already hard enough to prove that higher order mammals have consciousness, despite many experiments that seem to prove the
20 ability of non-human animals to learn and perform complex, non-instinctive behaviors. To contend that plants have some mechanism of mind-reading goes so far beyond the orthodoxy of modern scientific beliefs that anyone suggesting they might was instantly considered a heretic.

25 However, a steady flow of research over the next two decades would continue to revisit and replicate Clive Buckner's hypothesis. During his original experiment, Buckner noticed that his plant would produce a sharp and immediate response when he attempted to visualize the act of burning the plant's
30 leaves. Botanists at Kansas State found they could produce a similar response by cutting the leaves of an adjacent plant. Researchers in Wyoming discovered that plants respond to the distress signals of a spider in the room. A New Jersey scientist was able to cause a plant to trigger a switch on an
35 electric train set every time he gave himself a painful shock to the finger. One of Buckner's colleagues showed him how she was able to keep a detached leaf moist and lush for two months through daily positive encouragement while a control leaf which received no positive attention had completely
40 withered to a dry, brittle brown.

Although these experiments seem to add fuel to the flames of Buckner's speculations about plant consciousness, he is willing to acknowledge the scientific issues involved in replicating the experiments. "Many others have failed to
45 produce the same effects," he says. "The outcomes of the experiments seem very dependent on the experimenter's relationship to his plants."

Similarly, the interpretations of these experiments seem very dependent on the philosophical and metaphysical beliefs
50 of the interpreter. Many people without any botanical credentials are anxious to latch onto these experiments to support ideas they may have about the holistic interconnectivity of the universe. After all, if a plant in a lead box (shut off from all electromagnetic radiation) is able to react to a human
55 thought as it seemed to be able to do in one experiment, there must be some communication taking place between plant and human mind that is outside our normal scientific conception of cause and effect.

It is clear that plants are responsive to certain kinds of
60 interaction, but for what reason and by what means? Do plants grow better in the presence of music because they like it? Does their reaction to researchers' thoughts of harming them represent fear? Does their ability to react uniquely to someone who has previously killed a plant in front of them signify that
65 they have memory? Are experimenters merely interpreting the reactions of plants to agree with their premeditated goal of finding consciousness? (Scientists call this *confirmation bias.*) Are they ignoring the possibilities of alternative explanations for the sake of justifying their faulty hypotheses? (Scientists
70 call this *self-deception.*) As Cornell University professor Betty Wilkinson sees it, "Buckner's work opened up a Pandora's box of bad science."

Scientists interested in this emerging field of research, such as Eldon Byrd of the Naval Research Facility and Max
75 Crusella of a Marina Del Rey laboratory, think that there is a mountain of evidence that plants are sensitive to their environments in ways that traditional science is not equipped

to describe. "Perhaps some enthusiastic researchers have proposed overzealous explanations to their observations," says
80 Crusella, "but it is completely well-grounded to believe that there needs to be *some* kind of new scientific explanation for what are otherwise mysterious phenomena."

On the other side of this debate are resounding skeptics such as Professor Wilkinson and Steve Karnell, a writer for a
85 leading scientific journal. "Lacking in all these so-called 'experiments' are ingredients fundamental to the scientific method like control groups and blind studies." Karnell complains. "The fact that these experimenters freely admit to their observations being difficult to repeat by other, more skeptical scientists is
90 evidence that the phenomena upon which the crazy notion of mind-reading plants is based are unreliable from the start."

Clive Buckner and others continuing the pursuit of his inquiries merely chuckle at that line of argument. "We are trying to demonstrate the fact that plants develop subtle yet
95 meaningful connections with their caretakers, so the fact that the outcomes of experiments are varied is actually *support* for our notion that plant behavior is dynamic and responsive to a given individual."

11. The passage most strongly suggests that the current debate over research into plant consciousness was triggered by which of the following?

A. The invention of polygraph technology
B. An observed reaction of a plant to a spider in distress
C. Techniques introduced by the Boston Botanical Gardens
D. Experiments conducted by Buckner in the late 1960s

12. Clive Buckner's observation of his plant as mentioned in the fourth paragraph would most likely be described by Betty Wilkinson and Steve Karnell as which of the following?

F. Evidence that plants possess a sense of memory
G. A subtle connection between plant and caretaker
H. Something that other researchers may have trouble duplicating
J. An example of a plant's ability to perceive distress

13. The last paragraph primarily functions to:

A. provide specific examples of the body of evidence Clive Buckner would point to in defense of his theory.
B. suggest that Clive Buckner does not agree that one criticism offered by Steve Karnell is a legitimate one.
C. illustrate the complete indifference that Clive Buckner feels towards Steve Karnell's scientific concerns.
D. imply that Clive Buckner could counsel other experimenters on how to be better caretakers of plants in order to better replicate certain results.

14. According to the passage, lie-detectors are:

F. electric train trigger switches.
G. mechanisms of social reinforcement.
H. measurable distress signals.
J. polygraph galvanometer equipment.

15. The passage most strongly suggests that the social reinforcement required of Sheila Jennings at her job is designed primarily to do which of the following?

A. Condition the plants to be undisturbed by the sounds of visitors to the Botanical Gardens
B. Keep the employees alert during their monotonous work routines
C. Replicate the sounds of wildlife that the plants would hear in their natural habitats
D. Potentially lead to better plant growth than could be achieved without it

16. The main point of Steve Karnell's quotation in the ninth paragraph (lines 83–91) is that:

F. there are elements of how research is conducted that can make its findings less trustworthy.
G. some experimenters do not understand the function of control groups in the scientific method.
H. a blind study would have convincingly proven the existence of plant consciousness.
J. researchers working with plants are more likely to commit the error of confirmation bias.

17. The research examples provided in the fourth paragraph (lines 25–40) would potentially most undermine the position of:

A. Max Crusella.
B. the author of the passage.
C. Steve Karnell.
D. Clive Buckner.

18. According to the passage, the desire to affirm one's preconceived notions about an experimental observation is called which one of the following by scientists?

F. Control groups
G. Subtle yet meaningful connection
H. Confirmation bias
J. Self-deception

19. According to the passage, Clive Buckner believes that the potential outcome of an experiment measuring plant consciousness is:

A. highly unorthodox.
B. unfairly biased.
C. sometimes inconsistent.
D. scientifically sound.

20. The passage indicates that researchers in "this emerging field of research" (line 73) would be most likely to agree with which of the following statements?

F. The responsiveness of plants to their environment currently lacks an adequate traditional scientific explanation.
G. The results of many experiments have been tainted by self-deception on the part of the researchers.
H. There is currently some evidence to support plant consciousness but much more that contradicts it.
J. There are traditional scientific explanations that best account for the observations recorded in most of these experiments.

Passage III

HUMANITIES: This passage is adapted from the entry "How Songs Make Meaning" from the volume *How to Listen to Music Like a Conductor* (© 2007 by Air Guitar Press).

I used to have to feel pain in order to write songs.

Normally, this inspiration took the form of wanting or losing a girl. My heartsickness would reach a state of such unwieldy gloom that words and melodies would coalesce
5 and fall like raindrops to relieve the stress of carrying such a heavy cloud of misery. I think many of us mainly write songs for relief. It's unhealthy to keep swallowing unspoken words. Keep them on the tip of your tongue and they'll fester like bacteria. Stash them all in a song and you suddenly have an
10 emotional storage unit, which un-clutters your inner world.

The first "songs" we ever write are just exaggerated expressions of our stream of consciousness. We create theme songs while jostling with action figures, concoct mocking serenades to annoy our siblings, or narrate our inner lives
15 to a random tune. We have all been yelled at by a frustrated audience of our friends, acquaintances, and family members to cease our incessant noise making. While many learn to keep their songs to themselves as they master the rules of polite etiquette, songwriters apparently never learn. Instead, we begin
20 to turn our songs into something people will be happy to hear.

Music somehow makes people feel unashamed about being completely expressive. In speech, someone melodramatically complaining about all the injustices of his world would probably be chastised for lacking self-control. However,

25 in song, a proclamation of suffering is received as an almost heroic attempt to overcome adversity. Songs boldly broadcast a description of someone's inner world. Why do people want to tune into someone else's emotional episodes?

There's a balance of two opposing forces that we enjoy in
30 music. One force soothes, the other agitates. As music plays, the actual frequencies of the individual notes are constantly lining up in different mathematical relations to each other. When they are proportional to each other, we hear chords, harmony, and unison. Songs normally end on this sort of re-
35 lationship because it conveys closure, completion, resolution. Other combinations create a sense of tension, discomfort, and anticipation. Successful songs win over listeners just as successful stories do. They normally introduce a protagonist and take the listener along to experience some of his/her setbacks
40 and triumphs. Even instrumental pieces often introduce a central melody and then explore its travels through different passages of the song's structure.

Young children often enjoy hearing soothing lullabies as a way to be distracted from anxiety or coaxed into a peaceful
45 slumber. They take great pleasure in singing agitating songs, such as the "nenny nenny boo boo" melody that can be customized into any taunt. Similarly, adults have classical, smooth jazz, and easy listening styles of music when they want to be relaxed or distracted, and they have the more provocative
50 extremes of punk, rap, and metal when they want to use music to express irreverence or rebellion.

We become much more selective in our musical tastes as we age. As children, we passively accept and learn to love our parents' music just like we do their cooking. It's not that
55 a parent necessarily cooks "better" than other parents, but through sheer familiarity a child will greatly prefer her parents' cooking to that of others. Similarly, the cultural backdrop of a child's upbringing calibrates her listening tastes to a given set of rhythms, instruments, harmonic scales, and song structures.
60 As adolescents, though, we begin to choose our own songs just as we would choose our friends. We identify with artists based on their dress, their politics, their mood, their popularity. We look to find personal meaning in lyrics and to latch onto songs that seem to broadcast our private thoughts. Despite
65 not being the author of our favorite songs, we wear our songs like trinkets of personal expression, telltale accessories that describe to others important parts of our psychology. When we develop a kinship with a song, we feel waves of euphoria as it plays, the feeling of our inner world radiating out.

70 As songwriters, we must aspire to this private release in every song we write. However, sometimes we fear that if we express ourselves too specifically, we will deny listeners the opportunity to mold our song into something they can claim as their own. We often replace specific details with general
75 symbols, preserving for ourselves the original meaning of a lyric while infusing it with enough flexibility that someone else can derive a different significance.

The one thing we must be sure of as performers is that a song means *something* to us. Through observation of other artists, we learn to mimic expressions of joy and anguish. It becomes easy for us to write and perform songs without any genuine attachment to their emotional content. Nevertheless, just as audiences can distinguish between good and bad acting, so too will audience members feel a difference between a contrived and an authentic performance.

21. When the writer refers to "the rules of polite etiquette" in (lines 18–19), he is most likely referring to rules that:

    A. diminish the role of imagination in playing with action figures or other toys.
    B. are taught to children when they are enrolled in behavior modification classes.
    C. are too restrictive and demanding for songwriters to abide by.
    D. limit certain personal behaviors that others might find irritating or discomforting.

22. In the third paragraph (lines 11–20), the author says that a songwriter aspires to write songs people will be "happy to hear." It can reasonably be inferred that which of the following is NOT a characteristic of such songs?

    F. Mimicking joy and anguish
    G. Blending comfort and tension
    H. Fostering a kinship with the listener
    J. Allowing for different interpretations

23. It can be reasonably inferred that the primary purpose of this passage is to:

    A. explain to readers that expressing pain will enable them to be good songwriters.
    B. convince aspiring songwriters to stop giving in to polite etiquette and instead write catchy songs.
    C. discuss ideas concerning the goals and process of songwriting as well as the relationship to age and expectations of the audience.
    D. outline one author's argument that songwriters are too often limited by the cultural backdrop of their musical upbringing.

24. When the author states a songwriter must aspire to "this private release" (line 70), he is most directly referring to the idea that a songwriter must:

    F. describe her experiences with very specific details.
    G. outwardly project a genuine internal emotional state.
    H. force listeners to develop a kinship with the song.
    J. focus on the emotions of joy or anguish.

25. The author states that, unlike children, adolescents approach songs with a goal of:

    A. feeling a sense of belonging and familiarity.
    B. discovering new trends in fashion and politics.
    C. departing from the cultural backdrop of their upbringing.
    D. deriving some personal meaning from those songs.

26. The author states that our process of selecting songs can be compared to that of selecting all of the following EXCEPT:

    F. our friends.
    G. our parents' cooking.
    H. our favorite authors.
    J. personal trinkets.

27. Which of the following best describes the way the first sentence functions in relation to the passage as a whole?

    A. It introduces an idea that the author later explains is not true in the real world of songwriting.
    B. It is a claim that facilitates the author's anecdotal introduction to the topic of songwriting.
    C. It foreshadows the essay's contention that singing about one's problems is evidence of a lack of self-control.
    D. It is a vague idea that is not reinforced or clarified by the details that follow in subsequent paragraphs.

28. According to the passage, the divergent songwriting purposes of "soothes" and "agitates" (line 30) differ from one another in that:

    F. soothing songs, unlike agitating ones, have a mellowing effect that is often enjoyable to adults but annoying to younger audiences.
    G. soothing songs are associated with inducing sleep or reducing distress while agitating songs can be used to convey ridicule.
    H. agitating songs, unlike soothing songs, are often used by relatives to coax a child out of a state of slumber.
    J. agitating songs distract us from the things that we passionately hate, while soothing songs are very gentle to our ears.

29. According to the author's analogy, acting and performing music:

    A. are completely different.
    B. share at least one important characteristic.
    C. are more convincing expressing anguish than joy.
    D. are completely identical.

30. Based on the passage, the cultural backdrop of a child's upbringing is significant to her appreciation of music because it:

    F. predisposes the child to prefer the musical ingredients customary in that culture's music.

    G. gives the child a model of what to avoid in order to stand out as an original songwriter.

    H. instructs the child concerning the proper structure and political content of songs.

    J. will later be the primary basis through which the child is able to make friends.

Passage IV

NATURAL SCIENCE: This passage is adapted from "A Comment on Comets" by Dr. Anatole C. Thierry (© 2002 by Weak Alliteration Press).

Comets are solid masses of dust and frozen gases with diameters of only a few kilometers that revolve in highly eccentric orbits around the Sun. As a comet approaches the Sun, a very small portion of the frozen matter evaporates. This
5 creates a shroud of gas and dust, called a coma, enveloping an area up to a million kilometers around the solid nucleus of the comet. Solar winds and radiation pressure from the Sun can blow the material of the coma away from the comet's nucleus, creating a tail, which is sometimes longer than the
10 distance from the Earth to the Sun. However, the appearance of comets is misleading; they cast no light of their own. Though the comas and tails of the brightest comets can be seen with the naked eye in cities with heavy light pollution, the nucleus of a comet cannot be detected even with the most
15 powerful telescopes. This is not only because the solid portion of a comet is so small, but also because the highly reflective nature of the coma's material obscures the view to the nucleus.

The brightness of a comet depends primarily on two factors: its distance from the Sun and its distance from the
20 Earth. When comets are at their closest approach to the Sun, called perihelion, evaporation of the icy material occurs at a greater rate and volume, and the solar forces that scatter the gas and dust are stronger. However, when comets are far from the sun, they become less active and are often undetectable.
25 Because comets come from the farthest reaches of the solar system, most take over 200 years to orbit the sun, and most of the time they are so far away that the solar influence does not create a coma or tail, causing the comets to become invisible.

The stronger determinant of a comet's brightness is its
30 distance to Earth, especially in relation to its perihelion. If a comet passes its nearest point to Earth after the comet's perihelion, it will be much brighter than if it reaches its closest point to Earth while it is still relatively cold and solid, before the Sun evaporates much of the comet's matter. This explains
35 why Halley's Comet, which was very bright during its first observed pass near Earth in 1910, was so disappointing to

astronomers when it returned, this time much further from the Earth, in 1986. The distance from the Earth also determines a comet's speed as observed by astronomers—the closer a
40 comet comes to the Earth, the more quickly it moves across the sky. Typically, comets move about one or two degrees per day—much too slow to be perceived by the naked eye—and can remain visible for months. However, when comet IRAS-Araki-Alcock, the closest comet to pass the Earth in modern
45 times, appeared in 1983, it looked both very bright and very fast. This comet moved so quickly that observers compared its motion to that of the minute hand on a clock, and it had twice the apparent diameter of the Moon.

Even dedicated sky watchers and professional astrono-
50 mers are more likely to discover a comet by chance than by exacting calculations, because comets are only detectable for such a short portion of their orbits, and because it is so infrequent that the comets pass near enough to the Earth to be observed. However, astronomers' interest in comets lies in
55 characteristics beyond the novelty of these comets. Comets are believed to be remnants of the original disc of chemical material that formed the solar system about four billion years ago. Because comets spend most of their time in the very cold areas barely within the Sun's gravitation, they are believed to
60 have remained relatively unchanged during that time, and can thereby serve as a sort of "fossil record" of the solar system.

For this reason, planetary scientists have a great deal of interest in studying comets directly, rather than merely through telescopic observation. By studying the specific
65 chemical composition of comets, scientists hope to learn more about the chemical origins of the solar system. Explorations of comets can provide glimpses into this past. For example, a recent collection of tiny dust particles left in the Earth's stratosphere by the passage of comet 26P/Grigg-Skjellerup
70 has led to the discovery of a previously unknown mineral that had not been predicted by scientists to have been formed in the solar nebula. This highly unusual substance generates strong scientific interest because it, along with other new materials that may be found in comets, may cause scientists
75 to reconsider models of how the solar system formed. Future missions are planned to retrieve material directly from comets. Some scientists, who hypothesize that water and some organic compounds may have been delivered to Earth by collisions between comets and our planet in its earliest days, hope that
80 comet material may reveal information about the origins of life on Earth.

31. The primary purpose of the passage is to:

    A. persuade readers that astronomers have not yet done adequate studies to discover the origins of the solar system.

    B. encourage readers to learn to use telescopic equipment to aid in the search for new comets.

    C. describe the characteristics of comets currently known by astronomers and the motivation for their research.

    D. catalogue the experiments planetary scientists have done to determine the composition of comets.

32. The author would most likely agree with which of the following statements?

    F. There may be minerals in the solar system yet to be discovered by astronomers.

    G. Astronomers will not be able to observe comets brighter than IRAS-Araki-Alcock because their orbital periods are so long.

    H. Comets are older than the Earth as indicated by their greater distance from the Sun.

    J. Collections of samples directly from the surface of comets will be difficult because of comets' unpredictability.

33. According to the passage, which situation creates a comet's maximum brightness as observed from Earth?

    A. Its coma is much bigger than its nucleus.

    B. It is closer to the Earth and therefore moves more quickly.

    C. Its perihelion occurs after it passes the Earth.

    D. It is at its closest to the Earth after its perihelion.

34. Which of the following questions is NOT answered by information given in the passage?

    F. What do astronomers hope to learn by studying comets?

    G. What causes some comets to be trailed by such a long tail?

    H. What prevents astronomers from cataloging more new comets and predicting their approach to the Earth?

    J. Why do comets have such a highly eccentric orbit?

35. Information in the first paragraph indicates that "the appearance of comets" requires all of the following EXCEPT:

    A. the viewer to have a powerful telescope.

    B. solar winds and radiation pressure to scatter the coma.

    C. a portion of the surface material to evaporate.

    D. an envelope of gas and dust much larger than the nucleus.

36. The passage mentions astronomers observing all of the following about comets EXCEPT:

    F. unusual minerals in the chemical composition that have not been found on Earth.

    G. comets that emit bright light from their nuclei.

    H. changes in apparent brightness at different times and in different environments.

    J. orbits that take comets to the edges of the Sun's gravitational influence.

37. In the context of the third paragraph (lines 29–48), lines 34–38 primarily serve to emphasize the:

    A. relationship a comet's apparent speed has to its other visual characteristics, such as its apparent diameter.

    B. influence a comet's distance from Earth with regard to its perihelion has on a comet's apparent brightness.

    C. disappointment astronomers feel when highly anticipated celestial events do not live up to their expectations.

    D. difficulty in predicting when comets will be visible in the sky because of their highly eccentric orbits.

38. The passage most nearly indicates that attempts to study comets directly have been:

    F. prevented by technical difficulties.

    G. used to explain life on Earth.

    H. unsuccessful so far.

    J. promising, but incomplete.

39. As it is used in line 55, the phrase "characteristics beyond the novelty of these comets" most likely refers to:

    A. the likelihood of discovering new comets.

    B. the difficulty of detecting distant comets.

    C. comets' chemical composition.

    D. the age of comets.

40. The main purpose of the last paragraph is to:

    F. describe particular experiments that have been performed on comets as they pass near the Earth.

    G. convince readers that comets are responsible for the evolution of intelligent species.

    H. discuss the reasons planetary scientists are interested in pursuing direct study of comet material.

    J. contradict outdated information about the origin of the solar system.

Science Practice

SCIENCE REASONING TEST

35 Minutes—40 Questions

DIRECTIONS: There are seven passages in the following section. Each passage is followed by several questions. After reading a passage, choose the best answer to each question and blacken the corresponding oval on your answer document. You may refer to the passages as often as necessary.

You are NOT permitted to use a calculator on this test.

Passage I

A study was conducted regarding the fossil shells of a particular species of turtle that lives off the coast of the Opulasian Peninsula. Scientists discovered a continuous record of fossilized shells in the seabed off the coast dating back 120,000 years. In addition to examining the fossilized turtle shells, the scientists also examined the shells of living turtles.

From each layer of seabed, the scientists randomly selected five complete, unbroken fossilized shells. Each shell was carefully prepared, measured, and photographed. A bit of each shell was then clipped off and sent to a laboratory for radiocarbon dating to determine the precise age of each shell.

Table 1			
% shells with the following scute pattern:			
Age of shells (years)	M-m-M-M-m	M-M-m-m-M	M-m-M-m-M
120,000	46	44	10
90,000	42	54	4
87,000	30	67	3
85,000	21	72	7
80,000	20	66	14
50,000	76	21	3
27,000	100	0	0
15,000	100	0	0
8000	100	0	0
4000	100	0	0
1000	68	28	4
300	74	20	6
0	86	2	12

Study 1

All of the living turtles had a distinct band of hexagonal *scutes* (bony plates) running the length of their shells, from head to tail. The fossilized shells' scutes were not visible to the naked eye; however upon application of a particular dye, a similar band of scutes from head to tail was observed in every shell.

Scutes extending greater than $\frac{1}{8}$ of the length of the shell were labeled *major* (M), where scutes extending less than or equal to $\frac{1}{8}$ of the length of the shell were labeled *minor* (m). The pattern of scutes was recorded for each fossil. For each time period, the percent of fossils exhibiting each pattern is given in Table 1.

Study 2

For each shell, the surface area of the shell, the height of the shell's *bridge* (the part of the shell linking the upper and lower plates), and the total number of scutes were recorded (see Figure 1).

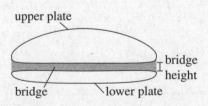

Figure 1

For the shells of each age, the average of each measurement was calculated. The results are presented in Figure 2.

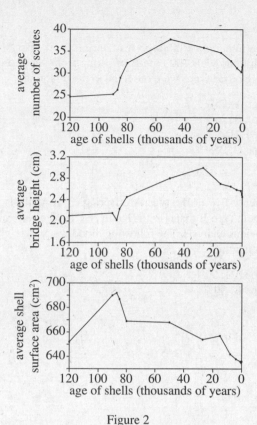

Figure 2

1. In a layer of seabed determined to be 250,000 years old, the scientists found fragments of twelve turtle shells, but no complete, intact shells. Which of the following is the most likely reason this layer of seabed was not included in the studies?

A. 250,000 years is too old to obtain an accurate radiocarbon date.
B. Shells that were 250,000 years old would have been irrelevant to the studies.
C. Accurate measurements of the dimensions of the shells could have been impossible to obtain.
D. The scientists would not have been able to accurately determine the color of the shells.

2. With regard to the descriptions given in Study 1, the shells with the M-M-m-m-M band of scutes probably most closely resembled which of the following?

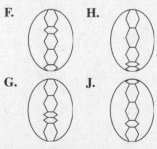

F.

H.

G.

J.

3. According to the results of Study 2, how do the average number of scutes and the average bridge height of living turtles of the Opulasian Peninsula compare to those of the turtles of the Opulasian Peninsula from 120,000 years ago? For the living turtles:

A. both the average number of scutes and the average bridge height are larger.
B. both the average number of scutes and the average bridge height are smaller.
C. the average number of scutes is larger, and the average bridge height is smaller.
D. the average number of scutes is smaller, and the average bridge height is larger.

4. Suppose, in Study 1, the scientists had found another seabed layer with fossilized shells that were radiocarbon dated and found to be 86,000 years old. Based on the results of Study 1, the scute pattern percents for the group of shells would most likely have been closest to which of the following?

	M-m-M-M-m	M-M-m-m-M	M-m-M-m-M
F.	100%	0%	0%
G.	50%	25%	25%
H.	36%	61%	4%
J.	26%	69%	5%

5. In Study 2, the average shell surface area of fossilized turtle shells that were 80,000 years old was closest to:

A. 670 cm²
B. 680 cm²
C. 690 cm²
D. 700 cm²

6. Which of the following statements best describes how Study 1 differed from Study 2 ?

F. In Study 1, the scientists examined 3 characteristics regarding the shape and size of turtle shells; but in Study 2, the scientists examined the frequency of occurrence of different patterns of scutes on turtle shells.
G. In Study 1, the scientists examined the frequency of occurrence of different patterns of scutes on turtle shells; but in Study 2, the scientists examined the environment in which turtles live.
H. In Study 1, the scientists examined the frequency of occurrence of different patterns of scutes on turtle shells; but in Study 2, the scientists examined 3 characteristics regarding the shape and size of turtle shells.
J. In Study 1, the scientists examined 3 characteristics regarding the shape and size of turtle shells; but in Study 2, the scientists examined the environment in which turtles live.

Passage II

The 4 different blood types in sheep are A, B, AB, and O. The blood type of an offspring is determined by the blood types of its parents. Each parent contributes a single gene to its offspring, forming a pair of genes. The *genotype* of an offspring refers to the arrangement of the offspring's new gene formed by the combination of the parents' genes.

There are three possible *alleles* (forms) of this gene: the type-A blood allele (I^A), the type-B blood allele (I^B), and the type-O blood allele (I^O). Both I^A and I^B are *dominant* to I^O, and I^O is *recessive* to I^A and I^B. This means that an individual with 1 I^A and 1 I^O will have type-A blood, and an individual with one I^B and one I^O will have type-B blood. When an individual has one I^A and one I^B allele, this individual will have type-AB blood, due to the *codominance* of the I^A and I^B alleles.

Table 1	
Blood Type	Possible Genotypes
A	$I^A I^A$ or $I^A I^O$
B	$I^B I^B$ or $I^B I^O$
AB	$I^A I^B$
O	$I^O I^O$

To explore the inheritance patterns of blood types in sheep, researchers conducted 4 analyses. In each analysis, male and female sheep of differing blood types were mated and the resultant blood types of their offspring recorded.

Analysis 1

One thousand males with type-O blood were mated with 1000 females with type-AB blood. The following blood types were observed in the offspring:

Type A: 50%
Type B: 50%

Analysis 2

Two hundred of the type-A offspring from Analysis 1 were mated with 200 type-O mates from no previous experiment. The following blood types were observed in the offspring:

Type A: 50%
Type O: 50%

Analysis 3

One hundred of the type-A offspring from Analysis 1 parented children with 100 type-B offspring from Analysis 1. The following blood types were observed in the offspring:

Type A: 25%
Type B: 25%
Type AB: 25%
Type O: 25%

Analysis 4

Twenty-five of the type-A offspring from Analysis 3 were mated with type-B mates with Genotype $I^B I^B$ who were not from any previous analysis. The following blood types were observed in the offspring:

Type AB: 50%
Type B: 50%

7. The ratio of blood types containing at least one I^A allele to the blood types containing at least one I^B allele produced in Analysis 3 was:

A. 1:0.
B. 1:1.
C. 2:1.
D. 3:1.

8. An offspring whose blood type exhibits codominance has which of the following genotypes?

   F. I^BI^B
   G. I^BI^O
   H. I^AI^B
   J. I^AI^O

9. To produce only offspring with AB blood, one would mate two sheep with which of the following sets of genotypes?

   A. $I^AI^B \times I^AI^B$
   B. $I^AI^B \times I^OI^O$
   C. $I^AI^A \times I^BI^B$
   D. $I^BI^B \times I^AI^O$

10. In Analysis 3, the offspring used from Analysis 1 most likely had which of the following genotypes?

   F. I^AI^O and I^BI^B
   G. I^AI^O and I^BI^O
   H. I^AI^A and I^BI^B
   J. I^AI^A and I^BI^O

11. Some or all of the offspring had 1 allele for type-O blood in Analyses:

   A. 1 and 2 only.
   B. 2 and 3 only.
   C. 1, 2, and 4 only.
   D. 1, 2, 3, and 4.

12. Suppose that 300 offspring were produced in Analysis 3. Based on the results, the number of offspring with type-B blood produced in Analysis 3 would most likely have been closest to:

   F. 25.
   G. 50.
   H. 75.
   J. 100.

Passage III

Vasoconstriction involves a narrowing of blood vessels that could lead to poor blood flow in the body if it persists over a long time. *Ergotamine* is a substance that can cause vasoconstriction. When ergotamine is injected into a normal blood vessel, vasoconstriction occurs quickly at the site of the injection (see Figure 1).

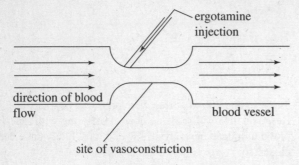

Figure 1

The diameter of the blood vessel at the site of vasoconstriction is less than the diameter of the normal blood vessel, so blood flow has a higher velocity through this narrow site. As a result, the blood pressure in the site of vasoconstriction is less than the blood pressure in the normal blood vessel. Moreover, the higher the velocity of the blood flow through the site of vasoconstriction, the lower the blood pressure at that site.

The percent change in blood pressure (%Δ*BP*) can be defined as:

$$\%\Delta BP = 100 \times \frac{\text{(Normal blood pressure – Pressure at site of vasoconstriction)}}{\text{Normal blood pressure}}$$

Blood vessel sections of similar diameters were isolated from laboratory rats and %Δ*BP* was measured over three experiments. When the researchers needed to create a site of vasoconstriction for some of the experimental trials, they would inject ergotamine to induce vasoconstriction within the blood vessel section.

Experiment 1

An artificial heart, which mimics a human's heartbeat, is used to move a constant volume of 500 mL of blood with each beat through four blood vessel sections. These four blood vessel sections were injected with the same amount of ergotamine, leading to sites of vasoconstriction of the same diameter. The rate at which the blood is pumped was varied for the four different blood vessel sections, and the %Δ*BP* values that resulted were measured.

Table 1	
Rate of artificial heart beat (beats per minute)	%Δ*BP*
60	1.2
90	9.3
120	22.3
150	45.1

Experiment 2

The artificial heart used in Experiment 1 was then used to pump a constant volume of 500 mL of blood with each beat at a constant rate of 90 beats per minute through five other blood vessel sections. These blood vessel sections were injected with different amounts of ergotamine, resulting in sites of vasoconstriction with different diameters. The %Δ*BP* values were then measured.

Table 2	
Diameter of site of vasoconstriction (cm)	%Δ*BP*
0.4	40.3
0.6	18.6
0.8	9.3
1.0	4.6
1.2	2.5

Experiment 3

The artificial heart used in Experiment 1 was used to pump different volumes of blood at a constant rate of 90 beats per minute through five blood vessel sections with the same diameter at the site of vasoconstriction. The %Δ*BP* values were then measured.

Table 3	
Volume of blood pumped (mL)	%Δ*BP*
400	8.4
450	8.8
500	9.3
550	9.7
600	10.2

13. Under the conditions described for Experiment 3, a %ΔBP of 9.0 would most likely be obtained if the entering volume of blood equaled:

   A. 350 mL.
   B. 475 mL.
   C. 550 mL.
   D. 650 mL.

14. Based on the results of Experiment 1, if the rate of the artificial heart beat had been less than 60 beats per minute, then the %ΔBP would most likely have been:

   F. less than 1.2.
   G. between 1.2 and 9.3.
   H. between 9.3 and 22.3.
   J. greater than 22.3.

15. Which of the following is the most likely explanation for the results of Experiment 1? As the rate of the artificial heart beat increases, %ΔBP:

   A. increases, because the velocity of blood through the site of vasoconstriction increases.
   B. increases, because the velocity of blood through the site of vasoconstriction decreases.
   C. decreases, because the velocity of blood flow through the site of vasoconstriction increases.
   D. decreases, because the velocity of blood flow through the site of vasoconstriction decreases.

16. Consider blood flow through three regions of the same blood vessel, each of which has a different diameter. The velocity of blood flow is measured in milliliters per minute (mL/min) and the blood pressure is measured in millimeters of mercury (mmHg), and their values for each of the blood vessel regions are shown in the following table:

Location	Velocity of blood flow (mL/min)	Blood pressure (mmHg)
A	500	31
B	1,000	29
C	900	30

Based on the information in the passage about blood flow, which of the following diagrams best represents the relative diameters of the three blood vessel regions?

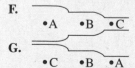
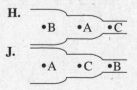

17. Based on the results of Experiments 1 and 2, what was the diameter of the site of vasoconstriction in the blood vessel section used in Experiment 3 ?

   A. 0.4 cm
   B. 0.6 cm
   C. 0.8 cm
   D. 1.0 cm

18. For the blood vessel sections used in Experiment 2 that had sites of vasoconstriction with diameters of 0.4, 0.8, and 1.2 cm, which of the following graphs best displays the comparison between blood pressure at each site of vasoconstriction and blood pressure in the normal region of the blood vessel leading to the site of vasoconstriction?

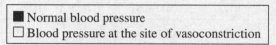

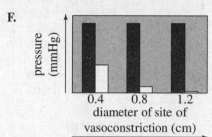

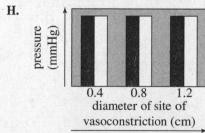

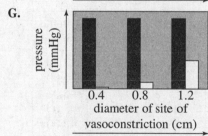

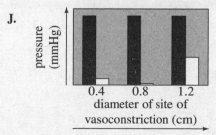

Passage IV

As the pressure on a gas is increased, the volume of that gas is expected to decrease by an inversely proportional amount. For example, if pressure is doubled the volume is halved. Under certain conditions, the volume of the gas will change by an amount that deviates from an inverse proportion. Various 10.00 L samples of gas were subjected to increases in pressure. Table 1 shows the resulting volume changes at 300°C, while Tables 2 and 3 show the volume changes at 25°C and –200°C, respectively. All pressures are measured in *atmospheres* (atm).

Table 1			
300°C	Initial pressure (atm)	Final pressure (atm)	Volume change (L)
Oxygen	1	2	–5.00
Oxygen	2	4	–5.00
Oxygen	3	6	–5.00
Argon	2	4	–5.00
Argon	4	5	–2.00
Carbon Dioxide	1	5	–8.00
Carbon Dioxide	3	6	–5.00
Carbon Dioxide	4	10	–6.00

Table 2			
25°C	Initial pressure (atm)	Final pressure (atm)	Volume change (L)
Methane	1	2	–5.00
Methane	2	4	–5.00
Helium	1	2	–5.00
Helium	1	5	–8.00
Helium	2	5	–6.00
Nitrogen	1	5	–8.00
Nitrogen	2	4	–5.00
Nitrogen	4	5	–2.00

Table 3			
–200°C	Initial pressure (atm)	Final pressure (atm)	Volume change (L)
Neon	1	2	–5.02
Neon	2	4	–5.03
Neon	4	8	–5.06
Helium	1	2	–4.98
Helium	2	4	–4.97
Hydrogen	1	2	–5.01
Hydrogen	1	5	–8.02
Hydrogen	1	10	–9.03

19. Which of the following gases shown in Tables 1–3 was compressed by the same amount each time the pressure was changed, regardless of its initial pressure?

   A. Helium
   B. Carbon Dioxide
   C. Neon
   D. Oxygen

20. Which of the following is the best explanation for the change in volume seen in any one of the samples of carbon dioxide in Table 1? As pressure on one sample of carbon dioxide was increased, the volume of that sample:

F. increased as the molecules of carbon dioxide were forced closer together.

G. increased as the molecules of carbon dioxide were forced farther apart.

H. decreased as the molecules of carbon dioxide were forced closer together.

J. decreased as the molecules of carbon dioxide were forced farther apart.

21. Based on Table 2, if the sample of nitrogen at a pressure of 4 atm were returned to its initial pressure of 2 atm, the volume would most likely be:

A. decrease by 5.00 L.
B. decrease by 8.00 L.
C. increase by 5.00 L.
D. increase by 8.00 L.

22. Based on Table 3, if the pressure on a 10.00 L sample of neon gas is increased from 8 atm to 16 atm at a temperature of –200°C, the change in volume will most likely be closest to which of the following?

F. –5.12 L
G. –5.06 L
H. –5.03 L
J. –5.02 L

23. A scientist concludes that whenever the pressure on helium is increased, its volume will decrease. Based on Tables 2 and 3, is this a valid conclusion?

A. Yes; in every trial that the pressure of helium was increased, the change in volume was negative.

B. No; in every trial that the pressure of helium was increased, the change in volume was positive.

C. Yes; when the pressure on helium was increased from 1 to 2 atm, its change in volume was positive at 25°C and negative at –200°C.

D. No; when the pressure on helium was increased from 1 to 2 atm, its change in volume was negative at 25°C and positive at –200°C.

Passage V

There are four planets in our solar system called gas giants: Jupiter, Saturn, Uranus, and Neptune. They are so named because they are composed largely of gases rather than solids. Figure 1 shows how temperatures of the atmospheres of Jupiter, Neptune, and Saturn vary with altitude above the cloud tops. Table 1 gives the composition of the planets in both relative abundance of gases and the altitude at which those gases are most abundant. Table 2 gives what the temperature at the cloud tops would be without greenhouse warming.

Table 2	
Planet	Temperature at cloud tops without greenhouse warming (K)
Jupiter	100
Neptune	50
Saturn	25

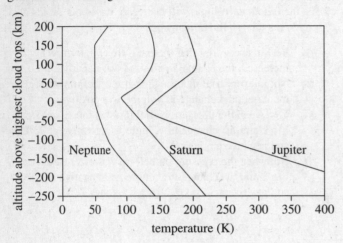

Figure 1

Table 1						
	Relative abundance (%)			Altitude above cloud tops where most abundant (km)		
Gas	Jupiter	Neptune	Saturn	Jupiter	Neptune	Saturn
H	86.1	79.0	96.1	−1,000 to −70,000	−10,000 to −23,000	−1,000 to −60,000
He	13.6	18.0	3.3	−500 to −1,000	−500 to −10,000	−500 to −900
CH_3	0.2	3.0	0.4	0 to 300	−100 to 0	0 to 200
NH_3	0.0045	0	0.0035	0 to −100	--	−50 to −200
H_2O vapor	0.0055	0	0.0065	−50 to −100	--	−200 to −300

24. According to Figure 1, the temperature of Neptune remains the same as altitude above the highest cloud tops increases from:

F. −250 km to −200 km.
G. −150 km to −50 km.
H. 0 km to 100 km.
J. 150 km to 200 km.

25. According to Figure 1, the temperature of Jupiter changes the most between:

A. −150 km and −50 km.
B. −50 km and 50 km.
C. 50 km and 100 km.
D. 100 km and 200 km.

26. Considering only the gases listed in Table 1, which gas is more abundant in the atmosphere of Jupiter than in the atmosphere of either Neptune or Saturn?

F. H
G. CH_3
H. NH_3
J. He

27. Based on Table 2, the average temperature at Saturn's cloud tops *without* greenhouse warming is how many degrees cooler than the temperature given in Figure 1 ?

A. 5 K
B. 25 K
C. 75 K
D. 150 K

28. Which of the following statements about H and He in the atmospheres of the 3 planets is supported by the data in Table 1 ?

F. Both Saturn and Neptune have a higher relative abundance of He than of H.
G. Both Saturn and Jupiter have a higher relative abundance of He than of H.
H. Both Jupiter and Neptune have an equivalent relative abundance of He and H.
J. Both Saturn and Neptune have a lower relative abundance of He than of H.

Passage VI

Nuclear fission occurs when the *nucleus* (central core) of an atom splits into multiple parts. This splitting is accompanied by the release of a large amount of energy, as in nuclear weapons and nuclear power plants.

A chemical element is said to be *radioactive* if it is prone to fission. Fission is often the result of the nucleus of a radioactive atom absorbing a *free neutron* (an uncharged nuclear particle). When a *fission event* occurs, the nucleus often splits into two new nuclei and produces free neutrons. This process generates the possibility of a chain reaction. If, on average, a fission event produces one neutron and that neutron causes another nucleus to fission, the reaction is said to be *critical*; that is, it will sustain itself, but not increase in magnitude. If one fission event releases more free neutrons than are required to initiate another fission event, the reaction is said to be *supercritical*; that is, it will sustain and increase in magnitude. If more neutrons are required to initiate a fission event than are released in fission, the reaction is said to be *subcritical*: the reaction will not sustain itself.

Many factors affect how many neutrons from each fission event will trigger another fission event. The most important factor is the mass (m) of the substance. The criticality of a substance also depends on the substance's purity, shape, density, temperature, and whether or not it is surrounded by a material that reflects neutrons.

In a nuclear weapon, a radioactive substance is made highly supercritical. One of the primary challenges in building a nuclear weapon is keeping the radioactive material subcritical prior to detonation, then upon detonation, keeping it supercritical for a long enough period of time for all of the material to fission before it is blown apart by the energy of the blast. A *fizzle* occurs when a nuclear weapon achieves supercriticality but is blown apart before all of the radioactive material fissions.

The first nuclear weapons were made of enriched uranium, or U-235. The density (ρ) of U-235 under normal conditions is 19.1 g/cm^3. For U-235 to attain a supercritical state, the product of its mass and density must exceed 10^6 g^2/cm^3. If it is assembled over too long a time (t), it will achieve slight supercriticality and then fizzle. Therefore, the speed of assembly (measured as t divided by ρ), must be less than 10^{-5} sec $\times$ cm^3/g (*Michelson's Criterion*).

Two schemes for the assembly of a supercritical amount of U-235 that avoid fizzle are discussed below.

Gun-Type Weapon

At one end of a tube, similar to a gun barrel, is a hollow, subcritical cylinder of U-235 with a mass of 48 kg; on the other end is a subcritical pellet of U-235 with a mass of 12 kg. The pellet is propelled by a small explosion down the tube and into the cylinder of U-235. The combined mass of the two pieces of

U-235 is great enough to induce a supercritical state. Since the combined cylinder of U-235 is at or near normal density, the assembly process must be completed in less than 2×10^{-4} sec to meet Michelson's Criterion.

Implosion-Type Weapon

A 15-kg sphere of U-235 is surrounded by explosives. When the explosives are simultaneously detonated, the U-235 is compressed in order to achieve supercriticality. The explosives are designed to compress the U-235 to a density of approximately 70 g/cm^3 in less than 10^{-7} sec.

---

29. For both types of weapon, avoiding fizzle is difficult because:

    A. the mass of U-235 must be large.
    B. 2 separate pieces of U-235 must be brought together.
    C. U-235 is highly unstable.
    D. of the speed with which the U-235 must be assembled.

30. Comparing the mass of uranium used in the two types of weapons reveals that:

F. the mass of U-235 used in the implosion-type weapon is less than the mass of U-235 used in the gun type weapon.

G. the mass of U-235 used in the implosion-type weapon is greater than the mass of U-235 used in the gun type weapon.

H. the mass of U-235 used in the implosion-type weapon is greater in some cases and less in some cases than the mass used in the gun-type weapon.

J. the mass of U-235 used in both weapons is approximately the same.

31. Both types of weapons use explosives in order to:

A. increase the heat of the U-235.

B. release the nuclear energy of the weapon from the confinement of the bomb's casing.

C. achieve supercriticality of U-235.

D. generate neutrons to start the chain reaction.

32. For an implosion-type weapon, when U-235 has reached criticality, to which of the following is the value of ρ closest?

F. 10^{-3} g/cm^3

G. 0.1 g/cm^3

H. 100 g/cm^3

J. 10^6 g/cm^3

33. In the implosion-type weapon, the explosives are used to:

A. trigger the first fission events.

B. heat the U-235 so it will become supercritical.

C. increase the density of U-235.

D. produce additional damage.

34. In order to achieve a supercritical state just before detonation, both methods:

F. increase the product of the mass and density of the U-235.

G. decrease the product of the mass and density of the U-235.

H. increase the amount of U-235 in the weapon.

J. decrease the time necessary for all the U-235 to fission.

35. Scientists are trying to build a bomb using only 8 kg of U-235. Presently they can achieve a ρ of 150 g/cm^3 with $t = 10^{-2}$ sec. Which of the following changes would be the most likely to get the weapon to meet Michelson's Criterion?

A. Decrease both t and ρ.

B. Decrease t and leave ρ the same.

C. Increase t and decrease ρ.

D. Increase t and leave ρ the same.

Passage VII

A scientist studying hemoglobin investigated the impact of temperature and carbon dioxide (CO_2) concentrations on the binding capacity of oxygen (O_2). The scientist observed the binding of oxygen to hemoglobin molecules as the pressure of oxygen was increased. The temperature and CO_2 were varied to identify their direct impact on the binding capacity of O_2.

Figure 1 displays the impact of changes in temperature on the binding (percent of hemoglobin saturated) of oxygen. Figure 2 displays the impact of varying carbon dioxide concentrations on oxygen binding. Under normal conditions, the core body temperature is 37°C and has carbon dioxide and oxygen concentrations of 40 mmHg and 100 mmHg respectively.

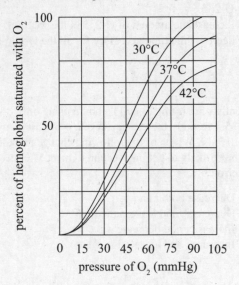

Figure 1

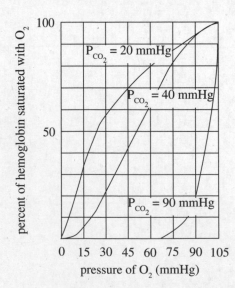

Figure 2

36. According to Figure 1, if the temperature is 42°C, which of the following changes in pressure of oxygen will cause the least increase in the percent of hemoglobin saturated with O_2?

    F. 0 – 15 mmHg
    G. 15 – 30 mmHg
    H. 30 – 45 mmHg
    J. 45 – 60 mmHg

37. According to Figure 1, which of the following sets of temperature and pressure of oxygen results in the lowest hemoglobin saturation with oxygen?

	Temperature (°C)	Pressure of Oxygen (mmHg)
A.	37	45
B.	37	60
C.	42	45
D.	42	60

38. According to Figure 1, if the pressure of oxygen is 100 mmHg and 65% of hemoglobin molecules are saturated with oxygen then the core body temperature is most likely within which of the following ranges?

    F. Less than 30°C
    G. 30°C – 37°C
    H. 37°C – 42°C
    J. Greater than 42°C

39. Based on Figure 2, if an individual has 70% of his hemoglobin molecules saturated at a pressure of 75 mmHg of oxygen, then the individual's carbon dioxide pressure is most likely closest to which of the following?

    A. 30 mmHg
    B. 50 mmHg
    C. 70 mmHg
    D. 90 mmHg

40. According to Figure 2, at a CO_2 pressure of 90 mmHg, as the pressure of O_2 is increased from 45 mmHg to 90 mmHg, the percent of hemoglobin saturated with oxygen:

    F. remains constant, then increases.
    G. remains constant, then decreases.
    H. increases, then decreases.
    J. decreases, then increases.

NO TEST MATERIAL ON THIS PAGE.

DIRECTIONS: There are seven passages in the following section. Each passage is followed by several questions. After reading a passage, choose the best answer to each question and blacken the corresponding oval on your answer document. You may refer to the passages as often as necessary.

You are NOT permitted to use a calculator on this test.

Passage I

The magnitude of seismic energy released from an earthquake is often described using the logarithmic and unit-less Richter scale. Originating at the *epicenter*, seismic energy travels through the earth via waves such as L-waves, S-waves, and P-waves. Earthquakes with a Richter scale magnitude of 5.0 or greater can typically be detected throughout the world. Figure 1 depicts the layers of the earth and typical travel patterns of seismic waves. Table 1 lists characteristics of those seismic waves. Figure 2 shows the number of earthquakes (by magnitude) detected at a particular seismic activity monitoring station in the past 30 years, as well as the percentage probability of future earthquakes (by magnitude) in that same region in the next 30 years.

Table 1		
Seismic wave	Depth range (km)	Crust velocity (m/s)
L-wave	0–10	2.0–4.5
S-wave	0–2921	3.0–4.0
P-wave	0–5180	5.0–7.0

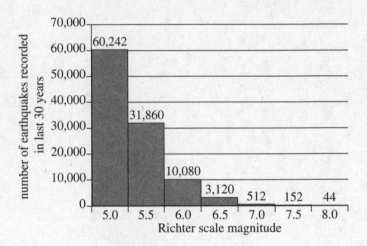

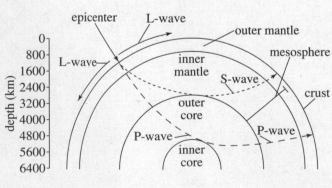

Figure 1

Figure 2

1. Figure 1 defines the mesosphere as a region of the Earth that overlaps which of the following atmospheric layers?

    I. Outer core
    II. Inner mantle
    III. Outer mantle

    A. II only
    B. I and II only
    C. II and III only
    D. I, II, and III

2. A series of seismic waves was observed from an observation station. The average crust velocity of these waves was 3 m/s, and their maximum depth occurred in the inner mantle. Based on Figure 1 and Table 1, the seismic waves observed were most likely:

    F. L-waves.
    G. S-waves.
    H. P-waves.
    J. K-waves.

3. Given the data in Figure 2, the future probability of an earthquake occurrence decreases by more than half when comparing which of the following 2 Richter scale magnitudes?

    A. 5.0 and 6.0
    B. 6.0 and 6.5
    C. 6.5 and 7.5
    D. 7.5 and 8.0

4. According to Figure 2, the probability of a future earthquake occurrence is lowest for which of the following ranges of Richter scale magnitude?

    F. 5.5 to 6.0
    G. 6.0 to 6.5
    H. 6.5 to 7.0
    J. 7.0 to 7.5

5. Based on Figure 2, the ratio of Richter scale 5.5 earthquakes to Richter scale 5.0 earthquakes in the last 30 years can be expressed approximately by which of the following fractions?

    A. $\dfrac{1}{3}$

    B. $\dfrac{1}{2}$

    C. $\dfrac{2}{3}$

    D. $\dfrac{3}{2}$

Passage II

In agriculture, soils can be classified based on *mineral content* (the amount of various metals present in the soil), and *organic content* (the percent of soil volume occupied by material made by living organisms). Ideal concentrations of various minerals are given in parts per million (*ppm*) in Table 1. If the levels of different minerals of a soil are all similar, relative to the optimal levels, the soil is said to be *well defined*. If the levels of different minerals in a soil vary widely relative to the optimal levels, the soil is said to be *poorly defined*.

Table 1	
Mineral	Ideal concentration (ppm)
Nitrogen	22
Phosphorus	14
Potassium	129
Chloride	12
Sulfur	88
Iron	6.9
Manganese	2.7

Study 1

Soil was taken from 5 different farms to a laboratory. The soils were *desiccated* (all water was removed), and a 1 L sample of each soil was prepared. In order to make sure that no minerals were trapped within the organic matter of a soil, the organic matter of each soil was burned by heating the soil to 500°C for 20 minutes. The ash of the organic matter was removed and the remaining soil analyzed for the concentration of various minerals. The results are shown, as percent of ideal concentration, in Table 2.

Table 2					
Mineral	Concentration of minerals (% of ideal concentration)				
	Farm 1	Farm 2	Farm 3	Farm 4	Farm 5
Nitrogen	89	112	160	78	210
Phosphorus	76	19	212	94	34
Chloride	124	106	64	87	65
Sulfur	290	97	189	102	112
Iron	57	26	73	91	165
Manganese	86	45	89	97	109

Study 2

To determine the percentage of the mass of each soil composed of organic matter, the above procedure was repeated, with the soil weighed before being heated to 500°C and after having the ash removed. The number of live cells (bacteria, fungi, etc.) in a cubic millimeter of each soil was determined by microscopic analysis. The results are presented in Table 3.

Table 3		
Farm	% organic matter	# living cells per mm³
1	7.1	2,964
2	8.9	3,920
3	4.8	1,642
4	6.6	2,672
5	18.9	9,467

6. Soils with more living cells per mm³ generally consume more oxygen than soils with fewer living cells. Based on this information, the soil of which farm would be expected to consume the most oxygen?

F. Farm 1
G. Farm 2
H. Farm 3
J. Farm 5

7. If, in Study 2, before and after heating a soil sample to 500°C for 20 minutes and removing the ash, the mass of the sample was approximately the same, which of the following is the most reasonable conclusion?

   A. There was little or no water in the soil.
   B. There was a large quantity of water in the soil.
   C. There was little or no organic matter in the soil.
   D. There was little or no mineral content in the soil.

8. In Study 2, before heating the sample to 500°C, it was necessary for the scientists to desiccate the soil in order to ensure that:

   F. the water was not mistaken for a mineral.
   G. the water was not consumed by the living cells.
   H. it was possible to count live cells by making sure the soil didn't stick together.
   J. the mass of the water was not mistaken for organic matter.

9. Based on Study 2, if the scientists took a soil sample from another farm, and the number of living cells per mm^3 was determined to be 2,100, the % organic matter in that soil would most likely be:

   A. less than 4.8.
   B. between 4.8 and 6.6.
   C. between 6.6 and 7.1.
   D. greater than 7.1.

10. Beans grow fastest in soils with high nitrogen and iron levels. If all other levels were equal, then based on the results of Study 1, which of the farms would be expected to produce the fastest growing beans?

    F. Farm 5
    G. Farm 4
    H. Farm 3
    J. Farm 2

11. The soil of which of the farms would likely be considered the most well defined, based on the information in Study 1 ?

    A. Farm 1
    B. Farm 2
    C. Farm 3
    D. Farm 4

Passage III

Rock candy was made by putting a mixture of 180 F water and an amount of sugar (S1) into an apparatus shown in Figure 1, inserting a string through the top, and allowing the mixture to stand and cool. The internal container was a jar made of glass, and the external container was made of plastic.

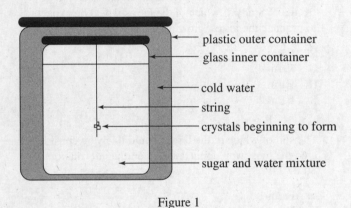

plastic outer container
glass inner container

cold water
string
crystals beginning to form

sugar and water mixture

Figure 1

Figure 2 shows how the temperature of S1 and the temperature of the cold water in the outer jar varied with time as the mixture was allowed to stand.

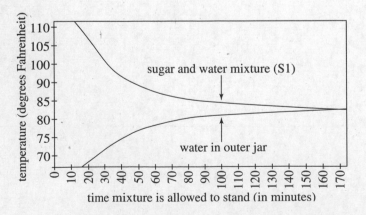

Figure 2

According to the *Second Law of Thermodynamics*, as the temperature of S1 *decreases*, the orderliness of the atoms in the solution must *increase*. This is why crystals form on the string, creating rock candy. Because of the Second Law of Thermodynamics, temperature of the sugar and water mixture can be monitored to measure orderliness of the atoms in the mixture. Two other sugar and water mixtures (S2 and S3) were monitored under standing conditions the same as those used for S1.

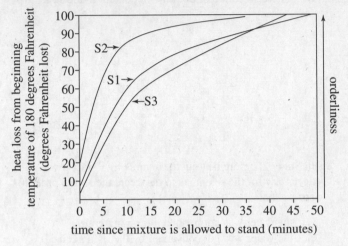

Figure 3

12. According to Figure 3, for S3, the heat lost from the beginning temperature of 180°F after being allowed to stand for 30 minutes is *closest* to which of the following?

   F. 10 degrees Fahrenheit
   G. 50 degrees Fahrenheit
   H. 80 degrees Fahrenheit
   J. 100 degrees Fahrenheit

13. According to Figures 2 and 3, as the temperature of the water in the outer jar increased, the heat loss from the beginning temperature of 180°F for S1:

    A. decreased only.
    B. increased only.
    C. decreased, and then increased.
    D. increased, and then decreased.

14. An additional sugar and water mixture (S4) was monitored under conditions identical to those used to gather the data in Figure 3. The heat lost after being allowed to stand 0 minutes was 15°F. How does the initial orderliness of the atoms in S4 compare with the orderliness of the atoms in mixtures S1, S2, and S3 ?

    F. The orderliness of S4 was greater than the orderliness of S1, S2, and S3.
    G. The orderliness of S4 was less than the orderliness of S1, S2, and S3.
    H. The orderliness of S4 was greater than the orderliness of S2 and S3, but less than the orderliness of S1.
    J. The orderliness of S4 was greater than the orderliness of S1 and S3, but less than the orderliness of S2.

15. Based on Figure 1, which of the following best explains the trends shown in Figure 2? In sum, as the time the mixture was allowed to stand increased, the heat was conducted by the:

    A. glass jar from the sugar and water mixture to the water outside the jar.
    B. glass jar from the water outside the jar to the sugar and water mixture.
    C. plastic container from the string to the water outside the jar.
    D. plastic container from the string to the sugar and water mixture.

16. Rock candy begins to form when the temperature of the sugar and water mixture has lost 100°F from its beginning temperature. Based on Figure 3, which mixture, if any, would begin to form rock candy first?

    F. S1
    G. S2
    H. S3
    J. All mixtures would begin to form rock candy at the same time.

Passage IV

The *Citric cycle* is an essential process used to transform carbohydrates, lipids, and proteins into energy in aerobic organisms. If yeast is unable to produce *succinate*, it cannot survive. The Citric cycle steps leading to the creation of succinate in yeast are shown in Figure 1. Each step in this cycle is catalyzed by an enzyme, which is essential to overcome the energy barrier between reactant and product. In the first step, Enzyme 1 is the enzyme, citrate is the reactant, and isocitrate is the product.

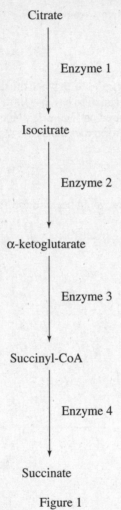

Citrate

Enzyme 1

Isocitrate

Enzyme 2

α-ketoglutarate

Enzyme 3

Succinyl-CoA

Enzyme 4

Succinate

Figure 1

Experiment

A scientist grew four strains of yeast on several different growth media. Each strain was unable to produce succinate because it lacked one of the enzymes required for the reaction pathway shown in Figure 1. Table 1 shows the results of the scientist's experiment: "Yes" indicates that the strain was able to grow in the basic nutrition solution (BNS) + the particular chemical. An undamaged strain of yeast would be able to grow in the basic nutrition solution without any additional chemical. If a strain was able to grow in a given growth medium, then it was able to produce succinate from the additional chemical added to the basic nutrition solution.

Table 1				
Growth Medium	Yeast Strain			
	W	X	Y	Z
BNS				
BNS + Isocitrate	Yes			
BNS + α- ketoglutarate	Yes	Yes		
BNS + Succinyl-CoA	Yes	Yes	Yes	
BNS + Succinate	Yes	Yes	Yes	Yes

If certain genes are damaged, the essential enzymes cannot be produced, which means that the reactions that the enzyme catalyzes cannot go. Table 2 lists the genes responsible for the enzymes in the steps of the Citric cycle leading to succinate production in yeast. If an enzyme cannot be produced, then the product of the reaction that enzyme catalyzes cannot be synthesized and the reactant in that reaction will become highly concentrated. If a gene is damaged, then it is notated with a superscript negative sign, as in $Cat3^-$; if a gene is not damaged it is notated with a superscript positive sign, as in $Cat3^+$.

Table 2	
Gene	Enzyme
Cat1	Enzyme 1
Cat2	Enzyme 2
Cat3	Enzyme 3
Cat4	Enzyme 4

17. Based on the information presented, the highest concentration of isocitrate would most likely be found in which of the following yeasts?

A. Yeast that cannot produce Enzyme 1
B. Yeast that cannot produce Enzyme 2
C. Yeast that cannot produce Enzyme 3
D. Yeast that cannot produce Enzyme 4

18. According to the information in the passage and Table 2, a strain of yeast that is $Cat1^+$ $Cat2^-$ $Cat3^-$ $Cat4^+$ CANNOT produce:

F. Enzyme 1 and Enzyme 4.
G. Enzyme 3 and Enzyme 4.
H. Enzyme 2 and Enzyme 3.
J. Enzyme 1 and Enzyme 2.

19. Which of the following statements best describes the relationships between citrate, isocitrate, and α-ketoglutarate as shown in Figure 1 ?

A. Isocitrate is a product of a reaction of α-ketoglutarate, and α-ketoglutarate is a product of a reaction of citrate.
B. α-ketoglutarate is a product of a reaction of isocitrate, and isocitrate is a product of a reaction of citrate.
C. α-ketoglutarate is a product of a reaction of citrate, and citrate is a product of a reaction of isocitrate.
D. Citrate is a product of a reaction of isocitrate, and isocitrate is a product of a reaction of α-ketoglutarate.

20. Strain X yeast was most likely unable to synthesize:

F. isocitrate from citrate.
G. α-ketoglutarate from isocitrate.
H. succinyl-CoA from α-ketoglutarate.
J. succinate from succinyl-CoA.

21. One of the growth media shown in Table 1 was a control that the scientist used to demonstrate that all four strains of yeast had genetic damage that prevented the reactions shown in Figure 1, the reactions which are responsible for the synthesis of succinate. Which growth media was used as a control?

A. BNS
B. BNS + succinate
C. BNS + isocitrate
D. BNS + succinyl-CoA

22. For each of the four strains of yeast, W–Z, shown in Table 1, if a given strain was able to grow in BNS + succinyl-CoA, then it was also able to grow in:

F. BNS.
G. BNS + isocitrate.
H. BNS + α-ketoglutarate.
J. BNS + succinate.

Passage V

Many viruses are known to persist more prevalently during certain times of the year. A study of four relatively unknown viruses was conducted to examine their annual rate of prevalence and mortality in a host population. A large survey was conducted of local populations for the presence of antigen markers indicative of viral exposures to the four virus types. Measurements were acquired monthly beginning in January of 2000 and concluding two years later. All monthly measurements were averaged for comparison.

Figure 1 shows the incidence (cases per 1,000 individuals studied) of viral infections attributed to each viral type over the duration of the study. Figure 2 shows the number of deaths (per 1,000 individuals studied) attributed to virus A and D infections.

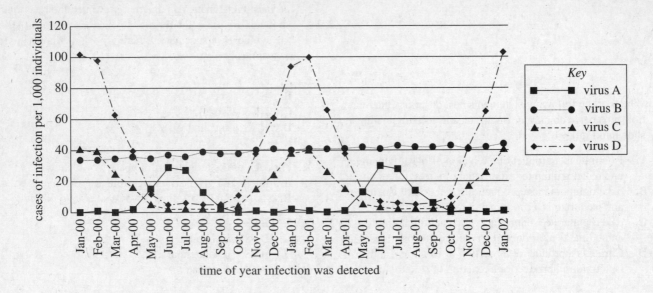

Figure 1

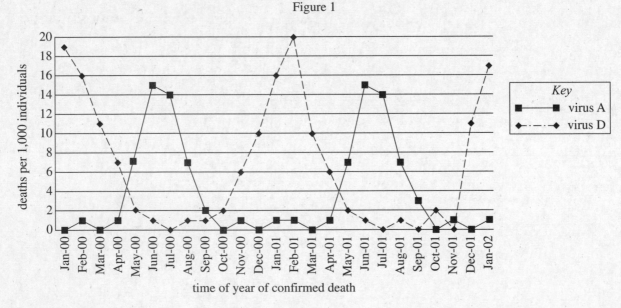

Figure 2

23. According to Figure 1, the incidence of virus A is *greatest* during which season of the year?

A. Spring (Mar–May)
B. Summer (Jun–Aug)
C. Fall (Sep–Nov)
D. Winter (Dec–Feb)

24. According to Figure 1, during April 2001, which virus was *least* prevalent in the studied population?

F. Virus A
G. Virus B
H. Virus C
J. Virus D

25. In a previous study, a virologist claimed that the incidence of virus B has always exceeded the incidence of virus C. As shown in Figure 1, the data for which of the following months is *inconsistent* with the virologist's claims?

A. January 2000
B. February 2001
C. August 2001
D. December 2001

26. According to Figure 1, the incidence of *at least 3* of the viruses is most alike during which of the following months?

F. April 2000
G. September 2000
H. November 2001
J. January 2002

27. During both years of the survey, in one month every year, 7 out of 1,000 individuals died as a result of infection with virus A and 2 out of 1000 individuals died as a result of infection with virus D. According to Figure 2, these data most likely were obtained during which of the following months?

A. January
B. March
C. May
D. October

Passage VI

The pH at which a protein is uncharged is called its *isoelectric point (pI)*. As the surrounding pH decreases, proteins gain an increasing positive charge. As the surrounding pH increases, proteins gain an increasingly negative charge. In *gel electrophoresis*, a mixture of proteins can be separated based on their relative charge. The proteins are first dissolved in a solvent and then placed at the starting point of an agarose gel. A current is applied to the gel and the proteins migrate different distances according to their charge (see Figure 1).

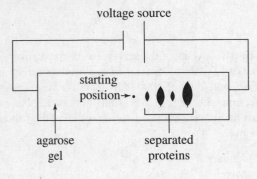

Figure 1

The following experiments were done to determine how varying the pH of a solvent affects the separation of proteins with gel electrophoresis. Table 1 shows the isoelectric points of the proteins and the pH values of the solvents used. The pH scale is logarithmic. Solutions with a pH less than 7.0 are acidic, while those with a pH more than 7.0 are basic.

Table 1	
Protein	*pI*
A	8.2
B	7.4
C	6.8
D	5.9
Solvent	pH
1	8.9
2	9.6
3	10.2

Experiment 1

A special paper 150 mm long is treated with an agarose gel. Electrodes were attached on each end and wired to a 100-volt source. A 150 μg mixture of proteins A–D was added to Solvent 1 to make a 200 μL solution. The solution was placed at the starting point of the gel and allowed to separate for 60 minutes. The density of the separated proteins was plotted as a percentage over their distance traveled. The procedure was repeated for Solvents 2 and 3 and the results presented in Figure 2.

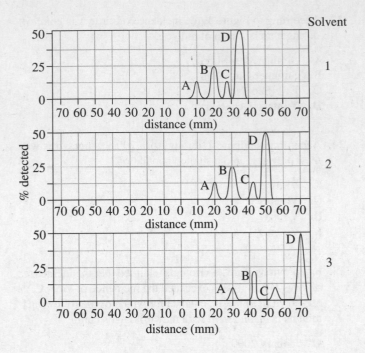

Figure 2

Experiment 2

The procedures of Experiment 1 were repeated after reversing the electrode attachments on the voltage source. Results are shown in Figure 3.

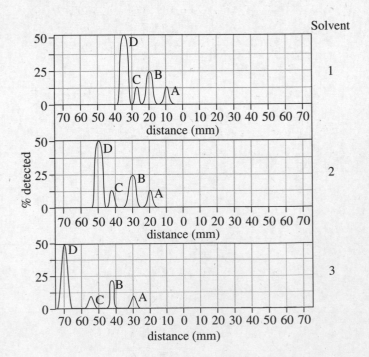

Figure 3

28. In Experiment 2, when Solvent 2 was used, the majority of Protein D migrated a distance from the starting point closest to:

F. 15 mm.
G. 35 mm.
H. 50 mm.
J. 65 mm.

29. Suppose that Experiment 1 were repeated using a solvent with a pH of 8.4. The migration distance of Protein A would most likely peak at:

A. less than 10 mm.
B. between 10 mm and 20 mm.
C. between 20 mm and 30 mm.
D. greater than 30 mm.

30. Protein L has an isoelectric point (pI) of 6.6. The results of Experiments 1 and 2 would be most similar to the plots shown in Figures 1 and 2 if, in each trial, Protein L were added to the protein mixture after removing:

F. Protein A.
G. Protein B.
H. Protein C.
J. Protein D.

31. The *resolution* of gel electrophoresis decreases as the overall distance between the peaks on the density plot decreases. Based on the results of Experiments 1 and 2, which of the following sets of conditions had the lowest resolution for the separation?

	Experiment 1	Experiment 2
A.	Solvent 1	Solvent 1
B.	Solvent 3	Solvent 3
C.	Solvent 2	Solvent 3
D.	Solvent 3	Solvent 1

32. Suppose that Experiment 1 will be repeated using Solvent 2, but Protein Y ($pI = 7.1$) is added to the overall mixture. Which of the following best predicts the order of migration distances of the 5 proteins, from shortest to longest?

F. D, C, Y, B, A
G. D, Y, C, B, A
H. A, B, Y, C, D
J. A, Y, B, C, D

33. In Experiment 2, for Solvent 2, at the migration distance where Protein B returned to its 0% migration detection, the percent of Protein A that migrated using Solvent 3 was closest to:

A. 0%.
B. 25%.
C. 50%.
D. 75%.

Passage VII

Students studying gravity and motion were given the following information:

- *Gravity* is an attractive force between two bodies that is directly related to their *mass* and indirectly related to the square of the *distance* between their centers.
- *Acceleration due to gravity* is the acceleration of an object that results from the *force* of gravity.
- *Weight* is the *force* on an object that results from *gravity*, and is not the same as *mass*.
- *Drag* is a force directly related to the *velocity* of a moving object and which results from air resistance and acts to *slow* an object down.
- When the *drag* on a free falling object is equivalent to the *weight* of that object, the object maintains a constant velocity called *terminal velocity*.

The students' teacher then described the following experiment:

The experimenter dropped a ball from a known height and recorded the time it took to hit the ground. In a second location, a second ball was dropped from the same height and the experimenter observed that it took a longer time to fall to the ground.

Providing no additional information, the teacher asked her three students to provide an explanation of the experimental conditions that would account for the different times it took the two balls to fall.

Student 1

Both trials were conducted in air with the same atmospheric properties. The balls had the same mass and weight, but the second ball had a larger radius and *surface area*. Therefore, the second ball was subjected to more drag and reached a lower terminal velocity than the first. This resulted in an increased fall time.

Student 2

Each ball had identical dimensions, but the first ball was made of a denser material giving it both greater mass and weight. Each ball was dropped through air with the same atmospheric properties. Since the second ball was subjected to less gravitational force and weighed less, it reached a lower terminal velocity compared to the first. Therefore, the second ball took more time to hit the ground.

Student 3

Both balls had the same dimensions and mass. The first ball was dropped above the Earth, while the second ball was dropped above the Moon. The first ball reached terminal velocity in the Earth's atmosphere. The second ball was not subjected to any atmosphere or air resistance. However, there was substantially less gravitational force on the second ball and subsequently it weighed less than the first ball. The overall net result was that the second ball fell more slowly and took longer to hit the ground.

34. Based on Student 1's explanation, the velocity of the first ball as it landed most likely equaled:

    F. the product of acceleration of gravity and the time it took to fall.
    G. the product of one-half the acceleration of gravity and the time it took to fall squared.
    H. the velocity of the ball directly before it landed.
    J. zero.

35. The teacher added another question to the students' assignment: Suppose the experimenter repeated the experiment by dropping two balls at the same time from the same height in a single *vacuum*, where no air resistance was present. The balls have different dimensions but identical weights, and they hit the ground at the same time. This new result is consistent with the explanations of which student(s)?

    A. Student 1 only
    B. Student 2 only
    C. Students 1 and 2 only
    D. Students 1, 2, and 3

36. According to Student 1, which of the following graphs demonstrates the velocity of the two balls as time increases?

F.

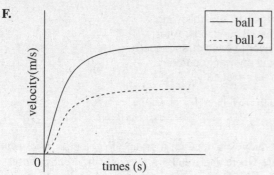

G.

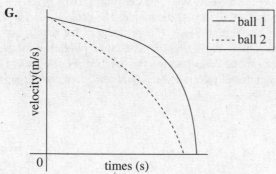

H.

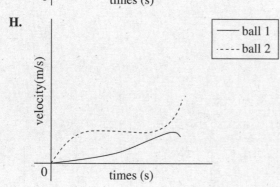

J.

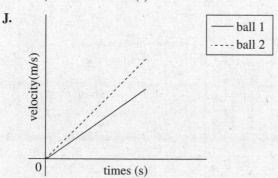

37. According to Student 1, did the surface area of the second ball have an effect on its terminal velocity?

   A. Yes; as the surface area of a ball decreases, its terminal velocity decreases only.

   B. Yes; as the surface area of a ball increases, its terminal velocity decreases only.

   C. No; as the surface area of a ball increases, its terminal velocity decreases, then increases.

   D. No; as the surface area of a ball increases, its terminal velocity is not affected.

38. Assuming that Student 3's explanation is correct, once the second ball starts falling, does it reach terminal velocity?

   F. Yes, because the weight of the ball was constant and drag force increased.

   G. Yes, because the weight of the ball decreased and no drag force was present.

   H. No, because the weight of the ball decreased and drag force was constant.

   J. No, because the weight of the ball was constant and no drag force was present.

39. The 3 explanations of the motion of the balls are similar to each other in that all 3 explanations suggest that:

   A. differences in the gravitational force are responsible for the change in falling times.

   B. increases in velocity result from gravity.

   C. drag plays only a small part in determining how long it takes an object to fall.

   D. a lead ball would have fallen faster.

40. Based on the explanations of the 3 students, what did all 3 students assume about the first ball?

   F. The velocity did not change.

   G. The velocity increased only.

   H. The velocity decreased only.

   J. The velocity increased for a time, and then reached terminal velocity.

DIRECTIONS: There are seven passages in the following section. Each passage is followed by several questions. After reading a passage, choose the best answer to each question and blacken the corresponding oval on your answer document. You may refer to the passages as often as necessary.

You are NOT permitted to use a calculator on this test.

Passage I

Sylvatic, or jungle, Yellow Fever is caused by a virus transmitted by mosquitoes from monkeys to humans. Figure 1 shows the life cycle of the mosquitoes who carry this disease. These mosquitoes' eggs do not hatch unless there is enough water for the next two stages of their life cycles. Yellow Fever is passed when an adult of these mosquitoes first bites a monkey that is infected with the virus and then bites a human.

A study was done on a group of ecologists who went into a jungle where the monkeys carrying the Yellow Fever virus live. These ecologists were divided into groups based on how frequently they went into the jungle. The ecologists were tested monthly for Yellow Fever. Figure 2 shows the number of new cases of Yellow Fever and the amount of rainfall in the jungle. For each group, Table 1 shows the number of ecologists in each group, number of mosquito bites, and percent of each group with Yellow Fever.

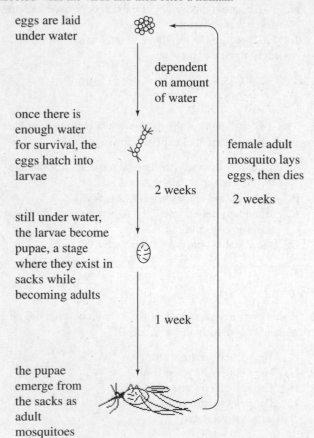

Figure 1

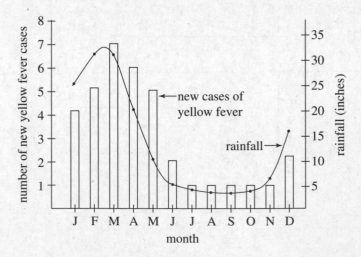

Figure 2

Table 1					
Group	Number of ecologists	Number of trips	Number of monkeys seen	Number of mosquito bites	Percent of group affected by yellow fever
A	10	0–5	36	100	10%
B	12	5–10	20	156	18%
C	10	10–15	43	210	29%
D	11	15–20	38	220	38%
E	13	20–25	58	338	52%

1. Based on Figure 1, what is essential in maintaining the mosquito population?

   A. Jungle
   B. Water
   C. Monkeys
   D. Humans

2. Based on Table 1, the average percent of ecologists affected by the yellow fever virus was closest to:

   F. 20%.
   G. 30%.
   H. 60%.
   J. 80%.

3. Suppose additional data had been gathered for Table 1 about the number of mosquito bites per month. Based on Figure 2 and Table 1, in which of the following months would you expect to have the largest total of mosquito bites per month?

   A. April
   B. June
   C. August
   D. November

4. According to Figure 2, the amount of rainfall was different for each of the following pairs of months EXCEPT:

   F. May and December.
   G. February and March.
   H. January and October.
   J. April and May.

5. Based on Table 1, as the number of trips into the jungle increased, the number of monkeys seen:

   A. increased only.
   B. decreased only.
   C. increased, then decreased.
   D. varied with no consistency.

Passage II

Ethanolamines are compounds which contain both alcohol (–OH or HO–) and amine (–NH_3, –RNH_2, –R_2NH, or –R_3N) subgroups. They remove weakly acidic gases from the atmosphere of enclosed spaces such as on a submarine. An example is the use of *monoethanolamine* (MEA) to remove CO_2 from the atmosphere as shown in Figure 1.

$$2\ MEA(liquid) + CO_2(gas) \xrightarrow{\ H_2O\ } (MEA)COO^-(aqueous) + (MEA)H^+(aqueous) + heat$$

Figure 1

If the temperature rises sufficiently, ethanolamines will release any absorbed acidic gases back into the environment, creating a potential hazard.

Scientists studied the absorption properties of 2 ethanolamines (MEA and DEA).

Experiment 1

At 0°C and 1 atmosphere (atm) pressure, 1 mole (6.02×10^{23} molecules) of MEA was spread at the base of a reaction vessel containing CO_2 gas at a concentration of 1,000 parts per million (ppm). As the CO_2 was absorbed, its ambient concentration decreased. The *scrub time* (time for CO_2 concentration to drop to at least 10 ppm) was measured. Longer scrub times indicate a slower rate of absorption. The experimental procedure was repeated at varying temperatures and for DEA, with results recorded in Table 1.

Temperature (°C)	Scrub time (msec)	
	MEA	DEA
0	11,400	8,600
5	11,150	8,410
10	11,025	8,315
15	10,925	8,240
20	10,850	8,190
25	10,790	8,145
30	10,740	8,105
35	10,700	8,075

Table 1

Experiment 2

The scrub times of MEA for different acidic gases were measured using the procedures of Experiment 1 at 26°C (see Table 2). Each of the gases listed is toxic and poses a significant safety hazard if its concentration becomes elevated within an enclosed space.

Table 2		
Gas	Formula	Scrub time (msec)
Hydrogen chloride*	HCl	8,500
Hydrogen cyanide	HCN	14,400
Hydrogen sulfide	H_2S	12,200
Sulfur dioxide	SO_2	8,930
Sulfur trioxide	SO_3	9,120

*Hydrogen chloride forms gaseous hydrochloric acid upon contact with atmospheric humidity.

6. In which of the following ways was the procedure of Experiment 2 different from that of Experiment 1? In Experiment 2:

F. temperature was varied; in Experiment 1, the temperature was held constant.

G. temperature was held constant; in Experiment 1, the temperature was varied.

H. only MEA was used; in Experiment 1, only DEA was used.

J. only DEA was used; in Experiment 1, only MEA was used.

7. In Experiment 1, during the DEA trial at 20°C, as the time progressed from 0 to 8,190 msec, the concentration of CO_2 in the vessel:

A. increased from 10 ppm to 1000 ppm.
B. increased from 1000 ppm to 10 ppm.
C. decreased from 10 ppm to 1000 ppm.
D. decreased from 1000 ppm to 10 ppm.

8. If, in Experiment 1, an additional trial were done at 12°C, the scrub times (in msec) for MEA and DEA would most likely be closest to which of the following?

	MEA	DEA
F.	10,805	8,370
G.	10,985	8,285
H.	11,000	8,365
J.	11,025	8,315

9. Based on the information in the passage, which of the following is a possible chemical formula for an ethanolamine?

A. $HO-(CH_2)_2-NH_3$
B. $HO-(CH_2CF_2)_2-CH_3$
C. $H^3C-(CH_2)_4-NH_3$
D. $H_3N-(CH_2CHCl)_2-NH_3$

10. A scientist claims that under the same conditions, DEA will always absorb CO_2 at a faster rate than will MEA. Do the results of Experiment 1 support this claim?

F. No; at all temperatures tested, the scrub time for DEA was more than that for MEA.
G. No; at all temperatures tested, the scrub time for MEA was more than that for DEA.
H. Yes; at all temperatures tested, the scrub time for DEA was more than that for MEA.
J. Yes; at all temperatures tested, the scrub time for MEA was more than that for DEA.

11. Based on the results of Experiment 2, which acidic gas had the slowest absorption by MEA at 26°C ?

A. HCl
B. HCN
C. H_2S
D. SO_2

Passage III

Taraxicum, the common dandelion, can reproduce both through spreading seeds and through vegetative reproduction. To spread its seeds, the dandelion grows seed pods shaped like globes, in which the seeds are loosely attached to a central ball; each seed grows a parachute-like tuft that lets it travel long distances on the wind (or when blown upon by humans). In vegetative reproduction, a new dandelion stalk and leaves can grow up from an existing root system. Two students discuss the spread of dandelion populations.

Student 1

In *Taraxicum*, vegetative reproduction and seed distribution make up the only means of growing new plants. Each accounts for 50% of the growth of new dandelions.

Taraxicum grows throughout North America. In many places there is very little wind. Therefore, *Taraxicum* must have a non-wind-based means of spreading itself. While blowing dandelion seeds is a common pastime among humans, this human influence is very recent in evolutionary terms; it is very unlikely that *Taraxicum* evolved to rely on humans to distribute its seeds.

The way *Taraxicum* grows in a typical field shows that both vegetative reproduction and seed distribution are at work. While seeds scatter over the whole field, the dandelions tend to grow together in clumps. This suggests that individual seeds sprout the first new dandelions, which then grow several more through vegetative reproduction.

Student 2

Seed distribution is the main way *Taraxicum* spreads itself. Without seed distribution, there are very few new dandelions. *Taraxicum* does use vegetative reproduction, sending new stalks from existing roots, but this is mainly to replace the aboveground plant if it has been cut or eaten. This allows the plant to survive threats in the environment but does not allow for the growth of new plants.

Plant studies show that plants which rely on vegetative reproduction to spread themselves tend to have large, complex root networks or underground root clusters. *Taraxicum* plants, however, each have a single large, deep taproot. This makes them very difficult to uproot, but it also means that their roots do not spread out underground, so any new plants growing from the roots would compete with each other for sunlight. Even a slight breeze or the brush of a passing animal is enough to spread dandelion seeds to a new area. Additionally, all known types of *Taraxicum* produce seed globes. If half the new dandelions grew from vegetative reproduction, then a seedless dandelion should not be at a competitive disadvantage and should be commonly observed in the wild.

Experiment

The students proposed 3 trials using an introduced *Taraxicum* population in three fields in a windy area where *Taraxicum* can naturally thrive (see Table 1).

Table 1	
Trial	Procedure
1	Several *Taraxicum* plants are planted in the soil of a field with no other *Taraxicum* plants. They are allowed to grow and spread normally.
2	*Taraxicum* specimens are planted in the soil of a similar field with no other *Taraxicum* plants. Their flowers are covered with plastic bags once they have grown seeds.
3	*Taraxicum* specimens are planted in large glass jars, which are then buried in a third similar field. Seeds are allowed to blow normally, but the plant roots cannot grow out of the glass jars.

12. Suppose an experiment were performed in which several new *Taraxicum* plants were planted in a field with their roots in glass jars and with plastic bags over the flowers. Assuming that Student 1's hypothesis is correct, the number of new dandelions in the field would most likely be what percent of the number in a control field?

F. 0%
G. 25%
H. 50%
J. 100%

13. Which of the following trials most likely provided the control group in the students' experiment?

   A. Trial 1, in which *Taraxicum* specimens are planted in the soil of a field with no other *Taraxicum* plants
   B. Trial 1, in which *Taraxicum* specimens are planted in large glass jars, which are then buried in the soil of a field with no other *Taraxicum* plants
   C. Trial 2, in which *Taraxicum* specimens are planted in the soil of a field similar to that of Trial 1
   D. Trial 3, in which specimens are planted in large glass jars in a field similar to that of Trial 1

14. Student 1 states that dandelions growing in clumps "suggests that individual seeds sprout the first new dandelions, which then grow several more through vegetative reproduction." Which of the following indicates why Student 2 believes this cannot be true? Student 2 says:

   F. *Taraxicum* tends to grow from a root network, while vegetative reproducers grow from single roots.
   G. *Taraxicum* tends to grow from a single root, while vegetative reproducers grow from root networks.
   H. *Taraxicum* has seeds which are attached loosely to the stem, a fact that suggests they are not important to *Taraxicum*'s reproductive strategy.
   J. *Taraxicum* has seeds which are attached loosely to the stem, but vegetative reproducers tend not to have seeds at all.

15. Student 2 would most likely agree with the statement that *Taraxicum:*

   A. uses vegetative reproduction to compensate for windless environments.
   B. improves its ability to survive by using vegetative reproduction to regenerate.
   C. has evolved a dependency on humans to distribute its seeds.
   D. tends to grow in clumps in fields to which it has spread itself.

16. With regard to the experiment described in the table, Students 1 and 2 would most likely agree that the increase in the *Taraxicum* population would be greatest in a field where:

   F. neither plastic bags nor glass jars were used.
   G. where plastic bags were used, but not glass jars.
   H. where glass jars were used, but not plastic bags.
   J. both plastic bags and glass jars were used.

17. Suppose Trial 3 of the experiment were performed as described. Based on Student 1's hypothesis, the resulting population would be closest to what percentage of a control population?

   A. 0%
   B. 25%
   C. 50%
   D. 100%

18. Suppose the 3 trials were performed as described. Student 2's hypothesis about the way *Taraxicum* reproduces would be best supported if the number of new dandelions fit which of the following patterns?

   F. The field in Trial 3 had roughly the same number of dandelions as the field in Trial 1, both of which had fewer dandelions than the field in Trial 2.
   G. The field in Trial 1 had more dandelions than the field in either Trial 2 or Trial 3, while the fields in Trials 2 and 3 had roughly equal numbers of dandelions.
   H. The field in Trial 2 had fewer dandelions than the field in Trial 3, which had more dandelions than the field in Trial 1.
   J. The field in Trial 3 had slightly fewer dandelions than the field in Trial 1, both of which had many more dandelions than the field in Trial 2.

Passage IV

Three studies were conducted to analyze the content of cake mix.

Study 1

Samples of 3 different cake mixes (X, Y, and Z) weighing 500.0 g were *desiccated* (thoroughly dried) in a 350ºF oven for 36 hours, and then passed through a sieve with 0.045 cm holes. Each sample was evenly spread in a trough 0.100 cm deep with a fan at one end and a secured piece of dark colored paper at the other end, downwind from the fan, as shown in Figure 1. Fan speed was slowly increased from 0 m/s until cake mix particles could be seen on the paper, the speed called the maximum immovable speed. The *maximum immovable speed* was recorded for each sample.

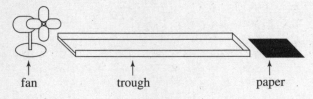

fan   trough   paper

Figure 1

This procedure was repeated with 35.0 g of cornmeal, a heavier ingredient, added to the cake mix prior to drying. The results are shown in Table 1.

Table 1		
Oven-dried cake mix	Maximum immovable speed (m/s)	
	Without cornmeal	With cornmeal
X	0.10	0.35
Y	0.13	0.38
Z	0.11	0.36

Study 2

Samples of each cake mix were prepared as in Study 1. Each sample was mixed with 500 mL of water then allowed to rest for 6 hours to ensure equal saturation of all particles in the sample. The samples were then evenly spread in a trough in an apparatus identical to that of Study 1. The fan was set to 10 m/s. Once the fan had dried the sample sufficiently, particles began to appear on the dark paper. At this point, water content of the sample was calculated. This procedure was repeated with 16 m/s fan speed. This set of procedures was then repeated with samples of each cake mix to which 35.0 g of cornmeal had been added. Figure 2 displays the results.

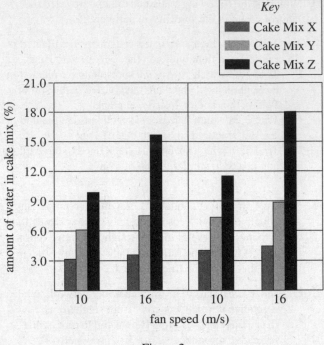

Figure 2

Study 3

Samples of each cake mix, without any preparation, were analyzed for flour particle, sugar particle, gelatin particle, and water content. The results are shown in Table 2.

Table 2				
Cake mix	Dry particle content (%)			Water content (%)
	Flour	Sugar	Gelatin	
X	77.4	20.3	2.3	3.3
Y	64.7	26.2	9.1	6.1
Z	58.5	28.3	13.2	10.1

19. Based on Study 3, the water content of cake mix Z after being allowed the 6 hours to saturate with water in Study 2 was most likely:

A. greater than 10%.
B. between 6% and 10%.
C. between 1% and 6%.
D. less than 1%.

20. Which of the following statements about the maximum immovable speed in the trials in which no cornmeal is added to the cake mix is best supported by the results of Study 1 for the three cake mixes?

F.　The maximum immovable speed for all cake mixes was 0 m/s.

G.　The maximum immovable speeds for all cake mixes were roughly equal.

H.　The maximum immovable speed for cake mix Y was three times the maximum immovable speed for cake mix X.

J.　The maximum immovable speed for cake mix Y was half the maximum immovable speeds of cake mixes X and Z.

21. Based on the results of Study 1 for a given cake mix, the addition of cornmeal to the cake mix caused a maximum immovable speed that was approximately:

A.　half as high as the maximum immovable speed when no cornmeal was added to the cake mix.

B.　twice as high as the maximum immovable speed when no cornmeal was added to the cake mix.

C.　between two and two and a half times as high as the immovable speed when no cornmeal was added to the cake mix.

D.　between two and a half and three and a half times as high as the immovable speed when no cornmeal was added to the cake mix.

22. If equal amounts of cake mixes Y and Z were blended and then prepared as in Study 1, then tested under the conditions of Study 1 with cornmeal added, the maximum immovable speed for this sample would most likely be:

F.　between 0.23 m/s and 0.25 m/s.

G.　between 0.28 m/s and 0.33 m/s.

H.　between 0.36 m/s and 0.38 m/s.

J.　between 0.39 m/s and 0.43 m/s.

23. A food scientist hypothesized that cake mixes with higher dry particle contents of gelatin will have a higher water content than cake mixes with lower dry particle contents of gelatin. Is this hypothesis supported by Study 3 ?

A.　Yes, because as gelatin content of cake mixes X, Y, and Z increased, water content decreased.

B.　Yes, because as gelatin content of cake mixes X, Y, and Z increased, water content increased.

C.　No, because as gelatin content of cake mixes X, Y, and Z increased, water content decreased.

D.　No, because as gelatin content of cake mixes X, Y, and Z increased, water content increased.

24. A fourth cake mix, cake mix Q, was analyzed as in Study 3. It was determined to contain 61% flour, 28% sugar, and 10% gelatin. Based on Study 3, what range would most likely be the water content of cake mix Q ?

F.　Less than 3.3%

G.　Between 3.3% and 6.1%

H.　Between 6.1% and 10.1%

J.　Greater than 10.1%

Passage V

Metals differ in their relative abilities to conduct electricity. *Resistance* is a measurement in ohms (Ω) of how much a metal opposes electric current at a particular voltage.

A scientist performed 3 experiments using the circuit shown in Figure 1.

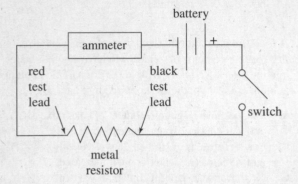

Figure 1

The *metal resistor* consisted of a coil of metallic wire with a known cross-sectional area and length (see Figure 2).

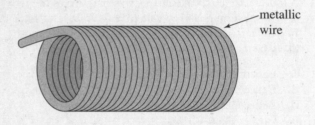

metallic wire

Figure 2

At the outset, the switch was open and no current flowed through the circuit. A 9-volt battery was used, and the black and red test leads of the circuit were attached to a metal resistor. When the switch was closed, electrons (negatively charged) flowed away from the negative battery terminal, through the circuit, and back to the positive battery terminal. The magnitude of current (charge per unit time) from this electron flow was measured by an *ammeter*, and was 1.0×10^{-3} coulombs/second for the first trial of each experiment. The resistance (R) of the metal resistor was calculated in ohms (Ω) from the resulting values for voltage (V) and current (I).

Experiment 1

Three nickel resistor coils, each with a cross-sectional area of 7.61×10^{-10} m^2 but with different lengths, were attached separately to the circuit. Results were recorded in Table 1.

Table 1		
Resistor length (m)	I (coulombs/second)	R (Ω)
100	1.0×10^{-3}	9,000
50	2.0×10^{-3}	4,500
25	4.0×10^{-3}	2,250

Experiment 2

Three gold resistor coils of varying cross-sectional area were tested. Each resistor coil had a measured length of 100 m. The results were recorded in Table 2.

Table 2		
Resistor cross-sectional area (m^2)	I (coulombs/second)	R (Ω)
2.7×10^{-10}	1.0×10^{-3}	9,000
8.0×10^{-10}	3.0×10^{-3}	3,000
2.4×10^{-9}	9.0×10^{-3}	1,000

Experiment 3

Three coils made of different metals were tested. Each resistor had a cross-sectional area of 2.67×10^{-10} m^2 and a length of 100 m. The value ρ is related to each metal's inherent *resistivity* to current flow. Results were recorded in Table 3.

Table 3			
Metal	ρ	I (coulombs/second)	R (Ω)
Gold	2.4×10^{-8}	1.0×10^{-3}	9,000
Nickel	6.9×10^{-8}	4.4×10^{-4}	25,690
Tin	1.1×10^{-7}	3.4×10^{-4}	41,250

25. In Experiment 2, the scientist varied which of the following aspects of the metal resistor?

A. Identity of the metal coil
B. Cross-sectional area of the coil
C. Length of the coil
D. Value ρ of the metal composing the coil

26. Assume that as ρ increases, a metal's ability to conduct current decreases. Based on the results of Experiment 3, which of the following correctly lists gold, nickel, and tin in order of increasing ability to conduct electrons when shaped as a wire coil?

F. Gold, nickel, tin
G. Gold, tin, nickel
H. Tin, nickel, gold
J. Tin, gold, nickel

27. In the first trial of Experiments 1–3, once the resistor was attached and the switch closed, what charge returned to the positive battery terminal every second?

A. -1.0×10^{-3} coulombs
B. -2.0×10^{-3} coulombs
C. -3.0×10^{-3} coulombs
D. -4.0×10^{-3} coulombs

28. Based on the results of the 3 experiments, the resistor with which of the following values of length, cross-sectional area, and metal type will have the highest current at a given voltage?

	Length (m)	Cross-sectional area (m²)	Metal
F.	100	2.00×10^{-10}	nickel
G.	50	2.00×10^{-10}	tin
H.	50	4.00×10^{-10}	gold
J.	50	2.00×10^{-10}	gold

29. In Experiment 1, the current across the circuit increased and the resistance of the resistor decreased as the:

A. value ρ of the metal resistor increased.
B. cross-sectional area of the metal resistor decreased.
C. length of the metal resistor increased.
D. length of the metal resistor decreased.

30. When the switch is closed in the circuit described in the passage, the battery caused electrons to flow in the direction(s) shown by which of the following diagrams?

F.

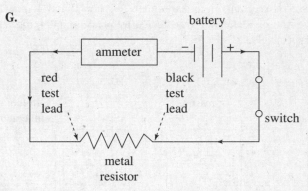

G.

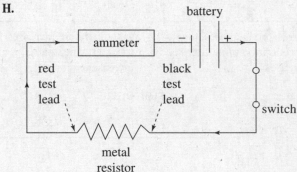

H.

J.

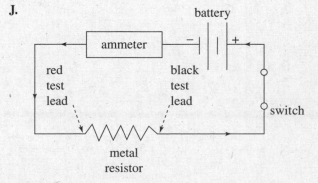

Passage VI

Pressure, temperature, volume, and amount of reactant are four variables that affect the rate at which a reaction in the gas phase occurs. A change in any of these variables changes the likelihood of particles running into each other and reacting: Increasing any one increases reaction rate; decreasing any one decreases reaction rate.

Pressure is measured in atmospheres, atm, where 1 atm is the sea level pressure of earth's atmosphere. Volume is measured in liters, L. The amount of reactant is measured in moles, where 1 mole is 6.02×10^{23} molecules.

Figure 1 shows how temperature and pressure affect the gaseous reactants in an experiment. Figures 2 and 3 show how the rate of Reaction A is affected by pressure and temperature, respectively.

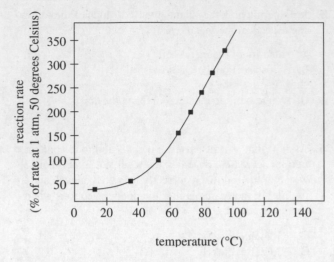

Figure 3

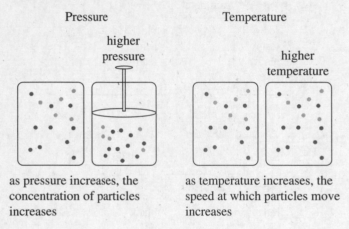

Figure 1

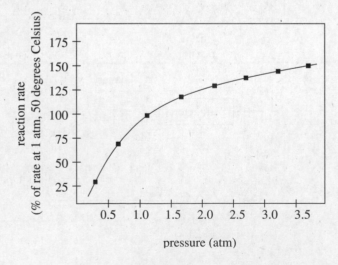

Figure 2

31. A scientist claimed that increasing temperature increases the rate at which Reaction A occurs and increasing pressure increases the rate at which Reaction A occurs. Is the scientist's claim supported by the passage and Figures 1–3 ?

A. Yes; the rate at which Reaction A occurred increased as temperature increased and increased as pressure increased.

B. Yes; the rate at which Reaction A occurred increased as pressure decreased.

C. No; the rate at which Reaction A occurred increased as temperature increased, but decreased as pressure increased.

D. No; the rate at which Reaction A occurred decreased as pressure increased.

32. According to Figures 2 and 3, the reactions occur at the same rate at what pressure and temperature?

F. 20°C and 2.0 atm
G. 40°C and 1.5 atm
H. 50°C and 1.0 atm
J. 70°C and 1.5 atm

33. The amounts of reactants in Reaction A are 1 mole/L of Compound Y and 2 mole/L of Compound Z. According to the passage, the number of molecules of Compound Y is:

A. one quarter of the number of molecules of Compound Z in the reactants.
B. one half the number of molecules of Compound Z in the reactants.
C. equal to the number of molecules of Compound Z in the reactants.
D. twice the number of molecules of Compound Z in the reactants.

34. A scientist tests a new Reaction B. This reaction is conducted with the same gas phase reactants, volume, pressure, and temperature as Reaction A, but the amounts (moles) of reactants are doubled. Based only on the information in the passage and Figures 1–3, how will the rate of Reaction B compare with the rate of Reaction A ?

F. Reaction B will be slower than Reaction A because temperature will be lower.
G. Reaction B will be faster than Reaction A because temperature will be lower.
H. Reaction B will be faster than Reaction A because the concentration of reactants is greater, so the likelihood of reactant molecules colliding and reacting is greater.
J. Reaction B will be slower than Reaction A because the concentration of reactants is greater, so the likelihood of reactant molecules colliding and reacting is greater.

35. A chemist wanted to measure Reaction A at the greatest possible reaction rate. She had the ability to change either the temperature or the pressure of the gaseous reactants. Based on the data in Figures 2 and 3, which property did she most likely alter to increase the rate of Reaction A ?

A. Pressure, which she decreased from 1 atm to 0.5 atm
B. Pressure, which she increased from 1 atm to 3 atm
C. Temperature, which she decreased from 50°C to 20°C
D. Temperature, which she increased from 50°C to 100°C

Passage VII

An experiment is set up to look at the physics of bouncing a ball, as shown in Figure 1.

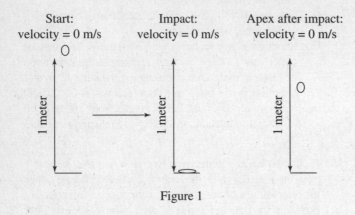

Start:
velocity = 0 m/s

Impact:
velocity = 0 m/s

Apex after impact:
velocity = 0 m/s

1 meter

1 meter

1 meter

Figure 1

When the ball is dropped, its initial velocity is 0 m/s. Velocity will increase until impact with the ground, at which point the ball's velocity immediately drops to 0 m/s again. After impact, velocity almost immediately increases to maximum post-impact velocity, and then begins to fall again as gravity works against it, slowing it down. The ball's velocity returns to 0 m/s when the ball is at its *apex*, or highest vertical point, post impact.

When a ball bounces, it deforms and becomes flatter. This is called *elasticity*. The more *elasticity* a material has, the better it is able to act like a spring and absorb force by being compressed, then use this force to "spring" back into the air. Post-impact velocity and the amount of time between velocity of 0 m/s at impact and velocity of 0 m/s at post-impact apex are affected by elasticity. Figure 2 shows the velocity of a ball versus time for balls with various elasticities and weights dropped from 1 meter height. Because gravity causes all objects to fall at the same speed regardless of weight, pre-impact velocities are identical for all balls.

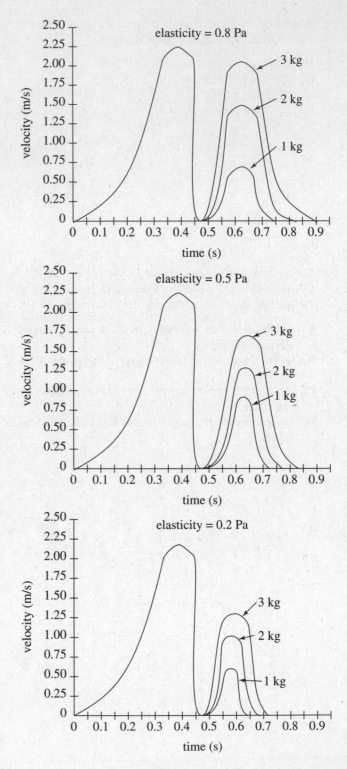

Figure 2

36. Based on the data in Figure 2, the maximum post-impact velocity of a ball will be smallest if the elasticity of the ball is:

F. 1.5 Pa.
G. between 1 and 1.5 Pa.
H. between 0.5 and 1 Pa.
J. 0.1 Pa.

37. Based on the information in Figure 2, a ball being dropped from 1 meter height with an elasticity of 0.2 Pa and a weight of 0.5 kg would have a maximum post-impact velocity of:

A. less than 0.50 m/s.
B. 0.75 m/s.
C. 1.0 m/s.
D. greater than 1.25 m/s.

38. Consider a ball as it completes one bounce, from drop to post-impact apex. If this ball has a weight of 2 kg and an elasticity of 0.50 Pa, based on the data in Figure 2, how many times does the ball have a velocity of 1.00 m/s ?

F. One time
G. Two times
H. Three times
J. Four times

39. Based on the data in Figure 2, how does the velocity of a ball change as it goes from impact to apex?

	Drop to Impact	Impact to Apex
A.	Increases only	Increases only
B.	Decreases only	Increases then decreases
C.	Increases then decreases	Increases then decreases
D.	Decreases then increases	Increases only

40. A ball will deform permanently and not spring back off the ground if the velocity with which it hits the ground exceeds the ball's *elastic limit*. Based on the data in Figure 2, if a ball is dropped from one meter and has a weight of 3 kg, an elasticity of 0.8 Pa, and an elastic limit of 2.75 m/s, will the ball deform permanently?

F. Yes, because the velocity with which the ball hits the ground is less than its elastic limit.
G. Yes, because the velocity with which the ball hits the ground is greater than its elastic limit.
H. No, because the velocity with which the ball hits the ground is less than its elastic limit.
J. No, because the velocity with which the ball hits the ground is greater than its elastic limit.

Essay Practice

Directions

This is a test of your writing skills. You will have thirty (30) minutes to write an essay. Before you begin planning and writing your essay, read the writing prompt carefully to understand exactly what you are being asked to do. Your essay will be evaluated on the evidence it provides of your ability to express judgments by taking a position on the issue in the writing prompt; to maintain a focus on the topic throughout your essay; to develop a position by using logical reasoning and by supporting your ideas; to organize ideas in a logical way; and to use language clearly and effectively according to the conventions of standard written English.

You may use the unlined pages in this test booklet to plan your essay. These pages will not be scored. *You must write your essay on the lined pages in the answer folder.* Your writing on those lined pages will be scored. You may not need all the lined pages, but to ensure you have enough room to finish, do NOT skip lines. You may write corrections or additions neatly between the lines of your essay, but do NOT write in the margins of the lined pages. *Illegible essays cannot be scored, so you must write (or print) clearly.*

If you finish before time is called, you may review your work. Lay your pencil down immediately when time is called.

DO NOT OPEN THIS BOOKLET UNTIL TOLD TO DO SO.

ACT Assessment Writing Test Prompt

Some colleges and universities, as part of the application process, have reviewed applicants' pages on social networking sites such as MySpace and Facebook. Many support this idea, arguing that schools can distinguish between true and false claims of extracurriculars listed on applications. Others disagree, arguing such use of social networking sites is unfair. In your opinion, should admissions' offices use the content of applicants' MySpace and Facebook pages in weighing their applications?

In your essay, take a position on this question. You may write about either one of the two points of view given, or you may present a different point of view on this question. Use specific reasons and examples to support your position.

The Princeton Review
Diagnostic ACT Form

ESSAY

Begin your essay on this side. If necessary, continue on the opposite side.

Continue on the opposite side if necessary.

The Princeton Review
Diagnostic ACT Form

Continued from previous page.

_____

_____

_____

_____

_____

_____

_____

_____

_____

_____

_____

_____

_____

_____

_____

_____

_____

_____

_____

_____

_____

PLEASE PRINT
YOUR INITIALS

First	Middle	Last

The Princeton Review
Diagnostic ACT Form

Continued from previous page.

_____

_____

_____

_____

_____

_____

_____

_____

_____

_____

_____

_____

_____

_____

_____

_____

_____

_____

_____

_____

_____

_____

_____

**PLEASE PRINT
YOUR INITIALS**

First   Middle   Last

The Princeton Review
Diagnostic ACT Form

Continued from previous page.

_____

_____

_____

_____

_____

_____

_____

_____

_____

_____

_____

_____

_____

_____

_____

_____

_____

_____

_____

_____

_____

Directions

This is a test of your writing skills. You will have thirty (30) minutes to write an essay. Before you begin planning and writing your essay, read the writing prompt carefully to understand exactly what you are being asked to do. Your essay will be evaluated on the evidence it provides of your ability to express judgments by taking a position on the issue in the writing prompt; to maintain a focus on the topic throughout your essay; to develop a position by using logical reasoning and by supporting your ideas; to organize ideas in a logical way; and to use language clearly and effectively according to the conventions of standard written English.

You may use the unlined pages in this test booklet to plan your essay. These pages will not be scored. *You must write your essay on the lined pages in the answer folder.* Your writing on those lined pages will be scored. You may not need all the lined pages, but to ensure you have enough room to finish, do NOT skip lines. You may write corrections or additions neatly between the lines of your essay, but do NOT write in the margins of the lined pages. *Illegible essays cannot be scored, so you must write (or print) clearly.*

If you finish before time is called, you may review your work. Lay your pencil down immediately when time is called.

DO NOT OPEN THIS BOOKLET UNTIL TOLD TO DO SO.

ACT Assessment Writing Test Prompt

In some high schools, administrators have limited students to participating in a maximum of two school-sponsored extracurricular activities each semester. Advocates believe that over-extended students lack sufficient time after school to devote to homework. Other educators disagree, arguing that extracurricular activities offer students vital experience and opportunities to explore additional interests. In your opinion, should schools limit the number of school-sponsored extracurricular activities?

In your essay, take a position on this question. You may write about either one of the two points of view given, or you may present a different point of view on this question. Use specific reasons and examples to support your position.

The Princeton Review
Diagnostic ACT Form

ESSAY

Begin your essay on this side. If necessary, continue on the opposite side.

The Princeton Review
Diagnostic ACT Form

Continued from previous page.

_____

_____

_____

_____

_____

_____

_____

_____

_____

_____

_____

_____

_____

_____

_____

_____

_____

_____

_____

_____

_____

_____

**PLEASE PRINT
YOUR INITIALS**

First	Middle	Last

The Princeton Review
Diagnostic ACT Form

Continued from previous page.

_____

_____

_____

_____

_____

_____

_____

_____

_____

_____

_____

_____

_____

_____

_____

_____

_____

_____

_____

_____

_____

_____

_____

The Princeton Review
Diagnostic ACT Form

Continued from previous page.

_____

_____

_____

_____

_____

_____

_____

_____

_____

_____

_____

_____

_____

_____

_____

_____

_____

_____

_____

_____

_____

_____

_____

**PLEASE PRINT
YOUR INITIALS**

First	Middle	Last

Directions

This is a test of your writing skills. You will have thirty (30) minutes to write an essay. Before you begin planning and writing your essay, read the writing prompt carefully to understand exactly what you are being asked to do. Your essay will be evaluated on the evidence it provides of your ability to express judgments by taking a position on the issue in the writing prompt; to maintain a focus on the topic throughout your essay; to develop a position by using logical reasoning and by supporting your ideas; to organize ideas in a logical way; and to use language clearly and effectively according to the conventions of standard written English.

You may use the unlined pages in this test booklet to plan your essay. These pages will not be scored. *You must write your essay on the lined pages in the answer folder.* Your writing on those lined pages will be scored. You may not need all the lined pages, but to ensure you have enough room to finish, do NOT skip lines. You may write corrections or additions neatly between the lines of your essay, but do NOT write in the margins of the lined pages. *Illegible essays cannot be scored, so you must write (or print) clearly.*

If you finish before time is called, you may review your work. Lay your pencil down immediately when time is called.

DO NOT OPEN THIS BOOKLET UNTIL TOLD TO DO SO.

ACT Assessment Writing Test Prompt

In some cities, restaurants must provide detailed nutritional information, including calorie, saturated and trans fat, carbohydrate, and sodium levels, on fast-food menu boards and printed menus. Supporters believe that consumers will make better food choices if educated about the nutritional content. Restaurant owners complain that a public display is unnecessary because the information is readily available if diners ask. In your opinion, should restaurants post nutritional information publicly?

In your essay, take a position on this question. You may write about either one of the two points of view given, or you may present a different point of view on this question. Use specific reasons and examples to support your position.

The Princeton Review
Diagnostic ACT Form

ESSAY

Begin your essay on this side. If necessary, continue on the opposite side.

The Princeton Review
Diagnostic ACT Form

The Princeton Review
Diagnostic ACT Form

Continued from previous page.

_____

_____

_____

_____

_____

_____

_____

_____

_____

_____

_____

_____

_____

_____

_____

_____

_____

_____

_____

_____

_____

_____

_____

_____

**PLEASE PRINT
YOUR INITIALS**

First	Middle	Last

The Princeton Review
Diagnostic ACT Form

Continued from previous page.

The Princeton Review
Diagnostic ACT Form

Continued from previous page.

_____

_____

_____

_____

_____

_____

_____

_____

_____

_____

_____

_____

_____

_____

_____

_____

_____

_____

_____

_____

_____

_____

Test 2

ACT ENGLISH TEST
45 Minutes—70 Questions

DIRECTIONS: In the five passages that follow, certain words and phrases are underlined and numbered. In the right-hand column, you will find alternatives for each underlined part. In most cases, you are to choose the one that best expresses the idea, makes the statement appropriate for standard written English, or is worded most consistently with the style and tone of the passage as a whole. If you think the original version is best, choose "NO CHANGE." In some cases, you will find in the right-hand column a question about the underlined part. You are to choose the best answer to the question.

You will also find questions about a section of the passage or the passage as a whole. These questions do not refer to an underlined portion of the passage but rather are identified by a number or numbers in a box.

For each question, choose the alternative you consider best and blacken the corresponding oval on your answer document. Read each passage through once before you begin to answer the questions that accompany it. For many of the questions, you must read several sentences beyond the question to determine the answer. Be sure that you have read far enough ahead each time you choose an alternative.

PASSAGE I

> The following paragraphs may or may not be in the most logical order. Each paragraph is numbered in brackets, and question 14 will ask you to choose where Paragraph 5 should most logically be placed.

A Window into History

[1]

One very long summer during high school, my mom volunteered me to help Grandpa research our family tree. Great, I thought, imagining hours spent pawing through dusty, rotting boxes and listening to boring stories about people I didn't know. "You'll be surprised," my mom promised. "Family histories can be very interesting."

[2]

It turned out Grandpa had more in mind than research. Hoping to also preserve our family memories. He'd discovered a computer program that helps digitally scan old pictures, and letters to preserve their contents before they crumble from old age. Grandpa wanted me to help him connect

1. Given that all the choices are true, which one best conveys the author's initial expectations and effectively leads into her mother's comments?
   A. NO CHANGE
   B. bonding with the grandfather I barely knew.
   C. remembering fun times I had with relatives.
   D. trying to operate an unfamiliar machine.

2. F. NO CHANGE
   G. research. Hope to also preserve
   H. research, that hope to also preserve
   J. research, hoping to also preserve

3. A. NO CHANGE
   B. pictures, and, letters
   C. pictures and letters,
   D. pictures and letters

GO ON TO THE NEXT PAGE.

1 ■ ■ ■ ■ ■ ■ ■ ■ ■ 1

the scanner and set up the computer program. He could type documents and send emails, but he had never used a scanner.
₄

[3]

[1] Instead of sorting through dusty boxes as I had imagined, we spent a lot of time in my grandpa's bright, tidy computer room. [2] The scanner hummed happily, turning my relatives precious memories into permanent digital images.
₅
[3] A scanner is a device which makes electronic copies of actual items. [4] I worked happily while Grandpa shared stories that turned out not to be boring at all. 6

[4]

Perusing through her belongings, I felt I was opening a
₇
window into the world of my relatives, a world long since gone.

Grandpa showed me a bundle of yellowed letters he had send
₈
to Grandma from the front lines of World War II, and I could almost smell the gunpowder. I turned the brittle pages of my great-grandmother's recipe book and could envision her sitting in her immaculate kitchen penning meticulously every entry. All
₉
of the people who had been merely names to me now had faces to match and lives lived.

[5]

I asked Grandpa to tell the story behind every picture and letter we scanned. Besides, the stories helped me not only
₁₀
understand but also relate to my relatives. Like me, they had celebrated achievements, overcome failures, pulled silly pranks, played sports, and, attended concerts. I became so hungry for
₁₁
more information that Grandpa needed additional props to keep

4. Which of the following choices is NOT an acceptable substitute for the underlined portion?
   F. emails but having
   G. emails, yet he had
   H. emails; however, he had
   J. emails but had

5. A. NO CHANGE
   B. relatives precious memory's
   C. relatives' precious memories
   D. relatives' precious memory's

6. Which of the following sentences in this paragraph is LEAST relevant to the progression of the narrative and therefore could be deleted?
   F. Sentence 1
   G. Sentence 2
   H. Sentence 3
   J. Sentence 4

7. A. NO CHANGE
   B. their
   C. one's
   D. there

8. F. NO CHANGE
   G. send
   H. has sent
   J. had sent

9. A. NO CHANGE
   B. kitchen, penning
   C. kitchen, which penned
   D. kitchen that penned

10. F. NO CHANGE
    G. Because the
    H. Therefore, the
    J. The

11. A. NO CHANGE
    B. sports, and
    C. sports and,
    D. sports and

GO ON TO THE NEXT PAGE.

me satisfied. He showed me a chest filled with random stuff, all

covered in dust. 12

[6]

As the new school year approached, Grandpa admitted, "I

probably could have done this project myself. I just wanted

someone to share it with." I can't thank him enough for sharing

the experience and making me appreciate the family members

who have made me the person I am. I will cherish family

memories and mementoes and hope that someday, I will be able
to pass them down to my own grandchildren.
   13

12. Which of the following true statements, if added at the beginning of this paragraph, would most successfully introduce readers to the information relayed in the paragraph?

   F. My family has been around for generations, so there were a lot of names to remember.

   G. My grandfather inundated me with items to catalogue on the computer.

   H. As I learned more about some relatives, I forgot about others.

   J. As the summer progressed, I became fascinated with my relatives' lives.

13. Which of the following provides the best conclusion to the paragraph and the essay as a whole?

   A. NO CHANGE

   B. My grandpa will teach me something new next summer.

   C. I never have to tell my mother she was right that family history isn't tedious and boring.

   D. I can figure out other ways to use my computer.

Questions 14 and 15 ask about the preceding passage as a whole.

---

14. Where should the author place Paragraph 5 in order to have a logical, coherent essay?

   F. Where it is now

   G. Before Paragraph 2

   H. Before Paragraph 3

   J. Before Paragraph 4

15. Suppose the writer's purpose had been to write an essay about some of the benefits of genealogical research. Does this essay succeed in achieving that purpose?

   A. Yes, because it describes the technological skills gained in the process of researching one's relatives.

   B. Yes, because it provides an example of how one person gained personal insights from her family history.

   C. No, because it provides only one person's research, which is susceptible to bias and cannot be reliable.

   D. No, because genealogical research require statistics in order to prove there were benefits.

PASSAGE II

Moving to a New Life

I stand on the corner of Elm Avenue and Main Street by

me, watching my parents walk away and feeling nothing but
  16

apprehension about adjusting to this new town. I try not to show

the passersby just how scared I really am, but it's not possible.

16. F. NO CHANGE
   G. me watching
   H. myself, watching
   J. myself. Watching

GO ON TO THE NEXT PAGE.

My tears start to flow, and I quickly run to my new, cold, bedroom.

I know I am making a complete spectacle of myself, but I can't help it. I am an only child whom has never been more than 30 minutes away from her parents, yet here I am, on the other side of the country, moving in to my new college dorm.

We all want to take responsibility for one's own lives. I just never realized that in order to do so, I would have to leave my family. No longer will I wake up to Mom's Sunday breakfast of non-pasteurized milk, and fresh orange juice, fluffy scrambled eggs and crisp bacon. I'll have to tackle the daily crossword puzzle on my own, without Dad's carefully veiled hints.

Everything is gone. ☐22 Can anyone understand what I'm going through?

As I lay crying into my pillow, hearing the door to the dorm suite open. It must be one of my two roommates. I quickly stop crying—I couldn't stand the embarrassment

17. A. NO CHANGE
  B. new, cold
  C. new cold
  D. new cold,

18. F. NO CHANGE
  G. completely spectacle about
  H. completely spectacle of
  J. complete spectacle about

19. A. NO CHANGE
  B. whom have
  C. who has
  D. who have

20. F. NO CHANGE
  G. their own life.
  H. our own lives.
  J. your own life.

21. A. NO CHANGE
  B. milk, and fresh orange juice, fluffy,
  C. milk and fresh orange juice fluffy
  D. milk and fresh orange juice, fluffy

22. The writer is considering revising the sentence "Everything is gone" in the preceding sentence to read:

> "It feels like everything I have ever loved is being ripped away from me."

Should the writer make this change, or keep the sentence as it is?

  F. Make the revision, because it conveys more vividly the type of emotions felt by the writer.
  G. Make the revision, because it describes the stages of emotion the writer faces as she mourns.
  H. Keep the sentence as it is, because it is already specific and does not need to be changed.
  J. Keep the sentence as it is, because it's short and more concise than the proposed revision.

23. A. NO CHANGE
  B. I was hearing
  C. I hear
  D. having heard

GO ON TO THE NEXT PAGE.

if she knew her new roommate was an emotional wreck! 24

Being full of surprise, I hear *her* crying as she runs to her room.
25

Curiosity overwhelming me and I tiptoe through the common
26
room to her still-open door.

    I stand in the doorway for merely a second before she

reacts. Slowly, her face jolts up, and her sudden shock at my
27
appearance is clearly written on her face. "Are you okay?" I

quietly ask. "I'm sorry," she stammers. "I thought I was alone.
28
I know this must seem very childish to you. I'm just very close

to my younger sister, and saying goodbye to her just now…."

Her sentence trails off as she turns her face away from me.

"I remember when she was born."
29

    "I completely understand," I say, and I really do. "Maybe

we can help each other get used to this new college life."

---

24. If the writer were to delete the phrase "—I couldn't stand the embarrassment if she knew her new roommate was an emotional wreck!" from the preceding sentence, the passage would primarily lose:

  F. a description of the uneasy relationship between the roommates.
  G. an insight into the reasons the writer stopped crying.
  H. a justification for her dissatisfaction with college.
  J. nothing at all, since the writer has already expressed her sadness.

25. **A.** NO CHANGE
     B. Since I was surprised,
     C. Being surprised,
     D. Much to my surprise,

26. **F.** NO CHANGE
     G. me, and I
     H. me, I
     J. me. I

27. Given that all the choices are true, which one provides the best transition by illustrating how quickly the roommate responded to the writer's presence?

  A. NO CHANGE
  B. Abruptly,
  C. After a few moments later,
  D. Sluggishly,

28. **F.** NO CHANGE
     G. asserts.
     H. quotes.
     J. screams.

29. Given that all the choices are true, which conclusion to this paragraph is most consistent with the writer's subsequent response?

  A. NO CHANGE
  B. "My sister has always been so fun to live with."
  C. "I wish that they would have left sooner."
  D. "It's going to be hard to adjust, that's all."

GO ON TO THE NEXT PAGE.

Question 30 asks about the preceding passage as a whole.

30. Suppose the writer's goal was to describe personal hardships first-time college students may experience. Does this essay successfully accomplish that goal?

F. Yes, because it gives an anecdotal account of separation anxiety experienced by the writer and her roommate.
G. Yes, because it focuses on the initial awkwardness between roommates who don't know each other.
H. No, because it focuses on the emotions of only one person instead of the experiences of many students.
J. No, because it fails to provide enough background information on the narrator's mental state before college.

PASSAGE III

The following paragraphs may or may not be in the most logical order. Each paragraph is numbered in brackets, and question 45 will ask you to choose where Paragraph 2 should most logically be placed.

Thrill Seekers Wanted

[1]

Like Indiana Jones, the staid college professor who undertakes daring adventures in his spare time, my father is a businessman by day and a thrill-seeking adrenaline fanatic by night. [31] His enthusiasm rubbed off on me, and I have been lucky to be his sidekick on many an adventure. We started out small by conquering America's fastest, most twisted rollercoasters. After that, a whitewater rafting excursion through

31. The writer is considering deleting the phrase "Like Indiana Jones, the staid college professor who undertakes daring adventures in his spare time," from the preceding sentence (and capitalizing the word *my*). Should the phrase be kept or deleted?

A. Kept, because it clarifies that the writer's father is also named Indiana.
B. Kept, because it adds a descriptive detail that heightens the thrill of the adventures described later in the passage.
C. Deleted, because it draws attention from the paragraph's focus on the father and places it on movies.
D. Deleted, because the information fails to specify if the writer's father is interested in archaeology.

GO ON TO THE NEXT PAGE.

the Grand Canyon on the <u>majestic, if murky</u> Colorado River
₃₂
jumpstarted our search for other extreme thrills across the globe.

[2]

Anyone who loves a challenging thrill should try

canyoning. ☐33 Our adventure began with a 90-foot rappel

down a canyon wall into a rushing, ice-cold <u>river, and without</u>
₃₄
wetsuits we surely would have become popsicles! Intrepidly, we
traversed the bone-chilling water toward the mouth of the river,
our final destination, where the reward for the journey would be
a panoramic <u>view of the natural wonder</u> of the lush Interlaken
₃₅
basin.

[3]

Spectacular thrills awaited us at every corner of the world.
A remarkable activity in its own right, <u>like skydiving was</u>
₃₆
especially momentous when performed from a helicopter over
the breathtaking Swiss Alps. We have gone spelunking in damp

and ominous Peruvian caves. ☐37 We have traveled to New
Zealand for *Zorb*, a strange activity in which participants enter
a giant, inflatable ball and roll down steep, grassy hills. Most

32. F. NO CHANGE
    G. majestic if murky
    H. majestic; if murky,
    J. majestic, if murky,

33. The writer is considering deleting the phrase "who loves
    a challenging thrill" from the preceding sentence. Should
    the phrase be kept or deleted?

    A. Kept, because it clarifies the term *anyone* and contrib-
       utes to the logic of the paragraph.
    B. Kept, because it indicates the paragraph's focus on
       people who love challenges.
    C. Deleted, because the term *anyone* describes all people
       and does not need clarification.
    D. Deleted, because the phrase is too long and confuses
       the focus of the sentence.

34. F. NO CHANGE
    G. river, without
    H. river without
    J. river and without

35. A. NO CHANGE
    B. view naturally of the wonder
    C. viewing of the wonderful nature
    D. view

36. F. NO CHANGE
    G. skydiving was
    H. skydiving,
    J. like skydiving

37. At this point, the writer is considering adding the follow-
    ing true statement:

    > We have bungee jumped from the world's highest
    > platform, Bloukrans Bridge in South Africa.

    Should the writer make this addition here?

    A. Yes, because it is an additional detail consistent with
       the main point of this paragraph.
    B. Yes, because it helps establish the main idea that
       Africa has the most exciting thrills in the world.
    C. No, because its focus is on a location and activity
       different than those in the rest of the paragraph.
    D. No, because the other activities in this paragraph do
       not involve the use of a bungee cord.

GO ON TO THE NEXT PAGE.

recently, in Interlaken, Switzerland, we attempted "canyoning,"
because of which was our most exhilarating adventure yet!
38

[4]

We had to navigate both the flowing river and the canyon
walls we became amphibious, moving seamlessly between
39
land and water. We slid over slick rocks at one moment,

leapt and descended from waterfalls and swam through
40
underwater tunnels the next. Back and forth we alternated,
scaling rope ladders before zooming down zip lines back into

the fresh mountain water. Certainly, danger from possible
41
miscalculations were lurking in each of these activities, but that
41
very danger provided the rush. Canyoning was indeed one thrill

after another, from beginning to end.
42

[5]

While canyoning is possible only in certain locales, thrills
and adventure can be found anywhere. Our humble beginnings
in the U.S. showed us just that. We continue to seek the big

thrills, but in doing so, we have learned to seek lesser forms of
43
excitement in daily life as well. After all, we can't go canyoning

every day, and small thrills are better than none for us thrill
44
seekers.
44

38. F. NO CHANGE
    G. and which was
    H. which was
    J. in which was

39. A. NO CHANGE
    B. walls, we
    C. walls so we
    D. walls, so we

40. F. NO CHANGE
    G. leapt
    H. leapt in the air and descended down
    J. leapt to descend

41. A. NO CHANGE
    B. miscalculations will be lurking
    C. miscalculations was lurking
    D. miscalculations lurking

42. Given that all the choices are true, which one best clarifies the distinction between the two types of activities mentioned in this paragraph?
    F. NO CHANGE
    G. both on rocky surfaces and in the chilly water.
    H. adventure after adventure.
    J. long after the waterfalls.

43. A. NO CHANGE
    B. and
    C. moreover,
    D. furthermore,

44. Given that all the choices are true, which one concludes the paragraph with a phrase that relates to the main topic of the essay?
    F. NO CHANGE
    G. and that's a shame.
    H. because we don't live near any canyons.
    J. but it's the last thrill I'll ever need!

GO ON TO THE NEXT PAGE.

Question 45 asks about the preceding passage as a whole.

45. For the sake of the logic and coherence of this essay, the best placement for Paragraph 2 would be:

   A. where it is now.
   B. before Paragraph 1.
   C. before Paragraph 4.
   D. before Paragraph 5.

PASSAGE IV

Enriching the American Tradition

The Mexican-American War, with its many conflicts and compromises, <u>represent</u> a largely overlooked part of the history of the United States, but its importance in the current shape and culture of the United States cannot be overstated. Certainly, it is difficult to imagine the present-day United States without the list of former Mexican territories, which <u>includes</u> Texas, Arizona, California, and others, but it is equally difficult to imagine America's vibrant multicultural society without the influence of Mexican-Americans.

But despite the obvious richness that Mexican-Americans have brought to American culture, one aspect of <u>their contributions, to American arts</u> is often overlooked: literature. Although the names of many famous Mexican-Americans are identifiable in film and music, many Americans are at a loss to name even a single Mexican-American author. <u>Carlos Santana, a musician born and raised in Mexico, has achieved widespread popularity in the United States.</u>

46. **F.** NO CHANGE
   G. represents
   H. have represented
   J. representing

47. **A.** NO CHANGE
   B. includes:
   C. included,
   D. included:

48. **F.** NO CHANGE
   G. their contributions, to American arts,
   H. their contributions to American arts,
   J. their contributions to American arts

49. **A.** NO CHANGE
   B. A musician who has achieved popularity in the United States is Carlos Santana, who was born and raised in Mexico.
   C. However, many Americans can easily identify Carlos Santana, a popular musician born and raised in Mexico.
   D. DELETE the underlined portion.

GO ON TO THE NEXT PAGE.

A major landmark in early Mexican-American literature came in 1885, when author, María Amparo Ruiz de Burton, published her second novel, *The Squatter and the Don*. In addition to being the first major novel written in English by an author of Mexican descent, *The Squatter and the Don* was also noteworthy for its revolutionary perspective. 51 María

Amparo Ruiz de Burton helped to acquaint American readers with and introduce them to an as yet unfamiliar group through her fictional family, the Alamars. A family of landed gentry

living in San Diego, nearly all is lost to the Alamars after

the American annexation of California during the Mexican-American War. As a result of the lopsided Treaty of Guadalupe Hidalgo, Mexico lost nearly forty percent of its previous territories and many, like Ruiz de Burton and her creations the Alamars, were uprooted from their previous comfort and made citizens of a new nation. Ruiz de Burton's wish that her works would speak for the many Mexican-Americans who felt

50. F. NO CHANGE
G. author María Amparo Ruiz de Burton
H. author, María Amparo Ruiz de Burton
J. author María Amparo Ruiz de Burton,

51. If the writer were to delete the phrase "In addition to being the first major novel written in English by an author of Mexican descent," from the preceding sentence, the essay would primarily lose:

A. an indication of Ruiz de Burton's command of the English language.
B. a fact that reveals that the novel was the first by a Mexican author to be read in the United States.
C. information that helps to strengthen the sense of the novel's historical importance.
D. a suggestion that María Amparo Ruiz de Burton considered writing the novel in her native Spanish.

52. F. NO CHANGE
G. give American readers a glimpse at
H. introduce American readers unacquainted with Mexican-American literature to
J. introduce American readers to

53. A. NO CHANGE
B. the Alamars lose nearly all that they own
C. losing all that they own
D. Ruiz de Burton describes a family that loses all that they own

54. F. NO CHANGE
G. within
H. throughout
J. through

55. A. NO CHANGE
B. being that
C. was that
D. being

GO ON TO THE NEXT PAGE.

the same concerns. [56] *The Squatter and the Don* marked an early and important exploration of many themes that Mexican-

American authors continue to explore, including themes of
 ___
 57
personal integrity, identity, and the relationships between individuals and collective history.

[1] Poet Ana Castillo has been publishing well-received novels and volumes of poetry prolifically since 1977, and her work has been essential in bringing issues of Mexican-American women, particularly those living in urban places such as Castillo's hometown of Chicago, to a larger audience. [2] Sandra Cisneros is the author of *The House on Mango Street*, which has sold over two million copies since its original publication in 1984, and her work, including the novel *Caramelo*, published in 2002, has helped give voice to the often difficult position of living between two cultures that Mexican-Americans face. [3] Ruiz de Burton's writings and that of other
 ___
 58

authors remain important parts of American literature today. [59]

56. At this point, the writer is considering adding the following true statement:

> After the Louisiana Purchase in 1803, many people of French descent living in the United States felt displaced as well.

Should the writer make the addition here?

F. Yes, because it provides historical information about another group that deepens the reader's understanding of the difficulties faced by Mexican-Americans.

G. Yes, because it links those with French descent with the characters in *The Squatter and the Don*.

H. No, because it does not provide a direct connection between the work of María Amparo Ruiz de Burton and the work of later Mexican-American authors.

J. No, because it is clear from the essay that the Louisiana Purchase had no importance to the Mexican-American authors discussed.

57. Which of the following alternatives to the underlined portion would be LEAST acceptable?

A. investigate
B. examine
C. look into
D. solve

58. F. NO CHANGE
G. by
H. those of
J. with

59. For the sake of the logic and coherence of this paragraph, Sentence 3 should be placed:

A. where it is now.
B. before Sentence 1.
C. before Sentence 2.
D. after Sentence 4.

GO ON TO THE NEXT PAGE.

[4] Along with many others, <u>these authors</u> continue to expand
                              60
the boundaries of American literature, just as Mexican-
Americans all over the country continue to enrich and challenge
accepted notions of what we call "American culture."

60. F. NO CHANGE
    G. the writers Ana Castillo and Sandra Cisneros and many
       other Mexican-American authors
    H. the Mexican-American authors being published today
    J. the many Mexican-American authors whose work as a
       whole represents them

PASSAGE V

A Simple but Complex Modern Vision

Ludwig Mies van der Rohe, typically cited alongside
Walter Gropius and Le Corbusier as a pioneer of modern
<u>architecture. Was</u> integral to the founding and proliferation of
        61
the "modern style" in architecture. Van der Rohe felt the design
of a building should be reflective of its age, as the Gothic and
Classical masterpieces surely were. Van der Rohe, called Mies
by friends and students, found many architects' attitudes toward
architectural design problematic, particularly these architects'
reliance on older, outdated architectural styles.

Van der Rohe, instead, sought to express through his
buildings what he <u>feels</u> to be the core tenets of modern
                    62
existence. The <u>buildings based on van der Rohe's designs,</u>
                                                    63
were primarily constructed <u>with</u> industrial steel and plate
                            64
glass—<u>that is,</u> only the materials of modern, twentieth-century
        65
life and industry. By using only the bare minimum materials
produced from American and German factories, Mies sought
to cast off what he found to be one of the main problems

61. A. NO CHANGE
    B. architecture. Being
    C. architecture, being
    D. architecture, was

62. F. NO CHANGE
    G. is feeling
    H. felt
    J. who felt

63. A. NO CHANGE
    B. buildings based on van der Rohe's designs
    C. buildings, based on van der Rohe's designs
    D. buildings based on van der Rohe's designs;

64. Which of the following alternatives to the underlined por-
    tion would NOT be acceptable?

    F. from
    G. using
    H. out of
    J. into

65. A. NO CHANGE
    B. that is
    C. this is,
    D. this is

GO ON TO THE NEXT PAGE.

with contemporary architecture, and overly decorative and
ornamental structures with no "function" were wasteful uses of
space and material. Through steel and plate glass, van der Rohe
felt that he could better practice the idea of "efficiency" that he
had pulled from his earlier readings of Russian Constructivism,
and using these materials as he did to create simple, planar,
rectilinear designs, Mies invested his buildings with a strange
intensity that conveyed at once the simplicity of design and
many of the buildings have been named National Historic
Landmarks.

Van der Rohe's architectural education was unique, and
many describe the architect as largely self-taught. From

1908 to 1912, under teacher Peter Behrens's guidance, Mies
became a proponent of many modern and avant-garde ideas in
architecture in Germany. From Behrens, van der Rohe began
to see the potential of developing an architecture of ideas, and
indeed, he was a "self-taught" expert in many ancient and
modern philosophical concepts. This helped him to understand
the character of the modern world, and with his maturing ideas
of this character, van der Rohe set out to create a style truly

of the twentieth century. While van der Rohe was committed
to creating a philosophical, theoretical basis for his works, he
helped to create a new vocabulary for the creation and study of
architecture.

[1] In order to escape the oppressive Nazi regime, van der
Rohe who left Germany for the United States in 1937. [2] Mies
was originally invited to become head of the school and to
contribute designs for the school's growing campus (which, as
the Illinois Institute of Technology, continues to grow today).

66. F. NO CHANGE
G. architecture that
H. architecture, which
J. architecture: that

67. Given that all the choices are true, which one would add the most effective detail to the description of the visual appeal of the buildings mentioned in the first part of the sentence?
A. NO CHANGE
B. the structure that had taken months, even years, to build.
C. the complex beauty of the free-flowing structures inside.
D. the buildings on display in many American and European cities.

68. F. NO CHANGE
G. teacher, Peter Behrens's guidance,
H. teacher Peter Behrens's guidance;
J. teacher, Peter Behrens's guidance

69. A. NO CHANGE
B. Studying philosophy
C. Something
D. This thing

70. F. NO CHANGE
G. Even though
H. Moreover
J. Because

71. A. NO CHANGE
B. left
C. leaves
D. leaving

GO ON TO THE NEXT PAGE.

[3] He had two commissions waiting for him there—one in Wyoming and <u>another</u> at the Armour Institute of Technology in
₇₂

Chicago. [4] <u>Pupils learning</u> his new method and architectural
₇₃
vocabulary, van der Rohe worked tirelessly as an educator, with only limited success. [5] While many students were initially

<u>enthusiastic,</u> Mies van der Rohe's influence was eventually
₇₄
eclipsed by the rise of Postmodern Architecture in the early

1980s. [75]

There can be no doubt, though, that van der Rohe has left a huge mark on the look of the North American city. Not only do his buildings help to create the skylines of Chicago, New York, and Toronto, but van der Rohe also gave architects from all over the world a new vocabulary and set of materials with which to create spaces for living and working, and he helped to make architecture one of the great arts of the twentieth century.

72. Which of the following alternatives to the underlined portion would NOT be acceptable?

   F. the other
   G. one
   H. this one
   J. the other one

73. A. NO CHANGE
   B. While pupils learn
   C. To teach pupils
   D. Pupils being taught

74. F. NO CHANGE
   G. enthusiastic and extremely excited,
   H. enthusiastic, overwhelmed with excitement,
   J. enthusiastic, thrilled,

75. For the sake of the logic and coherence of this paragraph, Sentence 3 should be placed:

   A. where it is now.
   B. after Sentence 1.
   C. after Sentence 4.
   D. after Sentence 5.

END OF TEST 1
STOP! DO NOT TURN THE PAGE UNTIL TOLD TO DO SO.

MATHEMATICS TEST
60 Minutes—60 Questions

DIRECTIONS: Solve each problem, choose the correct answer, and then darken the corresponding oval on your answer sheet.

Do not linger over problems that take too much time. Solve as many as you can; then return to the others in the time you have left for this test.

You are permitted to use a calculator on this test. You may use your calculator for any problems you choose, but some of the problems may best be done without using a calculator.

Note: Unless otherwise stated, all of the following should be assumed:

1. Illustrative figures are NOT necessarily drawn to scale.
2. Geometric figures lie in a plane.
3. The word *line* indicates a straight line.
4. The word *average* indicates arithmetic mean.

---

1. Violet is baking a mixed berry pie that contains blueberries, cherries, blackberries, and raspberries. She uses three times as many blackberries as cherries, twice as many blueberries as raspberries, and the same number of blackberries and raspberries. If Violet has 10 cherries, how many of each of the other berries must she use?

	Raspberries	Blueberries	Blackberries
A.	3	2	3
B.	30	2	3
C.	30	2	30
D.	30	60	10
E.	30	60	30

2. The expression $(3x - 5)(x + 2)$ is equivalent to:

   F. $3x^2 - 10$
   G. $3x^2 + x + 10$
   H. $3x^2 + x - 10$
   J. $3x^2 + 11x - 10$
   K. $3x^2 - 11x - 10$

3. A function f is defined by $f(x,y) = x - (xy - y)$. What is the value of $f(8,6)$?

   A. -46
   B. -34
   C. 46
   D. 50
   E. 62

4. What is $\frac{1}{7}$ of 28% of 8,000 ?

   F. $\quad$ 32
   G. $\quad$ 320
   H. $\quad$ 1,568
   J. $\quad$ 3,200
   K. $\quad$ 15,680

DO YOUR FIGURING HERE.

GO ON TO THE NEXT PAGE.

5. If $6x + 3 = 12 + 3x$, then $x = $?

DO YOUR FIGURING HERE.

A. 6

B. 5

C. 3

D. $\dfrac{5}{3}$

E. 1

6. The second term of an arithmetic sequence is –2, and the third term is 8. What is the first term?

(Note: An arithmetic sequence has a common difference between consecutive terms.)

F. –12

G. –10

H. $\dfrac{1}{2}$

J. 3

K. 10

7. Stacie has a bag of solid colored jellybeans. Each jellybean is orange, purple, or pink. If she randomly selects a jellybean from the bag, the probability that the jellybean is orange is $\dfrac{2}{9}$, and the probability that it is purple is $\dfrac{1}{3}$. If there are 72 jellybeans in the bag, how many pink jellybeans are in the bag?

A. 16
B. 24
C. 32
D. 40
E. 48

8. A cellular phone company unveiled a new plan for new customers. It will charge a flat rate of $100 for initial connection and service for the first two months, and $60 for service each subsequent month. If Bob subscribes to this plan for one year, how much does he pay in total for the year?

F. $600
G. $700
H. $720
J. $800
K. $820

GO ON TO THE NEXT PAGE.

9. A square and a regular pentagon (a 5-sided polygon with congruent sides and interior angles) have the same perimeter. One side of the pentagon measures 20 inches. How many inches long is one side of the square?

- **A.** 4
- **B.** 16
- **C.** 25
- **D.** 36
- **E.** 100

DO YOUR FIGURING HERE.

10. Two contractors bid on a job to build a brick wall in a yard. Contractor A charges a flat fee of $1,600 plus $2 per brick. Contractor B charges a flat fee of $400 plus $8 per brick. If x represents the number of bricks in the wall, which of the following equations could be solved to determine the number of bricks which would make B's charge to build the wall equal to A's charge?

- **F.** $1600 + 2x = 400 + 8x$
- **G.** $1600 + 8x = 400 + 2x$
- **H.** $2x + 8x = x$
- **J.** $2x + 8x = 1600$
- **K.** $2x + 8x = 400$

11. Given that $E = ABCD$, which of the following is an expression of B in terms of $E, A, C,$ and D ?

- **A.** $\dfrac{ACD}{E}$
- **B.** $E + ACD$
- **C.** $E - ACD$
- **D.** $\dfrac{E}{ACD}$
- **E.** $EACD$

GO ON TO THE NEXT PAGE.

DO YOUR FIGURING HERE.

12. Lines $\overline{XV}$ and $\overline{YV}$ intersect at point V on line $\overline{WZ}$, as shown in the figure below. The measures of 2 angles are given in terms of a, in degrees. What is the measure of $\angle XVZ$ in degrees?

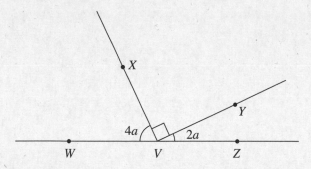

F. 30
G. 90
H. 120
J. 150
K. 180

13. An outdoor thermometer in Hanover, NH reads 70°F. The temperature in Hanover is 25°F cooler than in New Orleans, LA. What is the temperature, C, in degrees Celsius, in New Orleans?

(Note: $F = \dfrac{9}{5}C + 32$)

A. 21°C
B. 35°C
C. 68°C
D. 95°C
E. 113°C

14. If $3x + 2y = 5$, what is the value of the expression $6x + 4y - 7$?

F. −2
G. 3
H. 8
J. 10
K. 19

GO ON TO THE NEXT PAGE.

15. Mike sold $3\frac{2}{7}$ pounds of beef at his deli on Wednesday

    and $2\frac{1}{3}$ pounds of beef on Saturday. Which of the follow-

    ing ranges includes the total amount of beef, in pounds,

    Mike sold during these two days?

    A. At least 5 and less than $5\frac{1}{2}$

    B. At least $5\frac{1}{2}$ and less than $5\frac{2}{3}$

    C. At least $5\frac{2}{3}$ and less than 6

    D. At least 6 and less than $6\frac{1}{2}$

    E. At least $6\frac{1}{2}$ and less than $6\frac{2}{3}$

16. Dave leaves his house and bikes directly east for 3 miles.
    He then turns and bikes directly south for 4 miles. How
    many miles is Dave from his house?

    F. 3
    G. 4
    H. 5
    J. 6
    K. 7

17. A sensor records a piece of data every .0000000038
    seconds. The sensor will record 100,000,000,000 pieces of
    data in how many seconds?

    A. 3,800
    B. 380
    C. 38
    D. 3.8
    E. 0.0038

18. Alan has a rectangular photograph that is 20 centimeters
    wide by 30 centimeters long. Alan wants to reduce the area
    of the photograph by 264 square centimeters by decreasing
    the width and length by the same amount. What will be the
    new dimensions (width by length), in centimeters?

    F. 11 by 24
    G. 12 by 22
    H. 12 by 28
    J. 14 by 24
    K. 16 by 21

GO ON TO THE NEXT PAGE.

19. A quadrilateral has a perimeter of 36 inches. If the lengths of the sides are 4 consecutive, even integers, what is the length, in inches, of the shortest side?

   A. 2
   B. 4
   C. 6
   D. 7
   E. 8

DO YOUR FIGURING HERE.

20. In the standard (x,y) coordinate plane, what is the slope of the line with equation $7y - 3x = 21$?

   F. $-\dfrac{3}{7}$

   G. $\dfrac{3}{7}$

   H. $\dfrac{7}{3}$

   J. 3

   K. 7

21. In the figure shown below, points A, B, C, and D are collinear, and distances marked are in feet. Rectangle $ADEG$ has an area of 48 square feet. What is the area, in square feet, of the trapezoid $BCEF$?

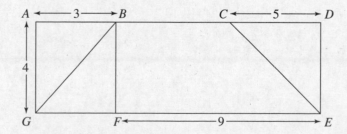

   A. 16
   B. 20
   C. 26
   D. 36
   E. 58

GO ON TO THE NEXT PAGE.

DO YOUR FIGURING HERE.

Use the following information to answer questions 22–24.

Quadrilateral *FGHJ* is shown below in the standard (*x*,*y*) coordinate plane. For this quadrilateral, $FG = 10$, $FJ = 6$, $HJ = \sqrt{136}$, and $GH = 12$.

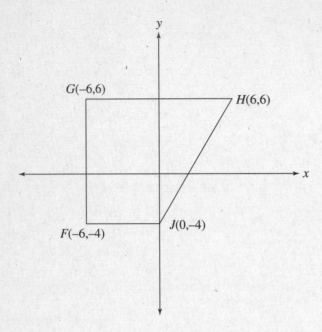

22. Which of the following is closest to the perimeter of quadrilateral *FGHJ*, in coordinate units?

   F.   28.0
   G.   39.7
   H.   60.0
   J.   108.0
   K.   120.0

23. What is the length of $\overline{GJ}$ in coordinate units?

   A.   4
   B.   8
   C.   16
   D. $\sqrt{108}$
   E. $\sqrt{136}$

GO ON TO THE NEXT PAGE.

24. Which of the following are the coordinates of the image of J under a 90° clockwise rotation about the origin?

DO YOUR FIGURING HERE.

- **F.** (−4,0)
- **G.** (0,−4)
- **H.** (0,0)
- **J.** (0,4)
- **K.** (4,0)

25. Which of the following geometric figures has at least 1 rotational symmetry and at least 1 reflectional symmetry?

(Note: The angle of rotation for the rotational symmetry must be less than 360°.)

A.

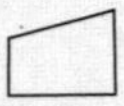

B.

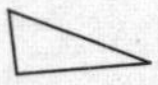

C.

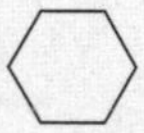

D.

E.

26. What is the coefficient of x^8 in the product of the polynomials below?

$$(-x^4 + 3x^3 - 5x^2 + x - 5)(5x^4 - 2x^3 + x^2 - 5x + 2)$$

- **F.** 0
- **G.** 5
- **H.** 4
- **J.** −2
- **K.** −5

GO ON TO THE NEXT PAGE.

Use the following information to answer questions 27–28.

The stem-and-leaf plot below shows the scores for each golfer in a recent tournament at the Lehigh Valley Golf Club. There were 13 golfers participating in the tournament.

Stem	Leaf
6	6, 7
7	1, 2, 2, 3, 5, 7, 9
8	2, 3, 3, 7

(Note: For example, a score of 72 would have a stem value of 7 and a leaf value of 2.)

27. Which of the following is closest to the mean score of all the golfers in the tournament?

   A. 72.0
   B. 74.4
   C. 75.0
   D. 75.9
   E. 83.0

28. If a score represented in the stem-and-leaf plot is selected randomly, what is the probability that the score selected is exactly 83 ?

   F. $\dfrac{2}{13}$

   G. $\dfrac{4}{13}$

   H. $\dfrac{83}{87}$

   J. $\dfrac{83}{987}$

   K. $\dfrac{166}{987}$

29. What is the least common multiple of 8, 2, 3a, 6b, and 4ab ?

   A. 16ab
   B. 24ab
   C. 24a^2b
   D. 54ab
   E. 60a^2b

GO ON TO THE NEXT PAGE.

DO YOUR FIGURING HERE.

30. Aleksandra began collecting model airplanes in May of 2008. The number of model airplanes that she owns in each month can be modeled by the function $A(m) = 2m + 2$, where $m = 0$ corresponds to May. Using this model, how many model airplanes would you expect Aleksandra to own in December of 2008 ?

   F.   2
   G.   12
   H.   14
   J.   16
   K.   18

31. In the standard (x,y) coordinate plane, line segment $\overline{CD}$ has end points $C(-3,5)$ and $D(11,-7)$. What is the midpoint of $\overline{CD}$?

   A.   (14,–12)
   B.   (8,2)
   C.   (7,1)
   D.   (7,–6)
   E.   (4,–1)

32. Given $x \neq \pm 4$, which of the following is equivalent to the expression $\dfrac{x^2 - 8x + 16}{x^2 - 16}$?

   F. $\dfrac{1}{2}x - 1$

   G. $-8x$

   H. $\dfrac{x-2}{2}$

   J. $\dfrac{1}{x+4}$

   K. $\dfrac{x-4}{x+4}$

33. Evan purchased 6 boxes of sugar cookies, each box containing 10 snack bags and each bag containing 12 cookies. Evan could have purchased the same amount of cookies by buying how many family-sized packs of 30 cookies each?

   A.   12
   B.   24
   C.   48
   D.   72
   E.   180

GO ON TO THE NEXT PAGE.

DO YOUR FIGURING HERE.

34. When $\dfrac{r}{s} = -\dfrac{1}{2}$, $16r^4 - s^4 = ?$

   F.   0
   G.   16
   H.   32
   J.   −16
   K.   −32

35. Emilia is going to bake cookies. She rolls out a square of dough that is 12 inches wide by 12 inches long and cuts 9 identical circular cookies from the dough, as shown in the figure below. Each circular cut-out is tangent to the circular cut-outs next to it and tangent to the edge or edges of the square piece of dough it touches. Approximately, what is the area, in square inches, of the remaining dough, as shown in the figure?

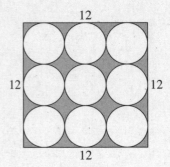

   A.   30.9
   B.   42.3
   C.   50.24
   D.   87.5
   E.   113.04

36. Which of the following lists contains only prime numbers?

   F.   63, 73, and 97
   G.   71, 87, and 91
   H.   73, 89, and 91
   J.   79, 89, and 97
   K.   81, 87, and 97

GO ON TO THE NEXT PAGE.

37. The costs of tutoring packages of different lengths, given in quarter hours, are shown in the table below.

Number of quarter hours	8	10	12	20
Cost	$200	$230	$260	$380

Each cost consists of a fixed charge and a charge per quarter hour. What is the fixed charge?

A. $15
B. $23
C. $80
D. $120
E. $380

38. At 3 p.m., the afternoon sun shines over a building and its rays hit the ground at a 34° angle. The building is 100 meters tall and is perpendicular to the ground. How long, to the nearest meter, is the building's shadow that is cast by the sun?

(Note: sin 34° ≈ 0.56, cos 34° ≈ 0.83, tan 34° ≈ 0.67)

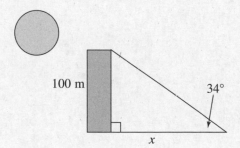

100 m

34°

x

F. 56
G. 67
H. 83
J. 120
K. 148

39. In the standard (x,y) coordinate system, circle O has its center at $(4,-3)$ and a radius of 12 units. Which of the following is an equation of the circle?

A. $(x-4)^2 + (y+3)^2 = 12$
B. $(x+4)^2 + (y+3)^2 = 12$
C. $(x+4)^2 - (y+3)^2 = 12$
D. $(x-4)^2 + (y-3)^2 = 144$
E. $(x-4)^2 + (y+3)^2 = 144$

GO ON TO THE NEXT PAGE.

40. What is the least integer value of x that makes the inequality $\dfrac{14}{21} < \dfrac{x}{12}$ true?

  F.   7
  G.   8
  H.   9
  J.   10
  K.   11

41. When $f(a) = a^2 + 2a + 5$, what is the value of $f(a+b)$?

  A. $a^2 + b^2 + 2ab + 5$
  B. $a^2 + b^2 + 2a + 2b + 10$
  C. $a^2 + b^2 + 2a + 2b + 5$
  D. $(a+b)^2 + a + b + 5$
  E. $(a+b)^2 + 2a + 2b + 5$

42. In the figure below, M is on $\overline{LN}$ and O is on $\overline{NP}$. $\overline{LP}$ and $\overline{MO}$ are parallel. The dimensions given are in feet. What is the length, in feet, of $\overline{NO}$?

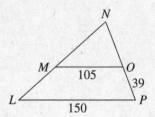

  F.   39
  G.   91
  H.   105
  J.   273
  K.   294

43. Gina watched as a plane took off from the runway and climbed to 30,000 feet. She calculated the plane's height, h feet, t seconds after takeoff to be given by $h = 1{,}200 + 32t$. To the nearest second, how many seconds did it take the plane to climb to a height of 2 miles? (Note: 1 mile = 5,280 feet)

  A.   37
  B.   128
  C.   293
  D.   900
  E.   1,264

GO ON TO THE NEXT PAGE.

44. In $\triangle ABC$, the measures of $\angle A$, $\angle B$, and $\angle C$ are $2x°$, $3x°$, and $5x°$, respectively. What is the measure of $\angle C$?

F. 18°
G. 36°
H. 54°
J. 90°
K. 180°

DO YOUR FIGURING HERE.

45. A basketball player has attempted 30 free throws and made 12 of them. Starting now, if he makes every free throw attempted, what is the *least* number of additional free throws he must attempt to raise his free-throw percentage to at least 55%?

(Note: Free-throw percentage =

$\dfrac{number\ of\ free\ throws\ made}{number\ of\ free\ throws\ attempted} \times 100$.)

A. 5
B. 10
C. 16
D. 17
E. 29

46. If y is a negative integer, which of the following has the least value?

F. $\sqrt[3]{y^2}$

G. 100^y

H. $\dfrac{\pi}{y}$

J. $\dfrac{1}{y^2}$

K. $\dfrac{1}{y^3}$

47. Jonathan, Ellery, and 3 other groomsmen are rehearsing for a wedding by walking down an aisle one at a time, one groomsman in front of the other. Each time all 5 walk down the aisle, the groom tells them to walk in a different order from first to last. What is the greatest number of times the groomsmen can walk down the aisle without walking in the same order twice?

A. 3,125
B. 720
C. 120
D. 100
E. 25

GO ON TO THE NEXT PAGE.

DO YOUR FIGURING HERE.

48. In the circle below, O is the center and measures 5 inches from chord $\overline{MN}$. The area of the circle is 169π square inches. What is the length of $\overline{MN}$, in inches?

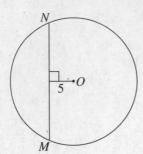

    F. 12
    G. 13
    H. 18
    J. 24
    K. 26

49. What is the x–intercept of the line that passes through points $(-3,7)$ and $(6,4)$ in the standard (x,y) coordinate plane?

    A. $(18,0)$

    B. $(0,\frac{1}{3})$

    C. $(0,6)$

    D. $(0,18)$

    E. $(\frac{1}{3},0)$

50. Which of the following equations represent a graph that intersects the x axis at $x = 7$?

    F. $y = (x + 7)^2$
    G. $y = (x - 7)^2$
    H. $y = (-x - 7)^2$
    J. $y - 7 = x^2$
    K. $y + 7 = x^2$

GO ON TO THE NEXT PAGE.

51. If $0° < \theta < 90°$ and $\tan \theta = \dfrac{2}{9}$, what is $\sin \theta + \cos \theta$?

A.　$\dfrac{11}{\sqrt{85}}$

B.　$\dfrac{-7}{\sqrt{170}}$

C.　$\dfrac{11}{\sqrt{170}}$

D.　$\dfrac{9}{\sqrt{85}}$

E.　$\dfrac{2}{\sqrt{85}}$

52. In the figure below, $\overline{OA} = \overline{AB}$, and $\overline{OB}$ is a radius of the circle, having a length of 8 inches. What is the area of $\triangle OAB$, in square inches?

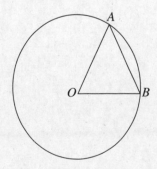

F.　$8\sqrt{3}$

G.　$16\sqrt{3}$

H.　32

J.　$32\sqrt{3}$

K.　64

GO ON TO THE NEXT PAGE.

DO YOUR FIGURING HERE.

53. In $\triangle XYZ$, shown below, $\overline{YZ} = 30$. Which of the following represents the length of $\overline{XY}$?

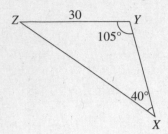

(Note: For a triangle with sides of lengths x, y, and z, and respective opposite angles measuring X, Y, and Z, it will be true that: $\dfrac{\sin X}{x} = \dfrac{\sin Y}{y} = \dfrac{\sin Z}{z}$, according to the law of sines.)

A. $\dfrac{30\sin 105°}{\sin 35°}$

B. $\dfrac{30\sin 105°}{\sin 40°}$

C. $\dfrac{30\sin 35°}{\sin 40°}$

D. $\dfrac{30\sin 105°}{\sin 40°}$

E. $\dfrac{30\sin 40°}{\sin 105°}$

54. Points P and Q lie on circle O with radius of 9 feet. The measure of $\angle POQ$ is 120°. What is the length, in feet, of minor arc $\overparen{PQ}$?

F. 3π
G. 6π
H. 9π
J. 18π
K. 27π

GO ON TO THE NEXT PAGE.

55. $\begin{bmatrix} w & x \\ y & z \end{bmatrix} - \begin{bmatrix} x & y \\ z & w \end{bmatrix} - \begin{bmatrix} \dfrac{1}{w+x} & \dfrac{1}{x+y} \\ \dfrac{1}{y+z} & \dfrac{1}{z+w} \end{bmatrix} = ?$

A. $\begin{bmatrix} 1 & 1 \\ 1 & 1 \end{bmatrix}$

B. $\begin{bmatrix} \dfrac{w-x}{w+x} & \dfrac{x-y}{x+y} \\ \dfrac{y-z}{y+z} & \dfrac{d-a}{d+a} \end{bmatrix}$

C. $\begin{bmatrix} w-x-\dfrac{1}{w+x} & x-y-\dfrac{1}{x+y} \\ y-z-\dfrac{1}{y+z} & z-w-\dfrac{1}{z+w} \end{bmatrix}$

D. $\begin{bmatrix} \dfrac{wx}{w+x} & \dfrac{xy}{x+y} \\ \dfrac{yz}{y+z} & \dfrac{zw}{z+w} \end{bmatrix}$

E. $\begin{bmatrix} \dfrac{1}{2w-2x} & \dfrac{1}{2x-2y} \\ \dfrac{1}{2y-2z} & \dfrac{1}{2z-2w} \end{bmatrix}$

56. If function f is defined by $f(x) = -2x^3$, then what is the value of $f(f(1))$?

F. −16
G. −8
H. 4
J. 8
K. 16

GO ON TO THE NEXT PAGE.

57. The function y varies directly as x for all real numbers in the (x, y) coordinate plane. Which of the following could be the graph of y ?

DO YOUR FIGURING HERE.

A.

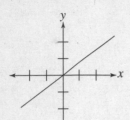

D.

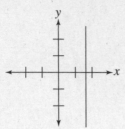

B.

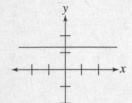

E.

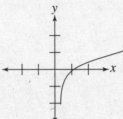

C.

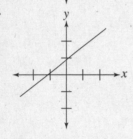

58. Gopi took 5 quizzes for which the scores are integer values ranging from 0 to 10. The median of her scores is 9. The mean of her scores is 8. The only mode of her scores is 10. Which of the following *must* be true about her quiz scores?

F. Her lowest score is 4.
G. Her lowest score is 5.
H. The median of the 3 lowest scores is 6.
J. The sum of the 5 scores is 50.
K. The sum of the 2 lowest scores is 11.

59. To make a cardboard table for her dollhouse, Ouisie uses a rectangular piece of cardboard measuring 40 inches wide and 60 inches long. She cuts four equal-sized squares from each corner and folds down the sides at a 90° angle. If the top of the table measures 800 square inches, how tall, in inches, is the table?

A. 40
B. 30
C. 25
D. 20
E. 10

GO ON TO THE NEXT PAGE.

60. Which of the following expressions gives the area, in square feet, of △*ABC*, shown below with the given side lengths in feet?

DO YOUR FIGURING HERE.

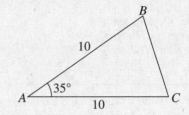

F. 50 tan 35°
G. 50 cos 35°
H. 50 sin 35°
J. 100 cos 35°
K. 100 sin 35°

READING TEST
35 Minutes—40 Questions

DIRECTIONS: There are four passages in this test. Each passage is followed by several questions. After reading each passage, choose the best answer to each question and blacken the corresponding oval on your answer document. You may refer to the passages as often as necessary.

Passage I

PROSE FICTION: This passage is adapted from the novel *Shipwreck* by Adam C. Thomas (© 2005 by Adam Thomas).

"Let the dead bury their dead."

The words rang in the boy's ears as he trudged through the inhospitable jungle, vines snarling around his ankles. Over and over again, he heard the captain shout, "Full speed ahead,
5 let the dead bury their dead."

Now the captain was gone and the boy felt alone despite his companions, now leading him through the alien jungle. He wondered what the words meant. How can the dead do anything? How can the dead have dead of their own?

10   These thoughts circled the boy's head, intermingled with the events of the last days. Again he heard the roar of the storm, felt the ship bucking and braying beneath his feet. The typhoon had come out of nowhere, it had seemed; even the captain, who surely knew everything, was taken aback by
15 its sudden appearance.

"Avast and hold the mainsail!" he shouted to the crew. "Stay fast and let the dead bury their dead!"

The boy had held fast, even as the ship had come apart. Even as the lightning lit up the sky like the fireworks the boy
20 had heard about, but never seen. Even as the thunder filled the air, shaking the very timbers of the ship with its bellowing ferocity. The walls of water rose up, crashing over the deck, then receded for an instant of calm before rising up as a dark mountain to once again besiege the small ship.

25   These memories would come to the boy in a split-second, filling his brain before he had a chance to consciously remember what had happened. Then they would recede, just as the storm had eventually receded, and the jungle would return, the monotonous trudging, day after day amid the vines and
30 trees that were nothing like his second home on the ocean.

Sometimes, the boy would think back to before the storm, and even before the ship, to his life on land—the stultifying life on the farm where he felt landlocked before he even understood what that word signified. He thought of his mother

35 and father, frail and worn-looking. He believed his parents did all they could to create a home for him, but his mother's sad, creased face and his father's cracked hands crowded out all other childhood memories. They filled the boy's sky, just as the thunder had, and were just as devastating, in their own
40 way, as the storm.

For the boy, his birthplace's rocky ground yielded only a life he could not live and a place he could not love. But the sea was softer, a malleable place in which an enterprising lad could reinvent himself. So the boy had run off to sea. He
45 vowed to leave the land forever to live atop the ocean. Now he had learned the hardness of the sea, he thought, as he jerked his mind back to the jungle.

Soon, his thoughts drifted back to his blissful days upon the ship. Although he had come aboard as a stowaway, the
50 captain took him in and gave him daily lessons in reading the stars and plotting the ship's course. "Ignorance is dangerous, not only aboard ship but also in life," the captain warned. The eager boy soon grew familiar with the night's sky and knew the maps in the captain's quarters as well as he knew his own
55 reflection. He had felt so secure in the captain's knowledge and in his own growing understanding.

But if the captain could be caught unawares, how could the boy ever feel safe again? How could he trust that everything the captain had said wouldn't lead to the same disastrous end?

60   "Let the dead bury their dead." Well, he had seen the dead after the storm. As the remaining crew members had urged him away from the wreckage, finally having to pull him by his arms to force his legs to move, the words "Let the dead bury their dead" appeared unbidden in his mind. But what
65 did those words mean? Searching his memory, the boy was shocked to find that after the shipwreck, his mind's eye could no longer distinguish the captain from any other man—the cook, the lowest deckhand, or even the boy's father. Was that what the captain meant by "their dead"—that all the dead
70 belonged to one another?

He walked mechanically, pace after pace, leading him away from the remains of his home and the only man he had ever loved. Toward what? He had no knowledge of what lay ahead. But still his legs moved, seemingly of their own

GO ON TO THE NEXT PAGE.

75 accord, his heart continued to beat, his lungs continued to fill
with air. His mind continued to retrace his life, and with the
beating of his heart and the filling of his lungs, still he walked.

1. As it is used in line 32, the word *stultifying* most nearly
means:

   A. stifling.
   B. strengthening.
   C. welcoming.
   D. productive.

2. The first seven paragraphs (lines 1–30) establish all of the
following about the boy EXCEPT that he:

   F. had companions on the walk through the jungle.
   G. had often watched fireworks light up the sky.
   H. respected the captain.
   J. often had his thoughts filled with memories of the
storm.

3. The passage states that the boy saw himself as:

   A. contented with life in the jungle.
   B. afraid of his mother.
   C. toughened by farm labor.
   D. at home on the sea.

4. The time sequence of the passage indicates that the shipwreck takes place:

   F. after the boy leaves the farm.
   G. after the boy walks through the jungle.
   H. before the boy meets the captain.
   J. before his mother tries to protect him.

5. How does the twelfth paragraph (lines 60–70) offer one
way to interpret the phrase "let the dead bury their dead,"
as implied by the passage?

   A. The boy remembers the captain's explanation of this
phrase.
   B. The dead cannot do anything, so one should trust only
the living.
   C. Death erases the distinctions that make the living
unique individuals.
   D. Without his experiences, the boy cannot expect to lead
a better life.

6. Compared to the captain's ideas, the boy's are:

   F. opposing; the captain is uncertain about the meaning
of the phrase, "let the dead bury their dead."
   G. opposing; the captain understood why the boy's father
was worn down.
   H. similar; the captain disliked the harsh life of the sea.
   J. similar; the captain valued learning and knowledge.

7. It is most reasonable to infer from the passage that the
ship's remaining crewmates accompanying the boy on his
walk through the jungle would agree with which of the
following statements about the boy?

   A. The boy's grief over the captain's death made him
unwilling to leave the scene of the shipwreck.
   B. The boy's grief over the captain's death made him run
away from his companions.
   C. The boy was constantly startled by loud noises.
   D. The boy hated his life on land and had escaped to the
sea to find freedom.

8. Which of the following statements best describes the
actions taken by the captain on finding the boy stowed
away on the ship?

   F. He scolds the boy because he did not pay the fare for
passage on the ship.
   G. He teaches the boy the meaning of the phrase "let the
dead bury their dead."
   H. He teaches the boy how to navigate using maps and
the stars.
   J. He ignores the boy, leaving him to fend for himself.

9. According to the passage, the storm features all of the
following EXCEPT:

   A. loud thunder.
   B. huge walls of water.
   C. bright lightning.
   D. ferocious hail.

10. Which of the following statements about the storm is supported by the passage?

   F. It blew up without warning, taking the captain by
surprise.
   G. It happened in the middle of the night.
   H. It was the most violent storm any of the crew had ever
seen.
   J. It was the storm the boy's father had warned him
about.

GO ON TO THE NEXT PAGE.

Passage II

SOCIAL SCIENCE: This passage is adapted from the article "Slang: Why It's Totally Sweet" by Patrick Tyrrell (© 2008 by Patrick Tyrrell).

Tony Thorne's email inbox is bloated with messages from teenagers and college students around the world explicating the meaning behind local terms such as "toop," "tonk," and "chung." Why would the Director of the Language Center at
5 King's College of London concern himself with seemingly nonsensical linguistic inventions?

Thorne is busy compiling a current dictionary of slang from around the English-speaking world. Although *neologisms*, new adaptations or inventions of words, are normally
10 born out of a specific geographic and cultural context, the ease of worldwide communication ushered in by the technological age has made slang an instantly exportable commodity. College students in Iowa are just as likely to use British slang like "bum" (one's posterior) as British homemakers are to employ
15 American slang like "dust bunny," since both groups are exposed to each other's movies, TV, music, and other media.

In the world of linguistics, slang is often viewed condescendingly as an affliction of vulgar speech, its users condemned for their intellectual laziness. Early 20th century
20 linguist Oliver Wendell Holmes described slang as "at once a sign and a cause of mental atrophy." Meanwhile, Thorne points out, some legendary authors such as Walt Whitman elevated the status of slang, referring to it as "an attempt by common humanity to escape from bald literalism, and express
25 itself illimitably."

What are the origins of most slang words? Many philologists, those who attempt to study and determine the meaning of historical texts, believe that slang is created as a response to the status quo, that its usage represents a defiant opposition
30 of authority. For example, many Americans use the phrase *a cup of joe* to refer to a cup of coffee; however, few know that it originated from one Admiral Joe Daniels who in 1914 denied his sailors wine. As a result, they decided their strict leader was a fitting namesake for the terribly acidic black
35 coffee they were forced to drink instead.

Thorne, however, would point out that most slang is derived for much more innocent purposes. For example, terms like "ankle-biters" (infants), "ramping up" (on the job training), and "Googling" (searching on the internet) do not involve
40 opposition to authority. Usually, slang evolves out of very insular groups with specific needs for informative or vibrant expressions that normal language does not encapsulate. It is the marriage of jargon, nuance, and effective imagery. While traditional hotbeds of slang have been the military, industrial
45 factories, and street markets, most modern slang comes from such arenas as corporate offices, college campuses, and users/designers of computers.

In determining the sources of slang terms, Thorne and his contemporaries repeatedly refine their definition of "slang"
50 as distinctive from "idioms," "euphemisms," "hyperbole," and other instances of conventional figurative language. Many linguists consider slang the polar opposite of formal speech, with other figurative language devices falling somewhere in between. Whereas a "colloquialism" still indicates a mea-
55 sure of respect owed to the expression's regional usefulness, "slang" brands a word as having fallen into a state of overused emptiness.

How do we know when a word has become overused or empty? Much slang is attached to some sense of style or fad
60 and therefore risks being as short-lived in nature as the trend upon which it is based. However, some terms such as "punk" and "cool" have been in common use for a century or more and have completely assimilated into the acceptable mainstream dialect. Clearly, then, some words fall into a gray area
65 between slang and proper language. Although lexicologists like Thorne attempt to define and apply standard principles in their classification of slang, there is definitely some subjectivity involved in determining whether a term deserves the maligning moniker.

70 Furthermore, intellectuals who would categorically denounce slang struggle with the fact that slang, when first conceived, involves as much inherent creativity and word play as the figurative language revered in poetry. It is ultimately how the word survives, or rather who continues to use it, that
75 determines its stature as artful rhetoric or the dreaded slang. If "respectable" people continue to use an expression for its conceptual vivacity, then the word was a clever invention worth enriching a nation's lexicon. If the "common man" uses a term and uses it too liberally, the word is deemed slang,
80 and an eloquent speaker will have the tastefulness to avoid it.

Whatever slang's level of social esteem, Thorne believes that it is an essential project to compile accurate modern dictionaries of its usage. When one considers the large amount of written artifacts our present world creates on a daily basis,
85 it is reasonable to also consider providing future generations (or civilizations) of humans with an effective way of decoding our meaning, which could easily be confused by our prevalent use of slang. Imagine how much less debate there would be over the meaning of some Shakespearean verses if we had a
90 detailed description of his contemporary slang. Because of this need to inform future scholars, Thorne's dictionary of slang attempts to not only define each term but also to explain its origins, connotations, and typical conversational uses.

GO ON TO THE NEXT PAGE.

11. Based on the passage, Thorne most likely describes some slang as *innocent* (line 37) to indicate his belief that not all slang is created to be:

A. rebellious.
B. informative.
C. nuanced.
D. accusatory.

12. The author includes the information in the last paragraph primarily to:

F. criticize Thorne for being too subjective with which words he chooses to include in his dictionary.
G. illustrate how a future scholar might be able to use Thorne's dictionary as a resource.
H. identify the ways Thorne uses Shakespearean slang to describe modern terms.
J. argue that Thorne's dictionary should be the primary focus of modern linguistics.

13. All of the following groups are mentioned in the passage as related to the academic study of slang EXCEPT:

A. philologists.
B. college professors.
C. linguists.
D. lexicologists.

14. The quotation marks around the phrase "common man" in line 78 primarily serve to:

F. emphasize the subjective and somewhat derogatory process of categorizing people and the words they use.
G. reveal the author's suspicion that the man in question is not common at all.
H. introduce a demeaning term the author believes is appropriate to describe users of slang.
J. show how an inventive term may enjoy popularity briefly but ultimately does not have the proper usage to survive.

15. As it is used in line 18, the word *vulgar* most nearly means:

A. sickening.
B. malicious.
C. unsophisticated.
D. profane.

16. The passage indicates that the efforts to compile current dictionaries of slang are viewed by some as essential because these dictionaries:

F. could possibly provide future scholars with a way of deciphering the meaning of today's writings.
G. are the only way that speakers of other languages can decode the subtle meaning of English texts.
H. currently do not exist except for those chronicling Shakepeare's era.
J. will provide modern English speakers with the correct conversational uses of each slang term.

17. According to the passage, Walt Whitman seems to view the use of slang as an attempt to:

A. show civility.
B. conform to traditions.
C. broaden expression.
D. defy authority.

18. The main purpose of the first paragraph in relation to the passage is to:

F. acquaint the reader with some examples of slang.
G. establish that British scholars are the leaders in slang research.
H. introduce slang as a possibly surprising topic of academic study.
J. outline Tony Thorne's problems with managing his email inbox.

19. The author's reference to groups like the military as being *hotbeds* of slang (line 44) most nearly means that such groups are:

A. prophetic.
B. old-fashioned.
C. innovative.
D. strict.

20. The passage suggests that of the following, which one encapsulates the greatest obstacle for intellectuals who would categorically denounce slang?

F. Their own invention of some slang terms
G. Disagreement on how certain slang terms are used
H. Respect for Thorne's academic interest and tireless determination.
J. Appreciation for the creativity involved in the origination of slang

GO ON TO THE NEXT PAGE.

Passage III

HUMANITIES: This passage is excerpted from the entry "Antonio Gaudi" in *Great Spanish Architects* (© 2006 by Teshigahara Press).

Most of the world's great cathedrals are impressive in their size and beauty, but the Sagrada Familia stands apart even from these architectural masterpieces because of its unique and startling design. This stunning cathedral tow-
5   ers above Barcelona like a strange, ornate sandcastle. With bright carvings of fruit baskets, a central nave that mirrors a forest of trees, bizarre spires, and beautiful spiral staircases, the iconic Sagrada Familia has become as well-known as the Eiffel Tower or Statue of Liberty. Moreover, the Sagrada
10 Familia captures the "freakish genius" of its designer Antoni Gaudi better than any of his other creations.

Today, crowds flock to Barcelona to witness Gaudi's great works, including Casa Mila, Casa Battlo, Palau Güell, Park Güell, and, of course, the Sagrada Familia. However,
15 the current popularity of Gaudi's work would not have been foreseen when he first unveiled his creations. Critics of his time described his work as hideous and compared his build-ings to monsters or dungeons; as recently as 50 years ago, the so-called genius of Gaudi was not well-recognized.

20 Antoni Gaudi I Cornet was born in 1852 to a family of artisans in a small town in northern Spain. When he was 16, he moved to Barcelona to finish his secondary education and study architecture. Even at this early age, he engendered controversy: often truant from class, he criticized the standard
25 architectural education of the day and complained that his classes were devoid of creativity. Ultimately, he was granted a degree, but just barely. His school director insightfully commented that Gaudi was either "a genius or a madman."

After graduation, Gaudi remained in Barcelona. The city
30 was growing, and rich benefactors were looking for artists to design modern, trendy buildings. In his mid-twenties, Gaudi met his lifelong patron Eusebi Guell, a wealthy industrialist and politician. For almost four decades, Güell would fund Gaudi's work for a wide array of venues, from Güell's private
35 mansion (the Palau Güell) to a massive public park (Park Güell) to the Guells' own crypt.

Nature was Gaudi's muse; many artists find inspiration in nature as he did, but few actually carved shapes found in nature such as trees, fruit baskets, lizards, and bones into
40 the physical architecture of his buildings. For example, the Sagrada Familia has huge carvings of fruit baskets amid its spires. Gaudi said that nature was "the Great Book, always open, that we should force ourselves to read." For Gaudi, nature was inspiration for the forms and motifs of his buildings
45 and for the colors he used liberally. In order to represent the limitless diversity of colors found in nature, he even forged a new architectural practice known as *trencadis*, in which tiles,

bottles, and pottery were smashed into small tiles to create abstract mosaics.

50 In 1883, Gaudi began work on his masterpiece, the Sagrada Familia. However, when the initial and substantial financial contributions for the church's construction fizzled out completely around the turn of the century, Gaudi had to sell his own home and even beg on street corners to raise funds.
55 As his health declined in later years, Gaudi moved into the Sagrada Familia to be closer to "his temple" and remained there for the rest of his life. At the time of his death, forty-three years after construction began, the church was only 15 percent complete.

60 Conflicting artistic vision and pesky finances have been the source of much grief for those who have hoped to finish Gaudi's vision for the Sagrada Familia. After his death, poli-ticians and architects clashed over whether other architects would be able to do his design justice. Eventually, the major
65 players agreed that the blueprints and plans Gaudi left behind would be sufficient to achieve his vision; unfortunately, bomb-ing during the Spanish Civil War destroyed Gaudi's crypt, workroom, and all the remaining designs. Construction on the church slowly resumed in the mid-1950s, in part due to
70 a lot more funding than in the past, but little progress was made until the 1980s, when steady donations began funding significant progress. However, the church will still take at least another three decades to realize Gaudi's complete design. It is likely, moreover, that there will always be grumblings that
75 modern architects ruined the purity of Gaudi's design.

In recent decades, the art world has experienced a renewed appreciation of the style known as Art Nuevo. As the most famous of all Art Nuevo architects, Gaudi has been showered with acclaim. In fact, Barcelona declared 2002 the Year of
80 Gaudi and held over 30 exhibitions and events in his honor. Buildings that had previously been closed to the public were opened for the first time, and over 90,000 people gathered in front of the Sagrada Familia to celebrate the 150th anniversary of Gaudi's birth.

85 Gaudi would most likely approve of such recognition. He never doubted his creative genius, did not allow his assistants to question him, and persevered with his fanciful designs despite harsh reviews by critics of his day. Current critics, however, see the gift of Gaudi as clearly as he did at the
90 time. After decades of functional designs in the architectural world, Gaudi's architecture-as-art is once more popular. As modern architect Norman Foster asserts, "Gaudi's methods, one century on, continue to be revolutionary." His genius is and will continue to be undisputed.

GO ON TO THE NEXT PAGE.

21. It can be most reasonably inferred from the passage that the author views the description of Gaudi as a "freakish genius" in line 10 as:

A. an overstatement of Gaudi's skill and contributions to modern architecture.
B. an inadequate explanation of a complex man and his controversial contributions to architecture.
C. a reasonable suggestion for how first-time viewers should explore Gaudi's work.
D. an accurate representation of the view of Gaudi's skill and artistic vision many current critics hold.

22. Based on information in the passage, when were donors LEAST likely to fund construction of the Sagrada Familia?

F. 1880s
G. 1900s
H. 1950s
J. 1980s

23. The passage's author indicates that compared to the world's other great cathedrals, the Sagrada Familia is:

A. more remarkable in terms of appearance and design.
B. less remarkable in terms of size and beauty.
C. more likely to be a part of the ongoing debate about how to construct a building after the original designer has died.
D. less likely to influence future architectural designs by new artists in Europe.

24. The main purpose of the third paragraph (lines 20–28) is to make clear that from a young age, and throughout his childhood, Gaudi:

F. was a controversial figure who caused a stir within traditional artist circles.
G. came from a family of artists and therefore was a natural artist, destined for great success.
H. was a mediocre and uninspired student who disliked learning about architecture, despite the later success he achieved.
J. was just one of many students who found the education of his day boring, unsatisfying, and unrelated to real artistic skill.

25. The word *array*, as it is used in line 34, could reasonably mean any of the following EXCEPT:

A. arrangement.
B. range.
C. selection.
D. variety.

26. As used in line 74, the word *grumblings* most nearly means:

F. churnings.
G. criticisms.
H. theories.
J. growling.

27. The passage suggests that in the late 19th century, compared to Gaudi, other contemporary artists were:

A. more reserved when trying new artistic forms and techniques.
B. less inhibited when trying new artistic forms and techniques.
C. more focused on perfecting architectural techniques.
D. less focused on perfecting architectural techniques.

28. According to the passage, one reason that politicians and architects agreed to continue construction of the Sagrada Familia after Gaudi's death was:

F. the survival of Gaudi's original designs to effectively guide ongoing work.
G. they witnessed the stunning design of the cathedral in person.
H. they wished to complete as much as possible before the impending Civil War.
J. the popularity of Gaudi's design inspired the public to demand its construction.

29. It can most reasonably be inferred from the passage that throughout his lifetime, from his schoolboy days to his years as a well-established artist, Gaudi:

A. successfully overcame harsh and damaging criticisms of his work to complete his lifetime dreams.
B. created both excitement and controversy over his non-traditional designs and techniques.
C. blurred the distinction between art and nature, using natural plants and animals as motifs.
D. adjusted a building's design to conform to its location, his patron's vision, and the environmental conditions.

30. It can most reasonably be inferred from the discussion of architecture-as-art's renewed popularity that in previous generations, some architects:

F. were never open to creative and unconventional designs.
G. preferred classic designs inspired by historical architecture.
H. created practical designs that were not necessarily aesthetically pleasing.
J. do not have one single design that they preferred and identified with.

GO ON TO THE NEXT PAGE.

Passage IV

NATURAL SCIENCE: This passage is excerpted from the article "Frank Drake and Project Ozma" by Arnold C. Topton (© 2004 by Crackpot Press).

On a cool April night in 1960, in Green Bank, West Virginia, Frank Drake became a scientific pioneer. Careful research had given him reason to believe that, if he tuned his radio to the correct frequency and aimed it at the correct
5 stars, he might pick up interstellar transmissions from another planet. Hoping for a breakthrough, he tuned the radio and began to listen.

So began Project Ozma, widely considered the first organized attempt to detect alien life by way of radio. Al-
10 though it was ultimately unsuccessful in its goal of finding other intelligent life in the universe, Project Ozma was hugely influential, inspiring the creation of many similar programs. The following fifty years would see a steady increase in both the sophistication and the scope of similar programs, ranging
15 from a wide-ranging but short-term program funded by NASA to the meticulously orchestrated Project Phoenix, designed to monitor carefully selected regions of space over a period of ten years. Today, many such programs are ongoing, in locations as august as the University of California at Berkeley and the
20 University of Western Sydney, both of which have reputations that draw respected scientists from around the world.

The scientists involved in the Search for Extraterrestrial Intelligence, or SETI, are far from the wide-eyed dreamers that many people associate with the field. The SETI scientists
25 are, in fact, esteemed academics, typically specializing in the areas of physics, astronomy, and engineering. Indeed, they have to be able to complete such complex tasks as calculating where to position the radios so as to achieve the best effect, deciding what messages are most likely to be understood
30 by an alien culture, and determining which stars to monitor.

Although these scientists' understanding of the origins of life on Earth is still imperfect, those involved in SETI do have some idea of what combinations of size, location, and chemical composition make a planet more likely to harbor
35 intelligent life. The general understanding is that there are two main factors that determine whether or not a planet is habitable (able to sustain life): temperature and mass. There are other factors that are often considered, such as the presence of certain chemicals, the proximity of other planets, and
40 planetary age, but temperature and mass are the initial, and most crucial, tests.

Liquid water is widely believed to be critical to the development of life, and this belief has led scientists to hypothesize that, in order to support life, a planet must experience tem-
45 peratures that fall within a range that allows for the presence of liquid water. This, in turn, suggests that hospitable planets must be located within a certain distance of their respective suns. If a planet is too far from the sun, its temperatures will fall below that range, as in the case of Saturn. If a planet is
50 too close to the sun, as in the case of Venus, its temperatures will be too high. Planets that fall within the range of appropriate temperatures are often called "Goldilocks Planets," since they are neither too hot nor too cold but instead "just right" to provide environments hospitable to life. However, even
55 when a planet is found that is within this range, there is still no guarantee that all of the related factors will be suitable. It is also necessary that the planet have an orbit that allows the planet to rotate at a speed and angle that prevents either side from freezing or boiling, ruling out most binary systems due
60 to their unstable orbits.

The other key to habitability is the mass of a planet. In order to sustain life, a planet must have sufficient mass to hold a gravitational field, while not having so much as to create an excessively heavy atmosphere. Truly massive planets also
65 tend to retain hydrogen gases and become "gas giants" with no solid surface. How large a planet can be, while retaining the ability to host living organisms, depends in part on that planet's distance from the sun. Larger planets have heavier atmospheres, so they also tend to retain more heat, creating a
70 greenhouse effect, wherein atmospheric gases absorb radiation, causing an increase in temperature. Therefore, a planet on the outer edge of the Goldilocks zone might be able to sustain life if its mass were great enough to hold in enough heat to bring the temperature back into the habitable zone, while a
75 smaller planet might be able to do the same on the inner edge.

The search for extraterrestrial life, and perhaps intelligence, that started in West Virginia back in 1960 continues today. The more knowledge scientists are able to gather about our own galaxy, the better equipped they will be when it comes
80 to seeking out similar planets outside our solar system. Perhaps someday Frank Drake's dream of a message from outer space will come true—once we know where to look for it.

31. According to the passage, Frank Drake:

    A. was one of the first scientists to use radio technology to look for alien life.
    B. successfully found signs of extraterrestrial life.
    C. ran Project Phoenix from his radio telescope in West Virginia.
    D. is a highly esteemed astronomer and physicist.

GO ON TO THE NEXT PAGE.

32. Which of the following would be the most appropriate characterization of Project Ozma, as portrayed by the author of the passage?

    F. Its unexpected success took the scientific community by surprise, altering the face of the field.

    G. Although it was a failure in one sense, it helped usher in a new era of interstellar research.

    H. Drake's goals were unrealistic, given his limited knowledge and resources.

    J. Without the financial support of institutions such as NASA, the Project was doomed to failure.

33. As it is used in line 19, the word *august* most nearly means:

    A. summery.

    B. elusive.

    C. esteemed.

    D. antique.

34. As conveyed in the passage, the author's attitude toward the search for life on other planets is:

    F. ironic yet sympathetic.

    G. scornful and angry.

    H. hopeful yet pragmatic.

    J. uncertain and fearful.

35. According to the passage, scientists involved in the search for life on other planets are likely to be:

    A. trained in scientific disciplines such as physics, astronomy, and engineering.

    B. wide-eyed dreamers prone to unrealistic expectations about space.

    C. employed at institutions such as universities or NASA.

    D. skilled radio mechanics, due to their work with radio telescopes.

36. The primary point of the fourth paragraph (lines 31–41) is that:

    F. even today scientists do not understand why life developed on our planet.

    G. liquid water is crucial to the evolution of intelligent life on any planet.

    H. only planets within a "Goldilocks Zone" are able to sustain life.

    J. there appear to be two crucial components in determining whether a planet may be habitable.

37. It can reasonably be inferred that, as it is used in line 46, the term *hospitable planets* is intended to mean:

    A. planets with cultures that are similar to those found on our planet.

    B. locations outside of our solar system that are in close proximity to the sun.

    C. binary planets with generally stable orbits and moderate temperatures.

    D. places with temperatures and masses that fall within the range able to support life.

38. Based on the information in the passage, Saturn is most likely unable to sustain life because:

    F. its close proximity to the sun causes a greenhouse effect.

    G. the atmosphere is too heavy to allow for liquid water to exist.

    H. its distance from the sun is too great for it to contain liquid water.

    J. it is an unstable gas giant, due to the chemical combinations present.

39. The passage indicates that any new planet discovered in a location that is comparable to Venus' location, relative to the sun, would most likely be:

    A. an overheated gas giant, due to its heavy atmosphere.

    B. incapable of supporting life due to its lack of a gravitational field.

    C. prone to the development of an unstable orbit.

    D. unable to sustain life unless it were small enough not to retain too much heat.

40. According to the passage, Goldilocks Planets are characterized by:

    F. temperatures that are moderate enough to allow for the existence of liquid water.

    G. heavy atmospheres that retain hydrogen gases, creating a greenhouse effect.

    H. either extremely hot or extremely cold temperatures, depending on proximity to the sun.

    J. the presence of both liquid water and a high concentration of hydrogen gases.

END OF TEST 3
STOP! DO NOT TURN THE PAGE UNTIL TOLD TO DO SO.
DO NOT RETURN TO A PREVIOUS TEST.

SCIENCE REASONING TEST

35 Minutes—40 Questions

DIRECTIONS: There are seven passages in the following section. Each passage is followed by several questions. After reading a passage, choose the best answer to each question and blacken the corresponding oval on your answer document. You may refer to the passages as often as necessary.

You are NOT permitted to use a calculator on this test.

Passage I

In recent years, the technology of magnetic levitation ("maglev") has been investigated to provide an alternative rapid transportation option. Using repulsion of magnetic fields, maglev trains can be pushed forward at speeds of up to 300 miles per hour. One specific type of magnetic levitation currently being investigated is electrodynamic suspension (EDS).

In EDS, magnetic rods are located at the bottom of the maglev train and within the track underneath the train. An electric current can induce a magnetic field in the magnets of the track. If this magnetic field can be induced to repel constantly the magnet in the maglev train, then the train will maintain a distance above the track known as an "air gap" and move forward. Theoretically, the maglev train in EDS should travel at least 4 inches above the track, so there would be virtually no energy lost to friction. If the system does lose energy, it will be in the form of thermal energy.

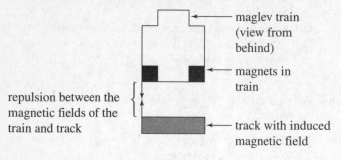

repulsion between the magnetic fields of the train and track

maglev train (view from behind)

magnets in train

track with induced magnetic field

Figure 1

Under controlled conditions, scientists conducted tests on an experimental maglev track oriented in an east-to-west direction.

Study 1

A maglev train with magnetic rods of fixed length was moved along the experimental track from east to west at various velocities v. The current I in the track required to induce these velocities was measured in amperes (A).

Table 1		
Trial	v (m/s)	I (A)
1	40	50
2	80	100
3	120	150
4	160	200
5	200	250

Study 2

The maglev train was run in five trials with varying lengths, L, of the magnetic rods, and run at a constant velocity of 40 m/s. The current I in the track required to induce this velocity given the different lengths of the rods was recorded.

Table 2		
Trial	L (m)	I (A)
6	0.6	50
7	0.8	67
8	1.0	84
9	1.2	100
10	1.4	116

Study 3

The magnetic field, B, measured in tesla (T), was varied in the maglev track. The current running through the maglev track was then measured in five new trials. Throughout these trials, the lengths of the magnetic rods and the maglev train velocities were kept constant.

GO ON TO THE NEXT PAGE.

Table 3		
Trial	B (T)	I (A)
11	5.90×10^{-4}	300
12	7.87×10^{-4}	400
13	9.84×10^{-4}	500
14	1.05×10^{-3}	600
15	1.20×10^{-3}	700

Study 4

The maglev train with magnetic rods of fixed length was moved along the experimental track from west to east at various velocities, and the current in the track required to induce these velocities was measured. The magnetic field was kept constant for each of these trials.

Table 4		
Trial	v (m/s)	I (A)
16	40	-50
17	80	-100
18	120	-150
19	160	-200
20	200	-250

1. In Study 1, I would most likely have equaled 500 A if v had been:

A. 40 m/s.
B. 125 m/s.
C. 200 m/s.
D. 400 m/s.

2. In Study 2, as the length of the magnetic rods in the maglev train increased, the amount of the current required to induce the train's velocity:

F. increased only.
G. decreased only.
H. remained constant.
J. varied, but with no consistent trend.

3. In Study 3, I would most likely have equaled 570 A if B had equaled which of the following?

A. 6.00×10^{-4} T
B. 8.00×10^{-4} T
C. 1.00×10^{-3} T
D. 1.50×10^{-3} T

4. During each trial, an electrical current moves through the magnetic track because a nonzero voltage was produced in the track. During which of the following trials in Study 3 was the voltage greatest?

F. Trial 11
G. Trial 12
H. Trial 13
J. Trial 14

5. In which of the studies, if any, did the electrical current flow in the opposite direction as compared with the other studies?

A. Study 1 only
B. Study 4 only
C. Studies 1, 2, and 3 only
D. None of these studies

6. The results of Study 3 are best represented by which of the following graphs?

F.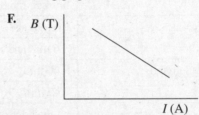

G.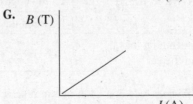

H.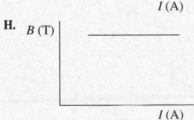

J.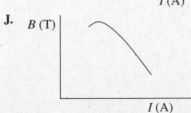

GO ON TO THE NEXT PAGE.

Passage II

Bats of the family *Vespertilionidae* (Vesper bats) are commonly found in North America. A guide for identifying Vesper bats found in Utah is presented in Table 1.

		Table 1	
Step	Trait	Appearance	Result
1	If the ears are:	longer than 25 mm	go to Step 2
		shorter than 25 mm	go to Step 5
2	If the dorsum (back) has:	3 white spots	*Euderma maculotum*
		no spots	go to Step 3
3	If the ears are:	separated at the base	*Antrozous pallidus*
		not separated at the base	go to Step 4
4	If the muzzle has:	well defined skin glands	*Idionycteris phyllotis*
		ill defined skin glands	*Corynorhinus townsendii*
5	If the uropatagium* is:	heavily furred	go to Step 6
		not heavily furred	go to Step 7
6	If the fur color is:	pale yellow at the base	*Lasiurus cinereus*
		dark with silver tips	*Lasionyceris noctivagans*
		brick red to rust	*Lasiurus blossevillii*
7	If the tragus** is:	< 6 mm and curved	go to Step 8
		> 6 mm and straight	go to Step 9
8	If the forearm length is:	> 40 mm	*Eptesicus fuscus*
		< 40 mm	*Pipistrellus hesperus*
9	If there is an obvious fringe of fur:	on the edge of the uropatagium	*Myotis thysanodes*
		between the elbows and knees	*Myotis volans*

*Wing-like tissue between hind legs
**Cartilage structure in the ear

Students observed Vesper bats in a Utah nature reserve and recorded descriptions of them in Table 2.

GO ON TO THE NEXT PAGE.

				Table 2			
Bat	Ears	Dorsum	Muzzle	Uropatagium	Fur	Tragus	Forearm
I	20 mm long, separate at base	no spots	ill defined skin glands	not heavily furred	brown	4 mm, curved	50 mm long
II	18 mm long	no spots	ill defined skin glands	not heavily furred; only an obvious fringe of fur on its edge	brown	7 mm, straight	25 mm long
III	30 mm long, joined at base	no spots	well defined skin glands	not heavily furred	olive	9 mm, curved	30 mm long
IV	15 mm long	no spots	ill defined skin glands	heavily furred	black with silver tips	4 mm, curved	20 mm long

7. Based on the given information, which of the following characteristics distinguishes bat IV from a *Pipistrellus hesperus*?

   A. 4 mm and curved tragus
   B. 15 mm long ears
   C. 20 mm long forearm
   D. Heavily furred uropatagium

8. Based on Table 1, Bats I and II share the same results through step:

   F. 1.
   G. 5.
   H. 7.
   J. 9.

9. Which of the following best describes the family *Vespertilionidae*?

   A. Mammals
   B. Protists
   C. Lampreys
   D. Birds

10. According to Table 1, *Lasiurus cinereus* and *Lasiurus blossevillii* could have all of the following traits in common EXCEPT:

    F. ears not separated at the base.
    G. 35 mm long ears.
    H. a heavily furred uropatagium.
    J. 20 mm long ears.

11. Based on Table 1, which of the following is likely to be most genetically similar to Bat II ?

    A. *Lasiurus blossevillii*
    B. *Idionycteris phyllotis*
    C. *Lasionyceris noctivagans*
    D. *Myotis volans*

GO ON TO THE NEXT PAGE.

Passage III

A heater was placed in a room with a measured initial temperature of 0°C. The heater was set to heat the room to 25°C, and a mercury thermometer recorded the change of the air temperature in the room over time. This process was then repeated with the heater set to heat the room to 37°C and 50°C (see Figure 1).

Next, a cooling device was placed in a tank filled with 50°C saltwater. For three separate tests, the cooler was set to cool the water to 25°C, 10°C, and 0°C, respectively, while a mercury thermometer recorded the temperature of the saltwater over time (see Figure 2).

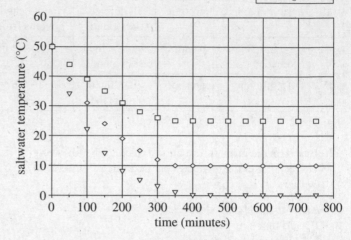

Figure 2

(Note: Assume that the temperature of the air was uniform throughout the room and the temperature of the saltwater was uniform throughout the tank in all tests and assume that at all times the heater and cooling device operated at full capacity.)

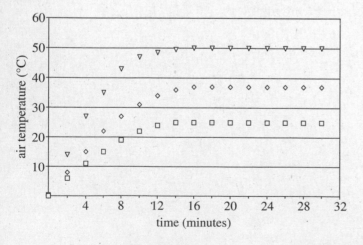

Figure 1

12. Based on the information presented in Figure 2, what was the most likely temperature of the saltwater in the 0°C setting at 220 minutes?

   F. 52°C

   G. 29°C

   H. 17°C

   J. 7°C

GO ON TO THE NEXT PAGE.

13. In the time interval from 8 minutes to 10 minutes, approximately how fast, in °C/min, was the temperature of the air changing when the heater was set to 37°C ?

   A.   0.5°C/min
   B.   2°C/min
   C.   27°C/min
   D.   31°C/min

14. When the cooling device was set to 0°C, for which of the following time periods represented in Figure 2 was the temperature of the water changing most rapidly?

   F.   0–100 min
   G.   100–200 min
   H.   200–300 min
   J.   300–400 min

15. According to Figure 2, when the cooling device was set to 25°C, at which of the following times was the average kinetic energy of the thermometer's mercury atoms the greatest?

   A.   150 min
   B.   350 min
   C.   550 min
   D.   750 min

16. Based on Figure 2, if another test were performed with the cooling device set to –10°C, approximately how long would it take for the saltwater to reach –10°C ?

   F.   Greater than 400 min
   G.   Between 100 and 350 min
   H.   Between 10 and 50 min
   J.   Less than 10 min

GO ON TO THE NEXT PAGE.

Passage IV

Pepsin is an enzyme in humans that catalyzes the digestion of proteins, like the milk protein *casein*, into smaller subunits called peptides. Pepsin is active only in acidic solutions.

The researchers prepared a solution of casein, a solution of *anserine* (a small peptide), a solution of pepsin, and various *buffer solutions* (solutions maintaining a constant pH). The following experiments were conducted using these solutions.

Experiment 1

Seven solutions were prepared in test tubes using a 5 mL solution buffered to pH 3.0. Different amounts of casein, anserine, and pepsin solutions were added to each tube, and then diluted to 10 mL with the buffer solution, so that the final pH in each test tube would be 3.0. Each tube was incubated at a constant temperature for 15 minutes, and then was monitored to determine whether there was any activity by pepsin (see Table 1).

		Table 1			
Trial	Casein (mL)	Anserine (mL)	Pepsin (mL)	Temperature (°C)	Pepsin Activity
1	1	1	1	30	No
2	1	1	1	35	Low
3	1	1	1	40	High
4	1	0	1	40	High
5	0	1	1	40	No
6	0	0	1	40	No
7	1	1	1	45	No

Experiment 2

Seven solutions were prepared in test tubes according to the same procedure as in Trial 3 of Experiment 1, and each test tube was diluted with different buffer solutions of varying pH (see Table 2).

	Table 2	
Trial	pH	Pepsin Activity
8	2.5	High Activity
9	3.0	High Activity
10	3.5	High Activity
11	4.0	Low Activity
12	4.5	Low Activity
13	5.0	Low Activity
14	5.5	No Activity

GO ON TO THE NEXT PAGE.

17. Pepsin is most likely to be found in which of the following organs?

    A. Kidney
    B. Heart
    C. Stomach
    D. Spinal cord

18. Suppose another trial had been performed in Experiment 2, and the results showed a high level of pepsin activity. Which of the following would be the most likely pH of the buffer solution used in this new trial?

    F. 2.0
    G. 4.0
    H. 6.0
    J. 8.0

19. Which of the following is the most likely reason that Trials 3 and 4 show high levels of pepsin activity while Trial 5 shows no pepsin activity?

    A. Pepsin activity is dependent on both casein and anserine.
    B. Pepsin activity is blocked by anserine.
    C. Pepsin is able to digest casein, but not anserine.
    D. Pepsin is able to digest anserine, but not casein.

20. According to the results from Experiment 1, which of the following trials are most likely to contain undigested casein?

    F. Trials 1, 3, 4, and 7 only
    G. Trials 1, 5, 6, and 7 only
    H. Trials 1 and 7 only
    J. Trials 5, 6, and 7 only

21. The experimental conditions for Trial 3 are most similar to those for which of the following trials?

    A. Trial 9
    B. Trial 11
    C. Trial 13
    D. Trial 14

22. According to the results from Experiments 1 and 2, which of the following best explains the relationship between pepsin activity, pH, and temperature?

    F. Pepsin digests proteins at a fast rate when the pH is greater than 4.0 and the temperature is about 40°C.
    G. Pepsin digests proteins at a fast rate when the pH is less than 4.0 and the temperature is about 40°C.
    H. Pepsin digests proteins at a fast rate when the pH is greater than 3.0 and the temperature is about 30°C.
    J. Pepsin digests proteins at a fast rate when the pH is less than 3.0 and the temperature is about 30°C.

GO ON TO THE NEXT PAGE.

Passage V

Chemical researchers studied the *viscosity* (a fluid's resistance to flow) for several liquids. Highly viscous fluids take more time to flow through a vessel than do low viscous fluids. They measured the viscosity in *centipoise* (cP) (.01 grams per centimeter per second). Some solutions were treated with chemical additives before the fluids were heated. The results are shown in Figures 1–3.

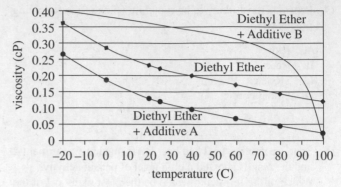

Figure 3

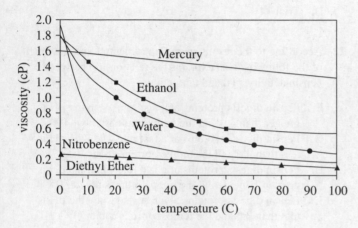

Figure 1

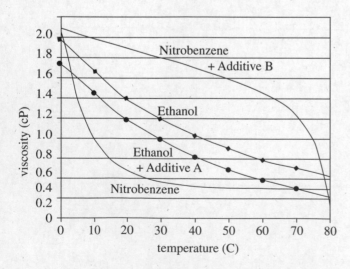

Figure 2

23. For which of the 3 figures did at least one sample fluid have a viscosity greater than 1.0 cP at a temperature of 0°C ?

A. Figure 1 only
B. Figure 3 only
C. Figures 1 and 2 only
D. Figures 1, 2, and 3

24. According to Figure 2, for the sample that contained nitrobenzene without Additive B, the greatest decrease in fluid viscosity occurred over which of the following intervals of temperature change?

F. From 0°C to 10°C
G. From 10°C to 20°C
H. From 30°C to 40°C
J. From 40°C to 50°C

GO ON TO THE NEXT PAGE.

25. According to Figure 1, after water was heated to reach a temperature of 70°C, the viscosity was closest to which of the following?

    A. 1.0 cP
    B. 0.6 cP
    C. 0.4 cP
    D. 0.2 cP

26. Based on the information given, which of the following best describes and explains the experimental results presented in Figure 2? As the temperature increased, the time required for the sample fluids to flow out of their containers:

    F. decreased, because heating the fluids increased each fluid's viscosity.
    G. decreased, because heating the fluids decreased each fluid's viscosity.
    H. increased, because heating the fluids increased each fluid's viscosity.
    J. increased, because heating the fluids decreased each fluid's viscosity.

27. A researcher hypothesized that a solution of nitrobenzene treated with Additive A would have a lower viscosity at 60°C than would untreated diethyl ether at that same temperature. Do the results in the figures confirm this hypothesis?

    A. Yes; according to Figure 2, at 60°C, nitrobenzene had a higher viscosity than did nitrobenzene treated with Additive B.
    B. Yes; according to Figure 3, at 60°C, diethyl ether had a higher viscosity than did diethyl ether treated with Additive A.
    C. No; according to Figure 2, at 60°C, nitrobenzene had a higher viscosity than did nitrobenzene treated with Additive B.
    D. No; according to Figures 1–3, samples of nitrobenzene treated with Additive A were not tested for viscosity.

GO ON TO THE NEXT PAGE.

Passage VI

Earthquakes disrupt the infrastructure of buildings and dwellings by displacing the ground beneath them as a result of surface waves. The origin of an earthquake is known as the *epicenter*. Surface waves propagate from the epicenter outward and are directly affected by the density of the ground through which they propagate. As seen in Figure 1, the strength of the wave may be characterized into three distinct types: strong, moderate, and weak.

Strong

Moderate

Weak

Figure 1

In order to study the effect of ground density on wave propagation, a seismologist has assembled a circular small-scale model with varying densities. Ground density and propagation duration were controlled in the experiment. In each study, earth and clay were laid down in a circular pattern with increasing density. Seismometers were positioned to detect the type of waves propagating at specific locations. A large speaker was placed 2 m below the surface of the epicenter to mimic an earthquake and each study was conducted over a period of 2 min with a fixed frequency of 10 Hz.

Study 1

The sound source was adjusted to 60 dB to mimic the impact of a magnitude 5 earthquake. The resulting *waveform plot* (exhibits wave type as a result of varying densities and distances from the epicenter) is shown in Figure 2.

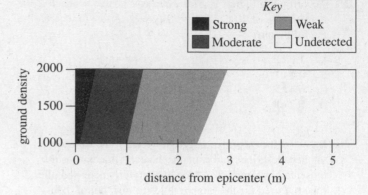

Figure 2

Study 2

Study 1 was repeated with the sound source adjusted to 80 dB to mimic the impact of a magnitude 7 earthquake. The resulting waveform plot is shown in Figure 3.

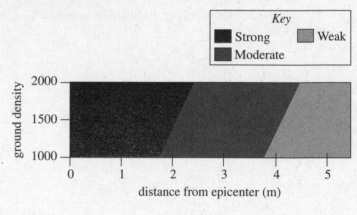

Figure 3

Study 3

The study was repeated with the sound source adjusted to 100 dB to mimic the impact of a magnitude 9 earthquake. The resulting waveform plot is shown in Figure 4.

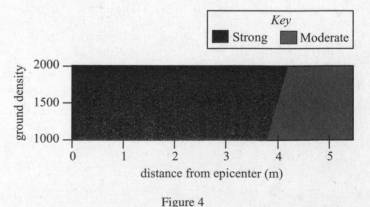

Figure 4

GO ON TO THE NEXT PAGE.

28. According to the results of Study 2, as the distance from the epicenter increases, the type of wave observed:

F. remained strong.
G. changed from strong to moderate.
H. changed from moderate to strong.
J. remained moderate.

29. According to the results of Studies 2 and 3, which of the following statements comparing the maximum distance from the epicenter for strong wave propagation and maximum distance for moderate wave propagation is true?

A. At all ground densities studied, the maximum distance from the epicenter at which strong waves may propagate was greater than the corresponding maximum distance from the epicenter at which moderate waves propagated.
B. At all ground densities studied, the maximum distance from the epicenter at which strong waves may propagate was less than the corresponding maximum distance from the epicenter at which moderate waves propagated.
C. For some of the ground densities studied, the maximum distance from the epicenter at which strong waves may propagate was greater than the corresponding maximum distance from the epicenter at which moderate waves propagated.
D. For some of the ground densities studied, the maximum distance from the epicenter at which strong waves may propagate was less than the corresponding maximum distance from the epicenter at which moderate waves propagated.

30. Which of the following factors in the seismologist's studies was NOT directly controlled?

F. Sound intensity (in dB)
G. Ground density
H. Propagation duration
J. Wave type

31. Consider the relative wavelengths of a moderate wave and a weak wave, as shown in Figure 1. Which, if either, is less than 100 cm ?

A. The wavelength of a moderate wave only.
B. The wavelength of a weak wave only.
C. Both the wavelength of the moderate wave and the wavelength of the weak wave.
D. Neither the wavelength of the moderate wave nor the wavelength of the weak wave.

32. Suppose Study 1 were repeated using a sound intensity of 70 dB. The resulting waveform plot would include which of the wave types referred to in the passage?

F. Strong only
G. Strong and weak waves only
H. Strong and moderate waves only
J. Strong, moderate, and weak waves

33. A study was conducted using a sound intensity between 75 dB and 85 dB. The minimum ground density where strong waves began propagating ranged from 1,000 kg/m^3 to 2,000 kg/m^3. Based on the information presented, the distance from the epicenter was most likely:

A. less than 2.5 m.
B. between 2.5 and 3.5 m.
C. between 3.5 and 4.5 m.
D. greater than 4.5 m.

GO ON TO THE NEXT PAGE.

Passage VII

A *solution* results from dissolving a *solute* into a *solvent*. The van 't Hoff factor (*i*) is the number of moles (1 mole = 6.02×10^{23} entities such as molecules, ions, or atoms) of particles produced in solution for every 1 mole of solute dissolved.

The temperature at which a solution changes state from liquid to solid is the *freezing point*. Two scientists observed that the freezing point of H_2O decreased after adding KCl to it. To explore this further, they conducted an experiment and each scientist provided separate explanations of the results.

Experiment

One mole each of fructose, KCl, and $MgCl_2$ were separately dissolved in 1 kg of pure water. The concentration of each solution was thus 1.0 mole/kg. In addition, 1 kg of pure water only was placed in a fourth container. The containers were placed in a cooling device. The temperature was gradually decreased and the freezing point of each solution was recorded. The results are shown in Table 1.

	Table 1			
Solution	Solute	*i*	Solution properties	Freezing point
1	—	—	Pure water only	0 °C
2	fructose	1	1 dissolved neutral particle	−1.9 °C
3	KCl	2	2 dissolved charged particles (K^+ and Cl^-)	−3.8 °C
4	$MgCl_2$	3	3 dissolved charged particles (Mg^{2+} and 2 Cl^-)	−5.7 °C

Scientist 1

For a solvent to freeze, its molecules must arrange in an orderly fashion relative to each other. When a solute is added, the dissolved solute molecules are attracted to the solvent molecules by the intermolecular force of charge. The attraction of the solute particles to the solvent particles interferes with the orderly arrangement of solvent molecules, and the net effect is that the freezing point is lowered. This decrease in freezing point is related only to the charge of the solute particles and occurs with solutes that form charged particles in solution.

Scientist 2

The freezing point of a solvent is the temperature at which the liquid and solid states of that solvent have equivalent energetic potentials. Below the freezing point, the solvent has a lower energetic potential in the solid state. When a solute is dissolved in a solvent, the energetic potential of the liquid phase is decreased more than the energetic potential of the solid phase. Because of the different energetic potentials, it takes a larger drop in temperature for the liquid to freeze. Thus, the size of the decrease in freezing point is in direct proportion with the van 't Hoff factor. This decrease in freezing point is related only to the concentration of particles, not to the identity or properties of each individual particle.

34. Based on the results in Table 1, how did the concentration of dissolved particles in Solution 4 compare with the concentration of dissolved particles in Solution 2? Solution 4 contained:

F. fewer particles in solution than did Solution 2, resulting in a lower freezing point.

G. more particles in solution than did Solution 2, resulting in a lower freezing point.

H. fewer particles in solution than did Solution 2, resulting in a higher freezing point.

J. more particles in solution than did Solution 2, resulting in a higher freezing point.

GO ON TO THE NEXT PAGE.

35. The freezing point of benzene is lowered with the addition of the solute naphthalene ($C_{10}H_8$), which has no charge. According to the information in the passage, this observation *disagrees* with the explanation provided by:

   A. Scientist 1, who argued that only charged particles can have an effect on the freezing point of a solution.
   B. Scientist 1, who argued that any solute is capable of increasing the stability of the liquid phase of a solvent.
   C. Scientist 2, who argued that only charged particles can have an effect on the freezing point of a solution.
   D. Scientist 2, who argued that any solute is capable of increasing the stability of the liquid phase of a solvent.

36. With which of the following statements about solutes would both scientists agree? Adding to a liquid a substance that has:

   F. a positive or negative charge will decrease the liquid's freezing point.
   G. a positive or negative charge will increase the liquid's freezing point.
   H. no charge will decrease the liquid's freezing point.
   J. no charge will increase the liquid's freezing point.

37. Suppose an experiment showed that adding the positively-charged solute $NaClO_4$ to the solvent H_2O but holding the concentration of the solution constant, the freezing point was significantly lower than an equally concentrated uncharged solution of $NaClO_4$ in pure H_2O. This finding would support the explanation(s) of which of the scientists, if either?

   A. Scientist 1 only
   B. Scientist 2 only
   C. Both Scientists 1 and 2
   D. Neither Scientist

38. Of the following diagrams, which best illustrates how Scientist 1 would describe the results after a charged solute (•) has been added to H_2O (×) ?

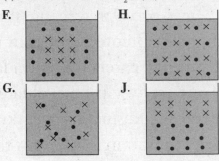

39. Do the scientists offer different explanations for the impact of a solute's physical properties, such as solute charge, on the decrease in freezing point of a solution?

   A. Yes, Scientist 1 states that solute physical properties have an impact but Scientist 2 states they do not.
   B. Yes, Scientist 2 states that solute physical properties have an impact but Scientist 1 states they do not.
   C. No, both scientists state that solute physical properties have an impact on solution freezing point.
   D. No, neither Scientist discusses the impact of solute physical properties on solution freezing point.

40. Assume the following for the addition of a substance to a pure liquid: k is a constant, ΔT is the decrease in freezing point, and i is the van 't Hoff factor. Which of the following equations is most consistent with Scientist 2's explanation?

   F. $\Delta T = k/i$
   G. $\Delta T = ki^2$
   H. $\Delta T = k/i^2$
   J. $\Delta T = ki$

END OF TEST 4
STOP! DO NOT RETURN TO ANY OTHER TEST.

Directions

This is a test of your writing skills. You will have thirty (30) minutes to write an essay. Before you begin planning and writing your essay, read the writing prompt carefully to understand exactly what you are being asked to do. Your essay will be evaluated on the evidence it provides of your ability to express judgments by taking a position on the issue in the writing prompt; to maintain a focus on the topic throughout your essay; to develop a position by using logical reasoning and by supporting your ideas; to organize ideas in a logical way; and to use language clearly and effectively according to the conventions of standard written English.

You may use the unlined pages in this test booklet to plan your essay. These pages will not be scored. *You must write your essay on the lined pages in the answer folder.* Your writing on those lined pages will be scored. You may not need all the lined pages, but to ensure you have enough room to finish, do NOT skip lines. You may write corrections or additions neatly between the lines of your essay, but do NOT write in the margins of the lined pages. *Illegible essays cannot be scored, so you must write (or print) clearly.*

If you finish before time is called, you may review your work. Lay your pencil down immediately when time is called.

DO NOT OPEN THIS BOOKLET UNTIL TOLD TO DO SO.

ACT Assessment Writing Test Prompt

Many schools have removed soda and unhealthy snack machines from school property. Some think this is a good way to combat the rising rates of childhood obesity because these machines feature high-calorie snacks with low nutritional value. Others argue that the machines are necessary sources of food and drink outside the hours the cafeteria is open. In your opinion, should schools ban soda and vending machines on school property?

In your essay, take a position on this question. You may write about either one of the two points of view given, or you may present a different point of view on this question. Use specific reasons and examples to support your position.

The Princeton Review

ACT Diagnostic Test Form

1. YOUR NAME: _____
(Print)　　　　　　　Last　　　　　　　First　　　　　　　M.I.

SIGNATURE: _____　**DATE:** _____ / _____ / _____

HOME ADDRESS: _____
(Print)　　　　　　　Number and Street

_____
City　　　　　　　State　　　　　Zip

E-MAIL: _____

PHONE NO.: _____
(Print)

SCHOOL: _____

CLASS OF: _____

IMPORTANT: Please fill in these boxes exactly as shown on the back cover of your tests book.

2. TEST FORM

_____

3. TEST CODE

⓪	⓪	⓪	⓪
①	①	①	①
②	②	②	②
③	③	③	③
④	④	④	④
⑤	⑤	⑤	⑤
⑥	⑥	⑥	⑥
⑦	⑦	⑦	⑦
⑧	⑧	⑧	⑧
⑨	⑨	⑨	⑨

4. PHONE NUMBER

⓪	⓪	⓪	⓪	⓪	⓪	⓪
①	①	①	①	①	①	①
②	②	②	②	②	②	②
③	③	③	③	③	③	③
④	④	④	④	④	④	④
⑤	⑤	⑤	⑤	⑤	⑤	⑤
⑥	⑥	⑥	⑥	⑥	⑥	⑥
⑦	⑦	⑦	⑦	⑦	⑦	⑦
⑧	⑧	⑧	⑧	⑧	⑧	⑧
⑨	⑨	⑨	⑨	⑨	⑨	⑨

5. YOUR NAME

First 4 letters of last name				FIRST INIT	MID INIT
Ⓐ	Ⓐ	Ⓐ	Ⓐ	Ⓐ	Ⓐ
Ⓑ	Ⓑ	Ⓑ	Ⓑ	Ⓑ	Ⓑ
Ⓒ	Ⓒ	Ⓒ	Ⓒ	Ⓒ	Ⓒ
Ⓓ	Ⓓ	Ⓓ	Ⓓ	Ⓓ	Ⓓ
Ⓔ	Ⓔ	Ⓔ	Ⓔ	Ⓔ	Ⓔ
Ⓕ	Ⓕ	Ⓕ	Ⓕ	Ⓕ	Ⓕ
Ⓖ	Ⓖ	Ⓖ	Ⓖ	Ⓖ	Ⓖ
Ⓗ	Ⓗ	Ⓗ	Ⓗ	Ⓗ	Ⓗ
Ⓘ	Ⓘ	Ⓘ	Ⓘ	Ⓘ	Ⓘ
Ⓙ	Ⓙ	Ⓙ	Ⓙ	Ⓙ	Ⓙ
Ⓚ	Ⓚ	Ⓚ	Ⓚ	Ⓚ	Ⓚ
Ⓛ	Ⓛ	Ⓛ	Ⓛ	Ⓛ	Ⓛ
Ⓜ	Ⓜ	Ⓜ	Ⓜ	Ⓜ	Ⓜ
Ⓝ	Ⓝ	Ⓝ	Ⓝ	Ⓝ	Ⓝ
Ⓞ	Ⓞ	Ⓞ	Ⓞ	Ⓞ	Ⓞ
Ⓟ	Ⓟ	Ⓟ	Ⓟ	Ⓟ	Ⓟ
Ⓠ	Ⓠ	Ⓠ	Ⓠ	Ⓠ	Ⓠ
Ⓡ	Ⓡ	Ⓡ	Ⓡ	Ⓡ	Ⓡ
Ⓢ	Ⓢ	Ⓢ	Ⓢ	Ⓢ	Ⓢ
Ⓣ	Ⓣ	Ⓣ	Ⓣ	Ⓣ	Ⓣ
Ⓤ	Ⓤ	Ⓤ	Ⓤ	Ⓤ	Ⓤ
Ⓥ	Ⓥ	Ⓥ	Ⓥ	Ⓥ	Ⓥ
Ⓦ	Ⓦ	Ⓦ	Ⓦ	Ⓦ	Ⓦ
Ⓧ	Ⓧ	Ⓧ	Ⓧ	Ⓧ	Ⓧ
Ⓨ	Ⓨ	Ⓨ	Ⓨ	Ⓨ	Ⓨ
Ⓩ	Ⓩ	Ⓩ	Ⓩ	Ⓩ	Ⓩ

6. DATE OF BIRTH

MONTH	DAY		YEAR	
◯ JAN				
◯ FEB				
◯ MAR	⓪	⓪	⓪	⓪
◯ APR	①	①	①	①
◯ MAY	②	②	②	②
◯ JUN	③	③	③	③
◯ JUL		④	④	④
◯ AUG		⑤	⑤	⑤
◯ SEP		⑥	⑥	⑥
◯ OCT		⑦	⑦	⑦
◯ NOV		⑧	⑧	⑧
◯ DEC		⑨	⑨	⑨

7. SEX

◯ MALE
◯ FEMALE

8. OTHER

1　Ⓐ Ⓑ Ⓒ Ⓓ Ⓔ
2　Ⓐ Ⓑ Ⓒ Ⓓ Ⓔ
3　Ⓐ Ⓑ Ⓒ Ⓓ Ⓔ

OpScan iNSIGHT™ forms by Pearson NCS EM-255315-1:654321　　Printed in U.S.A.

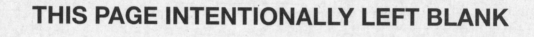
THIS PAGE INTENTIONALLY LEFT BLANK

The Princeton Review
Diagnostic ACT Form

Completely darken bubbles with a No. 2 pencil. If you make a mistake, be sure to erase mark completely. Erase all stray marks.

ENGLISH

1 Ⓐ Ⓑ Ⓒ Ⓓ	21 Ⓐ Ⓑ Ⓒ Ⓓ	41 Ⓐ Ⓑ Ⓒ Ⓓ	61 Ⓐ Ⓑ Ⓒ Ⓓ
2 Ⓕ Ⓖ Ⓗ Ⓙ	22 Ⓕ Ⓖ Ⓗ Ⓙ	42 Ⓕ Ⓖ Ⓗ Ⓙ	62 Ⓕ Ⓖ Ⓗ Ⓙ
3 Ⓐ Ⓑ Ⓒ Ⓓ	23 Ⓐ Ⓑ Ⓒ Ⓓ	43 Ⓐ Ⓑ Ⓒ Ⓓ	63 Ⓐ Ⓑ Ⓒ Ⓓ
4 Ⓕ Ⓖ Ⓗ Ⓙ	24 Ⓕ Ⓖ Ⓗ Ⓙ	44 Ⓕ Ⓖ Ⓗ Ⓙ	64 Ⓕ Ⓖ Ⓗ Ⓙ
5 Ⓐ Ⓑ Ⓒ Ⓓ	25 Ⓐ Ⓑ Ⓒ Ⓓ	45 Ⓐ Ⓑ Ⓒ Ⓓ	65 Ⓐ Ⓑ Ⓒ Ⓓ
6 Ⓕ Ⓖ Ⓗ Ⓙ	26 Ⓕ Ⓖ Ⓗ Ⓙ	46 Ⓕ Ⓖ Ⓗ Ⓙ	66 Ⓕ Ⓖ Ⓗ Ⓙ
7 Ⓐ Ⓑ Ⓒ Ⓓ	27 Ⓐ Ⓑ Ⓒ Ⓓ	47 Ⓐ Ⓑ Ⓒ Ⓓ	67 Ⓐ Ⓑ Ⓒ Ⓓ
8 Ⓕ Ⓖ Ⓗ Ⓙ	28 Ⓕ Ⓖ Ⓗ Ⓙ	48 Ⓕ Ⓖ Ⓗ Ⓙ	68 Ⓕ Ⓖ Ⓗ Ⓙ
9 Ⓐ Ⓑ Ⓒ Ⓓ	29 Ⓐ Ⓑ Ⓒ Ⓓ	49 Ⓐ Ⓑ Ⓒ Ⓓ	69 Ⓐ Ⓑ Ⓒ Ⓓ
10 Ⓕ Ⓖ Ⓗ Ⓙ	30 Ⓕ Ⓖ Ⓗ Ⓙ	50 Ⓕ Ⓖ Ⓗ Ⓙ	70 Ⓕ Ⓖ Ⓗ Ⓙ
11 Ⓐ Ⓑ Ⓒ Ⓓ	31 Ⓐ Ⓑ Ⓒ Ⓓ	51 Ⓐ Ⓑ Ⓒ Ⓓ	71 Ⓐ Ⓑ Ⓒ Ⓓ
12 Ⓕ Ⓖ Ⓗ Ⓙ	32 Ⓕ Ⓖ Ⓗ Ⓙ	52 Ⓕ Ⓖ Ⓗ Ⓙ	72 Ⓕ Ⓖ Ⓗ Ⓙ
13 Ⓐ Ⓑ Ⓒ Ⓓ	33 Ⓐ Ⓑ Ⓒ Ⓓ	53 Ⓐ Ⓑ Ⓒ Ⓓ	73 Ⓐ Ⓑ Ⓒ Ⓓ
14 Ⓕ Ⓖ Ⓗ Ⓙ	34 Ⓕ Ⓖ Ⓗ Ⓙ	54 Ⓕ Ⓖ Ⓗ Ⓙ	74 Ⓕ Ⓖ Ⓗ Ⓙ
15 Ⓐ Ⓑ Ⓒ Ⓓ	35 Ⓐ Ⓑ Ⓒ Ⓓ	55 Ⓐ Ⓑ Ⓒ Ⓓ	75 Ⓐ Ⓑ Ⓒ Ⓓ
16 Ⓕ Ⓖ Ⓗ Ⓙ	36 Ⓕ Ⓖ Ⓗ Ⓙ	56 Ⓕ Ⓖ Ⓗ Ⓙ	
17 Ⓐ Ⓑ Ⓒ Ⓓ	37 Ⓐ Ⓑ Ⓒ Ⓓ	57 Ⓐ Ⓑ Ⓒ Ⓓ	
18 Ⓕ Ⓖ Ⓗ Ⓙ	38 Ⓕ Ⓖ Ⓗ Ⓙ	58 Ⓕ Ⓖ Ⓗ Ⓙ	
19 Ⓐ Ⓑ Ⓒ Ⓓ	39 Ⓐ Ⓑ Ⓒ Ⓓ	59 Ⓐ Ⓑ Ⓒ Ⓓ	
20 Ⓕ Ⓖ Ⓗ Ⓙ	40 Ⓕ Ⓖ Ⓗ Ⓙ	60 Ⓕ Ⓖ Ⓗ Ⓙ	

MATHEMATICS

1 Ⓐ Ⓑ Ⓒ Ⓓ Ⓔ	16 Ⓕ Ⓖ Ⓗ Ⓙ Ⓚ	31 Ⓐ Ⓑ Ⓒ Ⓓ Ⓔ	46 Ⓕ Ⓖ Ⓗ Ⓙ Ⓚ
2 Ⓕ Ⓖ Ⓗ Ⓙ Ⓚ	17 Ⓐ Ⓑ Ⓒ Ⓓ Ⓔ	32 Ⓕ Ⓖ Ⓗ Ⓙ Ⓚ	47 Ⓐ Ⓑ Ⓒ Ⓓ Ⓔ
3 Ⓐ Ⓑ Ⓒ Ⓓ Ⓔ	18 Ⓕ Ⓖ Ⓗ Ⓙ Ⓚ	33 Ⓐ Ⓑ Ⓒ Ⓓ Ⓔ	48 Ⓕ Ⓖ Ⓗ Ⓙ Ⓚ
4 Ⓕ Ⓖ Ⓗ Ⓙ Ⓚ	19 Ⓐ Ⓑ Ⓒ Ⓓ Ⓔ	34 Ⓕ Ⓖ Ⓗ Ⓙ Ⓚ	49 Ⓐ Ⓑ Ⓒ Ⓓ Ⓔ
5 Ⓐ Ⓑ Ⓒ Ⓓ Ⓔ	20 Ⓕ Ⓖ Ⓗ Ⓙ Ⓚ	35 Ⓐ Ⓑ Ⓒ Ⓓ Ⓔ	50 Ⓕ Ⓖ Ⓗ Ⓙ Ⓚ
6 Ⓕ Ⓖ Ⓗ Ⓙ Ⓚ	21 Ⓐ Ⓑ Ⓒ Ⓓ Ⓔ	36 Ⓕ Ⓖ Ⓗ Ⓙ Ⓚ	51 Ⓐ Ⓑ Ⓒ Ⓓ Ⓔ
7 Ⓐ Ⓑ Ⓒ Ⓓ Ⓔ	22 Ⓕ Ⓖ Ⓗ Ⓙ Ⓚ	37 Ⓐ Ⓑ Ⓒ Ⓓ Ⓔ	52 Ⓕ Ⓖ Ⓗ Ⓙ Ⓚ
8 Ⓕ Ⓖ Ⓗ Ⓙ Ⓚ	23 Ⓐ Ⓑ Ⓒ Ⓓ Ⓔ	38 Ⓕ Ⓖ Ⓗ Ⓙ Ⓚ	53 Ⓐ Ⓑ Ⓒ Ⓓ Ⓔ
9 Ⓐ Ⓑ Ⓒ Ⓓ Ⓔ	24 Ⓕ Ⓖ Ⓗ Ⓙ Ⓚ	39 Ⓐ Ⓑ Ⓒ Ⓓ Ⓔ	54 Ⓕ Ⓖ Ⓗ Ⓙ Ⓚ
10 Ⓕ Ⓖ Ⓗ Ⓙ Ⓚ	25 Ⓐ Ⓑ Ⓒ Ⓓ Ⓔ	40 Ⓕ Ⓖ Ⓗ Ⓙ Ⓚ	55 Ⓐ Ⓑ Ⓒ Ⓓ Ⓔ
11 Ⓐ Ⓑ Ⓒ Ⓓ Ⓔ	26 Ⓕ Ⓖ Ⓗ Ⓙ Ⓚ	41 Ⓐ Ⓑ Ⓒ Ⓓ Ⓔ	56 Ⓕ Ⓖ Ⓗ Ⓙ Ⓚ
12 Ⓕ Ⓖ Ⓗ Ⓙ Ⓚ	27 Ⓐ Ⓑ Ⓒ Ⓓ Ⓔ	42 Ⓕ Ⓖ Ⓗ Ⓙ Ⓚ	57 Ⓐ Ⓑ Ⓒ Ⓓ Ⓔ
13 Ⓐ Ⓑ Ⓒ Ⓓ Ⓔ	28 Ⓕ Ⓖ Ⓗ Ⓙ Ⓚ	43 Ⓐ Ⓑ Ⓒ Ⓓ Ⓔ	58 Ⓕ Ⓖ Ⓗ Ⓙ Ⓚ
14 Ⓕ Ⓖ Ⓗ Ⓙ Ⓚ	29 Ⓐ Ⓑ Ⓒ Ⓓ Ⓔ	44 Ⓕ Ⓖ Ⓗ Ⓙ Ⓚ	59 Ⓐ Ⓑ Ⓒ Ⓓ Ⓔ
15 Ⓐ Ⓑ Ⓒ Ⓓ Ⓔ	30 Ⓕ Ⓖ Ⓗ Ⓙ Ⓚ	45 Ⓐ Ⓑ Ⓒ Ⓓ Ⓔ	60 Ⓕ Ⓖ Ⓗ Ⓙ Ⓚ

The Princeton Review
Diagnostic ACT Form

READING

1	Ⓐ Ⓑ Ⓒ Ⓓ	11	Ⓐ Ⓑ Ⓒ Ⓓ	21	Ⓐ Ⓑ Ⓒ Ⓓ	31	Ⓐ Ⓑ Ⓒ Ⓓ
2	Ⓕ Ⓖ Ⓗ Ⓙ	12	Ⓕ Ⓖ Ⓗ Ⓙ	22	Ⓕ Ⓖ Ⓗ Ⓙ	32	Ⓕ Ⓖ Ⓗ Ⓙ
3	Ⓐ Ⓑ Ⓒ Ⓓ	13	Ⓐ Ⓑ Ⓒ Ⓓ	23	Ⓐ Ⓑ Ⓒ Ⓓ	33	Ⓐ Ⓑ Ⓒ Ⓓ
4	Ⓕ Ⓖ Ⓗ Ⓙ	14	Ⓕ Ⓖ Ⓗ Ⓙ	24	Ⓕ Ⓖ Ⓗ Ⓙ	34	Ⓕ Ⓖ Ⓗ Ⓙ
5	Ⓐ Ⓑ Ⓒ Ⓓ	15	Ⓐ Ⓑ Ⓒ Ⓓ	25	Ⓐ Ⓑ Ⓒ Ⓓ	35	Ⓐ Ⓑ Ⓒ Ⓓ
6	Ⓕ Ⓖ Ⓗ Ⓙ	16	Ⓕ Ⓖ Ⓗ Ⓙ	26	Ⓕ Ⓖ Ⓗ Ⓙ	36	Ⓕ Ⓖ Ⓗ Ⓙ
7	Ⓐ Ⓑ Ⓒ Ⓓ	17	Ⓐ Ⓑ Ⓒ Ⓓ	27	Ⓐ Ⓑ Ⓒ Ⓓ	37	Ⓐ Ⓑ Ⓒ Ⓓ
8	Ⓕ Ⓖ Ⓗ Ⓙ	18	Ⓕ Ⓖ Ⓗ Ⓙ	28	Ⓕ Ⓖ Ⓗ Ⓙ	38	Ⓕ Ⓖ Ⓗ Ⓙ
9	Ⓐ Ⓑ Ⓒ Ⓓ	19	Ⓐ Ⓑ Ⓒ Ⓓ	29	Ⓐ Ⓑ Ⓒ Ⓓ	39	Ⓐ Ⓑ Ⓒ Ⓓ
10	Ⓕ Ⓖ Ⓗ Ⓙ	20	Ⓕ Ⓖ Ⓗ Ⓙ	30	Ⓕ Ⓖ Ⓗ Ⓙ	40	Ⓕ Ⓖ Ⓗ Ⓙ

SCIENCE REASONING

1	Ⓐ Ⓑ Ⓒ Ⓓ	11	Ⓐ Ⓑ Ⓒ Ⓓ	21	Ⓐ Ⓑ Ⓒ Ⓓ	31	Ⓐ Ⓑ Ⓒ Ⓓ
2	Ⓕ Ⓖ Ⓗ Ⓙ	12	Ⓕ Ⓖ Ⓗ Ⓙ	22	Ⓕ Ⓖ Ⓗ Ⓙ	32	Ⓕ Ⓖ Ⓗ Ⓙ
3	Ⓐ Ⓑ Ⓒ Ⓓ	13	Ⓐ Ⓑ Ⓒ Ⓓ	23	Ⓐ Ⓑ Ⓒ Ⓓ	33	Ⓐ Ⓑ Ⓒ Ⓓ
4	Ⓕ Ⓖ Ⓗ Ⓙ	14	Ⓕ Ⓖ Ⓗ Ⓙ	24	Ⓕ Ⓖ Ⓗ Ⓙ	34	Ⓕ Ⓖ Ⓗ Ⓙ
5	Ⓐ Ⓑ Ⓒ Ⓓ	15	Ⓐ Ⓑ Ⓒ Ⓓ	25	Ⓐ Ⓑ Ⓒ Ⓓ	35	Ⓐ Ⓑ Ⓒ Ⓓ
6	Ⓕ Ⓖ Ⓗ Ⓙ	16	Ⓕ Ⓖ Ⓗ Ⓙ	26	Ⓕ Ⓖ Ⓗ Ⓙ	36	Ⓕ Ⓖ Ⓗ Ⓙ
7	Ⓐ Ⓑ Ⓒ Ⓓ	17	Ⓐ Ⓑ Ⓒ Ⓓ	27	Ⓐ Ⓑ Ⓒ Ⓓ	37	Ⓐ Ⓑ Ⓒ Ⓓ
8	Ⓕ Ⓖ Ⓗ Ⓙ	18	Ⓕ Ⓖ Ⓗ Ⓙ	28	Ⓕ Ⓖ Ⓗ Ⓙ	38	Ⓕ Ⓖ Ⓗ Ⓙ
9	Ⓐ Ⓑ Ⓒ Ⓓ	19	Ⓐ Ⓑ Ⓒ Ⓓ	29	Ⓐ Ⓑ Ⓒ Ⓓ	39	Ⓐ Ⓑ Ⓒ Ⓓ
10	Ⓕ Ⓖ Ⓗ Ⓙ	20	Ⓕ Ⓖ Ⓗ Ⓙ	30	Ⓕ Ⓖ Ⓗ Ⓙ	40	Ⓕ Ⓖ Ⓗ Ⓙ

The Princeton Review
Diagnostic ACT Form

ESSAY

Begin your essay on this side. If necessary, continue on the opposite side.

The Princeton Review
Diagnostic ACT Form

Continued from previous page.

The Princeton Review
Diagnostic ACT Form

Continued from previous page.

_____

_____

_____

_____

_____

_____

_____

_____

_____

_____

_____

_____

_____

_____

_____

_____

_____

_____

_____

_____

_____

_____

_____

PLEASE PRINT
YOUR INITIALS

First	Middle	Last

The Princeton Review
Diagnostic ACT Form

Continued from previous page.

Test 3

ACT ENGLISH TEST
45 Minutes—75 Questions

DIRECTIONS: In the five passages that follow, certain words and phrases are underlined and numbered. In the right-hand column, you will find alternatives for each underlined part. In most cases, you are to choose the one that best expresses the idea, makes the statement appropriate for standard written English, or is worded most consistently with the style and tone of the passage as a whole. If you think the original version is best, choose "NO CHANGE." In some cases, you will find in the right-hand column a question about the underlined part. You are to choose the best answer to the question.

You will also find questions about a section of the passage or the passage as a whole. These questions do not refer to an underlined portion of the passage but rather are identified by a number or numbers in a box.

For each question, choose the alternative you consider best and blacken the corresponding oval on your answer document. Read each passage through once before you begin to answer the questions that accompany it. For many of the questions, you must read several sentences beyond the question to determine the answer. Be sure that you have read far enough ahead each time you choose an alternative.

PASSAGE I

Roast Done Right

Just like being the artist sculpting the Venus de Milo or
painting the Sistine Chapel, preparing a delicious meal is an art.
Even the seemingly mundane pot roast can be a true master-

piece. Nothing can be more rewarding to a cook than the sign of
a roast done right.

    Cooking a delicious roast with vegetables require three
things: the freshest ingredients, a slow-cooker, and good

timing. My friend Eric goes to the butcher shop just after its
5 a.m. delivery to snatch up the best cuts of meat, then heads
to the local farmer's market. He fills his canvas shopping bag
with ripe red tomatoes, crisp yellow onions, and thick russet
potatoes. The tastiest vegetables are the results of natural
sunshine and of a farmer's careful tending.

    With supplies in tote, Eric heads to the kitchen. While
the beef marinates in garlic and spices, he chops the colorful

1. A. NO CHANGE
   B. the artist
   C. one
   D. DELETE the underlined portion.

2. The writer would like to convey the distinct scent of a properly cooked roast. Given that all the choices are true, which best accomplishes the writer's goal?

   F. NO CHANGE
   G. the swirling rush of robust aromas
   H. the fine textures of vegetables and meats
   J. the diners' eager expectation

3. A. NO CHANGE
   B. has the requirements of
   C. requiring
   D. requires

4. Which of the following would be the LEAST acceptable alternative for the underlined portion?

   F. out to the butcher shop right before
   G. into the butcher shop just around
   H. at the butcher shop right after
   J. to the butcher shop close to

5. A. NO CHANGE
   B. sunshine, of which a farmer is
   C. sunshine, and a farmer is
   D. sunshine, which is a farmer's

GO ON TO THE NEXT PAGE.

array of fresh vegetables. Eric slowly places the vegetables
₆

around the meat in the slow-cooker's pot, he alternates rings of
₇
bright orange carrots and chunks of red potatoes. He sprinkles

in sliced onions and herbs until the ingredients nearly spill

over the top. Like with many cooks, Eric has a secret, final
₈
ingredient: a splash of red wine for flavor.

    At this point, it's time to cram the lid onto the heaping
₉
potful of ingredients and turn on the cooker. The temperature

inside the pot rises slowly as the contents stew in their natural
₁₀
juices. The roast will take six to eight hours to cook, but after

an hour or two, the first spicy scents start wafting through the
₁₁
kitchen. A few hours later, the rich, juicy smell of beef begins

to escape. Every half-hour, using a long, meat thermometer
₁₂
Eric reads the temperature of the roast and carefully examines

6. The writer wishes to emphasize Eric's attention to detail in making his pot roast. Given that all the choices are true, which one best accomplishes the writer's goal?

  F. NO CHANGE
  G. is very careful when pouring the vegetables
  H. meticulously layers the finely cut vegetables
  J. arranges the vegetables in a kind of order

7. A. NO CHANGE
  B. he has alternated
  C. alternates
  D. alternating

8. F. NO CHANGE
  G. Like many
  H. As most
  J. As many do

9. Which of the following alternatives to the underlined portion would be LEAST acceptable?

  A. Next,
  B. After that,
  C. Now,
  D. At least,

10. Given that all the choices are true, which one provides the most specific sensory detail and maintains the style and tone of the essay?

  F. NO CHANGE
  G. rises slowly but surely, stewing
  H. rises slowly to a lazy, bubbling boil, stewing the savory contents
  J. increases to about 200 degrees Fahrenheit to stew the contents

11. A. NO CHANGE
  B. drifting through the air to make the whole kitchen smell.
  C. wafting and floating through the whole kitchen.
  D. wafting through the air of the kitchen.

12. F. NO CHANGE
  G. half-hour, using a long meat thermometer,
  H. half-hour using a long meat thermometer
  J. half-hour, using a long meat thermometer;

GO ON TO THE NEXT PAGE.

the stewing contents. He doesn't want it overcooked or

undercooked, but "just right." 13

13. The writer is considering deleting the preceding sentence. Should it be kept or deleted?

    A. Kept, because it provides a reason for Eric's diligent attention to the temperature.

    B. Kept, because it reinforces that roasts are typically done cooking after 8 hours.

    C. Deleted, because it puts the focus on Eric and his cooking, rather than the roast.

    D. Deleted, because it doesn't provide enough information about temperature's effects on the roast.

Lift the finished roast out of the pot to serve, the tender

meat plops juicily onto our plates in generous servings. He tops

it off with zesty, steaming vegetables. Eric is obviously proud

to share his work of art, and his friends are more than willing to

eat it, this masterpiece of his.

14.   **F.** NO CHANGE

    G. As he lifts the finished roast

    H. When you lift the finished roast

    J. Lifting the finished roast

15.   **A.** NO CHANGE

    B. ready for us to eat.

    C. a masterpiece.

    D. DELETE the underlined portion, replacing the comma with a period after "it."

PASSAGE II

Growing Up On a Farm

Back in middle school, I went to live with my mother for

two years on her farm. Whenever people hear that I lived on a

farm, they immediately conjure up an image visualized in their

minds of dairy cows, tractors, hay, and overalls. Nothing could

be further from the truth.

16.   **F.** NO CHANGE

    G. assuming that they know what it was like

    H. of my life on the farm that consists

    J. DELETE the underlined portion.

To start, I wasn't on the kind of farm everyone imagines. I

17. Which of the following alternatives to the underlined portion would NOT be acceptable?

    A. First of all,

    B. To begin,

    C. For start,

    D. Firstly,

didn't feed cows or pigs; I didn't grow corn or wheat. I helped

my mother breed llamas.

[1] It is odd that such non-traditional livestock should

be raised on a long-established farm such as ours, which has

18.   **F.** NO CHANGE

    G. or, pigs

    H. or pigs,

    J. or pigs

GO ON TO THE NEXT PAGE.

been in the family for generations. [19] [2] Our family did indeed grow field crops, harvest orchards, and raise traditional

livestock for many decades. [3] He must of learned that wool
                                        ‾‾‾‾‾‾‾‾‾‾‾‾‾‾‾
                                              20
from llamas was more profitable than wool from sheep. [4] The

llama wool business turned out to be so successful in fact, that
                                         ‾‾‾‾‾‾‾‾‾‾‾‾‾‾‾‾‾‾‾‾
                                                 21
my great-grandfather converted the family business to a full-

fledged llama farm. [22]

Before I began to live on the farm, I had held naive
          ‾‾‾‾‾‾‾‾‾‾‾‾
              23
illusions of rural life. What could possibly be easier than

feeding and grooming some animals? After I had settled into my
                                     ‾‾‾‾‾‾‾
                                       24
new home, however, I realized that farm work was much more

19. The writer is considering deleting the phrase "which has been in the family for generations" (and ending the sentence with a period) from the preceding sentence. If the writer were to make this change, the essay would primarily lose:

   A. evidence of a broken relationship between the narrator and his mother.
   B. a transition into the discussion of traditional farm practices.
   C. a detail that reinforces the longevity of the family farm.
   D. an indication of what will eventually happen to the narrator.

20. F. NO CHANGE
    G. of learned of
    H. have learned that
    J. have learned about

21. A. NO CHANGE
    B. successful, in fact, that
    C. successful, in fact that
    D. successful in fact that

22. Upon reviewing this paragraph and realizing that some information has been left out, the writer composes the following sentence:

   Then, fifty years ago, my great-grandfather decided to buy a llama.

   This sentence should most logically be placed after Sentence:

   F. 1.
   G. 2.
   H. 3.
   J. 4.

23. Which of the following alternatives to the underlined portion would NOT be acceptable?

   A. started to live
   B. began living
   C. went to live
   D. begun to live

24. Which of the following alternatives to the underlined portion would NOT be acceptable?

   F. As soon as I
   G. When I
   H. Once I
   J. I

GO ON TO THE NEXT PAGE.

involved than I had expected. Collecting manure, for example,
doesn't seem so bad when someone else does it on TV, but I
had to get up before dawn every day to finish that chore before
catching the bus to school.

School in the country was also not what I had expected.
The school I attended had twenty students total: that's from
first to twelfth grade, and I was the only student in my grade.

We had one teacher who would occasionally educate us on a
specific academic study and methods of learning, but most of

my learning came from studying textbooks on my own.

I don't mean to say that my life on the farm was a bad
experience. I learned a lot about myself: for example, I'm not

a morning person. I also learned about llama's habits, such as
spitting when they are unhappy. Most importantly, my mother
and I got to spend a lot of time together during those years, for

which I'm so grateful. Although I doubt I'll pursue a career as
farming, I look forward to returning to the family farm for short
visits.

25. **A.** NO CHANGE
B. would expect.
C. would be expecting.
D. have expected.

26. Given that all the choices are true, which one most
effectively introduces the information that follows in this
paragraph?
F. NO CHANGE
G. Farming is a full-time job, taking up your entire day.
H. Llamas can grow to be six feet tall.
J. Life on the farm was tough but worthwhile.

27. **A.** NO CHANGE
B. verbally acknowledge how well the class was working
for us,
C. tell us how to learn about a specific academic study,
D. lecture about a specific topic,

28. Which choice provides the most specific and precise infor-
mation?
F. NO CHANGE
G. studying.
H. other things.
J. reading by myself.

29. **A.** NO CHANGE
B. llamas' habits,
C. llamas habits
D. llamas habits,

30. **F.** NO CHANGE
G. career of
H. career in
J. careers of

GO ON TO THE NEXT PAGE.

PASSAGE III

> The following paragraphs may or may not be in the most logical order. Each paragraph is numbered in brackets, and question 45 will ask you to choose where Paragraph 2 should most logically be placed.

Conjuring a Prophetic Literary Career

[1]

Born in Ohio in 1858, Charles W. Chesnutt was an author and essayist <u>whom,</u> during the Reconstruction era, spent much
₃₁
of his youth in North Carolina. Though his parents were free African-Americans, Chesnutt felt intensely the struggles of African-Americans in the United States in the period directly after the Civil War. ☐₃₂ Amid all the turmoil of the South of his boyhood, Chesnutt took solace in <u>literature, and he</u> had already
₃₃
decided, in his teens, that he would become a writer.

[2]

Although Chesnutt <u>continues</u> to write until his death in
₃₄
1932, it had become <u>as clear as day</u> that the work he completed
₃₅
after *The House Behind the Cedars* and *The Marrow of Tradition* (1901) had become too inflammatory to a society ever uneasy about the topic of race relations in the United States, particularly when authors had brought these problems as close to the surface as Chesnutt had. In recent years, however, Chesnutt's reputation has been restored and he has been treated as the pioneer that he most certainly was. Today as much as in the late nineteenth century, Chesnutt's works provide us with a

31. A. NO CHANGE
B. who,
C. which,
D. DELETE the underlined portion.

32. If the writer were to delete the last part of the preceding sentence (ending the sentence with a period after the word *States*), the paragraph would primarily lose:

F. a direct link to the following paragraph.
G. an unnecessary digression into historical details.
H. an important detail about the period of Chesnutt's youth.
J. a fact suggesting the extent of Chesnutt's historical writing.

33. Which of the following alternatives to the underlined portion would NOT be acceptable?

A. literature; he
B. literature, and he consequently
C. literature, he
D. literature. He

34. F. NO CHANGE
G. has continued
H. still continues
J. continued

35. A. NO CHANGE
B. so extremely clear
C. clear
D. clear to an incredible degree

GO ON TO THE NEXT PAGE.

number of literary masterpieces and a powerful and prophetic vision of race relations in the United States.

[3]

"The Goophered Grapevine," published in 1887 in *The Atlantic*, was Chesnutt's first major literary success, and this success encouraged Chesnutt to publish additional tales, which were eventually collected in *The Conjure Woman* (1899). *The Conjure Woman* was written in the tradition of earlier folklorists from a previous era Joel Chandler Harris
36

and Thomas Nelson Page. However, it presented a much
37
more frank treatment of race relations in the South during

slavery and Reconstruction. 38 *The Conjure Woman* and

it's narrator, Uncle Julius McAdoo, were clearly written in
39
response to the immensely popular Uncle Remus of Harris's tales, but the similarities between the two authors' works ended

36. **F.** NO CHANGE
 G. from a previous time
 H. from the years before
 J. DELETE the underlined portion.

37. **A.** NO CHANGE
 B. Page, however,
 C. Page. Consequently,
 D. Page, consequently,

38. At this point, the writer is considering adding the following true statement:

 The slaves were freed with the Emancipation Proclamation in 1862, but many conditions like those under slavery resurfaced after the collapse of Reconstruction efforts in 1877.

 Should the writer add the sentence here?

 F. Yes, because it shows how many of the gains made by ex-slaves were later taken away.
 G. Yes, because it is necessary to understand Chesnutt's motivation.
 H. No, because it provides information that is detailed later in this essay.
 J. No, because it would distract readers from the essay's main focus.

39. **A.** NO CHANGE
 B. their
 C. its
 D. its'

GO ON TO THE NEXT PAGE.

there. While Harris's tales used mostly animals and not voodoo,
conjure, and the injustices of slavery, which *The Conjure*
Woman did, also incorporating human characters instead of Brer
Rabbit and animals.

[4]

Chesnutt's true masterpiece, however, is *The House Behind*
the Cedars. The novel details the lives of an African-American

familys children who have chosen to "pass" as white, making
The House Behind the Cedars one of the first novels to talk

about racial passing. Chesnutt uses his characters' divided
status to travel back and forth between the black and white
worlds of the South, and in the process, Chesnutt manages to
show both the shocking disparity between the two worlds and
the insurmountable difficulties his characters, and those who
"pass" in real life, face. From the moment it was published in
1900, the novel was a sensation in American letters, garnering
the respect and admiration of such prominent white literary
critics as William Dean Howells and black intellectuals such as
W.E.B. Dubois.

40. Which choice provides the most logical arrangement of the parts of this sentence?

F. NO CHANGE

G. Humans were used as characters by *The Conjure Woman* and participated in tales relating to conjure, and the injustice of slavery and voodoo, which was different than Brer Rabbit and the animals from Harris's tales.

H. Conjure, voodoo, and the injustices of slavery and others were used by *The Conjure Woman*, along with real human characters instead of animals and Brer Rabbit from Harris's tales.

J. In the place of Brer Rabbit and the animals from Harris's tales, *The Conjure Woman* used human characters in stories that incorporated conjure, voodoo, and the injustices of slavery.

41. **A.** NO CHANGE
    B. families
    C. family's
    D. families's

42. **F.** NO CHANGE
    G. it.
    H. them.
    J. its topics.

43. Which of the following alternatives to the underlined portion would NOT be acceptable?

A. From the moment of its publication in 1900,

B. Having been first published in 1900,

C. Publishing it first in 1900,

D. In 1900, the year of its initial publication,

GO ON TO THE NEXT PAGE.

[5]

Author and essayist, Charles W. Chesnutt published two
books, *The Conjure Woman* and *The House Behind the Cedars*,
that were widely appreciated in his own time.

44. Given that all the choices are true, which one most effectively concludes and summarizes this essay?

F. NO CHANGE
G. Both author and essayist, Charles W. Chesnutt was a
pioneer in African-American literature whose novels
and tales are as meaningful today as they were when
first published.
H. Author of *The House Behind the Cedars*, Charles W.
Chesnutt already knew he wanted to be a writer in his
teens during the era of Reconstruction in the history of
the United States.
J. Author of *The Conjure Woman*, Charles W. Chesnutt
succeeded where earlier writers Joel Chandler Harris
and Thomas Nelson Page had failed in representing
the characters in their stories as people.

Question 45 asks about the preceding passage as a whole.

45. For the sake of the logic and coherence of this essay,
Paragraph 2 should be placed:

A. where it is now.
B. before Paragraph 1.
C. after Paragraph 3.
D. after Paragraph 4.

PASSAGE IV

Jackie Robinson: More Than a Ballplayer

When baseball resumes in America every spring, one April
day is always reserved to honor Jackie Robinson, the man who
broke the color barrier of America's national pastime. While
his accomplishments on the baseball field was numerous and

46. F. NO CHANGE
G. is
H. will be
J. were

impressive, his civil rights activism was according to his widow

47. A. NO CHANGE
B. was, according,
C. was, according
D. was—according

GO ON TO THE NEXT PAGE.

Rachel Robinson, equally important and often overlooked
<u>without being noticed.</u>
₄₈

The tenacious and spirited way <u>for the Brooklyn Dodgers</u>
₄₉
Jackie Robinson played baseball was a reflection of his focus
on civil rights. From the outset of the "Great Experiment"

of having African-Americans in <u>baseball; he</u> knew that his
₅₀
performance on the field would be a determining factor in
sports segregation. Jackie gradually converted jeers and

harassment into cheers and acceptance because white <u>spectators</u>
₅₁
could see his immense talent from any seat in the stadium.
Jackie became a highly respected figure by continually
succeeding on and off the field, all the while displaying stoic

restraint in the face of initial prejudice. ☐52

    [1] The vast amount of energy Jackie expended avoiding
a myriad of potential pitfalls could have caused an ordinary

man to wilt; <u>for example,</u> Jackie instinctively and relentlessly
₅₃
increased his efforts for positive civil rights changes, both in his
sport and in the African-American community at large.

[2] While many athletes today use <u>their</u> status to garner endorse-
₅₄
ments and live as celebrities, Jackie constantly utilized his

---

48. F. NO CHANGE
  G. while not being noticed.
  H. as no one notices.
  J. DELETE the underlined portion and end the sentence
    with a period.

49. The best placement for the underlined portion would be:

  A. where it is now.
  B. after the word *baseball.*
  C. after the word *focus.*
  D. after the word *rights.*

50. F. NO CHANGE
  G. baseball, and he
  H. baseball. He
  J. baseball, he

51. Which choice fits most specifically with the information at
  the end of this sentence?

  A. NO CHANGE
  B. people
  C. popcorn vendors
  D. pitchers

52. If the writer were to delete this paragraph from the essay,
  which of the following would be lost?

  F. A scientific explanation of the "Great Experiment"
  G. A description of the way Jackie influenced society's
    outlook on segregation in baseball
  H. A passionate plea to end prejudice around the world
  J. A comment on why the Brooklyn Dodgers were the
    best team in baseball

53. A. NO CHANGE
  B. as a result,
  C. rather,
  D. therefore,

54. F. NO CHANGE
  G. his
  H. its
  J. theirs

GO ON TO THE NEXT PAGE.

status to stimulate civil rights advancements. [55] [3] He often used his baseball travels as opportunities to speak publicly to blacks in U.S. cities about ending segregation and vigilantly defending their rights. [4] Post-baseball, Jackie became an

entrepreneur, but his focus did not stray as he found time to
56
write impassioned letters and telegrams to various U.S. presidents during the civil rights movement. [5] He had the status to demand that they too remain firmly focused on civil rights measures. [57]

Though Jackie Robinson's baseball exploits may be most widely known than his tireless efforts in the civil rights
58
movement his astonishing courage on the baseball field was it-
59
self a resounding stance against segregation and inequality. His numerous detractors consistently found that not only was Jackie undeterred, but he was excelling in his efforts. As a result, the
60
spark of positive change was ignited. Jackie turned that spark for civil rights into a torch and carried it his entire life.

55. The writer is considering deleting the preceding sentence. Should this sentence be kept or deleted?

   A. Kept, because it describes important information about Jackie Robinson's endorsement deals.
   B. Kept, because it helps the reader understand how Jackie Robinson sacrificed personal advancement in favor of civil rights work.
   C. Deleted, because it doesn't provide exact details about the civil rights laws that Jackie Robinson enacted.
   D. Deleted, because it draws focus toward other athletes and away from Jackie Robinson.

56. **F.** NO CHANGE
   G. entrepreneur,
   H. entrepreneur
   J. entrepreneur; and

57. If the writer were to divide the preceding paragraph into two shorter paragraphs in order to differentiate between Jackie's civil rights activism during and after his baseball career, the new paragraph should begin with Sentence:

   A. 2.
   B. 3.
   C. 4.
   D. 5.

58. **F.** NO CHANGE
   G. very widely known
   H. more widely known
   J. widelier known

59. **A.** NO CHANGE
   B. movement. His
   C. movement; his
   D. movement, his

60. Which of the following alternatives to the underlined portion would be LEAST acceptable?

   F. Consequently,
   G. Instead,
   H. Thus,
   J. Therefore,

GO ON TO THE NEXT PAGE.

PASSAGE V

Antarctica's Adaptable Survivors

Many inhabit sporadic green <u>patches of moss; fertilized</u>
₆₁
by excrement from migrating birds and sheltered by the
rocky mountainsides. Some hibernate in the winter, frozen

in ice under rocks and <u>stones, becoming active</u> again when
₆₂

the climate warms and the ice <u>is melting.</u> Extreme cold
₆₃

and wind are <u>all good to go for survival;</u> indeed, some
₆₄
species are able to endure temperatures as low as –30

degrees Celsius. These adaptable <u>invertebrates classified as</u>
₆₅
<u>arthropods;</u> are able to survive on a continent once thought
₆₅

<u>to arctic, to windy, and to icy,</u> to maintain any permanent
₆₆
land animals. The coldest place on earth, Antarctica is home
to great quantities of life that don't simply tolerate the lower

<u>temperatures; they</u> flourish in them.
₆₇

Microscopic mites, springtails, and wingless midges
<u>accompanied</u> lice and ticks as the most prevalent permanent
₆₈
land fauna on Antarctica. The tiny midges and mites tolerate
the cold due to the antifreeze liquid they carry in their bodies.
Parasitic lice and ticks seek shelter from the harsh climate in the

61. **A.** NO CHANGE
    B. patches, of moss
    C. patches, of moss,
    D. patches of moss

62. Which of the following options to the underlined portion would NOT be acceptable?

    F. stones, only to become active
    G. stones. Becoming active
    H. stones. Then they become active
    J. stones and then become active

63. **A.** NO CHANGE
    B. melting.
    C. melts.
    D. to melt.

64. **F.** NO CHANGE
    G. cool for survival;
    H. all right for survival;
    J. suitable for survival;

65. **A.** NO CHANGE
    B. invertebrates, classified as arthropods
    C. invertebrates, classified as arthropods,
    D. invertebrates classified as arthropods,

66. **F.** NO CHANGE
    G. to arctic, to windy, and to icy
    H. too arctic, too windy, and too icy
    J. too, arctic, too windy, and too icy,

67. Which of the following options to the underlined portion would NOT be acceptable?

    A. temperatures they
    B. temperatures; in fact, they
    C. temperatures. They
    D. temperatures—they

68. **F.** NO CHANGE
    G. accompany
    H. had accompanied
    J. were accompanying

GO ON TO THE NEXT PAGE.

warm fur of <u>seals, the waters of Antarctica teeming with marine</u>
<u>life,</u> and the feathers of sea birds and penguins.

⁶⁹

In the Dry Valleys located on the western coast of McMurdo
Sound in Antarctica, nematode worms feed on bacteria, algae,
and tiny organisms known as rotifers and tardigrades. [70] Here,

ice-covered land is not as abundant. Beneath the
⁷¹
moss-covered polar rock, nematodes thrive, coping ingeniously

by dehydrating themselves in the winter <u>with the low</u>
⁷²
<u>temperatures</u> and coming back to life with the summer and
⁷²
increasing moisture.

69. **A.** NO CHANGE
     B. seals, who return to land to breed,
     C. seals, six different types in all,
     D. seals

70. The writer is considering deleting the following phrase from the previous sentence (and adjusting the capitalization accordingly):

> In the Dry Valleys located on the western coast of McMurdo Sound in Antarctica,

Should this phrase be kept or deleted?

     F. Deleted, because this fact is presented later in this paragraph.
     G. Deleted, because it negates the preceding paragraph, which makes it clear that only insects live in Antarctica.
     H. Kept, because it clarifies that nematodes live both in Antarctica and McMurdo Sound.
     J. Kept, because it gives specific details about the "Here" mentioned in the subsequent sentence.

71. Given that all the choices are true, which one most explicitly and vividly describes the terrain of McMurdo Sound?

     A. NO CHANGE
     B. rocky land is colored vibrantly by green, yellow, and orange lichen, algae, and moss.
     C. there are signs that this is a place with extremely low humidity and no snow cover.
     D. the effects of low humidity are apparent in the presence of flora and orange lichen.

72. The best place for the underlined portion would be:

     F. where it is now.
     G. after the word *thrive*.
     H. after the word *coping*.
     J. after the word *moisture*.

GO ON TO THE NEXT PAGE.

Algae are another resilient life form of the Dry Valleys
of Antarctica. [73] In an effort to adjust to the strong winds and icy
temperatures, some algae live inside the rocks as opposed to on
top of them. Phytoplankton, the most common of Antarctica's
algae, is an important food resource within Antarctica's
ecosystem. These tiny free-floating plants are preyed upon
by copepods and krill, which then provide food for fish, seals,

whales and penguins. [74]

Excluding its aquatic life, Antarctica has a lower species diversity than any other place on earth. Nevertheless, Antarctica is
a haven for 67 documented species of insects and 350 species of
flora, proof that life persists in the most dramatic of conditions.

73. Given that all the choices are true, which one would
LEAST effectively introduce the subject of this paragraph?

A. NO CHANGE
B. Algae lack the various structures that characterize land
plants, such as the moss and lichen that inhabit Antarctica, which is why algae are most prominent in bodies
of water.
C. Algae are typically autotrophic organisms whose adaptive qualities enable them to live successfully in the
Dry McMurdo Valleys.
D. Although most often found in water, algae also inhabit
terrestrial environments such as the Dry Valleys of
Antarctica.

74. The writer is considering deleting the following phrase
from the preceding sentence:

which then provide food for fish, seals, whales and
penguins.

Should this clause be kept or deleted?

F. Kept, because it clarifies how phytoplankton support
Antarctica's ecosystem.
G. Kept, because it addresses the most important life
forms in Antarctica's waters, seals, penguins, and
whales.
H. Deleted, because it is irrelevant to the passage as a
whole, which addresses the smaller life forms living
on Antarctica.
J. Deleted, because it misleads the reader into thinking
that penguins, seals, and whales are among the permanent land dwelling life forms of Antarctica.

75. A. NO CHANGE
B. Indeed,
C. Consequently,
D. Therefore,

END OF TEST 1
STOP! DO NOT TURN THE PAGE UNTIL TOLD TO DO SO.

MATHEMATICS TEST
60 Minutes—60 Questions

DIRECTIONS: Solve each problem, choose the correct answer, and then darken the corresponding oval on your answer document.

Do not linger over problems that take too much time. Solve as many as you can; then return to the others in the time you have left for this test.

You are permitted to use a calculator on this test. You may use your calculator for any problems you choose, but some of the problems may best be done without using a calculator.

Note: Unless otherwise stated, all of the following should be assumed:

1. Illustrative figures are NOT necessarily drawn to scale.
2. Geometric figures lie in a plane.
3. The word *line* indicates a straight line.
4. The word *average* indicates arithmetic mean.

DO YOUR FIGURING HERE.

1. $|8-5|-|5-8| = ?$

   A. -6
   B. -5
   C. -3
   D. 0
   E. 6

2. A science tutor charges \$60 an hour to help students with biology homework. She also charges a flat fee of \$40 to cover her transportation costs. How many hours of tutoring are included in a session that costs \$220 ?

   F. $2\frac{1}{5}$
   G. 3
   H. $3\frac{2}{3}$
   J. 4
   K. $5\frac{1}{2}$

3. Train A averages 16 miles per hour, and Train B averages 24 miles per hour. At these rates, how many more hours does it take Train A than Train B to go 1,152 miles?

   A. 20
   B. 24
   C. 40
   D. 48
   E. 72

4. $33r^2 - 24r + 75 - 41r^2 + r$ is equivalent to:

   F. $44r^2$
   G. $44r^6$
   H. $-8r^2 - 24r + 75$
   J. $-8r^4 - 23r^2 + 75$
   K. $-8r^2 - 23r + 75$

GO ON TO THE NEXT PAGE.

5. Six equilateral triangles form the figure below. If the perimeter of each individual triangle is 15 inches, what is the perimeter of *ABCDEF*, in inches?

DO YOUR FIGURING HERE.

A. 18

B. 30

C. 60

D. $54\sqrt{3}$

E. 90

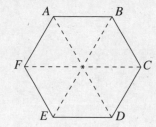

6. The expression $(5x + 2)(x - 3)$ is equivalent to:

F. $5x^2 + 13x - 6$
G. $5x^2 - 13x - 6$
H. $5x^2 - 4x + 5$
J. $5x^2 - 6$
K. $5x^2 - 5$

7. If 35% of a given number is 14, then what is 20% of the given number?

A. 2.8
B. 4.9
C. 7.0
D. 7.7
E. 8.0

8. The 7 consecutive integers below add up to 511,
$x - 2$, $x - 1$, x, $x + 1$, $x + 2$, $x + 3$, and $x + 4$.
What is the value of x ?

F. 71
G. 72
H. 73
J. 74
K. 75

9. In the standard (x,y) coordinate plane, point B with coordinates of $(5,6)$ is the midpoint of line $\overline{AC}$, and point A has coordinates at $(9,4)$. What are the coordinates of C ?

A. (13,2)
B. (7,5)
C. (1,8)
D. (14,10)
E. (−1,−8)

GO ON TO THE NEXT PAGE.

DO YOUR FIGURING HERE.

10. Isosceles trapezoid *ABCD*, with equal sides $\overline{AB}$ and $\overline{CD}$, has vertices *A* (3,0), *B* (6,6), and *D* (15,0). These vertices are graphed below in the standard (*x*,*y*) coordinate plane below. What are the coordinates of one possible vertex *C* ?

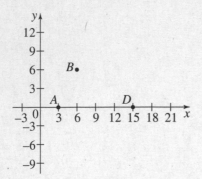

F. (11,7)
G. (13,6)
H. (12,6)
J. (13,5)
K. (12,7)

11. The town of Ashville has three bus stations (A, B, and C) that offer round-trip fares to its business district at both peak and off-peak rates. The matrices below show the average weekly sales for each station at each rate and the costs for both rates. In an average week, what are the combined peak and off-peak sales for Ashville's three bus stations?

	Peak	Off-peak
A	180	60
B	200	120
C	150	70

	Cost
Peak	$3
Off-peak	$2

A. $ 780
B. $1,590
C. $1,950
D. $2,090
E. $2,340

GO ON TO THE NEXT PAGE.

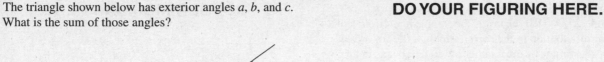
12. The triangle shown below has exterior angles a, b, and c. What is the sum of those angles?

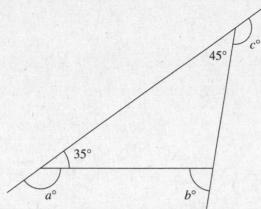

F.   360°
G.   315°
H.   225°
J.   180°
K.   Cannot be determined from the information given

Use the following information to answer questions 13–15.

A sample of 300 jellybeans was removed from a barrel of jellybeans. All of the jellybeans in the barrel are one of four colors: red, orange, green, and purple. For the sample, the number of jellybeans of each color is shown in the table below.

Color	Number of jellybeans
red	75
orange	120
green	60
purple	45

13. What percent of the jellybeans in the sample are green?

A.   15%
B.   20%
C.   25%
D.   40%
E.   60%

GO ON TO THE NEXT PAGE.

DO YOUR FIGURING HERE.

14. The sample of jellybeans was removed from a barrel containing 25,000 jellybeans. If the sample is indicative of the color distribution in the barrel, which of the following is the best estimate of the number of red jellybeans in the barrel?

    F.   3,750
    G.   5,000
    H.   6,250
    J.   10,000
    K.   18,750

15. If the information in the table were converted into a circle graph (pie chart), then the central angle of the sector for orange jellybeans would measure how many degrees?

    A.   54°
    B.   72°
    C.   90°
    D.   120°
    E.   144°

16. In rectangle *ABCD* shown below, *E* is the midpoint of $\overline{BC}$, and *F* is the midpoint of $\overline{AD}$. Which of the following is the ratio of the area of quadrilateral *AECF* to the area of the entire rectangle?

    F.   1:1
    G.   1:2
    H.   1:3
    J.   1:4
    K.   2:5

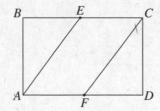

17. In the standard (*x,y*) coordinate plane, what is the slope of the line parallel to the line $y = \frac{1}{2}x - 3$?

    A.   −3

    B.   −2

    C. $-\frac{1}{2}$

    D. $\frac{1}{2}$

    E.   2

GO ON TO THE NEXT PAGE.

18. Aru watches a movie that is 120 minutes long in 2 sittings. The ratio of the 2 sitting times is 3:5. What is the length, in minutes, of the longer sitting?

F. 8
G. 15
H. 45
J. 60
K. 75

DO YOUR FIGURING HERE.

19. Which of the following could be a value of x if $11 < x < 12$?

A. $\sqrt{23}$
B. $\sqrt{121}$
C. $\sqrt{140}$
D. $\sqrt{145}$
E. $\sqrt{529}$

20. Susan is planning the layout of her garden. She wants to plant tomatoes in 3 plots, each 10 feet by 16 feet. Within the total area, she will leave a 4 foot by 6 foot rectangular plot for beans, and a $2\frac{1}{2}$ foot by 5 foot rectangular plot for lettuce. If each packet of tomato seeds will cover between 150 and 200 square feet of soil, which of the following is the minimum number of packets of seeds Susan needs to buy to plant tomatoes?

F. 5
G. 4
H. 3
J. 2
K. 1

21. What values of x are solutions in the equation $x^2 + 4x = 12$?

A. 8 and 12
B. 0 and 4
C. −2 and 6
D. −4 and 0
E. −6 and 2

GO ON TO THE NEXT PAGE.

22. For all $xy \neq 0$, and when both x and y are greater than 1, the expression $\dfrac{x^4 y^2}{x^2 y^4}$ equals which of the following?

DO YOUR FIGURING HERE.

F. $-\dfrac{x^2}{y^2}$

G. $-\dfrac{y^2}{x^2}$

H. 1

J. $\dfrac{x^2}{y^2}$

K. $\dfrac{y^2}{x^2}$

23. If point A has a non-zero x-coordinate and a non-zero y-coordinate and at least one of these coordinate values is positive, then point A *must* be located in which of the 4 quadrants labeled below?

Quadrants of the standard (x,y) coordinate plane

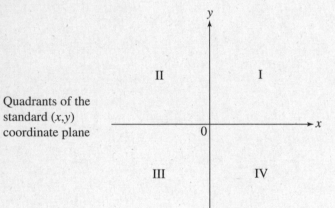

A. I only
B. I or II only
C. II or IV only
D. II, III, or IV only
E. I, II, or IV only

24. The variable cost to produce a box of paper is $4.75. The fixed cost for the paper production machinery is $1,600.00 each day. Which of the following expressions correctly models the cost of producing b boxes of paper each day?

F. $1,600\,b + 4.75$
G. $1,600\,b - 4.75$
H. $1,600 + 4.75\,b$
J. $4.75\,b - 1600$
K. $1,600\,b$

GO ON TO THE NEXT PAGE.

25. In the figure below, where $\triangle ABC \sim \triangle XYZ$, lengths are given in inches and the perimeter of $\triangle ABC$ is 576 inches. What is the length, in inches, of $\overline{AC}$?

(Note: The symbol ~ means "is similar to.")

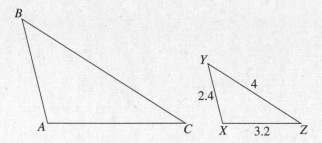

DO YOUR FIGURING HERE.

A. $126\frac{2}{5}$

B. 144

C. $168\frac{1}{5}$

D. 192

E. 240

26. Given that $\dfrac{\sqrt{11}}{x} \times \dfrac{6}{\sqrt{11}} = \dfrac{3\sqrt{11}}{11}$, what is the value of x ?

F. 6

G. 11

H. 121

J. $\sqrt{11}$

K. $2\sqrt{11}$

27. Natalie starts at the finish line of a straight 1,300 foot track and runs to the left toward the starting line at a constant rate of 12 feet per second while Jonathon starts 150 feet to the right of the starting line and runs to the right toward the finish line at a constant rate of 9 feet per second. To the nearest tenth of a second, after how many seconds will Natalie and Jonathon be at the same point on the track?

A. 483.3
B. 383.3
C. 63.7
D. 54.8
E. 10.9

GO ON TO THE NEXT PAGE.

28. Steve is going to buy an ice-cream sundae. He first must choose 1 of 3 possible ice-cream flavors. Next, he must choose 1 of 2 types of syrup. Finally, he must choose 1 of 6 kinds of candy toppings. Given these conditions, how many different kinds of sundaes could Steve possibly order?

- **F.** 162
- **G.** 36
- **H.** 18
- **J.** 9
- **K.** 6

DO YOUR FIGURING HERE.

29. The width of a rectangular cardboard box is half its length and twice its height. If the box is 12 cm long, what is the volume of the box in cubic centimeters?

- **A.** 72
- **B.** 216
- **C.** 252
- **D.** 1,296
- **E.** 1,728

30. At the end of each month, a credit card company uses the formula $D = B(1 + r) + 10m^2$ to calculate debt owed, where D is the cardholder's total debt; B is the amount charged to the card; r is the rate of interest; and m is the number of payments the cardholder has previously missed. If Daniel has charged $2,155 to his credit card with a 13% interest rate and has missed 2 payments, which value is closest to Daniel's total credit card debt?

- **F.** $2,195
- **G.** $2,435
- **H.** $2,455
- **J.** $2,475
- **K.** $2,495

GO ON TO THE NEXT PAGE.

31. In the figure below, a cone is shown, with dimensions given in centimeters. What is the total surface area of this cone, in square centimeters? (Note: The total surface area of a cone is given by the expression $\pi r^2 + \pi r s$ where r is the radius and s is the slant height.)

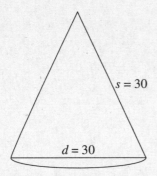

$s = 30$

$d = 30$

A. 225π
B. 450π
C. 465π
D. 675π
E. $18{,}000\pi$

32. Given the functions f and g are defined as $f(a) = 3a - 4$ and $g(a) = 2a^2 + 1$, what is the value of $f(g(a))$?

F. $6a^2 - 1$
G. $6a^2 - 3$
H. $2a^2 + 3a - 3$
J. $-2a^2 + 3a + 3$
K. $18a^2 - 48a + 33$

33. The table below shows the results of a recent poll in which 262 high school students were asked to rank a recent movie on a scale from 1 to 5 stars. To the nearest hundredth, what was the average star-rating given to this movie?

Stars given	Number of students who gave this rating
1	51
2	18
3	82
4	49
5	62

A. 0.31
B. 2.02
C. 3.06
D. 3.20
E. 18.8

GO ON TO THE NEXT PAGE.

34. Lines p, q, r, and s are shown in the figure below and the set of all angles that are supplementary to $\angle x$ is $\{1, 3, 8, 11\}$. Which of the following is the set of all lines that *must* be parallel?

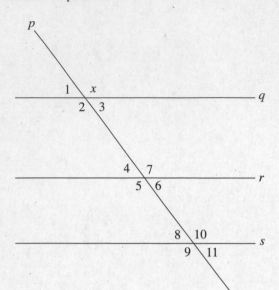

   F. $\{q, r\}$
   G. $\{q, s\}$
   H. $\{r, s\}$
   J. $\{p, q\}$
   K. $\{q, r, s\}$

35. $(4x^4 y^4)^4$ is equivalent to:

   A. xy
   B. $16x^8 y^8$
   C. $16x^{16} y^{16}$
   D. $256x^8 y^8$
   E. $256x^{16} y^{16}$

36. Which of the following expressions is equivalent to the inequality $6x - 8 > 8x + 14$?

   F. $x < -11$
   G. $x > -11$
   H. $x < -3$
   J. $x > -3$
   K. $x < 11$

GO ON TO THE NEXT PAGE.

DO YOUR FIGURING HERE.

37. As shown in the standard (x,y) coordinate plane below, A (2,4) lies on the circle with center L (10,–2) and radius 10 coordinate units. What are the coordinates of the image of A after the circle is rotated 90° counter-clockwise (↺) about the center of the circle?

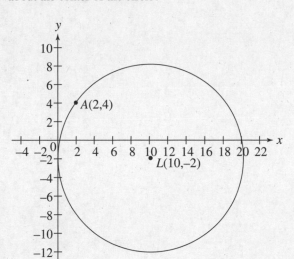

   A.   (10,2)
   B.   (–2,10)
   C.   (2,–8)
   D.   (0,–2)
   E.   (4,–10)

38. The length of the hypotenuse of the right triangle figured below is 16, and the length of one of its legs is 12. What is the cosine of angle θ ?

   F. $\dfrac{\sqrt{112}}{16}$

   G. $\dfrac{16}{\sqrt{112}}$

   H. $\dfrac{\sqrt{112}}{12}$

   J. $\dfrac{12}{16}$

   K. $\dfrac{16}{12}$

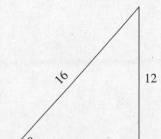

GO ON TO THE NEXT PAGE.

39. In the figure shown below, $\overline{CA}$ bisects $\angle BAD$, and $\overline{DA}$ bisects $\angle CAE$. What is the measure of $\angle CAD$?

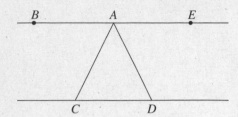

A. 30°
B. 45°
C. 60°
D. 90°
E. Cannot be determined from the given information

40. If the average number of carbon dioxide molecules per cubic inch in a container is 3×10^4 and there are 6×10^8 molecules of carbon dioxide in the container, what is the volume of the container in cubic inches?

F. 5×10^5
G. 2×10^2
H. 2×10^4
J. 18×10^{12}
K. 18×10^{32}

GO ON TO THE NEXT PAGE.

41. The figure below shows the screen of an automobile navigation map. Point *A* represents the car's starting point, point *B* represents the driver's intended destination, and point *C*, the origin of the circle, is the car's current position. Currently, point *A* is 15 miles from point *C* and 250° clockwise from due north, and point *B* is 20 miles from point *C* and 30° clockwise from due north. Which of the following represents the shortest distance (a straight line) between the car's starting point and the driver's desired destination?

(Note: For any △*ABC* in which side *a* is opposite ∠*A*, side *b* is opposite ∠*B*, and side *c* is opposite ∠*C*, the law of cosines applies: $c^2 = a^2 + b^2 - 2ab \cos \angle C$.)

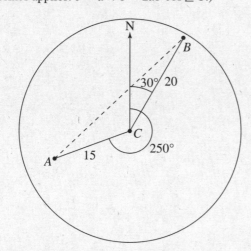

DO YOUR FIGURING HERE.

A. $\sqrt{15^2 + 20^2 - 2(15)(20)\cos 30°}$

B. $\sqrt{15^2 + 20^2 - 2(15)(20)\cos 140°}$

C. $\sqrt{15^2 + 20^2 - 2(15)(20)\cos 220°}$

D. $\sqrt{15^2 + 20^2 - 2(15)(20)\cos 250°}$

E. $\sqrt{15^2 + 20^2 - 2(15)(20)\cos 280°}$

42. What real number is halfway between $\frac{1}{4}$ and $\frac{1}{6}$?

F. $\frac{1}{6}$

G. $\frac{1}{5}$

H. $\frac{1}{2}$

J. $\frac{5}{24}$

K. $\frac{7}{24}$

GO ON TO THE NEXT PAGE.

43. In isosceles triangle △*ACE*, shown below, *B* and *D* are
the midpoints of congruent sides $\overline{AC}$ and $\overline{CE}$, respectively.
∠*ABE* measures 95°, and ∠*DAE* measures 35°. What is the
measure of ∠*DEB* ?

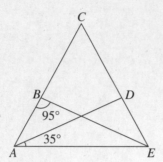

   A. 50°
   B. 30°
   C. 25°
   D. 15°
   E. 10°

44. A small square table and an L-shaped table fit together
with no space between them to create a large square table.
The area of the large square table is 108 square feet and is
nine times the area of the small square. What is *x*, the edge
of the L-shaped table labeled in the figure below in square
feet?

   F. $2\sqrt{3}$

   G.   4

   H. $4\sqrt{3}$

   J. $4\sqrt{6}$

   K.   12

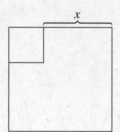

45. Which of the following is NOT an irrational number?

   A. $\sqrt{\pi}$

   B. $\sqrt{5}$

   C. $\sqrt{8}$

   D. $\sqrt{\dfrac{7}{49}}$

   E. $\sqrt{\dfrac{81}{25}}$

GO ON TO THE NEXT PAGE.

46. If $x < 0$ and $y < 0$, then $|x + y|$ is equivalent to which of the following?

   F. $x + y$

   G. $-(x + y)$

   H. $x - y$

   J. $|x - y|$

   K. $\sqrt{x^2 + y^2}$

47. Jane wants to bring her bowling average up to an 85 with her performance on her next game. So far she has bowled 5 out of 7 equally weighted games, and she has an average score of 83. What must her score on her next game be in order to reach her goal?

   A. 83
   B. 85
   C. 90
   D. 93
   E. 95

48. In a complex plane, the vertical axis is the *imaginary axis* and the horizontal axis is the *real axis*. Within the complex plane, a complex number $a + bi$ is comparable to the point (a,b) in the standard (x,y) coordinate plane. $\sqrt{a^2 + b^2}$ is the modulus of the complex point $a + bi$. Which of the complex numbers F, G, H, J, and K below has the smallest modulus?

   F. F
   G. G
   H. H
   J. J
   K. K

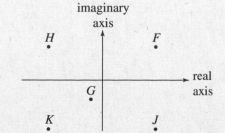

GO ON TO THE NEXT PAGE.

49. In the real numbers, what is the solution of the equation

$$9^{x-4} = 27^{3x+2} ?$$

A. $-\dfrac{6}{7}$

B. -2

C. -3

D. $-\dfrac{7}{2}$

E. -4

DO YOUR FIGURING HERE.

50. The graph of the trigonometric function $f(x) = 2 \sin x$ is represented below. Which of the following is true of this function?

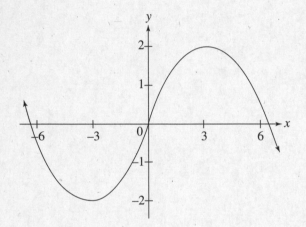

F. $f(x)$ is a 1:1 function (that is, x is unique for all $f(x)$ and $f(x)$ is unique for all x).

G. $f(x)$ is undefined at $x = 0$.

H. $f(x)$ is even (that is, $f(x) = f(-x)$ for all x).

J. $f(x)$ is odd (that is, $f(-x) = -f(x)$ for all x).

K. $f(x)$ falls entirely within the domain $-6 \le x \le 6$.

51. An integer from 299 through 1,000, inclusive, will be chosen randomly. What is the probability that the number chosen will have 1 as at least 1 of its digits?

A. $\dfrac{234}{1,000}$

B. $\dfrac{134}{702}$

C. $\dfrac{70}{702}$

D. $\dfrac{63}{702}$

E. $\dfrac{17}{702}$

GO ON TO THE NEXT PAGE.

52. In the figure below, side $\overline{MN}$ of isosceles triangle $\triangle NLM$ lies on the line $y + \dfrac{2}{3}x = 2$ in the standard (x,y) coordinate plane, and side $\overline{NL}$ is parallel to the x-axis. What is the slope of $\overline{LM}$?

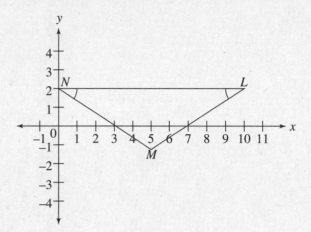

   F. $\dfrac{3}{2}$

   G. $\dfrac{2}{3}$

   H. $\dfrac{1}{3}$

   J. $-\dfrac{2}{3}$

   K. $-\dfrac{3}{2}$

GO ON TO THE NEXT PAGE.

53. In the figure below, $0 < y < x$. One of the angle measures in the triangle is $\sin^{-1}\left(\dfrac{x}{\sqrt{x^2+y^2}}\right)$. What is

$$\tan\left[\sin^{-1}\left(\dfrac{x}{\sqrt{x^2+y^2}}\right)\right]?$$

DO YOUR FIGURING HERE.

A. $\dfrac{x}{y}$

B. $\dfrac{y}{x}$

C. $\dfrac{x}{\sqrt{x^2+y^2}}$

D. $\dfrac{y}{\sqrt{x^2+y^2}}$

E. $\dfrac{\sqrt{x^2+y^2}}{x}$

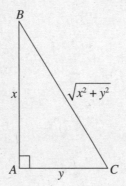

Use the following information to answer questions 54–56.

Melissa attaches her dog's leash to a metal anchor in the grass so that the dog can roam only within a radius of 12 feet in any direction from the anchor. A map of the area accessible to the dog is shown below in the standard (x,y) coordinate plane, with the anchor at the origin and 1 coordinate unit representing 1 foot.

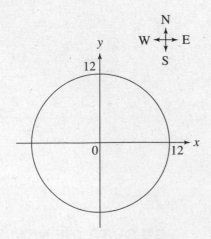

GO ON TO THE NEXT PAGE.

54. Which of the following is closest to the area, in square feet, the dog can roam?

    F.   75
    G.   144
    H.   452
    J.   904
    K. 1,420

DO YOUR FIGURING HERE.

55. Which of the following is an equation of the circle shown on the map?

    A. $(x - y)^2 = 12$
    B. $(x + y)^2 = 12$
    C. $(x + y)^2 = 12^2$
    D. $x^2 + y^2 = 12$
    E. $x^2 + y^2 = 12^2$

56. Joy brings her dog to the same park and anchors her dog 30 feet away from Melissa's anchor along a walking trail. Joy's dog can roam only within a radius of 20 feet in all directions from its anchor. For how many feet along the walking trail can *both* dogs roam?

(Note: Assume the leashes can't stretch.)

    F.   2
    G.   8
    H. 10
    J. 18
    K. 42

GO ON TO THE NEXT PAGE.

57. The graphs of the equations $y = -(x) + 1$ and
$y = -(x + 1)^2 + 4$ are shown in the standard (x,y) coordinate plane below. What real values of x, if any, satisfy the following inequality: $-(x + 1)^2 + 4 > -(x) + 1$?

DO YOUR FIGURING HERE.

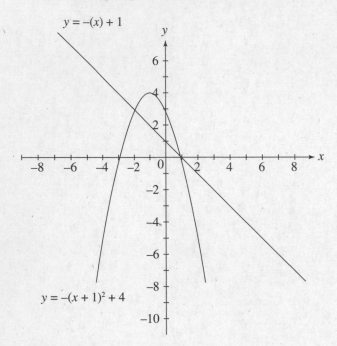

$y = -(x) + 1$

$y = -(x + 1)^2 + 4$

A. $x < -3$ and $x > 1$
B. $x < -2$ and $x > 1$
C. $-3 < x < 1$
D. $-2 < x < 1$
E. No real values

58. For any positive two-digit integer x, with tens digit t, units digit u, and $t \neq u$, y is the two-digit integer formed when the digits of x are reversed. What is the greatest possible value of $(y - x)$ when t is less than u ?

F. $u - t$
G. $ut - tu$
H. $t^2 - 10tu + u^2$
J. $9|u - t|$
K. Cannot be determined from the given information

GO ON TO THE NEXT PAGE.

59. In the figure below, the vertices of parallelogram $ABCD$ are A $(2,-4)$, B $(8,-4)$, C $(10,-2)$, and D $(4,-2)$. What is the area of the parallelogram?

DO YOUR FIGURING HERE.

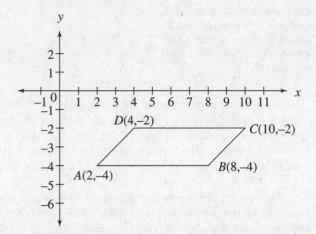

A.   6

B. $6\sqrt{2}$

C.   12

D. $12\sqrt{2}$

E.   16

60. The sum, S, of an arithmetic sequence with first term x_1 is given by $S = n\left(\dfrac{x_1 + x_n}{2}\right)$, where n is the number of terms in the sequence. The sum of 5 consecutive terms in a given arithmetic sequence is 145, and x_5 is 48. What is the sixth term of this sequence?

F.   49

G.   57.5

H.   77

J.   154.5

K.   174

END OF TEST 2

STOP! DO NOT TURN THE PAGE UNTIL TOLD TO DO SO.

DO NOT RETURN TO THE PREVIOUS TEST.

READING TEST
35 Minutes—40 Questions

DIRECTIONS: There are four passages in this test. Each passage is followed by several questions. After reading each passage, choose the best answer to each question and blacken the corresponding oval on your answer document. You may refer to the passages as often as necessary.

Passage I

PROSE FICTION: This passage is adapted from the short story "A Prisoner in His Castle" by Curtis Longweather (© 2008 by Curtis Longweather).

Since he returned from the hospital, he has been unable to reclaim his speaking voice. That is not to say that he can't make sounds, but that he often can't make his thoughts into sounds like words and sentences. Something is polluting the
5 chemistry that distills mental language into vocal output. His mind lights up with ideas just like mine does, but his ideas cannot escape. His thoughts are dispatched like knights to battle only to find they are unable to cross the moat that surrounds their castle. They are held prisoner in their own home,
10 quarantined in frustrated isolation from the outside world.

"I fear that I will eventually choke on my own thoughts," he worries aloud to me in one of his desperate letters.

"Then expel them all on to the page," I remind him. He is a volcano with no air vents to relieve the pressure of the heat
15 churning in his belly. His insides roil with fire, occasionally bubbling to the surface. His core vibrates with tightly coiled anticipation, the roof of his head eventually shedding off all shingles as a prelude to its propelling explosively into the atmosphere.

20 I tell him that his speaking voice may be like the oceanic cloud of dust and debris that the volcano spews into the air, but his writing can flow like omni-directional lava, indiscriminately absorbing everything in its path. Eventually, the continents that form as this lava cools will be fertile grounds
25 for his readers. Each of his letters stands proudly as an island within the sloshing seas of his mind, and his clarity of prose allows us explorers to navigate him.

"There is plenty of solace in writing," he acknowledges, but maintains, "never explain to someone who can't run that
30 at least he can drive a car."

He will always hear his thoughts as an echo, either reverberating within his own skull or as a crude imitation when transferred by pen.

I concede that the Page's shortcoming is a lack of dy-
35 namic human ears, but I optimistically point to the fact that written language has the potential to be seen by *countless*

human eyes. It has the potential to be richly revered classical music, not just catchy pop expressions that inspire bystanders to twitch in accordance. It has the advantage of being me-
40 thodically composed and purposefully orchestrated. However, it can be spontaneous and stream-of-consciousness as well.

"A verbal speech can be a symphony of thought just as an essay can be an improvisational blunder." He responds. "You are wrongly contrasting two styles of music when the more
45 appropriate comparison is two very different instruments."

His distinction is a valid one, but I continue to stubbornly assert the superiority of literary communication. When we *speak* to convey meaning, I argue, we can too easily get away with lazy word choice by using context, body language, tone,
50 and other non-verbal devices to supplement our stated words. In a piece of writing, the words exist in isolation from their author. They belong only to each other, like pirates who share a common destiny but no longer pledge allegiance to any sovereign entity. Judge them by your own standards
55 if you wish to be confused, but realize that the only telling diagnosis rests in the internal consistency of their ways. Do the various tensions created by the professed actions, ideas, and feelings of the writing allow the reader to vicariously behold the mental state of the author? If so, then the reader
60 has the satisfying experience of being simultaneously in the audience and backstage as well.

He enjoys coming to watch me during my trials. Sometimes I look over at him while I am delivering my closing arguments to a jury, and I see the mix of pride and pain in
65 his eyes as he listens to me express myself more lucidly than he may ever be able to again. If my profession would allow it, I would gladly yield my voice to him and become a mere puppet for his ideas, just so he could again experience the instant gratification of vocal persuasion. (I frequently wonder
70 if my friendship with him will ultimately venture into the territory of Cyrano de Bergerac, who so wished to woo the heart of a woman that he enlisted the help of a friend to speak his thoughts aloud to her.)

It is not the organization of thought that he treasures in
75 listening to my courtroom orations. It is the expressiveness that a human voice can add to the meaning of words that he deeply misses. He will occasionally have me rehearse my

GO ON TO THE NEXT PAGE.

speeches to him and never permits me to begin reciting my words too mechanically. The moment I begin *reading* and not
80 *speaking*, he will clap his hands and signal me to return back to the beginning of the idea.

In this way, just as I continue to remind him of the unspeakable value of written language, he continues to remind me of the irreplaceable value of the human voice.

1. As it relates to his friend's fear as described in the second paragraph, the narrator's description of a volcano (lines 13–19) most serves to:

   A. elaborate the friend's inner torment.
   B. speculate that his friend's thoughts will be unleashed.
   C. explain why the friend is unable to speak.
   D. imply the friend needs to be more patient.

2. Which of the following best describes the structure of the passage?

   F. A detailed character study of two close friends by means of describing one extended argument between them.
   G. A debate about a topic during which the two main characters take equal turns discussing their positions and reasons.
   H. An exploration of the author's experience of his friend's speech impairment using their verbal and written exchanges as a primary source.
   J. The depiction of a unique friendship that allows the narrator to explain his successes and struggles as a lawyer.

3. The erupting volcano simile refers to a dust cloud and a lava flow to portray:

   A. intuition and logic.
   B. simplicity and complexity.
   C. instinct and deliberation.
   D. vocal and non-vocal expression.

4. Based on the passage, which of the following statements most clearly portrays the respective attitudes of the narrator and his friend?

   F. The friend is argumentative and cynical; the narrator is jaded and indifferent.
   G. The friend is scornful and depressed; the narrator is apologetic and idealistic.
   H. The friend is anxious and despondent; the narrator is sympathetic and encouraging.
   J. The friend is shy and reclusive; the narrator is outgoing and nonchalant.

5. In the passage, the narrator most nearly describes Cyrano de Bergerac as:

   A. someone who was afraid of losing the love of his life.
   B. unable to produce any sound of his own due to a physical condition.
   C. someone who had reason to communicate indirectly with a woman.
   D. too caught up in the emotions of love to be able to describe them.

6. Which of the following statements about pirates is best supported by the narrator's characterization of them?

   F. They have no rules of conduct that they must follow.
   G. They succeed by means of confusing their enemies.
   H. They are not accountable to anyone other than themselves.
   J. They recognize the superior value of written language.

7. It can be most strongly inferred from the passage that the friend values which of the following in vocal speech?

   A. Meaningful expression
   B. Proper mechanics
   C. Rich vocabulary
   D. Clever humor

8. According to the passage, the friend is worried he may:

   F. say something embarrassing if he speaks.
   G. grow exasperated from his inability to vocalize thoughts.
   H. be damaging the narrator's chances of courtroom success.
   J. not be clever enough to compose a symphony of thought.

9. As it is used in (line 68), the word *puppet* most nearly means:

   A. entertainer.
   B. conversationalist.
   C. toy.
   D. mouthpiece.

10. Based on the narrator's account, the friend's reaction to watching the narrator during legal proceedings is:

   F. appreciative and yearning.
   G. confused and hopeless.
   H. awestruck and overbearing.
   J. bitter and resentful.

GO ON TO THE NEXT PAGE.

Passage II

SOCIAL SCIENCE: This passage is adapted from the entry "Larsen B" in *Down Off the Shelf: Recent Antarctic Natural Disasters* (© 2009 Subzero Publications).

Most people associate Antarctica with frigid temperatures, glaciers, and massive sheets of ice; however, recent geological events highlight not the cold, but issues of warming. Further, such events emphasize the ways in which human behavior
5　influences climactic and geological changes. Though scientists may disagree as to the extent of human influence, there is no doubt that our behavior does have significant and lasting outcomes. One of the most dramatic environmental events in recent years is the loss of ice shelves that float around much
10　of Antarctica; in particular, the collapse of the Larsen B ice shelf. This long, fringing mass was assumed to be the latest in a long line of victims of Antarctic summer heat waves linked to global warming; new research, however, calls this assumption into question.

15　In 2002, the northern section of the Larsen B ice shelf (a thick floating sheet of freshwater ice fed by glaciers) shattered and separated from the continent in the largest single event in a 30-year series of ice-shelf retreats in the peninsula. The Larsen B was about 220 meters thick and is thought to
20　have existed for at least 400 years prior to its collapse. The shattered ice from Larsen B set thousands of icebergs adrift in the Weddell Sea, east of the Antarctic Peninsula. A total of about 1,250 square miles of shelf area disintegrated in a 35-day period beginning on January 31 of 2002. The collapse
25　was perhaps foreshadowed when standing water appeared on the ice. (Scientists theorize that once melt-water appears on the surface of an ice shelf, the rate of ice disintegration increases; pooling water puts weight on the ice, filling small cracks that expand, eventually causing breakage.) The appear-
30　ance of standing water on ice shelves is generally attributed to global warming; thus, the collapse of the Larsen B ice shelf seemed to be one of the most obvious and stunning signs of worldwide climate change.

In support of this postulation, the *Journal of Climate*
35　published a 2006 study by Dr. Gareth Marshall of the British Antarctic Survey, providing the first direct evidence linking human activity to the collapse of Antarctic ice shelves. Scientists revealed that stronger westerly winds in the northern Antarctic Peninsula, driven principally by human-induced
40　climate change, are responsible for the significant increase in summer temperatures that led to the retreat and collapse of the Larsen B. They argue that global warming and the ozone hole have changed Antarctic weather patterns such that strengthened westerly winds force warm air eastward
45　over the natural barrier created by the Antarctic Peninsula's mountain chain. Elevated temperatures in the summer warm the area by approximately five degrees Celsius, creating the conditions that allowed melt-water to drain into crevasses on the Larsen ice shelf, a key process that led to its 2002

50　break-up. Dr. Marshall asserts that this is the first time anyone has demonstrated a process directly linking the collapse to human activity, and that climate change does not impact our planet evenly, as evidenced by the significant increase in temperatures in certain geographical areas, particularly the
55　western Antarctic Peninsula. According to his research, this icy region has shown the largest increase in temperatures observed anywhere on Earth over the past half-century.

Marshall's breakthrough research was followed, two years later, by new and somewhat contradictory information. In a
60　paper published in the Journal of Glaciology, Professor Neil Glasser and Dr. Ted Scambos assert that despite the dramatic nature of the break-up in 2002, observations by glaciologists and computer modeling by scientists at NASA pointed to an ice shelf in distress for decades. Glasser and Scambos contend
65　that the shelf was already teetering on the brink of collapse before the final summer, and though they acknowledge that global warming had a major role in the collapse, they emphasize that it is only one of a number of atmospheric, oceanic and glaciological factors. The amount of melt-water on the
70　Larsen B shelf just before the collapse caused many to assume that air temperature increases were primarily to blame, but Scambos and Glasser's research shows that ice-shelf breakup is not controlled simply by climate, citing, for example, that the location and spacing of crevasses and rifts on the ice do
75　much to determine its strength. Scientists in the field consider this study imperative, as the collapse of ice shelves contributes (albeit indirectly) to global sea-level rise.

Scientists agree that the break-up of Larsen B alone will not change sea level, but other glaciers previously restricted
80　by the ice shelf have surged forward, lowering their surfaces. Since lower elevations have warmer temperatures, these glaciers melt more quickly, causing more ice to flow into the sea, and levels to rise. If more and more ice shelves are lost in subsequent years, the concern is that the rise in sea
85　levels could affect ecosystems worldwide, generating such problems as widespread flooding, loss of coastal cities and island countries, decreased crop yields, and the possible extinction of millions of species. Determining the cause of ice shelf collapse, and the ways in which humans can contribute
90　to both the problem and the solution, may help to prevent such catastrophes in the future; it becomes clear, then, why researchers are compelled to continue their studies of ice shelves in the Antarctic.

GO ON TO THE NEXT PAGE.

11. The author most nearly characterizes the role of human activity in regard to the collapse of ice shelves as:

    A. a significant though previously unproven contributing factor.
    B. insignificant in comparison to glaciological influences.
    C. less of a contributor than initial evidence predicted.
    D. the primary and irreversible cause of all detrimental effects.

12. The author lists all of the following as possible effects of sea level rise EXCEPT:

    F. loss of island countries.
    G. extinction of millions of species.
    H. decreased crop yields.
    J. surging glaciers.

13. The author indicates that the common factor in Dr. Marshall's study (lines 34–57) and that of Doctors Scambos and Glasser (lines 58–77) is that both studies:

    A. cite global warming as a reason for the Larsen B ice-shelf collapse
    B. discredit climate change as a reason for the Larsen B ice-shelf collapse.
    C. found little compelling evidence to explain the Larsen B ice-shelf collapse.
    D. agree that structural weaknesses caused the Larsen B ice-shelf collapse.

14. In his statement in lines 50–55, the author most nearly means that human activity:

    F. is inconsequential compared to other factors influencing climate change.
    G. could eventually affect weather patterns worldwide, doing great harm.
    H. makes certain areas of the world much warmer than they would otherwise be.
    J. will cause sea level to rise, wiping out entire countries and species of animals.

15. The author calls which of the following a stunning sign of worldwide climate change?

    A. Worldwide sea-level rise
    B. Melt-water on the Larsen B ice shelf prior to its collapse
    C. The collapse of the Larsen B ice shelf
    D. Increased temperatures in the western Antarctic Peninsula

16. The author includes the findings in lines (64–75) primarily in order to:

    F. support the prevailing theory that global warming causes glacier break-up.
    G. encourage people to make environmentally-friendly choices in their daily lives.
    H. imply that ice shelf break-up is simpler than scientists originally thought.
    J. highlight the interaction between factors in a major environmental event.

17. The main idea of the third paragraph is that the Larsen B ice-shelf collapse:

    A. was not caused by global warming.
    B. was foreshadowed for years prior to the event.
    C. was caused by the uneven impact of climate change on the earth.
    D. was caused in part by direct human activity.

18. Which of the following is NOT listed in the passage as a cause of ice-shelf collapse?

    F. Global warming
    G. Human activity
    H. Spacing and location of crevasses and rifts
    J. Deep ocean currents

19. The author calls the increased westerly winds in the northern Antarctic Peninsula:

    A. irrelevant to the problem of ice-shelf collapse.
    B. responsible for an increase in summer temperatures.
    C. a common weather pattern in certain times of year.
    D. an unmistakable warning of sea-level rise.

20. The author uses the remark "largest increase in temperatures observed anywhere on Earth" lines (56–57) to:

    F. demonstrate how scientists are prone to exaggeration when talking about ice shelves.
    G. give a strong incentive for people to change their behavior.
    H. explain that global warming doesn't occur at the same rate in all regions.
    J. clarify a common misconception about weather patterns in cold areas.

GO ON TO THE NEXT PAGE.

Passage III

HUMANITIES: This passage is excerpted from the essay "Salman Rushdie: A Man of Multiple Worlds" by Paul Lopez (© 2010 by Paul Lopez). In this selection, the term *partition* refers to the British Empire's official relinquishment of its claim on India, at which point the area was divided into two self-governing countries: India and Pakistan. Also, the contemporary city of Mumbai was known as Bombay during the time this passage discusses.

As well-known for his life story as for his writing, Salman Rushdie is nonetheless a virtuosic author of the first degree. His books are filled with lyrical passages capable of transport-ing the reader to a kitchen in India, a mountain in Pakistan,
5 or a street corner in London. Although his plots often involve metaphysical or even magical elements, somehow they seem reasonable. He has the art of drawing the reader in, explaining each bizarre incident in such a way that, suddenly, it becomes plausible, if only for the moment.

10   Born in Bombay, on the Western coast of India, to Mus-lim parents during the year of the partition, Rushdie grew up amidst the India-Pakistan and Hindi-Muslim struggle. Each group strove to create a new identity and independence, apart from the colonial past, and Rushdie paid close attention to
15 each group's stories. Later, he immigrated to England to at-tend school, and there too he listened. As an author, he began to integrate these stories, and his books show the complex interplay that exists between these three cultures.

In his books, it is clear that each area has, for him, its
20 own unique beauty. Rushdie's India is a world of food; in one book, he spends pages discussing chutneys—their flavor, their coloring, and their preparation. His Bombay is described as a raucous place, filled with colors, scents that assault the nostrils, and people thronging the streets everywhere you
25 look. It is a place teeming with life and all that life entails. His Pakistan, on the other hand, is a place of stark beauty, and of dry, desert landscapes with communities centered on lakes scattered throughout the countryside. A people that has fought for its independence, filled with a ferocious pride of place,
30 but quiet, withdrawn. A private people, in stark contrast to the overflowing life of India. In Rushdie's Pakistan, it seems, they have room for quiet and have chosen that for themselves. It is also a world of hospitality, but on a personal scale. Instead of describing markets or streets, Rushdie dwells on families
35 and individuals, describing their appearances and behaviors minutely. And finally, there is Rushdie's England. Often, his characters in India and Pakistan long to be in England, causing the reader to wonder if Rushdie himself felt that longing at one time. Once they arrive, however, they often find England
40 disconcerting, its orderly chaos overwhelming to someone unaccustomed to the Western world. The colors too are miss-ing, along with the pungent spices in the air. Even when his characters are describing how happy they are to have made it to their promised land, they cannot seem to leave their
45 homelands completely behind.

It is this merging of three disparate cultures that makes Rushdie's writing stand out. Each culture is made to come alive for the reader, allowing his Western readers a chance to peer into a culture very different from their own. One
50 of his earlier books, written in 1981 and called *Midnight's Children*, takes as its focal point the partition of India. The main character is born at the stroke of midnight, drawing his first breath just as the partition becomes a reality. The book follows the many ways in which this coincidence affects the
55 character throughout his life, tying the events in his personal life to those in the larger life of the country and community, showing that neither one exists separate of the other. While Rushdie was not quite born at the stroke of midnight, he was born a mere month before the partition took place, and he
60 too would have grown up watching the people of India and Pakistan work to create new worlds for themselves. This experience permeates not only *Midnight's Children* but also all of his other works, as he describes characters striving to find a place for themselves in a world that doesn't always
65 make sense. He wants, it seems, for his readers to get a sense of the struggle to merge yet stay distinct.

In the end, many writers have discussed colonialism, independence, and migration, but none perhaps as engag-ingly as Rushdie. As interesting as his subjects are, certainly
70 the way his prose draws readers into his world has been the essential factor in making his work so enduring. His books may not be the first, but they are some of the most prominent books to deal with these subjects and, as such, have had a profound influence on the works of other writers, as well as
75 on the reading public. No matter what the future holds, the portraits of India and Pakistan drawn by Rushdie will continue to influence the literary world for years to come.

21. The first paragraph establishes all of the following about Rushdie EXCEPT:

   A. his intention to make Western readers more aware of what life in India and Pakistan is like.
   B. the kinds of elements that might be included in Rush-die's writing.
   C. whether or not he is well-known in his chosen profes-sion.
   D. some of the locations he tends to use in his writing.

GO ON TO THE NEXT PAGE.

22. The primary function of the second paragraph (lines 10–18) is to:

   F. discuss Rushdie's religious upbringing and personal faith.
   G. give some background information on Rushdie's childhood.
   H. contrast the Hindi and Muslim belief systems.
   J. list all the factors that led to Rushdie's emigration from India.

23. Which of the following statements most correctly identifies the main idea of the passage?

   A. Rushdie is a highly talented writer but his personal failings prevent readers from empathizing with his characters.
   B. The partition of India was a traumatic experience for the many people who were compelled to move in the years following the division.
   C. Rushdie uses his personal life experiences to describe for readers what life is like in the part of the world where he grew up.
   D. The book *Midnight's Children* is an insightful book about the events surrounding the official partition of India.

24. All of the following details are used in the passage to describe Rushdie's vision of Bombay EXCEPT that it:

   F. is filled with scents, some of which can be very pungent.
   G. is a place filled with many colors.
   H. is typically very hot and humid, with temperatures reaching uncomfortable levels.
   J. is overwhelmed with people and life.

25. One of the main points in the fourth paragraph is that, in his writing, Rushdie is trying to convey a sense of:

   A. futility.
   B. sadness.
   C. struggle.
   D. longing.

26. Which of the following questions is NOT answered in the passage?

   F. In general terms, which parts of the world tend to be prominently featured in Rushdie's works?
   G. How do Rushdie's descriptions of the Pakistani people differ from his descriptions of the Indian people?
   H. In which part of the world was Rushdie himself born?
   J. How many books had Rushdie, at the time of this essay's publication, written?

27. According to the passage, in which of the following countries did Rushdie attend school?

   A. Pakistan
   B. England
   C. India
   D. America

28. Which of the following words is the best characterization of Rushdie's Bombay, according to this passage?

   F. Frustrating
   G. Chaotic
   H. Vibrant
   J. Stark

29. The information in lines 69–71 is most likely included by the author in order to suggest:

   A. that it is Rushdie's skill as a writer, rather than his subjects alone, that has brought him lasting fame.
   B. Rushdie's tendency to rely too heavily on historical events for the plots of his novels.
   C. Rushdie's likelihood of remaining a literary icon well into the future is very uncertain.
   D. that the subjects that Rushdie writes about aren't actually very interesting to most people.

30. The passage suggests that Rushdie's most important contribution to literature is his:

   F. description of Pakistan's landscapes.
   G. portrayal of India's partition.
   H. ability to draw readers into his world.
   J. beautifully crafted prose.

GO ON TO THE NEXT PAGE.

Passage IV

NATURAL SCIENCE: This passage is excerpted from the article "Alternative Medicines: A New Perspective" by Audrey C. Tristan (© 2004 by Audrey Tristan).

The view of health as a holistic and integrative state of physical, spiritual, and emotional well-being is deeply rooted in mind-body philosophies that have survived thousands of years. Traditional *mindful movement* therapies found in
5 *yoga, tai chi,* and *qigong,* for example, couple aerobic and anaerobic exercise with mental focus. These practices, which originated in Eastern medicine, guide participants through a series of specialized movements synchronized to the breath and mental images. Involving more than cardiovascular activ-
10 ity, these exercise routines are said to improve overall health by bringing deeper awareness to the body and promoting strength, flexibility, and balance.

Modern Western biomedicine, on the other hand, has advanced largely by splitting the mind and body to allow for
15 the objective study of health and disease mechanisms, and thus has been slow to embrace the implications of mind-body health. However, as alternative and traditional therapies have become increasingly more popular and available in the West, researchers have begun to delve deeper into mind-body therapy
20 efficacy, that is, the ability to consistently produce a desired, therapeutic effect.

There is particularly solid research to support the use of mind-body therapy to counteract the debilitating effects of stress. Certain mind-body therapies may alter the way
25 we experience pain and manage stress through the use of conscious strategies to avert automatic responses. Stress, as defined in biomedical terms, is the physiological response to a perceived threat. It is not to be confused with the common usage of the term, which generally equates stress with those
30 activities that provoke a stress response (these are deemed *stressors*). When the central nervous system perceives a threat, the sympathetic division of the autonomic nervous system is engaged, signaling the release of stress hormones such as epinephrine and cortisol into the bloodstream that in
35 turn activate particular physiological responses: heart and respiratory rate acceleration, muscles tension, perspiration, indigestion, and pupil dilation.

This "fight-or-flight" response alludes to the conditions of ancestral humans and the presumed adaptive function of
40 such a response in evolutionary history. The response, how-ever, does not occur only in reaction to isolated incidences. Indeed, most stressors today, related to work, family, school, and interpersonal relationships, are prolonged, and the fight-or-flight responses are thus sustained. This continual state
45 of arousal results in deleterious effects on health over time, such as high blood pressure, cardiovascular disease, diabetes, digestive disorders, and suppressed immune response.

Mind-body therapies, such as guided imagery and medita-tion, essentially work by altering responses to stressors. The
50 simple act of breathing deeply and focusing on the breath will, in contrast to a stress response, engage the parasympathetic division of the autonomic nervous system, which lowers blood pressure, heart, and respiratory rates, and decreases muscle tension, thus countering the negative consequences of
55 fight-or-flight response.

Other mind-body therapies alter the experience of pain itself. Pain is a multidimensional experience that traverses four physiological pathways. *Transduction* occurs first, as sensory neurons, the *nociceptors*, detect potentially damaging stimuli
60 and transmit signals from affected tissue to neural activity. The next step is *transmission*, in which the pain messages are exchanged between the nociceptors and the spinal cord. *Central representation* follows as the information is relayed from the spinal cord through the thalamus to the limbic and cortical
65 structures of the brain, which identify the sensations relayed. *Modulation,* the last step, is a descending pathway in which the brain sends signals back to the spinal cord to moderate the sensation of pain, basically "numbing" the pain. Since the limbic system is also the brain center for emotion, memory,
70 and autonomic nervous system integration, the experience of pain is ultimately mediated by emotions, an individual's own past experiences, and present external environment.

In clinical hypnosis, or *hypnotic analgesia,* patients are taught alternative skills to alter the experience of pain.
75 Hypnotic analgesia produces psychophysiological effects as patients are taught to consciously re-evaluate and manage a painful stimulus, using visual imagery and positive emotional reinforcement. A recent review of controlled studies of hyp-notic analgesia suggests that the treatment can reduce pain
80 in chronic conditions resulting from osteoarthritis, cancer, fibromyalgia, and disability. The authors cautioned, however, that a number of questions remain unanswered.

Mind-body research has provided important insights into both the efficacy of such therapies and our understanding of
85 the cognitive and physiological perception of pain. More investigation is needed, however, to ascertain if outcome expectations influence the success of particular therapies, if response rates differ as a result of pain type or pain diagnosis, and to what degree variation in individual response, and if
90 research design should preclude broader inferences.

GO ON TO THE NEXT PAGE.

31. The studies reviewed in the seventh paragraph (lines 73–82) have shown that hypnotic analgesia may be effective in:

    A. restructuring the brain non-invasively.
    B. fighting cancer and fibromyalgia.
    C. decreasing depression in patients.
    D. altering the experience of pain.

32. According to the sixth paragraph, (lines 56–72), when a door slams on a person's hand, the detection of pain results from:

    F. the transmission of nerve signals from damaged tissue to the spinal cord and sympathetic nervous system.
    G. the transmission of nerve signals from damaged tissue to the spinal cord and brain.
    H. the sympathetic nervous system releasing chemical hormones, which reach the heart via the bloodstream.
    J. the sympathetic nervous system releasing chemical hormones, which reach the brain via the spinal cord.

33. According to the passage, overall health may be improved in part through any of the following EXCEPT:

    A. exercise combined with mental focus.
    B. cardiovascular activity combined with nutritious diet.
    C. awareness of the body.
    D. movement synchronized with breath and mental imagery.

34. As it is used in line 33, the word *engaged* most nearly means:

    F. stimulated.
    G. taken.
    H. obligated.
    J. destined.

35. According to the passage, the limbic system would be directly involved in all of the following EXCEPT:

    A. pain modulation.
    B. stress management.
    C. muscle movement.
    D. memory.

36. Information in the second paragraph indicates that mind-body therapies in Western medicine have been:

    F. increasingly used in place of biomedicine.
    G. rejected because there has not been enough clinical studies.
    H. an emerging field of scientific investigation.
    J. successful in curing many conditions and diseases.

37. The mind-body therapies mentioned in the fifth paragraph (lines 48–55) function by:

    A. preventing stress hormones from activating negative physiological responses.
    B. engaging the sympathetic nervous system to reduce stress responses.
    C. effectively eliminating emotional stressors.
    D. counterbalancing the effects of flight or fight responses.

38. According to the passage, stress responses with adaptive functions, as would have evolved in ancestral conditions, can be expected to:

    F. increase cortisol levels in the blood.
    G. suppress immune activity.
    H. perceive threats.
    J. decrease muscle tension.

39. In the last paragraph, the author expresses the belief that mind-body therapy should be further investigated because results from research are:

    A. carefully controlled to yield results consistent with expectations.
    B. valid only when analyzing Western-originating therapies.
    C. susceptible to external variables, the effects of which are yet to be determined.
    D. proof of the effectiveness in fighting stress and eliminating pain.

40. According to the passage, healthy mind-body therapies would have been deemed ineffective if which of the following effects occurred after patients engaged in positive meditation to manage work-related stress?

    F. Nociceptive signals were transmitted.
    G. Parasympathetic nervous system was engaged.
    H. Fight-or-flight response was prolonged.
    J. Spinal cord activity diminished.

END OF TEST 3
STOP! DO NOT TURN THE PAGE UNTIL TOLD TO DO SO.
DO NOT RETURN TO A PREVIOUS TEST.

SCIENCE REASONING TEST

35 Minutes—40 Questions

DIRECTIONS: There are seven passages in the following section. Each passage is followed by several questions. After reading a passage, choose the best answer to each question and blacken the corresponding oval on your answer document. You may refer to the passages as often as necessary.

You are NOT permitted to use a calculator on this test.

Passage I

In the solar system, solid planets and moons are made up of different layers, which have different compositions. The Earth's moon is surrounded by an outer crust, which is visible to observers on Earth. Beneath this crust is a solid *lithosphere*. Beneath the lithosphere is another layer called the *asthenosphere*. This layer is thought to have high temperatures, so the structure of this layer is said to be *plastic*, or easily changed. The innermost region of the moon is called the *core*, and it is thought to contain iron.

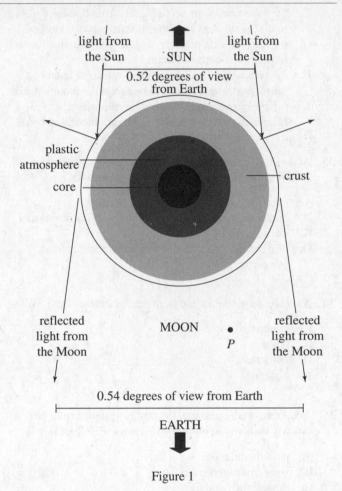

Figure 1

A solar eclipse occurs when the moon travels directly between the Earth and the Sun, temporarily blocking the transmission of sunlight to the earth and creating a shadow. Most solar eclipses are partial, because the moon does not always travel entirely within the path of the sunlight. However, complete solar eclipses are possible because the moon and the Sun have approximately the same diameter from the perspective of a viewer on the Earth. An observer on the Earth would view the sky as occupying 180 degrees. Of this entire distance, the moon takes up 0.54 degrees while the Sun takes up 0.52 degrees. Since the Sun appears to take up a smaller section of the sky, the Sun's rays can be blocked from traveling to the earth during a complete solar eclipse (see Figure 1).

The gravitational force exerted on the Earth by the moon, and by the Sun to a lesser extent, results in water *tides*, which are the changes in the level of the Earth's ocean surface. Figure 2 shows data collected by a tidal station on the western coast of the United States, showing the change in the ocean water level over a 60-hour period. During this period, the highest water level was 6 feet above mean sea level, while the lowest water level was 1 foot below mean sea level (represented by "–1" feet).

GO ON TO THE NEXT PAGE.

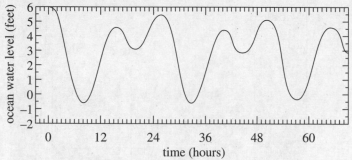

Figure 2

The highest and lowest ocean surface levels change over the course of a year. Figure 3 shows the change in the highest and lowest water levels measured by the same tidal station over a year.

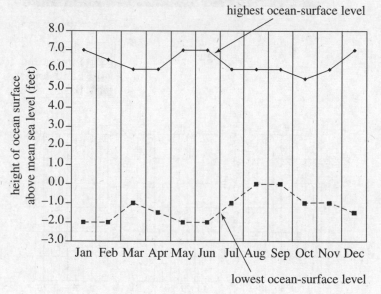

Figure 3

1. Figure 1 shows that a lunar orbiter at point *P* would be able to view which of the following?

    A. The moon only
    B. The Sun only
    C. The moon and the Earth only
    D. The moon, the Sun, and the Earth

2. According to Figure 1, when the Sun's rays encounter the surface of the moon during a solar eclipse, the rays most likely:

    F. stop transmitting forward and do not continue to the Earth's surface.
    G. enter the plastic asthenosphere and are absorbed.
    H. reflect off the surface of the moon, and then continue to the Earth.
    J. transmit unobstructed to the Earth's surface.

3. Based on Figure 2, for a given set of consecutive days, the time elapsed between the maximum values of the highest ocean-surface levels would most nearly be:

    A. 12 hours.
    B. 24 hours.
    C. 48 hours.
    D. 60 hours.

4. Based on the information provided in Figure 3, during what month was the data in Figure 2 most likely collected?

    F. January
    G. March
    H. June
    J. December

5. According to Figure 2, which of the following statements best describes the ocean surface level between $t = 0$ hours and $t = 12$ hours?

    A. The ocean surface level rises continuously during that entire time.
    B. The ocean surface level falls continuously during that entire time.
    C. The ocean surface level rises and then falls during that time.
    D. The ocean surface level falls and then rises during that time.

GO ON TO THE NEXT PAGE.

Passage II

Approximately 45,000 to 35,000 years ago, Lake Brussia straddled the boundary between modern Smith and Union counties. The lake was believed to have been formed as a result of seismic activity in the region. As seen in Figure 1, the cities of Middleton, West Union, and Basalt Valley rest over the sediment of the ancient lake. In order to test this hypothesis, a study examining the strata of the region was conducted using radioactive dating. Inconsistencies in the age of the rock layers indicate the presence of a fault in the region.

Radioactive dating is a technique which utilizes the amount of radiation exhibited by a distinct isotope within a sample to approximate its age. Uranium-235 is an isotope commonly found in varying types of strata with a half-life of approximately 700 million years. The half-life of an isotope is the time it takes for half of the isotope to decompose. 1,000 m core samples were acquired from three sites between the modern cities of Middleton and West Union as seen in Figure 2. Figure 3 shows the results of the Uranium-235 assays for each of the three sites. The age of the rock is determined using a ratio of the Uranium content in the sample to that of newly formed rock.

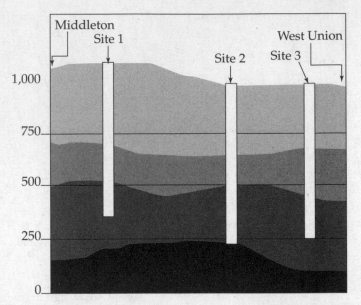

Figure 2

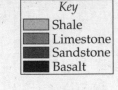

Key
- Shale
- Limestone
- Sandstone
- Basalt

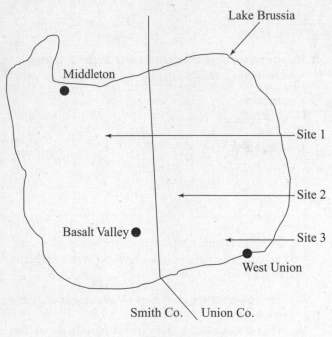

Figure 1

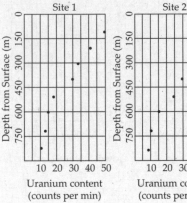

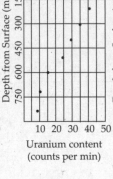

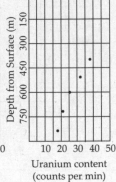

Figure 3

$$\frac{64}{\text{Counts per minute of Uranium -235 in Sample}} \times 700 = \text{approx. age of rock in millions of years}$$

Note:

GO ON TO THE NEXT PAGE.

6. According to Figure 2, the shale layer was thickest at which of the following cities or sites?

   F. Middleton
   G. Site 1
   H. Site 3
   J. West Union

7. According to Figure 2, as the thickness of shale decreases between Sites 2 and 3, the thickness of limestone residing below:

   A. increases.
   B. decreases.
   C. first decreases then increases.
   D. remains constant.

8. Based on Figure 2, which of the following graphs best displays the thickness of the shale layer at Sites 1, 2, and 3 ?

   F.
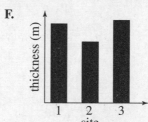

   G.
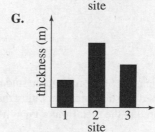

   H.
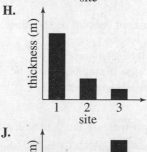

   J.
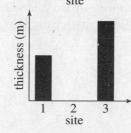

9. According to Figure 3, at Sites 1, 2, and 3 the highest number of counts of Uranium-235 detected were recorded at a depth of:

   A. less than 300 m below the surface.
   B. between 300 and 450 m below the surface.
   C. between 450 and 600 m below the surface
   D. greater than 600 m below the surface.

10. The uranium recorded in Sites 1, 2, and 3 is reduced by ½ roughly every 0.7 billion years. Based on Figure 3, and assuming no alteration of this uranium decay, the age of the rock with the greatest depth surveyed at Site 2 is closest to:

   F. 2.8 billion years old.
   G. 5.6 billion years old.
   H. 280 million years old.
   J. 560 million years old.

GO ON TO THE NEXT PAGE.

Passage III

For a science fair, a middle school student tested the hypothesis that bubbles in liquids would affect how far a water gun could shoot. To do this, she set up a holding device so that the water gun would always shoot at the same angle (the angle of inclination) and from the same place. She then measured the horizontal distance from the holding device to the furthest observable trace of liquid (see Figure 1).

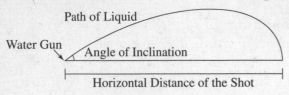

Figure 1

The angle of inclination was 30° in all experiments. The same metal water gun was used in Experiments 1 and 2.

Experiment 1

The student filled the metallic water canister of a water gun to 80% of its capacity with water from her tap (water with no bubbles in it) and measured how far from the holding device the water gun shot. Then, she again filled the canister to 80% of its capacity with tap water, shook the water gun, and immediately measured how far it shot. She repeated these tests with water mixed with laundry detergent, which contained many bubbles, and a flat-tasting cola beverage that showed no visible bubbles. Table 1 shows the results of these trials.

		Distance Shot	
Trial	Liquid	before shaking (meters)	after shaking (meters)
1	water	6.42	6.42
2	water with detergent	5.36	4.79
3	flat-tasting cola	6.42	5.49

Table 1

Experiment 2

Next, the student filled the water gun canister to 80% of its capacity with the flat-tasting cola, shook it to create bubbles and then let it sit, undisturbed. When 10 minutes had elapsed, she tested how far the water gun shot the cola, before and after shaking it (Trial 4). She then let it sit undisturbed for an hour before again testing how far it shot before and after shaking it (Trial 5). Table 2 shows the results of these trials.

	Distance shot	
Trial	before shaking (meters)	after shaking (meters)
4	5.98	5.49
5	6.42	5.61

Table 2

Experiment 3

For the third experiment, the student used an old-fashioned, plastic water gun, with transparent walls and the water container in the handle of the water gun. The student added the flat-tasting cola to fill the water container to 80% of its capacity, shot the water gun, and observed that no bubbles formed upon shooting. She then shook the water gun, which caused bubbles to form. After 10 minutes, there were still some visible bubbles in the cola; however, after an hour had passed, there were no visible bubbles.

11. In Experiment 3, what is the most likely reason the student chose to use an old-fashioned plastic water gun rather than a metal water gun? Compared to the metal water gun, the plastic water gun:

   A. exhibited different effects of bubbles on shooting distance.
   B. did not shoot as far as the metal gun.
   C. allowed the student to view the bubbles in the liquid.
   D. was easier to fit into the holding device.

12. Based on the results of Experiments 1 and 2, in which of the following two trials, before shaking the water gun, were the distances shot the same?

   F. Trials 1 and 4
   G. Trials 2 and 3
   H. Trials 3 and 4
   J. Trials 3 and 5

GO ON TO THE NEXT PAGE.

13. In Experiment 2, a result of shaking the water gun containing the flat-tasting cola was that the:

    A. density of the liquid increased.
    B. bubbles in the liquid disappeared.
    C. distance the liquid was shot increased.
    D. distance the liquid was shot decreased.

14. In Trial 5, is it likely that bubbles were present in large numbers in the cola immediately before the can was shaken?

    F. Yes; based on the results of Experiment 1, the bubbles generated in Trial 4 probably lasted for less than 10 minutes.
    G. Yes; based on the results of Experiment 1, the bubbles generated in Trial 4 probably lasted for more than 1 hour.
    H. No; based on the results of Experiment 3, the bubbles generated in Trial 4 probably lasted for less than 1 hour.
    J. No; based on the results of Experiment 3, the bubbles generated in Trial 4 probably lasted for more than 2 hours.

15. Suppose that in Experiment 2, the student had decided to measure the distance the water gun shot the cola one hour after finishing Trial 5 without shaking the water gun again. Based on the observations made in Trials 4 and 5, the horizontal distance the cola was shot would most likely have been:

    A. less than 5.49 meters.
    B. between 5.49 and 5.51 meters.
    C. between 5.52 and 5.98 meters.
    D. greater than 5.98 meters.

16. Based on the results of Trials 3–5, if the student filled the metal water gun to 80% of its capacity with the flat-tasting cola and shook it, the time it would take for the bubbles in the cola to disappear to the point that they would have no effect on the distance of the shot would most likely have been:

    F. greater than 1 hour.
    G. between 10 minutes and 1 hour.
    H. between 3 minutes and 9 minutes.
    J. less than 3 minutes.

GO ON TO THE NEXT PAGE.

Passage IV

An ecological study measured the reflection of light by different algae types and water samples. The study found that a water sample's reflectance of light is determined by the density of algae in it. As the density of algae in a water sample increases, the water sample's reflectance of light became more similar to the pure algae's reflectance of light.

Table 1 lists the wavelength range of the visible spectrum and the wavelength ranges of the colors of the visible spectrum.

Table 1	
Color	Wavelength (nm)
Violet	380–430
Blue	430–500
Green	500–565
Yellow	565–585
Orange	585–630
Red	630–750

Figure 1 shows the relative reflectance of light by pure samples of water and three types of algae versus the wavelength of light from 350 nm to 750 nm.

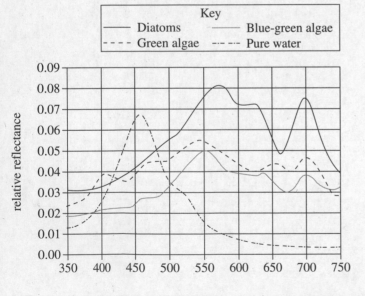

Figure 1

Figure 2 shows the relative reflectance light of a sample of lake water versus the wavelength of light from 350 nm to 750 nm.

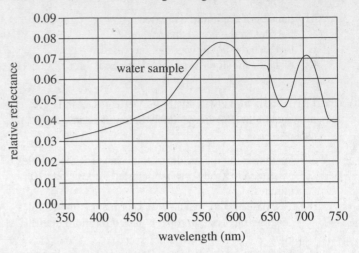

Figure 2

17. Based on Table 1 and Figure 1, which color of light is most reflected by blue-green algae?

A. Violet
B. Yellow
C. Red
D. Green

GO ON TO THE NEXT PAGE.

18. Autotrophic organisms, such as blue-green algae, absorb wavelengths using the molecule chlorophyll. Chlorophyll is typically associated with which of the following chemical reactions?

   F. Binary fission
   G. Condensation
   H. Photosynthesis
   J. Respiration

19. According to Figure 1, at which of the following wavelengths does the amount of light reflected by green algae exceed the amount of light reflected by diatoms?

   A. 400 nm
   B. 520 nm
   C. 670 nm
   D. 710 nm

20. Green algae is classified in which kingdom of organisms?

   F. Animalia
   G. Plantae
   H. Fungi
   J. Protista

21. Based on Figures 1 and 2, what type of algae has the greatest density in the lake water sample?

   A. Blue-green algae
   B. Diatoms
   C. Green algae
   D. No algae are in the water sample.

GO ON TO THE NEXT PAGE.

Passage V

Oceanographers conducted a series of experiments with water to explore the relationship between temperature, salinity (% salt by mass), and density (mass per unit volume).

Experiment 1

In a beaker, 35 g of NaCl and 965 g of distilled H_2O were mixed, and the solution was brought to a specific temperature. A graduated cylinder was then used to measure 150 mL of the solution. The mass of this 150 mL sample was measured with an electronic balance and the density (g/mL) was calculated. This procedure was repeated for 5 different temperatures with the results recorded in Table 1.

	Table 1		
Sample	Solution mass (g)	Temperature (°C)	Density (g/mL)
I	154.2	0	1.028
II	154.1	10	1.027
III	153.9	15	1.026
IV	153.8	20	1.025
V	153.3	30	1.022

Experiment 2

A graduated cylinder was placed on an electronic balance and a certain mass of NaCl was added. Distilled water at 10 C was added to make a 150 mL solution, and the total mass of this was noted. The density (g/mL) and salinity (%) of the solution were calculated. This procedure was repeated for 5 different quantities of NaCl with the results recorded in Table 2.

	Table 2		
Sample	Solution mass (g)	Salinity (%)	Density (g/mL)
VI	153.0	2.60	1.020
VII	152.7	2.35	1.018
VIII	152.4	2.10	1.016
IX	152.1	1.83	1.014
X	151.8	1.58	1.012

Experiment 3

Water samples from Experiments 1 and 2 were used individually to fill a test pool. For each sample, multiple prototypes of a newly designed instrument were placed in the pool. If a prototype stayed afloat, it was marked with a (+). If a prototype sank, it was marked with a (−). These data were then collected and recorded in Table 3.

Water Sample	Table 3 Prototype					
	R5	R6	U3	U4	X1	X2
I	+	+	+	+	+	+
II	+	+	+	+	+	+
III	−	+	+	+	+	+
IV	−	+	+	+	+	+
V	−	−	+	+	+	+
VI	−	−	−	+	+	+
VII	−	−	−	−	+	+
VIII	−	−	−	−	−	+
IX	−	−	−	−	−	−
X	−	−	−	−	−	−

22. In Experiment 1, if an additional sample were brought to 40°C and a density of 1.018 g/mL, what would its expected mass be in the graduated cylinder?

F. 150.9 g
G. 151.8 g
H. 152.7 g
J. 153.6 g

GO ON TO THE NEXT PAGE.

23. Based on Table 2, what is the most likely density of water at 10°C and 2.50% salinity?

    A. 1.019
    B. 1.017
    C. 1.013
    D. 1.010

24. An engineer states that prototype U3 is better suited than X2 for water surface data collection in a 10°C and 2.35% salinity environment. Do the results of the experiments support this claim?

    F. Yes, because prototype U3 will sink and X2 will float in these water conditions.
    G. Yes, because prototype U3 will float and X2 will sink in these water conditions.
    H. No, because prototype U3 will sink and X2 will float in these water conditions.
    J. No, because prototype U3 will float and X2 will sink in these water conditions.

25. A new prototype is tested in water samples IV through VII in a manner similar to Experiment 3. Which of the following results would NOT be possible?

	Water Sample		
	IV	V	VI	VII
A.	–	–	–	–
B.	+	+	+	+
C.	+	+	–	–
D.	–	–	+	+

26. In Experiment 1, samples were transferred to a graduated cylinder to obtain a more accurate and precise measurement of the:

    F. mass of the NaCl added to the H_2O.
    G. salinity after it reached the designated temperature.
    H. volume used to calculate the density.
    J. temperature used to determine the final salinity.

27. In a later analysis, the density of prototype U3 is manually determined. Which of the following values would be consistent with the results of Experiments 1 through 3 ?

    A. 1.021 g/mL
    B. 1.023 g/mL
    C. 1.026 g/mL
    D. 1.028 g/mL

GO ON TO THE NEXT PAGE.

Passage VI

Haloarchaea are single-celled microorganisms that can use light to generate energy, through a unique form of *photosynthesis*. To compare haloarchaeal photosynthesis with plant photosynthesis and bacterial fermentation, researchers performed two experiments in which they exposed plant haloarchaeal and bacterial cells to either red or green light. The researchers measured the growth of these cells by measuring how much acid and CO_2 were produced; more production of these indicated more growth.

Experiment 1

Water containing salt and sucrose was added to eight large test tubes. Next, *phenolphthalein* (a pH indicator that is colorless in the presence of acid and has a pink color in its absence) was added to each large test tube. A smaller test tube was then added, inverted, into each large test tube to collect CO_2; if CO_2 had been produced, a gas bubble would appear in this smaller tube (see Figure 1).

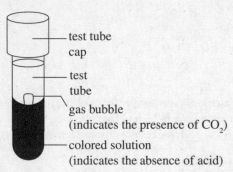

test tube cap

test tube

gas bubble (indicates the presence of CO_2)

colored solution (indicates the absence of acid)

Figure 1

The large test tubes were capped, heated until the solutions were sterile, and then cooled. Nothing was added to the first test tube (T1). Cells of the plant *Rosa carolina* were added to the second test tube (T2), cells of the haloarchaea *NRC-1* were added to the third test tube (T3), and cells of the bacterium *Bacillus anthracis* were added to the fourth test tube (T4). These four test tubes were exposed to red light, and incubated at 37°C for 48 hr. Then, the procedure was repeated with exposure to green light, using the four remaining test tubes: T5 (no cells), T6 (plant cells), T7 (haloarchaeal cells), and T8 (bacterial cells). In Table 1, + means presence and – means absence.

Table 1

Red light			Green light		
	Acid	CO_2		Acid	CO_2
T1: Control	–	–	T5: Control	–	–
T2: Plant	–	+	T6: Plant	–	–
T3: Haloarchaea	–	–	T7: Haloarchaea	+	–
T4: Bacterium	+	+	T8: Bacterium	+	+

Experiment 2

Some of the cells tested in Experiment 1 are thought to contain pigments that help them absorb light. To determine whether these cells absorbed light to generate energy, cells of the same species are exposed to red and green light in new test tubes. The researchers measure the *transmittance*, or the amount of light that transmits through the test tube. If the transmittance is low, then the cells in the test tube are assumed to contain pigments that absorb most of the light to generate energy. If the transmittance is high, then the cells are assumed to contain no pigment that could absorb light and generate energy. Instead, most of the light passes through the test tube.

Table 2

Red light		Green light	
	Transmittance		Transmittance
T9: Plant	Low	T12: Plant	High
T10: Haloarchaea	High	T13: Haloarchaea	Low
T11: Bacterium	High	T14: Bacterium	High

28. In Experiment 1, which cell types grew in the presence of green light?

F. Plant cells only
G. Plant and bacterial cells only
H. Plant and haloarchaeal cells only
J. Haloarchaeal and bacterial cells only

GO ON TO THE NEXT PAGE.

29. Suppose that plant cells and haloarchaeal cells that are situated close to each other do not interfere with each other's absorption of light and generation of energy. If a new test tube containing both plant and haloarchaeal cells were prepared, what would be the most likely results for Experiments 1 and 2 ?

	Red light			Green light		
	Acid	CO_2	Transmittance	Acid	CO_2	Transmittance
A.	–	–	High	–	–	High
B.	–	+	Low	+	–	Low
C.	+	–	Low	–	+	High
D.	+	+	High	+	+	Low

30. Suppose that a scientist isolates a cell type that is one of the four cell types used in Experiment 1. She finds that this cell type produces CO_2 in the presence of red light. She then tests the cell type in the presence of green light and finds that neither CO_2 nor acid is produced. Based on the results of Experiment 1, the cell type is most likely the:

F. control with nothing added.
G. plant *Rosa carolina*.
H. haloarchea *NRC-1*.
J. bacterium *Bacillus anthracis*.

31. What is the evidence from Experiments 1 and 2 that haloarchaea require green light to generate energy?

A. In the presence of red light, haloarchaea show low transmittance of light and produce acid.
B. In the presence of red light, haloarchaea show high transmittance of light and produce no acid.
C. In the presence of green light, haloarchaea show low transmittance of light and produce acid.
D. In the presence of green light, haloarchaea show high transmittance of light and produce no acid.

32. Which of the following best illustrates the results of Experiment 1 for the plant *Rosa carolina* in red light?

F.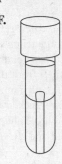

H.

G.

J.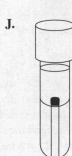

33. Do the results of Experiment 1 support the hypothesis that haloarchaea and bacteria use similar processes to generate energy?

A. Yes, because both haloarchaea and bacteria produce CO_2 in the presence of green light.
B. Yes, because both haloarchaea and bacteria produce CO_2 in the presence of red light.
C. No, because haloarchaea produce only acid in the presence of green light, while bacteria produce acid and CO_2 in both red and green light.
D. No, because neither haloarchaea nor bacteria produce CO_2 in the presence of either red or green light.

GO ON TO THE NEXT PAGE.

Passage VII

For most of the 20th century, scientists recognized two basic domains of living organisms, *prokaryotes* and *eukaryotes*. The presence of nuclei and other membrane-bound organelles within the cell primarily distinguished eukaryotes from prokaryotes. The possibility of revising this dichotomy resulted from the discovery of the *Archaea*, organisms with unique cell membrane and *ribosomal RNA (rRNA)* structure. Cell membranes are composed of *phospholipids* that have both water-insoluble and water-soluble subunits. *Ribosomes* are made of protein and rRNA and build new proteins within the cell.

Two scientists in the 1990s debate whether organisms should be classified into two or three domains.

2-Domain Hypothesis

The Archaea are prokaryotes because they lack intracellular membrane-bound organelles. Although they are found in extreme and unusual environments, the gross structure and life cycle of the Archaea are similar to prokaryotic bacteria. Like bacteria, their cells are usually surrounded by a cell wall, and they reproduce asexually through binary fission.

The structural and metabolic characteristics that are unique to the Archaea are not significantly different from other prokaryotes to warrant their separation into a third domain. Although the Archaea were distinguished very early on in the diversification of life, today they remain appropriately defined by the original definition of prokaryote.

3-Domain Hypothesis

The Archaea are a distinct form of life requiring a revision of the previously held dichotomy of prokaryote and eukaryote. Eukaryota should remain the same, but prokaryotes should be split into Archaea and Bacteria because of significant differences in genetics, structure, and metabolism.

Archaea as a domain is justified by detailed analysis. The genetic sequence of rRNA in the Archaea is so distinct from prokaryotes and eukaryotes that these groups of organisms likely diverged over 3 billion years ago. Archaea cell membranes contain more rigid *ether linkages* instead of the *ester linkages* found in eukaryotes and bacteria. This contributes to their survival in harsh environments. Finally, the Archaea are capable of exploiting a wider range of energy sources compared to eukaryotes and bacteria.

34. Which of the following statements is most consistent with the *3-Domain Hypothesis*? The time, in millions of years ago, when two groups of organisms diverge on the evolutionary tree increases as the:

F. similarities between rRNA gene sequences increases.
G. differences between rRNA gene sequences increases.
H. number of ester linkages in the cell membrane increases.
J. number of ether linkages in the cell membrane decreases.

35. By referring to the observation that the newly discovered organisms do not have membrane-bound organelles, the scientist supporting the 2-Domain Hypothesis implies that these new organisms do not have which of the following structures?

A. Phospholipids
B. Ribosomes
C. rRNA
D. Nuclei

36. According to the passage, a similarity between eukaryotes and prokaryotes is that both groups of organisms:

F. have ester linkages in their membranes.
G. contain membrane-bound organelles.
H. reproduce sexually.
J. are composed of cells.

37. According to the scientist who supports the 2-Domain Hypothesis, which of the following is the strongest argument *against* using a 3-Domain classification?

A. rRNA does not exist in prokaryotes.
B. Ether linkages are found in the cell membranes of the Archaea.
C. The Archaea meet the primary definition of prokaryotic.
D. The Archaea synthesize proteins in the cell cytoplasm.

GO ON TO THE NEXT PAGE.

38. It is shown that the Archaea have protein synthesis structures and mechanisms more like eukaryotes than prokaryotes. This observation contradicts arguments stated in which hypothesis?

    F. The 2-Domain Hypothesis, because the discovery would show that the new organisms and bacteria fundamentally differ in cellular metabolism.

    G. The 2-Domain Hypothesis, because the discovery would show that the new organisms and eukaryotes fundamentally differ in cellular metabolism.

    H. The 3-Domain Hypothesis, because the discovery would show that the new organisms and bacteria fundamentally differ in cellular metabolism.

    J. The 3-Domain Hypothesis, because the discovery would show that the new organisms and eukaryotes fundamentally differ in cellular metabolism.

39. The scientist who supports the 3-Domain Hypothesis implies that the 2-Domain Hypothesis is *weakened* by which observation?

    A. The Archaea have membrane-bound organelles.
    B. Microscopes cannot accurately describe organisms.
    C. The Archaea lack ester linkages in their cell membranes.
    D. Eukaryotes are not related to the Archaea.

40. Which of the following illustrations of a portion of a phospholipid cell membrane is consistent with the description in the passage?

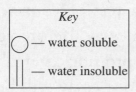

Key
◯ — water soluble
|| — water insoluble

F. Water
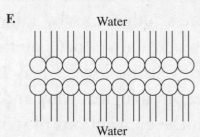
Water

G. Water
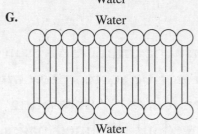
Water

H. Water
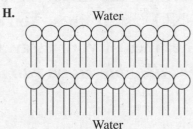
Water

J. Water
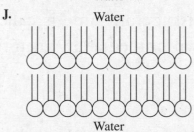
Water

END OF TEST 4
STOP! DO NOT RETURN TO ANY OTHER TEST.

Directions

This is a test of your writing skills. You will have thirty (30) minutes to write an essay. Before you begin planning and writing your essay, read the writing prompt carefully to understand exactly what you are being asked to do. Your essay will be evaluated on the evidence it provides of your ability to express judgments by taking a position on the issue in the writing prompt; to maintain a focus on the topic throughout your essay; to develop a position by using logical reasoning and by supporting your ideas; to organize ideas in a logical way; and to use language clearly and effectively according to the conventions of standard written English.

You may use the unlined pages in this test booklet to plan your essay. These pages will not be scored. *You must write your essay on the lined pages in the answer folder.* Your writing on those lined pages will be scored. You may not need all the lined pages, but to ensure you have enough room to finish, do NOT skip lines. You may write corrections or additions neatly between the lines of your essay, but do NOT write in the margins of the lined pages. *Illegible essays cannot be scored, so you must write (or print) clearly.*

If you finish before time is called, you may review your work. Lay your pencil down immediately when time is called.

DO NOT OPEN THIS BOOKLET UNTIL TOLD TO DO SO.

ACT Assessment Writing Test Prompt

Recently, one state has passed legislation making it illegal for anyone under the age of 18 to use a cell phone—including hands-free models—or any other electronic communications device while driving. Supporters argue that such devices distract drivers' attention from the road, and thus this law will lower the number of accidents and save lives. Opponents argue the law is discriminatory, since adults may use hands-free cell phones while driving. In your opinion, should all states pass a law banning drivers 18 and younger from using communication devices while driving?

In your essay, take a position on this question. You may write about either one of the two points of view given, or you may present a different point of view on this question. Use specific reasons and examples to support your position.

ACT Diagnostic Test Form

Use a No. 2 pencil only. Be sure each mark is dark and completely fills the intended oval. Completely erase any errors or stray marks.

1. YOUR NAME: _____
(Print)   Last   First   M.I.

SIGNATURE: _____   **DATE:** _____ / _____ / _____

HOME ADDRESS: _____
(Print)   Number and Street

_____
City   State   Zip

E-MAIL: _____

PHONE NO.: _____
(Print)

SCHOOL: _____

CLASS OF: _____

IMPORTANT: Please fill in these boxes exactly as shown on the back cover of your tests book.

2. TEST FORM

_____

3. TEST CODE

⓪	⓪	⓪	⓪
①	①	①	①
②	②	②	②
③	③	③	③
④	④	④	④
⑤	⑤	⑤	⑤
⑥	⑥	⑥	⑥
⑦	⑦	⑦	⑦
⑧	⑧	⑧	⑧
⑨	⑨	⑨	⑨

4. PHONE NUMBER

⓪	⓪	⓪	⓪	⓪	⓪	⓪
①	①	①	①	①	①	①
②	②	②	②	②	②	②
③	③	③	③	③	③	③
④	④	④	④	④	④	④
⑤	⑤	⑤	⑤	⑤	⑤	⑤
⑥	⑥	⑥	⑥	⑥	⑥	⑥
⑦	⑦	⑦	⑦	⑦	⑦	⑦
⑧	⑧	⑧	⑧	⑧	⑧	⑧
⑨	⑨	⑨	⑨	⑨	⑨	⑨

5. YOUR NAME

First 4 letters of last name				FIRST INIT	MID INIT
Ⓐ	Ⓐ	Ⓐ	Ⓐ	Ⓐ	Ⓐ
Ⓑ	Ⓑ	Ⓑ	Ⓑ	Ⓑ	Ⓑ
Ⓒ	Ⓒ	Ⓒ	Ⓒ	Ⓒ	Ⓒ
Ⓓ	Ⓓ	Ⓓ	Ⓓ	Ⓓ	Ⓓ
Ⓔ	Ⓔ	Ⓔ	Ⓔ	Ⓔ	Ⓔ
Ⓕ	Ⓕ	Ⓕ	Ⓕ	Ⓕ	Ⓕ
Ⓖ	Ⓖ	Ⓖ	Ⓖ	Ⓖ	Ⓖ
Ⓗ	Ⓗ	Ⓗ	Ⓗ	Ⓗ	Ⓗ
Ⓘ	Ⓘ	Ⓘ	Ⓘ	Ⓘ	Ⓘ
Ⓙ	Ⓙ	Ⓙ	Ⓙ	Ⓙ	Ⓙ
Ⓚ	Ⓚ	Ⓚ	Ⓚ	Ⓚ	Ⓚ
Ⓛ	Ⓛ	Ⓛ	Ⓛ	Ⓛ	Ⓛ
Ⓜ	Ⓜ	Ⓜ	Ⓜ	Ⓜ	Ⓜ
Ⓝ	Ⓝ	Ⓝ	Ⓝ	Ⓝ	Ⓝ
Ⓞ	Ⓞ	Ⓞ	Ⓞ	Ⓞ	Ⓞ
Ⓟ	Ⓟ	Ⓟ	Ⓟ	Ⓟ	Ⓟ
Ⓠ	Ⓠ	Ⓠ	Ⓠ	Ⓠ	Ⓠ
Ⓡ	Ⓡ	Ⓡ	Ⓡ	Ⓡ	Ⓡ
Ⓢ	Ⓢ	Ⓢ	Ⓢ	Ⓢ	Ⓢ
Ⓣ	Ⓣ	Ⓣ	Ⓣ	Ⓣ	Ⓣ
Ⓤ	Ⓤ	Ⓤ	Ⓤ	Ⓤ	Ⓤ
Ⓥ	Ⓥ	Ⓥ	Ⓥ	Ⓥ	Ⓥ
Ⓦ	Ⓦ	Ⓦ	Ⓦ	Ⓦ	Ⓦ
Ⓧ	Ⓧ	Ⓧ	Ⓧ	Ⓧ	Ⓧ
Ⓨ	Ⓨ	Ⓨ	Ⓨ	Ⓨ	Ⓨ
Ⓩ	Ⓩ	Ⓩ	Ⓩ	Ⓩ	Ⓩ

6. DATE OF BIRTH

MONTH	DAY		YEAR	
◯ JAN				
◯ FEB				
◯ MAR	⓪	⓪	⓪	⓪
◯ APR	①	①	①	①
◯ MAY	②	②	②	②
◯ JUN	③	③	③	③
◯ JUL		④	④	④
◯ AUG		⑤	⑤	⑤
◯ SEP		⑥	⑥	⑥
◯ OCT		⑦	⑦	⑦
◯ NOV		⑧	⑧	⑧
◯ DEC		⑨	⑨	⑨

7. SEX

◯ MALE
◯ FEMALE

8. OTHER

1 Ⓐ Ⓑ Ⓒ Ⓓ Ⓔ
2 Ⓐ Ⓑ Ⓒ Ⓓ Ⓔ
3 Ⓐ Ⓑ Ⓒ Ⓓ Ⓔ

OpScan *i*NSIGHT™ forms by Pearson NCS EM-255315-1:654321   Printed in U.S.A.

THIS PAGE INTENTIONALLY LEFT BLANK

The Princeton Review
Diagnostic ACT Form

ENGLISH

1 Ⓐ Ⓑ Ⓒ Ⓓ	21 Ⓐ Ⓑ Ⓒ Ⓓ	41 Ⓐ Ⓑ Ⓒ Ⓓ	61 Ⓐ Ⓑ Ⓒ Ⓓ
2 Ⓕ Ⓖ Ⓗ Ⓙ	22 Ⓕ Ⓖ Ⓗ Ⓙ	42 Ⓕ Ⓖ Ⓗ Ⓙ	62 Ⓕ Ⓖ Ⓗ Ⓙ
3 Ⓐ Ⓑ Ⓒ Ⓓ	23 Ⓐ Ⓑ Ⓒ Ⓓ	43 Ⓐ Ⓑ Ⓒ Ⓓ	63 Ⓐ Ⓑ Ⓒ Ⓓ
4 Ⓕ Ⓖ Ⓗ Ⓙ	24 Ⓕ Ⓖ Ⓗ Ⓙ	44 Ⓕ Ⓖ Ⓗ Ⓙ	64 Ⓕ Ⓖ Ⓗ Ⓙ
5 Ⓐ Ⓑ Ⓒ Ⓓ	25 Ⓐ Ⓑ Ⓒ Ⓓ	45 Ⓐ Ⓑ Ⓒ Ⓓ	65 Ⓐ Ⓑ Ⓒ Ⓓ
6 Ⓕ Ⓖ Ⓗ Ⓙ	26 Ⓕ Ⓖ Ⓗ Ⓙ	46 Ⓕ Ⓖ Ⓗ Ⓙ	66 Ⓕ Ⓖ Ⓗ Ⓙ
7 Ⓐ Ⓑ Ⓒ Ⓓ	27 Ⓐ Ⓑ Ⓒ Ⓓ	47 Ⓐ Ⓑ Ⓒ Ⓓ	67 Ⓐ Ⓑ Ⓒ Ⓓ
8 Ⓕ Ⓖ Ⓗ Ⓙ	28 Ⓕ Ⓖ Ⓗ Ⓙ	48 Ⓕ Ⓖ Ⓗ Ⓙ	68 Ⓕ Ⓖ Ⓗ Ⓙ
9 Ⓐ Ⓑ Ⓒ Ⓓ	29 Ⓐ Ⓑ Ⓒ Ⓓ	49 Ⓐ Ⓑ Ⓒ Ⓓ	69 Ⓐ Ⓑ Ⓒ Ⓓ
10 Ⓕ Ⓖ Ⓗ Ⓙ	30 Ⓕ Ⓖ Ⓗ Ⓙ	50 Ⓕ Ⓖ Ⓗ Ⓙ	70 Ⓕ Ⓖ Ⓗ Ⓙ
11 Ⓐ Ⓑ Ⓒ Ⓓ	31 Ⓐ Ⓑ Ⓒ Ⓓ	51 Ⓐ Ⓑ Ⓒ Ⓓ	71 Ⓐ Ⓑ Ⓒ Ⓓ
12 Ⓕ Ⓖ Ⓗ Ⓙ	32 Ⓕ Ⓖ Ⓗ Ⓙ	52 Ⓕ Ⓖ Ⓗ Ⓙ	72 Ⓕ Ⓖ Ⓗ Ⓙ
13 Ⓐ Ⓑ Ⓒ Ⓓ	33 Ⓐ Ⓑ Ⓒ Ⓓ	53 Ⓐ Ⓑ Ⓒ Ⓓ	73 Ⓐ Ⓑ Ⓒ Ⓓ
14 Ⓕ Ⓖ Ⓗ Ⓙ	34 Ⓕ Ⓖ Ⓗ Ⓙ	54 Ⓕ Ⓖ Ⓗ Ⓙ	74 Ⓕ Ⓖ Ⓗ Ⓙ
15 Ⓐ Ⓑ Ⓒ Ⓓ	35 Ⓐ Ⓑ Ⓒ Ⓓ	55 Ⓐ Ⓑ Ⓒ Ⓓ	75 Ⓐ Ⓑ Ⓒ Ⓓ
16 Ⓕ Ⓖ Ⓗ Ⓙ	36 Ⓕ Ⓖ Ⓗ Ⓙ	56 Ⓕ Ⓖ Ⓗ Ⓙ	
17 Ⓐ Ⓑ Ⓒ Ⓓ	37 Ⓐ Ⓑ Ⓒ Ⓓ	57 Ⓐ Ⓑ Ⓒ Ⓓ	
18 Ⓕ Ⓖ Ⓗ Ⓙ	38 Ⓕ Ⓖ Ⓗ Ⓙ	58 Ⓕ Ⓖ Ⓗ Ⓙ	
19 Ⓐ Ⓑ Ⓒ Ⓓ	39 Ⓐ Ⓑ Ⓒ Ⓓ	59 Ⓐ Ⓑ Ⓒ Ⓓ	
20 Ⓕ Ⓖ Ⓗ Ⓙ	40 Ⓕ Ⓖ Ⓗ Ⓙ	60 Ⓕ Ⓖ Ⓗ Ⓙ	

MATHEMATICS

1 Ⓐ Ⓑ Ⓒ Ⓓ Ⓔ	16 Ⓕ Ⓖ Ⓗ Ⓙ Ⓚ	31 Ⓐ Ⓑ Ⓒ Ⓓ Ⓔ	46 Ⓕ Ⓖ Ⓗ Ⓙ Ⓚ
2 Ⓕ Ⓖ Ⓗ Ⓙ Ⓚ	17 Ⓐ Ⓑ Ⓒ Ⓓ Ⓔ	32 Ⓕ Ⓖ Ⓗ Ⓙ Ⓚ	47 Ⓐ Ⓑ Ⓒ Ⓓ Ⓔ
3 Ⓐ Ⓑ Ⓒ Ⓓ Ⓔ	18 Ⓕ Ⓖ Ⓗ Ⓙ Ⓚ	33 Ⓐ Ⓑ Ⓒ Ⓓ Ⓔ	48 Ⓕ Ⓖ Ⓗ Ⓙ Ⓚ
4 Ⓕ Ⓖ Ⓗ Ⓙ Ⓚ	19 Ⓐ Ⓑ Ⓒ Ⓓ Ⓔ	34 Ⓕ Ⓖ Ⓗ Ⓙ Ⓚ	49 Ⓐ Ⓑ Ⓒ Ⓓ Ⓔ
5 Ⓐ Ⓑ Ⓒ Ⓓ Ⓔ	20 Ⓕ Ⓖ Ⓗ Ⓙ Ⓚ	35 Ⓐ Ⓑ Ⓒ Ⓓ Ⓔ	50 Ⓕ Ⓖ Ⓗ Ⓙ Ⓚ
6 Ⓕ Ⓖ Ⓗ Ⓙ Ⓚ	21 Ⓐ Ⓑ Ⓒ Ⓓ Ⓔ	36 Ⓕ Ⓖ Ⓗ Ⓙ Ⓚ	51 Ⓐ Ⓑ Ⓒ Ⓓ Ⓔ
7 Ⓐ Ⓑ Ⓒ Ⓓ Ⓔ	22 Ⓕ Ⓖ Ⓗ Ⓙ Ⓚ	37 Ⓐ Ⓑ Ⓒ Ⓓ Ⓔ	52 Ⓕ Ⓖ Ⓗ Ⓙ Ⓚ
8 Ⓕ Ⓖ Ⓗ Ⓙ Ⓚ	23 Ⓐ Ⓑ Ⓒ Ⓓ Ⓔ	38 Ⓕ Ⓖ Ⓗ Ⓙ Ⓚ	53 Ⓐ Ⓑ Ⓒ Ⓓ Ⓔ
9 Ⓐ Ⓑ Ⓒ Ⓓ Ⓔ	24 Ⓕ Ⓖ Ⓗ Ⓙ Ⓚ	39 Ⓐ Ⓑ Ⓒ Ⓓ Ⓔ	54 Ⓕ Ⓖ Ⓗ Ⓙ Ⓚ
10 Ⓕ Ⓖ Ⓗ Ⓙ Ⓚ	25 Ⓐ Ⓑ Ⓒ Ⓓ Ⓔ	40 Ⓕ Ⓖ Ⓗ Ⓙ Ⓚ	55 Ⓐ Ⓑ Ⓒ Ⓓ Ⓔ
11 Ⓐ Ⓑ Ⓒ Ⓓ Ⓔ	26 Ⓕ Ⓖ Ⓗ Ⓙ Ⓚ	41 Ⓐ Ⓑ Ⓒ Ⓓ Ⓔ	56 Ⓕ Ⓖ Ⓗ Ⓙ Ⓚ
12 Ⓕ Ⓖ Ⓗ Ⓙ Ⓚ	27 Ⓐ Ⓑ Ⓒ Ⓓ Ⓔ	42 Ⓕ Ⓖ Ⓗ Ⓙ Ⓚ	57 Ⓐ Ⓑ Ⓒ Ⓓ Ⓔ
13 Ⓐ Ⓑ Ⓒ Ⓓ Ⓔ	28 Ⓕ Ⓖ Ⓗ Ⓙ Ⓚ	43 Ⓐ Ⓑ Ⓒ Ⓓ Ⓔ	58 Ⓕ Ⓖ Ⓗ Ⓙ Ⓚ
14 Ⓕ Ⓖ Ⓗ Ⓙ Ⓚ	29 Ⓐ Ⓑ Ⓒ Ⓓ Ⓔ	44 Ⓕ Ⓖ Ⓗ Ⓙ Ⓚ	59 Ⓐ Ⓑ Ⓒ Ⓓ Ⓔ
15 Ⓐ Ⓑ Ⓒ Ⓓ Ⓔ	30 Ⓕ Ⓖ Ⓗ Ⓙ Ⓚ	45 Ⓐ Ⓑ Ⓒ Ⓓ Ⓔ	60 Ⓕ Ⓖ Ⓗ Ⓙ Ⓚ

The Princeton Review
Diagnostic ACT Form

READING

1 Ⓐ Ⓑ Ⓒ Ⓓ	11 Ⓐ Ⓑ Ⓒ Ⓓ	21 Ⓐ Ⓑ Ⓒ Ⓓ	31 Ⓐ Ⓑ Ⓒ Ⓓ
2 Ⓕ Ⓖ Ⓗ Ⓙ	12 Ⓕ Ⓖ Ⓗ Ⓙ	22 Ⓕ Ⓖ Ⓗ Ⓙ	32 Ⓕ Ⓖ Ⓗ Ⓙ
3 Ⓐ Ⓑ Ⓒ Ⓓ	13 Ⓐ Ⓑ Ⓒ Ⓓ	23 Ⓐ Ⓑ Ⓒ Ⓓ	33 Ⓐ Ⓑ Ⓒ Ⓓ
4 Ⓕ Ⓖ Ⓗ Ⓙ	14 Ⓕ Ⓖ Ⓗ Ⓙ	24 Ⓕ Ⓖ Ⓗ Ⓙ	34 Ⓕ Ⓖ Ⓗ Ⓙ
5 Ⓐ Ⓑ Ⓒ Ⓓ	15 Ⓐ Ⓑ Ⓒ Ⓓ	25 Ⓐ Ⓑ Ⓒ Ⓓ	35 Ⓐ Ⓑ Ⓒ Ⓓ
6 Ⓕ Ⓖ Ⓗ Ⓙ	16 Ⓕ Ⓖ Ⓗ Ⓙ	26 Ⓕ Ⓖ Ⓗ Ⓙ	36 Ⓕ Ⓖ Ⓗ Ⓙ
7 Ⓐ Ⓑ Ⓒ Ⓓ	17 Ⓐ Ⓑ Ⓒ Ⓓ	27 Ⓐ Ⓑ Ⓒ Ⓓ	37 Ⓐ Ⓑ Ⓒ Ⓓ
8 Ⓕ Ⓖ Ⓗ Ⓙ	18 Ⓕ Ⓖ Ⓗ Ⓙ	28 Ⓕ Ⓖ Ⓗ Ⓙ	38 Ⓕ Ⓖ Ⓗ Ⓙ
9 Ⓐ Ⓑ Ⓒ Ⓓ	19 Ⓐ Ⓑ Ⓒ Ⓓ	29 Ⓐ Ⓑ Ⓒ Ⓓ	39 Ⓐ Ⓑ Ⓒ Ⓓ
10 Ⓕ Ⓖ Ⓗ Ⓙ	20 Ⓕ Ⓖ Ⓗ Ⓙ	30 Ⓕ Ⓖ Ⓗ Ⓙ	40 Ⓕ Ⓖ Ⓗ Ⓙ

SCIENCE REASONING

1 Ⓐ Ⓑ Ⓒ Ⓓ	11 Ⓐ Ⓑ Ⓒ Ⓓ	21 Ⓐ Ⓑ Ⓒ Ⓓ	31 Ⓐ Ⓑ Ⓒ Ⓓ
2 Ⓕ Ⓖ Ⓗ Ⓙ	12 Ⓕ Ⓖ Ⓗ Ⓙ	22 Ⓕ Ⓖ Ⓗ Ⓙ	32 Ⓕ Ⓖ Ⓗ Ⓙ
3 Ⓐ Ⓑ Ⓒ Ⓓ	13 Ⓐ Ⓑ Ⓒ Ⓓ	23 Ⓐ Ⓑ Ⓒ Ⓓ	33 Ⓐ Ⓑ Ⓒ Ⓓ
4 Ⓕ Ⓖ Ⓗ Ⓙ	14 Ⓕ Ⓖ Ⓗ Ⓙ	24 Ⓕ Ⓖ Ⓗ Ⓙ	34 Ⓕ Ⓖ Ⓗ Ⓙ
5 Ⓐ Ⓑ Ⓒ Ⓓ	15 Ⓐ Ⓑ Ⓒ Ⓓ	25 Ⓐ Ⓑ Ⓒ Ⓓ	35 Ⓐ Ⓑ Ⓒ Ⓓ
6 Ⓕ Ⓖ Ⓗ Ⓙ	16 Ⓕ Ⓖ Ⓗ Ⓙ	26 Ⓕ Ⓖ Ⓗ Ⓙ	36 Ⓕ Ⓖ Ⓗ Ⓙ
7 Ⓐ Ⓑ Ⓒ Ⓓ	17 Ⓐ Ⓑ Ⓒ Ⓓ	27 Ⓐ Ⓑ Ⓒ Ⓓ	37 Ⓐ Ⓑ Ⓒ Ⓓ
8 Ⓕ Ⓖ Ⓗ Ⓙ	18 Ⓕ Ⓖ Ⓗ Ⓙ	28 Ⓕ Ⓖ Ⓗ Ⓙ	38 Ⓕ Ⓖ Ⓗ Ⓙ
9 Ⓐ Ⓑ Ⓒ Ⓓ	19 Ⓐ Ⓑ Ⓒ Ⓓ	29 Ⓐ Ⓑ Ⓒ Ⓓ	39 Ⓐ Ⓑ Ⓒ Ⓓ
10 Ⓕ Ⓖ Ⓗ Ⓙ	20 Ⓕ Ⓖ Ⓗ Ⓙ	30 Ⓕ Ⓖ Ⓗ Ⓙ	40 Ⓕ Ⓖ Ⓗ Ⓙ

The Princeton Review
Diagnostic ACT Form

ESSAY

Begin your essay on this side. If necessary, continue on the opposite side.

The Princeton Review
Diagnostic ACT Form

Continued from previous page.

_____

_____

_____

_____

_____

_____

_____

_____

_____

_____

_____

_____

_____

_____

_____

_____

_____

_____

_____

_____

_____

_____

PLEASE PRINT
YOUR INITIALS

First	Middle	Last

The Princeton Review
Diagnostic ACT Form

Continued from previous page.

_____

_____

_____

_____

_____

_____

_____

_____

_____

_____

_____

_____

_____

_____

_____

_____

_____

_____

_____

_____

_____

_____

_____

PLEASE PRINT
YOUR INITIALS

First	Middle	Last

The Princeton Review
Diagnostic ACT Form

Continued from previous page.

Test 1
Answers and
Explanations

TEST 1 ENGLISH ANSWERS

1.	D	48.	J
2.	F	49.	B
3.	B	50.	H
4.	H	51.	A
5.	C	52.	H
6.	J	53.	A
7.	D	54.	J
8.	J	55.	D
9.	A	56.	F
10.	F	57.	A
11.	B	58.	G
12.	G	59.	D
13.	C	60.	G
14.	H	61.	C
15.	B	62.	J
16.	F	63.	A
17.	D	64.	J
18.	J	65.	C
19.	B	66.	F
20.	H	67.	C
21.	A	68.	G
22.	J	69.	B
23.	B	70.	G
24.	J	71.	A
25.	B	72.	J
26.	F	73.	D
27.	D	74.	J
28.	F	75.	B
29.	D		
30.	F		
31.	D		
32.	G		
33.	D		
34.	H		
35.	C		
36.	J		
37.	A		
38.	G		
39.	C		
40.	F		
41.	B		
42.	F		
43.	D		
44.	G		
45.	D		
46.	H		
47.	C		

TEST 1 MATH ANSWERS

1.	A
2.	J
3.	B
4.	K
5.	D
6.	H
7.	A
8.	J
9.	C
10.	H
11.	A
12.	F
13.	D
14.	G

TEST 1 READING ANSWERS

15.	D	1.	C	
16.	G	2.	J	
17.	A	3.	B	
18.	G	4.	H	
19.	B	5.	B	
20.	H	6.	F	
21.	B	7.	A	
22.	F	8.	G	
23.	C	9.	C	
24.	K	10.	J	
25.	B	11.	B	
26.	F	12.	H	
27.	C	13.	D	
28.	J	14.	F	
29.	B	15.	D	
30.	H	16.	H	
31.	E	17.	A	
32.	H	18.	G	
33.	A	19.	C	
34.	J	20.	H	
35.	C	21.	C	
36.	J	22.	H	
37.	D	23.	A	
38.	J	24.	F	
39.	B	25.	B	
40.	F	26.	H	
41.	A	27.	B	
42.	K	28.	J	
43.	C	29.	C	
44.	G	30.	F	
45.	D	31.	A	
46.	J	32.	F	
47.	C	33.	C	
48.	J	34.	H	
49.	C	35.	B	
50.	K	36.	G	
51.	D	37.	D	
52.	G	38.	F	
53.	B	39.	B	
54.	F	40.	J	
55.	B			
56.	F			
57.	C			
58.	F			
59.	D			
60.	K			

TEST 1 SCIENCE ANSWERS

1. A
2. F
3. D
4. G
5. D
6. G
7. B
8. J
9. A
10. H
11. D
12. H
13. D
14. J
15. C
16. G
17. D
18. H
19. B
20. J
21. C
22. G
23. B
24. F
25. C
26. G
27. D
28. H
29. D
30. F
31. C
32. H
33. D
34. G
35. B
36. G
37. C
38. H
39. B
40. F

SCORING YOUR PRACTICE EXAM

Step A

Count the number of correct answers for each section and record the number in the space provided for your raw score on the Score Conversion Worksheet below.

Step B

Using the Score Conversion Chart on the next page, convert your raw scores on each section to scaled scores. Then compute your composite ACT score by averaging the four subject scores. Add them up and divide by four. Don't worry about the essay score; it is not included in your composite score.

Score Conversion Worksheet		
Section	Raw Score	Scaled Score
1	_____/75	_____
2	_____/60	_____
3	_____/40	_____
4	_____/40	_____

SCORE CONVERSION CHART

Scaled Score	Raw Score			
	English	Mathematics	Reading	Science Reasoning
36	75	60	39–40	40
35	74	59	38	39
34	72–73	58	37	38
33	71	57	36	—
32	70	55–56	35	37
31	69	53–54	34	36
30	67–68	52	33	—
29	65–66	50–51	32	35
28	62–64	46–49	30–31	33–34
27	59–61	43–45	28–29	31–32
26	57–58	41–42	27	30
25	55–56	39–40	26	29
24	52–54	37–38	25	28
23	50–51	35–36	24	27–26
22	49	33–34	23	25
21	48	31–32	21–22	24
20	45–47	29–30	20	23
19	43–44	27–28	19	22
18	40–42	24–26	18	20–21
17	38–39	21–23	17	18–19
16	35–37	18–20	16	16–17
15	32–34	16–17	15	15
14	29–31	13–15	14	13–14
13	27–28	11–12	12–13	12
12	24–26	9–10	11	11
11	21–23	7–8	9–10	10
10	18–20	6	8	9
9	15–17	5	7	7–8
8	13–14	4	—	6
7	11–12	—	6	5
6	9–10	3	5	—
5	7–8	2	4	4
4	5–6	—	3	3
3	3–4	1	2	2
2	2	—	1	1
1	0	0	0	0

TEST 1 ENGLISH EXPLANATIONS

1. **D** The phrase *left by the delivery man* is an unnecessary detail added to the sentence and should be off-set by two commas, making choice (D) the best answer. The semicolon in choices (A) and (C) creates a fragment in the second half of the sentence.

2. **F** The sentence uses *scrawled* as an adjective to describe the words, not as a verb, so you can eliminate (G). Choice (H) uses the wrong form of *scrawl*, and choice (J) is the wrong idiomatic expression.

3. **B** The phrase *my heart skipping a beat (or two)* is incomplete and cannot be linked to the complete phrase with *and*, eliminating choices (A) and (C). *When* changes the meaning of the sentence, making (B) the best answer.

4. **H** The two halves of this sentence are both complete, eliminating choice (J). Since the second half already uses the pronoun it to refer to the box, *that* and *which* are unnecessary, making choice (C) the best answer.

5. **C** Since the question asks you to make a contrast, you can eliminate choices (B) and (D). Choice (C) better describes the people for whom the record holds value than choice (A).

6. **J** The verb should be in past perfect tense to show that he made his living as a musician before marrying, making choice (J) the only possible answer. Choices (F), (G), and (H) all use *would*, which is the past perfect tense of will.

7. **D** The phrase *performing in music hall and local festivals* is incomplete and must be linked to the previous thought, eliminating choices (A) and (B). By using *which* to link the ideas, choice (C) makes it sound as if the grandfather performs the band, rather than the band performing.

8. **J** The best answer is (J) because it is the most concise of the choices. It is unnecessary to the meaning of the sentence to mention who produced the album.

9. **A** The phrase after the dash is adding further details to how rare the record truly is, making choice (A) the best answer. Choice (B) is a contrasting transition, and choices (C) and (D) use transition words that confuse the meaning of the sentence.

10. **F** The verb should be in past perfect tense because it is describing how long one copy had existed before the writer received the record in the mail, eliminating choices (H) and (J). Choice (G) uses the incorrect expression.

11. **B** The words *beg* and *plead* are synonyms, so it is redundant to use both. Choice (B) is the most concise answer.

12. **G** Since the question asks you to discuss the significance to the writer's upbringing, you can eliminate choices (F) and (H). Choice (G) is more personal to the writer than choice (J), making it the best answer.

13. **C** Choice (C) is the only answer that clearly expresses the writer's intended meaning. Choices (A), (B), and (C) all misplace phrases throughout the sentence, confusing who and what are being described.

14. **H** The punctuation should separate two complete ideas, eliminating choices (F) and (J). Choice (G) is an unnecessary transition word, because *however* is already used in the following sentence.

15. **B** The phrase *that he was still with me* is an incomplete thought and should be linked to the previous complete thought, eliminating choice (D). Since the sentence explains what the author feels reassured of, punctuation between *me* and *that* creates an unnecessary pause, making choice (B) the best answer.

16. **F** This question requires that you determine whether an apostrophe or additional punctuation mark is required. No apostrophe is needed because the word *lives* is not possessing anything, so eliminate choices (H) and (J). No pause is required between the words *lives* and *completely*, so eliminate choice (G), which interrupts the sentence unnecessarily. The sentence is correct as written, so the best choice is (F).

17. **D** The question asks for a line that indicates some similarity between the narrator and his friends. Choice (A) discusses only the narrator; choices (B) and (C) contain information that is much too general to discuss only the narrator and his friends. Only choice (D) has all the appropriate elements, particularly as presented in the words *palpable likeness*.

18. **J** This question requires that you determine whether an apostrophe or additional punctuation mark is required. No apostrophe is needed because there is no indication that owners are possessing anything (hint: don't get thrown off by the phrase *restaurant's owners* in which the word appears), so you can eliminate choice (H). Only choice (J) has the appropriate comma placement to situate *chat with the restaurant's owners* within a list (the other items in this list are *sit, drink a cup of coffee*, and *figure out which new and exciting place we'd be driving to next*). A semicolon is inappropriate here because the semicolon is a punctuation mark used to separate two complete ideas, and the context indicates that it is not used to separate the items in this list.

19. **B** The sentence as written contains the phrase *looking forward to it in anticipation*, which is redundant, so you can eliminate choice (A). Choices (C) and (D) contain the same error. Only choice (B) preserves the meaning in a concise, non-redundant way. In addition, the word *it* in choices (A) and (C) is ambiguous.

20. **H** This question asks whether the writer's proposed addition would be appropriately placed at the end of this paragraph. If you're not sure whether to answer Yes or No, look at the reasons. Choice (F) must be eliminated because the proposed addition is too general and is consequently not relevant to other, more personal information in the passage. Choice (G) must be eliminated because it is too general and gives no indication why the narrator should choose a *specific* diner. Choice (J) suggests that the primary focus of the paragraph up to this point has been *driving*, which it has not; rather, the primary focus of the paragraph is the stop at the diner and the things the narrator and his friends did there. Accordingly, only choice (H) appropriately recognizes the personal tone of the paragraph and correctly advises not to include the proposed addition.

21. **A** The first place you should look in this question is to whether *that* or *whom* is an appropriate first word. *Whom* is the objective form of who, which is used to refer only to people. The word here refers back to *something*, not a person, so eliminate choices (B) and (C). Choice (D) changes the meaning of the sentence to suggest that something is doing the ordering, rather than being ordered. The sentence is correct as written, so NO CHANGE is required.

22. **J** This question asks you to determine which word would be most appropriately modified by the phrase *from childhood*. To place the phrase after any of the words in choices (F), (G), or (H) is to break the flow of the sentence and to make the meaning of the sentence unclear. Only choice (H) establishes the proper link between the underlined and non-underlined portions of the sentence in the phrase *remembered from childhood*.

23. **B** In an earlier part of the sentence, the narrator refers to the food in the city as *too expensive*. Only choice (B) supports and modifies this idea. Read the question closely: While the other choices may be true, the best answer will be one that supports and modifies a specific part of the passage.

24. **J** In EXCEPT/LEAST/NOT questions, the underlined portion of the sentence is correct. Compare your answer choices. What do words like as and *when* do to the first part of the sentence? They make it an introductory idea and an incomplete thought. When the first part of the sentence is incomplete, the comma after the word *could* sets this first part off from the complete idea after it. By contrast, if the first part of the sentence is made complete as it is in choice (J), this creates a comma splice, wherein two complete ideas are insufficiently separated by a comma.

25. **B** Identify the subject of the verb. Although the word *restaurants* is closest to the verb, it is not the subject; rather, the subject is the word *place*, a singular subject that requires a singular verb. Since choices (A), (C), and (D) all contain plural verbs, eliminate them. Only choice (B) remains, and the verb *was* does agree in number with the word *place*.

26. **F** We need an idea that will signal the transition between the paragraph above, which is a recollection of the trips, and the paragraph below, which fast forwards to the present and discusses the narrator's life now. Only choice (F) contains this transition. Choice (G) deals only with the narrator's friends who are not mentioned in the last paragraph. Choice (H) deals only with the past, and choice (J) deals only with the narrator's life after graduation. Only choice (F) has both the past and present components it needs to transition from one paragraph to the next.

27. **D** This question asks you to determine whether you need a transition between the first and second sentences of this last paragraph. Choices (A) and (C) suggest a disagreement between the two ideas where none exists. Choice (B) suggests a cause-and-effect relationship between the two sentences where none exists. Only choice (D) makes sense in the context, where no transition is needed.

28. **F** In EXCEPT/LEAST/NOT questions, the underlined portion of the sentence is correct. To answer this question, you need to determine which prepositions work idiomatically with the verb *drive*. Choice (G) contains the same preposition, *about*, used in the underlined portion, and although not a particularly common usage, *drive about* is idiomatically correct. The same goes for the more familiar *drive around*, as it is used in choices (H) and (J). Accordingly, only choice (F) does not work in the context of the sentence, because it is incorrect usage to say to *drive among the town*.

29. **D** All the answer choices mean roughly the same thing; each just presents a different way to say it. In situations such as this one, the most concise answer that preserves the meaning is the best. Accordingly, choices (A), (B), and (C) are all too wordy in comparison with choice (D).

30. **F** This question too asks you to determine which choice presents the most concise alternative that preserves the meaning of the sentence. Eliminate choices (G) and (J) because each presents an awkward, wordy alternative to the original. Choice (H) is as concise as choice (F), but note the context: Your answer will need to be parallel to other verbs in the sentence. In this case, only *came back* is parallel with the tense and tone of *drove by*, making the best choice (F).

31. **D** In EXCEPT/LEAST/NOT questions, the underlined portion of the sentence is correct. The original sentence uses *even though* to introduce two contrasting ideas. Choices (A), (B), and (C) are all contrasting transition words and are acceptable. Choice (D) indicates that the ideas are similar and, therefore, is not an acceptable alternative.

32. **G** The best connecting statement should continue the previous idea that Siena has both ancient and modern elements, eliminating choices (F) and (J). The following sentence begins with *Another remnant*, which means the inserted sentence should already list specific examples, which makes choice (G) better than (H).

33. **D** It is redundant to describe the horse race as *biannual* and as *held twice a year*, eliminating choices (A) and (B). Choice (D) is better than choice (C) because it is more concise.

34. **H** The phrase *dreaded right-angle turns* describes an obstacle racers must face as they complete each lap, therefore it must immediately follow *laps* to clarify meaning. Choices (F), (G), and (J) do not provide logical sentences because the phrase does not describe *horses*, *track*, or *plaza*.

35. **C** Choice (C) correctly agrees with the present tense of the other verb in the sentence. Choices (A), (B), and (D) do not agree in tense and alter the meaning of the sentence.

36. **J** *Because* introduces an incomplete thought, so choice (F) creates a sentence fragment. Choice (G) suggests contrasting rather than similar ideas. Choice (H) is incorrect because the preceding sentence has already mentioned *financial* commitments, so voluntary taxation cannot be considered an additional act by members.

37. **A** The previous sentence illustrates the enormous cost to hire a jockey, which contrasts with the idea that it is a small price to pay, so the best transition word is choice (A). Choices (B), (C), and (D) all indicate a similar relationship, which is not consistent with the passage.

38. **G** The phrase *even more so than getting married* is an unnecessary description within the sentence and should be offset by either two commas or dashes, eliminating choice (F). Since the non-underlined portion uses a dash before *even*, the best answer is choice (G) not choice (H). Choice (J) creates a sentence fragment, since a semicolon can separate only complete ideas.

39. **C** The word *throughout* begins an incomplete idea, and the phrase cannot stand on its own as a sentence, eliminating choice (A). Choice (C) connects the incomplete phrase to the complete idea before it with the smoothest transition. The comma in choice (D) creates an unnecessary pause. Since a semicolon is generally used to separate two complete sentences, choice (B) is also incorrect.

40. **F** The word *Contrade* ends a complete thought, and *Contrada* begins a second complete thought, so you need a period making choice (F) the best answer. Choices (G), (H), and (J) all create run-on sentences because they do not separate complete ideas.

41. **B** The phrase *from baptisms to food festivals* is an unnecessary description within the sentence and should be offset by either two commas or dashes, eliminating choice (F). Since the non-underlined portion uses a comma after festivals, the best answer is choice (B) not choice (D). Choice (C) creates sentence fragments, since a semicolon can only separate complete ideas.

42. **F** The correct pronoun is *who* because *members* is the subject for the verb *become*. Choices (G) and (H) use possessive rather than subject case, and choice (J) is object case and does not indicate which noun become describes.

43. **D** The second half of the sentence is an incomplete idea and must be linked to the complete thought, eliminating choices (A), (B), and (C).

44. **G** The passage is written in the present tense, eliminating choices (F) and (H). Since the parties are *thrown* by the locals, you need the passive form for the verb (also called the past participle) not the past tense verb *threw*.

45. **D** The best location for Paragraph 3 is before Paragraph 5, choice (D), because Paragraph 4 introduces and defines the *contrada* discussed in the first sentence of Paragraph 3. There is also a logical sequence from winning the *Palio* at the end of Paragraph 3 to the celebration in the beginning of Paragraph 5.

46. **H** As written, the pronoun *it* in the underlined portion has no clear referent. Choices (G) and (J) do not fix the problem. Only choice (H) replaces the ambiguous pronoun with a clear referent.

47. **C** The sentence as written is a fragment. Choice (B) is also a fragment. Choices (C) and (D) both fix the sentence fragment, but choice (D) changes the meaning of the sentence.

48. **J** The sentence as written is incorrect because the adjective *tireless* cannot modify the verb *continued*. Choices (G) and (H) do not make sense in the given context. Only choice (J) links the word *tireless* with its appropriate noun *literary experimentation*.

49. **B** In EXCEPT/LEAST/NOT questions, the underlined portion of the sentence is correct. Since the verbs *to seem* and *to appear* are synonyms, look to other differences among the answer choices. Note that the original sentence and choices (A), (C), and (D) all contain the present tense, appropriately matched to the word *contemporary* used earlier in this sentence. Only choice (B) changes the tense to past, making choice (B) the LEAST acceptable substitution.

50. **H** The sentence as written is idiomatically incorrect. The prepositions *until* and *at*, as in choice (G), are incorrectly linked to the phrase *take a real step*. Only the word *toward* completes this phrase appropriately to create *take a real step toward*. Deleting the underlined portion, as in choice (J), makes the sentence unclear and changes its meaning.

51. **A** Choices (B), (C), and (D) all incorrectly separate the verb *fuse* from its objects. NO CHANGE is required here because no punctuation is necessary between the verb and its objects.

52. **H** In EXCEPT/LEAST/NOT questions, the underlined portion of the sentence is correct. Note the similarities between the words. *Encouraged*, *motivated*, and *emboldened*, in choices (F), (G), and (J) are all synonyms for the verb *inspired*. Only the word *forced* in choice (H) changes the meaning of the sentence and is thus the LEAST acceptable substitution.

53. **A** Since the phrase *as American writers living abroad were known* is a descriptive phrase that plays no essential role in determining the meaning of the sentence, it must be set off by a comma as it is in the sentence as written. Choices (B) and (D) introduce new punctuation that loses the clarity of the original sentence. Choice (C) suggests that the phrase is a portion necessary to preserve the meaning of the sentence and should not be set off from the rest. This is incorrect because *as American writers living abroad were known* is merely a phrase that clarifies and defines the word before it, *expatriates*.

54. **J** For two ideas to be separated by a comma and a coordinating conjunction such as *but*, the ideas on either side of this punctuation and conjunction must be complete. The sentence as written is incorrect because the phrase *but limited to those who were able to find copies of the book* is not a complete idea. Choice (H) is incorrect because a semicolon is also a punctuation mark that requires that the two ideas on either side of it be complete. Choice (G) creates an unnecessary pause in the sentence. Accordingly, only choice (J), which removes all punctuation marks, maintains the proper flow of the sentence and correctly treats *positive but limited to those who were able to find copies of the book* as a modifying phrase for the word *reception*.

55. **D** The sentence as written discusses the reception of a different book, not the one discussed in the previous sentence. Choice (C) refers to the current reputation of the book, and choice (B) is too general to be said to refer to only the specific book mentioned in this paragraph. Only choice (D) contains the reaction of critics to the appropriate work and the idea that the book was difficult to obtain.

56. **F** This question asks you to identify which answer best indicates that the novel *Beyond Desire* had presented something new in American literature. Choice (G) suggests that this book had other influences and does not say whether Anderson was the first to incorporate these influences. Choices (H) and (J) discuss the reactions of critics and readers to the book, not the book itself.

57. **A** Choice (B) is idiomatically incorrect—the preposition used with the word *contributions* in this context should be *to*, rather than *from*. Choices (C) and (D) are unclear in creating the phrases *the 1930s of the various writers* and *he influenced of the various writers*, respectively. Only choice (A) properly links the noun and the proper prepositional phrase in *works of the various writers*.

58. **G** To keep the sentence as written is to suggest the word *American* is not an essential piece of the sentence, but without this information, the words *the name* are undefined and unclear. Choices (H) and (J) omit the necessary comma before the conjunction *and*, which, in this case, is separating the items in a list: *the troubled relationship, the direct style*, and the idea are the main nouns used in this list. Only choice (G) indicates the importance of the word *American* to the meaning of the sentence and sets this portion of the sentence in a list appropriately.

59. **D** Pay close attention to the years discussed in each of these paragraphs. Paragraph 2 discusses Anderson's death in *1941* and his influence *today*. It should be logically placed after the paragraph discussing the time period most directly before that. Paragraph 5 is appropriate here because it discusses the 1920s and the 1930s, the periods closest to 1941 in this passage.

60. **G** Pay close attention to the reasons given in each of these answer choices. Choice (F) is too general and too reliant upon judgments about the content and does not accurately reflect the content of the passage. Choice (H) erroneously says that the passage is primarily about a difference between two large groups when in fact it is about only a single author and his influence on a group of other authors. Choice (J) suggests that the passage only discusses the 1920s and the 1930s when the years 1919 and 1941 are mentioned explicitly.

61. **C** Choice (C) is the clearest and most concise option. The verbs *retracted* and *diminished* essentially mean the same thing, thus choices (A) and (B) are redundant. Choice (D) is incorrect, because without a verb the sentence is incomplete.

62. **J** The passage is written in past tense, eliminating choices (G) and (H). The correct past tense form of *to begin* is *began*, making choice (J) the best answer. The form *begun* is used after a helping verb.

63. **A** *These responsibilities* refer to the previous sentence, which describes the responsibilities to be *traditionally assigned to men*. Choice (B), therefore, is redundant. Choice (C) creates a sentence fragment. Choice (D) does not agree in number with the plural *responsibilities*.

64. **J** Choice (J) eliminates the word *but*, fixing the sentence fragment that is created by the pronoun *that*. Choices (F), (G), and (H) incorrectly add conjunctions that create incomplete sentences.

65. **C** The two words *machinists* and *making* should be separated by a period because the sentence has two complete ideas, making choice (C) the best answer. Choices (A) and (D) create run-on sentences. A comma cannot separate two complete ideas, eliminating choice (B).

66. **F** The previous sentence already mentions factories and shipyards, making choices (G) and (H) redundant. Choice (J) changes the meaning of the sentence, therefore the best answer is choice (F).

67. **C** Choice (C) provides the correct verb, *was*, that agrees with the singular subject of the sentence, *presence*. Choices (A), (B), and (D) all incorrectly use a plural verb.

68. **G** Choice (G) is correct because the addition distracts the reader from the topic at hand, which is the changing role of women in the workforce during World War II. Choice (F) is wrong because although it suggests not adding the information, its reasoning is incorrect. The proposed sentence is consistent in style and tone with the rest of the essay. Choices (H) and (J) incorrectly recommend adding a sentence that is irrelevant to the essay.

69. **B** The rest of the essay is about the women's baseball league, therefore the best transition is choice (B). Choices (A) and (C) do not reflect the focus of the essay, and choice (D) is too extreme.

70. **G** *Philip K. Wrigley* is necessary to clarify who the *Founder* is and should not be off-set by commas, eliminating choice (J). Choices (F) and (H) have unnecessary pauses due to too many commas; therefore, choice (G) is the clearest answer.

71. **A** Choice (A) describes a specific visual with *pretty smiles* and *baseball mitts in their hands*. Choices (B), (C), and (D) are incorrect because the added information does not qualify as descriptive detail that helps the reader visualize the photographs.

72. **J** The sentence lists different feminine characteristics but does not make clear where the list ends, usually indicated by *and* before the last item. The best answer, therefore, is choice (J). Choices (F) and (G) don't list the items in parallel form. Choice (H) uses the wrong linkage for a list of things.

73. **D** The following sentence states that the photographs of the female players exemplify the *balance between feminine appeal and masculine labor* of women during WWII, making choice (D) the best explanation. Choice (A) is incorrect because the previous sentence suggests the physical attractiveness of the players but does not give specific details about what they look like. Choice (B) is incorrect because women's athleticism is not the focus of the paragraph. Choice (C) is incorrect because the captions of the photographs are never discussed.

74. **J** Choice (J) is the correct answer because the correct form of the possessive pronoun is *its*. The correct possessive form of the pronoun does not use apostrophes, eliminating choices (F) and (G). Choice (H) uses the plural pronoun *their*, which incorrectly replaces the singular antecedent *All American Girls Professional Baseball League*.

75. **B** The essay directly describes various jobs that women held during World War II, all of which were roles traditionally filled by men, eliminating choices (C) and (D). Choice (A)'s reasoning only addresses the *All American Girl's Baseball League*, which is the focus of Paragraph 4 but not the essay as a whole.

TEST 1 MATH EXPLANATIONS

1. **A**   Since $\overline{YZ}$ is $\frac{1}{3}$ the length of $\overline{XZ}$, $\overline{XZ}$ will be $3 \times 24 = 72$ kilometers. Since X is the halfway point of the trail, the trail's entire length will be twice $\overline{XZ}$, or $72 \times 2 = 144$ kilometers.

2. **J**   To find the value of x, first subtract 7 from both sides to get $\frac{4x}{5} = -1$. Next, multiply both sides by 5 to get $4x = -5$. Finally, divide both sides by 4 to give you choice (J). Choice (F) neglects the negative sign. Choice (G) is the reciprocal of the correct answer. Choices (H) and (K) are partial answers.

3. **B**   Determine how many minutes it takes each cyclist to make 9,760 pedal revolutions. Cyclist A takes 9,760 rev ÷ 80 rev/min = 122 minutes. Cyclist B takes 9,760 rev ÷ 61 rev/min = 160 minutes. So, Cyclist B takes 160 − 122 = 38 more minutes than Cyclist A. Notice that Choices (C) and (E) are partial answers. Choice (D) is the sum of each cyclist's rate, and Choice (A) is the difference of their rates.

4. **K**   The perimeter of a square is $4s$, so one side of this square is $\frac{36}{4} = 9$ inches. The area of the square is $s^2 = 9^2 = 81$. Choice (F) is the length of one side if the square had an *area* of 36. Choice (G) is the length of one side rather than the area. Choice (H) is the result of $9 + 9$. Choice (J) is the result of 6^2, rather than 9^2.

5. **D**   From the figure, you can see that the y-coordinate must be greater than 4, eliminating choice (C), and the x-coordinate must be less than 8, eliminating choice (E). Since the figure is a rectangle, opposite sides must be parallel and thus have the same slope. The slope from (2,0) to (8,3) is 3 units up and 6 units right. You can now calculate the fourth vertex from the point (0,4): (0+6, 4+3), which gives you (6,7). Choices (A) and (B) have an x-coordinate of 4, which is halfway between 0 and 8.

6. **H**   If Carla's brother has x notebooks, Carla has $5x$ notebooks, so $5x + x = 42$. Since $x = 7$ and Carla has $5x$ notebooks, she has $5(7) = 35$. You can also use the answer choices to solve this problem: divide the answer choices by 5 to calculate how many notebooks Carla's brother has and determine when Carla (the answer) and Carla's brother (the answer ÷ 5) add up to 42. A calculation error of $x = 6$ leads to choice (F). Choices (J) and (K) add and subtract numbers from the problem without answering the question asked.

7. **A**   A right angle has a measure of 90°; therefore, any angle contained within a right angle must be smaller than 90°, leaving only choice (A).

8. **J** You have to count the number of different ways Susie can choose her one T-shirt and her one pair of shorts. She has 3 options for her T-shirt and 3 options for her pair of shorts. She can combine any of the T-shirts with any of the pairs of shorts, so there are 3×3, or 9, combinations. Choices (F) and (G) do not account for all possible combinations. Choice (H) is 2^3 rather than 3^2.

9. **C** Use the words in the problem to create an equation: *percent* means "divide by 100," *of* means "multiply" and *what number* means "use a variable." The resulting equation is $\frac{20}{100} \times 20 = \frac{50}{100} \times y$. Solve to find that $y = 8$. Be careful of choices (B), which is 20% of 20, and (D), which is 50% of 20.

10. **H** The number of piano players exceeds the number of violin players; thus the number of musicians who play both instruments cannot exceed the number who play violin, eliminating choices (J) and (K). Since all 22 musicians who play the violin could also play the piano, choice (H) gives the maximum possible number.

11. **A** In order to make m^2 (and therefore m) as large as possible, make n^2 as small as possible. The square of any real number can't be negative, so the smallest that n^2 can be is 0. This makes $m^2 = 196$, so m equals either -14 or 14. Choices (B), (C), (D), and (E) are based on multiplication, division, or subtraction, not taking a square root.

12. **F** To solve this problem, break it down into manageable pieces. $\frac{1}{5} \times \$925 = \$185$, so the sale price of the drum kit is $\$925 - \$185 = \$740$. Since the sales tax is $.05 \times \$740 = \$37$, the total owed is $\$740 + \$37 = \$777$. Phil receives back the amount he gave the sales clerk minus the amount he owes: $\$800 - \$777 = \$23$. Choice (G) is the amount of tax paid. Choices (H) and (J) resemble numbers from steps within the problem and choice (K) calculates the taxed price without applying the sale discount.

13. **D** Taking the square root of a negative number yields an imaginary number. If you picked choice (C), be careful—this number is not *rationalized*, but that does not mean it is not a *real number*.

14. **G** The general quadratic expression $a^2 - b^2$ equals $(a - b)(a + b)$. In this question, take the square root of $25x^4$ and the square root of $16y^8$; thus $a = 5x^2$ and $b = 4y^4$. Choice (F) correctly factors the variables but not the coefficients, introducing an incorrect factor of the coefficients. Choices (H) and (K) incorrectly factor the coefficients. Choice (J) incorrectly factors the variables.

15. **D** Use the formula *Shaded Area = Total Area − Unshaded Area*. In this case, the *Total Area* is the area of the square, which is $4^2 = 16$. To find the *Unshaded Area*, add up the areas of the 4 unshaded triangles. Starting at the lower left of the figure and going clockwise, those areas are: $\frac{1}{2}(1 \times 2) + \frac{1}{2}(2 \times 2) + \frac{1}{2}(2 \times 1) + \frac{1}{2}(1 \times 2) = 5$. So, the *Shaded Area* = $16 - 5 = 11$.

16. **G** To find the percent P, substitute 20 for t to calculate $-0.001(20)^2 + 0.4(20) = 7.6$. Choice (F) is the rounded value of 0.076%, which is not equivalent to 7.6%. Choices (H) and (J) result if you don't pay attention to PEMDAS or distribution of the negative sign. Choice (K) results if t^2 and t are switched.

17. **A** Find the cost per grapefruit at each store by dividing the cost of each bag by the number of grape-fruits in each bag. The cost per grapefruit at Fatima's is $4.40 ÷ 8 = $0.55, while the cost per grapefruit at Ernie's is $1.86 ÷ 3 = $0.62. Find the difference: $0.62 − $0.55 = $0.07. Choice (B) comes from multiplying $0.07 by the difference in the number of grapefruits (8 − 3 = 5). Choice (C) comes from averaging $0.55 and $0.62. Choice (D) comes from adding $0.55 and $0.62. Choice (E) is the difference in costs of the two bags.

18. **G** In order to multiply factors, you need to FOIL (<u>F</u>irst, <u>O</u>uter, <u>I</u>nner, <u>L</u>ast). Remember to *add* ex-ponents when multiplying numbers with the same base and watch your signs carefully: $x^8 + 4x^4 − 4x^4 − 16 = x^8 − 16$. Choice (F) adds rather than multiplies the factors. Choice (J) multiplies the exponents instead of adding them. Choices (H) and (K) confuse the signs.

19. **B** First, calculate the number of tile pieces laid in the first period of work: $\frac{50 \text{ pieces}}{1 \text{ hour}}$ × 3.5 hours = 175 pieces. Next, since you are looking for the time Wade spends working after the interruption, you'll need to figure out how many tile pieces he laid during that time. Subtract 280 pieces − 175 pieces = 105 pieces. Calculate the number of hours he spends in the second work session by divid-ing $\frac{105 \text{ pieces}}{35 \text{ pieces per hour}}$ = 3 hours. If you chose choice (D), be careful—you may have included the 60 minutes during which Wade is interrupted, but the question is looking for the time it took Wade to complete his work *after he was interrupted*.

20. **H** To find the midpoint of a line, you must take the average of the *x*-coordinates, $\frac{x_1 + x_2}{2}$, and the average of the *y*-coordinates of the endpoints, $\frac{y_1 + y_2}{2}$. Choices (F), (G), and (K) incorrectly aver-age the *x*-coordinates. Choice (J) incorrectly averages the *y*-coordinates.

21. **B** You might want to draw a picture to see what is happening. Add the lengths of the two short sides of the backyard and one long side: 16 + 16 + 22 = 54. Choice (C) is the sum of two long sides and one short side. Choice (D) is the perimeter of the backyard but the problem says the fencing is needed only on 3 sides. Choice (E) is the area of the backyard.

22. **F** One way to solve this problem is to rewrite the equation in the slope-intercept form, $y = mx + b$, by subtracting 7*x* and dividing by −3 on both sides. The resulting equation is $y = \frac{7}{3}x − 7$, where −7 is the value of *b*, the *y*–intercept. Another way to solve this problem is to remember that the *y*–intercept occurs at *x* = 0 and calculate 7(0) − 3*y* = 21. Choice (H) is the slope of the line, and the other choices do not modify the equation correctly.

23. **C** Find the flower's growth rate by dividing the total growth by the number of days. This is the same thing as finding the slope: $\frac{17.4-15.0}{16-8} = \frac{2.4}{8} = 0.3$ cm per day. You want to know when the flower was 16.5 cm tall, which means it has grown 16.5 − 15.0 = 1.5 cm: 1.5 cm ÷ 0.3 cm/day = 5 days after April 8th, which is April 13th.

24. **K** To subtract, you must first distribute − 3 to each term in the second parentheses. You get $2x^3 - x - 1 - 3x^4 - 6x^3 + 6x^2 + 3x - 9$. Combine like terms to get $-3x^4 - 4x^3 + 6x^2 + 2x - 10$. Choices (H) and (J) incorrectly distribute the − 3. Choices (F) and (G) incorrectly combine terms and exponents.

25. **B** The slide makes a right triangle, as shown in the picture. Use the Pythagorean Theorem ($a^2 + b^2 = c^2$) to solve $7^2 = 6^2 + x^2$. $49 = 36 + x^2$, $x^2 = 13$, $x \approx 3.61$, which rounds to 4. Choice (A) is too small, and choice (C) is too large.

26. **F** You're looking for a set in which the mean (average), median ("middle" value), and mode (number that appears most often) all equal 8. All five answer choices have a median of 8, but you can eliminate (G) and (K), because their modes are not 8. You can then eliminate (H) and (J) by calculating their means—8.6 and 9, respectively. That leaves you with (F).

27. **C** The easiest approach to this problem is to test out the answer choices. For choice (C), if the 2nd term is 18, then the 3rd term is (18 + 2) × 3 = 60, and the 4th term is (60 + 2) × 3 = 186. You could also work backwards: if the 4th term is 186, then the 3rd term is (186 ÷ 3) − 2 = 60, and the 2nd term is (60 ÷ 3) − 2 = 18. Be sure to read the problem carefully. Choices (B) and (D) are the 1st and 3rd terms of the sequence, respectively.

28. **J** The easiest approach to this problem is to test all the answer choices. |9 − 3| ≥ 12 is false; thus the correct answer is choice (J). You could also solve algebraically by solving the equation where (x − 3) ≥ 12 and − (x − 3) ≥ 12. The other choices solve the inequality with wrong direction of signs, choice (K), or confusion of positive/negative values within the absolute value.

29. **B** Given that v is larger than s, then $t + u + v$ must be larger than $s + t + u$, since $t + u$ are equal in both expressions. Because $s + t + u = 29$, $t + u + v$ must be larger than 29. Choices (A), (C), (D), and (E) are not necessarily true, because you don't know anything about the relationships of t, u, and v. Another way to approach this question is to make up your own numbers for the variables: for example, let $s = 20$, $t = 5$, $u = 4$, and $v = 21$. Using these numbers, choices (A), (C), and (D) are false. Now make up different numbers: $s = 5$, $t = 4$, $u = 20$, and $v = 6$. Choice (B) is still true (30 > 29), but choice (E) is now false (15 > 29).

30. **H** You can eliminate choices (J) and (K) immediately since $\angle CBD$ is clearly less than 90° in the figure. Since $\overline{BE}$ is a straight line, $\angle CDE + \angle BDC = 180°$, $\angle BDC = 180° - 155° = 25°$. $\overline{AB}$ and $\overline{CD}$ are opposite sides of a rectangle, so the line segments are parallel. Extend line segments $\overline{AB}$, $\overline{CD}$, and $\overline{BE}$ to reveal that the two parallel lines are crossed by a transversal, which means $\angle BDC$ and $\angle ABD$ are congruent. Thus, $\angle ABD = 25°$. $\angle ABD$ and $\angle CBD$ make up one of the right angles of rectangle $ABCD$; thus $\angle CBD = 90° - 25° = 65°$. Choices (F), (J), and (K) are all angles within the figure, but do not answer the question.

31. **E** Test the prime numbers from the answer choices in the equation. Since all the numbers in the equation $a - b = c$ must be positive prime numbers, the only possible result for c can be 2 (e.g., $13 - 11 = 7 - 5 = 2$). The only exceptions to $c = 2$ are $5 - 2 = 3$, $13 - 2 = 11$, and $7 - 2 = 5$. Even so, the only number common to all of these equations is 2, answer choice (E).

32. **H** You can determine Pierre's average speed, in miles per hour, by dividing his total mileage by his total time. The total number of miles he covers is the distance from starting point S to finish line F, which is SF. You can eliminate choices (F), (G), and (J) because they don't include the entire length of the racecourse. The total elapsed time from point S to point F is t_F. You can eliminate choices (F), (G), and (K) because they don't use the elapsed time clocked at the end of the race.

33. **A** Since you know the hypotenuse of the triangle and need to find the adjacent side of $\angle ABC$, use SOHCAHTOA: $\dfrac{\overline{BC}}{13} = \cos(70°)$. So, $\overline{BC} = 13\cos(70°) \approx 4.4$. Choices (D) and (E) are the answers that you would get if you used either the sine or the tangent functions in the equation above. If you chose either choice (B) or (C), you might have assumed that the triangle was a 5:12:13 right triangle.

34. **J** When $x = -3$ and $y = -4$, then $\dfrac{8}{(-4)^2} - \dfrac{(-3)^2}{(-4)} = \dfrac{1}{2} - \left(-\dfrac{9}{4}\right) = \dfrac{11}{4}$. Choices (F), (G) and (J) all confuse the signs. Choice (K) switches x and y.

35. **C** The ramp forms a 30°-60°-90° triangle with side lengths in a ratio of $1 : \sqrt{3} : 2$. Since the shortest leg measures 4, the other leg of the triangle will be $\sqrt{3}$ times the short side: $4\sqrt{3} = 6.92 \approx 7$. Choice (D) gives the length of the ramp itself, not the horizontal length.

36. **J** $\triangle BCD$ is equilateral, so $\angle CBD$ is 60°. $\angle ABD$ must be larger than 60°, eliminating choices (F) and (G). Choice (J) would mean $\angle ABC$ is $96° - 60° = 36°$. Since $\angle ABC$ is half the measure of $\angle BAC$ and $\angle BAC = \angle BCA$, each base angle of the isosceles triangle would be $(180° - 36°) \div 2 = 72°$, which works within $\triangle ABC$: $36° + 72° + 72° = 180$. Choice (K) mistakenly calculates $\angle ABC$ to be twice, rather than half, the measure of $\angle BAC$.

37. **D** Use the standard slope formula with points $(8,0)$ and $(0,-4)$: $m = \dfrac{y_2 - y_1}{x_2 - x_1} = \dfrac{(-4) - (0)}{(0) - (8)} = \dfrac{-4}{-8} = \dfrac{1}{2}$. If you selected choice (E), you may have flipped the x and the y when you calculated the slope. If you selected choice (A), you may have confused some of the negative signs.

38. **J** Find the hypotenuse with the Pythagorean theorem: $a^2 + b^2 = c^2$. With the values given in the figure, this becomes $(8)^2 + (4)^2 = c^2$, and $c^2 = 80$, so $c \approx 8.9$. Accordingly, the sides of this triangle have lengths of 4, 8, and 8.9. To find the perimeter, add these sides together to get 20.9.

39. **B** The formula for cosine is as follows: $\cos\theta = \dfrac{adjacent}{hypotenuse}$. Since you are dealing with $\angle MNO$, the adjacent side will be 4, and the hypotenuse (the same whether you're dealing with sine or cosine) is $\sqrt{80}$. Accordingly, the cosine is $\dfrac{4}{\sqrt{80}}$. Choice (A) gives the sine of $\angle MNO$, and choice (C) gives the tangent.

40. **F** The fraction is equal to $\dfrac{\#\text{ of students who passed}}{\text{total \# of students}}$. If there are m students in the class, m must be the denominator, so you can eliminate choices (G), (H), and (J). The number of students who received a passing grade is calculated by subtracting the number who didn't pass the last exam, n, from the total number of students, m. Choice (K) would give a negative fraction, which is not possible.

41. **A** To solve the inequality, distribute the 2 on the right side of the inequality: $5x + 9 \geq 6x + 8 + 7$. Then combine like terms to get: $-x \geq 6$. Remember to flip the sign when you divide by -1 for x to give you the range $x \leq -6$. Choice (B) forgets to flip the sign. Choices (C) and (D) are the result if you forget to distribute 2 to the 4 in the first step. Choice (E) results if you missed a negative sign.

42. **K** The tiles must equal the surface area of the box, which is the sum of the areas of all 6 faces. There are three sets of faces: front/back, top/bottom, and the two sides: $2(4 \times 9) + 2(3 \times 9) + 2(3 \times 4)$ $= 24 + 72 + 54 = 150$. Because each tile covers 1 cm^2, the artist must have $150\text{ cm}^2 \div 1\text{ cm}^2 = 150$, choice (K). Choice (F) finds the area of only three faces, and choices (G) and (J) account for only two of the three pairs of faces. Choice (H) finds the volume of the box.

43. **C** Draw in $\overline{AD}$, which is parallel to both $\overline{BC}$ and $\overline{EF}$, to find $\angle BAD$. The interior angles of two parallel lines add up to $180°$, so you can subtract $\angle ABC$ ($130°$) from $180°$ to yield $\angle BAD = 50°$. Subtract $\angle BAE$ from the larger angle $\angle BAD$ to get $\angle EAD = 50° - 22° = 28°$. Since $\angle AEF$ and $\angle EAD$ are also interior angles of two parallel lines, subtract: $180° - \angle EAD = 180° - 28° = 152°$ $= \angle AEF$. You could also extend $\overline{AE}$ to $\overline{BC}$ and find the third angle of the triangle. The same rule will apply—the third angle of this triangle will be equal to $\angle AEF$ because $\overline{BC}$ and $\overline{EF}$ are parallel.

44. **G** To find the area of a trapezoid, multiply the height by the average of the bases. The bases are 6 and 14, so their average is 10. Don't confuse the height of the trapezoid with the length of one of the slanted sides, which would give you choice (J). Choices (F) and (H) are the results when you multiply the length of only one of the bases by the height. You can also solve this problem by breaking the trapezoid apart into one central rectangle and right triangles on either side.

45. **D** First, raise both sides of the equation to the fifth power to get rid of the fifth root: $\left(\sqrt[5]{x^2 + 4x}\right)^5 = 2^5$

becomes $x^2 + 4x = 32$. Then, subtract 32 from both sides to get a standard quadratic form: $x^2 + 4x$

$- 32 = 0$. Factor the quadratic to get $(x + 8)(x - 4) = 0$. So, $x = -8$ or $x = 4$. You could also test the

answers until you find all the numbers that satisfy the equation. Choice (A) gives only one of the

possible values for x. Choice (C) reverses the signs. Be careful of choice (E)—that's what you get if

you only square the 2 and use the quadratic formula!

46. **J** Since you know the length of the *hypotenuse* (the ramp) and are solving for the height *opposite* the

angle of 32°, use SOHCAHTOA: $\sin A = \dfrac{\text{opposite}}{\text{hypotenuse}}$. By process of elimination, you can get rid

of choices (F), (H), and (K). If $\sin 32° = \dfrac{\text{height}}{10}$, the height h is 10 sin 32°.

47. **C** Since average is $\dfrac{\text{sum}}{\text{\# of terms}}$, the sum of $j + j + k + n$ must equal 0 to make the average equal 0.

Combining like terms gives you $2j + k + n = 0$. Subtracting $2j$ from both sides, you get $k + n = -2j$.

Choices (A) and (B) are not necessarily true (for example, if $j = -3$, k could equal 4 and n could

equal 2). Choices (D) and (E) are only true when j is equal to 0.

48. **J** In the composite function $f(g(x))$, the value of $g(x)$ is the input x value in $f(x)$; therefore $f(x)$ is tak-

ing the square root of $g(x)$. When $g(x) = 4x^2 - 5$, its square root is $\sqrt{4x^2 - 5}$. Choices (G) and (K)

make errors in taking the square root of $4x^2 - 5$. Choices (F) and (G) reverse the composite and

use $g(f(x))$.

49. C Start with the rate formula: $d = rt$. In this problem, $t = 150$ s, and you'll want to set up equations for as much as you can. If r_r is Rusty's rate and d_r is Rusty's distance, the equation will be $d_r = r_r t$.

When the two cars meet, their combined distances will equal the length of the entire track, 6,000 m. Therefore, you can use the relationships given in the problem to set up an equation as follows: 6000 ft $= r_r t + (r_r - 8 \text{ ft/s})(t)$. Since t is constant at 150 s throughout this problem, substitute it into the equation to get 6000 ft $= (150 \text{ s})(r_r) + (150 \text{ s})(r_r - 8)$. The (150 s) is common to both terms so you can factor it out and divide both sides by 150 s to get this: $\dfrac{6,000 \, ft}{150 s} = r_r + r_r - 8$ and $40 \, ft/s = 2r_r - 8 \, ft/s$. Manipulate the equation to isolate and find $r_r = \dfrac{48 \, ft/s}{2} = 24 \, ft/s$. If you selected choice (A), be careful—this is Dale's rate!

50. K Since Rusty drove the first 7 laps at an average time of 180 s, you can multiply these values together to find that he drove the first 7 laps in a total time of 1,260 s. Complete the same operation for the second set of numbers: since Rusty drove 8 laps at an average time of 190 s, multiply these values together to find that he drove all 8 laps in a total time of 1,520 s. Since you know the two total times, you can simply find the difference between them to find the time of the last lap: 1,520 s – 1,260 s = 260 s. If you selected choice (H), be careful—this is the average of 180 and 190, but it doesn't take into account that Rusty drove 7 laps at an average of 180 s and only one lap at an average of 190 s.

51. D Dale drove 6 laps, each of which was 6,000 ft, for a total of 36,000 ft in 90 minutes. The question asks for this value in feet per hour, so convert the 90 minutes to 1.5 hours. 36,000 ft ÷ 1.5 hrs = 24,000 ft/hr. If you selected choice (A), you may have forgotten to change the 90 minutes to 1.5 hours.

52. **G**   The equation of a circle is $(x - h)^2 + (y - k)^2 = r^2$, where (h, k) is the center of the circle and r is the radius. Thus, circle B has its center at $(-4, 2)$ with a radius of 3. If you draw a diagram, you'll find that point $(-2, 2)$ lies outside circle A and inside circle B.

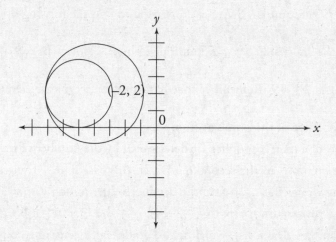

53. **B**   The perimeter is the distance of the shape's outline. There are two straight lines: from $(0,0)$ to $(0,4)$ and from $(0,0)$ to $(4,0)$, each with a length of 4. The straight lines total 8, eliminating choices (A), (D), and (E). The curved parts are two semicircles and two semicircles make one complete circle, so find the circumference of one circle with radius 2: $C = 2\pi r = 2\pi(2) = 4\pi$. Eliminate choice (C) and pick choice (B). If you picked choice (D), you may have found the area instead of the perimeter.

54. **F**   An even function is defined in the question as a function for which the value of $f(x) = f(-x)$. This means that $f(x)$ has the same value for both x and $-x$. If you fold the graph of an even function along the $f(x)$ axis, the two sides of the graph will be mirror reflections of each other. Choices (G), (J), and (K) are odd functions, in which $f(-x) = -f(x)$ for all values of x. Odd functions rotate $180°$ about the point $(0, 0)$. Choice (H) is not a function, because it does not pass the vertical line test; the same x value yields two values for $f(x)$.

55. **B**   Use the distance formula: $d = \sqrt{(x_2 - x_1)^2 + (y_2 - y_1)^2}$. $d = \sqrt{(4w - w)^2 + (w - 5 - (w + 5))^2} = \sqrt{9w^2 + 100}$.

56. **F**   In a right triangle with angle A, $\cos A = \dfrac{\text{length of adjacent side}}{\text{length of hypotenuse}}$. In this triangle, $\cos S = \dfrac{r}{t}$ and $\cos R = \dfrac{s}{t}$. So $\cos^2 S + \cos^2 R = \dfrac{r^2}{t^2} + \dfrac{s^2}{t^2}$, or $\dfrac{r^2 + s^2}{t^2}$. Since ΔRST is a right triangle, use the Pythagorean Theorem to determine that $r^2 + s^2 = t^2$. You're left with $\cos^2 S + \cos^2 R = \dfrac{t^2}{t^2} = 1$.

57.　C　Trapezoid *DECA* is isosceles because △*ABC* is isosceles and, since $\overline{DE}\,\|\,\overline{AC}$, line segments $\overline{AD}$ and $\overline{CE}$ have equal lengths. Since the trapezoid is isosceles, the diagonals are congruent. Thus, △*DFE* and △*AFC* are similar. Set up a proportion to find the missing side: $\dfrac{9}{6}=\dfrac{27}{FC}$. So, $\overline{FC}=18$. Choice (A) is the short side of △*DFE* multiplied by 2. Choice (B) is 9 + 6. Choice (D) is 27 + 6 and choice (E) is 27 + 9. Remember that hard problems typically require more work than just adding together some of the numbers from the problem!

58.　F　The dimensions of a matrix product are determined by the number of rows in the first matrix and the number of columns in the second matrix, in this case 2 × 1. Thus, choices (H), (J), and (K) have the wrong dimensions. To find the product value, multiply rows by columns and add the products of one row-column: (4 × 0) + (–2 × 2) = –4 and (3 × 0) + (–6 × 2) = –12.

59.　D　An ! symbol denotes a factorial, which is the product of decreasing consecutive integers starting from the integer in front of the ! sign. (For example, 5! = 5 × 4 × 3 × 2 × 1 = 120.) You can simplify this expression if you separate the two largest factors in the numerator; in other words, write $(n + 1)!$ as $(n + 1) \times (n) \times (n - 1)!$ Canceling $(n - 1)!$ from numerator and denominator leaves you with $(n + 1)(n)$. So $(n + 1)(n) = 20$, which means that $n + 1 = 5$ and $n = 4$. Finally, the question asks for $n! = 4! = 4 \times 3 \times 2 \times 1 = 24$. Choice (A) is 3! Choice (B) is half of 20. Choice (C) is half of 24. Choice (E) is 5!

60.　K　To simplify this abstract problem, substitute a value in for the circle's radius. If the radius is 3, the circumference is $2\pi r = 2(\pi)(3) = 6\pi$. $\dfrac{radius}{circumference} = \dfrac{3}{6\pi} = \dfrac{1}{2\pi}$. Choice (F) gives the ratio of the circumference to the radius. Choices (H) and (J) work with the diameter instead of the radius, and choice (G) finds the ratio of the diameter to the radius.

TEST 1 READING EXPLANATIONS

1. **C** Choice (C) points to the portion of the passage in which the narrator says that his grandmother had gained considerable stature in Robertson County and, more importantly, refers to information concerning the story's principle character. The main topic of the passage is Ruby and her diner, so you can safely assume there will be a connection between the main topic and the correct answer. Choice (A) focuses on information that occurs only in the beginning of the story and choices (B) and (D) are too general and not directly supported by information in the passage.

2. **J** The second paragraph begins by introducing the character of Ruby Sanders, the narrator's grandmother. This indicates that the paragraph will explain who she is and why she is important. Choices (F) and (G) point out topics in the beginning of the passage, but they do not serve to cover the character of Ruby. Finally, choice (H) is an overstatement, so we have to dismiss it as a viable choice in light of choice (J).

3. **B** Only choice (B) contains an answer that refers correctly to a part of the text—*If the diner were a sort of cell, then my grandmother was its nucleus; without the nucleus, the cell would surely perish.* The other answer choices contain words from the passage as well, but the things stated in those answer choices are either untrue or not supported by the passage.

4. **H** Choice (H) should be selected in this instance because the question asks you to make an inference, and inferences must always be supported by the facts within the area in question. The end of the paragraph directly states that the narrator was glad that he didn't know that he wouldn't return to the diner after his last summer there. Choices (F), (G), and (J) force us to make unfounded assumptions as to how the narrator would feel.

5. **B** Locate where the author talks about working at the diner (paragraph 8). The narrator mentions that the work was *hard but never dull*. Therefore, you should select choice (B). Although each of the others contains individual characteristics that may be true, both characteristics listed in the correct answer must be true.

6. **F** Note the sentence at the end of the second paragraph: *It didn't take long before my grandmother was a person of considerable stature in and around Robertson County, just like the restaurant that bore her name.* From this sentence, you can easily infer that both Ruby and her restaurant were popular in and around the community. If you chose one of the other answers, be careful—these refer to either Ruby or the restaurant, but never to both.

7. **A** The lines in question provide the introduction to this paragraph, which details the ways in which Ruby's was significant to the community in ways other than as a restaurant—choice (A). Choice (B) is not supported in the text, and choice (D) gives a too literal interpretation of the lines referred to in the passage and misreads the word *expect*. Choice (C) is deceptive—the passage does suggest that Ruby herself had risen to prominence, but it does not mention anyone else in this regard.

8. **G** The author speaks of choices (F), (H), and (J) in the sixth paragraph. He mentions football leagues in the last paragraph, but as something he had to forego to continue to work at the restaurant. Accordingly, the passage mentions all of the things as being available at the diner EXCEPT the football leagues, choice (G).

9.　C　In the seventh paragraph, the author vividly describes the physical details of the restaurant. In this paragraph, he gives a detailed description of the grounds, down to the furniture and the locations of some minor items. Choices (A), (B), and (D) use words from the passage, but the information in these choices is not supported.

10.　J　In the last paragraph, the narrator says, *After all, the woman who built Ruby's was strong enough to make me forget those things, if only for the summer.* It can therefore be inferred that the narrator is impressed by his grandmother's strength. None of the other answer choices are supported by evidence in the passage.

11.　B　The passage is about studies on several different factors that contribute to happiness. According to the second paragraph, Tellegen and Lykken state that genes play a part in happiness, but no specific genes have been found that cause hedonic adaptation, eliminating choice (A). Although an account of Lyubomirsky and Sheldon's studies indicates that there may be ways to improve happiness levels (lines 70–80), there is no discussion of the cure for depression mentioned in choice (C). No scientist in the passage disagrees that genes have an influence on happiness levels, eliminating choice (D).

12.　H　All the studies in the passage involve subjects telling researchers how happy they are, which is the same as *subjective well-being* as defined in lines 8–11. Only Lyubomirsky and Sheldon's study made specific note of studying their subjects' levels of happiness *over time* (lines 64–67), eliminating choice (F), or involved subjects engaging in acts of *kindness* (line 75), eliminating choice (G). Only Tellegen and Lykken's study mentioned using *identical twins* (lines 13–14), eliminating choice (J).

13.　D　Tellegen and Lykken's study of twins that had been *separated and raised in different families* (line 15) does not indicate whether separated twins were less happy. The question presented by choice (A) can be answered by the statistic on line 52, which says *10 percent is influenced by circumstances.* Descriptions of Lyubomirsky and Sheldon's studies suggest that people who *varied their acts of kindness* (line 75) and who wrote *a list of things to be grateful for* (line 78) can improve their subjective well-being, which answers the question posed in choice (B). In lines 43–44, Sheldon explains that scientific literature suggests that behaviors such as choosing the right goals *provide only a temporary increase in subjective well-being,* answering the question in choice (C).

14.　F　Lyubomirsky hopes to show how *conscious strategies counteract genetic forces* (lines 63–64)—in other words help people to overcome their genetic predispositions. You can eliminate choice (J) because the passage never indicates that hedonic adaptation can be eliminated entirely. Sheldon and Lyubomirsky also agree that *50 percent of subjective well-being is predetermined by the genetic set point* (lines 50–51), which confirms, rather than contradicts, Tellegen and Lykken's study, eliminating choice (G). Determining which intentional act is more effective is not the primary purpose of their research, eliminating choice (H).

15.　D　The statistics cited in the last sentence of the passage best support choice (D). Though the passage indicates that some psychologists' emphasis caused them to *suspect that overall levels of subjective well-being are low* (line 85), this does not summarize the University of Chicago studies, so eliminate choice (A). Though Americans are mostly happy people, this does not mean that depression is *uncommon,* as choice (B) states. You can also eliminate choice (C), because it suggests that happiness levels are actually harmed by attempts to improve them.

16. **H** Lines 73–74 states that intentional activity can improve happiness, and line 75 cites *acts of kindness* as a specific example of intentional activity. Choice (F) alludes to the woman mentioned in the first paragraph, who did return to her natural level of happiness. Choice (G) is a trap, referring to factors that improve *heart disease* (line 62), not necessarily mental health. Choice (J) can be eliminated because the lottery winners are described as being no happier than average after a year passed.

17. **A** Hedonic adaptation is useful because it benefits people who experience adverse conditions in their lives (line 25). Although these adverse conditions may include *permanent disability or sudden loss of income* (lines 26–27), hedonic adaptation does not cause people to *forget* about these problems, as indicated in choice (B). It is not useful to adjust to the higher level of happiness caused by *winning the lottery,* eliminating choice (C). Hedonic adaptation helps people to adjust their levels of happiness back to their own genetic set point, not to identify better with family members, eliminating choice (D).

18. **G** If you deleted the first paragraph, you wouldn't get a detailed story about a particular person whose life shows that happiness and life events, in this case the Holocaust, are not necessarily correlated, as in choice (G). The passage mentions in the third paragraph that circumstances are not a large contributor to happiness, so eliminate choice (F). The first paragraph includes an example that is relevant to establishing the main idea of the passage, eliminating choice (H). Lines 26–27 mention *permanent disability or sudden loss of income* as specific examples of adverse conditions people may experience, so you can eliminate choice (J).

19. **C** The topic sentence of the last paragraph suggests that its purpose is to focus on people's generally positive assessment of their own happiness. The researchers mentioned in the paragraph had an incorrect suspicion, which is different from making *many errors*, so you can eliminate choice (A). Choice (B) can be eliminated because Ross's anecdote in the first paragraph is not meant to suggest that Americans are unhappy. Lyubomirsky and Sheldon's findings that certain behaviors may improve happiness are still valid even if people are already generally happy, eliminating choice (D).

20. **H** Lines 64–65 state that Lyubomirsky and Sheldon *are currently expanding their study*. Though it is possible that the researchers mentioned in choices (F), (G), and (J) may still collaborate, the passage never explicitly gives this information, making choice (H) the best answer.

21. **C** This question asks what the author has learned. Since the author ended the passage by explaining her new theory of the connectedness of fiction and biography, you want something that agrees with that, which choice (C) does nicely. Choices (A) and (D) both use deceptive language from the passage but do not reflect what the author has learned. Choice (B) is extreme.

22. **H** The passage states that studying literature in college involved *scouring personal letters for hints of relationship problems, familial tragedies, or even fond memories that seemed reminiscent of storylines.* Since the prior part of the sentence discussed the intensive research that the author did, *scouring* is being used to mean something like *researching*. Choice (F), *purifying*, is not supported. The author is studying, so choice (G), *obliterating*, is not supported. Choice (J), *cleansing*, is one meaning for *scouring*, but it is not supported in this context.

23. **A** The author states, *since I've been a Nathaniel Hawthorne fan since junior high, a side trip to the building that had inspired one of his greatest works seemed to be in order.* While the passage states that the author was visiting Salem's tourist attractions, choice (A) is better supported by the text than choice (B). The author had not originally sought to learn the personal details of Hawthorne's life, making choice (C) incorrect. Choice (D) is deceptive, since there is no proof that Hawthorne lived during the Salem Witch Trials.

24. **F** While the college professors are mentioned in line 21, we do not learn until the last paragraph that the author has finally understood that *when we weave the threads of the author's life around that base, we are able to see the interactions between text and author, as they join to create a pattern more complete than either would be on its own.* The passage does not state that one is more necessary than the other, as choices (G) and (J) do. Choice (H) is too strong, since the professors are referring to understanding, not enjoyment.

25. **B** The passage tells us that the author *opted to major in literature, assuming that this would involve reading scores of wonderful books.* Although the author disagrees with her professors, there is no evidence that she chose her field of study in order to disprove their theories, as stated in choice (C), and choices (A) and (D) incorrectly state that she agrees with the professors' approach.

26. **H** The author's ultimate conclusion regarding the purpose of literary studies is most clearly outlined in the final paragraph, as quoted in choice (J), but that does not answer this question. Choice (F) refers to her earlier aim when reading, and choice (G) refers to what she gleaned in inspired moments. Choice (H) correctly refers to what the author experienced *more often* and thus was the most likely result of completing her professors' assignments.

27. **B** The House of the Seven Gables is discussed mainly in the fourth and fifth paragraphs. The passage does not state precisely who lived there, just that Nathaniel Hawthorne did not, eliminating choice (A). Although it may have been an important historical site, the passage does not tell us if anything actually took place there, as choice (C) states. The garden is described as *desolate* due to the season but there is no evidence that the house is in poor repair, as in choice (D). Since the author must buy tickets and take part in a tour in order to visit the house, it is reasonable to infer that it is now a tourist attraction, as in choice (B).

28. **J** The passage closes with the statement that *The work itself is indeed the frame, but when we weave the threads of the author's life around that base…* In this context, the *frame* is referring to the novel, which the author believes is the *base* of our understanding. Choice (F) incorrectly states that the novel is the *isolated goal.* Choice (G) likewise treats the novel as the *purpose* as opposed to the *base.* Choice (H) refers to the novel as extra, or *auxiliary,* information. Choice (J) correctly identifies the novel as the *focal,* or central, point.

29. **C** Choice (C) most closely matches the author's final opinion of studying authors' lives as discussed in the final paragraph, where she states that *we are able to see their interactions,* as they join to become something *more complete than either would be on its own.* Choice (A) does not address the author's ultimate conclusion that this study can be worthwhile. Neither *timidity,* choice (B), nor *frustration,* choice (D), is supported by the passage.

30.   **F**   The third paragraph tells us what happened after the author finished school, connecting the second paragraph, which details her childhood and schooling, to the fourth paragraph, which brings us back to the visit to Salem. The reasons for her trip, choice (G), are mentioned in the first paragraph. The study of literature, choice (H), was discussed in the second paragraph as well as the third, and the evidence for the author's final conclusion, choice (J), is found in the last paragraph.

31.   **A**   Although the passage mentions that the frogs' calls concern mating behavior, it doesn't specify how often they mate, so choice (A) is the best answer. Choice (B) is addressed in line 17, choice (C) is answered in lines 29–43, and choice (D) is answered in lines 54–57.

32.   **F**   Lines 15–16 state that the coqui faces almost no ecological competition because there are no other native amphibians; thus, choice (F) is the best answer. Choice (G) is contradicted in lines 58–62.

33.   **C**   Paragraph 4 (lines 29–43) states that the *volume of the frog's call is compounded by two other factors*, one of which is the *wall of sound* produced by overlapping calls, making choice (C) the best answer. Choice (A) is contradicted by lines 4–5. Choices (B) and (D) refer to facts that aren't supported by the passage.

34.   **H**   This paragraph states that the coqui thrives because it doesn't need as much water as it would if it were born a tadpole. The end of the paragraph also implies that the coqui faces little predatorial threat before it has matured. The paragraph does describe the environmental conditions in Hawaii, but description of the habitat isn't the primary purpose of the paragraph, eliminating choices (F) and (G). Choice (J) is not the primary purpose of the paragraph, nor does it accurately describe the coqui.

35.   **B**   The first paragraph is a descriptive, evocative passage that attempts to capture the sound of the frog calls in the night. By contrast, the sixth paragraph explains specifically how scientists believe these frogs could endanger the local environment, so choice (B) is the best description of the change in the language's tone. Nothing in the passage suggests the *author's* opinion, so choice (A) doesn't fit. The sixth paragraph talks about the frogs as a potential threat, so you wouldn't select choice (C) or (D) as the best option.

36.   **G**   Earlier in the sentence, the coqui populations are described as *threatening the survival of arthropods*, which indicates that the arthropod population is struggling, eliminating choices (H) and (J). The word *pursuit* doesn't fit as well as *extinction*, making choice (G) the best answer.

37.   **D**   The last sentence of the fifth paragraph (lines 54–57) begins with the phrase *Ornithologists fear*, which means that the potential outcome hasn't happened yet. Choice (A) is stated as factual information in lines 33–34, choice (B) in lines 71–73, and choice (C) in lines 81–82.

38.   **F**   The passage states that *nematodes and other types of vertebrate parasites could be transported with coquis and infect indigenous fauna*, making choice (F) the best answer. Choices (G) and (H) refer to the frogs' food sources, not parasites; *arachnids* in choice (J) aren't mentioned specifically in the passage, although they are a member of the arthropod class.

39. **B** The fifth paragraph states that *another quieter genus of the frog—the greenhouse frog—represents an equal threat to the biodiversity of the island*, which is best summarized by choice (B). Choice (C) incorrectly states that the greenhouse frog is less, rather than equally, dangerous. It is true that the greenhouse frog is relatively quiet, but that characteristic isn't necessarily what makes the frog hard to eliminate, eliminating choice (D). Although the name *greenhouse frog* points to an indoor habitat, the passage doesn't support that assumption, so you can rule out choice (A).

40. **J** The last paragraph mentions *1,000 acres* in the first sentence and continues in the next sentence to describe the land as the habitat in which the coqui has adopted as its home in Hawaii, making choice (J) the best answer. There is no evidence in the passage to support choices (F), (G), and (H).

TEST 1 SCIENCE EXPLANATIONS

1. **A** The data in Table 3 indicate that for every increase of 25°C, there is a corresponding increase in θ of approximately 3.5 degrees. A temperature of 62.5°C falls halfway between 50°C and 75°C, so the corresponding angle should fall halfway between 25.4 and 29.0 degrees. Only choice (A) has a value anywhere within this range.

2. **F** According to Table 1, the object made of brick required the largest ramp angle θ before any movement took place. Therefore, it is the most resistant to movement. Raising the angle of the ramp accomplishes the same thing as applying increasing force to the object to eventually overcome friction.

3. **D** In Experiments 1 and 4, the angle θ where the wooden object starts to move stays the same, no matter how many objects are stacked on top of each other. Since any change to this angle will signal a change to the coefficient of static friction, you can confidently say that if the angle doesn't change, the coefficient of friction will not change.

4. **G** The interaction of interest is between the various objects and the polymer coating of the ramp. The polymer coating is what comes into contact with the objects, while the underlying plastic board is not participating, eliminating choice (F). Objects of different material are not brought into contact during the experiment, eliminating choice (H). Objects are not stacked until Experiment 4, eliminating choice (J).

5. **D** The object with the largest angle θ is the object that is most resistant to movement. According to Table 1, this is brick. Only choice (D) ranks brick as the most resistant to movement, eliminating all other answer choices.

6. **G** The data in Table 3 indicate that when temperature increases, the corresponding θ increases. The passage states that the *tangent of this angle represents the coefficient of static friction between the object and the polymer surface.* The experiment is not exploring the interaction between wood and wood, eliminating choice (F). The mass of the object is constant, eliminating choice (H). Only wooden objects are used in Experiment 3, eliminating choice (J).

7. **B** The transition from April to May shows a small increase in the number of reported polio infections, and the transition from November to December shows a decrease, so neither choices (C) nor (D) would be the correct answer. There are large increases in the number of reported cases from January to February and from February to March, but upon close inspection, the transition from February to March is larger. Therefore, choice (B) is the best answer.

8. **J** In June 2004, 80 cases of polio infection were reported, so $80 \times 200 = 16,000$ people would have been at risk for contraction of the infection.

9. **A** In all the Indian cities, there are more reported cases of polio virus infections in August than in June. Choices (B) and (D) are consistent with *decreases*, not increases, in the reported polio cases. The study described by Figure 2 only covers the dry summer and rainy monsoon season, not the autumn or winter, so the explanation given in choice (C) is unsupported. Choice (A) is the best answer because the month of August is expected to have more rainfall, and therefore is more likely to feature water contamination.

10. **H** Figure 2 presents findings that are applicable only to India, not Nigeria, so (F) is incorrect. The findings only present information on reported infections during June and August 2007, not on unreported infections (choice (G) is wrong) nor on winter months (choice (J) is wrong). The findings do, however, show a stark contrast between the small number of reported cases in the cities in western and southern India (Mumbai, Chennai, and Hyderabad) and the large number of cases in the northern cities (New Delhi and Kolkata), making (H) the best answer.

11. **D** The passage states that the polio virus is most often transmitted through water contaminated with human waste and makes no mention of the role (or the lack thereof) that other life forms play in the transmission of the virus. The answer that summarizes this is choice (D).

12. **H** In June 2007, there were between 10 and 15 reported polio infections in Kolkata, while in August 2007, there were between 20 and 25 reported polio infections. This is an approximate doubling of the number of reported infections, so choice (H) is the best answer.

13. **D** The solution with the *least osmotic pressure* will have the smallest value from Figure 1. The pressure for choice (A) is 85 atm; choice (B) is 70 atm; choice (C) is 90 atm; choice (D) is 50 atm. Therefore, a 2.0 M sucrose solution has the least osmotic pressure.

14. **J** The introduction states that *higher van't Hoff factors correlate with greater dissociation or ionization.* According to Table 1, $FeCl_3$ exhibits the greatest van't Hoff factor, which means the highest degree of ionization.

15. **C** Examine the equation given in the introduction: $\Pi = iMRT$. Since the values of R and T remain constant among all the answer choices as seen in the question, osmotic pressure is determined by the product of M and i. The product of concentration of solute particles and van't Hoff factor for a 1.5 M NaCl solution is $1.5 \times 1.9 = 2.85$. The product for the solution in choice (A) is $1.0 \times 1.9 = 1.9$; choice (B) is $2.0 \times 1.9 = 3.8$; choice (C) is $2.9 \times 1.0 = 2.9$; choice (D) is $3.5 \times 1.0 = 3.5$. Choice (C) has the closest product to 2.85.

16. **G** The pressure required to maintain solvent equilibrium across a membrane is the solution's osmotic pressure, as discussed in the introduction. Figure 1 shows a linear relationship between solute concentration and osmotic, eliminating choices (H) and (J). As concentration of solute decreases, the osmotic pressure will also decrease, eliminating choice (F).

17. **D** Comparing different solutes in Figure 1 at a given concentration greater than $M = 0$, you will determine that $FeCl_3$ always has greater osmotic pressure than sucrose, eliminating choices (B) and (C). The trend in Figure 1 predicts that a substance with $i = 3.8$ would have a greater osmotic pressure than $FeCl_3$, which does *not* support the scientist's findings.

18. **H** Examine the relationship between the line for Sample 1 and the line for Sample 4. Between the 30–60-cm depth range and the 60–90-cm depth range, the line for Sample 1 crosses over to become higher than the line for Sample 4. Choices (F) and (G) suggest that the lines would never cross over, while choice (J) incorrectly states that Sample 4's shallower sodium concentrations were lower than Sample 1's.

19. **B** On the line for Sample 3 in Figure 2, the second data point most closely matches 17%. Choice (A) would describe the earliest data point for Sample 3, from a soil depth of 0–30 cm; choices (C) and (D) describe Samples 4 and 5 at this depth, respectively.

20. **J** Use Sample 4, because the question asks you for soil 40 m away from the river. Remember the definitions given for EC and ESP: EC is the total electrical conductivity of the soil, while ESP is the percentage of that amount which is due to sodium ions. To find the total EC due to sodium ions, you would need to multiply the total EC by the percentage due to sodium. Since the total EC for Sample 4 is significantly less at the 90–120-cm depth than at the 60–90-cm depth, while the ESP is roughly the same, (H) is incorrect; similarly, the low total EC at the 0–30-cm depth rules out the possibility of it having the greatest total EC due to sodium ions. Since the EC at the 0–30-cm depth and 30–60-cm depth are nearly the same, the much lower ESP at the 0–30-cm depth makes (J) the correct answer.

21. **C** This question is essentially asking you to convert one set of data points on a line graph into a bar graph. Choice (C) does this correctly, while choice (A) inverts the values, making small values large and large values small. Choice (B) measures the wrong data point—it would be accurate for a sample depth of 60–90-cm, not 90–120-cm. Choice (D) is very close, but mixes up the values for Sample 4 and Sample 1.

22. **G** Compare all five samples in Figure 1 using a common depth such as 30–60-cm. In Sample 1, the EC is approximately 1 mS/cm; 20 mS/cm in Sample 2; 1 mS/cm in Sample 3; 0.5 mS/cm in Sample 4; 8 mS/cm in Sample 5. Thus, there is no consistent trend in the electrical conductivity, which means salinity does not increase with consistency with distance from the river, eliminating choices (H) and (J). The explanation in choice (F) is also not supported by passage.

23. **B** Examine the conditions associated with each group in Table 1. Group 6 is the only group which does not include data from an area affected by habitat loss or declines in prey population. It therefore allows the researchers to compare areas affected by these factors to one unaffected by them. Choices (A), (C), and (D) suggest that Group 6 provides information to the researchers that is not included in the passage.

24. **F** Examine the conditions associated with Group 2. These areas have additional seaweed which is consumed by marine mammals, the likely prey of the primarily carniverous polar bear. Choice (G) implies that polar bears may prefer to eat seaweed, but there is nothing in the passage to support this statement. Choice (H) is eliminated because the study does not directly measure the population density of prey animals. Choice (J) would require additional information which links the population of prey animals to Arctic sea ice.

25. **C** A greater average population density ratio for a certain group indicates that more polar bears are living in areas that are a part of that group. Choice (C) correctly lists the groups by average population density ratio as given in Figure 1.

26. **G** Group 1 exhibits declines in the number of marine mammals consumed by polar bears. Choices (F) and (H) are not mammals so they are eliminated. Choice (J) is eliminated because the population of polar bears is the outcome being studied as a result of some other environmental change, and there is nothing in the passage to suggest that polar bears consume other polar bears. Only choice (G) is a marine mammal that is likely consumed by a polar bear.

27. **D** You can use the process of elimination with the definitions in Table 1 to find the correct answer for this problem. Choice (A) includes Groups 1 and 2; these are likely to cause effects in opposite directions, not the same direction. Choices (B) and (C) each include Group 4; as Group 4 is simply a combination of Groups 1 and 3, the researchers are never directly comparing the effects of Group 4 conditions to any other conditions. Choice (D) lists Groups 1 and 3, both groups where there have been conditions likely to make it difficult for polar bears to survive. This is confirmed by data in Figure 1.

28. **H** Choices (F) and (J) are both true. As seen in Figure 1, average polar bear population ratios for both Groups 1 and 3 are not equal to 1. If they were equal to 1, this would indicate that there is no difference between those areas with the conditions listed and those without. Choice (H) reverses the relationship between Groups 1 and 3 in Figure 1, which means it is not supported. Choice (G) states the relationship from (H) correctly, which means (G) is supported and therefore not the correct answer.

29. **D** Scientist 2 says "*the •OH generated by Reactions 1 and 4 will react rapidly with any H_2CO,*" indicating that she does agree those reactions occur; the dispute is what formaldehyde decomposes to after Reaction 3. So according to both scientists, O_3 leads to the formation of •OH (Reaction 1), and OH leads to the formation of •CH_3 (Reaction 2).

30. **F** As methane (CH_4) levels increase, CH_3 levels will increase (Reaction 2). As •CH_3 levels increase, H_2CO levels will increase (Reaction 3). Therefore the correct graph should show low levels of H_2CO when methane levels are low, and high levels of H_2CO when methane levels are high. Choice (F) is the only graph that reflects this direct relationship.

31. **C** Remember: reactants on the left; products on the right. From that you can eliminate answer choices (B) and (D). For choice (A), it is true that H_2CO is composed of atoms (it *is* a molecule); however, composition is not mentioned in the question. Since there are no other reactants, the mass of H_2CO (the reactant) must be exactly the mass of the products (H_2 and CO). Therefore, the molecular mass of each of the products must be less than that of H_2CO.

32. **H** According to Scientist 1, the first step in the production of formaldehyde requires ozone (O_3). Follow the reactions: if O_3 levels decrease, •OH levels would decrease (Reaction 1), leading to a decrease in •CH_3 levels (Reaction 2), which in turn would lead to a decrease in H_2CO levels (Reaction 3). Thus, both •CH_3 and H_2CO levels would decrease.

33. **D** Scientist 2 says Reactions 1–4 do occur, which support choices (A) and (C). Choice (B) is Scientist 2's central argument: that the •OH produced by Reactions 1 and 4 can react with H_2CO to form CO (Reaction 6). While Scientist 2 does say that some H_2CO may form from CH_4 and O_3, she says that "H_2CO quickly decomposes" and that the chain reaction of Reactions 2–4 is inhibited. Thus, she would *not* expect an increase in CH_4 levels to cause levels of H_2CO to rise dramatically.

34. **G** If Reaction 4 were inhibited, the amount of H_2CO generated would be reduced, and therefore, according to Scientist 2, the amount of CO generated would be reduced, not increased, so choice (F) is incorrect. •OH can react with H_2CO to form CO, but there is no evidence of HO_2 reacting with H_2CO, as in choice (H). O_2 is not involved in the generation of CO, so choice (J) cannot be correct. Answer choice (G) is Scientist 2's hypothesis: the H_2CO generated in Reaction 3 will react in Reactions 5 and 6 to produce CO.

35. **B** Reaction 6 shows •OH reacting with H_2CO in the atmosphere, which weakens Scientist 1's hypothesis in 2 ways: it reduces the level of H_2CO, which Scientist 1 says is *increasing* in the atmosphere, and consumes •OH, inhibiting the chain reaction (Reactions 2–4), which is central to Scientist 1's hypothesis. Thus, choice (B) is the best explanation. The •OH produced in Reaction 4 reacts with CH_4 (in Reaction 2) agrees with Scientist 1's argument, so choice (A) is incorrect. The H_2O produced in Reaction 6 may react with light and O_3, as in Reaction 1, but again, does not weaken Scientist 1's argument, so choice (C) is incorrect. For choice (D), •OH is not produced in Reaction 6, it is a reactant.

36. **G** To solve this problem, you must be sure to read the question carefully: you are looking at the section of the graph where V is *decreasing* from its largest value. First, find the largest value of V; this is the point on the curve that is furthest to the right, since V increases left to right. Once you are looking in the right place, you just draw a line up from 1.5 mL. on the V-axis to where it meets the curve, then draw a line over to the P-axis to get your answer: 30 Pa., choice (G).

37. **C** From the passage and Figures 1 and 2, you know that both ends of the second half of the curve must meet the ends of the first half to complete the cycle, so P must be higher on the left side than on the right side. Choices (A) and (B) cannot be correct because P is higher on the right side than on the left side. Choice (D) is simply the wrong shape to complete the cycle, so it cannot be correct. Choice (C) has P higher on the left side than on the right side, so it must be correct.

38. **H** Looking at Figure 1, all you need to do is find the lowest point on the curve, then draw a line down to the V-axis. Choice (H), 3.5 mL. is the closest answer.

39. **B** To solve this question, you must first locate the approximate lowest and highest values of V on Figure 2. The lowest value is about 0.75 mL. and the highest value is about 2.25 mL., so the lowest value is about 1/3 times the highest value, choice (B). Another way to solve this problem is to check the answer choices against the graph. Choice (A) cannot be correct because there are no negative numbers on the graph. Choice (C) doesn't really make sense because if the lowest value were 1 times the highest value, it would have to be the same number as the highest value, and then there wouldn't be a highest or lowest. Choice (D) doesn't make sense either because if the lowest value were 2 times the highest value, the lowest value would have to be higher than the highest value. Choice (B) is the only choice which could work because it is the only choice which is not negative and would make the lowest value actually lower than the highest value.

40. **F** This question is actually just an easy question with tricky wording. All it asks is this: What is the value of V when P is at its highest value? Find the highest value of P, and then find the value of V: 1.0 mL, choice (F).

WRITING TEST

Essay Checklist

1. The Introduction
   Did you
   ○ start with a topic sentence that paraphrases or restates the prompt?
   ○ clearly state your position on the issue?

2. Body Paragraph 1
   Did you
   ○ start with a transition/topic sentence that discusses the opposing side of the argument?
   ○ give an example of a reason that one might agree with the opposing side of the argument?
   ○ clearly state that the opposing side of the argument is wrong or flawed?
   ○ show what is wrong with the opposing side's example or position?

3. Body Paragraphs 2 and 3
   Did you
   ○ start with a transition/topic sentence that discusses your position on the prompt?
   ○ give one example or reason to support your position?
   ○ show the grader how your example supports your position?
   ○ end the paragraph by restating your thesis?

4. Conclusion
   Did you
   ○ restate your position on the issue?
   ○ end with a flourish?

5. Overall
   Did you
   ○ write neatly?
   ○ avoid multiple spelling and grammar mistakes?
   ○ try to vary your sentence structure?
   ○ use a few impressive-sounding words?

English Practice
Answers and
Explanations

ENGLISH PRACTICE 1 ANSWERS

1.	C	48.	G
2.	F	49.	A
3.	A	50.	G
4.	J	51.	A
5.	B	52.	F
6.	J	53.	D
7.	C	54.	G
8.	H	55.	A
9.	D	56.	H
10.	G	57.	D
11.	B	58.	H
12.	G	59.	C
13.	D	60.	J
14.	J	61.	D
15.	A	62.	F
16.	F	63.	D
17.	C	64.	G
18.	H	65.	C
19.	B	66.	F
20.	F	67.	A
21.	A	68.	J
22.	G	69.	D
23.	C	70.	F
24.	H	71.	A
25.	D	72.	F
26.	J	73.	A
27.	B	74.	H
28.	F	75.	C
29.	B		
30.	G		
31.	A		
32.	H		
33.	B		
34.	J		
35.	A		
36.	G		
37.	B		
38.	H		
39.	A		
40.	F		
41.	D		
42.	G		
43.	C		
44.	H		
45.	B		
46.	H		
47.	A		

ENGLISH PRACTICE 1 EXPLANATIONS

Passage I

1. **C** In EXCEPT/LEAST/NOT questions, the underlined portion of the sentence is correct. The original word was *proclaim*. Which answer choice would NOT have roughly the same meaning as proclaim? Choice (A), *announce*, and choice (B), *declare*, have the same meaning. Choice (D), *advertise*, is a little different, but still quite close. Choice (C), *compare*, suggests making a statement about similarities between two things rather than simply expressing something.

2. **F** The sentence in question signals the main idea of the paragraph, so it should be kept, choice (F). It does not, however, establish the narrator's love for hats, which eliminates choice (G). It does not contradict information in the preceding sentence, which eliminates choice (H). Finally, a primary theme of the essay is to explain the author's personal interpretation of hats, which eliminates choice (J).

3. **A** The sentence follows after, and expands on, the point made more narrowly by the preceding sentence, so it should not be separated into a new paragraph. This eliminates choices (C) and (D). The sentence contrasts the narrow and specific meaning of top hats and mortarboards with the more general symbolism of cowboy hats and berets, but does not propose a general rule or system, which eliminates choice (B).

4. **J** The beret suggests something directly about the wearer, so there should be no comma between *suggests* and *you*. This eliminates choices (F) and (H). *And* joins the two adjectives on its own, so there should be no comma in the list. This eliminates choice (G).

5. **B** The correct idiom is "show up," choice (B). Things do not *show way up* which eliminates choice (A). The phrase *show features in* is idiomatically incorrect and changes the meaning of the sentence, which eliminates choice (C). Finally, omitting way up leaves only *show in*, which is also incorrect usage, eliminating choice (D).

6. **J** The author's attitude towards hats is highly positive, stressing their versatility and many symbolic uses and applications. Choice (J) captures this best. Choice (F) would stress hats' negative effects on hair style, something not introduced to date and counter to the author's positive attitude towards hats. Choice (G) stresses the high price of hats, something not previously discussed and that would be a negative aspect of hats, not a positive one. Choice (H) discusses losing hats in restaurants, a new topic and one that would not be positive.

7. **C** As written, the sentence makes it sound as though the author *was deserving congratulations* rather than the people to whom he takes off his hat. The underlined portion needs to be changed to include clear identification of the individuals who should be congratulated. Only choice (C) does this.

8. **H** The underlined portion as written, choice (F), creates a run-on sentence: There are two separate thoughts expressed, each with its own subject and verb. This needs to be corrected by separating the text into two distinct sentences. Only choice (H) does this.

9. **D** The proposed addition is a sudden and unsignaled shift from the approach of the essay up until this point, away from metaphoric and symbolic meanings of hats; instead, the author would abruptly insert a detailed historical and scientific basis for hat-related figures of speech. Only choice (D) accurately conveys this. Choice (A) claims that it shows the author's affection for hats, but the statement reflects the author's knowledge of hat history, not his personal fondness for them. Choice (B) claims that the addition usefully demonstrates Lewis Carroll's interest in hats, but there is no evidence he had any such interest, and the essay is not about Lewis Carroll. Choice (C) claims that the problem is that many people in the nineteenth-century other than hat-makers were exposed to toxic fumes, but that is not relevant to the question of whether the proposed added text is consistent with the central ideas of the essay.

10. **G** The text as written uses a comma to separate the *possibility of using a hat* from what the hat would actually be used to do—*to make myself more like someone very different*. Because this is vital information that directly concludes a thought, it should not be split off. The comma after *hat* should therefore be removed. Only choices (G) and (H) do so. However, choice (H) inserts another comma after *possibility*, separating that word from its own direct conclusion, *of using a hat*. This introduces a new error, eliminating choice (H).

11. **B** In the original sentence, who is doing the thinking? The author. The topic of the author's thoughts is also the author. For this reason, since he both originates and receives the action, the author would need to use the reflexive pronoun *myself*, rather than *me*. This is choice (B).

12. **G** In the text, the daring adventurer is the one who is launching a search for treasure. Thus, that would make him a daring adventurer *whose* search for fabulous treasure is sure to succeed. This corresponds with choice (G). Choices (H) and (J) would turn the sentence into a garbled statement that would require ending the sentence with *that will succeed against all odds*, rather than simply *will succeed against all odds*.

13. **D** As written, the *that* after *my family* indicates that the author has more than one family, and the sentence would also require another verb. This eliminates choice (A). Omitting *that* reduces the sentence to its clearest form, making choice (D) the preferred option. Choices (B) and (C) can be eliminated on the basis that *family* is a collective noun and should take a singular verb, not the plural verbs *are* and *were*.

14. **J** The proposed conclusion does indeed praise hats, consistent with the author's attitude, but it does so on the basis that hats make the wearer personally happy. This was not a central theme of the essay, which stressed the symbolism and communication uses of hats. Because the concluding sentence should restate or comment on the central themes of the essay, and because this does not, it should not be used as a concluding sentence. Choice (J) accurately depicts this recommendation and reasoning. Choice (F) incorrectly claims the proposed conclusion restates the central idea. Choice (G)'s claim that hats have many uses is irrelevant to the question of whether to use the sentence as a conclusion. Choice (H)'s claim that the prior sentence expressed the same ideas is incorrect.

15. **A** The author talks about the ways in which he uses hats to express his feelings and convey to others what kind of person he sometimes wishes to be. Counting hats as items of clothing, this would seem to be enough to judge that the essay succeeded in demonstrating that clothing can be used to communicate things about the wearer. This corresponds to choice (A). Choice (B) claims incorrectly that the essay establishes that hats (crowns) have been symbols of royalty. Choice (C) states mistakenly that the essay failed to establish this key idea, giving as its reason the unsupported assertion that the author prefers modern-day to historical hats. Choice (D) incorrectly claims the essay does not support the proposed idea and cites the irrelevant fact that the author's family and friends think his interest in hats is odd.

Passage II

16. **F** This is correct use of the past perfect tense (the had tense). It refers to an event in the past that precedes another event in the past. Some songs *had been* undocumented until the cassette recorder became available. Choice (G) changes the verb tense to present perfect (the has/have tense), which is used to talk about a currently ongoing phenomenon or an unspecified time period. Choices (H) and (J) incorrectly change this sentence to present tense.

17. **C** Since the question specifically asks that you choose the most stylistically effective and *concise* wording, you should start by checking the shortest answer choice. Choice (C) works well and therefore becomes a better choice than choices (B) and (D). Choice (A) is incorrect because it is more appropriate to say that Diamond the songwriter was influenced by other artists than to say that his *songs* were influenced.

18. **H** There are two complete ideas in this sentence: *another song is the opposite* and *the song sounds like the straightforward rock of Buddy Holly*. Choice (H) uses a semicolon to separate the two complete ideas. Choices (F) and (G) incorrectly and awkwardly connect the two ideas with the word *of*. Choice (J) uses nothing to connect the ideas, which results in a run-on sentence.

19. **B** Choice (B) is the only option that conveys any detail about lyrical subject matter, telling you that the lyrics to these songs involved subjects like dating and automobiles. Choice (A) is just speculation about what inspired the lyrics. Choices (C) and (D) refer to the way Diamond wrote or performed the lyrics, but they do not tell you anything about the subject matter of the lyrics.

20. **F** There is nothing incorrect about choice (F), so there can only be a better answer if it is more concise than choice (F). However, choices (G), (H), and (J) are all more lengthy, awkward, and redundant, making choice (F) the best pick.

21. **A** Based on the context of the previous sentence's mention of *an upbeat* verse, this sentence is using the possessive form of the singular noun verse. Choice (A) indicates the correct 's to use. Choice (B) would change the original intended meaning. Choice (C) is the possessive form of the plural noun *verses*. Choice (D) is just the plural noun *verses*.

22. **G** Since *conflicted* is being used to describe Diamond, make sure the pronoun you use agrees with this singular, masculine noun. This is choice (G). Choices (F) and (H) are not specific, and choice (J) changes the meaning of the sentence.

23. **C** Content should only be added if it seems to flow well with the purpose and tone of the paragraph. In this case, this sentence does not contribute anything new to a paragraph that has as its main theme a discussion of Diamond's unique songwriting voice. Only choice (C) correctly states that the sentence should not be included in the paragraph and gives the correct reason.

24. **H** The two clauses of the sentence provide a contrast: there is abundant music knowledge about New Orleans, Detroit, and Nashville but little known about Lexington. The use of *while* indicates a contrast, as do choices (F), (G), and (J). Choice (H) makes the first clause of the sentence sound as if it is the cause of the second clause, which is incorrect.

25. **D** The previous sentence is a transition to begin discussing what interests musicologists about Diamond's songs. This sentence explains that there were very few other recordings from Lexington artists. Choices (A), (B), and (C) offer details about the cassette recording process that are irrelevant to the point of the sentence. If a question offers you the choice of deleting or omitting something, it is asking you if there is any reason that something NEEDS to stay in order for the sentence to make sense. If not, omit!

26. **J** The intended meaning of the sentence is that there was little known about the music culture of Lexington, Kentucky in the 1960s. The rest of the paragraph provides context to clarify that idea. Choice (J) correctly identifies the *music culture in a city like Lexington* as the topic. Choice (F) incorrectly makes the songs belong to Lexington, choice (G) incorrectly makes the historians belong to Lexington, and choice (H) incorrectly makes the taste belong to Lexington.

27. **B** When you are describing the action of one thing influencing another, the correct verb is *to affect*. The convention is to say you are affected by something, not that you are affected *with* something, which makes choice (C) incorrect. Choices (A) and (D) incorrectly use the noun *effect*, which is used to discuss a specific influence or reaction. For example, cat hair *affects* me negatively; one of the *effects* I feel is an itchy nose.

28. **F** Choice (F) is the best answer because it is the most concise, correctly written option. The parallelism of the sentence is naming two places Diamond performed: *at a local blues bar* and *at a jazz dance hall*. Choices (G) and (H) add extra wording to say the same thing as choice (F). Choice (J) adds an *-ing* that breaks the parallelism of the sentence.

29. **B** The beginning of the passage establishes the setting of Bruce Diamond's recording as occurring during the 1960s. The correct verb tense for this sentence is the past tense, which choice (B) uses. Choices (A) and (C) are present tense forms, and choice (D) is the present perfect.

30. **G** The essay's focus was the interest that musicologists have taken in Diamond's recordings. Choice (G) effectively ties the conclusion back to the intro. Since the passage deals with present study of Diamond's work, it is not consistent to make a prediction about Diamond's future popularity as choice (F) does. Choices (H) and (J) offer useless speculation about whether Diamond ever bought another recorder or performed in another city, neither of which were topics of discussion in the passage.

Passage III

31. **A** The underlined portion as it stands gives an appropriate amount of information without becoming redundant or long-winded. Both choice (B) and choice (C) convey similar information but with more unnecessary words. Choice (D) leaves out the crucial point that the narrator is talking about riding the subway, as opposed to a horse or a motorcycle, for example.

32. **H** The underlined portion adds an unnecessary comma between *neighbor* and *named*; the comma interrupts the phrase *a neighbor named Sasha*. If *named Sasha* were to be omitted from the sentence, the meaning of the sentence would be unclear, so it is incorrect to set it off with commas. For similar reasons, you can eliminate choice (J), which also contains an unnecessary comma. In choice (G), the semicolon is an even more pronounced division of this phrase, so that answer is also incorrect.

33. **B** The sentence is incorrect in its original form because *intricacy* is a noun serving as an adjective (modifying *subway routes*). *Intricate* is the adjective form of the word, so choice (B) is the best one. Choice (C) uses the adverb form *intricately* in place of the adjective, so you can get rid of that answer, and choice (D) doesn't address the part-of-speech problem merely by omitting the comma.

34. **J** This sentence contains a redundant phrase in the underlined portion; *During his childhood* becomes unnecessary when *as a child* appears later in the sentence. The best answer choice will eliminate any reference to childhood early in the sentence, which gets rid of choices (F) and (H). Choice (G) uses an incorrect verb tense.

35. **A** When you have a singular noun, like *family* here, use an apostrophe followed by an *s*. In choice (B), the apostrophe appears in the wrong place, and choices (C) and (D) both change the word to its plural form, so you can eliminate them.

36. **G** The most important clue for this question is the phrase *overcome this fear* in Sentence 2. Note that in the passage as it stands, Sentence 1 doesn't contain a clear reference to the narrator's fear, so the phrase *this fear* doesn't make sense. If you move Sentence 5 to the spot following Sentence 1, you'll place the direct allusion to the narrator's fear BEFORE the reiteration of *this fear*, a move that lends more logical coherence to the paragraph as a whole. Placing Sentence 5 anywhere AFTER Sentence 2 makes the reference to *this fear* confusing, so you can eliminate choices (F), (J), and (H).

37. **B** Check for pronoun agreement; the noun that "them" refers to is either *the woman on the left* or *the woman on the right*. The either/or rule makes the noun singular, so because choices (A) and (D) are both plural, you can eliminate those. Choice (C) offers the singular *her*, but that pronoun doesn't unambiguously refer to one woman or the other, so you wouldn't choose that option. Choice (B) provides the phrase *the one on the left*, which avoids both number and ambiguity problems.

38. **H** The two thoughts the narrator conveys are different enough to require a more definite stop between them; consequently, *if* is not an appropriate connector, so get rid of choice (F). *Even though* could work in this position, but that word would need a form of punctuation that separates two independent clauses such as a period or semicolon, so eliminate choice (J). *Which* needs to refer back to some other noun, and this sentence doesn't have one that makes sense, so choice (G) is wrong. Choice (H) has the proper punctuation to shift from one thought to the other in the same sentence.

39. **A** To use a colon, you need to have a complete idea in front of it, which *After a little searching though* is not, so eliminate both choice (B) and choice (D). To decide whether a word or phrase needs to be set off with commas both before and after that word, try removing it entirely from the sentence. If the sentence still makes sense, you'll want to set that word or phrase off with commas. In this case, *though* is an adverb meant to emphasize the contrast this sentence makes with the previous sentence, but *though* is not a word essential to preserving the meaning of this sentence.

40. **F** Since you need to select an answer that expresses the narrator's discomfort, you should rule out choices (G) and (J), which don't relate to that perspective. Choice (H) is fairly neutral in describing what the narrator sees, so choice (F), which describes how the narrator feels *conspicuous*, is the best answer.

41. **D** As in question 31, this question hinges on how much information is truly necessary and how much is repetitious. Once the narrator says he is *confused*, other indications of this confusion become redundant. Thus, choices (B) and (C), which talk about *uncertainty* and *lack of understanding*, both contain unnecessary language and should be ruled out. As for choice (A), the phrase *in my mind* is also redundant, and *like a whirlwind* sets up a faulty comparison.

42. **G** This question involves verb tense. You can get rid of choice (F) and choice (J) because they use the incorrect *of* instead of the correct *have* in their verb forms. Choice (H) changes the meaning of the sentence, leaving choice (G) as the best answer.

43. **C** This sentence is actually two complete sentences: *When we were seated on the train, Sasha looked at me with a pleased expression* and *I suppose he was proud of how well he had served as a guide*. A comma between these two sentences creates a comma splice, so you'll need something stronger to separate them. That leaves out choices (A), (B), and (D). Only choice (C), with the period after *expression*, contains the proper punctuation.

44. **H** *Which* is a relative pronoun, so the noun to which it refers (here, the noun is *side*) should be the main subject of the second part of the sentence. Because the *side* doesn't have anything to do with the second part of the sentence, eliminate choices (F) and (G). *Where* would fit if the narrator somehow shrugged his side, but that doesn't make sense either, so leave out choice (J). Only choice (H) sets the two complete ideas in the appropriate relation to one another.

45. **B** The narrator is employing a metaphor to describe how it felt to complete her first subway experience, but in the form of the original sentence it sounds as though the experience is literally about coming out of the *fantastic caverns*. Choices (C) and (D) move parts of the sentence around, but both place them in an order that is choppy and perhaps even misleading. Because choice (B) begins with the phrase *I might just as well*, it clarifies that the entire description is clearly metaphorical, and this choice is also the best answer in grammatical terms.

Passage IV

46. **H** *Likely* means "something reasonable to be believed," as does *possibly*. Therefore, it would be redundant to include both in the same sentence. Only choice (H) offers a concise choice that is idiomatically correct.

47.   **A**   The sentence is discussing events that occurred in the past, so choices (B) and (D) can be eliminated since they use present tense and present perfect tense, respectively. Choice (C) is also incorrect because *have* is the plural form of the verb, but the subject *he* is singular.

48.   **G**   The first part of the sentence highlights information that is true in spite of the second part of the sentence. Therefore, choices (F) and (H) are both wrong, since they both feature conjunctions that connect the two clauses as if they agree. Choice (J) is incorrect, because if the underlined section were deleted, the remaining sentence would be a run-on.

49.   **A**   This underlined portion of the sentence is modifying *diameter*, so it is appropriate to use *small* as it is written. Choices (B) and (C) are incorrect because no direct comparison is being made in this sentence. Choice (D) changes the meaning of the sentence to imply the diameter is too small.

50.   **G**   The primary purpose of the reference sentence is to demonstrate in understandable terms the extremely small size of the black hole in comparison to items of similar mass. Only choice (G) articulates this purpose. The sentence explains nothing about why black holes are studied or how they are formed, nor is the information reiterated later in the passage. Therefore, choices (F), (H), and (J) are all incorrect.

51.   **A**   The underlined portion is correct, because it is the only answer that correctly introduces the topic of how black holes are formed, which will be the focus of the rest of the passage. All the other answer choices raise interesting questions; however, none of them are actually answered.

52.   **F**   *Their* is the possessive pronoun, which shows ownership. As there is no case of ownership in the underlined portion of the sentence, both choices (G) and (H) are incorrect. *They're* is the contraction *they are*, which does not fit the context of the sentence. Therefore, choice (J) is also incorrect.

53.   **D**   As written, the sentence is a fragment, so choice (A) is incorrect. Choice (C) is incorrect because it is written in the future tense. Choice (B) is also incorrect because the sentence needs simple present tense, not present progressive. Choice (D) is the only option written in the correct tense and parallel to the other verb in this sentence, *suggests*.

54.   **G**   In EXCEPT/LEAST/NOT questions, the underlined portion of the sentence is correct. Choices (F), (H), and (J) are all reasonable substitutes for the underlined portion in that they are grammatically correct and preserve the meaning of the original sentence. Choice (G) can't work because, while *close* and *near* are synonyms, the correct idiom in this situation requires the word *to*, as in *close to the end*. Consequently, choice (G) is NOT acceptable.

55.   **A**   As written, the sentence is correct. Choices (B) and (D) are incorrect because you can connect only two complete thoughts with periods or semicolons. The comma and coordinating conjunction *and* in choice (C) function in the same way—this combination can separate only two complete thoughts. Only choice (A) can separate the first part of the sentence, an independent clause or complete thought, from the last part, a dependent clause or incomplete thought.

56.   **H**   Choices (F) and (G) are incorrect because the underlined portion is using *star* as a possessive form, not as a plural. Choice (J) is incorrect because no comma is necessary after *exterior*.

57.   **D**   As written, the sentence is a fragment, so choice (A) is incorrect. Choice (C) is incorrect because it is written in the future tense. Choice (B) is also incorrect because *has* is the singular form of the verb, but the subject *theorists* is plural.

58. **H** This sentence needs a transition which shows a contrast from the previous sentence. Choices (F), (G) and (J) are incorrect because they all indicate that a new concept is being introduced.

59. **C** Choice (C) is the only answer choice that succinctly states that the scientific community cannot explain the formation of mini black holes. Choices (A), (B), and (D) all introduce redundancies into the underlined portion.

60. **J** If the author's goal were to show that Einstein's skepticism slowed or stopped scientific inquiry into black holes, specific examples would have to be provided showing that to be the case. Nothing of the sort is provided; in fact, clearly research did continue or black holes would not have been discovered at all. Only choice (J) correctly explains this point of view. Choices (F) and (G) are factually correct, but have no bearing on whether the passage successfully fulfilled the intended goal. Choice (H) includes information not mentioned in the passage.

Passage V

61. **D** The clause *that have become companions to America's trashcans* is necessary information insofar as its omission would change the meaning of the sentence, so eliminate choice (C), because *which* is for unnecessary information. You can also eliminate choices (A) and (B) because necessary information should not be set off by commas. Only choice (D) has the proper omission of punctuation and, with the word *that*, the recognition that this part of the sentence is essential to the meaning of the sentence as a whole.

62. **F** Only choice (F) provides a form of the verb with a tense consistent with the preceding sentence. Since the word *has* is not underlined, you know that the underlined verb must be in the present perfect tense, as in *has become*. The word *became* is not compatible with the word has.

63. **D** The first sentence indicates that the passage is talking about the way things are *today* (and how they've progressed to this point from the way things were in the past). The most direct way to talk about what people think today would be to use present tense here: *extends*.

64. **G** The question asked for an answer that emphasizes lack of awareness. Choices (F) and (J) say people don't often encounter or pay attention to the problem, not that they aren't aware of it. It's a small difference, but it's a difference that means you can cross these two choices out because choice (G) is better. Choice (H) refers to governments' attempts to study it, which means they are aware, so cross that one out, too. Only choice (G), which matches *realize* in the answer choice with *awareness* in the question, is consistent with what you are asked to emphasize.

65. **C** The first half of the sentence (*E-waste...devices*) is a complete idea or independent clause, as is the second half of the sentence (*the majority...landfills*). Only choice (C) correctly joins two complete ideas with a comma and coordinating conjunction. Choices (A), (B), and (D) are all punctuation marks and relative pronouns used to join only an incomplete idea with a complete one, so cross them all out.

66. F When you are using a relative pronoun, *people*—such as *Activists*—should nearly always be referred to using *who* (rather than *which* or *that*), so eliminate choice (H). You need the phrase *who track such waste* to specify which activists are doing the estimating, and information essential to the meaning of the sentence such as this should not be separated out from the rest of the sentence with commas (only do that with information not essential to the meaning of the sentence), so eliminate choices (G) and (J).

67. A The phrase *such as* indicates that these are examples of toxins being released. Choice (A) is consistent with that description. Choice (B) is never touched on by any information in the passage, nor does it accurately describe the phrase the author is considering adding, so eliminate it. Choice (C) is not something this phrase needs to accomplish and can therefore be eliminated as well. Choice (D) is simply false. The passage has not already mentioned these things.

68. J Because the underlined word modifies the verb *contaminates*, you need to choose an answer that provides an adverb, rather than an adjective. Adjectives modify nouns and pronouns; adverbs modify verbs, adjectives, and other adverbs. Choices (F), (G), and (H) provide adjectives and can therefore be eliminated. The proper adverb is *dangerously*, which choice (J) provides.

69. D *Consequently* would indicate that the *reusable silver, gold, and other electrical conductors* in the motherboards were a consequence of how burning *contaminates the air*. Cross out (A) because nothing indicates that this is true; instead, the positive sentiment expressed in the first sentence of this paragraph is a marked shift from the negative sentiment at the end of the previous paragraph. Choices (B) and (C) would reflect a consistent flow—so eliminate those. Choice (D), on the other hand, accurately signals the shift occurring between these two paragraphs.

70. F You can cross off choice (G) because the second half of the sentence (*by reducing...destroy ecosystems*) is not a complete idea, meaning a semicolon is not an acceptable way to join it with the first half of the sentence, which is a complete idea. In choice (H), *so* creates a cause-and-effect relationship between the two halves of the sentence that is not consistent with what the paragraph describes, so eliminate it, too. Choice (J) creates a sentence that means the opposite of what the author is actually trying to convey, so leave the sentence as-is and select choice (F).

71. A Leave the sentence as-is and pick choice (A). Each of the other options changes the meaning of the sentence.

72. F Choice (F) accurately describes the flow of this paragraph. While choice (G) is true—though, to be fair, it's a single statistic, not *statistics* as the answer choice says—choice (F) is more comprehensive and attuned to the big picture, making it a better answer than choice (G). Choice (H) simply isn't true (it provides the statistic), and choice (J) isn't much better: *Redundant* would mean that it provided the same information, and you know it provides more than that (the statistic), so knock out both of these.

73. A Eliminate choice (D) first, as there's nothing tangential about this point. It addresses disposal of e-waste, the same thing the author's been talking about all along. Next, cross out choice (C), because the word *Nevertheless* in the following sentence acknowledges the change in flow choice (C) describes—which means you should get rid of the answer choice, not the proposed addition. Choice (A) is preferable to choice (B) because you need to be concerned more about the specifics of why these organizations are bad—not the mere fact that they are bad.

74. **H** Since *progress* and *a step forward* mean the same thing in this context, it is redundant to use them both, so you can eliminate choices (F), (G), and (J), some of which change the meaning of the sentence in addition to being redundant. Only choice (H) provides a concise substitute for the underlined portion that preserves the meaning.

75. **C** The passage discusses e-waste and its effect on the environment when it isn't properly recycled. The new information about government regulations on pollution isn't wholly unrelated, but it is off-topic in this essay, as choice (C) suggests. Neither choice (A) nor (B) correctly describes what this sentence accomplishes, so eliminate both of those choices. Cross out choice (D), since the subject of *government regulation* as *complicated and complex* is not addressed anywhere else in the passage.

ENGLISH PRACTICE 2 ANSWERS

1. A
2. F
3. C
4. J
5. C
6. H
7. C
8. G
9. D
10. J
11. C
12. F
13. D
14. G
15. C
16. H
17. A
18. H
19. C
20. H
21. C
22. G
23. C
24. H
25. B
26. F
27. C
28. G
29. C
30. F
31. A
32. J
33. B
34. F
35. C
36. G
37. D
38. G
39. D
40. H
41. C
42. J
43. B
44. H
45. A
46. G
47. D
48. J
49. D
50. F
51. D
52. F
53. C
54. G
55. C
56. H
57. C
58. H
59. A
60. H
61. D
62. J
63. B
64. F
65. C
66. H
67. A
68. J
69. C
70. G
71. D
72. G
73. C
74. F
75. B

ENGLISH PRACTICE 2 EXPLANATIONS

Passage I

1. **A** For this answer choice, you need to recognize the appropriate idiom for this expression. The correct choice depends on which word matches up most effectively with the verb *born*; in this case, a daughter is born TO her parents, so this is the correct answer.

2. **F** Here, you should be able to eliminate some answer choices because they're unnecessarily wordy or redundant. You can get rid of answer choice (G) because it contains the repetitive phrase *as a child at the age of six years old* and choice (H) because of the phrase *leaving her to be an orphan as a young child*. Choice (J) contains the redundant phrase *the young age of six years old* (as opposed to the original's more concise *at age six*), so select choice (F) as the best answer choice.

3. **C** To answer this question correctly, you'll need to read a bit further to get a clear idea of the main subject of the essay. Once you reach a certain point, you should recognize that *Madame* Sarah Breedlove Walker is the focus of the essay. Whether the writer should add the sentence about Louis Armstrong depends on whether doing so will add to the reader's understanding of Madame Walker. Choices (A) and (B) don't do this, so eliminate them. Choice (D) correctly argues that the writer shouldn't add this sentence, but its reason for leaving it out doesn't connect with the rest of the essay.

4. **J** One way to decide how to punctuate the possessive word *its*—as in *belonging to it*—is to remember that *it's* always means *it is*. If you substitute *it is* in place of *it's* here, the sentence doesn't make sense, so you can eliminate choice (G). There's no such word as *its'*, so choice (F) doesn't work. And you can eliminate choice (H) because of a noun/pronoun agreement problem. The noun for which the plural pronoun *their* would stand in is *St. Louis*, a singular noun. Consequently, choice (J) is the correct answer choice.

5. **C** This question tests the correct idiom to express the passage of time. Choices (A), (B), and (D) are all idiomatically incorrect; only (C) uses the correct expression.

6. **H** As it stands, the sentence beginning with *As well as* is a fragment, so eliminate choice (F). Looking at choice (G), you should keep in mind that you use a semicolon only when both sides of the punctuation form complete sentences. Because the *as well as* part is still a fragment, a semicolon isn't the correct form of punctuation to use, so choice (G) can't be right. In choice (J), the ideas are separated by a colon, which is an appropriate form of punctuation either when you're beginning a list, a definition, or an example. Since *as well as in churches and lodges* is none of these, you're left with choice (H).

7. **C** This question again concerns conciseness. Generally, if you see two *who* phrases—*who worked in the newspaper publishing business and who also lived in St. Louis*—look to condense the two ideas. Choice (C) does that, conveying the same information in far fewer words. The other choices are just as wordy as the original and don't add important details, so choice (C) is the best answer.

8. **G** The original sentence is a type of run-on sentence sometimes called a *comma splice*, in which a comma separates two complete sentences or *independent clauses*. Fixing this problem requires either using a stronger form of punctuation or making one of the clauses *dependent* on the other. Answer choice (J) makes the same mistake as (F); (G) and (H) both rely on the second strategy, using pronouns to begin the second clause, so your goal is to decide which pronoun is right. And the women are performing the action in the second clause, so you wouldn't use the object form *whom* but rather the subject form *who*, choice (G).

9. **D** This is another idiomatic expression; to get the right answer, you'll need to know what preposition is appropriate with *her supervision*. The idiomatically correct preposition with *supervise* is *under*, as in *under her supervision*. Choice (D) works.

10. **J** The sentence is composed of a complete idea and an incomplete idea, which need to be joined together with punctuation. A semicolon may only be used to separate two complete ideas, so eliminate choice (G). A colon in this situation would require a subject in the second idea in order to make sense. There is no subject, so eliminate choice (H). The phrase *using these terms to emphasize...*is not describing *culturists;* it's explaining why Walker employed those terms, so a comma is needed to make that clear—select choice (J).

11. **C** Transitional sentences between paragraphs should connect an idea or ideas from the previous paragraph to an idea or ideas in the following paragraph. Only choice (C) refers to the action that took place in the preceding paragraph. The others have no clear connection to the context.

12. **F** When a sentence begins with a modifying clause, as is the case here, the verb should appear in its *past participle* form—e.g., *understood, seen, begun*. The verb in the modifying phrase here is *choose*, so look for the past participle form in your answer choices. Choice (G) is in simple past tense, choice (J) is the present participle, and choice (H) isn't a word. *Chosen* is the right form, so choice (F) is the correct answer choice.

13. **D** The key phrase in this sentence is *these charitable acts*. The word *these* indicates that the passage has discussed charitable acts before this sentence, and that this sentence is referring back to that prior mention. Therefore, only choice (D) makes logical sense, because the paragraph doesn't mention charity until Sentence 4.

14. **G** As in question 10, this question requires you to notice the change of direction in this sentence and punctuate that change appropriately. You will need some form of punctuation, so choice (J) doesn't work, and choice (H) uses a semicolon, which is incorrect because the clauses following the punctuation don't form a complete sentence. Choice (F) adds an unnecessary comma after *maintaining*, which interrupts the connection between that word and what is being maintained. Choice (G) has the proper form.

15. **C** This essay doesn't stray very far at any point from the life and actions of Madame Walker, so if this passage is meant to discuss the broader subject of the beauty industry in the early twentieth century, it's too narrowly focused to be successful. Choice (C) most accurately presents the correct judgment—that this essay isn't effective on these terms—and the most convincing reason for that judgment.

Passage II

16. **H** Each answer choice will be followed by *we were hardly saying a word*, which is a complete idea or independent clause. Choices (F) and (J) begin with an incomplete idea and a comma, which are properly followed by a complete idea. Choice (G) is a complete idea followed by a comma and the coordinating conjunction *but*, which is also properly followed by another complete idea. Choice (H), on the other hand, connects two complete ideas with a comma, which is incorrect.

17. **A** The shortest correct way of saying something is usually the best answer choice. If you are considering adding words, make sure they say something of added value. In this case, the original sentence indicates that this is an *ordinary birthday*. Choices (B), (C), and (D) are just different ways of redundantly restating that the occasion was typical. They add nothing to the original meaning of the sentence, which gives us no reason to prefer any of them to the original wording.

18. **H** The paragraph is focused on the fact that the narrator and his uncle are having their traditional celebration of the narrator's birthday, but the uncle's mood is unusually depressed. Choices (F), (G), and (J) all contribute towards developing that context. Choice (H) is the least relevant to this paragraph, mentioning the narrator's predilection for a banana split with chocolate ice cream.

19. **C** The intended meaning of the sentence is that the uncle is uneasy about the narrator joining the army rather than going to college. Choice (C) provides the correct placement to achieve that meaning. Choices (A) and (B) incorrectly apply the phrase *joining the army* to the uncle, whereas the context of the sentence before and after this makes it clear that the narrator is the one joining the army. Choice (D) would make an extremely clumsy ending to the sentence, saying *reservations about me rather than joining the army going to college*.

20. **H** The fact that the narrator's father was in the Polish army is necessary to the rest of the paragraph, as the narrator and uncle debate what the narrator's late father would think of his decision to join the army. This makes choice (H) correct. Choices (F), (G), and (J) are irrelevant or unsupportable ideas.

21. **C** As written, the sentence gets incorrectly divided into two separate clauses. However, the two clauses are part of one continuous idea and should not have punctuation dividing them. The error is similar to writing: *My uncle asked me; a question*. There should be no punctuation interrupting the idea, which makes choice (C) correct and choices (A), (B), and (D) incorrect.

22. **G** When you use the word *as* in a sentence, you make a comparative statement that requires another *as* to introduce the second idea of the comparison. Also, the idiom *as _____ as _____* implies that the things being compared are equal. Choice (G) uses the *as/as* idiom correctly. Choice (F) is incorrect because you can only use *than* when comparing unequal things: e.g., *more/greater/less/fewer than*. It is never correct to use *as/than* together. Choice (H) introduces more confusion by using an inappropriate homonym of *than*. The word *then* is used in conditional statements like *if _____, then _____* or when referring to time periods. Choice (J) would produce a sentence that is incomplete by starting the *as _____ as _____* idiom without finishing it.

23. **C**   Any time you are considering adding something, consider first the purpose of the paragraph. This paragraph is a list of memories the narrator and his uncle shared during the narrator's childhood in Poland. The sentence in consideration provides a general fact about carnivals in Poland, but it does nothing to add to the list of shared experiences being discussed in this paragraph. Therefore, choice (C) is correct. Choice (A) is incorrect because the topic of the essay is the relationship of the narrator to his uncle. Choice (B) is incorrect because this rather boring detail about carnivals is not crucial information about a Polish upbringing. Choice (D) is incorrect because this detail is NOT explained elsewhere.

24. **H**   Use the context of the paragraph to determine which pronoun would be most appropriate. The sentence before this one and other sentences in the paragraph describe things that the narrator and his uncle did together, and this sentence contains the word *ourselves*. For the sake of consistency, choice (H) would be correct because it identifies the subject as the narrator and his uncle. Choices (F), (G), and (J) refer to a person or persons in general. However, this sentence is a memory that belongs to the narrator and his uncle specifically, which makes those choices incorrect.

25. **B**   When you are attaching a phrase to a noun in order to specifically describe it, you do not need to use any punctuation. The sentence is specifically identifying *sleeping bags my grandmother had bought*. Therefore, choice (B) is correct. It would have also been acceptable to say *sleeping bags that my grandmother had bought*. However, adding a comma, as choice (D) does, is not acceptable. Choices (A) and (C) also incorrectly separate the clause *my grandmother had bought* from the noun it modifies, *sleeping bags*.

26. **F**   The two verbs in the underlined portion need to be the same tense as the verb *lie* in the passage, because all three are things the narrator and his uncle used to do—*lie, drink,* and *listen*. Choices (G) and (H) use the incorrect tense *drank,* and choice (J) uses the incorrect *listening*. Thus, the sentence is correct as written—choice (F).

27. **C**   Just as verb tense has to be consistent within a sentence listing several actions, so too should it be consistent within a paragraph listing several ideas. This paragraph is a list of memories the narrator and his uncle shared during the narrator's childhood in Poland. Choice (A) is present tense, so it must be incorrect. Because other ideas in this paragraph are expressed in the tense of *he would take me, we would go, he and I would race,* etc., the consistent and correct verb tense is *he would tell me*. This makes choice (C) correct, and choices (B) and (D) incorrect.

28. **G**   Use the context of the paragraph to determine where this information is most relevant. Sentence 6 discusses the narrator and his uncle *rowing canoes and swimming from our dock out to a rock formation and back*, so it would be helpful to add the new sentence before this idea in order to let the reader know what body of water they are on. Choice (G) correctly places the sentence before sentence 6. Choices (F), (H), and (J) incorrectly put the sentence in places that do not add any logical clarity.

29. **C**   Choice (C) is correct because *its* is the possessive pronoun that stands in for *Poland's* influence. Choice (A) is incorrect because that contraction means *it is*. The sentence should not read *I will never lose track of it is influence on who I am*. Choice (B) does not exist in English grammar; *its'* is always incorrect. Choice (D) is incorrect because Poland is a singular noun, and therefore it should not be replaced with the plural possessive pronoun *their*.

30. **F** The question asks you to make the best logical bridge from the preceding sentence, describing the job opportunity that enticed the narrator and his uncle to come to America, and the current sentence, which describes the effect the experience of living in America has had on the narrator. Choice (F) effectively identifies that bridge, transitioning from the uncle being offered a job to the two of them immigrating into the U.S. Choices (G), (H), and (J) include less relevant details about cities in Pennsylvania and the uncle's status as an engineer. None of these details transition as smoothly as choice (F) into a discussion of the narrator's experience in America, and therefore they are incorrect.

Passage III

31. **A** The act of studying occurred in the past prior to the other past tense verb *struggled*, so it should be in the pluperfect tense to demonstrate this, as with choice (A). Choices (B), (C), and (D) do not agree with the past tense of *struggled*.

32. **J** The phrase *as difficult as* initiates a comparison. The item following the phrase must correctly agree with *enduring*, as with choice (J). Choices (F) and (H) contain verb tenses that do not agree with *enduring*. Choice (G) creates an incorrect phrase of comparison.

33. **B** Choice (B) is the most concise answer that conveys the correct meaning. Choices (A), (C), and (D) skew the intended meaning through excessive wordiness.

34. **F** The phrase *under my nose* correctly conveys the meaning of "obvious," so choice (F) is correct. Choice (G) is not quite strong enough to convey the correct meaning. Choices (H) and (J) convey meanings opposite of the intended one.

35. **C** The word *liking* is a gerund, so it requires an adjective to modify it, eliminating choices (A) and (D), which contain adverbs. Choice (C) correctly modifies the gerund with an adjective and properly completes the idiom *take a liking to*. Choice (B) improperly completes the idiom.

36. **G** In this sentence, the author accepts the invitations from the previous sentence. This direct relationship between the two sentences negates the need to begin a new paragraph at this point, thus eliminating, choices (H) and (J). Choice (F) is unnecessarily wordy. Thus, choice (G) is correct.

37. **D** Choice (D) is the most concise answer that conveys the correct meaning. Choices (A), (B), and (C) skew the intended meaning through excessive wordiness.

38. **G** The remainder of the sentence following the word *surprised* is part of the same complete thought. Choice (G) correctly identifies this without extra punctuation. Choices (F) and (H) create unnecessary pauses with commas. Choice (J) creates a sentence fragment.

39. **D** The additional sentence is not consistent with the main point of the essay, so it is distracting and should not be added. Thus, choices (A) and (B) are eliminated. Since this idea is not mentioned earlier in the essay, choice (C) can be eliminated as well. Choice (D) is correct because the additional sentence is not necessary to the development of the paragraph.

40. **H** The phrase *as karaoke often is* is unnecessary information, so it should be offset by commas, thus choice (H) is correct. Choice (F) has no pauses to offset this information, which confuses the flow of the sentence. Choices (G) and (J) do not properly utilize commas to offset the phrase, creating sentence fragments.

41. **C** Since the word *number* belongs to the word *song* in the sentence, a possessive is required. Choice (C) correctly uses an apostrophe to show the possession of *number* by the song. Choice (A) does not contain any possessive. Choice (B) incorrectly pluralizes the song when there should be only one. Choice (D) contains *songs's*, which is never used.

42. **J** Choice (J) is correct because the sentence reveals what the rest of the party thought in reaction to the narrator's gaffe. Choice (F) is incorrect because the miscommunication example is not the main point of the essay; rather, it supports the main point. Choice (G) incorrectly identifies the sentence as an extra example when it is in fact the completion of the only example. The sentence has no contrasting relationship with the initial sentence of the paragraph, so choice (H) cannot be correct either.

43. **B** Choice (B) is the most concise answer that conveys the correct meaning. Choice (A) is wordy because of the use of passive voice. Choice (C) skews the intended meaning by removing the person who has learned the lesson. Choice (D) creates a sentence fragment.

44. **H** Choice (H) emphasizes the existence of other slang differences in the context of the main idea of the essay, so it is the correct choice. Choices (F), (G), and (J) do not create an emphasis on other slang differences among cultures, so they do not answer the question correctly.

45. **A** Choice (A) correctly indicates the author's main point of learning to understand a foreign culture through interaction. Choice (B) incorrectly identifies the miscommunication as intentional. Choice (C) too narrowly focuses the main point to only the enjoyment of night life. Choice (D) portrays an idea opposite to the main point that involves isolating oneself in a foreign environment rather than interacting.

Passage IV

46. **G** The compound noun in this instance is *Pennsylvania hills and mountains*. In this sense, since *daunting* is the only adjective modifying this compound noun, no commas are necessary.

47. **D** Although each of the answer choices suggests the same meaning out of context, in this context, answer choice (D) is the least acceptable alternative, because the phrase *in following* is not idiomatically correct.

48. **J** As written, this sentence suggests that the *old bike* belongs to the *page*, when in fact the *old bike* belongs to the narrator. Since this essay is written in the first person, only the first-person *my* is an acceptable substitution, as in choice (J).

49. **D** Since there are no specific grammatical errors in any of the answer choices, choose the most concise answer that preserves the meaning of the sentence. Choices (A), (B), and (C) all contain redundant wording—only choice (D) appropriately removes the redundancy.

50. **F** The reflexive pronoun *myself* is not necessary in this context and changes the meaning of this sentence. Since the narrator is discussed as living in a specific place in the earlier paragraphs, and this paragraph signals a shift, it must be correct that the narrator is moving *out*, as in choice (F), rather than moving *in*, as in choice (J).

51. **D** Choices (B) and (C) change the meaning of the sentence, so they should be eliminated immediately. Since the subject of this sentence is the plural noun *bundles* (not the singular noun *money*), the verb in this sentence must be plural as well, as in choice (D).

52. **F** In this sentence, the narrator contrasts *a quick 30-minute drive where I grew up* with *a two-hour drive…in this new place*. While the *30-minute drive* is a part of this contrast, this specific part of the sentence cannot be said to contrast with *in this new place*, as choice (H) suggests; rather, *30-minute drive* is in a contrasting relationship with *two-hour drive*. Choices (G) and (J) are not supported by information in the passage.

53. **C** Choice (B) changes the meaning of the sentence, so it should be eliminated immediately. Choices (A), (C), and (D) contain no specific grammatical errors and mean roughly the same thing, so you should pick the most concise answer that preserves the meaning of the sentence. Since *resolved* and *decided* mean roughly the same thing in this context, it is redundant to use them both in the same sentence. Only choice (C) fixes this redundancy error.

54. **G** The dependent clause in this sentence is used adjectivally to describe the author's visit to the attic. Accordingly, the participle *fighting* is required at the beginning of the clause. The conjunctions listed in choice (F), (H), and (J) obscure the meaning of the sentence.

55. **C** In this sentence, the noun *gold-rushers* is followed directly by a verb *must*. No ownership is indicated in the sentence, so eliminate choices (A) and (B). Moreover, you never want to separate the subject and verb with a comma unless there is some appositive clarifying the subject, which there is not in this case, so you can eliminate choice (D).

56. **H** In this context, when the verb *began* is linked with a second verb, the second verb must be in its infinitive form. Only choice (H) satisfies this condition. Choice (G) contains the word *to*, but the *-ing* form of a verb is not part of its infinitive.

57. **C** This sentence gives a list of items: *four-dollar-a-gallon gas*, *traffic jams*, and *the interminable wait*. In any list, the items must be listed in a parallel fashion. Use the non-underlined portions as context. Choices (A), (B), and (D) all introduce elements to the third item in this list that are not consistent with the first two items.

58. **H** As written, this sentence is a run-on. Given the answer choices, the best way to fix this sentence is to separate the two independent clauses with the appropriate punctuation. Only choice (H) does this, while choices (F), (G), and (J) preserve the run-on.

59. **A** The word *Now* at the beginning of the following sentence indicates that some contrast is being set up at the end of the sentence in question with the word *freedom*. Since only choice (A) gives the word *freedom* and signals the time-contrast with the word *anymore*, it provides the best substitute.

60. **H** This essay discusses the writer's decision to begin riding a bike instead of driving, and it gives some details about the role of biking in parts of the narrator's life. The essay does not discuss any means of transportation in detail, as in choice (F). The essay does not give any predictions as to the effects of large-scale bike-riding, as in choice (G). Choice (J) is factually incorrect, considering that this essay is more inclined toward biking than driving. Only choice (H) correctly indicates that this essay does not achieve the goal stated in the question and gives the correct reason why not.

Passage V

61. **D** The portion of the sentence before the comma is an introductory, dependent clause starting with *Where once it was considered...*Therefore, the second part of the sentence will have to be an independent clause if the sentence is to be complete. Choices (A), (B), and (C) all create sentence fragments with the various words they insert. Only choice (D) correctly removes the conjunction and relative pronoun and maintains the comma to show the dependent/independent relationship.

62. **J** Try each answer choice in the sentence. Notice (F), (G), and (H) are all idiomatically correct forms of the verb *to benefit*. Only choice (J) creates an awkward sentence fragment—it is therefore NOT an acceptable alternative.

63. **B** Paragraph 2 is about the archaeological details regarding the earliest dogs, and Paragraph 3 is about some of the early historical uses people had for domesticated dogs. Choice (A) does not address historical questions; choices (C) and (D) do address historical questions, but they suggest that the following paragraph will discuss the horse and the wolf, respectively. Only choice (B) is appropriately general to relate to both Paragraph 2 and Paragraph 3.

64. **F** Choices (G) and (J) obscure the meaning of the sentence, so they can be eliminated right away. To decide whether you need *Although* or *Because*, figure out the relationship between the two parts of the sentence. As you can see, the first part of the sentence talks about *many* reasons where the second part talks about the *primary* reason, so the two parts of the sentence are in a contrasting relationship with one another. Only (F), *Although*, can work.

65. **C** Read the sentence carefully. Notice what comes directly after the underlined portion—*primary responsibility*. Since this is referring to the primary responsibility that certain dogs had at this time, the correct answer will have to show a possessive relationship. Only choice (C) does this. If you chose (D), be careful—this is the contraction for "who is."

66. **H** Paragraph 4 gives a brief sketch of how dogs' relationship to humans changed in the eighteenth century, and thus sets up a contrast with the previous paragraph. Only choice (H) adequately expresses this contrast. Choice (F) cannot work because no example is given; choice (G) cannot work because dogs' new treatment is not discussed as a *consequence*; and choice (J) cannot work because *moreover* is a word that indicates similarity rather than contrast or difference.

67. **A** Without the phrase *as hunters or guardsmen*, the noun *roles* is not clearly defined. Thus, *roles as hunters or guardsmen* should not be separated with any punctuation.

68. **J** Because the number of owned dogs is given as a quantity (74 million), you must use *fewer* instead of *less* or *lesser*, and you can eliminate choices (G) and (H). Now, you need to decide between *than* and *then*—*than* is a comparison and *then* is a time or transition word. In this situation, you are comparing *74 million* to *fewer than 74 million*, so you need the comparison word as in choice (J).

69. **C** Because this is talking about an event in the past, you'll need a past tense verb; therefore, you can eliminate choices (A) and (B). Choice (D) is an incorrect use of the past perfect tense—if past perfect is to be used, the correct form is *had begun*. Only choice (C) gives the correct tense and conjugation.

70. **G** The phrase gives further modification to the word *attitudes*, indicating the way these attitudes have shifted. It does not give any description of dog-breeding, as in choice (F), or any discussion of dogs' historical importance, as in choice (H). Furthermore, it is a necessary part of the sentence and paragraph because it gives the reader a more precise sense of the character of the change in humans' attitude toward dogs, so you can eliminate choice (J).

71. **D** Notice the phrase *this point in time* at the beginning of Sentence 2. This indicates that the preceding sentence will need to mention a specific time, so you can eliminate choice (B). Now note the specific times in each sentence. Sentence 1 speaks generally about the 18th century, and Sentence 4 speaks about the year 1855, and the following paragraph discusses dogs in the present tense. Note how Sentence 2 contains the word *currently* and is written in the present tense. Because of this, the sentence will have to appear after Sentences 1 and 4, which discuss earlier times, and in proximity to the following paragraph, which is written in the present tense, so only choice (D) works.

72. **G** Because both *indispensable* and *underappreciated* are used to describe dogs in this sentence, there is no need to set either word off with commas—eliminate choices (F) and (J). Choice (H) contains a semicolon, but this cannot work because a semicolon can be used only when the two sentences on either side of it are complete (or independent clauses). Only choice (G) preserves the meaning of the sentence without introducing any unnecessary punctuation.

73. **C** Because the first part of the sentence begins with the word *Although*, you need something to contrast with the verb *seem*. Of all the choices, only (C) gives the appropriate contrast with the word *actuality*. Choices (A) and (D) both seem to indicate contradictions, but they do not contrast adequately with the word *seem*, and moreover, choice (A) suggests that this is part of an extended contrast (i.e., that there will be an *other hand* later on). Choice (B) does not signal a contrast, so it can be eliminated.

74. **F** This sentence issues a command which means that *Have* is actually the main verb of this sentence with an implied *You* as its subject. Choices (G), (H), and (J) do not use the verb properly, nor do they maintain appropriate parallel structure with the later part of the sentence beginning with *and you'll find*.

75. **B** This sentence best fits in Paragraph 3, which discusses the historical uses of domesticated dogs before dogs became primarily house pets in the 18th century. Since the proposed insertion gives an additional example of a way dogs were used before the 18th century, it should be included in Paragraph 3.

ENGLISH PRACTICE 3 ANSWERS

1. D
2. F
3. B
4. G
5. C
6. F
7. C
8. J
9. D
10. J
11. C
12. J
13. A
14. H
15. B
16. G
17. D
18. H
19. B
20. J
21. B
22. G
23. A
24. F
25. A
26. J
27. C
28. H
29. B
30. F
31. B
32. H
33. A
34. H
35. A
36. G
37. C
38. F
39. B
40. H
41. A
42. G
43. D
44. J
45. D
46. G
47. A
48. H
49. D
50. G
51. B
52. F
53. A
54. J
55. C
56. G
57. B
58. F
59. C
60. J
61. B
62. H
63. D
64. F
65. D
66. G
67. C
68. J
69. D
70. F
71. B
72. G
73. B
74. J
75. C

ENGLISH PRACTICE 3 EXPLANATIONS

Passage I

1. **D** Bazin is described in this sentence as being the premier intellectual who belongs to or is part of a city. Since you need to show this possessive relationship, you can eliminate choices (A) and (B). To decide between choices (C) and (D), you need to figure out whether you're dealing with a singular *city* or plural *cities*. In this situation, the city is Paris and none other, so the best answer is (D).

2. **F** Don't insert a comma into this sentence if you don't need to. In this sentence, there is nothing in the sentence that has to be set off as unnecessary or interruptive, so no commas are necessary. Note how choices (G), (H), and (J) all break the flow of the sentence.

3. **B** All the words in the answer choices can be synonyms for the word *exploded*, but in this case, the word *release* does not make sense. The films *were released*, but it doesn't make sense to say that *the films released*, making choice (B) the LEAST acceptable alternative.

4. **G** Note the context on either side of the punctuation. Before the comma, you have *Bazin published his first piece of film criticism in 1943 and pioneered a new way of writing about film* and after the comma you have *he championed the idea that cinema was the seventh art*. Since both of these are complete ideas, choices (F) and (H) cannot work because neither separates these complete ideas appropriately. Choice (J) introduces a period but, with the word *although*, turns the part after the period into a sentence fragment. Only choice (G) has the appropriate punctuation.

5. **C** *Architecture* is the first word in a series here, and every word in a series must be succeeded by a comma, so you can eliminate choice (D). If you are to use a colon to introduce a list, the words directly before it must form a complete sentence, which *every bit as deserving as the more respected arts of* does not—eliminate choice (A). Choice (B) introduces an unnecessary pause before the word *architecture*. Only choice (C) preserves the flow of the sentence and properly situates the word *architecture* in a list.

6. **F** Without the proposed addition, the sentence does not have any clear connection to its context. To include the proposed addition is to tie the sentence to the previous sentence's mention of the word *theatre*. Because you'll want to include the sentence, you can conclusively eliminate choices (H) and (J). You can also eliminate choice (G) because this sentence is not discussing Bazin's own writing; rather, it is discussing the work of authors of *many early writings about film*. Only choice (F) advises that the writer add the clause and indicates that the writer do so because this will make this sentence more clear and precise.

7. **C** The end of this paragraph introduces the concept of *auteur* theory, a subject taken up by the next paragraph. Accordingly, any sentence that does not discuss *auteur* theory directly should not be added at this point, eliminating choices (A) and (B). There is nothing in the rest of the essay that discusses either *What is Cinema?* or anything about Film Studies classes, so you can also eliminate choice (D). Only choice (C) advises that the writer omit the proposed sentence for the reason that it strays from the topic of the current paragraph.

8. **J** Notice you've got a list of things here: *style, perspective, and voice*. All elements in this list must have a structure parallel to one another. To introduces extra words such as *his* or *the director's*

throws off the parallel structure of the list as written. Since you must keep the word *voice* parallel with *style* and *perspective*, choice (J) is the best answer.

9. **D** When you get DELETE as an answer choice, as you do here, always give it special attention. Omitting a few words can often make a piece of writing more clear and concise. In this case, choices (A), (B), and (C) all indicate some kind of contrast in this sentence where no contrast is present. Accordingly, choices (A), (B), and (C) are incorrect, and only choice (D) preserves the flow and tone of the sentence by opting to DELETE the underlined portion.

10. **J** Look at the sentence as a whole. Notice there is a dash after the word *Renoir*. A dash in this context suggests that a certain part of the sentence is being set off as with commas or parentheses. Accordingly, since the phrase that is set off ends with a dash, it must also begin with a dash as in choice (J).

11. **C** This paragraph is about Bazin's influence on film criticism, and the next paragraph is about his influence on filmmaking. Because you'll need some mention of his role in both, you can eliminate choices (A), (B), and (D). Since the last paragraph indicates that Bazin's most important influence was on later generations of filmmakers, choice (C) provides the best transition with its indication that Bazin's influence lay *elsewhere* (i.e., somewhere other than film criticism).

12. **J** As in Question 9, always give DELETE special attention. Choices (F), (G), and (H) are all redundant because the sentence already contains the word *international*. Accordingly, the clearest and most concise fix for this sentence is to DELETE the underlined portion entirely.

13. **A** Choices (B), (C), and (D) give details about the films but no indication of why these films were important. Only choice (A) gives some indication of the films' importance to the international film community.

14. **H** The verbs in this sentence are in the present tense, so any time words you use will have to indicate the present. Eliminate choices (F) and (G) which indicate the past, and eliminate choice (J) because what *the end* would be in this sentence is unclear, particularly given that the process is discussed as ongoing. Only choice (H) appropriately indicates the present tense with the word *now*.

15. **B** Choice (B) encapsulates this essay well: the first few paragraphs are about Bazin's role and influence in film criticism, and the last paragraph is about his influence on filmmaking. Choice (A) is incorrect—the part of the text to which it refers discusses Bazin as wanting to show that cinema was a *seventh art*, not his influence on the other six. Choice (C) is untrue because the essay is primarily about Bazin, not *auteur* theory or French filmmaking in general. Finally, there is no support for the idea that Bazin was a filmmaker, only that he was a film critic, so choice (D) cannot be the answer.

Passage II

16. **G** Choice (G) creates a subject for the verb, which we need, in a concise manner. The non-underlined part of the sentence already has a verb (*will be*) so the underlined portion functions as a noun. Choice (J) incorrectly makes it a verb, while choices (F) and (H) are both awkward and wordy.

17. **D** The three words (*unwillingly, sadly,* and *painfully*) are all adverbs describing the author's feelings about returning her library books. They are all unhappy words, and choice (D) does the best job of linking these ideas. Choice (A) goes against the passage, choices (B) and (C) incorrectly focus on the author's move and motives, respectively.

18. **H** The word being replaced is *plenty*, used in the phrase *plenty of other books*. All of the answers are words that describe a good quantity, but choice (H), numerous, cannot be followed by the preposition *of*.

19. **B** Only choice (B) addresses the run-on problem in the original sentence. The previous sentence explains what a *biblioemergency* is, while the sentence after the underlined portion explains how problematic this is for the author. Since they are both complete sentences, they need to be separated with appropriate punctuation. Choice (C) adds only the word *that*, while choice (D) adds a comma, which changes the run-on to a similarly unacceptable comma splice.

20. **J** The original sentence uses the word *its* but the context of the sentence shows that the meaning is intended to be "it is." Choice (J) contains the correct formation of that, *it's*. Choices (G) and (H) complicate the problem by incorrectly making the pronoun plural.

21. **B** This question is testing punctuation, so you can use the non-underlined parts of the sentence to determine what kind you need. The underlined phrase refers to the *books* that are mentioned later in the sentence. You don't want to end a sentence before getting to the end of your description, so you can eliminate choices (C) and (D). The underlined part also comes immediately before the descriptive phrase *sometimes two or more*. Because there is a comma after that phrase, and it's additional information that does not change the basic meaning of the sentence, you need to have a comma before it as well. Choice (B) includes that comma.

22. **G** As written, this sentence has a pronoun that doesn't really refer to anything, and even if properly singular could refer either to the book or the bag. Choice (G) replaces the pronoun with a short phrase that makes it clear what the author is discussing. Choices (H) and (J) repeat the initial pronoun problem.

23. **A** Choice (A) correctly uses the apostrophe at the end of a word to show possession. *Parents'* is both plural and possessive, which is what the sentence needs. Choices (B) and (D) don't have apostrophes, and choice (C) is not a correct formation.

24. **F** Choice (F) correctly uses the descriptive phrase *as soon as* to show the timeline of events in the sentence. The author, as a kid, got fidgety and then the mother gave her books to keep her quiet. Choice (G) takes away the time words, turning this into two complete sentences without anything linking them. Choices (H) and (J) also take away the pronoun, making it seem as though the mom is the one getting fidgety.

25. **A** The sentence that the author is considering adding makes sense in the context and is relevant. Choices (C) and (D) are incorrect because the new sentence doesn't contradict anything, nor is it irrelevant (or offensive, for that matter). Choice (B) goes a bit too far—you can understand the rest of the paragraph without this sentence.

26. **J** This sentence is going into the present-day, explaining how the author's childhood experiences still affect her as an adult. Since the childhood stuff is causing the adult reaction, you need a conjunction that shows this cause-effect relationship. That eliminates choices (F), (G), and (H).

27.   **C**   Only choice (C) correctly creates a parallel sentence and makes the second half of the sentence complete by adding a subject. Choice (B) adds a lot of unnecessary words that ruin the parallelism, while choice (D) repeats the problem in the original sentence.

28.   **H**   As written, this sentence is not parallel, nor does it contain the correct idiom. The phrase *plan to* needs to be followed by the rest of the infinitive in order to be correct. Only choice (H) contains the correct part of the infinitive and nothing else. Choice (G) is in the past tense, which does not agree with the other verbs in the sentence (*plan* and *do*). Choice (J) does have the infinitive, *be*, but is unnecessarily wordy compared to choice (H).

29.   **B**   When you have to reorder sentences, it's best to see if there are any sentences that are clearly linked or that have to go first or last. In this case, Sentence 3 refers to an unpleasant experience, which is itself described in Sentence 1. Therefore, Sentence 1 needs to come directly before Sentence 3, which means you can eliminate choices (A), (C), and (D).

30.   **F**   When you are asked whether to keep or delete a paragraph, the best thing to do is just try to determine what the gist of that paragraph is and then focus on elimination. In this case, the final paragraph refers back to the topic of the first paragraph then proposes a plan based on her expected actions and past experiences. Choice (F) recognizes this. Choice (G) incorrectly states that the author is refusing to return the books. Choice (H) is incorrect because the paragraph doesn't move away from the focus of the passage. Choice (J) is incorrect because the final paragraph does give new details.

Passage III

31.   **B**   The first part of the sentence clearly states that Heinlein was a political writer. Therefore it is redundant to repeat this information, which is why choices (A), (C), and (D) are incorrect.

32.   **H**   Adding this phrase would be redundant, because the phrase *race to the moon* already conveys the same information.

33.   **A**   The underlined portion is correct as written, because *our inner world* both correctly describes our current location on Earth, and is parallel to the phrase *outer space* which appears later in the sentence. The other choices change the meaning of the sentence and are not parallel.

34.   **H**   As written, the underlined portion contains the contraction *it is*, which is not appropriate in this sentence, so choice (F) is incorrect. Only choice (H) correctly uses the possessive pronoun. Choice (G) is not a real word, and choice (J) uses a plural pronoun where a singular is necessary.

35.   **A**   Since *the very first space station launched in 1971 by the Russians* is not a complete thought or independent clause, it cannot be preceded by a semicolon or a period. This eliminates choices (C) and (D). However, some punctuation is needed to separate it from the rest of the sentence, so choice (B) is wrong as well.

36.   **G**   In this sentence, the phrase *before plummeting to Earth* is an introductory phrase and must be set off by commas (also note the comma after the first introductory phrase *For example*). Accordingly, you can eliminate choices (H) and (J) because they use the wrong type of punctuation to link the independent clauses. Choice (F) gives too many commas by creating an unnecessary break within the introductory clause.

37. **C** This clause provides extraneous information that is not essential to the passage. Therefore, it should not be included.

38. **F** Only choice (F) describes aspects of *Mir* which can be deemed successful. Choice (G) provides only the origin of the name. Both choices (H) and (J) focus on negative aspects of the space station.

39. **B** Since the sentence begins with the phrase *Hit by debris,* the first noun in the next clause needs to refer to space station. Choice (B) is the only option provided in active voice that doesn't change the meaning of the sentence that implies the launch created the damage to the space station. Choice (A) doesn't begin with the space station, and it is in passive voice. Both choices (C) and (D) imply that the space station was already damaged prior to launch.

40. **H** The adverb *mainly* should be moved to modify the verb *focused*, as in choice (H).

41. **A** The underlined portion is correct as written. To remove the period creates one long run-on sentence.

42. **G** This sentence requires an adverb to modify *launched*, which eliminates choices (F) and (J). No *and* is required between an adverb and the verb it is modifying, so choice (H) can also be eliminated.

43. **D** All the choices listed besides choice (D) can be used interchangeably to refer to a country.

44. **J** Sentence (3) needs to come first in the paragraph because it introduces the main topic. Sentences (2) and (1) logically follow, as they offer additional detail about how the Russians and Americans worked together to create the space station.

45. **D** This essay does not focus on Robert Heinlein. It uses only one of his quotations to frame a broader discussion of the development of space stations starting in the 1960s.

Passage IV

46. **G** Choice (G) corrects the idiom error in the sentence as written. Choices (F), (H), and (J) all give idiomatically incorrect prepositions that do not match with *made history* in this context.

47. **A** The underlined portion is correct as written; the phrase *in order to* should be coupled with the infinitive form of the verb. Choices (B), (C), and (D) all employ incorrect prepositions and conjugations of the verb.

48. **H** All choices preserve the meaning of the sentence, so none can be eliminated on those grounds. Only choice (H) is wordy and incorrectly conjugated by adding the phrase *in which*. Choice (H) is therefore NOT acceptable. Note: If you chose choice (J), you may have been on the right track—choice (J) is in the passive voice, to which active is always preferable, but in this case, choice (H) is far worse.

49. **D** The second paragraph continues the same line of thought as the preceding one. The transitional word *however* shows contrast, and is incorrect here. Likewise, choices (B) and (C) show disagreement, and would not be acceptable replacements. Eliminating a transition word altogether best preserves the agreement between the two paragraphs.

50. **G** Choice (G) corrects a punctuation error. The models are of today, which is to say, the models are today's, in contrast to the model of Anderson, or Anderson's. Choice (H) puts the apostrophe in the wrong place: today is singular not plural. Choice (J) is incorrect because it removes the comma before the linking word though.

51. **B** Choice (B) fixes the redundancy of the underlined portion, and is also the most concise of the answer choices, which is preferable. The wording in choice (D) is as redundant as the original, and adds the unnecessary phrase *that is*. Choice (C) changes the meaning of the sentence.

52. **F** The underlined portion of the sentence is correct as written. Choices (G), (H), and (J) all introduce unnecessary commas that break the flow of the sentence.

53. **A** The underlined portion is correct as written; the wipers were Mary Anderson's invention, so the possessive pronoun *her* should be used. The possessive pronouns in choices (B) and (D) are incorrect, while *it's* in choice (C) is the contraction of "it is."

54. **J** The introductory sentence as written does not provide a smooth transition between the two paragraphs; it refers only to the previous paragraph. You should look for a sentence that links the two discussions—Mary Anderson and other female inventors. Choice (J) makes that transition, and is the best choice. Choices (G) and (H) do not add anything to link themselves to the new paragraph.

55. **C** Choice (C) corrects a punctuation problem. An introductory phrase, such as *at first not a huge success*, should be set off by a comma. Because *at first not a huge success* is not an independent clause or complete idea, choices (A), (B), and (D) can all be eliminated.

56. **G** *Prevented* and *stopped* may be slightly stronger than *discouraged*, but they would be in keeping with the original meaning of the sentence. *Disturbed* changes the meaning of the sentence and does not fit with the preposition from. Therefore, choice (G) is NOT an acceptable substitute for the underlined portion.

57. **B** Choice (B) corrects an error in the verb conjugation. Any verb following the main verb of this sentence, *compelled,* must be in its infinitive form.

58. **F** The underlined portion is correct as written. Choices (G), (H), and (J) do not add any new meaning to the sentence and are unnecessarily wordier than the original.

59. **C** Choice (C) corrects the subject/verb agreement error in the underlined portion. The subject *genius* is singular and should not be confused with the prepositional phrase *behind their innovations*. Choices (A), (B), and (D) are all verb forms for plural subjects.

60. **J** The primary subject of this essay is Mary Anderson and her invention of windshield wipers. Although there are some minor references to Henry Ford and the Model T, the focus of this essay could not be said to be advancements in the auto industry. While choice (H) is true, it does not address the question regarding the goals of this essay and advancements in the auto industry.

Passage V

61. **B** Since the previous sentence is *The program was different from virtually any other in the world*, you'll need something that shows how Chicago's recycling program was unique. Choices (A) and (C) show similarity more than difference, and choice (D) is not relevant to the passage. Only choice (B) shows how the program was unlike other programs.

62. **H**   Notice this sentence: *Many embraced the city's program because they felt it wouldn't inconvenience residents.* So, the city's logic is driven by the convenience of the program. Choices (F), (G), and (J) do not deal with the idea of convenience. Only choice (H) discusses how residents can participate in the program *without the hassle*.

63. **D**   The punctuation in question introduces a list, so a colon is the best fit. The main restriction on the colon is that it must be preceded by a complete thought or independent clause, as this one is. Choice (D) works. Choices (B) and (C) create excessively long and wordy sentences with no strong breaks. Choice (A) uses a semicolon, which requires independent clauses both before and after it—(A) can't work because the second part of the sentence, starting with the word *collecting*, is not complete.

64. **F**   This sentence has two introductory phrases: *In 2005* and *according to a report by city officials.* Both introductory sections should be punctuated the same way—that is, both should be set off from the rest of the sentence by commas, as in choice (F). Choice (G) omits the pause and breaks the flow of the sentence. Choices (H) and (J) introduce a period and semicolon, respectively, both of which must be preceded by an independent clause, which *In 2005, according to a report by city officials* is not.

65. **D**   Although it is asked differently, this question tests many of the same concepts tested in questions 63 and 64. Recall that if you use a period or semi-colon between two clauses, then both of those clauses must be independent or complete. The first begins with *According to their estimates*, and the second begins with *In other words*—both of these full clauses are independent, so choice (C) works interchangeably with the sentence as written. A colon functions similarly to a semicolon, but it must have an independent clause preceding it (which this one does) and must be closely connected to the later part of the sentence. In this case, the part of the sentence beginning with *in other words* is an extension of or elaboration upon the first part of the sentence. Choice (B) works. Now the last two choices involve the use of commas. The only time a comma can be used to link two independent clauses is when that comma is accompanied by a coordinating conjunction, such as *and*, *but*, or *so*. Since choice (A) has the comma and coordinating conjunction, it works, leaving only choice (D) as the alternative that is NOT acceptable.

66. **G**   Note the tense of the verbs in the preceding sentence—*were* and *was*. Accordingly, this sentence will have to be in the past tense as well, eliminate (F) and (H). Choice (J) changes the meaning of the sentence, leaving only choice (G).

67. **C**   Determine which preposition goes idiomatically with the word *wrong*. It must be *with*, as in *what was wrong with this program*. Choice (A), (B), and (D) use the incorrect idiom.

68. **J**   Choices (F), (G), and (H) all mean roughly the same thing as *running* in this context. Only choice (J) gives a word that, although somewhat similar to the others, does not work in this context, so choice (J) is the LEAST acceptable alternative.

69. **D**   Since all answer choices are trying to say roughly the same thing, start with the most concise, choice (D). It works well in the sentence, and as you go through the others, you'll find that they either change the meaning of the sentence, as in choice (B), or do not make logical sense, as in choices (A) and (C).

70. **F** As in question 69, since all answer choices are trying to say roughly the same thing, start with the most concise, choice (F). The meaning in the sentence as written is clear, and the ideas presented are complete. As you go through the others, you'll find they either change the meaning of the sentence, as in choices (H) and (J), or do not make logical sense, as in choice (G).

71. **B** The sentence cannot remain where it is, because it makes the word *these* in Sentence 5 ambiguous, so you can eliminate choice (A). Sentences 5, 6, and 7 seem to form a unit—primarily as a discussion of the mechanics of running the program, not any of the difficulties posed by the residents, so you can eliminate choices (C) and (D). If you place the sentence after Sentence 1, you'll see it becomes an answer to the rhetorical question posed in Sentence 1 and leads in to what is discussed in Sentence 2.

72. **G** While choice (F) is probably the best substitute for the underlined portion, your task in this question is to find the worst. Choices (H) and (J) preserve the meaning of the sentence. Only choice (G) introduces the word *they've* and makes the sentence a run-on. Accordingly, choice (G) is NOT an acceptable alternative.

73. **B** First, determine the tense of the sentence. The phrase *during the Blue Bag program* indicates that the verb will have to be past tense, eliminate choice (C). Now determine the subject of the sentence. Although *centers* is right next to the verb, the subject of this sentence is actually *trip*, a singular subject which will require a singular verb. Only choice (B) can work.

74. **J** The writer says he had to go to other centers that were less full, suggesting that this recycling center was extremely full. Choices (F), (G), and (H) all suggest that there were few or no recyclables at these centers. Only choice (J) suggests that the recycling centers were full.

75. **C** The sentence as written uses the possessive pronoun *whose*, creating a sentence fragment, and choice (D) cannot work because the sentence explicitly refers to people. In this case, you need the subject *who*, as in *many of us who hope that…*, instead of the object *whom*.

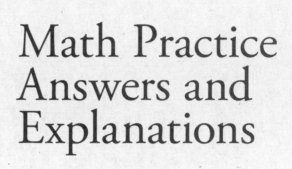

Math Practice
Answers and
Explanations

MATH PRACTICE 1 ANSWERS

1.	B		48.	H
2.	J		49.	E
3.	E		50.	K
4.	G		51.	A
5.	C		52.	J
6.	H		53.	A
7.	A		54.	K
8.	K		55.	A
9.	D		56.	G
10.	G		57.	E
11.	D		58.	J
12.	F		59.	A
13.	E		60.	H
14.	G			
15.	D			
16.	G			
17.	A			
18.	G			
19.	A			
20.	J			
21.	B			
22.	J			
23.	D			
24.	G			
25.	A			
26.	J			
27.	A			
28.	H			
29.	E			
30.	J			
31.	C			
32.	H			
33.	D			
34.	H			
35.	B			
36.	G			
37.	D			
38.	F			
39.	E			
40.	H			
41.	E			
42.	F			
43.	E			
44.	G			
45.	D			
46.	J			
47.	C			

MATH PRACTICE 1 EXPLANATIONS

1. **B** The magician receives 4($120) + 3($25) = $555 in payment for performances and light shows, leaving $635 – $555 = $80 in payment for additional goodie bags. Since each costs $2.50, she provides $\frac{80}{2.5} = 32$ bags. Choice (A) calculates all 4.75 hours worked at the $120 rate. Choice (C) divides the $120 and $2.50 from the problem without answering the question and choice (D) miscalculates based on three performances instead of four. Choice (E) assumes the entire $635 is for additional goodie bag payment.

2. **J** Subtract the number of miles run at or faster than marathon pace during 2004 from the number of total miles run in 2004. 4,982 – 1,150 = 3,832 .

3. **E** 60 seconds is 1 minute. There are 60 minutes in 1 hour, so there are 60 × 24 = 1,440 minutes in 24 hours.

4. **G** The total pages read by the student equals the number of pages read per day times the number of days at each rate. $(a \times d) + (b \times 2d) = ad + 2bd$. Choice (F) omits the d in the second term and choice (H) applies the 2 to both terms. Choice (J) drops the addition sign between the terms. Choice (K) multiplies the two terms instead of adding them.

5. **C** To find the area of the trapezoid, split it into a rectangle with dimensions of 12 and 6 and a triangle with a height of 12 and a base of 5, then add the areas of the two smaller shapes: $(6)(12) + \frac{1}{2}(5)(12) = 72 + 30 = 102$. Choice (B) gives only the area of the rectangular portion and choice (A) gives the perimeter of the whole figure. Choice (E) doubles the area. Choice (D) finds the hypotenuse of the triangle and multiplies it by the height of the triangle.

6. **H** Estimating should help you eliminate choices (F), (J), and (K). Find the mean (or average) of the first five months by finding the total number of visitors and dividing by 5: (200 + 300 + 200 + 350 + 200) ÷ 5 = 1,250 ÷ 5 = 250. Now try out the answer choices and see which one gives a six-month average equal to 250. Choice (F) doesn't work because you need to divide the total by 6 this time. Choice (G) is the mode. Choice (H) gives you 1,500 ÷ 6 = 250. Choice (J) is double what it should be. Choice (K) is the total of the first five months.

7. **A** Substitute 3 seconds into the equation $f = 60(3) – 17(3)^2$ and solve. $f = 180 – 153 = 27$ feet.

8. **K** To find the test-score range for each student, subtract the highest test score from the lowest. Emily's score range is 89 – 70 = 19 points. The range for Cleo's and David's scores are 18 points each, and Alicia's score range is 17 points. Brandon's score range is 12 points.

9. **D** Subtract Craig's and Chris's fish to determine how many fish Nita catches. For Chris, 45% of 300 = .45 × 300 = 135 fish. 300 – 135 – 25 = 140 fish that Nita catches. $\frac{140}{300} = \frac{7}{15}$

10. **G** Find the value of $g(4)$ and substitute it into the function given for $f(x)$. $g(4) = 3 - \dfrac{4}{2} = 3 - 2 = 1$ and $f(1) = 4(1)^2 = 4$, choice (G). Choice (F) stops at the value of $g(4)$ and choice (K) finds $f(4)$. The other choices make small math errors within each function.

11. **D** Estimate by calculating the area of a 6 × 6 square surrounding the shaded figure, then counting and subtracting the unshaded squares within that 36 unit area: roughly 18 squares. Subtract $36 - 18 = 18$. Answer choice (D) is closest.

12. **F** The slope of the ramp is $6 \div 24 = \dfrac{1}{4}$. The rise is $\dfrac{1}{4}$ of the run, so the rise is $\dfrac{1}{4} \times 62 = 15\dfrac{1}{2}$. Choice (G) uses a slope of $\dfrac{1}{3}$. Choice (H) is $62 - (24 - 6)$. Choice (J) is $62 + (24 - 6)$. Choice (K) is 4×62.

13. **E** Substitute the given values of x and y into the expression and simplify, using the rules of order of operations (PEMDAS). $(-3)^2 + [(2 \times 2) - (2 \times -3)] = 9 + [4 - (-6)] = 9 + (4 + 6) = 19$. Choice (C) drops the second negative sign in the final term, subtracting 6 from 4 instead of adding. Choice (B) subtracts 9 from 10 in the last step instead of adding. Choice (A) negates the value of $2x - 2y$. Choice (D) finds the value of xy in the first term of the expression instead of y^x.

14. **G** Extend lines $\overline{BD}$, $\overline{AE}$ and $\overline{DE}$. Using the rule of 180 for a line, the supplementary angle to $\angle BDE$ measures 105°. The supplementary angle to $\angle DEA$ measures 75°. Since the supplement of $\angle BDE$ equals $\angle DEA$ (and the supplement of $\angle DEA$ equals $\angle BDE$), $\overline{DE}$ is a transversal and $\overline{BD}$ and $\overline{AE}$ are parallel. Eliminate any answer that does not contain II. That leaves choices (G), (J), and (K). Since there is no way to determine the measures of $\angle ABD$ and $\angle BAE$, it cannot be concluded that $\overline{AB}$ and $\overline{DE}$ are parallel. So, eliminate choices (J) and (K).

15. **D** Multiply the price by the number of shirts sold. The price of the shirts will be the original price: $4.10 – the $0.02 discount × the number of discounts (x). The number of shirts sold is the original 95 shirts + 1 shirt for each day the price is reduced: (x). Multiply $(4.10 - 0.02x)(95 + x)$ to get the number of shirts sold on any given day. If you're stuck on a problem like this or if you can't figure out exactly what the answer should be, use process of elimination: you know that the price of the shirts goes down but the number sold goes up. Therefore, you'll want a (–) in your first set of parentheses and a (+) in your second set of them—this allows you to eliminate choices (A) and (C). Then, notice that the $0.02 will be a change in the price, not the number of items sold, so you can eliminate (E). Compare choices (B) and (D) and consider which contains numbers from the problem—in no part of the problem is there a 2, only $0.02, so choice (D) is the best answer choice.

16. **G** To factor $x^2 - 7x + 12$, find two numbers that multiply to +12 and add to –7. Those numbers are –4 and –3. The factored expression is $(x - 4)(x - 3)$.

17. A Substitute the values given for x and y in the equation. $\dfrac{5(2)}{70} + \dfrac{9}{5(5+2)} + \dfrac{1}{5+2} = \dfrac{10}{70} + \dfrac{9}{35} + \dfrac{1}{7}$.

Find a common denominator for all of the fractions by looking at the smallest multiple of 70, 35, and 7. 70 is the smallest denominator. The equation becomes $\dfrac{10}{70} + \dfrac{18}{70} + \dfrac{10}{70} = \dfrac{38}{70} = \dfrac{19}{35}$. If you're not sure how to simplify all of these fractions, plug the values in to your calculator to see that your answer will be roughly 0.543. Check the answer choices against this value to find that choice (A) is the only one that works.

18. G To find the greatest possible product, first determine the largest number of minutes and seconds possible, which is 59:59. After that, the timer will roll over to its maximum value of 60:00. $(5)(9)(5)(9) = 2{,}025$. Choice (F) results from $(5 \times 9) + (5 \times 9)$ and choice (H) takes the product of $(59)(59)$ instead of separating the values into digits first. Choice (J) finds the number of seconds in an hour and choice (K) assumes the largest display to be 99:99 which it cannot be because, as the problem states, this is only a 60-minute timer.

19. A Since you are looking for 2 numbers, one of which is bigger by 6, that add up to 42, set up an equation: $2x + 6 = 42$, and solve for x, which is the lesser of the 2 numbers, 18. If you chose (E), be careful! That's the *greater* of the two numbers and you're looking for the *lesser* of the two numbers.

20. J The area of the square is 324, so each side is 18. Since the two right triangles are isosceles, their respective bases and heights are congruent. For each of the triangles, $A = \dfrac{1}{2}bh = \dfrac{1}{2}(18)(18) = 162$. There are two triangles, so the total area is $162 \times 2 = 324$. Choice (G) gives the area of only one triangle, and choice (K) gives the area of the entire figure. Choice (F) assumes 324 to be the area of the entire figure and divides by three, assuming that the three smaller shapes are equal in area. Choice (H) doubles the value of choice (F).

21. B Since the triangles are similar, set up a proportion: $\dfrac{8}{17} = \dfrac{x}{85}$. So, $x = 40$. Choice (A) is $17 + 8 = 25$. Choice (C) is $85 + 17 = 102$. Choice (D) is $85 + 17 + 8 = 110$. Choice (E) flips one side of the proportion: $\dfrac{8}{17} = \dfrac{85}{x}$.

22. J Rewrite the equation as $(x - 1)(x - 1) = (x - 7)(x - 7)$ and multiply everything out: $x^2 - 2x + 1 = x^2 - 14x + 49$. Subtract x^2 from each side: $-2x + 1 = -14x + 49$. Add $14x$ to each side: $12x + 1 = 49$. Subtract 1 from each side: $12x = 48$. Divide both sides by 12: $x = 4$. If you try the answer choices in the equation, $x = 4$ gives you $(4 - 1)^2 = (4 - 7)^2$. This simplifies to $(3)^2 = (-3)^2$ or $9 = 9$, making the equation true.

23. **D** Draw a horizontal line at point A to split $\angle BAC$ in half, creating two 30°-60°-90° triangles. The y value at point A, which is w, is equal to the y value halfway between points B and C, so the y value at point C is twice as big: $2w$. Eliminate choices (A), (C), and (E), where the y value is not $2w$. The ratio of the sides of a 30°-60°-90° triangle is $1 : \sqrt{3} : 2$ from smallest to largest, so the length of the leg adjacent to the 30° angle is $\sqrt{3}$ times the length of the shorter leg, or $w\sqrt{3}$. Choice (B) neglects to multiply the x value by $\sqrt{3}$.

24. **G** The diagonal of a square makes two triangles with angle measures 45°, 45°, and 90°, and sides in the proportion $x : x : x\sqrt{2}$. Since we know that the hypotenuse of one of the triangles is $4\sqrt{2}$, we know that the legs of that triangle, which are also the sides of the square, measure 4 feet. The area of the square is $\text{side}^2 = 16\,\text{feet}^2$.

25. **A** SOHCAHTOA tells you that $\sin\theta = \dfrac{opposite}{hypotenuse} = \dfrac{15}{x}$. Eliminate choices (B) and (C), which confuse the sides of a right triangle. $\dfrac{\sin\theta}{\cos\theta} = \tan\theta$, so choice (E) can also be eliminated. Choice (D) refers to the angle measure of θ itself, rather than the trigonometric relationship between the sides of the triangle.

26. **J** Since 15 is a whole number, $\sqrt{a}$ will most likely be a whole number, and a a perfect square. Try some perfect squares to see which yields 15 in the equation. $\sqrt{45 + 36} + \sqrt{36} = \sqrt{81} + 6 = 9 + 6 = 15$.

27. **A** Use the Pythagorean theorem to find the length of $\overline{EF}$. The midpoints cut each side of the rectangle in half, so $AF = 6$ and $AE = 8$. Right triangle AFE, then, is a 6:8:10 triangle, and $EF = 10$. FG is also 10, and the perimeter of the pentagon is $10 + 10 + 8 + 12 + 8 = 48$ inches. Choice (B) is the perimeter of the rectangle. Choice (C) is the area of a triangle with the same base and height as the rectangle. Choices (D) and (E) are the areas of the pentagon and rectangle, respectively.

28. **H** In 2004, there were 60 million female workers age 16 or over and there were 130.9 million total such workers. The percent of the workers who are female is found by $\dfrac{60}{130.9} \times 100 \approx 46\%$.

29. **E** Since the chart shows that 8.4% of the workers took *public transportation*, the degree measure of the central angle for the "Public" sector must also be 8.4% of the 360° in a circle: $\dfrac{8.4}{100} \times 360 \approx 30°$. Choice (A) is the percent of workers who took public transportation in 2006. Choice (B) is the measure of the central angle for the workers who walked in 2006. Choice (D) is the central angle that would result from using the public transportation percentage from 2004.

30. J In 2006, there were 63.6 million female workers. In 2004, there were 60.0 million female workers. The total growth was 3.6 million. The growth happened over a 2-year period so the average growth per year is 3.6 ÷ 2 = 1.8 million female workers per year. Choice (F) is the difference between the number of female workers in 2004 and 2005 divided by 2. Choice (G) is the result of dividing 3.6 by 4 years rather than 2 years. Choice (H) is the average growth in the number of male workers between 2005 and 2006. Choice (K) is the difference between the number of female workers in 2004 and 2006.

31. C To solve, enter the data into the given equation and solve using a common denominator. $\frac{1}{20}+\frac{1}{60}=\frac{3}{60}+\frac{1}{60}=\frac{4}{60}=\frac{1}{15}$, so T_c, the combined time, is 15 minutes. Choice (A) divides the two numbers given while choice (E) finds their average. Choices (B) and (D) make calculation errors. Choice (E) is also unreasonable because the combined time must be less than the time of either hose working alone.

32. H The numbers 2, 3, and 5 are prime, while 6 and 4 are not. The probability that the die will NOT land on a prime number is 2 non-prime numbers out of 5 total numbers, or $\frac{2}{5}$. If you picked choice (G), you left out the NOT.

33. D Find y by substituting $x = 3$: $y = \left(\frac{5}{3}\right)^2 = \frac{25}{9}$. Now find the value of $7x + 9y$: $7 \times 3 + 9 \times \frac{25}{9} = 21 + 25 = 46$. If you chose (A) or (B), you may have forgotten to square the fraction or to multiply it by 9. Choice (C) comes from not squaring the $\frac{5}{3}$. Choice (E) comes from squaring only the 5 in the numerator.

34. H Sketch a graph of points (0,0), (4,0) and (4,4). You'll notice that the fourth point of the square is at (0,4). Since you need to find a diagonal, draw a line from (0,0) to (4,4), and notice you now have two 45°-45°-90° triangles, with the square's sides as their legs and the diagonal as their hypotenuse. The hypotenuse will be the length the question asks for, and you can use the Pythagorean theorem to find it: $a^2+b^2=c^2$; $(4)^2+(4)^2=c^2$, $c=4\sqrt{2}$. If you chose (G), you selected the length of a side of the square, not one of its diagonals. If you chose either (J) or (K), you may have been using the ratio of sides in a 30-60-90 triangle rather than that of a 45-45-90 triangle.

35. B The question is asking, *4 raised to the 3rd power = ?* $4 \times 4 \times 4 = 64$.

36. G An easy way to do this problem is to test each answer choice to find the pair of numbers that satisfies the given equation. For choice (G), $y = 18 - 0.2(1) = 17.8$ or 0.2 quarts of water have boiled away. None of the remaining answers makes the provided equation true.

37. **D** The second figure shows that the small and large diameters of the coffee cup are 4 and 6 respectively, so the radii are 2 and 3. Plugging the numbers into the equation given, $V = \frac{1}{3}\pi 5.5(3^2 + 2^2 + 3 \cdot 2) = \frac{1}{3}\pi 5.5(19) \approx 109$. Choice (A) is the portion of the equation inside the parentheses and choice (C) neglects to multiply by $\frac{1}{3}\pi$. Choice (B) uses a height of $\frac{5}{2}$ instead of $5\frac{1}{2}$, or 5.5. Choice (E) plugs the diameters into the equation instead of the radii.

38. **F** Simplify the right side of the equation: $3(3x+4) = 9x + 12$. What can x be in the equation $9x + 12 = 9x + 12$? Any real number.

39. **E** First, figure out $\dfrac{\frac{3}{4}}{\frac{3}{4}-\frac{2}{3}}$: the big fraction bar means division, so this is $\frac{3}{4} \div \left(\frac{3}{4} - \frac{2}{3}\right)$. To subtract $\frac{3}{4}$ and $\frac{2}{3}$, get a common denominator of 12: $\frac{9}{12} - \frac{8}{12} = \frac{1}{12}$. Now you have $\frac{3}{4} \div \frac{1}{12}$, but you divide fractions by flipping the fraction on the right and multiplying, so this becomes $\frac{3}{4} \times \frac{12}{1}$. This is $\frac{36}{4}$ or 9. Now combine the three remaining fractions: $\frac{9}{12} - \frac{8}{12} + \frac{6}{12} = \frac{7}{12}$. You now have $9 \div \frac{7}{12}$, which becomes $9 \times \frac{12}{7} = \frac{108}{7}$. If you chose one of the other answers, be careful—watch your order of operations, and be careful putting these fractions into your calculator.

40. **H** To find the area of the shaded empty space, you must first find its radius. Since the width of the bagel from the center to the edge is 56 mm, the width, or diameter, of the space, is the total diameter of the cross-section minus the width of the bagel itself on both sides. $144 - 2(56) = 32$. The radius of a circle is half its diameter, so $r = 16$ mm. $Area = \pi r^2 = \pi (16)^2 \approx 800$. Choice (J) calculates the area using the diameter of 32 instead of the radius. Choice (K) finds the area of the entire bagel including the shaded space. Choice (F) finds the circumference of the shaded space, and choice (G) finds the outer circumference of the bagel.

41. **E** Any non-zero number raised to the 0 power $= 1$. So $a^0 = 1$, $b^0 = 1$, and $c^0 = 1$. $1 + 1 + 1 = 3$.

42. **F** Use SOHCAHTOA: $\tan = \dfrac{opposite}{adjacent}$. For each of the angles, the opposite side is AB. Since AB is constant for each angle, the length of the adjacent side is all that matters when determining which angle has the greatest tangent value. The angle with the shortest adjacent side, $\angle BEA$, has the greatest tangent.

43. **E** The y-intercept of a graph is the point where the graph meets up with (intercepts) the vertical (y) axis. This graph meets up with the y-axis at point $(0,1)$. Choices (B) and (D) are the two x-intercepts of the graph. Choices (A) and (C) do not lie on either axis.

44. **G** This graph is symmetrical with a vertex at point X. The squared term of a quadratic equation gives it the smooth curve about the vertex. If you have a graphing calculator, you can enter a simple quadratic equation like $y = x^2$ to confirm your choice. Choice (F) would require a wave-like graph and choice (H) would form a graph with a sharp V shape. Cubic functions, as in choice (J), do not create symmetrical graphs. Choice (K) refers to a function that is a straight line, which this is clearly not.

45. **D** To reflect a graph over the line $y = x$, switch the x and y coordinates of each point on the graph. For this graph, Point $V (-2, 1)$ becomes $(1, -2)$ and point $Z (0, 1)$ becomes $(1, 0)$. Eliminate any graph that does not include these three points. Note that point $X (-1, -1)$ remains the same. You can also visualize the reflection by drawing the line $y = x$ on the graph and imagine folding the paper along that line. Where the graph meets the other half of the page is where the reflection will be. Choice (A) reflects the graph across the x-axis and choice (C) reflects it across the y-axis. Choice (B) shifts the graph up two places. Choice (E) moves the vertex to $(1, 1)$.

46. **J** Factor 32 and 45. 32 has factors 32, 16, 8, 4, 2, and 1. 45 has factors 45, 15, 9, 5, 3, and 1. Answer choice (F) is 32×45, (G) is 32×9, (H) is 16×5, (K) is 1×1, and (J) cannot be made by multiplying 1 number from the set of factors of 32 by 1 number in the set of factors of 45.

47. **C** $17_o = 15 + 13 + 11 + 9 + 7 + 5 + 3 + 1 = 64$ and $4_o = 3 + 1 = 4$. So $17_o \times 4_o = 64 \times 4 = 256$. Choice (A) is $17_o \div 4_o$. Choice (B) is 72×2; this would be correct if you were adding all *even* integers less than k, instead of the odd ones. Choice (D) is 81×4; this would be correct if the problem said "less than or equal to k." Choice (E) is 136×6; this would be correct if you were adding *all* integers less than k, not just the odd ones.

48. **H** There's no need to graph the equation or to put it into $y = mx + b$ form. Substitute a into the equation for x and -3 into the equation for y. So, $a - 4(-3) = 14$ or $a + 12 = 14$. So, $a = 2$. Choice (F) is the result of substituting a for y and -3 for x. Choice (K) is the result of a sign error when substituting to get $a - 12 = 14$.

49. **E** Substitute values to see what happens as t grows larger. When $t = 2, \dfrac{2^2 - 1}{2 - 1} - 2 = 1$. When $t = 3, \dfrac{3^2 - 1}{3 - 1} - 3 = 1$. Even when $t = 1,000, \dfrac{1,000^2 - 1}{1,000 - 1} - 1,000 = 1$. Choices (A), (B), (C), and (D) mirror terms from the question but do not accurately describe what happens as t changes. If you work this problem algebraically, it will give you the same result: $f(t) = \dfrac{t^2 - 1}{t - 1} - t = \dfrac{(t - 1)(t + 1)}{(t - 1)} - t = (t + 1) - t = 1$.

50. **K** Since there are 180° in a straight line, the sum of the two angle measures must be equal to 180. $(3x + 2) + (x + 28) = 180$. Simplify the equation: $4x + 30 = 180$, $4x = 150$, $x = 37\dfrac{1}{2}$. To find the measure of $\angle YXZ$, substitute $37\dfrac{1}{2}$ for x in the expression $3x + 2$, and solve. If you picked choice (G), make sure you read the question more carefully.

51. **A** Use the formula for the slope of a line, $m = \dfrac{y_1 - y_2}{x_1 - x_2}$. You can start with either point, so long as you start with the same point in both the numerator and denominator. In this case, $m = \dfrac{10 - (-2)}{3 - 2} = \dfrac{10 + 2}{1} = \dfrac{12}{1} = 12$. Watch your signs and remember to put the y values on top. Slope measures how steep something is; how quickly the height rises. Choice (C) reverses the x and y values. Choice (E) confuses signs when dividing. Choices (B) and (D) confuse signs in calculating the numerator.

52. **J** One radian $= \dfrac{180°}{\pi}$, or $180° = \pi$ radians. Multiply $\dfrac{7\pi}{15}$ radians $= \dfrac{7(180°)}{15} = 84°$.

53. **A** The equation of a circle with center (h,k) and radius r is defined as $(x - h)^2 + (y - k)^2 = r^2$. Here, $h = 4$ and $k = -8$. Eliminate choices (C), (D), and (E), which all flip the values of h and k. To find the radius, use the circumference 10π given in the problem. $C = \pi d = 10\pi$, so the diameter is 10. The radius is half of that, or 5, so to complete the equation, $r^2 = 25$. Choice (B) squares the diameter instead of the radius.

54. **K** Choose values for x and y that make $xy = -x^2$ true. For example, $x = 2$ and $y = -2$. Choices (F), (G), (H), and (J) are all true with these numbers. However, choice (K) is false because $(2)^3 - (-2)^3 = 16$.

55. **A** Compare the points of the original rectangle with the first matrix to see that the x values of A, B, C, and D run along the top row and their y values run along the bottom row. For the translated rectangle $ABCD$, plot the points you know: $B(3, -3)$, $C(-2, -6)$, and $D(-4, -3)$. When you've got those points, note the relationship between them. In your figure, it should be clear that the distance from point C to point D will be the same as the distance from point B to point A. From C to D, the point shifts to the left 2 and up 3. Now do the same thing to point B to get $A(1, 0)$ and $n = 0$, choice (A). Choices (B), (C), (D), and (E) are in the range of numbers of the problem, but do not translate properly.

56. **G** Start from the output 0. Since a CHANGE function needs to have input 1 to get output 0, the output of the IF function needs to be a 1. A 1 is the output of an IF function either if the first input is 1 and the second input is 1, or if the first input is 0 and the third input is 1. The first input could be 1 if both p and q are 1; however, no answer choices contain p and q values which are both 1. Therefore, p and q could be either 0 and 1, or 1 and 0, or 0 and 0, to yield an output of 0. This doesn't narrow any answer choices. Since you know that the first input of the IF function is 0, the second input could be either 1 or 0, so the input of the next CHANGE function doesn't matter. s and t, however, must both be 1, since the output of the BOTH function must be a 1 in order to make the third term in the IF function a 1. Answer choice (G) is the only answer choice that has s and t both as 1.

57. **E** To solve this equation, you'll need to remove the absolute value signs. Remember, since absolute value means only the "positive distance from 0," the value inside the absolute value signs can be either positive or negative. To solve $|x - a| \le 3$, therefore, remember that when you remove the absolute value sign, this becomes two separate inequalities: $x - a \le 3$ and $x - a \ge -3$. Don't forget to flip the inequality sign in the second equation when you introduce the negative! These expressions simplify to $x \le a + 3$ and $x \ge a - 3$. Combine these two equations to get $a - 3 \le x \le a + 3$, which is represented in choice (E).

58. **J** First, scientific notation requires that the first term be a number less than 10. (F), (G), and (H) are out. Multiply the terms in the given expression: $30 \times 10^{x+y} = 3.0 \times 10^{x+y+1}$. Remember that when you multiply exponents with the same bases the base remains the same and the exponents are added together. The exponent 1 is added because 10 is being multiplied by itself one more time, to make up for taking a factor of 10 out of 30.

59. **A** The midpoint of a line segment divides that line segment in half; therefore, if the length of $\overline{QR}$ is x, the length of $\overline{QS}$ is $2x$. The question also states that the midpoint of $\overline{PS}$ is Q, so $\overline{PQ} = \overline{QS}$. Substitute for the lengths to get $4x - 16 = 2x$. ($4x - 16$ is given in the problem as the length of $\overline{PQ}$.) Solving for x, you get $2x = 16$, or $x = 8$. The length of $\overline{PS}$ is $x + x + 4x - 16 = 8 + 8 + 32 - 16 = 32$. To understand this problem, draw a straight line, mark points P, Q, R, and S along it, and label the lengths as you find them. Choice (D) gives the value of x, not the length of $\overline{PS}$. Choice (C) finds the length of $4x - 16$. Choice (B) miscalculates x to be 4, and choice (E) is the value of the miscalculated x.

60. **H** Find the radius of the circle using the area formula: $A = \pi r^2$. So, $64\pi = \pi r^2$ and $r = 8$. To find the length of a minor arc, first find the circumference of the circle: $C = 2\pi r = 2\pi(8) = 16\pi$. The minor arc is $\dfrac{24}{360} = \dfrac{1}{15}$ of the circumference of the circle. So, the length of the minor arc is $\overset{\frown}{CD} = \left(\dfrac{1}{15}\right)(16\pi) = \dfrac{16}{15}\pi$. Choice (F) attempts to use the radius of the circle, 8, to find the fractional part of the circle. Choice (G) is similar to (F) but uses half of the radius. Choice (J) is the area divided by the central angle. Choice (K) is the radius multiplied by the central angle.

MATH PRACTICE 2 ANSWERS

1.	E	48.	H
2.	H	49.	B
3.	D	50.	H
4.	K	51.	D
5.	D	52.	J
6.	H	53.	D
7.	E	54.	F
8.	J	55.	C
9.	C	56.	K
10.	F	57.	C
11.	B	58.	K
12.	H	59.	C
13.	A	60.	K
14.	F		
15.	C		
16.	H		
17.	D		
18.	F		
19.	E		
20.	F		
21.	B		
22.	G		
23.	E		
24.	K		
25.	B		
26.	K		
27.	D		
28.	G		
29.	E		
30.	J		
31.	C		
32.	G		
33.	D		
34.	H		
35.	C		
36.	F		
37.	C		
38.	J		
39.	B		
40.	J		
41.	C		
42.	J		
43.	C		
44.	J		
45.	A		
46.	K		
47.	D		

MATH PRACTICE 2 EXPLANATIONS

1. **E** Simplify the expression by taking a factor of 2 out of each term. The distributive property guarantees that $2(a + 2b + 3c) = 2a + 4b + 6c$.

2. **H** "The square of the product" means you must multiply a by b before squaring the result. Choice (H) is the only choice that represents this. If you chose (G), be careful—by the order of operations, in ab^2, the b will be squared before it is multiplied together with a, thus precluding the "product of a and b."

3. **D** In order to get the total distance traveled, subtract the original mileage from the final mileage to find a difference of 18,130 km – 16,450 km = 1,680 km. Then, divide the change in mileage over the number of hours traveled to get the average driving speed during that week. 1,680 km ÷ 30 hr = 56 km/hr.

4. **K** To solve, use the formula: *Volume = length × width × height*. Here, our dimensions are 12 by 3 by 3, so the volume is $12 \times 3 \times 3$, which equals 108. Choice (F) is the sum of the three dimensions. Choice (G) is the area of one of the sides. Choices (H) and (J) are the results of adding two of the sides before you multiply.

5. **D** $3^4 = 81$, so $x = 4$. Plug $x = 4$ into the given expression to get $3 \times 2^4 = 3 \times 16 = 48$. Choice (B) gives one 2^4, and choice (C) miscalculates x as 3. Choices (A) and (E) are distracting numbers from the problem and do not answer the question.

6. **H** The ratio of folk songs to rock songs is 3 to 11, which means that for every 3 folk songs, there are 11 rock songs. Hence, there are more rock songs on the mp3 player than folk songs. I is true, which eliminates choices (G) and (J). II is also true, which eliminates choice (F). Ratios compare parts to parts, however, not parts to wholes as do fractions. The fraction of the songs that are folk songs is actually $\frac{3}{3+11} = \frac{3}{14}$. So, III is false. Eliminate choice (K).

7. **E** Subtract $5\frac{1}{9}$ gallons – $3\frac{1}{3}$ gallons. Convert each mixed number into a fraction: The equation becomes $\frac{9 \times 5 + 1}{9} - \frac{3 \times 3 + 1}{3} = \frac{46}{9} - \frac{10}{3}$. To subtract, both fractions need to have common denominators, so make $\frac{10}{3}$ into $\frac{30}{9}$. $\frac{46}{9} - \frac{30}{9} = \frac{16}{9} = 1\frac{7}{9}$.

8. **J** The point of intersection represents the midpoint between points F and H. You can use the midpoint formula, $\left(\dfrac{x_1 + x_2}{2}, \dfrac{y_1 + y_2}{2}\right)$ to determine the coordinates of point H. Solving for the x-coordinate gives $\left(\dfrac{-7 + x_2}{2} = -2\right)$. The x-coordinate of point H equals 3, eliminating choices (F), (G), and (K). Solving for the y-coordinate gives $\left(\dfrac{-2 + y_2}{2} = -4\right)$. The y-coordinate of point H equals –6, eliminating choice (H).

9. **C** First, factor out the numerator to get $\dfrac{9(x+5)}{9}$. The nines cancel out, and the $x + 5$ remains. Choices (A) and (B) divide only one of the terms in the numerator by the denominator. Choice (D) adds the integers in the numerator to get $\dfrac{54x}{9} = 6x$.

10. **F** To solve this question, remember to follow the order of operations. First, distribute the $-6f$ to the $(5f + 3g)$ and get $-30f^2 - 18fg$. Now simplify $23fg - 30f^2 - 18fg$ and get $5fg - 30f^2$. Choice (G) is the result of adding $5f$ and $3g$ and then distributing the 6. Choice (J) is the result of adding $23fg$ and $18fg$ instead of subtracting. Choice (K) is the result of switching the signs.

11. **B** Set a variable for the number of pints of strawberries, which is equal to the number of quarts. The number of pints at \$3 each plus the number of quarts at \$5 each is equal to the total of \$120, so you can write an equation: $3x + 5x = 120$. Solve for x to find that $8x = 120$ and $x = 15$. Choice (E) gives the total sales in dollars of the pints of strawberries. Choice (C) assumes all sales were at \$5, and choice (D) assumes all the sales were at \$3. Choice (A) makes a calculation error in solving for x. You can also test the answer choices to see which fits the requirements of the problem. When there are 12 pints sold at \$3, there are also 12 quarts sold at \$5: $12(3) + 12(5) = 120$.

12. **H** The formula for the area of a rectangle is $A = lw$. So, the actual area of the cloth is $A = (6)(1.5) = 9$ ft². To find the percent *greater* for the estimate use the percent change formula: $\%change = \dfrac{difference}{original} \times 100$. So, $\%change = \dfrac{12 - 9}{9} \times 100 \approx 33\%$. If you chose (F), be careful—you may have calculated what percent of 12 is 9. If you chose (J), you may have found the percent change from 12 to 9, rather than the percent change from 9 to 12.

13. **A** Use the definition provided by the problem: $\sqrt[3]{2 \times 4 \times 27} = \sqrt[3]{216} = 6$. Choice (B) is the arithmetic mean or average of the three numbers. Choice (C) is $27 - 4 - 2$. Choice (D) is the product of the three numbers, 216, divided by 3 rather than the cube root of the product. Choice (E) is the product of the three numbers.

14. **F** Plug the given values for p and q into the equation. $q = \dfrac{(80)^2}{50} = \dfrac{6,400}{50} = 128$ questions.

15. **C** You can eliminate choices (A) and (B) immediately because these are not binomial expressions. The fastest way to do this problem is to factor the quadratic equation $x^2 + 2x - 15 = (x + 5)(x - 3)$; thus, the other binomial will be $(x - 3)$. If you're not sure how to factor, FOIL the answer choices with $(x + 5)$ and see which gives you the quadratic expression from the problem. When you multiply $(x + 5)$ by choice (C), $(x - 3)$, you find it equals $x^2 + 2x - 15$. Eliminate choices (D) and (E).

16. **H** The equation for production cost is $P(x) = 175x + 150{,}000$. After plugging in 465,000 for $P(x)$, solve for x. First subtract 150,000 and then divide by 175 to obtain 1,800 for $x = 1{,}800$ computers. If you chose (K), be careful—you may have added 150,000 + 465,000 rather than subtracting 465,000 − 150,000.

17. **D** To solve this question, substitute the value of x, in this case $\frac{1}{3}$, wherever x is in the equation. This results in $\dfrac{(\frac{1}{3})^2 + \frac{7}{9}}{(\frac{1}{3})^3 + \frac{11}{27}}$ which equals 2. Choice (A) is the result of multiplying the terms instead of dividing. Choice (B) is the result of dividing the $\frac{7}{9}$ by $\frac{11}{27}$ and ignoring the x terms. Choices (C) and (E) are the results of calculation mistakes.

18. **F** Hannah is 5 years younger than Nora, so she is $x - 5$ years old. To find her age in 2 years, add two to this term. $x - 5 + 2 = x - 3$. The other answer choices all make calculation errors in simplifying this expression.

19. **E** The formula for the area of a rectangle is $A = lw$. This rectangle has a length of x, a width of $5x$, and an area of 320. So, $320 = (x)(5x) = 5x^2$. Therefore, the length is 8, the width is 40, and the perimeter is $2 \times (8 + 40) = 96$. Choice (A) is the length of the rectangle. Choice (B) is the width of the rectangle. Choice (C) is the sum of the length and the width. Choice (D) is the area divided by 5.

20. **F** $\angle ACD \cong \angle ADC$, so their supplements, $\angle ACB$ and $\angle ADE$, are also congruent. Since the question tells you that $\angle BAC \cong \angle DAE$, you can see that all three angles in triangles ABC and AED are congruent to one another. Similar triangles are defined as triangles that have three congruent angles and three proportional sides. Because all the angles in these two triangles are congruent, you can determine that $\triangle ABC$ is similar to $\triangle AED$, choice (F). Because $\angle ACD \cong \angle ADC$, you know that $\overline{AC} \cong \overline{AD}$, but you cannot conclude anything about the relationship of either of these sides to $\overline{AB}$. You don't have enough information to compare $\triangle ACD$ and $\triangle ADE$, eliminating choices (G) and (J). You do not know the measure of $\angle CAD$, eliminating choice (K).

21. **B** If an exponent is a fraction, raise the base to the value of the numerator and use the value of the denominator to take the root of the base. Take these steps one at a time in either order. First take $8^1 = 8$, then take $\sqrt[4]{8}$.

22. **G** The graph tells you that admission plus five events costs $90. If you subtract the $30 admission fee from $90, you are left with $60 as the total cost for 5 events. If you divide $60 by 5, you will see that the cost of one event is $12, choice (G).

23. **E** If $16\sqrt{3}$ is the measurement of the longer leg, that means that it is opposite to the 60° angle. Using 30-60-90 triangles, we know that the side opposite to the 30° angle is 16, and so the hypotenuse is double that, which is 32 centimeters. Choices (B) and (D) confuse this triangle with a 45-45-90 triangle. And choice (C) finds the length of the shorter leg, not the hypotenuse.

24. **K** The smallest consecutive odd integers greater than 15 are 17, 19, 21, 23, and 25. These five integers add up to 105. Choice (F) is the product of 5 and 15. Choice (G) is the sum of the smallest consecutive integers, including the evens. Choice (H) includes 15. Choice (J) is the sum of the five smallest consecutive even integers.

25. **B** Use SOHCAHTOA. You are looking for the side adjacent to the 43° angle and you know the hypotenuse, so use $C = \dfrac{A}{H}$. $\cos 43° = \dfrac{?}{25}$. Multiply both sides of the equation by 25 to get $? = 25 \cos 43°$. Notice you don't even have to solve any further than this. The other answer choices use the wrong trigonometric functions.

26. **K** Since $x - 15 = |-5|$ is equivalent to $x - 15 = 5$, then $x = 20$. Choice (H) is the result of solving the equation $x - 15 = -5$ and attempting to divide both sides by -15. Choice (J) results from solving the equation $x - 15 = -5$.

27.   **D**   Let x equal the number of blueberry packages, and let y equal the number of strawberry packages. Construct two equations to solve: $x + y = 9$, which says that the total number of packages is nine, and $4x + 6y = 40$, which says that the total price is $40. Solve using a system of equations.

Multiply the first equation by 4 to get $4x + 4y = 36$. Subtract the second equation from the result

$$\begin{aligned} 4x + 6y &= 40 \\ - \ \ 4x + 4y &= 36 \\ \hline 2y &= 4 \end{aligned}$$. So, $y = 2$. But this represents the number of strawberry packages. There are nine

packages total, so there must be 7 blueberry packages. Be careful with choice (A)—it represents the number of strawberry packages. If you chose choice (B), you probably added 6 and 4 in the second equation to get $10x = 40$.

28.   **G**   To solve this question, remember that the sum of the interior angles of a triangle is 180°; therefore $a + b + 45 = 180$ and $c + d + 45 = 180$. Thus, since $a + b + c + d + 90 = 360$, $a + b + c + d = 270$. Choice (F) is the difference of 360 and 45. Choice (H) is the sum of 180 and 45. Choice (J) is the sum of either a and b or c and d.

29.   **E** $\triangle ACE$ is isosceles with base $\overline{AE}$, so $\angle CAE \cong \angle AEC$. Since both angles are bisected, the four smaller angles created are all congruent: $\angle CAD \cong \angle DAE \cong \angle AEB \cong \angle BEC$. Choice (E) compares two of these congruent angles. Choices (A) and (B) compare one of the triangle's angles to one of the bisected angles, which are half as large. Choices (C) and (D) compare the bisected angles with the third side of the isosceles triangle, a relationship it is impossible to know without any actual angle measures.

30.   **J**   To find the area of a trapezoid, multiply the average of the bases by the height. The formula for the area of a trapezoid is $A = \dfrac{(b_1 + b_2)}{2} \times h$. Plugging in the values given, find $A = \dfrac{(3 + 9)}{2} \times 6 = 36$.

31.   **C**   You can eliminate answer choices by substituting the number of years after 2001 for x. If you substitute 3 for x, you should get approximately 547 because 3 years after 2001, in 2004, there were 547,000 book club members. Choice (C) gives $\dfrac{8}{3}(3) + 539 = 547$, eliminating choices (A), (B), (D), and (E). Note that these choices all confuse years with actual values in the problem (the year 2001 becomes 2,001 in choices (A), (B), and (E), for example)—make sure you are reading carefully and not falling into these traps.

32. G From 1997 to 1998 the percent of U.S. citizens who had consumed the soda rose from 57.8% to 58.2%, 58.2 – 57.8 = 0.4%, which is the smallest increase among the years listed. If you picked choice (J), be careful—(J) gives the LARGEST increase. You're looking for the smallest.

33. D Look at the graph. Line D roughly approximates the scatterplot, beginning and ending at the same values. Thus, Line D most closely matches what would be the ideal average line of the scatterplot data. Line E is completely above the scatterplot, and Line C is completely below it. Lines A and B don't come close to matching the diagonal scatterplot line.

34. H The table states that by 2002 63.4% of all U.S. soda consumers had consumed the brand-name soda. Set up an equation: 63.4% of the total number of U.S. soda consumers = 74,672,120 U.S. citizens who had consumed the brand-name soda. Round the numbers since the question asks for an approximate answer: $.634 \times x = 74{,}672{,}120$, $\dfrac{75{,}000{,}000}{.63} = 119{,}000{,}000$ people.

35. C You may be familiar with this format, known as scientific notation, from your science classes, but you don't need to understand scientific notation to be able to complete this problem. All you need to know is that $10^5 = 100{,}000$ and $0.0001 = 10^{-4}$. Therefore, the full expression looks like this: $\dfrac{(y \times 10^5)(z \times 10^{-4})}{(y \times 10^5)(z \times 10^{-4})} = 1$.

36. F To solve this equation use the slope-intercept formula: $y = mx + b$. To find the slope, use the two points that you know: $(-1, 3)$ and $(2, -21)$. $\dfrac{-21 - (3)}{2 - (-1)} = -8$; thus the slope is -8. Now put the slope into the value for m and get $y = -8(x) + b$. Now, plug one of the points, say $(-1, 3)$, into the equation and get $3 = -8(-1) + b$, which reduces to $b = -5$. Another way to find the y-intercept is even easier: just look on the graph. The graph clearly shows that line h crosses the y-axis at $(0, -5)$. So either way, the equation for h is $y = -8x - 5$. Choice (G) is using the wrong y-intercept. Choices (H), (J), and (K) miscalculated the slope.

37. C To change 2.25π radians into degrees, multiply by $\dfrac{180}{\pi}$ to get $405°$. Choices (A) and (B) are fractions of 405. Choices (C) and (E) are multiples.

38. J Calculate the area of the triangular sail using the formula for the area of a triangle: $A = \dfrac{1}{2}$ (base)(height). Area = $\dfrac{1}{2}$ (50ft)(120ft) = $3{,}000\,\text{ft}^2$. Divide $\dfrac{3{,}000}{150}$ to find the number of 150 square foot pieces of material required = 20 pieces. Multiply 20 pieces × \$8.99 per piece = \$179.80 ≈ \$180.00. Don't be distracted by the *in any quantity* part of this question—the numbers divide evenly.

39. B This triangular sail happens to be a version of a 5-12-13 right triangle. If you had the dimensions of this triangle memorized already you would know that the hypotenuse must be 130 feet long. 130 + 120 + 50 = 300 feet. You also could have used the Pythagorean theorem: $a^2 + b^2 = c^2$, where a and b are the two legs of the triangle and c is the hypotenuse.

40. J Since the 10° angle is across from the 120-foot side and adjacent to the 50-foot side, you can use

$\tan 10° = \dfrac{\text{Opposite side}}{\text{Adjacent side}}$. The problem states that $\tan 10° \approx .18$, so substitute this value for $\tan 10°$.

$0.18 = \dfrac{120 - x}{50}$. Subtract x, which is the value by which the 120-foot side will be shortened, from

120 feet, and divide by the adjacent side, 50 feet. Solve the equation: $9 = 120 - x$, $x = 111$ feet . If

you chose choices (F) or (G), you may have found only a partial answer—make sure you read the

problem closely and complete all its steps.

41. C Since all the rectangles are congruent, you can find some relationships between their lengths and widths. For example, since $\overline{AD} \cong \overline{JI}$, $\overline{AD}$ is equal to three times the width of each rectangle ($\overline{BH}, \overline{HE}$, or $\overline{EC}$). $\overline{AD}$ represents one length (or three widths), and $\overline{AK}$ represents one length and two widths combined (or the equivalent of five widths). The ratio of the two sides is therefore (five widths):(three widths) or 5:3. If you're not sure how to find the relationships in this problem, use the figure: $\overline{AD}$ is smaller than $\overline{AK}$, so eliminate choices (A), (D), and (E). $\overline{AK}$ is not double the length of $\overline{AD}$, so eliminate choice (B).

42. J To solve average questions remember that the average is the sum of all the members of the set divided by the total number of members in the set. Here, since there are a total of 12 games, 12 is the divisor. The sum will be (10 games × 90 points per game) + (2 games × 102 points per game), which equals 1104 total points. Now divide 1,104 by 12 and get the average points per game of 92. Choices (F) and (K) are partial averages for the first 10 and next 2 respectively; neither includes all 12 games. Choice (H) is the average of 90 and 102.

43. **C** The ferry starts at its maximum distance from the island then travels towards the island. As the time moves from left to right from the start of the graph, the distance should decrease. Eliminate choices (B) and (D) in which the distance increases. The graph should dip to a distance of 0, then rise again as the ferry sails away. Choice (E) does not show the return trip. According to choice (A), the boat is at **two** distances from the island at the same time, which is impossible. If you chose (A), you may have confused the two axes. Choice (C) accurately represents the data given.

44. **J** The cosine of an angle is equal to the adjacent side over the hypotenuse, which in this triangle is $\frac{12}{37}$. Since you know the longest side is always the hypotenuse, draw a figure and work this problem visually. Choices (F), (G), (H), and (K) represent the cotangent, sine, tangent, and secant, respectively.

45. **A** Don't be thrown off by the vocabulary in this question. Adjacent simply means "next to," and noncommon rays are simply rays that do not overlap. Accordingly, if the two noncommon rays form a straight angle (or a 180° angle), it is probably simplest to think of one of these rays pointing to the right and the other pointing to the left. That takes care of your noncommon rays; now the common ray will just be one ray set at an angle to the straight line such that it creates one large angle which is four times larger than its supplement (the angle with which it adds to form a straight or 180° angle). Since the two angles are supplementary, you can create the following equation if x is the smaller angle: $4x + x = 180°$; $5x = 180°$; $x = 36°$, choice (A). If you picked choice (E), be careful—this is the measure of the larger angle.

46. **K** To solve this question you have to remember the axis to which each of the numbers in the coordinates refer. Since the system is x, y, z, the coordinate (–1, 3, 0) means that vertex M is "back" one on the x-axis, "right" three on the y-axis, and "up" zero on the z-axis. Thus, since vertex N is "forward" two, "left or right" zero, and "up" two, the coordinates are (2, 0, 2). Choice (F) would be correct if vertex M were on the y-axis. Choice (G) mixes up the y and z coordinates. Choice (J) mixes up the x and y coordinates.

47. **D** The median of a set of numbers is the one in the middle when the data are listed in numerical order. Resort the data to read: 18, 19, 19, 23, 25, 29, 35, 41. Since there is an even number of terms, find the average of the two numbers closest to the middle to get the median. $\frac{23 + 25}{2} = 24$. Choice (A) calculates the average of the two middle numbers in the set without reordering. Choice (B) is the mean, or average, and choice (E) is the mode, or most common number. Choice (C) chooses the median if the list of numbers includes 19 only once.

48. **H** Use the definition for the $\otimes$ function provided by the problem: $-5 \otimes 3 = (-2(-5) - 3)^2 = (10 - 3)^2 = 7^2 = 49$. Choice (F) is -5×3. Be careful! Although the symbol looks a little like a multiplication sign, you still need to use the definition in the problem. Choice (G) is $-5 + 3$. Choice (J) is $10^2 - 3^2$ and choice (K) is $10^2 + 3^2$.

49. **B** Substitute a value for x in the given terms to find their order. For example, if $x = -4$, $x^x = -4^{-4} = \dfrac{1}{(-4)^4} = \dfrac{1}{256}$, $((-x)!)^x = ((4)!)^{-4} = (4 \times 3 \times 2 \times 1)^{-4} = \dfrac{1}{24^4} = \dfrac{1}{331,776}$, $((-x)!)^{(-x)!} = (4 \times 3 \times 2 \times 1)^{(4 \times 3 \times 2 \times 1)} = 24^{24}$. $24^{24} \geq \dfrac{1}{256} \geq \dfrac{1}{331,776} \geq -4$. If you chose (E), be careful—note the direction of the inequality signs.

50. **H** Start by plotting out the figure to determine the distance between each point. You can find the distance between each point by using the distance formula: $d = \sqrt{(x_2 - x_1)^2 + (y_2 - y_1)^2}$. From point S to point R, for example, find $d = \sqrt{(4 - 0)^2 + (-2 - 0)^2} = \sqrt{16 + 4} = \sqrt{20} = 2\sqrt{5}$. As you compute the other sides, you'll notice that they all equal $2\sqrt{5}$, so the perimeter will be $4 \times 2\sqrt{5} = 8\sqrt{5}$.

51. **D** First, manipulate the equation given to get $y = \dfrac{4}{5}x + 4$. Then graph this line, with a slope of $\dfrac{4}{5}$ and a y-intercept of 4. The graph lies in the first, second, and third quadrants, and not in the fourth quadrant, Choice (D).

52. **J** To solve this use the formula for triangular numbers: $\dfrac{n^2 + n}{2}$ where n represents the number you wish to find, i.e. for the first triangular number, n would equal 1, for the second, n equals 2, and so on. Here, since the question asks for the 24th triangular number, n equals 24. Using n equals 24, we get $\dfrac{24^2 + 24}{2}$, which equals 300. Choice (F) is the result of $(\dfrac{n}{2})^2$. Choice (G) is $(\dfrac{n}{2})^2 + n$. Choice (H) is $\dfrac{n^2}{2}$. Choice (K) is $n^2 + n$.

53. **D** Use a picture to see what's happening here. First, draw a square and label its midpoints. Carefully draw a circle connecting these points. It should fit exactly inside the square, touching the square at the square's four midpoints. Draw diagonals in the square to connect the opposite corners. Then count the number of regions created. Each quarter of the square is cut into one large region inside the circle and two smaller regions outside the circle, so thus 12 total. Choice (B) neglects to draw the diagonals and choice (C) miscounts the number of areas created. Choice (A) would mean that only one line ran through the square. Choice (E) includes many overlapping shapes that the question excludes with the words "non-overlapping regions."

54. **F** The formula for the circumference of a circle is $C = 2\pi r$. So, $50 = 2\pi r$ and, therefore, $r = \dfrac{25}{\pi}$. Choice (G) is the result of forgetting to divide by the 2 in the formula. Choice (H) could result by mistakenly multiplying 50 by 2 rather than dividing when using the formula. Choices (J) and (K) incorrectly solve for the radius.

55. **C** Use the distance formula: $d = \sqrt{(x_2 - x_1)^2 + (y_2 - y_1)^2}$. So, $d = \sqrt{(-6-0)^2 + (1-9)^2} = \sqrt{100} = 10$. Note that the radius of the circle is the hypotenuse of a 6-8-10 right triangle that includes the given points as two of its vertices. So, the radius of the circle is 10 and its diameter is 20. Choice (A) is the radius of the circle. Choice (B) is the sum of the two sides of the triangle. Choice (D) is the sum of the two sides of the triangle multiplied by 2. Choice (E) is the radius squared—probably a result of forgetting to take the square root when using the Pythagorean theorem.

56. **K** To find the vertical asymptote, set the denominator equal to 0 and solve: $x - 1 = 0$, $x = 1$. If x is 1 the denominator is 0 and the function is undefined, therefore the graph cannot reach $x = 1$, and $x = 1$ is the graph's vertical asymptote.

57. **C** In order to produce an even number using the answer choices, you must multiply by 2. Eliminate choice (A). One less than $2 \times 3 = 6$ is 5, which is prime. Eliminate choice (B). One less than $2 \times 5 = 10$ is 9, which is not prime. Eliminate choices (D) and (E).

58. **K** The midpoints of any quadrilateral, when connected, create a four-sided figure, which eliminates Choices (F), (G), and (H). If you chose any four points in a rectangular coordinate system, and found the midpoints, the slopes of the lines connecting the midpoints are not perpendicular, but the slopes of the opposite sides are parallel, which makes the shape a parallelogram.

59. **C** To solve this question you need to use simultaneous equations:

$$b(x) = 3x^2 - 8x + 113$$
$$+c(x) = -3x^2 + 18x + 7$$

$$\overline{}$$
$$b(x) + c(x) = 10x + 120$$
$$a(x) = 10x + 120$$

Thus, since x must be an integer, $10x + 120$ must be a multiple of 10, since both terms are themselves multiples of 10.

60. **K** First, find the area of the original triangle T_1. $A = \frac{1}{2}(12)(20) = 120$. The sum of the triangles must be larger than 120, so eliminate choices (F), (G), and (H). Draw T_1 with T_2 inside it, with the vertices of T_2 at the midpoints of each of the sides of T_1. T_2 points in the opposite direction of T_1, and T_1 is now split into four congruent triangles. Since congruent triangles have equal areas, $T_2 = \frac{1}{4}(120) = 30$. $T_1 + T_2 = 120 + 30 = 150$, so choice (J) is also too small. The full sum of this geometric sequence is $120 + 30 + 7.5 + 1.875 + 0.46875 + \ldots \approx 160$.

MATH PRACTICE 3 ANSWERS

1. C
2. G
3. B
4. J
5. D
6. K
7. E
8. G
9. E
10. F
11. E
12. G
13. D
14. H
15. A
16. H
17. D
18. K
19. C
20. J
21. C
22. J
23. B
24. G
25. E
26. G
27. D
28. K
29. A
30. J
31. A
32. G
33. C
34. J
35. C
36. G
37. E
38. J
39. C
40. F
41. B
42. J
43. D
44. F
45. D
46. F
47. E

48. K
49. C
50. H
51. D
52. H
53. A
54. J
55. D
56. K
57. A
58. H
59. B
60. G

MATH PRACTICE 3 EXPLANATIONS

1. **C** Divide the total number of miles the runner ran in 2005 by the number of runs she ran in that year to find the average number of miles per run: $\frac{1,255}{395} = 3.177$, which rounds to 3.2 miles.

    There's a lot of extra information in this table—make sure you're using only what you need.

2. **G** Because the angles in the polygon are 90°, find the unlabeled lengths by subtracting the shorter labeled sides from the longer labeled sides opposite them (parallel). Calculate 30 − 25 = 5, and 15 − 5 = 10, so the two missing lengths are 5 and 10, and the perimeter is 30 + 15 + 25 + 10 + 5 + 5 = 90, or (G). Choice (F) adds the given values but forgets to calculate the missing sides, while (H) assumes the missing sides are equal to the given values 5 and 15. Choice (J) calculates the *area* correctly, while (K) calculates the area incorrectly (30 × 15).

3. **B** Start by looking at the endpoints on the number line and match those up with the inequality signs in the answer choices. The left circle at 0 is an open circle, so this corresponds to < or >, eliminating choices (D) and (E). The right circle at 4 is a closed circle, so this corresponds to ≤ and ≥, eliminating choice (A). Now look at the range of values covered in the line: 0 to 4—a range that does not include −2 as choice (C) suggests.

4. **J** Plug In the values given into the expression, using order of operations (PEMDAS). Start with the exponent: $4 + 3^{(3 − (−1))} = 4 + 3^4 = 4 + 81 = 85$. Choice (F) confuses the signs in the exponent, and choice (G) multiplies 3 × 4 instead of finding 3^4. Choice (H) subtracts 1 from the whole expression, instead of treating it as part of the exponent. Choice (K) adds 3 + 4 before raising it to the exponent.

5. **D** To determine which cannot be a value of x, try to use each of the answer choices as values for x and find a value for y for which $xy = 14$. In choice (A), if $x = 2$, $y = 7$. In choice (B), if $x = 1$, $y = 14$. In choice (C), if $x = −7$, $y = −2$. In choice (E), if $x = −14$, $y = −1$. Only choice (D) does not have a complementary integer value for y.

6. **K** The formula for the volume of a cube is as follows: $V = s^3$. In this case, $s = 6$, so the volume is 216. Choice (F) finds $s × 3$; choice (G) finds the area of a square with sides of 6; choice (H) makes a calculation error; and choice (J) finds $s^2 × 3$.

7. **E** Add the products of 80 pies sold at $25 each and B pies sold at $10 each: $(80 × 25) + (B × 10) = 2,000 + 10B$. Choice (D) finds the price of 50 pies instead of 80 and choice (C) gives the number of baked goods sold. Choice (A) finds the price of B loaves of bread and B apple pies. Choice (B) multiplies 10B by the sum of all other numbers in the problem.

8. **G** The sum of the two angles will be 180°, since together they make a straight line, and there are 180° in a straight line. To find $\angle WXY$, first find the value of a. $4a° + 11a° = 180°$, $a = 12$. $\angle WXY = 4a°$, $4(12) = 48°$. If you chose (F), you found the correct value for a but did not answer the question, which asks for $\angle WXY$ or $4a°$.

9. **E** Probability is represented by a proper fraction, and (A), (B), (C), and (D)—even the small numbers—can be converted into proper fractions (e.g., .00004 becomes $\frac{4}{100,000}$). Choice (E) $\frac{5}{4}$ is correct because it is the only fraction here greater than one, which makes it an impossible probability (more than 100%). Something cannot happen 5 out of 4 times.

10. **F** Teddy's standardized test scores do not decrease at any point, so you can eliminate choices (G) and (J). Nor do they *only* increase—at the end, his scores leveled off and neither increased nor decrease, so you can eliminate (K). And since these scores level off at the end, not in the middle, you can eliminate choice (H). Only choice (F) gives an accurate representation of scores that increase slowly, then increase quickly, then remain constant.

11. **E** First multiply the dimensions of the base of the sandbox to find its volume, then divide by the number of cubic inches per bag to get the number of bags needed. $60 \times 72 \times 18 = 77,760$. $77,760 \div 3,600 = 21.6$. Round up, since part of a 22nd bag will be needed. Choice (D) rounds down.

12. **G** When you are applying scales as the one given in this problem, ensure that you apply the same scale to both dimensions. Since the scale you are given is $\frac{1}{3}$ inch = 1 foot, simply multiply each of your values by $\frac{1}{3}$. You don't need to convert the values to inches because the scale is given from feet to inches. Accordingly, $\frac{1}{3} \times 9 = 3$ in, and $\frac{1}{3} \times 16 = 5\frac{1}{3}$ in, answer choice (G). If you chose (F), you may have changed the scale value to $\frac{1}{4}$ in, and if you chose (H), you may have applied different scale values to each of the dimensions.

13. **D** First find what percentage of students are seniors. Since the percentage of students who are not seniors is $25 + 35 + 20 = 80$, the remaining 20% of the students are seniors. Since there are 150 seniors, 150 is 20% of the total number of students. Now put the numbers into an equation: $150 = .20 \times total$. Divide both sides by .20 to find that the total is 750. Choice (C) miscalculates 150 to be 25% of the total, and choice (B) miscalculates it to be 30% of the total. Choice (A) adds all numbers in the problem, and choice (E) resembles the number of students but does not use the information given.

14. **H** For every single revolution, the tire will travel a horizontal distance equivalent to that tire's circumference. To find how many revolutions this tire makes, simply divide 2,700 in $\div$ 75 in = 36 rev. If you chose (F), be careful—you may not have converted the horizontal distance into inches and simply divided $225 \div 75$. If you chose (K), you may have multiplied an extra 12 to the 2,700 in—but this value is already in inches!

15. **A** Distribute the minus sign throughout the parentheses before combining like terms: $(2 - 4t + 5t^2) - (3t^2 + 2t - 7) = 2 - 4t + 5t^2 - 3t^2 - 2t + 7 = 2t^2 - 6t + 9$. The other choices all confuse signs in calculating. Choices (C) and (E) also add the exponents of the terms.

16. **H** Set up an equation with x as the total amount of money the gift certificate is worth. Subtract $\frac{1}{3}$ of the total amount for the niece's entrée and drink, and $6.00 for the niece's desert, from the total gift certificate value. Set the equation equal to the amount of money Cliff will have left over: $18.00 for his regular entrée: $x - \frac{1}{3}(x) - \$6.00 = \$18.00$. Solve for x: $\frac{2}{3}\$x = \$24.00$, $x = \$36.00$.

17. **D** To solve, check some possible fractions of books read (out of a possible 15): $\frac{10}{15} = 66.6666\%$; $\frac{11}{15} = 73.33333\%$; $\frac{12}{15} = 80\%$; $\frac{13}{15} = 86.6666\%$; and $\frac{14}{15} = 93.3333\%$. Only choice (D) gives a possible percentage. Alternatively, you can try all the percentages in the answer choices and see which gives you an integer value.

18. **K** A geometric sequence is one that has a constant factor between its terms. To find this constant multiple, divide the second term by the first (or the third by the second, the fourth by the third, etc.). In this case, the constant factor between all terms is $1 \div (-0.125) = (-8) \div 1 = -8$. To find the 5th term, simply multiply the fourth term by -8 : $64 \times (-8) = -512$. If you forget what a geometric sequence is, look at what the numbers are doing. First and foremost, they're alternating between negative and positive, so the fifth term must be negative—this enables you to eliminate choices (F) and (G). Next, notice that the magnitude of each number (ignoring its sign) is getting larger, so eliminate choice (H). From there, make sure that you've got a relationship of multiplication (geometric sequence) rather than addition (arithmetic sequence). If you chose (J), be careful: you added the second through third terms of the sequence—making them all negative—to get $(-1) + (-8) + (-64) = -73$.

19. **C** The square refers to everything inside the parentheses, so use FOIL (*First Outer Inner Last*). $(a - 5b)(a - 5b) = a^2 - 5ab - 5ab + 25b^2 = a^2 - 10ab + 25b^2$. Choices (D) and (E) miscalculate the middle term, and choice (B) squares each term individually. Choice (A) adds the binomials instead of multiplying them.

20. **J** Use similar triangles. Since $\angle FGK$ is congruent to $\angle HGJ$, and angles F and H are both right angles, you know the remaining angles are equal as well. Because they share three congruent angles, $\triangle FKG$ and $\triangle HJG$ are similar. You know, therefore, that the sides are proportional. Set up the following proportion to find the length of the longer ramp $\overline{GK}$:

$$\frac{\overline{FK}}{\overline{HJ}} = \frac{\overline{GK}}{\overline{GJ}}$$

$$\frac{20}{6} = \frac{\overline{GK}}{9}$$

$$\frac{(20)(9)}{6} = \overline{GK}$$

$$\overline{GK} = 30$$

21. **C** First distribute the minus sign through the parentheses to get $9x - 3x + 1 = 3$. Combine the terms on the left and subtract 1 from both sides: $6x = 2$. Divide both sides by three to find that $x = \dfrac{1}{3}$. Choice (B) and (D) do not distribute the parentheses and choices (A) and (E) divide incorrectly.

22. **J** Since you have the full area of the triangle and its height, or altitude, $\overline{BD}$, you can find its base $\overline{AC}$ by rearranging the area formula $A = \dfrac{1}{2}bh$ to be $b = \dfrac{2A}{h}$. Simply enter the numbers from the problem to find the base: $b = \dfrac{2(54)}{9} = 12$. If you chose (G), be careful—you may have forgotten the $\dfrac{1}{2}$.

23. **B** Plug -5 into the expression given for $g(x)$ and watch your signs. $g(-5) = 4(-5)^2 - 8(-5) + 2 = 4(25) - (-40) + 2 = 100 + 40 + 2 = 142$. Choice (A) squares the value of $4x$ and choice (C) omits the 4 in calculating. Choices (D) and (E) confuse signs.

24. **G** For the first $100.00 spent, multiply $100.00 \times \$0.80 = \$80.00$ that the company will reimburse. For the next $200.00 spent, multiply $200.00 \times \$0.70 = \$140.00$. So far, for $300.00 spent, the company will have reimbursed $80.00 + \$140.00 = \$220.00$. Subtract $400.00 - \$220.00 = \$180.00$ that the employee was reimbursed. To find the additional amount of money the employee must have spent, set up an equation with x as the additional number of dollars. $\$0.60(x) = \$180.00$, $x = \$300.00$. Finally, add all of the dollars spent: $100.00 + \$200.00 + \$300.00 = \$600.00$.

25. **E** The campers who are *at least 11 years old* include the 11-, 12-, and 13-year-olds. Because all the values in the chart represent percents of the same number, you can simply add them together to get $21 + 37 + 8 = 66\%$, or choice (E). Choice (A) counts only the 9 and 10 year old percentages; choice (B) counts the percentage of everyone older than 11 (12 and 13 year olds); and choice (D) counts ages up to and including 11. Choice (C) incorrectly guesses 50% because 11 is the median of the 5 numbers.

26. **G** Although this question is short, it gives the terms in an order that might be unfamiliar to you. It might help to rearrange the terms in the question to this: $\dfrac{1}{8}$ is what percent of $\dfrac{5}{8}$? To find the answer simply divide $\dfrac{\frac{1}{8}}{\frac{5}{8}} = \dfrac{1}{5} = 0.2$ or 20%. Choice (F) is $\dfrac{1}{8}$ converted to a percent, and choice (J) is $\dfrac{5}{8}$ converted to a percent. If you chose (K), be careful—you switched your terms to find that $\dfrac{5}{8}$ is 500% of $\dfrac{1}{8}$.

27. **D** Multiply the number of residences times the fraction affected by the outage to find the total number of people affected. $(63{,}000)(\frac{2}{3}) = 42{,}000$. Choice (B) tells the number of residences not affected. Choice (C) finds $\frac{1}{2}$ of the residences. Choice (A) divides the number of residences by the product of 2 and 3, while choice (E) subtracts 2 and 3 from the number of residences.

28. **K** Since you know that the sides of a square are always equal, pay close attention to the numbers given in the problem. Use them as you draw square X and rectangle Y. In this case, that means the sides of square X are both 3, and the sides of rectangle Y are 2 and 4. Since you know that the area of a square is $A = s^2$ and the area of a rectangle is $A = lw$, find the area of each figure with the numbers from the problem. The area of square X is 9, and the area of rectangle Z is 8, so the (area of square X):(area of rectangle Z) is 9:8. Note, you can choose different numbers for the sides of square X and rectangle Z as long as these numbers are in the proportion outlined in the problem. As long as they are, you'll see that whatever ratio you find between the areas will reduce to 9:8.

29. **A** Take the statement in small pieces, and don't worry, you don't need to know how the constant of proportionality works to answer this question correctly. Since a varies inversely as the product of b^2 and c, make sure that these values are both in the denominator of the right side of the equation. This eliminates choices (B), (C), (D), and (E). In case you are interested, the standard forms of direct and inverse variation with k as the constant of proportionality are $y = kx$ (direct) and $y = \dfrac{k}{x}$ (inverse).

30. **J** The base angles of any isosceles triangle are equal, the sum of the angles of any triangle is 180°, and the vertex angle of this triangle is 4 times its base angles, so $4x + x + x = 180$. $6x = 180$, or $x = 30$. The question asks for the vertex angle, which is $4x = 4(30) = 120$. Choice (F) gives the base angles (or the partial answer x you found in your equation), choice (H) gives the sum of the base angles, and choice (K) only subtracts the value of one base angle from 180. Choice (G) finds the value of x when $4x$ is equal to 180, omitting the base angles.

31. **A** Set $N = 0$ and factor the equation into $(x - 800)(x + 200)$, because $-800 \times 200 = -160{,}000$ and $-800 + 200 = -600$. Set each factor equal to 0 and solve for x. Either $x = 800$ ounces or $x = -200$ ounces. Since -200 ounces is not possible, $x = 800$ ounces. You could also try substituting the numbers in the answer choices for the x values in the given equation. You would have found that only 800 ounces used yields 0 new ounces that need to be purchased.

32. **G** If Fresco finally broke even, his cost should be the same as the revenue. The point where the $C(x)$ and $R(x)$ functions cross represents 5 sculptures sold, or choice (G). Choice (F) shows a revenue that's still less than the cost, while (H) and (J) show a profit for the company because the revenue is greater than the cost. If you're reading the y-axis numbers instead of the x-axis, you might be misled to choice (K).

33. **C** The cost function, or $C(x)$, begins at the $10,000 mark on the y-axis, so this is its fixed cost, or choice (C). Choice (A) calculates the cost per sculpture, or fee paid each celebrity ($1,000). If you're mistakenly looking at the x-axis you might guess choice (D) or (E).

34. **J** To determine the cost of each trash sculpture, consider a point on the revenue function line, $R(x)$, and divide the money by the number of sculptures sold ($\frac{y}{x}$). A convenient point shows 5 sculptures sold for $15,000, which is $3,000 per sculpture, or choice (J). Choice (F) calculates the cost per sculpture, or fee paid each celebrity ($1,000). If you're mistakenly reading the $C(x)$ line, you might calculate that 10 sculptures cost $20,000, or choice (H) $2,000 per sculpture; or that 15 sculptures cost $25,000, or roughly choice (G), $1,667.

35. **C** As you factor, take out one piece at a time, and remember that if you factor something out of the equation, you must be able to factor it out of every term: $12b^2c + 6bc + 3b = b(12bc + 6c + 3) = 3b(4bc + 2c + 1)$. Choice (A) omits the $3b$ you've factored out of the other terms; choice (B) erroneously calculates $12 - 3 = 9$ instead of $12 \div 3 = 4$ for the first term in the parentheses; choice (D) omits the $3b \div 3b = 1$ term (the last in the parentheses); and choice (E) is factored correctly but it is not *completely* factored as the problem asks.

36. **G** Use the two points given to find the slope of the line. $m = \frac{y_1 - y_2}{x_1 - x_2} = \frac{17 - (-7)}{2 - (-2)} = \frac{24}{4} = 6$. Manipulate the answer choices to match the slope-intercept form of a line, where $y = mx + b$. For choice (G), add y and subtract -5 from both sides to get $6x + 5 = y$, or $y = 6x + 5$. $m = 6$, which is the slope you need. None of the other lines have this slope, so you don't need to find the value of b. Choice (H) confuses signs in calculating the slope. Choice (K) confuses the slope and y-intercept. You can also answer this question by plugging the two given points into answer choices, but make sure both points work. Choice (F) works only for the first point given, and choice (J) works only for the second point.

37. **E** The perimeter of a square is equal to the sum of its sides. For this square, $64 = 4s$, $s = 16$. The radius of the circle is thus also 16. To find the area of the circle, use $A = \pi r^2 = \pi (16)^2 = 256\pi$. Choice (A) gives the radius of the circle and choice (C) gives its circumference. Choice (D) mistakes the perimeter of the square for its area, and choice (B) uses that calculation to find the circumference of the circle.

38. **J**   You can solve this problem at least three different ways. The fastest way, if you know how to do it,

is to set up simultaneous equations like this:

$8x + 4y = 96$

$8x + y = 30 \Rightarrow -1(8x + y = 30) \Rightarrow -8x - y = -30$, and when you've got opposite coefficients for

one of your variables, add the two equations together like this: $\begin{array}{r} 8x + 4y = 96 \\ -8x - y = -30 \\ \hline 0 + 3y = 66 \end{array}$, and with $3y =$

66, find $y = 22$. If you're not sure how to use simultaneous equations, you can also solve for one

variable in one equation: $8x + y = 30 \Rightarrow 8x = 30 - y \Rightarrow x = \dfrac{30 - y}{8}$, and then substitute it into the

other equation: $8x + 4y = 96 \Rightarrow 8\left(\dfrac{30 - y}{8}\right) + 4y = 96 \Rightarrow 30 - y + 4y = 96 \Rightarrow 3y = 66$ and again,

$y = 22$. Finally, since you know that your x-coordinate and y-coordinate must be the same in each

equation, you can substitute possible y-coordinates and see which one produces the same x-coor-

dinate in both equations. If you chose (F), be careful—this is your x-coordinate, and the problem

asks for the y-coordinate.

39. **C**   Substitute the numbers in the diagram for the variables in the formula given for the area of a trap-

ezoid: $A = \dfrac{1}{2}(40)(50 + 30) = 1{,}600 \text{ ft}^2$. If you chose (A), be careful—you may have forgotten the

$\dfrac{1}{2}$.

40. **F**   Make a right triangle by drawing in a perpendicular line from R to $\overline{MQ}$. This new line will be the

same height as $\overline{LM}$. Since $\overline{LR}$ is 30 feet, the base of the new triangle will be 50 − 30 = 20 feet.

To find $\overline{QR}$, use the Pythagorean theorem: $a^2 + b^2 = c^2$, where a and b are the two legs of a right

triangle, and c is the hypotenuse. $20^2 + 40^2 = \overline{QR}^2$, $2{,}000 = \overline{QR}^2$, $\overline{QR} = \sqrt{2{,}000}$.

41. **B** $\overline{MN}$, which is 40 feet, limits the diameter of the circle. If you chose (A), be careful—this is the

radius.

42. **J** To find the height of the ramp you'll need to use the tangent of 10°, since tangent is equal to length of side opposite the angle (unknown ramp height) divided by length of side adjacent to the angle (length of the base, or 25 feet). Calculate 0.176 × 25, and you'll get approximately 4.4, or choice (J). If you use the sine of 10°, you'll get 4.3, or (H); cosine will give you 24.6, or (K). If you multiply all three given numbers (cos, sin, tan) by 25, you'll get 2.3, or (F).

43. **D** Draw the circular clock and mark twelve evenly spaced points on it, and start trying out the numbers for n in the given problem. Choose any starting point—let's say two for this example. If you start at 2 and every two numbers are painted, as in choice (A), then in the first revolution, the numbers painted will be 4, 6, 8, 10, 12; in the second revolution, they will be 2, 4, 6, 8, 10, 12. In other words, if the integer n is 2, then there is no way that all of the numbers on the face of the clock will be painted. Choices (B), (C), and (E) all create the same issue. Only choice (D), $n = 7$, will fill in all of the numbers on successive revolutions.

44. **F** Since $(x + 1)$ will never be a negative exponent, increasing this exponent will always increase the value of a number greater than 1 and decrease the value of a real number between 0 and 1. The problem stipulates that p must be positive, so if y decreases as x increases, p must be a fractional constant less than 1.

45. **D** Plug In the x and y values of the two given points into the distance formula. You can start with either point as long as you start with the same point each time. $distance=$

$$\sqrt{(x_1 - x_2)^2 + (y_1 - y_2)^2} = \sqrt{[1-(-5)]^2 + [-3-5]^2} = \sqrt{6^2 + (-8)^2} = \sqrt{36+64} = \sqrt{100} = 10.$$

Choice (A) does not square the differences of the x and y values. Choice (B) confuses signs in subtracting in the first step. Choice (E) makes this same error and omits the square root sign as well.

Choice (C) gives the amount of change along the x axis, which neglects the vertical distance.

46. **F** To solve this problem, use the distance formula $d = rt$. If both runners start from the point at which Carl had to stop to tie his shoes, and both d represent the distance at which they meet, then Carl will run $d = 9.2s$ and Melissa will run $d = 8s + 20$ because she has a 20 foot head start. Because the d is the same for each equation, simply set these equations equal to each other to find $8s + 20 = 9.2s$. If you chose (G), be careful—you may have given Carl the head start instead of Melissa. Choices (J) and (K) give the time it takes Carl and Melissa to run 20 feet, respectively.

47. **D** Manipulate the first given inequality to get x alone on one side. $-3x > -6$, or $x < 2$. Don't forget to flip the inequality sign when dividing both sides by a negative number. Combine the first inequality with the second to get $-4 < x < 2$. Choice (B) gives the solution to only the first inequality and choice (A) repeats the second inequality. Choices (C) and (D) make errors in manipulating the first inequality.

48. **K** To solve this problem, use the group formula: *Total = Group₁ + Group₂ − Both + Neither*. In this problem, that means 110 employees = (35 sales) + (50 operations) − (15 both) + Neither. Solve for Neither = 40, choice (K). Choice (F) erroneously subtracts all the smaller values from the total number of employees; choice (G) subtracts sales employees from operations employees; choice (H) subtracts employees working in both departments from the number of employees in sales; and choice (J) subtracts employees working in both departments from the number of employees in operations.

49. **C** The slope of a perpendicular line is the negative reciprocal of the slope of the line to which it is perpendicular.

50. **H** If (24, 3) is the midpoint of the other two points, then the average of the two x values should be 24; calculate $\dfrac{z+15z}{2} = 24$, and $z = 3$, or (H). Choice (G) mistakenly calculates $z + 15z = 24$ (where $z = 1.5$). The other choices mistakenly set point values equal to each other. Choice (F) calculates $2z + 1 = 3$ (where $z = 1$); (J) calculates $z - 4 = 3$ (where $z = 7$); and (K) simply sets z equal to 24.

51. **D** The word BADGERS has 7 letters, and you are looking for combinations of four letters with no repeats. There are four letter-slots to fill, so you need to figure out how many letters can go in each of these four slots. Since there are 7 letters in BADGERS, you can choose any of them for the first slot. Since there are no repeats, and one of your letters will be in the first slot, you have 6 options for the second slot, 5 options for the third, and 4 options for the fourth. Multiply these numbers together to get $(7)(6)(5)(4) = 840$. Choice (A) gives only the number of slots; choice (B) gives only the number of letters in the word BADGERS; choice (C) gives 4^4; and choice (E) gives 7^4.

52. **H** Compare point O to the answer choices, watching the order of the three axes. Point O shifts neither to the left nor right in the y direction, so the y value will be 0, eliminating choices (G) and (K). The height of the cube is 2 units and side $\overline{OS}$ starts where z is 0, so the z coordinate of O is 2, eliminating choice (J). The distance along the x axis from Q to S is the diagonal of square $PQRS$. The diagonal of a square is the length of its side $x\sqrt{2}$, or $2\sqrt{2}$, so the x value of O is $2\sqrt{2}$, eliminating choice (F).

53. **A** To combine logarithms (logs), the bases must be the same, so eliminate choice (C). Group the first and last terms together, since they have common bases, to get $\log_4 a + \dfrac{1}{2}\log_4 c - 2\log_8 b$. The laws of logarithms state that $c\log_b x = \log_b x^c$, so $\log_4 a + \log_4 c^{\frac{1}{2}} - \log_8 b^2$. Eliminate choices (B) and (D) which multiply b by 2 instead of squaring it. A fractional power represents a root, so $\log_4 a + \log_4 \sqrt{c} - \log_8 b^2$. Eliminate choice (E), which does not include $\sqrt{c}$. You are left with choice (A). The laws of logs also state that $\log_b x + \log_b y = \log_b xy$, so $\log_4 a + \log_4 \sqrt{c} = \log_4 a\sqrt{c}$.

54. J   Since you're dealing with absolute value, all solutions of the problem will be positive, so work with the extremes of each inequality until you find the greatest value. The greatest value results when $a = -6$ and $b = 7$: $|a - 2b| = |-6 - 14| = |-20| = 20$. Choice (H) gives the value if $a = -4$ and $b = 7$. Choice (K) gives the absolute value of ab if $a = -6$ and $b = 7$.

55. D   Octagons have 8 sides, so using the formula in the question, the sum of the interior angles measures $(8 - 2)180 = 1,080$. The angles of regular polygons are equal, so divide by 8 to find the measure of each angle: $\frac{1,080}{8} = 135°$. The designated angle in the figure is an exterior angle, and there are 360° in a circle, so subtract the interior angle from 360° to find the measure of the designated angle: $360° - 135° = 225°$. If you chose (A), the measure of one of the *interior* angles, be careful— make sure you're answering the right question.

56. K   First, tan x does not have an amplitude: Answer choice (J) is out. Second, multiplying the entire function by a constant stretches the graph vertically and changes the amplitude. Both sin x and cos x alone have amplitudes of 1. Multiplying the functions sin x or cos x by a constant will make the amplitude equal to that constant. Altering the *angle*, as in choices (G) and (H) does not change the amplitude of the function—it changes the *period*.

57. A   To solve this algebraically, you need to work with the original equation, $A = \frac{xy - 2}{x - y}$, and try to isolate the x variable. First multiply both sides by $(x - y)$, and you'll get $A(x - y) = xy - 2$. If you distribute the left side of the equation, you get $Ax - Ay = xy - 2$. Now subtract and add terms from each side so that all the terms with x are on one side; you should get $Ax - xy = Ay - 2$. Pull the x from each term on the left side and you have $x(A - y) = Ay - 2$. Divide both sides by $(A - y)$ and you have the answer: $x = \frac{Ay - 2}{A - y}$, or choice (A). If you try to solve by substituting numbers and you pick tricky numbers such as $x = 1$ and $y = 0$ (for which $A = -2$), you'll be misled to choices (D) and (E), since both will seem correct ($x = 1$). If you mistakenly set the answer choices equal to the original equation (and again try to solve using 0 and 1 for the variables), you may be misled to choices (B) and (C).

58. H To complete this problem, extend the left transversal to form a triangle with *a* as one of its angles:

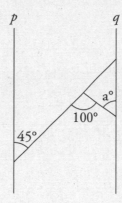

First, find that the supplement of 100° will be 80°. Note that because lines *p* and *q* are parallel, the uppermost angle of this triangle will be 45°. Now you can find *a* by subtracting your two known angles from the total angle measure of this triangle: 180° – 45° – 80° = 55°. Choice (F) erroneously subtracts the 45° and 100° angles from 180°. Choice (G) cannot work because *a* does not lie along the same transversal as 45°; choice (J) cannot work because the 100° angle and *a* do not share any parallel lines; and choice (K) cannot work because the value can be determined.

59. B Use SOHCAHTOA, eliminating answer choices that are not supported by the figure. Notice that the third angle of the triangle is 50° to reveal that $\sin 50° = \dfrac{x}{9}$, or $x = 9 \sin 50°$. The remaining choices confuse the sides of the figure in finding sine, cosine, and tangent of the two angles.

60. G There are 360° in a circle, so each time you add or subtract 360° from an angle measure, you get another angle with the same terminal side. In the case of this problem, every time you find an angle with same the terminal side as 1,314°, you can eliminate it because this problem asks for the angle that does NOT share a terminal side with 1,314°. 1,314° – 360° = 954°. This is not an answer choice, so keep going. 954° – 360° = 594°, so eliminate choice (F). 594° – 360° = 234°, eliminating choice (H). 234° – 360° = – 126°, so eliminate choice (J). –126° – 360 = –486, eliminating choice (K). Choice (G) resembles the angle in the problem, but does not land at the same point.

Reading Practice
Answers and
Explanations

READING PRACTICE 1 ANSWERS

1. A
2. F
3. D
4. F
5. C
6. J
7. B
8. G
9. C
10. J
11. A
12. H
13. D
14. G
15. C
16. J
17. C
18. J
19. B
20. G
21. B
22. H
23. A
24. H
25. A
26. J
27. B
28. F
29. C
30. J
31. B
32. J
33. C
34. G
35. D
36. F
37. B
38. H
39. D
40. G

READING PRACTICE 1 EXPLANATIONS

Passage I

1. **A** The first paragraph describes the narrator's arrival at the local airport. She refers to herself as *dressed for an overly air-conditioned office climate*, in contrast to her later description of her mother's faded dress. It also mentions her rental car and her delayed flight, all things that relate to her life in the city. The next paragraph describes her drive home, and the rest is set in a rural area, with screen doors instead of air conditioners and an old tire swing. Therefore, choice (A) is the best answer, since it addresses the switch from modern, city conditions to old-fashioned, rural ones. Choice (B) is incorrect because it is too general. The narrator does state that the weather puts her in a bad mood, but she associates her eventual anger with past behavior, not present weather. This answer also does not address the change in tone from the airport to the country. Choice (C) is incorrect because the first paragraph does not describe the setting of the bulk of the passage. Choice (D) is incorrect because nowhere does the narrator describe herself as abandoned.

2. **F** The narrator compares the weather upon her arrival in Alabama to a *woolen blanket that had been soaked in water* and claims that the walk to the car rental agency was *like a trek through the jungle*. In other words, the climate is described as hot, humid, and stuffy. Choice (F) is the best match for these descriptions. Choice (G) might have looked appealing, but the weather isn't described as *unbearable*. It certainly sounds unpleasant, but the narrator remembers bearing it during her childhood. Choice (H) says the opposite of what you want. Choice (J) is incorrect because, while the weather is indeed *familiar*, the narrator does not consider it at all *pleasant*.

3. **D** The second paragraph describes the narrator's arrival at her childhood home. According to the passage, very little about the appearance has changed since she left, and she recognizes several familiar objects, such as the tire swing and rocking chair. She also comments that she had to calm her nerves and that she grabbed her bags anxiously, suggesting that she is nervous. Therefore, choice (D) is the best answer. Choice (A) is incorrect because she describes the house as virtually unchanged. Choice (B) is incorrect because the second paragraph describes only the outer appearance of the house, not the narrator's feelings about her mother. Choice (C) is incorrect because the only thing the passage tells us about the author's feelings is that she has to get ready to go inside. The description of her tiredness was in the first paragraph.

4. **F** The narrator of the passage is the daughter, and she describes visiting her family home after having moved away ten years earlier. She mentions moving away for college and working in an office, making choice (F) the best answer. Choice (G) incorrectly focuses on the narrator's childhood, which is mentioned only briefly and is not the main theme of the passage. Choices (H) and (J) incorrectly identify the mother as the narrator.

5. **C** The word braced is used here in the line ending "I grabbed my bags anxiously, trying to calm my nerves, and braced myself." The author is preparing to enter her mother's house, after getting lost in her thoughts during the drive. Choice (C), prepared, is a good synonym for braced in this context and is the best answer. Choices (B) and (D) might look tempting if you were thinking about braces for teeth or legs, but the meaning in this context is closer to prepared.

6. **J** The relationship between the narrator and her mother is most clearly expressed in the final two paragraphs, when the narrator arrives at her childhood home. She is angry because her mother doesn't seem to care that her daughter has finally come home, then she realizes that this is due to her mother's understanding of the daughter's need to be independent. Therefore, choice (J) is the best answer, since it encompasses both the mother's seeming unconcern and her underlying motivation. Choice (F) is too extreme; although the narrator expresses anger toward her mother, she does not describe her mother as *harsh*. Choice (G) is not supported by the passage because the mother's education is never discussed. Choice (H) does not adequately address the distance between the two characters.

7. **B** The passage describes the narrator's experience of returning home after a long absence. The beginning of the passage focuses on her frustration and feelings of anger toward her mother, but the end of the passage finds her coming to a better understanding of her mother's motivations. Therefore, choice (B) is the best answer. Choice (A) is too strong, since it does not reflect the narrator's final acceptance of and realization about her mother. Choice (C) is too narrow; the narrator's comments about her mother's aged appearance are only in one part of the passage. Choice (D) is incorrect because it focuses on the mother's feelings instead of the narrator's.

8. **G** Although the passage deals with the reunion of a mother and daughter, there is very little dialogue. Even in the reflective portions, the narrator describes previous conversations with her mother in very brief terms, and then mentions that they no longer speak with any frequency. When she arrives at the house, the two characters barely speak, but the daughter is able to understand her mother's feelings based on her body language and responds through action of her own. Therefore, they seem to have a relationship that is based more on actions than words, making choice (G) the best answer. Choice (F) is incorrect because it describes the relationship as *built on frank emotional openness*, which is in direct contradiction with the largely unspoken bond between the two characters. Choice (H) goes too far—although the relationship appears strained, the daughter's final actions are not at all antagonistic. Choice (J) is contradicted by the events discussed in the passage.

9. **C** Most of the passage is told from the point of view of the narrator, as she reflects on her journey, so her own emotions are conveyed in her own thoughts. When she first encounters her mother, however, she notices her mother's clothing, and the shaking of her hands, and from those sights determines her mother's emotions. Therefore, choice (C) is the best answer. The emotional states of the characters are not conveyed primarily through the setting, making choice (A) incorrect. Choice (B) is incorrect because the dialogue is limited to two lines. Choice (D) is incorrect because the narrator speaks of her own emotional experiences and thus cannot be said to be *objective*.

10.   J   It is when the narrator notices her mother's hands shaking as she shells peas that the narrator realizes that her mother *must have understood on some level* why the daughter had to leave and tried to give the daughter as much independence as possible. This goes against the narrator's earlier comments regarding her mother's attitude toward the author's decision to go away for school, implying that this is a new discovery for the author. Therefore, choice (J) is the best answer. Choice (F) is incorrect because in the previous paragraph the narrator does express a wish that her mother be more expressive. Choice (G) is incorrect because there is no evidence that the daughter had trouble recognizing her mother. Choice (H) is incorrect because the problem of not being able to visit was mentioned in a previous paragraph, meaning this was not a new discovery.

Passage II

11.   A   The answer can be found in lines 46–49; the author begins the paragraph by arguing that the social character of coffeehouses was in place for centuries before such establishments appeared in the United States, but that they soon took on an American character. The author continues by giving credit to returning soldiers from World War II for introducing the concept but credits the rise of the automobile for the uniquely American development that followed. Choice (B) is wrong because it refers to the character of coffeehouses in London in the seventeenth and eighteenth centuries. You can eliminate choice (C) because it misstates a comment the author makes about the current number of coffeehouses. Similarly, choice (D) is wrong because it refers to the current time, long after the author indicates the United States had marked its influence on the coffeehouse.

12.   H   The passage as a whole concerns the way in which examining coffeehouses can shed light on cultural developments, whether social or architectural, in a society—hence its main idea is well summarized in the sentence, *Understanding how coffeehouses developed as social sites can permit a greater appreciation for the diverse ways that social communication occurs* (lines 5–7) and the concluding sentence, *But one thing is clear: The coffeehouse has proven to be remarkably flexible in adapting to its cultural environs* (lines 88–90). Choices (F) and (G) are too narrow, and choice (J) isn't a good fit because much of the passage is devoted to illustrating how coffeehouses change to reflect the changing values of different cultures and time periods.

13.   D   The passage mentions listening to music or poetry as one of the activities Middle Eastern customers thought suitable for the coffeehouse (see line 16). The Ottoman Empire is mentioned only in reference to its influence on Venice's import industry, and the passage implies that the Ottoman Empire was still going strong in 1645, so choice (A) doesn't fit. Choice (B) is an opposite answer, and choice (C) is wrong because the local population had access to coffee long before the sixteenth century, at least as far back as 1475 at the opening of Kiva Han, so *introduced* is incorrect.

14. **G** Only choice (G) is broad enough to capture the full range of discussion in this paragraph. Although the paragraph does mention that a trader's servant ran the first coffeehouse in London, there's no indication that other servants did the same, so eliminate choice (F). Choice (H) isn't the best choice because although a penny may well have been an inexpensive price to pay for the London coffeehouse experience, there is no specific mention that the beverage was popular among university students. The question of coffeehouses' authenticity doesn't arise in this passage, nor are the positions of Venice and London relative to trade routes ever discussed, so eliminate choice (J).

15. **C** Lines 40–45 discuss late eighteenth-century British coffeehouses. This part of the passage relates how groups that shared certain values began to congregate in certain establishments, a movement that in turn created a growing sense of exclusivity in coffeehouses. Choices (A) and (B) aren't mentioned in the passage, and choice (D) refers to the drive-in coffee shops discussed in the fourth paragraph.

16. **J** The author describes American coffeehouses as *offering a visual emblem of a nation's desire to shake off the past and plunge into the future*, thus making (J) the best answer. Choices (F) and (H) are not supported by the passage, and choice (G) is contradicted by the passage.

17. **C** When the fourth paragraph introduces the description of googie architecture, it mentions that it *eschewed* (avoided) the usual coffeehouse décor of mahogany booths and brass railings, so choice (A) must be eliminated. Similarly, googie architecture is referred to as having *replaced the sedately darkened rooms of the European coffeehouse* (lines 67–68), so choice (B) must be eliminated. Regarding choice (D), Las Vegas is referred to as a *playground* in line 62, but there is no indication that googie architecture has influenced the architecture of actual playgrounds in Las Vegas. Only choice (C) is supported by the passage.

18. **J** Note that the question asks about *drive-in* coffeehouses, so the best answer will mention something regarding the automobile, as only choice (J) does. *Business people* are not mentioned until the next paragraph, eliminating choice (F). No *new laws* are discussed in the passage, eliminating choice (G). Finally, the passage merely mentions that Americans had come to use space in different ways, not that there was any shortage of space in urban areas, eliminating choice (H).

19. **B** Choice (B) is the only critique that the final paragraph raises. Choices (A) and (D) are too focused on the practicality of working in coffee shops, and choice (C) sets up a comparison that the passage doesn't make.

20. **G** Choices (F), (H), and (J) are all too extreme in different ways. *Unique* means *one-of-a-kind*, and the passage doesn't argue that no other institutions can be examined in this way, so strike out choice (F). Choice (H) refers to the comparison made in line 22, but the passage doesn't go so far as to say that coffee surpasses tea or tobacco in this respect, so that choice doesn't fit. The passage implies that coffeehouses gave architects who were interested in developing new styles an opportunity to see them realized, but again, it doesn't contend that architects would have been unable to do so if coffeehouses didn't exist. Therefore, you should eliminate choice (J).

Passage III

21. B The context following this sentence states that *The rational decision-making process* is *a demonstration of self- and environmental analysis*. The first paragraph's banana example explores how an economic decision is based on several comparative and relative factors. By saying *no choice is made in a vacuum*, the author is stressing the effect of context on any decision. Choice (B) describes something with no environmental influence. Choice (A) uses trap language based on the association of *vacuum* to *cleaning*. Choices (C) and (D) do not correctly identify the use of *vacuum*, and they make unsupported claims; the author does not discuss the influence of our subconscious, and a choice *made in a vacuum* would presumably have no opportunity cost whatsoever.

22. H Choice (H) correctly identifies the purpose of the yin-yang metaphor. The author says that his peers viewed his best friend and him as a *single unit* and *fused together as one entity*. Choice (F) involves name-calling, which the passage does not support; choice (G) contains an unsupportable mention of Eastern mysticism. The yin-yang metaphor is not used to discuss people in general as choice (J) suggests but rather to describe how the author and his best friend might be seen by others.

23. A The final sentence of the fourth paragraph identifies the respective chosen professions of the three brothers as filmmaker, musician, and novelist. Choice (A) correctly names one of these. Choices (C) and (D) are pulled from hypothetical examples brought up in the final paragraph (lines 75–91). Choice (B) is contradicted by the information that the author's older brother stopped playing piano at age 9 (line 51).

24. H Choice (H) is correct because the only time that a *journalist* is brought up in the passage involves an analogy to something hypothetical. The author indicates in the second paragraph that he has considered pursuing law, choice (G), and he indicates in the final paragraph that some alternate visions of his life include his being an *astrophysicist*, choice (J), and *raising a family*, choice (F).

25. A The context of the previous sentence matches up the term *gimmick* most directly with *selecting our personalities*. Combined with the sentence before that which stresses Americans' need for the *expression of individuality*, choice (A) is well supported and a reasonable paraphrase of the meaning. Choice (B) uses trap language based on the aforementioned advertisers but they have nothing to do with the usage of *gimmick* in this context. Choice (C) is close, but there is no way to support its claim that being individualistic is *uniquely* American. There is no discussion of *hastily* chosen opportunities, making choice (D) unsupported.

26. J Toward the end of the first paragraph, the author states that *the same thought process takes place as each of us carves out his personality and ambitions*. Therefore, the author clearly suggests that choice (J) is true. Choice (F) contains extreme wording; it is never stated or implied that these two concepts are *central* to *any* economic theory. The author did not say he opened a barber shop, which eliminates choice (G). The concept of *comparative advantage* requires that one compare oneself to others, which eliminates choice (H) as a possibility.

27. B The preceding paragraph ascribes a quality to all Americans and uses *We* in line 62. Therefore, the *We* used in the final paragraph must also refer to all Americans, making choice (B) correct. The author is not restricting his generalizations here to his family, his friends, or himself, so choices (A), (C), and (D) cannot be correct.

28. **F** The passage states that the author's older brother abandoned the piano because the alternative was *sharing the instrument with his younger brother*. This means the author was younger than eight when he began playing piano, making answer choice (F) correct. Choices (G) and (H) relate to the author's older brother's age when he started and finished playing piano. Choice (J) is impossible unless the author was in high school at age 7 or so, which, aside from being extremely unlikely, is not supported by the text.

29. **C** The previous sentence suggests some hypothetical examples of people whose current identities would not suggest their hidden potentials. The final sentence cautions that oversimplifying people, *acknowledging only what we currently see them doing*, amounts to equating their current activities with their whole being. Choice (C) correctly identifies an example in which someone's main occupation would lead us to assume that there is nothing else to his/her personality. Choice (A) would be the opposite of oversimplifying our view of a physician. Choice (B) refers to whether or not someone likes his job, which is not supported, and choice (D) assumes that someone wants to be something other than his outward identity.

30. **J** Choice (J) is supported by the fact that in choosing separately to be a *filmmaker, musician, and novelist,* the author and his two brothers were attempting to more easily distinguish themselves from one another. Choice (F) describes something the author did with his best friend, and there is nothing about having done this to avoid *communicating*. Choice (G) is too extreme in wording to be supported by saying *every* hobby was ruined. Choice (H) is unsupported by the passage.

Passage IV

31. **B** Answer choice (B) is directly supported by the second paragraph with the phrase (in reference to color created through structure) *producing the brilliant single wavelength of iridescent color, brighter and more luminous than any color produced by pigmentation*. Choice (A) is the opposite of what the passage says. Choices (C) and (D) are incorrect because neither is supported by the passage.

32. **J** Choice (J) is the correct answer because you could easily replace the word *employ* with *use* and keep the intended meaning of the passage. Answer choices (F), (G), and (H) all provide the more common definitions of the word *employ*, but they would not be appropriate synonyms in the context of this passage and therefore can't be the best choices.

33. **C** Choice (C) is the best answer because the sentence talks about a claim that these products will create *surrealistic effects they could never attain with traditional makeup*. This supports both the unique qualities and the previously unattainable element. There is no evidence for choice (A) or choice (D); though they might be likely to happen, there's nothing in the text to support those inferences. There is no evidence that Dr. Vukusic's research can't be applied to more than one product; in fact, the opposite is stated several times throughout the passage, so choice (B) cannot be your answer.

34. **G** The question asks how the phrase functions. The phrase comes right after a sentence that says iridescent light is more brilliant and luminous than color created by pigments. So the phrase in question is meant to qualify or explain that idea. Choice (F) is incorrect because there's no evidence that iridescent light looks any different to Dr. Vukusic than to any other person, nor is that the purpose of the phrase. Choices (H) and (J) are incorrect for the same reason. They both state unlikely answers that do not discuss the function of the phrase as much as the meaning of it. There is no evidence that fish and plant life use iridescence, and the phrase is not suggesting an appreciation for nature; it is expanding on the idea that iridescence provides a deeper, more complex view than just what appears on the surface, supporting choice (G) only.

35. **D** Paragraph six is dedicated almost exclusively to a discussion of how swallowtails use fluorescence to signal each other. Choice (A) is the opposite of what you're looking for; they want to be seen, not camouflaged. Choice (B) could be tempting because ultraviolet light is reflected to create fluorescence, but it is not specific enough to be correct. The paragraph talks about the butterflies signaling each other through the use of fluorescence and how that fluorescence is produced. Choice (C) is an element of an LED that mimics a butterfly's wing; the butterfly is not dependent on it, so that answer cannot be correct either.

36. **F** The passage says that most light from LEDs cannot escape, but does not say why it cannot escape. Therefore choice (F) is the correct answer. Choice (G) is answered in paragraph three (lines 27–36) where it states the morpho butterfly uses color to signal its peers; choice (H) is addressed in paragraph six (lines 59–80), where there is a detailed discussion of how swallowtails emit light; and choice (J) is found in the beginning of paragraph two (lines 10–19) in the discussion.

37. **B** The context of the paragraph tells you that in standard LEDs light can't escape, and the paragraph goes on to say that without the photonic crystal most light would be lost, or useless; the wing with holes keeps light from being trapped inside which supports answer choice (B). Choice (A) is the most common definition for *lost* but the word is not used in that context in this sentence. Choices (C) and (D) are neither secondary definitions of lost nor do they work as synonyms in this case.

38. **H** Choice (H) is the best answer because it supports the idea that the wing works *like* the crystal. Butterfly wings don't contain the crystal, so you must cross off both choices (F) and (G). Answer choice (J) can't be right because the comparison is incorrect. Scales of the wing work like the Bragg reflector. The holes in the wing work like a photonic crystal.

39. **D** Choice (D) is supported by the sentences, *When light strikes these structures, each wavelength is reflected at different angles… Eventually, only one wavelength is reflected back in the direction of the viewer.* Answer choices (A), (B), and (C) present all of these elements, but in the incorrect order.

40. **G** The passage states that *most light emitted from standard LEDs cannot escape, resulting in what scientists call a low extraction efficiency of light.* This supports choice (G), because high extraction of light is usually not observed with the standard LED. Choice (H) may be tempting because most LEDs do have a low extraction of light, but that is the opposite of what the question asks. Choice (F) is wrong for the same reason: most LEDs do have fluorescent light. Choice (J) is incorrect because there is nothing in the passage to support the idea that pigmentation is related to LEDs.

READING PRACTICE 2 ANSWERS

1. A
2. J
3. A
4. F
5. B
6. H
7. B
8. G
9. C
10. F
11. A
12. J
13. B
14. H
15. C
16. F
17. B
18. J
19. B
20. J
21. A
22. G
23. A
24. H
25. D
26. G
27. B
28. H
29. C
30. H
31. C
32. F
33. A
34. H
35. B
36. G
37. D
38. H
39. D
40. H

READING PRACTICE 2 EXPLANATIONS

Passage I

1. **A** Although the narrator calls the memory of her grandmother *almost painfully* (lines 66–67), she goes on to note that her grandmother's image was one to which the narrator has *often come back whenever I've needed consolation or company* (lines 69–70). This description doesn't match the words featured in choices (B), (C), or (D), so choice (A) is the best selection here.

2. **J** Choice (J) takes note of the narrator's desire to *seek the patterns of our life in India, including my daily morning visits to the market to do the day's food shopping* (lines 12–13), so that's the best answer. The time at which the produce arrives at the market isn't mentioned in the passage, so you should eliminate choice (F). Although the information in choice (G) is true according to the passage, that fact doesn't influence the narrator's shopping time. Choice (H) presents information not contained in the passage.

3. **A** We know the narrator is initially intimidated by the strangeness of her new environment—the *unfamiliar streets and landmarks of our new city* (line 18)—but near the end of the passage she mentions that she has learned to combine products from both the specialty market and the supermarket, which implies that she has become more comfortable. The fact that she puts on a sweatshirt and uses *quick prep* sauces near the end of the passage confirms this reading; therefore, choice (A) is appropriate. Choice (B) is wrong on both counts: The narrator is not excited to learn new ways at the outset of her stay, and the only person she encounters (the grocery clerk) leaves her only temporarily annoyed, not disillusioned. Eliminate choice (C) because the first part of the answer suggests that the couple *enjoyed* eating out at restaurants; lines 17–20 make clear that the narrator and her husband are eating at restaurants because they're intimidated by their new surroundings, not because they like to dine out. Choice (D) isn't a good choice because the narrator specifies that she had been to the specialty market earlier in the day, when she had seen the old woman who reminded her of her grandmother (lines 66–67), so she is clearly not refusing to leave her apartment.

4. **F** This question provides a good opportunity for you to eliminate wrong answers. Choices (G), (H), and (J) all rely on information not presented in the passage, so you can get rid of all three. The narrator writes that she promised to go to the supermarket *so we could both have a taste of the home we'd been aching for* (lines 25–26), so choice (F) is the best answer.

5. **B** You can start by eliminating choice (A), because the narrator says explicitly that the produce section is missing items she considers staples (lines 34–35). Choice (C) is too extreme and, while the narrator is surprised to see the produce section *tucked away*, she does not make any statement regarding *Indian supermarkets* or suggest that the produce sections are *always* out in the open. Choice (D) refers to an event that takes place elsewhere in the store. The narrator comments that the produce section is *surprisingly tucked away* (lines 32–33), a description that suggests she had expected the produce section to be more centrally situated. Thus, choice (B) is the best option.

6. **H** Note that although the clerk stares at the narrator, he immediately replies to her question and displays a *wide, unexpectedly amiable grin* (line 47), so you can get rid of the answers that describe the clerk as unfriendly or unhelpful—i.e., choices (G) and (J). Choice (F) depicts the clerk correctly, but the narrator tells us that she was irritated, not pleased. Choice (H) is the best answer.

7. **B** First, find the reference to fluorescent lighting; the narrator says that it *bleached out* the packages' colors, making them *flat and lifeless* (line 59). Choice (D) is nearly an opposite answer, whereas choice (A) refers to a contrast the narrator doesn't draw in the passage. Choice (C) points to an earlier part in the passage; by the time the narrator describes the lighting, she is no longer intimidated by the store (and terrified is certainly too strong in any case). Choice (B) correctly references the passage's description of the fluorescent lights: *I observed that the supermarket's fluorescent ceiling bulbs effectively bleached out the shelves' contents. The bottles and boxes no longer seemed exotic or glamorous* (lines 53–56).

8. **G** *Unfriendly* is a strange word to apply to an inanimate object such as a jar of curry powder, so examine the context to try to make sense of that term here. The narrator has just been thinking about the different spices—*each with its own…subtle but memorable color*—that her grandmother used to make homemade curry powder (lines 77–78). In the next lines, the narrator sets up a contrast between the unfamiliar curry powder in the supermarket and the *familiar result* of her *grandmother's efforts*. Consequently, choice (G) is the best option. Choices (H) and (J) don't work because the narrator doesn't mention either the curry powder's ingredients or its country of origin. And you can eliminate choice (F) because the clerk in fact tells the narrator where to find the product.

9. **C** The passage tells us that the old woman is noteworthy for handing out *sample pieces of fruit* and *explaining how adding one more ingredient will perfect the planned dish* (lines 64–66), so she's neither nervous nor stingy. Thus, you can eliminate choices (B) and (D). The passage refers to the grandmother's *swift, sure knife* (line 76), a portrait that is at odds with the idea that she is frail, so you can get rid of choice (A). Only *sociability*, choice (C), really describes how kind and welcoming the narrator's grandmother seemed, even to strangers.

10. **F** You can eliminate choice (G) because the narrator describes putting on a college sweatshirt before starting to prepare the meal (lines 86–88). The passage says that the narrator's grandmother does get along easily with others, so choice (H) is inaccurate. And you should avoid picking choice (J) because the passage doesn't say whether the narrator's grandmother or mother liked or disliked air conditioning. In fact, the passage mentions the narrator's mother only once; in line 86, the narrator says that she uses a combination of the specialty market items and the supermarket's *quick prep* materials, so *making dinner isn't the all-day task it often was for my grandmother and even my mother*. This observation closely reflects choice (F), so that's your best response.

Passage II

11. **A** The passage states that more than *900 independent record stores have perished since the rise of digital music sales in 2003* (lines 11–13). This supports choice (A). Choice (B) features percentages from the passage which refer to the impact on CD sales, not the number of record stores that specialize in older formats. Choice (C) states that fewer than 2000 stores were in business prior to 2003, but the passage tells us only that this is the current number of stores in business. Choice (D) makes a prediction that is not found in the passage.

12. **J** The *silver lining* refers to the gray-haired older men that are the *largest segment* of the record store consumer base and gives reasons why they *don't seem to be lured away* by the alternatives (lines 79–80). The fact that a trip to the record store allows older men to *escape* their careers and *reconnect* with their childhoods is support for choice (J)'s claim that they savor the experience. Choice (F) describes the opposite of what this paragraph reports about older men. Choice (G) is incorrect because the passage says that older men are not lured away by superstores, not that record stores have lured customers back. Choice (H) uses words from the paragraph like *posters* (line 84) and *album covers* (line 85) to make an unsupportable claim about their effects on downloaded music.

13. **B** *Prehistoric* is used figuratively to mean *old-fashioned*. The context of this paragraph describes the growing trend of downloadable music and describes its appeal to younger consumers, saying *recent technology* allows *thousands of songs* to fit onto a small, portable device and questions why anyone would want a CD instead (lines 31–35). Choice (B) correctly identifies the implication that CDs are no longer a preferred choice among some consumers. Choice (A) is not supported by the passage. Choice (C) refers to download speeds, which the passage does not discuss. Choice (D) suggests that size is the only problem with CDs, when the passage also specifically mentions how few songs CDs can carry.

14. **H** Spelling concedes *the greater affordability of superstore prices* (line 69), making choice (H) a valid inference. He believes superstore shoppers miss out on mingling with record store clientele with similar interests, not that they share no similar interests as choice (F) states. He does not say anything about the online music purchasing process lacking *any* sense of community, so you can eliminate choice (G). He does not blame consumers as choice (J) states but rather struggles to come up with a reason why they should want to go to a record store.

15. **C** The passage as a whole is an analytical look at the troubles facing the record store industry. Introducing the passage with the anecdote of Spelling's store is intended to give one illustration of a store that is suffering because of industry conditions, not because the store is inherently flawed. This supports choice (C). Choice (A) is incorrect because the passage does not ever try to criticize record stores for a lack of modernization. Choice (B) is incorrect because the passage never mentions whether consumers are or are not interested in rare musical commodities. Choice (D) is incorrect because the passage does not suggest that record store owners lack real estate knowledge but rather that they are increasingly forced to relinquish their stores due to lagging business.

16. **F** The context of this paragraph discusses digital music as a growing trend, saying consumers are *increasingly likely* to buy their music this way. Therefore, if digital music since 1999 has reduced CD sales by *twenty to thirty percent*, it can be reasonably inferred that prior to 1999 the percentage was lower. Choices (G), (H), and (J) all suggest that the impact of digital music was the same prior to 1999 as it is now or even larger.

17. **B** The passage states that *because superstores expect to sell a higher volume of goods than that of a specialized store* (lines 44–45), superstores can afford to make prices very low. This supports choice (B). A large initial amount of investment, a wide variety of merchandise, and a warehouse-sized facility are all mentioned as characteristics of superstores but do not in and of themselves give a reason for why prices can be made low, making choices (A) and (C) incorrect. The ambitiousness of the economic planners of superstores is not mentioned, making choice (D) unsupportable.

18. **J** Sam Walton is identified as the creator of the superstore business model, and superstores are mentioned throughout the passage as one of the two main economic forces creating a decline in business for record stores. This makes choice (J) the correct answer. Record stores do not use the superstore business model as choice (F) states. Sam Walton is not mentioned as having any direct goals or criticisms towards the record store industry as choices (G) and (H) state.

19. **B** Choice (A) is supported by numerous references to the fact that superstores sell CDs at lower prices than do record stores. Choice (C) is mentioned in the discussion of digital downloads, explaining that a CD is *harder to put in one's pocket than an MP3 player and holds less than 1% as much music* (lines 34–35). Choice (D) is supported by saying that *superstores hold the allure of allowing a shopper to make* music, clothing, and grocery *purchases at the same cash register* (lines 42–43). The fear of being unwelcome, as choice (B) states, is never mentioned in the passage.

20. **J** The author states that superstores have to keep prices so low when they open that *it will be years before a superstore recovers the initial money put into building it.* This supports choice (J). Since choices (F), (G), and (H) are all steps mentioned that come before this point, they cannot be correct.

Passage III

21. **A** The narrator discusses her childhood feelings toward Mexican art in the first paragraph. She describes herself as having grown up *surrounded by art* (line 1) at home and bored by art while on vacation, when her parents would shop at roadside stands. Therefore, the best answer is choice (A). Choice (B) incorrectly mentions *geometric designs*, which are not discussed in the passage. Choice (C) incorrectly refers to a phrase used later in the passage, in reference not to Mexican art but to the European art the narrator studied in school. Choice (D) incorrectly attributes the feelings of the narrator's parents, who do in fact like the art because it reminds them of home, to the narrator herself.

22. **G** The second paragraph deals with the narrator's decision to study art in college and her growing preference for European art. At the end of the paragraph, she describes bringing European prints home to her parents, who respond by smiling, then putting the new prints in the narrator's bedroom. Therefore, although they do accept the gift, they do not seem very excited about it, making choice (G), *tolerant,* the best answer. Choice (F) is incorrect because although the parents might be *grateful,* no evidence of this is given in the passage. Choices (H) and (J) both suggest negative reactions where none is suggested in the passage—there is no evidence that the parents are *horrified* or *perplexed.*

23. **A** This passage is told in past tense: the narrator is looking back on events from her past. Therefore, choice (A) is the best answer. Choice (B) incorrectly identifies the narrator as a child during all of the events in the passage, which is incorrect because it describes her college experiences. Choice (C) incorrectly identifies the narrator as an artist, as opposed to the art student that she actually is. Choice (D) is incorrect because the narrator's parents are explicitly mentioned during the passage and are not themselves the narrators.

24. **H** The narrator's comment that describes her parents' collection as *almost shameful* is mentioned as part of the discussion comparing the art of the narrator's childhood to the art that she studied at school. She sees her parents' art as inferior and tries to bring them European art, which she prefers. Therefore, choice (H) is the best answer. Choice (F) is incorrect because the passage does not address her parents' finances. Choice (G) is incorrect because the passage never discusses how the narrator feels about bringing friends to her home. Choice (J) is incorrect because the narrator herself advocates displaying art—she just prefers art of a different style.

25. **D** The word *victorious* is used in the phrase *our victorious arrival in California.* At this point, the passage has just described the difficulties that the narrator has encountered on her road trip but she is still planning to end at her parents' house in California. Choice (D), *successful,* is the best match for this description and best aligns with the idea that the arrival in California will signify a successful end to that leg of the trip. Choices (A), (B), and (C) give alternatives to the word *victorious* but these words do not make sense in the context of the passage.

26. **G** The passage begins with the narrator describing her childhood, surrounded by but not appreciating the Mexican art loved by her parents. She then begins to study art in college, where she begins to prefer European art, and considers it superior. At the end of the passage, however, she has an encounter with a Mexican artist that changes her perceptions and helps her to begin to appreciate Mexican art. Therefore, choice (G) is the best answer, as it addresses this shift from disdain to appreciation. Choice (F) is incorrect because it describes a change in the opposite direction. Choice (H) is too strong—there is no evidence that the narrator decides to reject European art. Choice (J) makes a claim that is unsupported by the passage, particularly because of the claim made earlier in the passage that the narrator wants to be the curator of a museum.

27. **B** The old man is discussed in the sixth and final paragraphs, after the narrator wanders into the studio where he is painting. He is described as *slightly hunched over, seeing something else entirely,* and *otherwise occupied.* The narrator sees him as focused on his painting to the exclusion of anyone else in the room. Moreover, the narrator's decision to leave the studio silently, out of respect for his mastery, demonstrates that she is impressed by his abilities. Therefore, choice (B) is the best answer, as it best encompasses both the painter's attention to his work and his artistic abilities. Choice (A) is incorrect because nowhere does the passage discuss the old man's level of education. Choice (C) incorrectly describes the old man as rude. Although he does not acknowledge the presence of the narrator, the passage explains this in terms of his focus, and specifically states that he does not appear unfriendly. Choice (D) is incorrect because the passage does not support the idea that the old man is forgetful.

28. **H** The phrase *launched himself at the canvas* is used to describe the old man's actions once he decides what to paint. It transitions him from sitting, lost in thought, to *adding details to the face at a furious pace.* Therefore, a good translation of the phrase would be *went into action.* Choice (H), the correct answer, does the best job of capturing this transition. Choice (F) is incorrect because the old man does not literally attack the canvas. Choice (G) is incorrect because the old man is later described as having a great deal of skill. Choice (J) is incorrect because the old man's hesitation ended with the action that is being described.

29. **C** At the end of the passage, the narrator expresses a desire to speak with the painter but explains her decision not to because *he looked like he was otherwise occupied, his thoughts on some past time.* She then leaves the studio silently, *as anyone would when leaving the presence of a master,* showing her newfound respect for the old man. Therefore, choice (C) is the best answer, as it correctly identifies the narrator's decision as due primarily to this feeling of respect. Choice (A) incorrectly describes the narrator as afraid, an idea that is not supported by the passage. Choice (B) is incorrect because it does not address the narrator's expressed feelings of respect. Choice (D) is incorrect because it does not address the narrator's change of heart, as shown in the latter portion of the passage.

30. **H** The final paragraphs of the passage describe the narrator's recognition that the old man she sees painting has a great deal of talent. Therefore, choice (H) is the best answer, as it correctly identifies the author's feelings of respect and her decision to leave the studio without making noise. Choice (F) is incorrect because the narrator is not described as *condescending* after her encounter. Choice (G) incorrectly describes the narrator as *bored,* which is not supported by her actions in the passage. Choice (J) is incorrect because the passage does not support the claim that the narrator is either *annoyed* or *offended.*

Passage IV

31. **C**   The passage discusses many influences on the timing of birds' migration periods. Though one specific research study is described, this is not the main idea of the passage, as choice (A) indicates. The distance traveled by the wandering albatross is mentioned, but the distances of other birds are not specified, as suggested by choice (B). Weather is only one of several factors mentioned that influences birds' decisions to migrate, so eliminate choice (D).

32. **F**   The author mentions that many birds do not migrate to prevent a misinterpretation that the 50 million birds cited as migratory in the previous sentence may indicate the total number of birds in the world. The author agrees that the biological mechanism for migration is complex; therefore, he does not want to *undermine* this idea, as indicated by choice (G). There is no suggestion in the passage of a disagreement among ornithologists, so eliminate choice (H). There is no support that the migration cycle is changing, as stated in choice (J).

33. **A**   The passage states that Dolnik and Blyumental's work focuses only on chaffinches, which are a type of diurnal migratory land bird. The last paragraph indicates that chaffinches have a shorter migration path than many other species. The focus on a particular geographical area is not cited as a weakness, as indicated by choice (B). Though the passage indicates that Dolnik and Blyumental did destroy birds in their research, the passage does not identify this as a limitation, so eliminate choice (C). The passage states that Dolnik and Blyumental were able to establish the *total* population (line 41), so eliminate choice (D).

34. **H**   The purpose of the third paragraph is to provide explanations of several ways that food supply influences the timing of bird migration. Though some sources of food are listed, their specification is not the primary purpose of the paragraph, as stated in choice (F). Weather conditions are mentioned, but the paragraph does not mention the way weather affects bird flight, so eliminate choice (G). The passage does not indicate that any general scientific principles have been discovered through the observation of migratory birds, as suggested by choice (J).

35. **B**   Dolnik and Blyumental measured the fat content of all the birds they captured, so their description of some as *very fat* (line 45) must be based on a comparison between the captured birds. There is no indication of the sample size in the researchers' experiment, so eliminate choice (A). The fact that Dolnik and Blyumental examined *the carcasses of birds* (line 39) means that they were not merely observing the birds in flight to make their assessment, as indicated in choice (C). The passage does not indicate that the scientists conducting the study had any preference as to the fat content of the birds, so eliminate choice (D).

36. **G**   The passage states that wandering albatrosses travel hundreds of thousands of kilometers each year, and these are a species of sea bird. Chaffinches are the example of land birds, which the passage indicates have shorter migration paths, so eliminate choice (F). The first paragraph mentions that tropical birds often do not migrate at all, so eliminate choice (H). Temperate birds' migration times and distances are not clearly indicated, so eliminate choice (J).

37. **D** The example of caged birds is used to indicate that birds have an internal ability to sense the time at which their species migrate. The passage indicates that caged birds experience *migratory restlessness* (line 20) because they cannot migrate, so eliminate choice (A). Stores of body fat are discussed in the passage only in relation to chaffinches, so eliminate choice (B). There is no suggestion in the passage that a bird in a cage loses its ability to tell the difference between night and day, as indicated in choice (C).

38. **H** The passage states that chaffinch *migration volume peaked* (lines 50–51) in the afternoon of the second day. Choice (F) indicates the time at which *only very fat birds flew* (line 45). Choice (G) includes the time right before the volume peaked. Choice (J) notes the time at which *all the birds that began to migrate were very lean* (lines 53–54), but does not indicate the number of birds that fit this description.

39. **D** The passage says that healthy birds influenced *the remaining population that was not as physically fit for migration* (lines 43–44), explaining why more and more lean birds flew after the fat birds. The passage contains no comparison of the numbers of healthy versus unhealthy birds, as indicated by choice (A). The passage states that the lean chaffinches ate before flying, whereas the fat chaffinches flew without eating, so eliminate choice (B). There is no indication that Dolnik and Blyumental monitored the health of individual chaffinches over the entire migration, which would be necessary to come to the conclusion stated in choice (C).

40. **H** The phrase *few species* indicates that the extreme distances traveled by wandering albatrosses is unusual in migratory birds. The *coastal birds* in choice (F) would include chaffinches, which migrate much shorter distances than wandering albatrosses. The passage does not indicate whether wandering albatrosses are *temperate migrants*, so eliminate choice (G). Wandering albatrosses are long-distance migratory sea birds, so their behavior cannot be considered *unusual* for this type of bird, as indicated in choice (J).

READING PRACTICE 3 ANSWERS

1. B
2. G
3. B
4. F
5. C
6. J
7. A
8. G
9. B
10. J
11. D
12. H
13. B
14. J
15. D
16. F
17. C
18. H
19. C
20. F
21. D
22. F
23. C
24. G
25. D
26. H
27. B
28. G
29. B
30. F
31. C
32. F
33. D
34. J
35. A
36. G
37. B
38. J
39. C
40. H

READING PRACTICE 3 EXPLANATIONS

Passage I

1. **B** The narrator relates that she thinks of the hens as *slumbering ladies* (line 65), which is a metaphorical way of thinking that connects with her imagination. By contrast, the farmhouse is described merely as *neat* and *white* (lines 30–31), so those terms don't signal anything in particular about the narrator's imagination, so you can get rid of choice (A). Similarly, Essie's narratives of how Aunt Millie braids her hair (line 72) and how the earth smells (lines 50–51) are straightforward, rather than imaginative. Therefore, choice (B) is the best answer.

2. **G** Look for the context clues that suggest Essie has never visited the farm before, such as her reference to the *unfamiliar farm country* in line 24, or her description of the *red barn* as looking *just like my mother's descriptions and the pictures in books I'd seen when I was younger* (lines 31–33). In the passage, Essie doesn't characterize her life in New York as preferable to any of her farm experiences, so you should eliminate choice (F). As for choice (H), you could argue that her experiences on the farm are important enough for her to remember vividly, but she doesn't say that her visit was the *most* important event of her life, so reject this answer choice. Choice (J) is not supported by the passage.

3. **B** Essie mentions that she and her brother had made a pact to take note of all the details that differed from their life at home in New York, which suggests that their unfamiliar surroundings made their perceptions more acute. Thus, choice (B) is the best answer. The passage doesn't mention any trauma Essie has suffered, and we don't know that she can't speak, so choice (A) doesn't work. The passage doesn't indicate that Essie is more perceptive than Kiran is, nor that she is especially shy, so eliminate choice (C). And nothing Essie describes indicates that her relationship with Aunt Millie increases her awareness of her surroundings, so choice (D) isn't accurate.

4. **F** The narrator uses the term *blurred* to suggest a contrast between Aunt Millie and her own mother, who is *all sharp lines and tight angles* (lines 34–35), so choice (F) is the best fit. Elsewhere in the passage, Essie seems to have keen powers of observation and eyesight, as in the sections where she looks out of the bus windows (lines 18–37), so choice (H) isn't a good fit, and the passage doesn't indicate that Aunt Millie's personality is either more or less distinctive than is the narrator's mother's, so choice (J) doesn't work well. Choice (G) doesn't come up in this passage.

5. **C** Essie does say that there was a lot of work to do on the farm, but the passage doesn't suggest that this work was unappreciated by her aunt and uncle, so choice (A) should be eliminated. Instead, Essie talks about how much she enjoys the work, particularly collecting eggs from the farm's chickens (lines 60–61), so choice (C) is a better fit. The narrator neither contrasts farm life with any *difficulties* in New York nor argues that boys and girls have different roles on the farm, so get rid of choices (B) and (D).

6. **J** As it says in lines 8–10, *I had never been outside of New York City before, so I was nervous about moving, not to mention that I had never met my aunt and uncle before.* Thus, choice (J) gives the event that took place first in the narrator's life.

7.   **A**   The paragraph in question is an account of how Aunt Millie would braid and treat the narrator's hair. The fact that Aunt Millie takes time away from other responsibilities to make time for this activity implies that she is not cut off from or indifferent toward Essie, so choices (B) and (D) don't agree with the passage. Choice (C) focuses on the different worldviews of Aunt Millie and the narrator and how these differences might drive them apart, but that possibility isn't supported either here or elsewhere in the passage.

8.   **G**   In depicting the food at the farm, Essie says that the food is similar but not identical to the food she has eaten in New York, so you can eliminate choice (F), which doesn't account for the subtle differences she explains. At the other end of the scale is choice (H), which implies that the food is entirely unfamiliar compared to the food she's eaten before. Choice (J) is an overly literal rendering of the narrator's connection between the meal and the farm that produced it. This leaves choice (G) as the most accurate description.

9.   **B**   The two most important details that suggest the mother's sadness are the tear Essie spots in the corner of her mother's eye (line 14), and the fact that her mother waves to Essie and Kiran for a long time after the bus pulls away (line 15). The passage doesn't contain any details that connote the mother's desire for the children to have a good time, so choice (A) doesn't work. The reason the narrator's mother sends the children to the North Carolina farm is that her new job would require them to stay by themselves too much (lines 5–7); she doesn't indicate that learning self-discipline on the farm is important to her, so you shouldn't select choice (C). Finally, although the mother is described as *wary* of leaving the children at home while she is at her job, the passage doesn't signal that she has any fears about the bus ride, so eliminate choice (D).

10. **J**   All of the answer choices besides choice (J) contain information not covered specifically in the passage: nothing suggests that the narrator is sickly. Although Essie and Kiran might learn new skills on the farm, we don't know whether these skills will be valuable, nor does anyone give this as the reason for the trip, and whereas the children's cousin Ike is mentioned in the passage, the relationship among the cousins is not given as a reason for the trip. Only choice (J) refers to information that appears in the passage (lines 5–7).

Passage II

11. **D**   The first paragraph describes plant consciousness attaining scientific credibility *mainly since the work of Clive Buckner came to light* (lines 10–11). Professor Wilkinson also says that *Buckner's work opened up a Pandora's box of bad science* (lines 71–72). The second paragraph identifies that his shocking work took place forty years ago, and the blurb indicates that the passage was written in 2007. These details support choice (D). The polygraph was involved in Buckner's early experiments, but the invention of the polygraph is not mentioned in the passage which makes choice (A) incorrect. Choice (B) describes one of the experiments which followed Buckner's work, so it could not be the original catalyst. Choice (C) makes an unsupportable claim that the scientists at the Boston Botanical Gardens were innovators in their field and sparked subsequent controversy.

12. H   Buckner observed a reaction taking place in his plant as soon as he had a thought of burning the plant. While Buckner takes this to mean that plants can perceive human thoughts, Wilkinson and Karnell are referred to in the passage as skeptics who believe that the *crazy notion of mind-reading plants* is partly a result of poorly conducted experiments that are *difficult to repeat by other, more skeptical scientists*. This supports choice (H). Choices (G) and (J) represent interpretations sympathetic to Buckner's. Choice (F) would not be appropriate to this experiment nor would it appeal to the skeptical point of view of Wilkinson and Karnell.

13. B   Buckner's response to Karnell's line of criticism is that the *varied outcomes* of plant consciousness experiments are actually supportive of Buckner's scientific predictions that plants have a unique response to a given caretaker. Therefore, choice (B) is supportable because Buckner thinks Karnell's point strengthens the plant consciousness theory, not weakens it. There are no specific examples offered, as choice (A) states. While Buckner disagrees with Karnell's criticism, there is nothing to suggest that he is *completely indifferent* to this criticism, as choice (C) states. Rather, Buckner thinks Karnell's concerns are relevant support of Buckner's theory. There is nothing to support choice (D)'s idea that Buckner plans to train other experimenters.

14. J   In the second paragraph, *lie-detectors* are defined as *polygraph galvanometer equipment,* which supports choice (J). Choices (F), (G), and (H) contain familiar wording from elsewhere in the passage but not attributable to *lie-detectors*.

15. D   The reference to *social reinforcement* is followed by a comment that the idea behind this seems to be *that interacting with these plants will help them flourish*. This makes choice (D) an acceptable choice. There is nothing in the paragraph or the passage to support the goals stated in choices (A) and (C). The rationale stated in choice (B) is referred to in the passage as what a casual observer might mistake as the purpose of Sheila's behavior.

16. F   By referring to parts of the scientific method that some of the plant experiments lacked, Karnell is trying to demonstrate that the observed results that some experimenters have interpreted as plant-consciousness are *unreliable from the start* because of flawed methodology. This supports choice (F), which paraphrases that poorly conducted studies can make for less trustworthy findings. Karnell's point does not specifically accuse researchers of not understanding the point of a control group, as choice (G) states. He would not necessarily believe a well-conducted study *would* prove that there is plant consciousness as choice (H) states. He does not make a distinction about confirmation bias being more likely in plant related experiments, which makes choice (J) unsupportable.

17. C   The fourth paragraph discusses the *steady flow of research* that attempts to *revisit and replicate Buckner's hypothesis*. Because Steve Karnell maintains that other researchers have had a hard time duplicating evidence of plant consciousness, these experiments would undermine Karnell's position. The positions of Crusella, choice (A), and Buckner, choice (D), are in line with the research being conducted. The author's position on this issue is never revealed, which makes choice (B) unsupportable.

18. **H**   The passage defines confirmation bias as researchers *interpreting* experimental observations to agree with their *premeditated goals*, what they're trying to prove or discover. This makes choice (H) correct. Choices (F) and (G) involve familiar wording that is not explicitly defined in the passage, and choice (J) describes a concept defined as *ignoring potential alternative explanations to justify a faulty hypothesis*. That is not a fair paraphrase for what this question is asking, which makes choice (J) incorrect.

19. **C**   In the fifth paragraph, Buckner acknowledges that *many experiments fail to replicate the same results* and says that the outcome is very dependent on the researcher. This statement makes choice (C) the most supportable answer choice because the likelihood of having different results means the outcome is inconsistent. Choice (A) relates to the third paragraph but not to Buckner's specific words. Choice (B) relates to the skeptics' point of view. Choice (D) is unjustifiably confident and not supported by Buckner's quotation.

20. **F**   Researchers in this field *think that there is a mountain of evidence that plants are sensitive to their environments in ways that traditional science is not equipped to describe* and *believe that there needs to be some kind of new scientific explanation*. This supports the idea of choice (F) that there is currently no sufficient traditional scientific explanation for the observed evidence. Choices (G) and (J) are points of view that belong to skeptics who do not think this is worthwhile or well-conducted scientific research. Choice (H) characterizes the available evidence in a way that is not supported anywhere in the passage.

Passage III

21. **D**   The context before this sentence explains that we all get yelled at by others to *cease our incessant noise making*. In other words, we are being a nuisance by singing our songs. This behavior is lessened as we learn the rules of etiquette, so choice (D) is correct in saying that these rules instruct us to refrain from behavior like singing that may annoy others. Choice (A) is incorrect because the rules of etiquette do not necessarily pertain to playing with toys, particularly if one was playing alone. Choice (B) is incorrect because it is not supportable to assume the author is referring to specific etiquette classes, as opposed to maturing through ordinary socialization. Choice (C) is incorrect because it is unfairly assuming that songwriters will not abide by rules of etiquette, whereas the author explains that songwriters will attempt to adjust their songs so that they are no longer a nuisance, which would be a polite gesture.

22. **F**   Although the concept of *happy to hear* is not defined precisely, you should expect that anything the author discusses with a positive tone is something songwriters use to approach this goal. Choice (F) is correct because the mimicry of joy and anguish is brought up by the author as a potentially negative capacity of a songwriter, contrasted with songwriting that is infused with genuine emotional meaning (lines 79–86). Choice (G) is discussed in paragraph five; *there's a balance of two opposing forces we enjoy in music...one soothes, the other agitates*. Choice (H) is discussed in paragraph seven. Choice (J) is discussed in the final few paragraphs as something songwriters aspire to do so that audience members can more personally identify with songs.

23. C The passage is mainly a descriptive discussion of songwriting, including how we approach and absorb music as children, adolescents, and adults, and some of the considerations songwriters face in their craft. Choice (C) effectively captures the scope and tone of the passage. The other three choices present too narrow a purpose and/or critical tone. Choice (A) is incorrect because much of the passage had nothing to do with expressing pain. Choice (B) is incorrect because the author does not specifically endorse catchy music. Choice (D) is incorrect because the author mentions cultural upbringing only as an influence on songwriting, not as a negative limitation.

24. G Whenever you see a pronoun as in *this private release,* the explanation of what *this* is should be the preceding idea. The sentence before this one describes the feeling of one's inner world radiating out. Choice (G) is the closest paraphrase to that idea. Choice (F) is incorrect because the author explains why refraining from specific details is sometimes helpful to a songwriter. Choice (H) is incorrect because the tone of forcing a listener to develop a kinship is too strong and unsupportable. Choice (J) is incorrect because the author never says a songwriter must focus on these two emotions.

25. D The passage states that as adolescents *we look to find personal meaning in lyrics.* This makes choice (D) correct. Choice (A) is incorrect because a sense of belonging and familiarity is identified as something children also look for in songs, similar to preferring their parents' cooking due to its familiarity. Choice (B) is incorrect because of the unsupportable language that adolescents are seeking to *discover new trends* rather than just to identify with the dress and politics of certain artists. Choice (C) is incorrect because the passage never mentions adolescents rebelling against their cultural upbringing.

26. H Choice (H) is correct because one's favorite authors are never mentioned; the closest mention is that *successful songs win over listeners just as successful stories do.* Choices (F), (G), and (J) are all comparisons made in paragraph seven.

27. B Choice (B) is correct because the author proceeds to discuss personal details of what influenced his early songwriting. Choice (A) is incorrect because the author never contradicts this first idea. Choice (C) is incorrect because the author contends that expressing one's troubles is only frowned upon as a lack of self-control in speech. Choice (D) is incorrect because the idea of the first paragraph is reinforced throughout the first few paragraphs.

28. G Choice (G) is correct because soothing songs are *often used to distract from anxiety or coax into slumber,* while agitating songs can be *customized into any taunt.* Choice (F) is incorrect because the passage says nothing about soothing songs being preferred by adults. Choice (H) is incorrect because agitating songs are not mentioned as a way to wake up a sleeping child. Choice (J) is incorrect because agitating songs are not mentioned as a way to distract us from things we hate.

29. B The last sentence states that just as audiences can discern between good and bad acting, they can discern between authentic and contrived performances of music. Choice (B) is therefore supported and correct. Choice (A) is incorrect because the author mentions something that acting and performing music have in common. Choice (C) is incorrect because the author never makes a comparative statement about which is more convincing, anguished or joyful acting/music. Choice (D) is incorrect because it is too strong. Although the author states one thing acting/singing have in common, it is unsupportable to say that they are *completely identical.*

30. **F** The passage states that the cultural backdrop *calibrates her listening tastes,* and it is connected to the previous sentence's notion that a child will naturally prefer her parents' cooking just because of its familiarity. These ideas support choice (F) and make it correct. Choice (G) is incorrect because the passage does not mention songwriters striving to avoid their cultural upbringing. Choice (H) is incorrect because the tone of the paragraph suggests the surrounding culture influences musical tastes but does not necessarily *instruct the proper structure.* Choice (J) is incorrect because of extreme and unsupportable language about a cultural context being the *primary basis* of how a child makes friends.

Passage IV

31. **C** The passage describes current information about comets and provides an explanation for why astronomers are interested in comets. Though there are still some things unknown about the origins of the solar system, pointing this out is not the primary purpose of the passage, as choice (A) indicates. The passage does not indicate that readers should *aid in the search* for comets as choice (B) suggests. Only one specific mineral in the composition of comets is mentioned in the passage, so eliminate choice (D).

32. **F** The mention of *other new minerals that may be found* on lines 73–74 indicates that the author believes that there are still some undiscovered minerals in the solar system. Though comet IRAS-Araki-Alcock was the brightest comet in recent times, the passage does not make any predictions about future bright comets, eliminating choice (G). The passage indicates that comets were made at the same time as the rest of the solar system on lines 55–58, so you can get rid of choice (H). Line 76 talks about scientist's plan to *retrieve material* but the passage does not indicate any possible reasons for difficulty in completing the mission, so eliminate choice (J).

33. **D** The third paragraph states that the comet's nearness to Earth in relation to perihelion, or closest approach to the sun, strongly affects a comet's apparent brightness. All comets are described as having large comas compared to their nuclei, so eliminate choice (A). Though comets do seem to move more quickly when they are closer to the Earth, this is not the cause of the apparent brightness, eliminating choice (B). If a comet's perihelion occurs after it is closest to earth, it will be *relatively cold and solid* (line 33), not bright, so you can eliminate (C).

34. **J** The passage describes comets' orbits as erratic, but does not explain *why.* The last paragraph answers the question in choice (F). The first paragraph describes the *solar winds and radiation pressure from the Sun* (line 7) that form the tail, answering the question in choice (G). Comets are most often *invisible* (line 28), which explains why new ones are difficult to discover, answering choice (H).

35. **A** Lines 12–13 state that the *brightest comets can be seen with the naked eye,* so no telescope is needed to detect comets. The information in choice (B) in line 7 indicates that *solar winds and radiation pressure* are required to make a comet's tail visible. The comet is created when *frozen matter evaporates* (line 4), eliminating choice (C). The material in the comet can fill *an area up to a million kilometers around the solid nucleus* (line 6) supporting the information in choice (D).

36. **G**   According to line 11, comets *cast no light of their own*. Line 70 discusses the *discovery of a previously unknown mineral*, supporting the information in choice (F). The example of the two appearances of Halley's comet in the third paragraph support the *changes in apparent brightness at different times* mentioned in choice (H). Line 59 states that comets come from *areas barely within the Sun's gravitation,* so eliminate choice (J).

37. **B**   The example of Halley's comet is used to show how a comet's distance to *Earth, especially in relation to its perihelion* (line 30) affects its brightness. Choice (A) discusses speed which is not related to the example of Halley's comet, but rather comet IRAS-Araki-Alcock (lines 43–44). Though the second pass of Halley's comet was a *disappointment* (line 36), this information is not what the example is used to emphasize in the passage, so eliminate choice (C). Choice (D) incorrectly suggests that comets are unpredictable with regard to *when* they will be visible, rather than how bright they will be.

38. **J**   The last paragraph discusses interesting results of examination of dust from a comet as well as future missions that have not yet been completed. There was no mention of *technical difficulties*, so eliminate choice (F). Though some scientists *hope* (line 65) that information gained from direct study of comets might explain life on Earth, this has not yet happened as indicated in choice (G). Lines 68–70 state that samples of comet dust have been collected and successfully examined, contradicting choice (H).

39. **C**   The quotation refers to the aspects of comets that interest astronomers. These are discussed in detail in the next paragraph as primarily chemical differences between comets and the Earth, and in this paragraph, it is mentioned that comets are thought to represent remnants of many of the chemical materials from which the social system was created. Choice (A) indicates the interest in *novelty* of the comets, not the characteristics *beyond* novelty. The *difficulty of detecting* comets is explained in the passage, but is not described as being of particular interest to astronomers, so eliminate choice (B). Though comets are said in the passage to provide a *fossil record* (line 61) of the solar system, this is because they are unchanged, not because they are older.

40. **H**   The last paragraph is mainly about the reasons scientists study comets. Choice (F) suggests that many experiments have been performed on passing comets, but the paragraph mentions only one, and indicates that many planned experiments have yet to be tried. Though some scientists *hope that comet material may reveal information about the origins of life on Earth* (lines 79–81), the passage does not suggest that comets caused evolution, as stated in choice (G). Although lines 72–75 mention that information about comets may cause scientists to *reconsider new models* for the origins of the solar system in the future, the passage does not *contradict* current models, so eliminate choice (J).

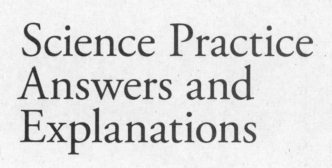

Science Practice
Answers and
Explanations

SCIENCE PRACTICE 1 ANSWERS

1. C
2. G
3. A
4. J
5. A
6. H
7. B
8. H
9. C
10. G
11. D
12. H
13. B
14. F
15. B
16. J
17. C
18. G
19. D
20. H
21. C
22. F
23. A
24. H
25. A
26. H
27. C
28. J
29. D
30. F
31. C
32. H
33. C
34. F
35. B
36. F
37. C
38. J
39. B
40. F

SCIENCE PRACTICE 1 EXPLANATIONS

1. **C** Nothing is mentioned in the passage about how far back radiocarbon dating is accurate, so choice (A) is incorrect. You are not told what motivation caused the scientists to perform the study, and there is nothing to suggest that they are only interested in a certain time period, so choice (B) can be eliminated. For choice (D), the scientists do not try to determine the color of the shells; rather, they use a dye to visualize the scutes so that they can determine their sizes and patterns. Without any complete shells, it would be very difficult for the scientists to determine any of the measurements used in Study 2—choice (C).

2. **G** M hexagons are the longer ones; m hexagons are the smaller ones. Choice (G) shows a band with two large, then two small, and another large hexagon in a band down the middle of the shell.

3. **A** 120,000 years ago, the average number of scutes was about 25, and now (at 0—the furthest right point on the graph), it is about 32, so the average number of scutes is larger. 120,000 years ago, the average bridge height was about 2.1 cm, and now it is about 2.5 cm, so the average bridge height is also larger.

4. **J** The hypothetical 86,000-year-old data point falls between the 85,000 and 87,000-year-old data points. Therefore, you should expect the percent of shells having each pattern to be between the percentages at 85,000 and 87,000 years old. For the first column (M-m-M-M-m), 25.5 is the average of 21 and 30, so choice (J) looks like a good fit. To be sure, check the other columns as well. The value in the second column (M-M-m-m-M) should be about 67–72, and the value in the third column should be around 3–7. (J) works well.

5. **A** The third graph in Figure 2 shows average shell surface area. Find the 80 thousand years point on the *x*-axis and move vertically to the data point. Move horizontally to the y-axis to find the answer: 670 cm².

6. **H** The first study examines the relative frequency of occurrence of different patterns of scutes (M-m-M-M-m, etc.). The second study looks at shell diameter, shell bridge height and the number of scutes on shells—3 shape and size characteristics of turtle shells, making choice (H) the best answer.

7. **B** Since all four blood types were produced in equal measure in Analysis 3, refer back to Table 1 to determine your ratio. There are two blood types that contain at least one I^A allele: A and AB. Similarly, there are two blood types that contain at least one I^B allele: B and AB. Since there are two possible blood types for each allele, the ratio of possibilities must be 1:1.

8. **H** If you're not sure what *codominance* is, look to the description of the experiment: *When an individual has 1 I^A and 1 I^B allele, this individual will have type-AB blood, due to the codominance of the I^A and I^B alleles.* Consequently, an offspring whose genotype exhibits *codominance* must have type-AB blood. Look to Table 1 to see that the genotype for type-AB blood is $I^A I^B$, answer choice (H).

9. **C** Table 1 indicates that the only genotype that can produce type AB blood is $I^A I^B$. For this to happen in every offspring, and because each parent contributes only a single allele, one parent must only be capable of contributing I^A while the other parent is only capable of contributing I^B. The cross of $I^A I^A \times I^B I^B$ will *always* produce offspring with $I^A I^B$ genotypes and type AB blood phenotypes. If you chose choice (A), be careful—think of all possible combinations of these two genotypes. If one parent contributes I^B and the other parent contributes I^B, the offspring will have type-B blood.

10. **G** Since both parents come from Analysis 1, refer back to the description there: *One thousand males with type-O blood were mated with 1,000 females with type-AB blood.* In Analysis 1, the males had only Genotype $I^O I^O$ and the females had only Genotype $I^A I^B$. The only possible combinations of these genotypes are $I^A I^O$ and $I^B I^O$. Since it is these offspring who are mated in Analysis 3, their blood types must be $I^A I^O$ and $I^B I^O$.

11. **D** If you're not sure how to find the answer, use process of elimination. The easiest place to look for blood-types containing I^O alleles would be in analyses that produced offspring with type-O blood. This includes Analyses 2 and 3, so any answer choice that does not contain both can be eliminated—eliminate choices (A) and (C). Since one of the parents in Analysis 1 has type-O blood (Genotype $I^O I^O$), one of these alleles must have been passed on to each of the offspring—eliminate choice (B). This leaves only (D), so even if you're not sure about Analysis 4, (D) is the only answer that contains all the others about which you are sure. Note: Analysis 4 works because the parents had genotypes $I^A I^O$ and $I^B I^B$, so their offspring could only have genotypes $I^A I^O$ and $I^A I^B$.

12. **H** Analysis 3 had offspring with 4 possible phenotypes in equal frequency. If 300 offspring were identified, then 25% of 300 or 75 of them would be expected to have type B blood.

13. **B** Table 3 shows that a pumped blood volume of 450 mL yields a %ΔBP of 8.8, while a pumped blood volume of 500 mL yields a %ΔBP of 9.3. The %ΔBP of 9.0 is between these other two %ΔBP values, so it was likely produced by a pumped blood volume between 450 and 500 mL. Only choice (B) fits this requirement.

14. **F** Table 2 shows that when the artificial heartbeat pumps blood at 60 beats per minute, the %ΔBP is 1.2. As the rate at which the blood is pumped increases, so does the %ΔBP, so it follows that as the rate decreases, so would the %ΔBP. Therefore, choice (F) is the best answer.

15. **B** Experiment 1 shows that as the artificial heart beat rate increases, so does the %ΔBP, and only choices (A) or (B) show this. The passage states that a lower blood pressure follows from faster blood flow through the site of vasoconstriction. Therefore, an increasing blood pressure would follow from slower blood flow through the site of vasoconstriction. Choice (B) summarizes this.

16. **J** According to the passage, a faster velocity of blood flow and a lower blood pressure are consistent with a narrow region of a blood vessel, while a slower velocity of blood flow and a higher blood pressure are consistent with a wide region of a blood vessel. Therefore, the measurement at location A would have been taken at the region with the widest diameter, while the measurement at location B would have been taken at the region with the narrowest diameter. Choice (J) best illustrates this. Note: Since the values in the chart are not listed in a consistent order, you can safely eliminate choices (F) and (G), which show the three diameters consistently increasing from A–C or decreasing from A–C, respectively.

17. **C** Experiments 2 and 3 use an artificial heart that pumps blood at a constant rate of 90 beats per minute. In Experiment 3, the %ΔBP is measured as 9.3 for a blood volume of 500 mL, the amount that was used in Experiment 1 for a heart rate of 90 beats per minute. In Experiment 2, a %ΔBP of 9.3 was measured when the diameter of the site of vasoconstriction was 0.8 cm. Therefore, it follows that the diameter of the site of vasoconstriction used throughout Experiment 3 was also 0.8 cm, so choice (C) is the best answer.

18. **G** As the diameter of the site of vasoconstriction increases, the %ΔBP decreases. Refer back to the passage for the %ΔBP formula. From this formula, you can deduce that a larger %ΔBP will result from a larger difference between normal pressure and pressure at the site of vasoconstriction. Only the graph in choice (G) shows this pattern across the three given diameters. If you chose (F), be careful—you may have chosen them in the opposite order.

19. **D** For every trial involving oxygen in Table 1, the volume decreased by exactly 5.00 L. All the other choices had volume changes that varied.

20. **H** In Table 1, each trial involving carbon dioxide showed a negative volume change, or decrease in volume. Therefore, choices (F) and (G) are eliminated. The molecules will occupy less volume only if they are pushed closer together, eliminating choice (J).

21. **C** The passage states that increases in pressure lead to decreases in gas volume. Therefore, decreases in pressure would be expected to result in increases in gas volume, eliminating choices (A) and (B). In Table 2, the volume of carbon dioxide decreased by 5.00 L when the pressure was increased from 2 atm to 4 atm. Therefore, the volume would be expected to increase by 5.00 L upon returning to its initial pressure.

22. **F** In Table 3, the volume of neon decreases by an increasingly larger factor as the pressure changes increase. The question proposes an even larger pressure increase than those listed in Table 3, so the resulting volume change would also be expected to be larger, eliminating all choices except (F).

23. **A** No trials on any of the tables have positive changes in volume, so you can eliminate choice (B). Choices (C) and (D) can be eliminated because while the pressure changes at different temperatures produced differing results for volume, the volume was always decreasing.

24. **H** Choice (H) is the correct answer for this problem because it is the straightest part of the Neptune line. To solve this problem you should look at which answer choice represents no temperature change, so which answer choice represents a section of the line that is straight up and down. Choices (F), (G), and (J) all represent sections of the line that represent relatively large changes in Neptune's temperature.

25. **A** Compare the changes in temperature for each range in the answer choices. The question does not specify an increase or decrease, so you'll want to pick the answer choice containing the largest range of temperatures. (A) ranges from about 150 K to 300 K; (B) ranges from about 150 K to 200 K; (C) does not have a range any wider than about 30 K; (D) has a range similarly small to that of (C). Choice (A) clearly contains the largest range of temperatures and so can be said to change the most.

26. **H** Compare the relative abundances of each gas in the answer choices. NH_3, Choice (H), is the only gas that has a higher relative abundance in Jupiter than in either Neptune or Saturn. Choice (F) cannot be correct because H has a higher relative abundance in Saturn than in Jupiter. Similarly, (G) cannot be correct because Neptune has a higher relative abundance of CH_3 than Jupiter, as is the case with He in choice (J).

27. **C** To solve this problem, you must look at Figure 1 and see what temperature Saturn is when the altitude above cloud tops equals 0 km, then compare to Table 2. Saturn is about 100 K at a 0 km altitude above the cloud tops, so the answer must be choice (C), because 100 K − 25 K = 75 K.

28. **J** Read the answer choices carefully. Since each answer choice is comparing the relative abundance of He and H on the three planets, see if you can identify any general trends in Table 1. You'll notice that for each planet, the H values are much higher than the He values, so in no case will the relative abundance of He be greater than or equivalent to that of H. Only choice (J) has He and H in the proper relationship to one another.

29. **D** In the middle of the fifth paragraph is this sentence: *If it [the U-235] is assembled over too long a time (t), it will achieve slight supercriticality and then fizzle.*

30. **F** The implosion-type weapon uses 15 kg of U-235. The gun-type weapon uses a 48-kg cylinder and a 12-kg pellet for a total of 60 kg of U-235.

31. **C** In the fifth paragraph of the passage, notice that to achieve supercriticality, the product (multiplication) of the mass and density of U-235 must be a large value. Therefore, supercriticality could be achieved by increasing either the mass or the density of the U-235. In the gun-type weapon, the explosives are used to propel one piece of U-235 into another (increasing the total mass). In the implosion-type weapon, the explosives are used to increase the density of the U-235. In both cases the goal is to increase the product of mass and density in order to achieve supercriticality.

32. **H** ρ stands for density. Read the implosion-type weapon paragraph and notice that the density after compression is 70 g/cm³, which is closest to 100 g/cm³.

33. **C** In the section on implosion-type weapons, the passage says that explosives are used to compress the U-235. To compress is to decrease the amount of space a substance occupies while preserving its mass, which is to increase its density.

34. **F** Again, the passage says that to achieve a supercritical state the product of mass and density must be *greater than* some value. This is why the gun-type weapon combines two pieces of U-235 to increase the mass, and it is why the implosion-type weapon compresses the U-235.

35. **B** Michelson's Criterion says that t divided by ρ must be *less than* some number. Therefore to meet this criterion, t could be decreased or ρ could be increased. Choice (B) is the only answer choice that fits with this.

36. **F** Examine Figure 1; the least increase in the percent of hemoglobin saturated with O_2 occurs at the lowest temperatures where lines just begin to increase. Answer choice (F) results in a change of approximately 5%. Choices (G) through (J) will all result in changes greater than 10%, and since you are looking for the range of pressures that gives the *least increase*, choice (F) is the best answer. If you picked choice (J), be careful—this one has the *greatest* increase.

37. **C** First, examine Figure 1 closely. At higher temperatures, oxygen binding decreases, so answer choices (A) and (B) may be eliminated since their binding will be greater at 37°C than at 42°C for the same oxygen pressures. Furthermore, at lower pressures of oxygen, less hemoglobin binding occurs, so you can eliminate choice (D). Choice (C) has the best match of a high temperature and a low pressure.

38. **J** Look at Figure 1. At 65% saturation of the hemoglobin, any pressure of oxygen greater than 75 mmHg requires a temperature greater than 42°C. Subsequently, at a pressure of 100 mmHg, the temperature must be considerably greater than 42°C, correlating to answer choice (J).

39. **B** Examine Figure 2. The closest data point you have to those given in the problem is 75 mmHg pressure of O_2 at approximately 80% hemoglobin saturation. Since the problem asks for a 70% saturation, note the relationship between CO_2 pressures and percent of hemoglobin saturation—it is clear from the graph that as oxygen is kept at constant pressure, hemoglobin saturation increases with decreasing CO_2 pressures. You will need something slightly larger than 40 mmHg, so you can eliminate choice (A), and you can eliminate choices (C) and (D) because they go too far in the other direction. Only (B) is appropriately close to the given data point.

40. **F** Look at the curve for a carbon dioxide pressure of 90 mmHg in Figure 2; the hemoglobin fails to saturate at oxygen pressures below 70 mmHg. This means that the percent of hemoglobin saturated remains constant at any pressure below 70 mmHg. This question asks for how the percentage changes as O_2 pressure changes from 45 mmHg to 90 mmHg, and hemoglobin binding remains constant at first and then increases.

SCIENCE PRACTICE 2 ANSWERS

1. C
2. G
3. C
4. J
5. B
6. J
7. C
8. J
9. B
10. F
11. D
12. H
13. B
14. J
15. A
16. G
17. B
18. H
19. B
20. G
21. A
22. J
23. B
24. F
25. A
26. G
27. C
28. H
29. A
30. H
31. A
32. H
33. A
34. H
35. D
36. F
37. B
38. J
39. B
40. J

SCIENCE PRACTICE 2 EXPLANATIONS

1. **C** Look at Figure 1: The shallow boundary of the mesosphere lies somewhere in the outer mantle. The deep boundary lies at the interface between inner mantle and outer core, but the outer core is not included. This eliminates I and choices (B) and (D). The mesosphere includes only parts of the inner and outer mantle.

2. **G** A K-wave does not appear in Figure 1, and velocity data is not included in the passage, so choice (J) can't work. Given that the waves have an average velocity of 3 m/s, they could either be L-waves or S-waves according to Table 1, and choice (H) should be eliminated. Between L-waves and S-waves, only S-waves can travel to a depth that spans the inner mantle as depicted in Figure 1, so eliminate choice (F).

3. **C** The bottom chart of Figure 2 refers to future probability. The percentage probability of a 6.5 magnitude earthquake is 70%, and that of a 7.5 magnitude earthquake is 32%. This is the only comparison among the answer choices that represents a decrease of more than one half.

4. **J** The likelihood of an earthquake of any particular magnitude refers to future probability as depicted in the bottom chart of Figure 2. This chart illustrates that as Richter scale magnitude increases, the probability of occurrence decreases. Therefore, an earthquake between Richter scale 7.0 and 7.5 has the lowest probability of occurrence.

5. **B** According to Figure 2, there were 31,860 Richter scale 5.5 earthquakes and 60,242 Richter scale 5.0 earthquakes in the past 30 years. Therefore, the ratio is 31,860/60,242, which is approximately 1/2.

6. **J** You need to determine which farm's soil has the greatest number of living cells per mm^3. To do that, look at Table 3. Farm 5 has the greatest number of living cells per mm^3, so it must also consume the most oxygen. If you chose (F), be careful—you may have switched the information given in the question.

7. **C** The soil has all the water removed before it is heated to 500°C, so neither choice (A) nor (B) is correct. The reason the scientists heat the soil to 500°C for 20 minutes is to burn off all the organic matter. In other words, the minerals remain, and the organic matter disappears. Therefore, if there is little or no organic matter, there will be little or no change in mass of the soil.

8. **J** The mass of organic matter was determined by heating the sample to 500°C, removing the ash, and calculating the difference in mass before and after the heating. If any water had been present, it would have evaporated, and its mass would have been included in calculating the mass of organic matter. Including water in the initial weight would have made the estimation for the weight of the organic matter artificially high, which is correctly explained by choice (G).

9. **B** In Table 3, notice that as % organic matter increases, number of living cells per mm^3 also increases. With 2,100 living cells per mm^3, the hypothetical sample would fall somewhere between Farms 3 and 4. Therefore, the % organic matter should also fall between farms 3 and 4, or between 4.8 and 6.6%.

10. **F** Looking at the levels of nitrogen and iron in Table 2, we find that the amounts in the soil of Farm 5 (210 and 165, respectively) are the highest.

11. **D** At the end of the first paragraph in the passage, we find that a well-defined soil has similar levels of minerals, relative to the minerals' ideal levels. In other words, you are looking for similar percentages in Table 2. The soil of Farm 4, with all values within 24 percent of each other, is the most well defined.

12. **H** Choice (H), 80 degrees Fahrenheit, is the only correct choice. To solve this question, draw a line from 30 minutes on the x-axis to the S3 curve, then a line from that point on the S3 curve to the y-axis. If you look where S3 is at 30 minutes and just estimate that point on the y-axis, you can see it is between 70°F and 90°F. Now look at the answers: 10°F is practically at the bottom of the axis, so it is much too low; 100°F is the very top of the y-axis, so much too high; 50°F is roughly in the middle, but not quite as high as it should be; 80°F is just about right.

13. **B** Figures 2 and 3 have an x-axis in common. Since this axis for both shows an increase in *time mixture is allowed to stand,* the y-axes are easy to compare. In Figure 2, the temperature of the water in the outer jar increases as the time allowed to stand increases. In Figure 3, the heat loss of S1 increases as the time allowed to stand increases. Therefore, as the temperature of water in the outer jar increases, the heat loss of S1 will also increase.

14. **J** According to the arrow on the right side of the graph, the *Orderliness* increases as the *Heat loss* increases. To compare the orderliness of the four mixtures, therefore, all you need to do is compare the heat loss of the four mixtures at the given point. Choice (J) correctly compares the temperatures of the four mixtures at 0 minutes. Because the mark at 15°F is higher than that of S1 or S3, the solution must be more orderly than S1 and S3, but because the mark is lower than S2, it must be less orderly than S2.

15. **A** Since you have no data about the behavior of heat in the string, you can eliminate choices (C) and (D). Look at the relationships given to you in choices (A) and (B), and note how those relationships correspond to those in Figure 2. In this figure, the sugar and water mixture decreases in temperature and the water outside the jar increases in temperature until the temperatures of the two things are equal. It must be the case, therefore, that the Mixture is losing heat and the Water Outside the Jar is *gaining* heat—in other words, heat is being conducted by some material from the Mixture to the Water Outside the Jar, choice (A).

16. **G** Choice (G) is correct because S2 reaches 100°F lost from the beginning temperature of 180°F at around 35 minutes standing, before S1 or S3. To solve this question, look at which line gets to 80°F earliest, which would indicate that the mixture has cooled from 180°F to 100°F.

17. **B** Note this from the passage: If an enzyme cannot be produced, then the product of the reaction that the enzyme catalyzes cannot be synthesized and the reactant in that reaction will become highly concentrated. In other words, if a particular chemical cannot produce the appropriate enzyme, that chemical then becomes highly concentrated. Look at Figure 1 to see which enzyme catalyses the reaction of which isocitrate is the reactant: Enzyme 2. Therefore, since yeast that cannot produce Enzyme 2 will have the highest concentration of isocitrate, choice (B) is the correct answer.

18. **H** The passage tells you that a gene notated with a superscript positive sign is not damaged and that a gene notated with a superscript negative sign is damaged. The passage tells you that if one of the four genes in Table 2 is damaged, then the enzyme it is responsible for cannot be produced. Therefore Cat1$^+$ Cat2$^-$ Cat3$^-$ Cat4$^+$ means that Enzyme 1 and Enzyme 4 can be produced and Enzyme 2 and Enzyme 3 cannot be produced, so the correct answer is choice (H).

19. **B** The passage tells you that in the first reaction, citrate is the reactant and isocitrate is the product. Based on this, you know that the reactant is what the arrow points away from and the product is what the arrow points to. Now, take a look at the relationship shown in Figure 1 between the three chemicals in the question (citrate, isocitrate, and α-ketoglutarate). You can see that α-ketoglutarate is a product of a reaction involving isocitrate, and isocitrate is a product of a reaction involving citrate, choice (B).

20. **G** Based on Table 1, you know yeast strain X grows in growth media where α-ketoglutarate, succinyl-CoA, and succinate are added, but cannot grow when citrate or isocitrate are added. This means that the succinate synthesis reaction pathway can happen only if α-ketoglutarate or any reactant after that in the pathway is added, so there is something which prevents the reaction pathway from proceeding from isocitrate to α-ketoglutarate. Therefore, choice (G) is the correct answer.

21. **A** A control is anything in a given experiment that is left alone. Note in Table 1 that BNS appears in all instances, once by itself and then with a number of chemicals added to it. It can be reasonably inferred, then, that the basic nutrition solution (BNS) alone is the control.

22. **J** To answer this question, figure out which strains of yeast have a *Yes* in the row where succinyl-CoA is the added chemical: strains W, X, and Y. Now, all you need to do is look at which other basic nutrition solution + additional chemical all three strains grew in. The only other medium that all three grow in as well is BNS + succinate as well, so choice (J) is the answer.

23. **B** Examine Figure 1: the incidence of virus A cycles annually with the greatest incidence around June and July of each year. Therefore, the incidence of virus A is greatest during the summer season.

24. **F** From Figure 1, the rate of incidence is least where the number of cases is least for the population. During April 2001, virus B and virus D exhibit the greatest number of cases. Therefore, answer choices (G) and (J) may be eliminated. Between viruses A and C, virus C exhibits the greater amount eliminating answer choice (H).

25. **A** Examine the data for viruses B and C closely in Figure 1. Virus B, unlike the other viruses, gradually increases in prevalence over the time of the survey. Virus C, however, cycles seasonally. During the first two months of the survey, the incidence of virus C exceeds that of virus B. Following February 2000, the incidence of virus B is consistently greater than that of virus C. Consequently, only answer choice (A) provides data that contradicts the virologist's statement.

26. **G** Examine each of the months given as answers. During April 2000 and November 2001, the incidences of virus B and virus D are similar; however the incidences of virus A and C differ considerably. In contrast, during September 2000, three of the lines appear to meet at about 5 cases per 1,000 individuals surveyed with only one incidence value differing considerably. Answer choice (J) is similar to choices (F) and (H), in that only two lines appear to intersect. Therefore, answer choice (G) exhibits the most similar incidences of viral infection.

27. **C** Look at Figure 2: The number of deaths attributed to virus A is approximately 7 per 1,000 individuals during May and August. Looking at the number of deaths attributed to virus D during May and September, the number is approximately 2 per 1,000 individuals, which is consistent with the values given in the context of the question. Of the answer choices, only May is present as a choice. Therefore, the answer should be (C).

28. **H** The results of Experiment 2 are shown in Figure 3. Looking at the middle row for Solvent 2, the peak for Protein D is found at a distance of approximately 50 mm from the starting position.

29. **A** The data in Table 1 combined with the results shown in Figure 2 demonstrate that as the solvent pH decreases, the migration distance of Protein A decreases. For Solvent 1 (pH 8.9), Protein A migrated about 10 mm. A solvent with a pH of 8.4 is less than that of Solvent 1. Therefore, Protein A would be expected to migrate less than it did with Solvent 1.

30. **H** The isoelectric point of Protein L is closest to that of Protein C. Protein C appears between Proteins B and D in Table 1, Figure 1, and Figure 2. Since 6.6 is between the isoelectric points of Proteins B and D, the results would be most similar if Protein L replaced Protein C in the mixture.

31. **A** The more crowded the peaks appear, the lower the resolution. Therefore, the trials should display the most crowded plots. In each experiment, Solvent 2 produces intermediate resolution plots, so choice (C) can be eliminated. Solvent 1 always results in peaks that are close together, and Solvent 3 always results in peaks that are far apart in both experiments. Since you're looking for the set of solvents with the lowest resolution, choice (A), which gives Solvent 1 in both experiments, is the best choice.

32. **H** The isoelectric point of Protein Y is between that of Proteins B and C. Given the data in Table 1 and Figure 2, the peak for Protein Y is expected to fall between that of B and C. This eliminates choices (G) and (J). Protein B always migrates less than Protein C in Figure 2, eliminating choice (F).

33. **A** In Figure 3, Protein B returns to 0% detection at approximately 35 mm for Solvent 2. Looking down at Solvent 3, a distance of 35 mm corresponds to 0% detection for Protein A.

34. **H** The explanation of Student 1 implies that both balls reach terminal velocity. Therefore, before the first ball lands, it is falling at a constant velocity, and its velocity a split second before landing would be the same as it lands, which would be choice (H). Choices (F) and (G) are based on formulas for velocity and displacement of projectiles which assume drag is negligible (no air resistance), which contradicts Student 1's explanation. If the velocity were zero when it landed, the ball never would have collided with the earth (J).

35. **D** By placing the two balls in a vacuum, it eliminates the effect of drag. This suggests that air resistance had an effect on the results, supporting Student 1. This eliminates choice (B). The new experiment also uses balls with identical weights, suggesting that weight can affect the results (even though this is really only true when air resistance is present), supporting Student 2. This eliminates choice (A). This experiment also placed both balls in the same location with the same force of gravity. This suggests that gravitational force can play a role and supports the views of Student 3. Only choice (D) indicates all students can potentially explain the new result.

36. **F** Choice (F) is better than choices (G), (H), and (J) because it matches Student 1's description of the two balls by showing a slow increase in velocity that tapers off into a constant velocity, with the second ball having a lower terminal velocity than the first. Choice (G) shows velocities decreasing to zero. Choice (H) shows a very unusual trend, and while the velocity of the second ball is lower than that of the first, it does not match the description of Student 1. Choice (J) does not account for terminal velocity, and the velocity of the second ball is higher than that of the first, suggesting it would land first.

37. **B** Student 1 states a different surface area accounts for the difference in fall times, implying some effect and eliminating choices (C) and (D). Specifically, the student argues that the second ball has a greater surface area, which results in a lower terminal velocity, eliminating choice (A).

38. **J** Student 3 states that the second ball falls on the Moon where there is no atmosphere or air resistance. According to the introduction of the passage, drag force results from air resistance. Therefore, there is no drag force on the Moon, and choices (F) and (H) are eliminated. Weight is the force on an object that results from gravity and is constant, eliminating (G). Terminal velocity occurs only when there is a drag force equal and opposite to the weight of a free falling object.

39. **B** Choices (A) and (C) are not supported by the claims of Student 1. Choice (D) is not supported by the experimental data. Choice (B) is correct because all 3 students assume that it is gravity that is increasing speed, but differences in the magnitude of gravity, or differences in drag, are the cause of the difference in falling times.

40. **J** Choice (F) would suggest that the ball does not move at all. All three students acknowledge some form of acceleration. Choice (G) does not take into consideration the concept of terminal velocity, and choice (H) suggests that the ball's velocity would reach a negative number, as it starts at zero. Choice (J) acknowledges terminal velocity, and still explains that for all of the time that the ball has not reached terminal velocity, it is increasing.

SCIENCE PRACTICE 3 ANSWERS

1. B
2. G
3. A
4. G
5. D
6. G
7. D
8. G
9. A
10. J
11. B
12. F
13. A
14. G
15. B
16. F
17. C
18. J
19. A
20. G
21. D
22. H
23. B
24. H
25. B
26. H
27. A
28. H
29. D
30. J
31. A
32. H
33. B
34. H
35. D
36. J
37. A
38. J
39. C
40. H

SCIENCE PRACTICE 3 EXPLANATIONS

1. **B** Choice (B) is correct because it is the only choice that Figure 1 says is necessary for the mosquito life cycle to progress. If there is no water then the eggs will not hatch.

2. **G** To solve this problem, you need to average the five numbers in the *Percent of Group Affected by Yellow Fever* column. 10% + 18 % + 29% + 38% + 52% = 147%. 147%÷5 = 29.4% which is closest to 30%.

3. **A** This question asks you to look at trends in Table 1 and Figure 2 to determine amounts of mosquito bites per month. Figure 2 tells you about trends in cases of Yellow Fever. Table 1 tells you that as the number of mosquito bites increases, cases of Yellow Fever increase. Now look at Figure 2: if you know that more mosquito bites means more cases of Yellow Fever, then the month with the most mosquito bites must also be the month with the most cases of Yellow Fever. April has 6 cases, June has 2 cases, August and November each have 1 case, which means that choice (A), April, is the correct answer.

4. **G** Choice (G) is the correct answer because February and March had different amounts of rainfall. To solve this problem you must compare the amounts of rainfall for each of the 2 months in the answer choices. Only one answer, choice (G), has the same amount for the 2 months in the pair. This question tests your ability to read a graph with 2 *y*-axes; be sure to check which axis you're getting your information from. For this question you should use the one on the right *Rainfall (inches.)*

5. **D** To solve this problem, you must determine the trend of the numbers in the *Number of Monkeys Seen* column. This question is tricky because the numbers increase some and decrease some but don't do either consistently. If the answer is not entirely right, it must be wrong, so you can eliminate choice (A) because the numbers don't only increase, choice (B) because the numbers don't only decrease, and choice (C) because the numbers did not increase then decrease, they partially decreased, then increased, then decreased again, then increased again. It's intimidating to choose choice (D), varied with no consistency, but it is the only correct answer.

6. **G** The results in Table 1 for Experiment 1 indicate that the temperature varied for that experiment, eliminating choice (F). Table 1 also indicates that both MEA and DEA were used in Experiment 1, eliminating choices (H) and (J). The description of Experiment 2 states that all trials were done at a constant temperature of 26°C.

7. **D** Concentration cannot increase from 1,000 ppm to 10 ppm or decrease from 10 ppm to 1,000 ppm, eliminating choices (B) and (C). The description of Experiment 1 states that CO_2 concentration started at 1,000 ppm and decreased as it absorbed, eliminating choice (A).

8. **G** In Table 1, as temperature is increased, scrub times for both MEA and DEA decrease. Therefore, if an additional trial were done at 12°C, the scrub times would be expected to fall between the values listed for 10°C and 15°C for MEA and DEA. Only choice (G) has values that lie between these limits for both compounds.

9. **A** The first paragraph of the passage states that ethanolamines are compounds with both an alcohol and an amine subgroup. Choices (A) and (B) both have alcohol subgroups, and choices (A), (C), and (D) each have at least one amine subgroup. Only choice (A) has both.

10. **J** Experiment 1 compares MEA and DEA. The results in Table 1 indicate that the scrub times for DEA are always less than MEA at each temperature tested, eliminating choices (F) and (H). The passage states that *longer scrub times indicate a slower rate of absorption*. Therefore, DEA must have a faster rate of absorption at all temperatures.

11. **B** The passage states that *longer scrub times indicate a slower rate of absorption*. The results of Experiment 2 are shown in Table 2. The acidic gas with the longest scrub time is HCN, so it must have the slowest rate of absorption.

12. **F** Student 1 hypothesizes that vegetative reproduction and seed distribution together make up the only ways that *Taraxicum* reproduces. The experiment described would prevent vegetative reproduction (glass jars) and seed distribution (plastic bags), so if Student 1 is correct, no daughter plants should ever grow.

13. **A** Trials 2 and 3 both describe instances in which the experimenters have interfered with one of the ways that dandelions spread themselves. The first trial, in which *Taraxicum* specimens are left to grow naturally, provides the control for this experiment, meant to establish what happens without any change in the variables being investigated.

14. **G** Choice (G) is correct, while choice (F) states the opposite of what Student 2 claims—the actual claim was that dandelions have a single taproot, unlike vegetative reproducers. Choice (H) is wrong: the plant holds the seeds loosely not because they are not important, but because they must be distributed for the plant to spread. Choice (J) is wrong because no claim is made that vegetative reproducers never produce seeds.

15. **B** Student 2 says that *Taraxicum does use vegetative reproduction...to replace the above-ground plant if it has been cut or lost,* and that this allows *Taraxicum* to survive threats in the environment. Choice (A) is Student 1's argument, which Student 2 rejects. Choice (C) is rejected by Student 1 and never mentioned by Student 2. Choice (D) is an observation made by Student 1, but Student 2 does not comment on whether it is accurate.

16. **F** Student 1 and Student 2 believe that dandelions spread through both seed distribution and vegetative reproduction; they disagree only on the relative importance of the two means. Thus, choice (F) is correct because neither means of reproduction is limited. Choices (G) and (H) both describe situations in which some part of the dandelion's reproductive ability is experimentally tampered with, while choice (J) describes a situation in which both the dandelion's reproductive strategies were negated.

17. **C** Student 1 asserts that vegetative reproduction and seed distribution each make up equal parts of *Taraxicum's* reproduction. Experiment 3 is meant to remove vegetative reproduction from the picture, while leaving seed distribution. If choice (D) is true, then student 2 is right; if choice (A) is true, then dandelions do not rely on seed distribution at all. If you chose Choice (B), you may have misread Student 1 to say that the two methods together account for 50% production.

18. **J** Student 2's hypothesis is that seed distribution is the main reproductive strategy for *Taraxicum,* while some incidental vegetative reproduction is possible. For this to be true, the control field (experiment 1) would have the largest population, followed closely by the field in experiment 3 (which has no vegetative reproduction), with only very few dandelions in field 2 (which eliminated seed distribution). Choice (F) describes a scenario where vegetative reproduction alone resulted in more dandelions than seed distribution and vegetative reproduction together, which would be mysterious. Choice (H), similarly, claims that the control experiment would have fewer offspring than the experiment which eliminated vegetative reproduction. If the results in Choice (G) were obtained, then removing dandelion's seed distribution and vegetative reproduction would have roughly equal effects, which would mean student 1 was correct.

19. **A** Based on the information in Table 2, you know that plain, unprepared cake mix Z has a water content of 10.1%. The question asks what the water content is after water is added, so the amount of water in the sample must have increased. Therefore, you know that the answer must be greater than 10.1%, so choice (A) is the only possible correct answer.

20. **G** The first thing you should do is locate the study and the data that this question asks about: Study 1 and the column in Table 1 refer to maximum immovable speed without cornmeal. Once you have done this, go through each answer to select the best one. Choice (F) cannot be right because none of the cake mixes has a maximum immovable speed of 0 m/s. Choices (H) and (J) cannot be correct because none of the cake mixes has a maximum immovable speed two or three times larger than any other. Choice (G), therefore, must be correct: even though the maximum immovable speeds aren't exactly the same, they are approximately the same, so it is the best answer.

21. **D** This question asks you to compare the two columns of data for each cake mix in Table 1. Mix X is exactly 3.5 times greater, Mix Y is just under 3 times as great, and Mix Z is over 3 times greater. Among the answers, (D) is the best answer.

22. **H** Look at Study 1, the column for maximum immovable speed with cornmeal, and the speeds for cake mixes *Y* and *Z:* 0.38 m/s and 0.36 m/s, respectively. If you mix equal amounts of cake mixes *Y* and *Z,* then you would expect the maximum immovable speed for the mixture to be somewhere between the maximum immovable speeds for the individual mixes, so the answer is choice (H), between 0.36 m/s and 0.38 m/s.

23. **B** In short, this question asks whether increasing the amount of gelatin in a cake mix means increasing the water content. Look at Table 2 and you can see that as gelatin content increases, water content increases. Now look at your answer choices: You want a choice that says yes because the hypothesis is supported by Study 3 and you want the reason to be that as gelatin content increases, water content increases. The only correct choice is choice (B). Be sure to pick the choice that is totally right: Choices (A) and (D) are only half right!

24. **H** Each of the three components of cake mix Q falls between the comparable components of cake mixes Y and Z. Therefore, the water content of cake mix Q should likewise fall between that of cakes mixes Y and Z, specifically 6.1 to 10.1. Choice (H) is correct.

25. **B** In Experiment 2, all of the metal resistors were gold and 100 m in length, eliminating choices (A), (C), and (D). The description of the experiment and data in Table 2 indicates that cross-sectional area was varied across trials.

26. **H** The results of Experiment 3 shown in Table 3 indicate that as ρ increases, resistance increases and current decreases. Since gold has the lowest ρ value, it should be the best conductor and the third item in your list, eliminating choices (F), (G), and (J).

27. **A** According to the passage, electrons are negatively charged and return to the positive battery terminal. This explains why each answer choice is negative. The passage introduction states current is charge per unit time measured in coulombs/second, and that the magnitude of this current was 1.0×10^{-3} coulombs every second for the first trial of each experiment. Therefore, a charge of -1.0×10^{-3} coulombs returned to the positive battery terminal each second the switch was closed.

28. **H** The results in Table 1 indicate that current increases with decreasing length of the metal resistor, making choice (F) the least favorable by this factor. The results in Table 2 indicate that current increases with increasing cross-sectional area of the metal resistor, making choice (H) the most favorable by this factor and eliminating choice (J). The results in Table 3 indicate that gold has the highest conductance with all other factors being equal, again making choice (H) the most favorable, and eliminating choices (F) and (G).

29. **D** In Experiment 1, only the length of the metal resistor was varied, eliminating choices (A) and (B). The results in Table 1 indicate that as the length of the metal resistor decreased, current increased and resistance decreased, eliminating choice (C).

30. **J** The passage states that when the circuit was closed, electrons flowed away from the negative battery terminal, through the circuit, and back to the positive battery terminal. This describes flow in one direction only, eliminating choices (F) and (G). In Figure 1, the negative battery terminal is on the left and the positive battery terminal is on the right. The only way that electrons could flow from negative to positive while passing through the circuit is to go counter-clockwise, eliminating choice (H).

31. **A** Choice (A) is the only correct answer. You can see in Figure 2 that increasing pressure increases the rate of reaction and you can see in Figure 3 that increasing temperature increases the rate of reaction. The scientist's claim is true based on these two things so the answer is choice (A). Be careful of choices like choice (B) which are only half right. Choice (B) says that the scientist is right, but gives an incorrect reason.

32. **H** To solve this problem, compare the reaction rates for each answer choice, which shows that choice (H) is the only correct answer. Be sure to look at the y-axis in problems like these to be sure both charts are measuring the same thing.

33. **B** This is a deceptive question—you don't need to convert mole/L back to number of molecules, and you don't need to use 6.02×10^{23} at all! Because the units for the amount of Compound Y and Compound Z are the same, you can just divide the amount of Compound Y by the amount of Compound Z, [1 mole/L]/[2 mole/L] to get the correct answer, choice (B).

34. **H** Choice (H) is the only correct answer. You know from the passage that the rate of a gaseous reaction is changed by changing temperature, pressure, volume, or amount of reactants. Figure 1 shows that increasing temperature and pressure increases the likelihood of particles running into each other. Figure 2 shows that increasing pressure increases the rate of reaction and Figure 3 shows that increasing temperature increases the rate of reaction. Putting all of this together, you know that increasing the likelihood of a collision increases the rate of reaction. This means that increasing the concentration of reactants increases the rate of reaction, so choice (H) is correct. For the same reason, choice (J) must be incorrect. You can eliminate choices (F) and (G) right away because they talk about changing temperature and nothing in the passage or Figures 1–3 tells you that changing the amount of reactants will change temperature.

35. **D** The best way to solve this problem is to look at each answer choice and see how the reaction rate changes. Looking at choice (A) and Figure 2, decreasing pressure would cause a decrease in reaction rate so it cannot be the correct answer. Choice (C) and Figure 3 show the same, so that cannot be correct either. Choice (B), increasing pressure from 1 atm to 3 atm, would increase the reaction rate to between 125% and 150% of the reaction rate at 50°C and 1 atm. Looking at Choice (D) and Figure 3, you can see that increasing temperature from 50°C to 100°C will increase the reaction rate to 350% of the reaction rate at 50°C and 1 atm. Since choice (D) represents the biggest increase in reaction rate, it is the correct answer.

36. **J** Looking at Figure 2, you can see that the maximum velocity post-impact, the second peaks on the graphs, decreases as elasticity decreases. The answer to this question must therefore be the smallest elasticity, or 0.1 Pa., choice (J).

37. **A** Looking only at the graph in Figure 2 that shows balls with an elasticity of 0.2 Pa., you can see that as weight increases, maximum post-impact velocity increases. This question asks about a ball with a weight of 0.5 kg. The smallest ball in this graph has a weight of 1 kg and a maximum post-impact velocity between 0.50 and 0.75 m/s, so you know your 0.5 kg ball must have a smaller maximum post-impact velocity. Choice (A) is the only choice that satisfies that requirement.

38. **J** To solve this problem, you should first locate the graph and the line on the graph that matches the ball in the problem. Then, the easiest way to solve this is to draw a line from 1.00 m/s on the y-axis all the way across the graph and count how many times it hits the line that represents the 2.0 kg ball: 4 times, choice (J).

39. **C** You know from the passage and Figure 2 that drop is the very beginning when time is 0 s and velocity is 0 m/s the first time, impact is when velocity is 0 m/s the second time, and apex is when velocity is 0 m/s the third time. Looking at the graphs in Figure 2, you can see that velocity increases after drop then decreases to impact, then increases after impact, and then finally decreases to the apex, so choice (C) is the only correct answer. This question could be tricky if you forgot that apex refers to vertical height, not maximum velocity. Be careful of partial answers like choices (A), (B), or (D); if the answer says *only*, be sure that it's really the only thing that happens.

40. **H** Look at Figure 2, and find the graph and the line on the 0.8 Pa graph, which matches the 3.0 kg ball. The passage tells you that at impact, the ball has a high velocity, then almost immediately slows to 0 m/s, then almost immediately increases to a high velocity again, so you know to look at the maximum velocity prior to impact. This velocity is about 2.25 m/s, which is less than the elastic limit, 2.75 m/s, of the ball in the question, so the only correct answer is choice (H). Note: Be sure to read the entire answer in questions like this. There are two answers that correctly say *No,* but only one that gives the correct reason.

WRITING TEST

Essay Checklist

1. The Introduction
   Did you
   o start with a topic sentence that paraphrases or restates the prompt?
   o clearly state your position on the issue?

2. Body Paragraph 1
   Did you
   o start with a transition/topic sentence that discusses the opposing side of the argument?
   o give an example of a reason that one might agree with the opposing side of the argument?
   o clearly state that the opposing side of the argument is wrong or flawed?
   o show what is wrong with the opposing side's example or position?

3. Body Paragraphs 2 and 3
   Did you
   o start with a transition/topic sentence that discusses your position on the prompt?
   o give one example or reason to support your position?
   o show the grader how your example supports your position?
   o end the paragraph by restating your thesis?

4. Conclusion
   Did you
   o restate your position on the issue?
   o end with a flourish?

5. Overall
   Did you
   o write neatly?
   o avoid multiple spelling and grammar mistakes?
   o try to vary your sentence structure?
   o use a few impressive-sounding words?

Test 2
Answers and
Explanations

TEST 2 ENGLISH ANSWERS

1.	A		48.	J
2.	J		49.	D
3.	D		50.	G
4.	F		51.	C
5.	C		52.	J
6.	H		53.	B
7.	B		54.	F
8.	J		55.	C
9.	B		56.	H
10.	J		57.	D
11.	B		58.	H
12.	J		59.	B
13.	A		60.	F
14.	J		61.	D
15.	B		62.	H
16.	H		63.	B
17.	B		64.	J
18.	F		65.	A
19.	C		66.	J
20.	H		67.	C
21.	D		68.	F
22.	F		69.	B
23.	C		70.	J
24.	G		71.	B
25.	D		72.	H
26.	H		73.	C
27.	B		74.	F
28.	F		75.	B
29.	D			
30.	F			
31.	B			
32.	J			
33.	A			
34.	F			
35.	D			
36.	H			
37.	A			
38.	H			
39.	D			
40.	G			
41.	C			
42.	G			
43.	A			
44.	F			
45.	C			
46.	G			
47.	A			

TEST 2 MATH ANSWERS

1.	E
2.	H
3.	B
4.	G
5.	C
6.	F
7.	C
8.	G
9.	C
10.	F
11.	D
12.	H
13.	B
14.	G

15.	B	1.	A	
16.	H	2.	G	
17.	B	3.	D	
18.	J	4.	F	
19.	C	5.	C	
20.	G	6.	J	
21.	C	7.	A	
22.	G	8.	H	
23.	E	9.	D	
24.	F	10.	F	
25.	C	11.	A	
26.	K	12.	G	
27.	D	13.	B	
28.	F	14.	F	
29.	B	15.	C	
30.	J	16.	F	
31.	E	17.	C	
32.	K	18.	H	
33.	B	19.	C	
34.	F	20.	J	
35.	A	21.	D	
36.	J	22.	G	
37.	C	23.	A	
38.	K	24.	F	
39.	E	25.	A	
40.	H	26.	G	
41.	E	27.	A	
42.	G	28.	F	
43.	C	29.	B	
44.	J	30.	H	
45.	B	31.	A	
46.	H	32.	G	
47.	C	33.	C	
48.	J	34.	H	
49.	A	35.	A	
50.	G	36.	J	
51.	A	37.	D	
52.	G	38.	H	
53.	C	39.	D	
54.	G	40.	F	
55.	C			
56.	K			
57.	A			
58.	K			
59.	E			
60.	H			

TEST 2 SCIENCE ANSWERS

1. D
2. F
3. C
4. J
5. B
6. G
7. D
8. G
9. A
10. G
11. D
12. J
13. B
14. F
15. A
16. F
17. C
18. F
19. C
20. H
21. A
22. G
23. C
24. F
25. C
26. G
27. D
28. G
29. B
30. J
31. D
32. J
33. A
34. G
35. A
36. F
37. A
38. G
39. A
40. J

SCORING YOUR PRACTICE EXAM

Step A

Count the number of correct answers for each section and record the number in the space provided for your raw score on the Score Conversion Worksheet below.

Step B

Using the Score Conversion Chart on the next page, convert your raw scores on each section to scaled scores. Then compute your composite ACT score by averaging the four subject scores. Add them up and divide by four. Don't worry about the essay score; it is not included in your composite score.

Score Conversion Worksheet		
Section	Raw Score	Scaled Score
1	_____ /75	_____
2	_____ /60	_____
3	_____ /40	_____
4	_____ /40	_____

SCORE CONVERSION CHART

Scaled Score	Raw Score			
	English	Mathematics	Reading	Science Reasoning
36	75	60	39–40	40
35	74	59	38	39
34	72–73	58	37	38
33	71	57	36	—
32	70	55–56	35	37
31	69	53–54	34	36
30	67–68	52	33	—
29	65–66	50–51	32	35
28	62–64	46–49	30–31	33–34
27	59–61	43–45	28–29	31–32
26	57–58	41–42	27	30
25	55–56	39–40	26	29
24	52–54	37–38	25	28
23	50–51	35–36	24	27–26
22	49	33–34	23	25
21	48	31–32	21–22	24
20	45–47	29–30	20	23
19	43–44	27–28	19	22
18	40–42	24–26	18	20–21
17	38–39	21–23	17	18–19
16	35–37	18–20	16	16–17
15	32–34	16–17	15	15
14	29–31	13–15	14	13–14
13	27–28	11–12	12–13	12
12	24–26	9–10	11	11
11	21–23	7–8	9–10	10
10	18–20	6	8	9
9	15–17	5	7	7–8
8	13–14	4	—	6
7	11–12	—	6	5
6	9–10	3	5	—
5	7–8	2	4	4
4	5–6	—	3	3
3	3–4	1	2	2
2	2	—	1	1
1	0	0	0	0

TEST 2 ENGLISH EXPLANATIONS

1. **A** The mother says that the author will be surprised to find that *family histories can be very interesting*, which implies that the author currently believes the opposite. Choice (A) is the best answer, expressing boredom and disinterest. Choices (B) and (C) are too optimistic, and choice (D) is irrelevant in this paragraph.

2. **J** Choices (F) and (G) create sentence fragments because *hoping* begins an incomplete thought. Choice (J) is the best answer because it corrects the sentence fragment error by connecting the incomplete thought to the complete one before it with a comma. Choice (H) confuses the meaning of the sentence.

3. **D** *Pictures and letters* is a list of only two items, so no commas are needed before the *and*, eliminating choices (A) and (B). Choice (C) also has an unnecessary comma after *letters*, interrupting the flow of the sentence.

4. **F** In EXCEPT/LEAST/NOT questions, the underlined portion of the sentence is correct. Choice (G) has the same structure and meaning as the original, since *yet* and *but* are both coordinating conjunctions, which, with a comma, can join two complete ideas. Choice (H) is acceptable because a semicolon is an appropriate punctuation to separate two complete thoughts. Choices (F) and (J) eliminate the need for punctuation by deleting he and making the second half of the sentence incomplete. However, choice (F) uses an incorrect tense and is NOT acceptable.

5. **C** Choice (C) correctly uses the apostrophe to show possession. An apostrophe after *relatives* is necessary to indicate more than one relative has the memories, eliminating choices (A) and (B). *Memory* does not possess *into;* thus choice (D) is incorrect.

6. **H** Sentences 1 and 2 continue the narrative by providing a setting and the scanner's activity. Sentence 4 shows an important shift in the author's attitude from reluctance to happiness. Sentence 3 offers information that can be figured out from the context and is therefore the least relevant to the telling of the story.

7. **B** The word *belongings* refers to the relatives, which is plural, so you can eliminate choices (A) and (C). The correct answer is choice (B), not (D); *there* refers to a place and *their* is the plural possessive pronoun.

8. **J** Choice (J) gives the past perfect form of the verb *to send*; this form is needed because the letters were sent in the distant past. Choices (G) and (H) are in the wrong tense, and choice (F) does not use the proper past participle form of the verb *send*.

9. **B** A pause is necessary between *kitchen* and *penning* to clarify that the great-grandmother not the kitchen was *penning* the entries, which makes choice (B) better than choice (A). Choices (C) and (D) can also be eliminated because *which* and *that* refer to the closest preceding noun, which is *kitchen*, and create the same error in meaning.

10. **J** This sentence continues the same attitude about stories that is expressed in the previous sentence, so you can eliminate choice (F) for incorrect direction. *Because* makes the phrase after incomplete, so choice (G) is incorrect because it creates a sentence fragment. *Therefore* indicates the correct direction but doesn't link the ideas in a logical way. The best answer is (J).

11. **B** A comma should precede the last *and* in a list of 3 or more things, eliminating choices (C) and (D). Choice (A) has an unnecessary comma after the *and*, so the correct answer is (B).

12. **J** The best answer is (J) because it clearly introduces the paragraph's focus on the author's growing interest in her family. Choices (F) and (H) mention the relatives; however, the focus is not on how many names and relatives the writer needs to keep track of. Choice (G) revisits the idea of using the computer to preserve family memories but does not match this paragraph's main idea.

13. **A** Paragraph 6 discusses what the writer gained from her experience, and the conclusion should continue that idea. Choice (A) is the best choice because it discusses what the writer plans to do with what she gained and emphasizes the important relationship between grandfather and grandchild seen in this narrative. Choices (B), (C), and (D) digress from the main point of the essay about the significance of the experience.

14. **J** Paragraph 5 discusses the writer's positive view of her grandfather's stories. Her change in attitude is first introduced at the end of Paragraph 3. Paragraph 5 then concludes by introducing the chest of stuff, which explains what the *belongings* are in the beginning of Paragraph 4. Therefore, the best placement of Paragraph 5 should be between Paragraphs 3 and 4.

15. **B** The writer concludes the essay by stating how much she appreciates family memories and mementoes after helping her grandfather research their family lineage; thus her purpose has been achieved, eliminating choices (C) and (D). Choice (A) is not true because the computer skills are not the benefit the writer gained from her experience.

16. **H** The writer is trying to state that she is standing alone; thus the correct pronoun is *myself* not *me*, eliminating choices (F) and (G). The phrase after *myself* is incomplete and cannot be separated by a period, eliminating choice (J). A comma can be used to connect a complete thought to an incomplete thought.

17. **B** The words *new* and *cold* are both adjectives describing *bedroom* and should be separated by a comma, eliminating (C) and (D). A comma after *cold* is unnecessary and disruptive to the flow of the sentence, eliminating choice (A).

18. **F** The writer is trying to describe *spectacle,* which is a noun, so *complete* should be an adjective, eliminating choices (G) and (H). The correct idiomatic expression is *to make a spectacle of,* so choice (F) is better than choice (J).

19. **C** Since the action *has never been more than 30 minutes away...* refers to *only child,* the pronoun should be in subject case *who,* eliminating choices (A) and (B). Choice (D) incorrectly uses the plural verb form, rather than the singular.

20. **H** The pronoun *one's* does not agree with the subject *we* earlier in the sentence. Only choice (H) uses the correct possessive pronoun of *we,* which is *our.*

21. **D** The sentence is listing two different pairs of breakfast items—milk and juice, eggs and bacon. There should not be a comma after *milk* because the *and* is used to connect two nouns, *milk* and *juice,* not to list 3 or more items. You can eliminate choices (A) and (B). The comma is necessary between *juice* and *fluffy* in order to separate the two different pairs of items.

22. **F** Choice (F) clearly articulates the angst she feels and clarifies that she misses her old way of life. Choice (G) is incorrect because the different stages of mourning are not described. Although the original sentence is short and concise, it is too literal and does not accurately describe her emotional state.

23. **C** Because the first half of the sentence is an incomplete thought, the underlined portion must include a subject to make the second half a complete thought, eliminating choices (A) and (D). Choice (C) uses the present tense of the verb, which fits better in the context of the story than the present perfect tense in choice (B).

24. **G** Choice (G) is correct, because the phrase does clarify why the writer stops crying in the first half of the sentence. There is no evidence to support a strained roommate relationship, so choice (F) is incorrect. Choice (H) is incorrect because the phrase does not show that the writer is right to feel sad. The phrase does give new understanding into what the author is thinking and feeling, so choice (J) is incorrect.

25. **D** Choices (A), (B), and (C) imply that the writer hears her roommate crying because she is surprised, which is not the intended meaning. The writer is surprised to hear her roommate cry, making choice (D) correct.

26. **H** The conjunction *and* is not the correct link between the incomplete thought *Curiosity overwhelming me* and the complete second half the sentence, eliminating choices (F) and (G). Choice (J) is incorrect because a period cannot come after an incomplete thought.

27. **B** Choice (B) is the only transition listed that suggests a quick, unexpected reaction from the roommate. Choices (A), (C), and (D) all indicate that some time passes before the roommate responds.

28. **F** Choice (F) is the only appropriate verb that is consistent in meaning with the description of the roommate as shaken up and surprised by the presence of the writer. Choice (G) means to state confidently, choice (H) means to use another person's words, and choice (J) means to yell loudly.

29. **D** Choice (D) both captures the roommate's emotion and explains why the writer responds by suggesting they adjust to college life together. Choices (A) and (B) are not consistent with the writer's response. Choice (C) completely disagrees with the emotions of both the writer and the roommate.

30. **F** The passage is a personal account of the writer, a first-time college student who is worried after moving away from home, and of the writer's roommate, who feels similar emotions. Thus, choice (F) is the best answer.

31. **B** Choice (B) is the best answer here because the analogy provides vivid detail. The reasons provided in choices (A), (C), and (D) are not compelling.

32. **J** The phrase *if murky* is unnecessary information, so it should be offset by commas. Thus choice (J) is correct. Choice (G) has no pauses to offset this information, which confuses the flow of the sentence. Choices (F) and (H) create sentence fragments.

33. **A** The phrase clarifies the term *anyone* by describing the kind of people who should try canyoning, so choice (A) is correct. Choice (B) is incorrect because the paragraph focuses on canyoning, not people. Choice (C) is extreme and not logical. Choice (D) is incorrect because the phrase does not confuse the focus of the sentence in any way.

34. **F** The word *river* ends a complete thought, and the word *without* begins a second complete thought. Choice (F) correctly uses a comma with a coordinating conjunction to link two complete thoughts. Choices (G), (H), and (J) create run-on sentences and do not provide proper punctuation to link two complete thoughts.

35. **D** Choice (D) is the most concise answer that conveys the correct meaning. Choices (A), (B), and (C) are wordy and unclear.

36. **H** Because *A remarkable activity in its own right* is a modifier, the *activity*—skydiving—must be named immediately after the modifier. Thus, choices (F) and (J) are wrong. Choice (H) omits the sentence's verb and also treats skydiving as unnecessary information by setting it off with commas. Choice (H) is the answer.

37. **A** Choice (A) is correct because the statement describes an additional thrilling activity in an exotic location, which is the focus of this paragraph. Choice (B) does not correctly describe the main idea of the paragraph. Choice (C) is incorrect because the locations and activities are different in each scenario, not just this one. Choice (D) is too narrowly focused and strays from the main idea.

38. **H** The phrase *because of which was our most exhilarating adventure yet* is intended to describe (modify) *canyoning*. Thus, the phrase should begin with the word *which*, as in choice (H). The remaining answer choices are unclear and create fragments.

39. **D** The word *walls* ends a complete thought, and the word *we* begins a second complete thought. Choice (D) correctly uses a comma with a coordinating conjunction to link two complete thoughts. Choices (A), (B), and (C) create run-on sentences and do not provide proper punctuation to link two complete thoughts.

40. **G** Choice (G) is the most concise answer that conveys the correct meaning, since *leaping* naturally implies a following descent. Choices (F), (H) and (J) are redundant.

41. **C** The subject of the sentence is the word *danger*, so its verb must be singular to agree with it, as with choice (C). Choice (A) contains a plural form of the verb, so it does not agree with the subject. Choice (B) contains a future tense, so it does not agree with the past tense of this sentence and of the passage. Choice (D) uses a gerund form incorrectly.

42. **G** A clear distinction between water and land activities is made in this paragraph, so choice (G) best clarifies this distinction with its mention of *rocky surfaces* and *chilly water*. Choices (F) and (H) do not address the distinction at all.

43. **A** The word *thrills* begins a complete thought that switches the direction of the sentence, so an opposite direction conjunction is necessary at the beginning of the thought preceding it. Choice (A) provides the correct conjunction. Choices (B), (C), and (D) provide same direction conjunctions.

44. **F** The essay focuses on the enjoyment of thrills, so choice (F) is correct. Choices (G) and (H) do not mention thrills at all. Choice (J) mentions thrills but with a tone opposite to that of the entire essay.

45. **C** The best location for Paragraph 2 is before Paragraph 4, choice (C), because Paragraph 3 introduces the activity of *canyoning* discussed in the first sentence of Paragraph 2. There is also a logical sequence from the introduction and description of the river in Paragraph 2 to its navigation in the beginning of Paragraph 5.

46. **G** Note that the subject of this sentence—*Mexican-American War*—is singular. Don't be thrown off by the words *conflicts* and *compromises*, which, although closer to the verb, are not the main subjects of the sentence. Since *Mexican-American War* is singular, you can eliminate choices (F) and (H), and (J) creates a sentence fragment. Only (G) works.

47. **A** Two main things are changing in the answer choices here. First, the verb in the sentence changes from the present *include* to the past *included*, but this sentence discusses the Mexican-American War as being *overlooked* in the present (and note the mention of the *current shape and culture* in the following sentence), so you'll want to keep *include*. Moreover, if you're going to use a colon (:), you must have, at the very least, a complete idea before it, which you do not in this case.

48. **J** Choices (F) and (H) break the flow of the sentence unnecessarily, so they can be eliminated easily, but to determine whether you need the commas around the phrase *to American arts,* determine whether the sentence makes sense without this piece of information. As you can see, without this phrase, the word *contributions* is not clearly defined in the text. Accordingly, *to American arts* is an essential part of the sentence and should not be set off by commas.

49. **D** Choices (A), (B), and (C) are all rewriting the same sentence—only (D) gives a completely different option. If you check (D) first, you can save yourself a lot of work. In this case, you can DELETE this sentence because it is inappropriately placed in the paragraph. While Mexican-American musicians are mentioned earlier in the paragraph, the previous sentence represents an important transition to the following paragraphs discussing Mexican-American authors.

50. **G** To determine whether or not a selection should be set off by commas as *María Amparo Ruiz de Burton* is in this sentence, see if the sentence makes sense without that selection. In this case, it does not make sense to say, *A major landmark in early Mexican-American literature came in 1885, when author published her first novel…* The author's name is an essential part of this sentence and so cannot be set off by commas.

51. **C** Answers (A) and (D) are out, because neither is indicated elsewhere in the passage. (B) is deceptive—the paragraph says this novel was the first to be written in English by an author of Mexican descent, not that it was the first by a Mexican author to be read in the United States. Only choice (C) captures the historical importance of the novel having been the first written in English by an author of Mexican descent.

52. **J** Since all of these answer choices ultimately say the same thing, pick the most concise answer that preserves the meaning of the original sentence. This definitely eliminates (F) and (H), and while choice (G) seems similar in length to choice (J), choice (G) is unclear and awkward in its construction, not least because *give a glimpse at* is idiomatically incorrect.

53. **B** Because *A family of landed gentry living in San Diego* is a modifier, the *family*—the Alamars—must be named immediately after the modifier. Thus, Choices (A), (C), and (D) are wrong, and choice (B) is the answer.

54. **F** The sentence discusses a single event that took place during the Mexican-American War, so choice (H), which implies that the event was continuous, must be eliminated. Choices (G) and (J) alter the meaning of the sentence and are idiomatically incorrect. Only choice (F) works appropriately.

55. **C** Choices (A), (B), and (D) all create sentence fragments. Only choice (C) contains a verb, *was*, that can make this sentence complete.

56. H You need to determine here whether the sentence should be added to or kept out of the paragraph. If you're not sure whether to answer Yes or No, look at the reasons in each answer choice. Choice (F) can't work because the sentence discusses individuals of French descent, and there is no indication that the writer is drawing any kind of parallel between individuals of French descent and those of Mexican descent. Choice (G) can't work because the sentence does not give any indication that it is meant to be connected to *The Squatter and the Don*. Choice (J) can't work because the reaction of Mexican-Americans to the Louisiana Purchase is never discussed. Only choice (H) indicates that the sentence does not provide information relevant to this paragraph.

57. D In EXCEPT/LEAST/NOT questions, the underlined portion of the sentence is correct. In this case, the words in choices (A), (B), and (C)—*investigate, examine,* and *look into*—are all roughly synonyms for *explore*. Choice (D), *solve*, has a meaning different than *explore* and its synonyms and changes the meaning of the sentence. Thus, choice (D) is the LEAST acceptable solution and the correct answer to this question.

58. H Choices (G) and (J) are both idiomatically incorrect and change the meaning of the sentence, so all you really need to decide is whether to use the relative pronoun *that* or *those*. To determine this, find which word or words the pronoun will be replacing. In this case, the word replaced is *writings*, a plural noun, which can be replaced only by the plural pronoun *those*.

59. B Sentence 3 introduces *other authors* for the first time in the passage. Sentences 1 and 2 provide examples of two other authors who are important. Therefore, Sentence 3 must come before Sentence 1. Choice (B) is correct.

60. F Because all four answer choices have the same meaning, select the most clear and concise. Choice (F) is the most clear and concise.

61. D Note the context of this sentence. The underlined portion ends a portion of the sentence that should be set off by commas—*typically cited alongside Walter Gropius and Le Corbusier as a pioneer of modern architecture*, so you can eliminate choices (A) and (B). The word *being*, as in (C), creates a sentence fragment, so the best answer is (D).

62. H Note the other verb in this sentence, *sought*. Since this is in the past tense, the other verbs in this sentence must be in the past tense. For the underlined portion, only choices (H) and (J) are written in the past tense, and choice (J) creates a sentence fragment with its use of the relative pronoun *who*.

63. B The easiest answer to eliminate is choice (D), as the semicolon would improperly separate two incomplete ideas. The phrase *based on van der Rohe's designs* is a necessary part of the sentence, so it should not be set off by commas. Likewise, it is not part of an introductory clause, so it should not be followed by a comma. Choice (B) correctly omits any commas.

64. J In EXCEPT/LEAST/NOT questions, the underlined portion of the sentence is correct. Choice (J) is NOT acceptable, because it changes the meaning of the sentence by suggesting that something is being made *into* steel and glass, when in fact the buildings are constructed *out of* steel and glass.

65. **A** The phrase *that is* is an introductory clause and therefore is properly followed by a comma. The part of the sentence after the dash serves to elaborate upon the sentence's earlier mention of the materials, and *that is* (an idiomatically shortened form of *that is to say*) functions in the same way that expressions like *for example* or *in this case* might in another sentence.

66. **J** Of the choices available here, only the colon is appropriate. The latter part of the sentence gives an example of *one of the problems* mentioned earlier in the passage. Accordingly, only choice (J) can be appropriate. Also note, when using a colon, make sure there is a complete sentence before it as there is in choice (J).

67. **C** Choices (A) and (B) don't directly discuss the visual elements of the buildings, merely how long they took to construct or their historical importance. Choice (D) gets closer by mentioning that the buildings are *on display* in various cities, but only choice (C) really discusses the buildings' *visual appeal* in its description of the buildings' *complex beauty*.

68. **F** The easiest answer to eliminate is choice (H), as the semicolon would improperly separate two incomplete ideas. Because the phrase *under teacher Peter Behrens's guidance* is unnecessary to the sentence as a whole, it should be set off by commas. Therefore, choice (F) is correct. Choice (J) is wrong because it eliminates the comma needed at the end of an unnecessary phrase and it incorrectly inserts a comma after *teacher*. Choice (G) is wrong because, while the entire phrase as a whole may be unnecessary, *Peter Behrens's guidance* is a necessary part of the phrase, so the comma following *teacher* is inappropriate.

69. **B** In the sentence as written, it is unclear what the pronoun *This* refers to, so to fix this pronoun ambiguity, you'll need a substitute that is more specific. Choices (C) and (D) are no more specific than is (F); only choice (B) fixes the problem by giving a specific subject.

70. **J** First, consider whether the last sentence of the paragraph provides a contrast to or a continuation of the prior sentence. Both sentences concern van der Rohe's development of a new style, so contrasting choices (F) and (G) are wrong. Choice (H) is wrong because it would transform an incomplete sentence followed by a comma and a complete sentence into two complete sentences separated by a comma. Choice (J) is grammatically correct and clear.

71. **B** Since this sentence refers to an event that occurred in 1937, the sentence must be in the past tense (note, also, that the other sentences in the paragraph are in the past tense). Only (A) and (B) satisfy this condition, but (A) creates a sentence fragment by introducing the relative pronoun *who*.

72. **H** In EXCEPT/LEAST/NOT questions, the underlined portion of the sentence is correct. Choices (F), (G), and (J) all preserve the meaning of the original sentence. Choice (H) changes the meaning of the sentence and, moreover, contains a pronoun, *this,* that does not refer to any noun. Choice (H) is thus NOT an acceptable substitution.

73. **C** Choices (A) and (D) create a misplaced modifier—since *van der Rohe* comes directly after the introductory phrase must be modifying this subject in some way. The word *while* in choice (B) suggests that a contradiction will come later in the sentence, but none does. Only choice (C) functions properly to modify the actions of van der Rohe.

74. **F** Since all the answer choices are roughly synonymous, choose the most concise that preserves the meaning. Choices (G), (H), and (J) all contain some redundancy and do not contain any essential information beyond the word *enthusiastic*.

75. **B** Look for clues in Sentence 3 that might give you some hints as to its proper placement. The main clue is the word *there*, which suggests that a previous sentence will contain some mention of a place. Sentence 2 discusses the Illinois Institute of Technology, but look closely, the end of Sentence 3 indicates that this is one of the commissions awaiting him there, so we still don't have a clear idea of what *there* is. In Sentence 1, however, you see that the architect is discussed as moving from Germany to the United States, so Sentence 3 should clearly be placed after Sentence 1 because the *there* in this situation clearly refers to the United States.

TEST 2 MATH EXPLANATIONS

1. **E** Use Process of Elimination aggressively. Since Violet has 10 cherries, she uses *three times* 10 = 30 blackberries, eliminating choices (A), (B), and (D). Thus, she also uses 30 raspberries and *twice* 30 = 60 blueberries. Choice (C) lists 2 rather than 2 × 30 for the number of blueberries.

2. **H** Expand the equation with FOIL (first, outside, inside, last): $(3x)(x) + (3x)(2) + (-5)(x) + (-5)(2) = 3x^2 + 6x + (-5x) + (-10)$. Combine the middle terms to get the simplified expression $3x^2 + x - 10$. Choices (G), (J), and (K) are the results of confusing the signs. Choice (F) only multiplies the first terms and the last terms, which is not the correct way to multiply binomials.

3. **B** Substitute 8 and 6 for x and y, respectively, into the equation $f(x,y)$, to get $f(8,6) = 8 - [(8 \times 6) - 6] = 8 - 42 = -34$. Choices (A), (C), (D), and (E) are wrong because they do not distribute the negative correctly.

4. **G** Use the words in the problem to create an equation: *percent* means "divide by 100," *of* means "multiply" and *what number* means "use a variable." The equation is $x = \frac{1}{7} \times \frac{28}{100} \times 8,000$. So, $x = 320$. Choice (H) is $7 \times \frac{28}{100} \times 8,000$, a common fraction mistake.

5. **C** When you have numbers in the answer choices and variables in the question, you can plug the answer choices into the variables in the question to find out which answer choice makes the equation true. Start with answer choice (C) when plugging in the answer choices because it is the middle value and will sometimes tell you whether you need a bigger or smaller number if answer choice (C) is not the correct answer. Does $6(3) + 3 = 12 + 3(3)$, or, $21 = 21$? Yes, and you're done!

6. **F** First, calculate the difference of the third and second terms: $8 - (-2) = 10$. The first term, therefore, is the second term minus the difference: $(-2) - 10 = -12$. Choices (G) and (K) are variations of the actual common difference, rather than the value of the first term. Choice (H) calculates the first term in a geometric, rather than arithmetic, sequence. Choice (J) incorrectly calculates –2 as the first term, rather than the second.

7. **C** Probability is equal to $\frac{number\ of\ favorable\ outcomes}{number\ of\ total\ possible\ outcomes}$. If you find a common denominator between the two probabilities, you can determine the number of unfavorable outcomes. The least common denominator between $\frac{2}{9}$ and $\frac{1}{3}$ is 9. The probability that the jellybean is NOT pink is $\frac{5}{9}$, so the probability that the jellybean is pink is $\frac{4}{9}$. Now, multiply $\frac{4}{9}$ by the total number of jellybeans, 72, to find the bag contains 32 pink jellybeans, choice (C).

8. **G** Because the flat rate of $100 includes the first two months, Bob will be billed $60/month for only 10 months out of the year. The total cost is $100 + $60 (10) = $700, so choice (G) is correct. Choice (F) results if you incorrectly charge $100 for every two-month period. The flat rate applies only for the first two months. Choice (H) calculates the total without the flat rate. Choice (J) incorrectly charges the flat rate twice for the first two months. Choice (K) adds 12, rather than 10, months of service charges to the flat rate.

9. **C** If one side of the pentagon measures 20 inches, the perimeter of the pentagon is 100 inches (20 × 5). Because the pentagon and the square have the same perimeter, the square also has a perimeter of 100 inches. Each side of the square is then 25 inches (100 ÷ 4). Choice (E) is wrong because it is equal to the perimeter of both the square and the pentagon, which is not what the question asks for. Choices (A), (B), and (D) give a perimeter that is not equal to our target of 100 inches.

10. **F** Translate the words into an equation, making x the number of bricks. Contractor A charges $1,600 *plus* $2 *times* the number of bricks, $1,600 + 2x$. Contractor B charges $400 plus $8 times the number of bricks, $400 + 8x$. Set the expressions equal to each other to get $1,600 + 2x = 400 + 8x$. Choice (G) sets each contractor's flat rate plus the other contractor's per brick charge equal. Choice (H) sets the sum of each contractor's per brick charges and the number of bricks equal. Choices (J) and (K) set the per brick charges equal to Contractor A's and B's flat rates, respectively.

11. **D** Solve for B. Divide both sides of the equation by ACD to get $B = \dfrac{E}{ACD}$.

12. **H** You need to remember some things about angles and lines: A straight line, in this case $\angle WVZ$, measures 180°, and $\angle XVY$ measures 90° because it is marked as a right angle. The sum of the measures of $\angle WVX$ and $\angle YVZ = 180° - 90° = 90°$. Since $\angle WVX$ and $\angle YVZ$ measure $4a$ and $2a$ respectively, $6a = 90°$ so $a = 15°$. Therefore, $\angle YVZ = 30°$ and $\angle XVY = 90° + 30° = 120°$. Choice (F) is the value of $\angle YVZ$. Choice (J) is the sum of $\angle WVX$ and $\angle WVY$. Choice (K) is too big because we know that $\angle VVZ$ is not a straight line.

13. **B** First find the temperature of New Orleans in °F by adding 25°F to 70°F to get 95°F. Your answer choices give you different values of °C. You can start with the middle answer choice, 68°C, and substitute this value for C in the equation to see if you get 95°F. Choice (C) gives $\dfrac{9}{5}(68) + 32 = 154$ °F. Since this value is too large, you can eliminate choices (C), (D), and (E). Choice (B) gives $\dfrac{9}{5}(35) + 32 = 95$ °F.

14. **G** The factored form of the expression is $2(3x + 2y) - 7$, so you can substitute 5 for $3x + 2y$ to get $2(5) - 7 = 3$. Choice (F) results if you forget to multiply $3x + 2y$ by 2, and choice (J) forgets to subtract 7. Choices (H) and (K) incorrectly use the coefficients of x and y to determine the value.

15. **B** The total amount of beef in pounds would be $3\frac{2}{7} + 2\frac{1}{3} = 5\frac{13}{21}$. This number falls in the range "At least $5\frac{1}{2}$ and less than $5\frac{2}{3}$." Choices (A), (C), (D), and (E) are incorrect because $5\frac{13}{21}$ does not fall within those ranges.

16. **H** Draw a picture. Since Dave went directly east and then directly south, the distance to his house can be found using a right triangle. The distance is $d = \sqrt{3^2 + 4^2} = 5$. Careful not to choose (K), which is the sum of the two legs of the triangle!

17. **B** The rate at which the sensor records—1 piece of data every .0000000038 seconds, or $\frac{1}{.0000000038}$

   —is constant, and therefore the ratio of pieces of data recorded per second will be equal for any given number of pieces of data or seconds. Set $\frac{1}{.0000000038}$ equal to the ratio 100,000,000,000 pieces of data every x seconds: $\frac{1}{.0000000038} = \frac{100,000,000,000}{x}$. Solve for x by multiplying diagonally across the equation: $x \times 1 = 100,000,000,000 \times .0000000038$. $x = 380$.

18. **J** Use the answers: Since the width and length are reduced by the same amount, you can eliminate any that do not use the same difference between original and new dimensions, answers (F), (H), and (K). Then, calculate the original area of the photograph: $A = l \times w = 20 \times 30 = 600$ cm². The final area of the photo, therefore, equals $600 - 264 = 336$ cm². Choice (G) gives you $12 \times 22 = 264$ cm². The correct answer is choice (J), $14 \times 24 = 336$.

19. **C** The perimeter is the sum of all 4 side lengths of the quadrilateral. The answer choices give you the length of the shortest side, so you can work backwards by adding the three larger consecutive even numbers to each answer choice. You can immediately eliminate choice (D) because 7 is not an even number. Choice (C) correctly gives you 6 + 8 + 10 + 12 = 36. Choices (A), (B), and (E) do not give you a sum of 36.

20. **G** Rearrange the equation into the slope-intercept form, $y = mx + b$. The resulting equation is $y = \frac{3}{7}x + 3$, with slope m of $\frac{3}{7}$. Choice (F) confuses the signs. Choice (H) results if you rearrange the equation into "$x =$" form, which does not indicate slope. Choice (J) is the y-intercept of the line.

21. **C** To find the area of the trapezoid *BCEF*, subtract the area of triangle *CDE* from rectangle *BDEF*. The area of rectangle *BDEF* is 36 square feet (9 × 4), and the area of triangle *CDE* is 10 square feet [(5 × 4) ÷ 2]; therefore, the area of the trapezoid *BCEF* is 26 square feet (36 – 10). Choice (A) is incorrect because it finds the area of the square with sides *BC* and *BF*. Choice (D) is incorrect because it is only solving for the area of the rectangle *BDEF*.

22. **G** Make sure you read the given information carefully. You don't have to do any figuring aside from approximating $\sqrt{136}$ because all the other values are given to you. Because $\sqrt{136} \approx 11.7$, to find the perimeter, simply add the sides: $11.7 + 10 + 6 + 12 = 39.7$. If you chose (F), you may have forgotten to include the diagonal in your calculation. If you chose (J), you did too much work—this is the area!

23. **E** Use the Pythagorean theorem $a^2 + b^2 = c^2$. Since $FG = 10$ and $FJ = 6$, $(10)^2 + (6)^2 = \overline{GJ}^2$, and $\overline{GJ} = \sqrt{136}$. If you chose (B), you may have confused this with a 6:8:10 triangle, but be careful—FG and FJ are just the legs in this triangle. If this were a 6:8:10 triangle, the longest side would have to be 10. Also note, that because point J shares a y-coordinate with the midpoint of GH, $\overline{GJ} = HJ$.

24. **F** Since the graph is rotating clockwise, the point will be moving 90° and will have a new point on the x-axis. Any point on the x-axis must have a y-coordinate of 0, so you can eliminate choices (G) and (J) immediately. If you chose choice (K), be careful—you may have rotated the graph in a *counter*clockwise direction rather than a clockwise direction.

25. **C** A geometric figure has rotational symmetry if it looks the same after a certain amount of rotation. A geometric figure has reflectional symmetry when one half is the reflection of the other half. Choice (C) is the only figure that has rotational and reflectional symmetry.

26. **K** Expand the equation with FOIL (first, inside, outside, last) and you will see that only the first term in each polynomial has exponents that add together to become x^8: $-x^4 * 5x^4 = -5x^8$. Choice (F) wrongly assumes the absence of a x^8 term. Choice (G) confuses the sign; choice (H) incorrectly adds the coefficients; choice (J) multiplies the wrong terms.

27. **D** To find the mean, add up all the scores: $66 + 67 + 71 + 72 + 72 + 73 + 75 + 77 + 79 + 82 + 83 + 83 + 87 = 987$. Divide this number by the total number of scores, 13, to find $\frac{987}{13} \approx 75.9$. If you chose (C), be careful—this is the median. If you chose (B), you may have taken the means of the stems and leaves separately and added them together.

28. **F** To find the probability, determine the number of desirable outcomes divided by the number of total possible outcomes. Since you want a score of exactly 83, go to the stem-and-leaf plot to see that two of the golfers had a score of 83. Since there were 13 total golfers, the probability that an 83 would be selected out of the whole group is $\frac{2}{13}$. If you chose either choices (J) or (K), be careful—this question is asking about the probability of selecting a certain score; the actual numerical value of that score is not relevant.

29. **B** First, factor each number. In this problem, the given numbers are all products of 2, 3, a, and b. To find the lowest common multiple of the given values, you need to figure out the maximum number of times each component (2, 3, a, and b) appears in any one of our given values. $8 = 2 \times 2 \times 2$, so the lowest common multiple must have $2 \times 2 \times 2$ as a factor. No value has more than one factor of 3, so our number is only required to have one factor of 3. Finally, our least common multiple must have one a and one b. Multiply the mandatory factors together, $2 \times 2 \times 2 \times 3 \times a \times b$, to get $24ab$.

30. **J** To solve for the function, you need to determine the value of m in December. Since December is 7 months after May and $m = 0$ in May, $m = 7$ in December. Substitute 7 for m in the function to get $A(7) = 2(7) + 2$, so Aleksandra will have 16 model airplanes. Choice (F) is the number of airplanes she had in May. Choices (G), (H), and (K) result if you use the wrong value of m for December.

31. **E** The midpoint of a line is $(\frac{x_1 + x_2}{2})$, $(\frac{y_1 + y_2}{2})$. Thus, the x-coordinate of the midpoint = $\frac{-3+11}{2} = 4$, eliminating choices (A), (B), (C), and (D). The only remaining choice is (E), which also has the correct y-coordinate = $\frac{5-7}{2} = -1$. Be careful not to subtract x_2 from x_1, which would give you an x-coordinate of 7. Choices (A) and (B) merely add or subtract the x- and y-coordinates, rather than finding their averages.

32. **K** Factor the numerator and denominator separately: $\frac{(x-4)(x-4)}{(x+4)(x-4)}$. The factor $(x-4)$ on both the top and the bottom of the fraction cancel each other out, so you're left with choice (K). Choices (F), (G), and (H) are all the result of incorrectly canceling out terms without factoring. Choice (J) cancels both factors from the numerator, which is not possible with only one $(x-4)$ in the denominator.

33. **B** If Evan purchased 6 boxes, with 10 bags in each box, and 12 cookies in each bag, he will have purchased 720 cookies ($6 \times 10 \times 12$). Dividing 720 by 30 will give us the number of family packs with 30 cookies that he could have purchased instead. $720 \div 30 = 24$. Choices (A), (B), (C), and (E) are wrong because they do not result in the target amount of total cookies.

34. **F** If $\frac{r}{s} = -\frac{1}{2}$, then $s = -2r$. Substitute $-2r$ for s in the given expression: $16r^4 - (-2r)^4 = 16r^4 - 16r^4 = 0$. If you choose (H) you may have made a sign error.

35. A   Because the nine circles fit into the square "as shown," quickly estimate the area that remains to eliminate any answer choices that couldn't possibly be correct. Roughly, it appears that $\frac{1}{4}$ of the square remains. Since the total area of the square is 144 square inches, and $144 \div 4 = 36$, answer choices (C), (D), and (E) are out because they are too big. Answer choice (A) is slightly closer to our estimate than answer choice (B), but if you have time, do the math. Since the circles are identical and are tangent to all adjacent circles and to the edges, the diameter of any circle must be $\frac{1}{3}$ of a 12-inch side, or 4 inches, and the radius of any circle must be 2 . The area of each circle is $\pi \times$ the radius squared, or 3.14×4, or 12.56 . Multiply 12.56 square inches by 9 cookie cut-outs to get 113.04 square inches cut out, and 30.96 square inches remaining. You can also make this problem fast if you know that the area of a circle inscribed in a square is always equal to $\frac{\pi}{4} \times$ the area of the square, and can see that the area remaining in each of the small squares is proportional to the area remaining in the big square. $144 - (\frac{\pi}{4} \times 144) = 30.9$.

36. J   Use the answer choices and Process of Elimination. Remember that a prime number has only two distinct factors, itself and 1. 63 is divisible by 3, 7, 9 and 21, eliminating choice (F). 91 is divisible by 7 and 13, eliminating choices (G) and (H). 81 is divisible by 3, 9, and 27, eliminating choice (K).

37. C   First determine the cost per quarter hour using the rate formula: $rate = \dfrac{change \ in \ cost}{change \ in \ quarter - hours}$. Pick two different packages: $\dfrac{\$230 - \$200}{10 - 8} = \dfrac{\$30}{2}$ to find the rate that is \$15 per quarter-hour. Now use the 8 quarter-hour package: fixed cost + $\$15 \times 8 = \$200$ to find that the fixed cost is \$80. Choices (A) and (B) find the rate for the 8-quarter-hour and 10-quarter-hour package without a fixed cost. Choice (D) is a partial answer.

38. K   Because you know the height of the building *opposite* the angle and want to find the shadow length *adjacent* the angle, use SOHCAHTOA: $tan(45°) = 1 = \dfrac{Opposite}{Adjacent} = \dfrac{100}{x}$, thus $x = 100/\tan$ $34° \approx 100/0.67 \approx 148$. Choices (F), (H), and (J) are the result if you use the wrong trigonometric function. Choice (G) is the result if you incorrectly set up $\tan \theta = \dfrac{adjacent}{opposite}$.

39. **E** The general equation for a circle with center (h,k) and radius r, is $(x-h)^2+(y-k)^2=r^2$. Because $h=4$, $k=-3$, and $r=12$, the equation for this circle is $(x-4)^2+(y+3)^2=144$. Choices (A), (B), and (C) are incorrect because they do not square r. Choice (D) is incorrect because it does not distribute the negative in the $(y-k)^2$ term.

40. **H** Use your calculator to make the comparisons easier: $\dfrac{14}{21}=0.\overline{66}$. Now, test the answers. Choice (F) is $\dfrac{7}{12}=0.58\overline{3}$, which is less than $0.\overline{66}$, and choice (G) is $\dfrac{8}{12}=0.\overline{66}$, which makes the two fractions equal. Choice (H) is $\dfrac{9}{12}=0.75$, which makes the inequality true. Choices (J) and (K) also make the inequality true but neither is the *least* integer that makes the inequality true.

41. **E** Substitute $(a+b)$ for a. Square the quantity $(a+b)$, distribute the 2 within $(a+b)$ by multiplying a and b both by 2, and add 5.

42. **G** Since lines $\overline{MO}$ and $\overline{LP}$ are parallel, $\angle NMO\cong\angle NLP$ and $\angle NOM\cong\angle NPL$. Thus, ΔMNO and ΔLNP are similar triangles with congruent angles and proportional sides. To find the length of $\overline{NO}$, set up a proportion: $\dfrac{\overline{MO}}{\overline{LP}}=\dfrac{\overline{NO}}{\overline{NP}}$. Using x for $\overline{NO}$, solve for x: $\dfrac{105}{150}=\dfrac{x}{x+39}$. $\overline{NO}=91$ feet. Choice (F) gives the length of $\overline{OP}$. Choice (K) is the sum of the three side lengths.

43. **C** First, convert 2 miles to feet, $2\,miles\times\dfrac{5{,}280\,feet}{1\,mile}=10{,}560\,feet$, because height, h, is given in feet in the equation. Now, substitute the answer choices for the value of t to see which choice equals 10,560 feet. Choice (C) gives, $1{,}200+32(293)=10{,}576$. The precise answer is 292.5 seconds, but the question asked for the nearest second.

44. **J** The three angles of a triangle will always equal 180°, so $2x+3x+5x=180$. Since $\angle C=5x$ and $x=18°$, $\angle C=5(18°)=90$. Choices (F) and (K) are partial answers. Choices (G) and (H) give the measures for the wrong angles.

45. **B** If the basketball player made 12 out of his 30 shots, he currently has a free-throw percentage of 40%. Use the answers to calculate the least number of additional free throws he must make. Make sure you add the number to both the numerator and denomination, since any addition free throws are both attempted and made. Choice (B) gives you $\dfrac{12+10}{30+10}\times100=55\%$. Choice (A) is the result of adding 5 only to the numerator. Choices (C) and (D) approximate 55% to 56% of 30 free throws. Choice (E) incorrectly raises the percentage *by* 55% rather than *to* 55%.

46. **H** Pick a number in the provided range and try out the answers. If $y = -2$, choices (F), (G), and (J) yield positive results. Choice (H) is approximately $-\frac{3}{2}$, which is less than the result of choice (K), $-\frac{1}{8}$.

47. **C** Draw five placeholders for the positions of each of the 5 groomsmen: ___ ___ ___ ___ ___. How many groomsmen could possibly walk in the first position? Five. Write a 5 in the 1st position. Next, if one groomsman takes the first position, how many possible groomsmen are left to take the second position? Four. Write a 4 in the second position, and multiply the 5 possibilities for the first position by the 4 possibilities for the second position (each of the 5 possible groomsmen in the 1st position could be with 4 different other groomsmen in the 2nd position). After another of the groomsmen is chosen for the 2nd position, there are 3 possible groomsmen for the 3rd position, then 2 possible groomsmen for the 4th position, and finally only 1 possible groomsman for the 5th position. _5_ × _4_ × _3_ × _2_ × _1_ = 120 total possible orderings.

48. **J** As with all circle problems, it is helpful to first calculate and draw the radius. Given the area of the circle is 169π square inches, use the area formula: $A = 169\pi = \pi r^2$, so $r = 13$. Radii $\overline{MO}$ and $\overline{NO}$ form two right triangles with chord $\overline{MN}$, so you can use the Pythagorean theorem to find the length of the two missing legs: $5^2 + b^2 = 13^2$, so $b = 12$. The length of the chord is $2 \times 12 = 24$ inches. Choice (F) gives only half the length of the chord. Choices (G) and (K) give the radius and diameter of the circle, rather than the chord. Choice (H) is the sum of 5 and 13, which is not the correct operation to calculate lengths of a right triangle.

49. **A** The x-intercept occurs where $y = 0$, eliminating choices (B), (C), and (D). Next, find the slope of the line: $\frac{rise}{run} = \frac{4-7}{6+3} = -\frac{3}{9}$, or $-\frac{1}{3}$. The line to the x-intercept must have the same slope. The slope between choice (A) and $(-3,7)$ is $\frac{7-0}{-3-18} = -\frac{1}{3}$. Careful not to choose (C), which is the y-intercept.

50. **G** Intercepting the x axis at $x = 7$ means the equation must satisfy the coordinate (7,0). The only equation that does this is choice (G). Choices (F) and (H) incorrectly give x-intercepts at $(-7,0)$. Choice (J) gives the y-intercept at $y = 7$, and choice (K) gives the y-intercept at $(0,-7)$.

51. **A** If the $\tan \theta = \frac{2}{9}$, the side opposite to θ is 2, and the side adjacent is 9. Therefore the hypotenuse is $\sqrt{85}$ ($h = \sqrt{2^2 + 9^2}$), so $\cos \theta = \frac{9}{\sqrt{85}}$ and $\sin \theta = \frac{2}{\sqrt{85}}$. $\cos \theta + \sin \theta = \frac{11}{\sqrt{85}}$

52. **G** Triangle OAB is equilateral since OA and OB are both radii of the circle and $OA = AB$. The formula for the area of a triangle is $A = \dfrac{1}{2}bh$. The base of $\triangle OAB$ is 8. To find the height of $\triangle OAB$, draw a line from A that is perpendicular to OB, creating two 30°-60°-90° triangles. Using the relationship $a : a\sqrt{3} : 2a$, the height of $\triangle OAB$ is $4\sqrt{3}$. So, $A = \dfrac{1}{2}(8)\left(4\sqrt{3}\right) = 16\sqrt{3}$. Choice (F) uses 4 for the base. If you chose (J), you probably forgot the $\dfrac{1}{2}$ in the area formula. Choice (H) uses 8 for both the base and the height of the triangle.

53. **C** Use the formula given and replace variables with values from the diagram. You will also need to find the degree measure of angle Z, since the problem asks for the length of the side opposite Z. Given that there are 180° in a triangle, subtract 105° and 40° from 180° to get 35° for angle Z. Now Plug In all of the information in the equation: $\dfrac{\sin 40°}{30} = \dfrac{\sin 35°}{z}$. Solve for z by multiplying both sides by z and by 30 to get: $z \sin 40° = 30 \sin 35°$. Divide both sides by $\sin 40°$.

54. **G** To find arc length, use a ratio of $\dfrac{sector}{circle} : \dfrac{central\ angle}{360°} = \dfrac{arc\ length}{circumference}$. Since the radius is 9 ft., the circumference is $C = 2\pi(9) = 18\pi$. Now, fill known values into the ratio: $\dfrac{120°}{360°} = \dfrac{arc\ PQ}{18\pi}$. Cross-multiply and solve to find the length of the arc is 6π. Choice (J) is a partial answer that gives the circumference rather than arc length. Choice (K) is the sector's area, rather than arc length.

55. **C** In order to subtract these matrices, you must combine the corresponding elements from each matrix. That is, you subtract the first row, first column numbers in the second and third matrices from the first row, first column number in the first matrix. Thus, the matrix $\begin{bmatrix} w - x - \dfrac{1}{w+x} & x - y - \dfrac{1}{x+y} \\ y - z - \dfrac{1}{y+z} & z - w - \dfrac{1}{z+w} \end{bmatrix}$, choice (C), is the best answer. Choices (A), (B), and (E) all improperly subtract fractions and integers. Choice (D) uses multiplication rather than subtraction.

56. K To deal with compound functions, the trick is to work inside out. First, determine the value of the inside $f(1) = -2(1)^3 = -2$. The value of $f(1)$ becomes the new x-value for the outside f function, so determine $f(-2) = -2(-2)^3 = -2(-8) = 16$. Remember that a negative number raised to an odd integer stays negative; thus choices (F) and (G) are wrong because they confuse the signs. Choice (H) is the value of $-x^3$, rather than $-2x^3$. Choice (H) is the result of multiplying $f(x)$ by $f(x)$, which is not the same operation as compound functions.

57. A If a function y varies directly with x, this means that as x increases, y increases proportionally, eliminating choices (B) and (D). This proportionality means that the function must be a straight line, eliminating choice (E), with the equation $y = kx$, where k is a constant. This line must then pass through the origin, because if $x = 0$, then $y = 0$. Choices (C) is incorrect because it does not pass through the origin.

58. K If the quiz scores are listed from lowest to highest, the middle score, the median, is 9. The two highest scores are both 10. Since the only mode of the quiz scores is 10, the remaining two scores must be distinct integers. The mean of the 5 scores is 8, so the sum of the five scores is $8 \times 5 = 40$. The sum of the two lowest scores must be $40 - (9 + 10 + 10) = 11$. Choices (F), (G) and (H) *could* be true because the quiz scores could be (3, 8, 9, 10, 10), (4, 7, 9, 10, 10) or (5, 6, 9, 10, 10). Choice (J) is the number of scores multiplied by the mode.

59. E First, draw a picture and fill in as much information as you can from the problem. Two opposite sides of the cardboard are 60 inches, and two opposite sides are 40 inches. Since you're looking for the height of the table and the answer choices are numbers, not variables, representing the height of the table, use the answer choices to fill in the diagram further. Try labeling the height of the table starting with choice (C), the middle value. Given that the width of the cardboard is 40 inches, a height of 25 inches on either side of the tabletop is not possible—50 inches is greater than the size of the paper. Try the next smallest number, 20 inches, in answer choice (D). 20 inches is too big: If the paper table were 20 inches tall on either side, the top of the table would be a line. Choice (E), 10 inches, must be the correct answer.

60. H To find the area of a triangle, use the formula $A = \dfrac{1}{2} base \times height$. You already know the base is 10, but you need to find the height. Draw a line from point B that is perpendicular to line $\overline{AC}$.

Use SOHCAHTOA: $\sin 35° = \dfrac{height}{AB}$, so the height of this triangle is $10 \sin 35°$. The area is $A = \dfrac{1}{2}(10)(10 \sin 35°) = 50 \sin 35°$. Choices (F), (G), and (H) use the wrong trigonometric functions. Choice (K) does not take $\dfrac{1}{2}$ the product of $\overline{AB}$ and $\overline{AC}$.

TEST 2 READING EXPLANATIONS

1. **A** The use of the word *stultifying* refers to the boy's experience of life on his family's farm; later in the sentence, the passage tells us that the boy felt *landlocked* by this life, so something like trapped would fit well. Therefore, you can eliminate choices (B) and (C), because *strengthening* and *welcoming* don't match this description. Choice (D) is incorrect because nothing in the passage implies productivity.

2. **G** Line 20 shows that the boy had only heard about but never seen fireworks. Line 7 shows that the boy has companions who lead him through the jungle, so choice (F) is incorrect; choice (H) is negated by line 55, which implies that the boy respects the captain's knowledge; line 25 shows that memories of the storm often intruded in the boy's thoughts, so choice (J) doesn't work.

3. **D** Line 30 refers to the boy's second home on the ocean, the idea presented in choice (D). Line 3 refers to the jungle as *inhospitable* and mentions the *snarling* vines in the jungle, making choice (A) incorrect; choice (B) is incorrect because the passage portrays the boy's mother only as *frail and worn-looking* (line 35), not frightening; and choice (C) is incorrect because the passage doesn't note that the boy feels positive about any aspect of farm life.

4. **F** This choice is correct because the passage about the boy leaving the farm is a flashback, as shown in line 44. Choice (G) is incorrect because the boy is remembering his past life while he continues to walk through the jungle; choice (H) doesn't work because the boy meets the captain and sets sail before the captain is killed and the ship is destroyed in the wreck; choice (J) is incorrect because his parents *create a home for him* (line 36) on the farm, before he goes off to sea.

5. **C** This choice is correct because the boy follows his question about what the phrase means with an acknowledgment that he can't distinguish the captain from the other men in his mind (lines 63–67). Choice (A) is incorrect because the passage up to this point has shown the boy wondering about the meaning behind the captain's words, implying that the captain hadn't explained the phrase previously; choice (B) is incorrect because, although the boy wonders what the dead can do earlier in the passage, his thoughts here are focused on the captain; choice (D) is incorrect because there is no indication that the boy's experiences will lead him to a better life.

6. **J** Choice (J) is correct because the boy was eager to learn about navigation from the captain, as seen in lines 52–55, and the passage shows us the captain's dislike of ignorance, which he sees as *dangerous* (line 51). Choice (F) is incorrect because the boy wonders what the words mean at the beginning and end of the passage (lines 60–70); choice (G) is incorrect because the passage contains no evidence that the captain even knew the boy's father was worn down; choice (H) is incorrect because the passage contains no evidence about the captain's view of life at sea.

7. **A** Choice (A) is correct because lines 61–63 show the crewmates urging the boy (and finally pulling him) away from the scene of the wreck, showing his reluctance to leave. Choice (B) is incorrect because lines 6–7 shows the boy continuing to walk with his companions—no running away here; choice (C) is incorrect because, although lines 10–12 say that unpleasant memories of the storm often filled his thoughts, there is nothing in the passage that describes his reaction to loud noises; choice (D) is incorrect because the passage contains no evidence that the crewmates know about the boy's feelings about life on the farm.

8. **H** This choice is correct because the passage shows the captain teaching the boy about navigation (lines 49–51). Choice (F) is incorrect because the passage never describes the captain scolding the boy for stowing away; choice (G) is incorrect because the boy wonders what the phrase means even at the end of the story, as shown in lines 68–70; choice (J) is incorrect because lines 48–56 show the captain paying attention to the boy by teaching him navigation.

9. **D** This choice is correct because the passage does not mention hail. Thunder is described in lines 20–22, the *walls of water* are mentioned in line 22, and lightning is described in lines 19–20, making choices (A), (B), and (C) incorrect.

10. **F** This choice is correct because lines 13–15 shows the unexpectedness of the storm. Choice (G) is incorrect because the passage does not mention the time at which the storm arrived; choice (H) is incorrect because the passage does not mention how the crew responded to the storm; choice (J) is incorrect because the passage does not contain any reference to the boy's father mentioning a storm.

11. **A** The *however* at the beginning of this sentence tells you that Thorne's comment is in direct contrast to the paragraph that came before, which identified the typical understanding of slang as something that is said in *defiant opposition of authority*. Choice (A) is most relevant to undermining that generalization. Choices (B) and (C) do not relate to defying authority, and rather they represent Thorne's attempts to provide counterexamples to the claim that all slang is intended to be against the status quo. Choice (D) is unsupportable anywhere in the passage; it is a trap answer based on the normal association of the contrast between *accusing* someone of guilt and his/her *innocence*.

12. **G** The final paragraph establishes the need to compile a slang dictionary so that people of future eras will have a way to understand our current forms of communication. The details regarding how Thorne's dictionary will explain each term and the analogy to modern attempts to decipher Shakespearean slang support choice (G). There is nothing critical in tone in this paragraph to support choice (F). The passage does not say that Thorne uses Shakespearean slang in his dictionary as choice (H) states. While the author does agree that a dictionary of slang would be useful to future generations, he does not argue that the project of compiling such a dictionary is the *primary* goal of modern linguistics as choice (J) states.

13. **B** Choice (B) is correct because college professors, while possibly involved in the study of slang, are never mentioned in the passage. Choices (A), (C), and (D) are all mentioned in the passage.

14. **F** The quotation marks around *common man* highlight the fact that this is a questionable term that is being applied by someone else's point of view. This paragraph discusses how a word becomes viewed as slang based on a very subjective assessment of the people who use that word. The parallelism of the two sentences tells you that *common man* must be the opposite of the *respectable* people mentioned in the previous sentence. Choice (F) correctly relates the derogatory classification of slang to its less respected users. Choice (G) is not supported anywhere in the passage. Choice (H) incorrectly identifies a point of view held by *intellectuals who would categorically denounce slang* as the author's own. Choice (J), while related to this paragraph, is too extreme in wording and does not answer the question of the intended effect of adding quotation marks around a certain term.

15. **C** The context of this sentence tells you that slang is viewed *condescendingly* and as a signal of *intellectual laziness*. Choice (C) reinforces these ideas by identifying vulgar speech as containing something (slang) that sophisticated speech would not include. Choices (A), (B), and (D) are all correctly negative in tone but to an unfairly severe and specific degree. Certain uses of slang may be *sickening, malicious,* or *profane*, but this sentence is concerned with the way linguists view ALL slang as being uneducated in tone.

16. **F** According to the final paragraph, Thorne believes that in order for *future generations* or *civilization* to be able to decode the meaning contained in all our written artifacts, we need to provide them with a way of understanding our usage of slang. Choice (F) correctly identifies this purpose. Choice (G) suggests the purpose is for foreign language learners, choice (H) suggests the purpose is to write the first-ever slang dictionary, and choice (J) suggests the purpose is to provide a current how-to-use manual of slang. All three are unsupported and do not address the stated need for this sort of resource.

17. **C** The quote from Whitman describes slang as an attempt to escape from *bald literalism*, meaning an attempt to find more colorful ways of saying what one means, and as humanity's attempt to *express itself illimitably*, meaning to have limitless expression. Choice (C) is a fair paraphrase of those ideas. Choice (A) is irrelevant and unsupportable. Choices (B) and (D) are stated elsewhere in the passage as reasons for slang but not attributable to Whitman or related to his quote.

18. **H** The first paragraph attempts to make a contrast between unscholarly sounding words and a man of great academic distinction. The rhetorical question at the end of the paragraph attempts to invite the reader's curiosity as to why these two things would go together. Choice (H) effectively ties the first paragraph's anecdote to the purpose of the passage as a whole, discussing the academic treatment of slang. Choices (F) and (J) are too narrow in scope, failing to explain the first paragraph's relation to the passage as a whole. Choice (G) has an extreme claim that British scholars are the *leaders*, which is unsupported by the passage.

19. **C** The parallelism of this sentence indicates that while *most modern slang comes from* groups like corporate office workers, students, and computer users, previously most slang came from groups like the military. In describing groups such as the military as *hotbeds of slang*, the author is saying that such groups are likely inventors of slang. Choice (C) correctly matches this concept. Choice (A) means to predict the future, which is not supported by the passage. Choices (B) and (D) are unsupportable and make use of the trap language association between *traditionally* and *old-fashioned* as well as *the military* and *strict*.

20. **J** The passage indicates that most intellectuals do not completely reject slang because they *realize almost all slang* initially *involves as much inherent creativity* as the admired word play of poetry. Choice (J) addresses this detail. Choices (F), (G), and (H) are not supported anywhere in the passage.

21. **D** The author says *his genius is and will continue to be undisputed* (lines 93–94), so she does not think it is an *overstatement* or inadequate to suggest Gaudi's work is *genius,* eliminating choices (A) and (B). It is reasonable to assume that the author views the description of Gaudi's work as *freakish genius* as a correct interpretation of how current critics and viewers understand his contributions to architecture (choice D). Choice (C) is wrong because it is directed only at first-time viewers and is only a suggestion.

22. **G** The harsh images of Gaudi begging on the street suggest that the 1900s (choice G) were a time of great need, and when funders were least likely to fund construction. The passage also says, *financial contributions for the church's construction fizzled out completely around the turn of the century.* Choice (F) is incorrect because Gaudi began construction in the 1880s and there was "significant funding." The progress of the 1950s, choice (H) is due to increases in funding and construction picked up in the 1980s because of steady donations to fund that work, choice (J).

23. **A** The passage says that the Sagrada Familia stands apart from the rest of the world's cathedrals because of its *unique and startling design* (line 4), supporting the claim that it is more remarkable because of its unique appearance and design, choice (A). Choice (B) is incorrect because the passage does not indicate that the Sagrada Familia compares unfavorably to other cathedrals. There is no information in the passage to support choices (C) or (D), and neither is mentioned in comparison to other great cathedrals.

24. **F** The primary objective of the third paragraph is to tell the reader about Gaudi's childhood and show that he caused controversy from an early age choice (F). The reference to his family is not the primary point of the paragraph, choice (G). The education of the day was boring and unsatisfying because he was looking for more creativity, so choice (H) and choice (J) take excerpts of the paragraph out of context.

25. **A** The passage says that Guell funded a wide *array* of structures, including a mansion, park, and crypt, meaning a wide range choice (B), a broad selection choice (C) or large variety choice (D). *Arrangement* choice (A) does not capture a similar idea.

26. **G** In context of the sentence, *grumblings* refers to the reasons the finished Sagrada Familia may receive criticism, thus choice (G) is the best answer. Choices (F) and (J) are more literal, common usages of the word.

27. **A** When compared to his contemporaries and artists since his time, Gaudi used controversial methods, developed unique designs, and pioneered his own techniques like *trencadis* (line 47). Therefore Gaudi was less inhibited, eliminating choice (B), and other contemporaries were more reserved, making choice (A) the best answer. The passage never mentions technique, and it cannot be assumed that either Gaudi or his peers were more focused on technique, eliminating choices (C) and (D).

28. **F** The passage says that politicians and architects *agreed that the plans Gaudi had left behind were sufficient to achieve his vision* and that, therefore, they would continue with the construction (choice (F)). There is no evidence to suggest that viewing the Sagrada Familia in person (choice (G)), the impending civil war (choice (H)), or the popularity of Gaudi's design (choice (J)) influenced their decision.

29. **B** The passage says that *even at this early age, he engendered controversy* (lines 23–24), which supports choice (B). While it is true that Gaudi was able to withstand harsh criticisms (choice A), he was unable to complete the Sagrada Familia. His inspiration from Nature also influenced his work (choice C), but it not clear when he started using natural inspiration. Moreover, there is no support in the passage that his creations ever *blurred* the distinction between art and nature—no one mistook his buildings for nature itself. There is also no evidence in the passage to suggest that Gaudi changed his building's design (choice D) according to surroundings or other people's desires.

30. **H** In the passage, the discussion of the architecture-as-art includes the statement that *functional designs dominated the architectural world* for years, suggesting that the most recent generations preferred pragmatic designs, supporting choice (H). There is no mention of historical architecture or modern unconventional designs in the passage, eliminating choices (F) and (G). Choice (J) is also weaker than choice (H), since the passage mentioned functional designs.

31. **A** Frank Drake is primarily discussed in the first paragraph and briefly mentioned during the conclusion. He is described as the person in charge of Project Ozma, which is in turn called *the first organized attempt to detect alien life by way of radio*. The correct answer, choice (A), correctly summarizes this information. The project was unsuccessful in its search for alien life, making choice (B) incorrect. Choice (C) confuses Project Ozma with Project Phoenix, which is not mentioned in connection with Drake. The passage does not explicitly state Drake's education or position, as in choice (D).

32. **G** Project Ozma is discussed in the second paragraph, immediately after the description of Frank Drake's experiment. The passage tells us that the project was a failure in the sense that it failed to find signs of intelligent life but a success in terms of leading to other similar programs. Therefore, choice (G) is the best answer. Choice (F) is incorrect because the project was not a success. The passage does not call Drake's goals unrealistic, as in choice (H), nor does it discuss NASA at this time, as in choice (J).

33. **C** The word *august* is used to describe two colleges, the University of California at Berkeley and the University of Western Sydney. Those programs are then described as having *reputations that draw respected scientists from around the world*. Therefore, a good word to replace *august* would be respected. Choice (C), *esteemed*, is a good synonym for respected. Choice (A), *summery*, might sound like it's related to *august*, but it doesn't mean respected.

34. **H** The author concludes the passage by stating that *Perhaps someday Frank Drake's dream of a message from outer space will come true once we know where to look for it*. This implies a certain hopefulness about the search while acknowledging that there are difficulties yet to be overcome. Therefore, the best answer is choice (H). There is no evidence that the author is *ironic*, as in choice (F), or *angry*, as in choice (G). Choice (J) goes too far, since the author is inclined to be hopeful, not fearful.

35. **A** The passage describes scientists in this field in the third paragraph. They are described as *esteemed academics, typically specializing in the areas of physics, astronomy, and engineering*. Choice (A), the best answer, is a good paraphrase of this information. Choice (B) includes words from the passage, but goes against the information given. Choice (C) mentions specific places of employment. Although the passage does mention such institutions, it does not discuss these researchers as specifically employed there. Choice (D) incorrectly focuses on radio mechanics, instead of interstellar research.

36. **J** The fourth paragraph serves as a bridge between the introductory paragraphs, which discuss the search for extraterrestrial life in general terms, and the rest of the passage, which goes into greater detail about two of the relevant factors in determining various planets' habitability. Choice (J) is the best answer because it correctly identifies the shift to the two factors as the primary point of the paragraph. Choice (F) incorrectly identifies a minor point in the first sentence as the main idea. Liquid water is not discussed until paragraph five, ruling out choice (G). *Goldilocks Zones* are not mentioned until paragraph six, ruling out choice (H).

37. **D** The term *hospitable planets* is used in the fifth paragraph, during the discussion of temperature and liquid water. The sentence states that *hospitable planets must be located within a certain distance of their respective suns.* This sentence falls in the middle of the discussion of what conditions will allow for life, so a good phrase to replace *hospitable planets* with would be *life-supporting* or, to use another term introduced in the passage, *life-sustaining.* Choice (D) is the best answer, since it is the best match for *life-supporting.* Choice (A) refers to cultures, which are not within the scope of this passage. Choice (B) incorrectly focuses on distance from the sun, which does not necessarily mean *life-supporting.* Choice (C) goes against the information in the passage.

38. **H** Saturn is mentioned in paragraph five, as an example of a planet that is too far from the sun to have temperatures conducive to life. Choice (H) correctly connects this statement to the earlier statement that planets too far away from the sun cannot sustain liquid water, making it the best answer. Choice (F) incorrectly states that Saturn is too close to the sun. Choice (G) incorrectly associates distance from the sun with a heavy atmosphere, a link not discussed in this passage. Choice (J) mentions *gas giants,* which the passage does not discuss until the following paragraph, and not in connection with Saturn.

39. **D** This question asks you to find a situation analogous to that of Venus. The passage mentions Venus in the fifth paragraph, as an example of a planet that is too close to the sun, and thus too hot, to support life. Later in the passage, the author also notes that the size of a planet may alter this rule, since smaller planets retain less heat and can thus be closer to the sun. The correct answer, choice (D), correctly connects these facts. The passage never describes Venus as a *gas giant*, as in choice (A), nor does it state that Venus lacks a gravitational field, as in choice (B). Choice (C) incorrectly identifies Venus as having an unstable orbit.

40. **F** Goldilocks Planets are discussed in the fifth paragraph and are described as *planets that fall within the range of appropriate temperatures.* Therefore, choice (F) is the best answer. Choice (G) incorrectly discusses atmospheres, while choice (H) has the opposite information as the passage. Choice (J) incorrectly mentions hydrogen gases, which are not mentioned in this part of the passage.

TEST 2 SCIENCE EXPLANATIONS

1. **D** In Table 1, when the current doubles, the velocity of the train also doubles. Therefore, a current of 500 A must be associated with a train velocity of 2×200 m/s = 400 m/s.

2. **F** Table 2 shows that the current consistently increases as the length of the magnetic rods increases, so choice (F) is the best answer.

3. **C** When $B = 9.84 \times 10^{-4}$ T, I = 500 A, and when $B = 1.05 \times 10^{-3}$ T, I = 600 A. Therefore, I = 570 A would be produced by a magnetic field with a values in between these two B values. Choice (C) is the only option that fits.

4. **J** The question suggests that an increasing electrical current results from an increasing voltage. Of the options listed, Trial 14 has the greatest electrical current, so it must also have the greatest voltage.

5. **B** Study 4 stands out because all of the values for electrical current are negative. Therefore, choice (B) is the correct answer.

6. **G** In Study 3, both current (I) and magnetic field (B) increase with a direct relationship. Choice (G) shows this direct increasing linear relationship.

7. **D** Using Figure 1, you determine the features of a *Pipistrellus hesperus* starting at Step 8 and work backwards. Step 8 describes it to have a *forearm length < 40 mm*. Step 7 describes it to have a *tragus < 6 mm and curved*. Step 5 describes it to have a *uropatagium not heavily furred*, and Step 1 describes it to have *ears shorter than 25 mm*. Only choice (D) refers to a feature of Bat IV, *uropatagium heavily furred*, that differs from those of *Pipistrellus hesperus* found using the above method. Alternatively, you could use the features of bat IV from Table 1 and find the point on Figure 1 where the result differs from the path necessary to get to *Pipistrellus hesperus*.

8. **G** Follow Figure 1 step by step using the descriptions for bats I and II from Table 1 until you find the last step with the same result. Starting at Step 1, both bats have ears *shorter than 25 mm* making Step 5 next. Therefore, choice (F) must be wrong. Both bats have a uropatagium that is *not heavily furred*, making Step 7 next. Bat I has a *4 mm, curved* tragus, and bat II has a *7 mm, straight* tragus. Therefore, the results of Step 7 differ making choices (H) and (J) wrong. This leaves choice (G), Step 5, as the last point where the bats had similar traits. Note that the *obvious fringe of fur* on the uropatagium of bat II does not come into play until Step 9 of Figure 1.

9. **A** All of the choices are in the kingdom Animalia and phylum Chordata. Vesper bats, like all bats, belong to the class Mammalia. Mammals are vertebrates with sweat glands, hair, and similar middle ear structures that give birth to live young (except monotremes which lay eggs).

10. **G** Both species are found at Step 6 in Figure 1. Step 6 can only be reached from having *heavily furred* uropatagium in Step 5, eliminating choice (H). Step 5 can only be reached from having *shorter than 25 mm* ears in Step 1, eliminating choice (J). Choice (F) refers to Step 3 which is not part of the path for either species, meaning it may or may not be a common trait. Choice (G) is more definitive because it refers to the only feature that neither species can have according to Figure 1. It is not possible to get to Step 6 if the ears are greater than 25 mm long.

11. **D** Using the features listed in Table 1 for bat II, follow the steps in Figure 1. Bat II's *18 mm long* ears lead from Step 1 to Step 5 in Figure 1. The uropatagium overall is *not heavily furred*, which then leads to Step 7. The tragus is *7 mm* and *straight*, leading next to Step 9. Since there is an *obvious fringe of fur* on the edge of the uropatgium, bat II is *Myotis thysanodes*. Choice (D), *Myotis volans*, is most likely the closest genetic relative because it is in the same genus, has very similar features, and is adjacent on Figure 1.

12. **J** Looking at Figure 2, the 0°C setting is the lowest curve, represented by triangles. At 200 min. the saltwater temperature is about 8°C, and at 250 min. the temperature is about 5°C. Therefore, at 220 min., you should expect the temperature to be between 5°C and 8°C.

13. **B** Since we are asked about a heater and a 37°C trial, Figure 1 will be the relevant chart. At 8 min. the air temperature is about 27°C, and at 10 min. the temperature is about 31°C. If the air changes 4°C in 2 minutes, divide 4 by 2 to get the answer: 2°C/min.

14. **F** For every temperature setting in each figure, the temperature changes fastest in the beginning and slower as time progresses. The 0°C cooling trial is no different: from 0–100 min. the saltwater temperature goes from 50°C to about 22°C, a change of 28°C, a much greater change than those recorded in any of the other 100 minute intervals listed in the answer choices.

15. **A** Average kinetic energy is directly proportional to temperature. That is, when temperature is high, average kinetic energy is high, and when temperature is low, average kinetic energy is low. Choice (A) corresponds to the highest temperature. However, you don't need to know what kinetic energy is to answer the question. Answers (B), (C), and (D) all yield the same temperature (25°C), and since there is no other variable in either figure to which average kinetic energy could be related, if one of them were correct, they would all have to be correct. Therefore, by process of elimination, choice (A) is the only possibility.

16. **F** The lower the cooling device's temperature setting, the longer it takes for the saltwater to reach that temperature. It takes the cooling device about 300 min. to reach the 25°C setting; about 350 min. to reach the 10°C setting, and about 400 min. to reach the 0°C. Therefore, you should expect the cooler to take more than 400 min. to reach an even lower setting, such as –10°C.

17. **C** Pepsin is described as an enzyme that is involved with protein breakdown, and that is active in an acidic environment. Of the choices listed, only choice (C) is a component of the digestive system, which is responsible for the breakdown of nutrients. Also, the stomach is an organ with a highly acidic environment.

18. **F** Note where the Pepsin Activity in Table 2 is High. There is no evidence on the table that Pepsin activity is high at any pH higher than 3.5, so you can only be sure of choice (F).

19. **C** Pepsin is capable of high activity in the absence of anserine in Trial 4, thus choice (B) cannot be correct. Pepsin activity is also high in the presence of anserine in Trial 3, thus choice (B) cannot be correct. Casein is described as a protein that can be digested by pepsin, so choice (D) cannot be correct. This leaves choice (C) as the only possible answer. Another way to approach this problem is to notice that what makes Trial 5 different from Trials 3 and 4 is that it does not contain casein. If no pepsin activity is seen when casein is absent, it would follow that casein is a substance that can be digested by pepsin, supporting Choice (C).

20. **H** In order for casein to remain undigested, casein must first be present in the solution. Trials 5 and 6 do not contain casein, so choices (G) and (J) can be eliminated. Choice (H) is a better choice than choice (F) because the high pepsin activity in Trials 3 and 4 would break casein down into the smaller peptides.

21. **A** Trial 3 in Experiment 1 is conducted at a pH of 3.0 and at a temperature of 40°C. While all of answer choices feature Experiment 2 trials conducted at a temperature of 40°C, only Trial 9 is conducted at a similar pH of 3.0. Therefore, choice (A) is the best answer.

22. **G** The results from Experiment 1 show high activity of pepsin, meaning a fast rate of protein digestion by pepsin, at a temperature of 40°C, which excludes choices (C) and (D). The results from Experiment 2 show high activity of pepsin at pH values that are less than 4.0, so choice (B) is the best answer.

23. **C** Read the vertical axes in all 3 figures when $T = 0°C$. The only fluid whose viscosity is less than 1.0 cP is diethyl ether, eliminating choices (B) and (D). Ethanol, water, mercury, and nitrobenzene are all found in both Figures 1 and 2, so the correct answer is choice (C).

24. **F** The nitrobenzene line in Figure 2 has a sharp initial decrease and then plateaus. Thus, choice (F) has the greatest decrease in viscosity of approximately 1.1 cP. Choice (G) has only a decrease of approximately 0.25 cP. Choices (H) and (J) both decreases less than 0.1 cP.

25. **C** Figure 1 shows that the viscosity of water at 70°C is approximately 0.4 cP. Although choices (A), (B), and (D) provide values that are represented in the figure, they are all values for temperatures other than the specified 70°C.

26. **G** Figure 2 demonstrates that viscosity decreased with an increase in temperature, eliminating choices (F) and (H). The introduction states that the greater the viscosity, the greater the resistance to flow, thus the greater time it would take for a fluid to move out of its container. Given Figure 2 shows decreasing viscosity, the time for the fluids to leave their containers would also decrease. Thus, choice (G) is the correct answer.

27. **D** To assess the hypothesis, you would require values for viscosity at 60°C for nitrobenzene with Additive A and untreated diethyl ether. Although Figure 2 provides the viscosity for nitrobenzene treated with Additive B, no figure shows the viscosity value for nitrobenzene blended with chemical additive A. Figure 1 shows that nitrobenzene has a viscosity higher than that of diethyl ether, and Figures 2 and 3 show that Additive A lowers the viscosity of both ethanol and diethyl ether; however, you cannot assume that treatment of nitrobenzene with Additive A would lower its viscosity below 0.07cP. Thus, choice (D) is the best option.

28. **G** Examine Figure 3 along the x-axis. Notice how the farther you go to the right along the x-axis, the weaker the wave type becomes. Only choice (G) accurately describes this phenomenon.

29. **B** First, examine Figures 3 and 4 closely. In both figures, the transition lines show that at densities between 1,000 and 2,000 kg/m³, strong waves appear always to begin to propagate at shorter distances from the epicenter than moderate waves. Thus, answer choices (C) and (D) may be eliminated. Since the maximum distance from the epicenter is less for strong waves than moderate waves, answer choice (A) may also be eliminated.

30. **J** Look at the passage closely, the passage states that *ground density and propagation duration were controlled in the experiment.* Thus, answer choices (G) and (H) may be eliminated. Answer choice (F) may be eliminated because in each experiment, the sound intensity was controlled. The wave type formed in the experiments was not controlled as it varied with distance and density.

31. **D** Examine Figure 1 closely. A wavelength constitutes the distance from one hump to the next. The moderate wave is approximately 150 cm, and the weak wave is approximately 500 cm. Subsequently, neither wave type exhibits a wave length of less than 100 cm.

32. **J** From the passage, Studies 1 and 2 were conducted using sound intensities of 60 and 80 dB, respectively. Accordingly, the resulting waveform plot of study using 70 dB should exhibit wave types reminiscent of Figures 2 and 3. Both figures exhibit all three types of waves; therefore choice (J) is the best answer. The waveform plot of Study 3 does not include weak waves, but its sound intensity was set to 100 dB, well above the sound intensity of 70 dB given in this question.

33. **A** Use the range of sound intensities given in the passage to determine which waveform plot you need to use. Since this range is 75 dB to 85 dB, you can confidently use the waveform plot from Study 2, which has as its sound intensity 80 dB. Using Figure 3 (Study 2), therefore, note the range of distances from the epicenter for strong waves: roughly 0 m to 2.3 m. Accordingly, any distance from the epicenter for strong waves between sound intensities of 75 dB and 85 dB can be reasonably expected to have a distance shorter than 2.5 m.

34. **G** The information in Table 1 indicates that Solution 4 contained three dissolved particles, where Solution 2 contained only one dissolved particle. Solution 4 thus had more dissolved particles, enabling you to eliminate choices (F) and (H). Now compare the respective freezing point of each solution. The freezing point of Solution 2 was –1.9°C while the freezing point of Solution 4 was lower at –5.7°C. Be careful here—a large negative number is smaller than a small one!

35. **A** Scientist 2 states that the change in freezing point is NOT related *to the identity or properties* of the solute dissolved. The observation that a solute with no charge such as naphthalene can still lower the freezing point of a solvent does not contradict Scientist 2's viewpoint, so choices (C) and (D) are incorrect. Scientist 1 specifically states that a change in freezing point *only occurs with solutes that form charged particles in solution.* Therefore, the fact that naphthalene causes a change in the freezing point of benzene directly contradicts Scientist 1's viewpoint as stated in choice (A).

36. **F** Use process of elimination. Scientist 2 argues that any increase in the concentration of a solution will lower its freezing point, so you can eliminate choices (G) and (J). Scientist 1 argues that only charged solvents can have an influence on the freezing point, so you can eliminate choice (H) as well. This leaves you only with choice (F), which agrees with the hypotheses of both scientists.

37. **A** Scientist 2 states that only the concentration of a solution can change its freezing point, and since the concentration here is held constant, choices (B) and (C) are not the best answers. Scientist 1 states that *the decrease in freezing point is related only to the charge of the solute particles,* a hypothesis which is supported by the observations in the question.

38. G Scientist 1 states that *solute molecules are attracted to the solvent molecules by intermolecular forces* and interfere *with the orderly arrangement of solvent molecules*. Choices (F) and (J) are eliminated because they do not depict attraction between solute and solvent molecules, and both show a very orderly arrangement of solvent molecules. Choice (G) and choice (H) demonstrate attraction between solute and solvent, but only choice (G) illustrates interference with an orderly arrangement of solvent molecules.

39. A Only Scientist 1 states that the physical properties (charge) of the solute have an impact on changing the freezing point of a solvent. This eliminates choices (B) and (D). Scientist 2 states that the physical properties of the solute do not have an effect on freezing point depression. Therefore, choice (C) is eliminated and choice (A) is correct.

40. J Scientist 2 states that the decrease in temperature *is in direct proportion with the van 't Hoff factor*. Choices (F) and (H) show the decrease in temperature and the van 't Hoff factor in an inverse proportion, so they can be eliminated. Choice (G) can also be eliminated because there is no indication that the van 't Hoff factor should be squared in the proportion. Only choice (J) shows decrease in temperature (ΔT) and the van 't Hoff factor (i) in direction proportion with one another.

WRITING TEST

Essay Checklist

1. The Introduction
   Did you
   o start with a topic sentence that paraphrases or restates the prompt?
   o clearly state your position on the issue?

2. Body Paragraph 1
   Did you
   o start with a transition/topic sentence that discusses the opposing side of the argument?
   o give an example of a reason that one might agree with the opposing side of the argument?
   o clearly state that the opposing side of the argument is wrong or flawed?
   o show what is wrong with the opposing side's example or position?

3. Body Paragraphs 2 and 3
   Did you
   o start with a transition/topic sentence that discusses your position on the prompt?
   o give one example or reason to support your position?
   o show the grader how your example supports your position?
   o end the paragraph by restating your thesis?

4. Conclusion
   Did you
   o restate your position on the issue?
   o end with a flourish?

5. Overall
   Did you
   o write neatly?
   o avoid multiple spelling and grammar mistakes?
   o try to vary your sentence structure?
   o use a few impressive-sounding words?

Test 3
Answers and Explanations

TEST 3 ENGLISH ANSWERS

1.	D	48.	J
2.	G	49.	B
3.	D	50.	J
4.	H	51.	A
5.	A	52.	G
6.	H	53.	C
7.	D	54.	F
8.	G	55.	B
9.	D	56.	F
10.	H	57.	C
11.	A	58.	H
12.	G	59.	D
13.	A	60.	G
14.	G	61.	D
15.	D	62.	G
16.	J	63.	C
17.	C	64.	J
18.	F	65.	C
19.	C	66.	H
20.	H	67.	A
21.	B	68.	G
22.	G	69.	D
23.	D	70.	J
24.	J	71.	B
25.	A	72.	H
26.	F	73.	B
27.	D	74.	F
28.	F	75.	A
29.	B		
30.	H		
31.	B		
32.	H		
33.	C		
34.	J		
35.	C		
36.	J		
37.	A		
38.	J		
39.	C		
40.	J		
41.	C		
42.	F		
43.	C		
44.	G		
45.	D		
46.	J		
47.	C		

TEST 3 MATH ANSWERS

1.	D
2.	G
3.	B
4.	K
5.	B
6.	G
7.	E
8.	G
9.	C
10.	H
11.	D
12.	F
13.	B
14.	H

TEST 3 READING ANSWERS

15.	E
16.	G
17.	D
18.	K
19.	C
20.	H
21.	E
22.	J
23.	E
24.	H
25.	D
26.	K
27.	D
28.	G
29.	B
30.	J
31.	D
32.	F
33.	D
34.	G
35.	E
36.	F
37.	E
38.	F
39.	C
40.	H
41.	B
42.	J
43.	D
44.	H
45.	E
46.	G
47.	E
48.	G
49.	B
50.	J
51.	B
52.	G
53.	A
54.	H
55.	E
56.	F
57.	D
58.	J
59.	C
60.	G

1.	A
2.	H
3.	D
4.	H
5.	C
6.	H
7.	A
8.	G
9.	D
10.	F
11.	A
12.	J
13.	A
14.	H
15.	C
16.	J
17.	D
18.	J
19.	B
20.	H
21.	A
22.	G
23.	C
24.	H
25.	C
26.	J
27.	B
28.	H
29.	A
30.	H
31.	D
32.	G
33.	B
34.	F
35.	C
36.	H
37.	D
38.	F
39.	C
40.	H

TEST 3 SCIENCE ANSWERS

1. C
2. F
3. B
4. G
5. D
6. G
7. A
8. H
9. A
10. G
11. C
12. J
13. D
14. H
15. D
16. G
17. D
18. H
19. D
20. J
21. B
22. H
23. A
24. H
25. D
26. H
27. A
28. J
29. B
30. G
31. C
32. G
33. C
34. G
35. D
36. J
37. C
38. F
39. C
40. J

SCORING YOUR PRACTICE EXAM

Step A

Count the number of correct answers for each section and record the number in the space provided for your raw score on the Score Conversion Worksheet below.

Step B

Using the Score Conversion Chart on the next page, convert your raw scores on each section to scaled scores. Then compute your composite ACT score by averaging the four subject scores. Add them up and divide by four. Don't worry about the essay score; it is not included in your composite score.

Score Conversion Worksheet		
Section	Raw Score	Scaled Score
1	_____/75	_____
2	_____/60	_____
3	_____/40	_____
4	_____/40	_____

SCORE CONVERSION CHART

Scaled Score	Raw Score			
	English	Mathematics	Reading	Science Reasoning
36	75	60	39–40	40
35	74	59	38	39
34	72–73	58	37	38
33	71	57	36	—
32	70	55–56	35	37
31	69	53–54	34	36
30	67–68	52	33	—
29	65–66	50–51	32	35
28	62–64	46–49	30–31	33–34
27	59–61	43–45	28–29	31–32
26	57–58	41–42	27	30
25	55–56	39–40	26	29
24	52–54	37–38	25	28
23	50–51	35–36	24	27–26
22	49	33–34	23	25
21	48	31–32	21–22	24
20	45–47	29–30	20	23
19	43–44	27–28	19	22
18	40–42	24–26	18	20–21
17	38–39	21–23	17	18–19
16	35–37	18–20	16	16–17
15	32–34	16–17	15	15
14	29–31	13–15	14	13–14
13	27–28	11–12	12–13	12
12	24–26	9–10	11	11
11	21–23	7–8	9–10	10
10	18–20	6	8	9
9	15–17	5	7	7–8
8	13–14	4	—	6
7	11–12	—	6	5
6	9–10	3	5	—
5	7–8	2	4	4
4	5–6	—	3	3
3	3–4	1	2	2
2	2	—	1	1
1	0	0	0	0

TEST 3 ENGLISH EXPLANATIONS

1. **D** The phrase *just like* introduces a comparison to *preparing a meal*, which means the correct answer must also start with an *-ing* word to compare two like items, eliminating choices (B) and (C). Choice (D) is a better answer than (A) because it is more concise.

2. **G** Choice (G) addresses the writer's goal by describing the robust aromas and provides sensory detail of *swirling rush*. Choices (F), (H), (J) do not describe the richness of smell.

3. **D** Don't be fooled by the stuff in between! *Cooking,* one activity, is the subject of the underlined plural verb *require*, so you need the singular form of the verb. This means you can eliminate choices (A) and (C). Choice (D) is more concise than choice (B).

4. **H** In EXCEPT/LEAST/NOT questions, the underlined portion of the sentence is correct. All the choices use correct prepositions for going to the store, except choice (H) which implies that Eric is attacking the store.

5. **A** Two things caused the vegetables to be tasty: *natural sunshine and the farmers' careful tending,* which should be separated by *and,* eliminating choices (B) and (D). To be consistent, the two causes should both be introduced with the preposition *of* making choice (A) the best answer. The comma preceding *and* in choice (C) is not necessary because it doesn't separate two complete thoughts.

6. **H** Choice (H) describes how Eric precisely cuts his vegetables and arranges the vegetables in layers. Just because Eric *slowly* places the vegetables does not necessarily mean he is paying attention to detail, eliminating choice (F). Choices (G) and (J) are weaker descriptions, because *pours* is less meticulous than *layers* and *kind of order* is vague.

7. **D** Commas cannot join two complete ideas. Because the first half of the sentence is complete, the underlined phrase must begin an incomplete thought, eliminating choices (A) and (B). Choice (C) is the wrong form of the verb for adding an incomplete, descriptive thought: *alternating* is the correct form, which is choice (D).

8. **G** Since you're comparing people, *Eric* to *many cooks*, the best answer is choice (G). Choice (F) confuses the phrases *like* and *as with*, creating an incorrect idiomatic expression. A verb needs to immediately follow *as* in order to compare Eric's actions to those of many cooks, eliminating choices (H), which doesn't have a verb, and (J), which has the verb *do* in the wrong place.

9. **D** In EXCEPT/LEAST/NOT questions, the underlined portion of the sentence is correct. In the original sentence, the phrase *At this point* introduces the next step in a sequence of actions. Choices (A), (B), and (C) all indicate what Eric is going to do after splashing red wine into the cooker. Choice (D) is the incorrect expression, confusing *at least* with *at last*.

10. **H** Choice (H) adds detail to help readers visualize what the roast looks like as the pot heats up. Choices (F), (G), and (J) describe the slow rise in temperature, but provides no sensory detail.

11. **A** Choice (A) is the most concise answer, as choices (B), (C), and (D) add words but not any additional information.

12. G The introductory phrase *Every half-hour* must be followed by a comma, and the incomplete idea *using a long meat thermometer* must also be followed by a comma to link it to the complete idea, *Eric reads the temperature…*Choice (G) is the only option that provides a pair of commas around this phrase. Choice (F) offsets the wrong phrase *using a long,* confusing the meaning of the sentence. The lack of commas in choice (H) creates a run-on sentence. Choice (J) uses a semicolon instead of a comma, incorrectly separating an incomplete thought from a complete one.

13. A What choice (B) describes is redundancy, which would mean the sentence should be deleted, not kept, so cross this one off. The overall essay describes both Eric and the roast he cooks, so the reasoning in choice (C) is incorrect. You can eliminate choice (D) because the previous paragraph already described the relationship between rising temperature and stewing vegetables. Choice (A) maintains consistent flow and focus within the paragraph and overall essay.

14. G Choice (F) incorrectly has a comma separating two complete ideas. You can also eliminate choice (H) because *you* is inconsistent with the third-person *he* the author has been using throughout the rest of the essay. Choice (J) has a misplaced modifier, suggesting that the *plump meat* is lifting itself. Choice (G) is the most clear and consistent answer, describing Eric lifting the meat.

15. D Choices (A), (B), and (C) all reiterate what has been already stated in the sentence: that the roast is a work of art. Choice (D) is the most concise answer.

16. J Choice (J) is the most concise and doesn't omit necessary information. Choices (F), (G), and (H) make the sentence wordy and redundant; they describe the speculation that the narrator already mentions *(people conjure up an image)*.

17. C In EXCEPT/LEAST/NOT questions, the underlined portion of the sentence is correct. The writer uses *to start* to introduce his argument about people's misconceptions of the type of farm he was on. Choices (A), (B), and (D) are acceptable substitutions to achieve the same effect. Choice (C) is unacceptable because the correct expression is *For starters*, not *For start*.

18. F Choice (F) uses a semicolon to divide the sentence into two complete thoughts. Choices (G), (H), and (J) create run-on sentences.

19. C The writer is trying to illustrate the contrast between the unconventional livestock and the conventions expected of a farm that has existed as long as that of her family. Therefore, the phrase is used to emphasize the longevity of the farm. The sentence gives no indication of the narrator's relationship with her mother (A), nor does it indicate that anything bad is going to happen, (D). The following sentences also discuss the untraditional practices of her family farm, eliminating choice (B).

20. H The correct expression to express a person's assumption is *must have* not *must of,* eliminating choices (F) and (G). Choice (J) uses *about,* which is idiomatically incorrect; therefore, (H) is the best answer.

21. B The phrase *in fact* is unnecessary and should be offset with commas, making choice (B) the best answer. The single comma in choices (A) and (C) creates a disruptive pause within the sentence.

22. G Sentences 1 and 2 describe the farm before the introduction of the llamas. Choice (F) interrupts this description. Choice (G) makes it clear that the he referred to in Sentence 3 is the narrator's great-grandfather. Choices (H) and (J) introduce the narrator's great-grandfather too late, leaving the reader to wonder who Sentence 3's *he* is.

23. **D** In EXCEPT/LEAST/NOT questions, the underlined portion of the sentence is correct. Choices (A) and (C) use appropriate synonyms for the past tense verb *began*. *Living* can replace *to live*, making choice (B) also acceptable. Choice (D) is incorrect because it uses the wrong verb form *begun*, which should always be preceded by a helping verb to indicate past perfect tense rather than past tense.

24. **J** In EXCEPT/LEAST/NOT questions, the underlined portion of the sentence is correct. Choices (F), (G), and (H) use appropriate synonyms for *after*. Without an introductory conjunction, choice (J) creates a run-on sentence.

25. **A** Choice (A) correctly puts the verb in the past perfect tense because the narrator's expectation came before his realization. Choices (B) and (C) make the action hypothetical by using *would*. Choice (D) puts the action in the present perfect tense, but the story takes place in the past tense.

26. **F** Choice (F) correctly introduces the topic of school, which is the focus of the remainder of the paragraph. Choices (G), (H), and (J) provide information that strays from the topic of this paragraph.

27. **D** Choice (D) is the most clear and concise answer. Choices (A), (B), and (C) are all too wordy and confusing.

28. **F** Choice (F) makes it clear that she learned from reading textbooks on her own, rather than the instruction from the teacher. Choices (G), (H), and (J) are vague in comparison.

29. **B** Because the habits describe all llamas, the apostrophe should show plural possessive, making choice (B) the best answer. Choice (A) uses the singular possessive. Choices (C) and (D) do not use the possessive form at all.

30. **H** The correct expression is to *make a career in farming*, making choice (H) the best answer. Choices (G) and (J) would be correct if the expression were *make a career out of farming*. Choice (F) would be correct if the expression were *make a career as a farmer*.

31. **B** This can't be *which* because it refers to a person, and the portion can't be omitted because the sentence doesn't make sense without the relative pronoun; eliminate choices (C) and (D). The question now is whether to use *who* or *whom*. Look at the other parts of the sentence, noticing what you need to connect it to: *who/whom spent much of his childhood*. You need the subjective *who* form here. Would you say *he spent much of his childhood,* or *him spent much of his childhood*? The best answer is choice (B).

32. **H** Choice (F) can't work because the following paragraph doesn't talk about the Civil War. Choice (G) can't work because the underlined portion is not an *unnecessary digression*; it's merely a mention of the Civil War. Choice (J) can't work because there is no mention in this essay that Chesnutt was a historical writer. Only choice (H) agrees with the main theme of this paragraph, which is a discussion of Chesnutt's childhood.

33. **C** In EXCEPT/LEAST/NOT questions, the underlined portion of the sentence is correct. Note the differences between what separates the words *literature* and *he* in each of the answer choices. Since *literature* ends a complete thought and *he* begins a new one, only choices (A), (B), and (D) can work—choice (A) because it has a semicolon separating the two complete thoughts, choice (B) because it has a comma and coordinating conjunction separating the thoughts (as in the original sentence), and choice (D) because it has a period separating the two complete thoughts. Choice (C), however, creates a comma splice, and without a coordinating conjunction (such as, *and* or *but*), a comma cannot be used to separate two complete thoughts.

34. **J** Because the sentence indicates that action ended with the author's death in 1932, the underlined verb must be in the past tense, which only choice (J) is.

35. **C** Since all choices are roughly synonymous, choose the most concise answer that preserves the meaning of the sentence. Choice (C) is the most concise, and it preserves the meaning of the sentence.

36. **J** Note that in the part of the sentence before the underlined portion, the author refers to *earlier folklorists*. The word *earlier* makes choices (F), (G), and (H) redundant. Only choice (J) correctly opts to DELETE the underlined portion.

37. **A** Begin by determining whether the sentence beginning with *However* provides a continuation of the prior sentence or a contrast to the prior sentence. Because the author illustrates a difference between the work of earlier folklorists and that of Chesnutt, eliminate the continuation words, choices (C) and (D). Choice (B) is wrong because two complete sentences may not be separated by a comma. Choice (A) properly uses a period.

38. **J** The proposed addition does not relate to or flow from the paragraph, which is about Chesnutt's works. Eliminate choices (F) and (G). The substance of choice (H) is incorrect. Choice (J) correctly observes that the addition is distracting.

39. **C** This pronoun refers to *The Conjure Woman*, a singular noun, so it cannot be *their* as in choice (B). Choice (D) is not a word, so that can be eliminated as well. Choice (A) gives the contraction *it is*, which is not used to show possession. Choice (C) shows the appropriate possession. Remember: possessive pronouns don't have an apostrophe (think of hers, yours, and ours).

40. **J** Because the underlined portion is difficult to follow, don't try to rewrite it on your own. Rather, read all four answer choices to determine which one is the clearest. Choice (J) clearly articulates the author's meaning and does so without wordiness.

41. **C** Since the sentence is referring to only a single *family*, eliminate choices (B) and (D). Between choices (A) and (C), remember that although a family includes many people, it is actually a singular noun, and its possessive should thus be punctuated as *family's*, as in choice (C).

42. **F** While choices (G), (H), and (J) all make the sentence shorter, each makes the meaning of the sentence unclear. Choice (G) gives an ambiguous pronoun with no clear antecedent. Choice (H) is also ambiguous, although it probably refers to the children, changing the meaning of the sentence. Choice (J) suggests that the novel was the first to talk about itself, which does not make logical sense. Only choice (F) gives a clear, unambiguous indication of what the novel was the first to talk about.

43. **C** In EXCEPT/LEAST/NOT questions, the underlined portion of the sentence is correct. The underlined portion is a modifier, properly followed by what the modifier describes: *the novel*. Choices (A), (B), and (D) are also modifiers describing *the novel*. Choice (C), however, is a modifier describing the person or company that published the novel. Thus, choice (C) would have to be followed by that person or company, not *the novel*.

44. **G** Choices (F), (H), and (J) are all too narrow to be described as summarizing the essay. Choice (F) refers only to the two books discussed in the text, but the last paragraph indicates that Chesnutt's influence extends beyond these two books and beyond his lifetime. Choice (H) refers to only the first paragraph. Choice (J) refers only to the paragraph about *The Conjure Woman*. Only choice (G) is general enough to encapsulate the entire essay.

45. **D** Notice the time periods in each paragraph. Paragraph 2 talks about the end of Chesnutt's life, his death in 1932, and his current reputation. Accordingly, it must come after discussions of earlier points in his biography but before Paragraph 5, which is meant to conclude and summarize the essay. Also note that *The House Behind the Cedars* is mentioned as if the reader already has some familiarity with it, so the paragraph must come after Paragraph 4, which discusses *The House Behind the Cedars*.

46. **J** The subject of the sentence is *accomplishments*, so the verb must be plural to agree with it. Choice (J) provides a plural verb in the correct past tense. Choices (F) and (G) are singular. Choice (H) can be either singular or plural, but it uses a future tense, which does not agree with the tense of the passage.

47. **C** The sentence makes sense if you remove the phrase *according to his widow Rachel Robinson*. Since the phrase is not essential to the meaning of the sentence, it should be offset by commas. Thus, choice (C) is correct. Choice (A) has no pauses to offset this information, and choice (B) has an additional and unnecessary comma. Both choices confuse the flow of the sentence. Choice (D) uses a long dash incorrectly because the non-underlined portion uses a comma instead of a second long dash to indicate that the phrase must be offset.

48. **J** Choice (J) is the most concise answer that conveys the correct meaning, and it removes the redundancy of the original sentence. Choices (F), (G), and (H) are wordy and redundant. Note, when DELETE is offered as an answer choice, always give it serious consideration—omitting an unnecessary part of the sentence can often make it more clear and concise.

49. **B** The underlined phrase describes the team for which Jackie Robinson played baseball, so choice (B) is correct. Choices (A), (C), and (D) confuse the meaning of the sentence or disrupt its flow.

50. **J** The word *baseball* ends an incomplete thought, and the word *he* begins a complete thought. Choices (F), (G), and (H) all contain punctuation that can only be used to separate two complete thoughts. Choice (J) is the only answer choice that uses a comma to correctly link an incomplete thought to a complete one.

51. **A** The end of the sentence details the seats in the stadium, so the most specific type of person to fill them is a spectator, choice (A). Choice (B) is not specific enough. Choices (C) and (D) describe types of people that would be at a baseball game but not occupying the seats in the stadium.

52. G Choice (G) is correct because the paragraph describes how Jackie's excellent play changed the attitudes of whites toward having blacks in baseball. Choices (F), (H), and (J) do not accurately describe the point of the paragraph, so they are not things that would be lost with its deletion.

53. C First, determine whether the sentence following *for example* provides a continuation of the prior sentence or a contrast to the prior sentence. Because the prior sentence explains that an ordinary man who did what Jackie did would wilt, and the sentence following *for example* describes Jackie's increased efforts, a contrasting term is needed. Thus, eliminate choices (A), (B), and (D). Choice (C) is correct.

54. F The noun being referred to is *athletes*, so the possessive pronoun relating to it must agree in person and number, as it does in choice (F). Choices (G) and (H) do not agree because the possessive pronouns in these choices are singular. Choice (J) contains the proper agreement, but it incorrectly acts as a noun instead of an adjective.

55. B The sentence should be kept because it provides important information about Jackie Robinson's personality, eliminating choices (C) and (D). Choice (B) is correct because the mention of other athletes using their status for personal gain emphasizes Jackie's personal sacrifice and dedication to civil rights advancement. Choice (A) is incorrect because there is no indication in the passage that Jackie had any endorsement deals.

56. F The word *entrepreneur* ends a complete thought, and the word *his* begins a second complete thought. Choices (G) and (H) contain punctuation that can not be used to connect complete thoughts. Choice (J) incorrectly uses a semicolon instead of a comma with the coordinating conjunction *and,* causing the second thought to become incomplete.

57. C Sentence 3 contains the description of Jackie's civil rights activism during his baseball career, and Sentence 4 describes his activism after his baseball career, so choice (C) is correct. Choices (A), (B), and (D) do not correctly separate the two periods of his activism.

58. H The word *than* indicates a comparison between two things, as with choice (H). Choice (F) contains a superlative, which is used for three or more things. Choice (G) does not contain any words of comparison. Choice (J) contains a word that is not proper English.

59. D The word *movement* ends an incomplete thought, and the word *his* begins a complete thought. Choice (D) correctly uses a comma to link an incomplete thought to a complete one. Choice (A) creates a run-on sentence. Choices (B) and (C) contain punctuation that can only be used to separate two complete thoughts.

60. G In EXCEPT/LEAST/NOT questions, the underlined portion of the sentence is correct. This sentence agrees in tone with the one preceding it. Therefore, a transition word that indicates that agreement is required, as with choices (F), (H), and (J). Choice (G) provides a transition word that indicates an opposing tone, so it is the LEAST acceptable alternative and thus the correct answer.

61. D Choice (D) corrects the punctuation error in the passage. A semicolon should not be used if it separates essential parts of a sentence (the verb *fertilized* should not be separated from its subject *patches of moss*). Choices (B) and (C) incorrectly insert a comma between a preposition and its object.

62. **G** In EXCEPT/LEAST/NOT questions, the underlined portion of the sentence is correct. Choice (G) inserts a period, incorrectly separating the dependent clause from the independent clause. The dependent clause *becoming active again when the climate warms and the ice is melting* cannot stand on its own as a complete sentence.

63. **C** Choice (C) provides a verb form that is parallel in structure to the preceding verb, *warms*. Choices (A), (B), and (D) are not parallel, and choice (B) also creates a sentence fragment.

64. **J** Choice (J) presents wording that is consistent with the style and tone of the rest of the essay. Choices (F), (G), and (H) are all too informal.

65. **C** Because the phrase *classified as arthropods* is not necessary to the sentence, it needs to be set off by commas, as in choice (C). Choices (B) and (D) are incorrect because each omits one of the required commas. Choice (A) is incorrect because a semicolon may be used only in between two complete ideas.

66. **H** Choice (H) provides the correct usage of the adverb *too*, which means to an excessive degree, and removes the improper comma after *icy*. Choices (F) and (G) incorrectly use the preposition *to*. Choice (J) improperly inserts a comma after *icy*.

67. **A** In EXCEPT/LEAST/NOT questions, the underlined portion of the sentence is correct. Choice (A) incorrectly omits a necessary comma, thereby creating a run-on sentence.

68. **G** Choice (G) correctly uses the present tense (*accompany*), which is in accordance with the use of the present tense in the rest of this paragraph. Choices (F) and (J) incorrectly use the past tense and choice (H) uses the past perfect tense.

69. **D** Choice (D) is the clearest, most concise answer. Choices (A), (B), and (C) all provide information that is not relevant to the passage.

70. **J** Choice (J) is correct because without the inclusion of the modifying phrase, the *Here* in the following sentence does not refer to anything. Choice (F) incorrectly suggests removing the phrase, and the modifying phrase does not include a fact that is provided later in the paragraph. Choice (G) incorrectly proposes removing the phrase and wrongly states that the above paragraph mentions insects as the only life forms in Antarctica. While it's true that the clause should be kept, choice (H) incorrectly assumes that Antarctica and McMurdo Sound are two different places; the phrase clearly specifies that McMurdo Sound is part of the continent of Antarctica.

71. **B** Choice (B) is the most descriptive and relevant of the answer choices. Choice (C) provides no visual detail besides snow cover, and choices (A) and (D) lack the vivid detail of choice (B), which adds description to the flora with the adjectives green, yellow, and orange. In addition, only choice (B) directly addresses the *terrain* in its description of the *rocky land*.

72. **H** Choice (H) is the most logical place to move this prepositional phrase. The nematode worms are not *thriving with the low temperatures*, or *dehydrating themselves with the low temperatures*, or *increasing moisture with the low temperatures*, they are *coping with the low temperatures*. In addition, note that Choices (F), (G), and (J) all match verbs with prepositions in idiomatically incorrect ways.

73. B Choice (B) does not effectively address the central point made in Paragraph 4: namely, that algae exist not only in the water, but also on land. Choices (A), (C), and (D) all effectively introduce the subject of Paragraph 4, signaling that the paragraph will discuss the ways in which algae adapt to the harsh climate of Antarctica, both on land and in the sea.

74. F Choice (F) correctly suggests keeping the phrase and ties it back into the point made in the preceding sentence: that phytoplankton help maintain the equilibrium of Antarctica's ecosystem. While Choice (G) is correct to propose keeping the clause, it incorrectly identifies seals, whales, and penguins as the most important creatures in Antarctica's seas, a debatable topic. Choices (H) and (J) incorrectly suggest removing the clause.

75. A Choice (A) correctly fits between the preceding sentence and the sentence that follows, because it indicates a contrasting relationship between the two ideas; while *Antarctica has the lowest species diversity of anywhere on earth,* the numbers of those species that do exist are staggering considering the harsh climatic conditions of the environment. Choices (B) wrongly inserts *indeed,* which is incorrect because the writer is presenting a contrasting relationship, not emphasizing a point made in the preceding sentence. Choices (C) and (D) each suggest a cause-effect relationship that is not indicated in the passage.

TEST 3 MATH EXPLANATIONS

1. **D** Treat absolute value bars like parentheses and evaluate what's inside the absolute value bars first:

    $|8-5| - |5-8| = |3| - |-3| = 3 - 3 = 0$. Remember that absolute value is a measure of distance so the

    result is always nonnegative. Choice (E) is 3 − (−3) = 6.

2. **G** First, subtract the flat fee from the total cost to determine how much the tutor charged exclusively for tutoring: $220 − $40 = $180. $180 = $60/hr × 3 hours, so choice (G) is correct. Choice (F) incorrectly uses $40 + $60 = $100 as the hourly rate. Choices (H) and (K) divide $220 by $60 and $40, respectively, without subtracting the flat fee. Choice (J) calculates the session with a $60 flat fee and $40 hourly rate.

3. **B** The time it takes Train A can be found by dividing the number of miles it goes by the speed,

    $\frac{1152}{16} = 72$. Train B then takes 48 hours, $\frac{1152}{24} = 48$. To find how many more hours it takes,

    subtract the hours it takes Train B to go from the hours it takes Train A, 72 − 48 = 24, choice (B).

    Choice (A) is the result of averaging the miles per hour values, and choice (C) from adding them.

    Choice (D) and (E) are the hours that each train takes, not the difference.

4. **K.** The question is asking you to simplify the expression by combining like terms. $33r^2 - 41r^2 = -8r^2$, $-24r + r = -23r$. The simplified expression is $-8r^2 - 23r + 75$. Choices (F) and (G) combine all coefficients between unlike terms. Choice (H) forgets that r is actually $1r$. Choice (J) incorrectly multiplies variables rather than just adding the coefficients.

5. **B** Since the triangles are equilateral and each one's perimeter is 15, each side is 5. Figure *ABCDEF* has six sides, so its perimeter is 6(5) = 30. Choice (D) finds the area of the figure rather than its perimeter. Choice (E) treats the sides of each triangle, rather than the perimeter of each triangle, as 15. Choice (A) miscalculates the side of the triangle as 3 inches and choice (C) includes the dotted interior lines in calculating the perimeter.

6. **G** Use the FOIL method. Multiply the First, Outside, Inside, and Last terms together, and then add

    the results. $(5x + 2)(x - 3) = 5x^2 - 15x + 2x - 6 = 5x^2 - 13x - 6$.

7. **E** Use the words in the problem to create an equation: *percent* means "divide by 100," *of* means "mul-

    tiply" and *what number* means "use a variable." The first equation is $\frac{35}{100}x = 14$ and $x = 40$. The

    second equation is $y = \frac{20}{100}(40) = 8$. Choice (A) is 20% of 14. Choice (B) is 35% of 14. Choice

    (D) is (20% + 35%) of 14.

8. **G** The list of integers adds up to $7x + 7$. Set that equal to 511 then solve, and you'll get choice (G); 72. Choice (H) divides 511 by 7 without first subtracting 7, and choice (J) mistakenly adds 7 to the sum. Choices (F) and (K) are both incorrect estimates.

9. **C** The easiest approach to this problem is to test all the answer choices. If point B is the midpoint of line A, you can use the midpoint formula $(\frac{x_1 + x_2}{2}, \frac{y_1 + y_2}{2})$ by plugging in the answer choices into the equation along with the values given for point A. When Plugging In answer choice (C), the equation is $(\frac{1+9}{2}, \frac{8+4}{2})$ which gives you the correct midpoint of (5,6). The other answer choices do not use the midpoint formula correctly.

10. **H** Because the trapezoid is isosceles, its two vertical halves are mirror images of each other. To get from A to B requires adding 3 to the x value, and 6 to the y value of A, so to get from D to C, instead subtract 3 from the x value and add 6 to the y value of D.

11. **D** To find the total average sales at each bus station, multiply the values of each column of the first matrix by the relevant row in the second matrix. 180(3) + 200(3) + 150(3) + 60(2) + 120(2) + 70(2) = 2,090. Choice (A) finds the number of tickets sold and choice (C) multiplies that total by $2.50, the average of the two fare rates. Choice (B) gives only the peak fare sales. Choice (E) finds the total if all of the fares were bought at the peak $3 price.

12. **F** The sum of the exterior angles of a regular polygon = 360°. If you have trouble remembering this rule, use the supplemental angles in the problem. Because $a° + 35° = 180°$, $a = 145°$. Find angle b the same way: $b° + 45° = 180°$, so $b = 135°$. You can now find the third angle in the triangle: $180° - 35° - 45° = 100°$. Now you know that $c° + 100° = 180°$, so $c = 80°$. $a + b + c = 145° + 135° + 80° = 360°$.

13. **B** Use the words in the problem to create an equation: *percent* means "divide by 100," *of* means "multiply," and *what number* means "use a variable." The equation is $\frac{x}{100} \times 300 = 60$, so $x = 20\%$. Choice (A) is the percent of purple jellybeans. Choice (C) is the percent of red jellybeans. Choice (D) is the percent of orange jellybeans. Choice (E) confuses the number of green jellybeans and the percent of the sample consisting of green jellybeans.

14. **H** Set up a proportion: $\frac{75 \, red}{300 \, total} = \frac{x}{25,000 \, total}$ and $x = 6250$. Choice (F) is the estimate for the number of purple jellybeans in the barrel. Choice (G) is the estimate for the number of green jellybeans. Choice (J) is the estimate for the number of orange jellybeans. Choice (K) assumes that the 75 red jellybeans in the sample is the same as the percentage of red jellybeans and finds 75% of 25,000.

15. **E** To find the central angle, first find what fraction of the sample is composed of orange jellybeans: $\frac{120}{300} = \frac{2}{5}$. The central angle for the orange sector is $\frac{2}{5} \times 360° = 144°$ Choice (A) is the central angle for the purple sector. Choice (B) is the central angle for the green sector. Choice (C) is the central angle for the red sector. Choice (D) confuses the number of orange jellybeans with the degree measure of the central angle.

16. **G** Because E and F are both midpoints, draw a line between them and you divide the rectangle into 4 equal parts. Quadrilateral $AECF$ contains 2 of these 4 parts, or (G). Choice (J) shows the ratio using $\triangle ABE$ instead of quadrilateral $AECF$, while choice (F) shows the ratio of the quadrilateral to the other half of the rectangle. Choice (H) assumes the 3 parts in the original diagram are equal. Choice (K) divides the rectangle into 5 parts.

17. **D** In the slope-intercept form, $y = mx + b$, the slope of the line is $m = \frac{1}{2}$. Parallel lines have the same slope, so the answer is choice (D). Choice (B) is the slope of the perpendicular line to the given line. Choice (A) is the y-intercept. Choices (C) and (E) are the opposite and reciprocal, respectively, of the correct slope.

18. **K.** Given that the ratio of the two sittings is 3:5, you can make the equation: $3 \times x$ minutes + $5 \times x$ minutes = 120 minutes, so $8x = 120$, and $x = 15$. The longer sitting is $5x = 5 \times 15 = 75$ minutes. Careful not to choose choice (H), which is the shorter sitting.

19. **C** Find the square root of each answer choice on your calculator until you find a value between 11 and 12. $\sqrt{140} \approx 11.83$. Choice (B) is 11 exactly; the question asks for something greater. The value of choice (D) is just more than 12, too big. Choice (A) adds the numbers from the problem without answering what is asked for, and choice (E) = 23, the sum of the numbers in the problem.

20. **H** The area of the entire space of the garden is $10 \times 16 \times 3 = 480$ ft². The rectangular plot for beans is $4 \times 6 = 24$ ft², and the rectangular plot for lettuce is $2\frac{1}{2} \times 5 = 12.5$ ft². Subtract the spaces for beans and lettuce from the total space for tomatoes. $480 - 24 - 12.5 = 443.5$ ft². Since the maximum number of square feet that can be covered by a packet is 200, estimate $\frac{443.5 \text{ ft}^2}{200 \text{ ft}^2 \text{ per packet}} > 2$, packets. Susan will need to buy a minimum of 3 packets.

21. **E** First, bring the 12 to the left side of the equation, so the whole equation is equal to 0 (i.e., $x^2 + 4x - 12 = 0$). Factor the equation by thinking of what two numbers when multiplied together = –12 and when added together = 4. 6 and –2 satisfy those conditions. Make the equation $(x + 6)(x - 2) = 0$, then set $(x + 6) = 0$ and $(x - 2) = 0$ and solve for x in both cases. x is either = –6 or 2. You can also try the numbers from the answer choices and see which ones satisfy the equation.

22.   J   To divide, subtract the exponents of common terms. To visualize what's happening, you can write

out the expression as $\dfrac{x \cdot x \cdot x \cdot x \cdot y \cdot y}{x \cdot x \cdot y \cdot y \cdot y \cdot y}$. Cancel matching terms in the numerator and denominator

to get $\dfrac{x \cdot x}{y \cdot y}$, or $\dfrac{x^2}{y^2}$. Choices (F) and (G) negate the value of the entire expression, and Choice (K)

flips the numerator and denominator. Choice (H) incorrectly assumes $x^2 = y^2$.

23.   E   If point A must have at least one positive coordinate value, it could be located in any quadrant except for III, or choice (E). Points in quadrant III have negative x-coordinates and negative y-coordinates. Choice (C) incorrectly assumes the point has exactly 1 positive coordinate. Choice (A) assumes the point has exactly 2 positive coordinates, while (D) assumes it cannot have 2 positive coordinates.

24.   H   If the fixed cost each day of the company is $1,600 and the variable cost is the additional cost each day of producing each box. The equation then would be the fixed cost plus the variable cost, which is $1600 + 4.75b$, or choice (H). Choices (F) and (K) switch the fixed and variable costs. Choices (G) and (J) find the difference between the variable costs and the fixed cost instead of adding them to form the total cost.

25.   D.   The sides of similar triangles are proportional in length. To find how many times larger the larger

triangle's perimeter is than the smaller triangle's, divide the two known perimeters $\dfrac{576"}{9.6"} = 60$

times larger. $\overline{AC}$ will also be 60 times larger than $\overline{XZ}$: $3.2" \times 60" = 192"$.

26.   K   Multiply the fractions on the left so that $\dfrac{6\sqrt{11}}{x\sqrt{11}} = \dfrac{3\sqrt{11}}{11}$. You can then cross multiply to get

$66\sqrt{11} = 33x$, which simplifies to $x = 2\sqrt{11}$. You can also substitute the answer choices in for x

and see which works in the equation. Choice (J) is half the value needed and choice (G) is its

square. Choice (H) is 11^2. Choice (F) is a number from the problem that does not answer the

given question.

27. **D** Set up an equation for each runner, with the number of seconds to get to the crossing point, as well as the number of feet from point "0 feet" being equal for both runners. Jonathan starts 150 feet in from what we will say is "0 feet" on the track, or at the 150 ft. point, and he runs at a speed of 9 ft./second for x seconds, covering y feet: 150 ft. + 9 ft./second × (x seconds) = y feet. Natalie starts at 1,300 feet and runs in the opposite direction at 12 ft./second for x seconds, covering y feet: 1,300 ft. – 12 ft./second × (x seconds) = y feet. Since both equations = y, set them equal to each other and solve for x seconds. $150 + 9x = 1,300 – 12x$, $21x = 1,150$, $x = 54.8$ seconds. If you're not sure how to set up the equation, try working backwards from the answer choices. In this case, each of the answers is a possible value for the time—use this time to figure out how far along each runner is on the track, and pick the answer that gets them the closest. It won't give you the exact answer, but it can help you to eliminate some answers that give values that are either much too large or much too small.

28. **G** For each of the 3 possible ice-cream flavors, there are 2 possible types of syrup: so multiply 3 × 2. For each of those 6 possible orders, there are 6 possible kinds of candy toppings, so multiply 6 × 6 = 36 total possibilities.

29. **B** The width of the box is half its length, so if its length is 12 cm, its width is 6 cm. The width is also twice the box's height, so the height is 3 cm. To find the volume, you multiply all three dimensions ($V = lwh$): 12(6)(3) = 216. Choice (D) incorrectly calculates the sides as *6, 12,* and *24,* and choice (E) incorrectly calculates the sides as *12, 24,* and *48.* Choice (A) neglects to multiply by the depth. Choice (C) finds the surface area of the box.

30. **J** Substitute the values into the equation given, and you'll get $D = \$2,155(1 + 0.13) + 10(2)^2$, which is equal to $2,475.15, or approximately choice (J). Choice (F) forgets to calculate the interest rate. Choice (G) forgets to add the $10(2)^2$, while choice (H) adds only 20. Choice (K) incorrectly calculates the interest rate at 14%.

31. **D** The equation for surface area is given as the expression $\pi r^2 + \pi r s$ where r is the radius and s is the slant height. The radius in the figure is half of the diameter, which is given as 30. The height is 30. By plugging these into the equation you get $(15)^2 \pi + (15)(30)\pi$, or 675π, choice (D). Choice (C) is the result of forgetting to square the radius. Choice (E) uses the diameter instead of the radius in the equation. Choices (A) and (B) are the result of only solving half of the equation.

32. **F** To solve a composite function, work inside out starting with the value of $g(a)$, then taking the function f of $g(a)$. $g(a)$ is given as $2a^2 + 1$, so $f(g(a)) = f(2a^2 + 1)$. Substitute $2a^2 + 1$ for a in the $f(a)$ equation to get $f(2a^2 + 1) = 3(2a^2 + 1) – 4$. Distribute the 3 within the parentheses to get $6a^2 + 3 – 4$, which simplifies to $6a^2 - 1$.

33. **D** To find the average, you need to find the total of all stars given to the movie and divide by the number of students surveyed. $\dfrac{1(51)+2(18)+3(82)+4(49)+5(62)}{262} \approx 3.20$. If you don't have time for the calculations, cross out answer choices that are too large or too small to be the average and take a reasonable guess. Choice (A) is much too small and choice (E) is much too large. Choice (A) flips the numerator and the denominator. Choice (E) divides 262 by the sum of the column on the left and its answer is rounded to only the nearest tenth. Choices (B) and (C) each drop one of the components of the numerator when calculating.

34. **G** Two angles are supplementary if the sum of their degrees measures is 180°. To create supplementary angles when two lines are intersected by a third line, the two lines must be parallel. Since $\angle x$ is supplementary to angles 8 and 11, lines q and s must be parallel. Since angles 4 and 6 are not necessarily supplementary to $\angle x$, lines q and r need not be parallel, eliminating choices (F) and (K). Since angles 7 and 5 are not necessarily parallel to angles 8 and 11, lines r and s need not be parallel, eliminating choice (H). Lines p and q intersect so they cannot be parallel, eliminating choice (J).

35. **E** Choice (E) reflects the correct rules of exponents: The numeral inside the parentheses (4) gets *raised to the power* of 4, then the exponents inside the parentheses are *multiplied by* 4. Choices (B) and (C) incorrectly multiply the numeral by 4, and (D) incorrectly adds 4 to the variables' exponents. Choice (A) divides all the numbers by 4.

36. **F** In order to solve this problem you need to isolate x. By doing this you get the equation $x < -11$, thus the correct answer is (F). The other choices solve the inequality with the wrong direction of signs (choice (G)) or incorrect algebra.

37. **E** Since you are looking for a point that is rotated counter-clockwise, the point should be in Quadrant IV with a positive x-value and negative y-value, eliminating choices (A) and (B). A 90° rotation means you can use the line perpendicular to $\overline{AL}$. Find the slope of $\overline{AL}$ by counting the rise over the run from A to $L = \dfrac{6}{-8}$. The perpendicular slope will be the negative reciprocal $\dfrac{8}{6}$, so you want to go 8 units down and 6 units left from the center of the circle: $(10 - 6, -2 - 8) = (4, -10)$.

38. **F** First, use the Pythagorean theorem to find the third side of the triangle. $(12)^2 + b^2 = 16^2$, so $b = \sqrt{72}$. SOHCAHTOA tells you that $Cosine = \dfrac{Adjacent}{Hypoteneuse}$, or $\dfrac{\sqrt{72}}{16}$. Choice (J) is the sine of the angle, and choices (G), (H), and (K) all find other trigonometric functions of the angle.

Also, note that to solve this problem, you don't need to solve for the angle θ.

39. **C** Since $\overline{CA}$ bisects $\angle BAD$, $\angle BAC$ and $\angle CAD$ are equal, and since $\overline{DA}$ bisects $\angle CAE$, $\angle DAE$ and $\angle CAD$ are equal. Since $\angle BAC$ and $\angle DAE$ are both equal to $\angle CAD$, $\angle BAD = \angle DAE = \angle CAD$. Given that there are 180° in a straight line, $\angle CAD = \frac{1}{3}(180°) = 60°$.

40. **H** To find the volume of the container, set up the equation $\frac{6 \times 10^8 \text{ molecules}}{x \text{ cubic inches}} = 3 \times 10^4 \text{ molecules / cubic inch}$ $= 3 \times 10^4 \text{ molecules / }$ per cubic inch. So, $x = \frac{6 \times 10^8}{3 \times 10^4} = 2 \times 10^4$. Remember to subtract the exponents when dividing quantities with like bases. Choice (F) is $\frac{3 \times 10^4}{6 \times 10^8}$. Choice (G) is the result of dividing the exponents.

Choice (J) is the result of multiplying the numbers in the problem. Choice (K) is $(3 \times 6) \times (10^{4 \times 8})$.

41. **B** Choice (B) correctly calculates the value of $\angle C$, which is $360 - 250 + 30 = 140$. Choices (A) and (D) use the wrong angles, 30 and 250 respectively. Choice (C) incorrectly calculates $250 - 30$, while choice (E) calculates $250 + 30$.

42. **J** The number halfway between $\frac{1}{4}$ and $\frac{1}{6}$ can be found by averaging the two numbers. $\frac{\frac{1}{4} + \frac{1}{6}}{2} = \frac{5}{24}$, which is a real number, making Choice (K) the correct answer. The other answer choices are real numbers but are not halfway between the two values. Choice (G) is between the two values, but it is not halfway.

43. **D** Find $\angle DEB$ by subtracting all other angles in $\triangle ADE$ from 180°. $\triangle ADE$ and $\triangle ABE$ are congruent because they have congruent sides: both triangles share $\overline{AE}$, $\overline{BA}$ and $\overline{DE}$ are each half the length of congruent sides, and diagonals $\overline{DA}$ and $\overline{BE}$ are equal. Therefore, $\angle ABE = \angle ADE = 95°$, and $\angle DAE = \angle BEA = 35°$. $\angle DEB = 180° - \angle ADE - \angle DAE - \angle BEA = 95° - 35° - 35° = 15°$. Choice (A) simply subtracts the two angles given from 180°.

44. **H** x is the side of the large square table minus the side of the small square table. Since $A = s^2$, $\sqrt{A} = s$. The side of the large square table is $\sqrt{108} = \sqrt{36 \cdot 3} = 6\sqrt{3}$. The area of the small square table is $\frac{108}{9} = 12$, so its side is $\sqrt{12} = \sqrt{4 \cdot 3} = 2\sqrt{3}$. $x = 6\sqrt{3} - 2\sqrt{3} = 4\sqrt{3}$. Choice (F) gives the side of the small square table instead of x, and choice (K) gives the area of the small square table. Choice (G) subtracts terms with a common radical incorrectly. Choice (J) subtracts the two areas and then takes the square root of the result, instead of first taking the square root of each area and then subtracting the results.

45. **E** A rational number is one which can be expressed as a fraction. Only (E) can be reduced to integer values in the numerator and denominator: $\sqrt{\frac{81}{25}} = \frac{\sqrt{81}}{\sqrt{25}} = \frac{9}{5}$.

46. **G** Pick a value for both x and y. If $x = -5$ and $y = -3$, then $|-5 + (-3)| = |-8| = 8$. Choice (G) is also 8. Choice (F) is –8. Choice (H) is –2. Choice (J) is 2 and choice (K) is $\sqrt{34}$.

47. **E** In order to figure out what Jane must get on her next game, you need to figure out how many points total she has earned on the first 5 games and how many points total she must get in order to average 85 in 6 games. To find the total points she needs on the six games, multiply her desired average by the number of games: $85 \times 6 = 510$. To find the number of points she has already gotten, multiply her average on the first 5 games by the number of games which is $5 \times 83 = 415$. The difference between these numbers is the score she must get in order to get an average of 85 on the 6 games, which is 95, or choice (E). Choice (C) is the score she would have to get in the next two games for an average of 85. You could use Process of Elimination to rule out choices (A) and (B) since she wants her average to go up, and thus, she must get a higher score on the next test.

48. **G** Since the modulus is $\sqrt{a^2 + b^2}$, then the quadrant that the point is found in is negligible since all points are squared. Thus, the point with the greatest distance from the origin will have the greatest modulus, and the point with the shortest distances from the origin will have the smallest. To see this you could use sample points to test this. Thus, choice (G) is the answer since it is the closest to the origin, and thus has the smallest modulus.

49. **B** Since $9 = 3^2$ and $27 = 3^3$, make $9^{x-4} = 27^{3x+2}$ into $3^{2(x-4)} = 3^{3(3x+2)}$. The equation now reads: "3 to some power = 3 to some power." Therefore, the exponents are equal: $2(x - 4) = 3(3x + 2)$. Distribute the 2 and the 3 to get $2x - 8 = 9x + 6$. Subtract $9x$ and add 8 to both sides of the equation to get $-7x = 14$. Divide by –7, $x = -2$.

50. **J** A sine curve is an odd function, so choice (J) is correct. If you didn't know this, test each answer choice against the graph and the function, eliminating those not supported. If you can draw a horizontal line through the function that crosses it at two or more points, you have found multiple x values for the same y value, meaning the function is not 1:1 as defined. The horizontal line $y = 0$ crosses the graph of the function three times, eliminating choice (F). This also tells us that y, another name for $f(x)$, is 0 at $x = 0$, eliminating choice (G). The arrows at either end of the function's graph tell you that the domain (set of all x values) extends infinitely in both directions beyond –6 and 6 respectively, eliminating choice (K). Test values to find the remaining incorrect answer. You can approximate that (–3, –2) and (3, 2) lie close to function. $f(-3) \neq f(3)$ because $-2 \neq 2$, eliminating choice (H). You are left with choice (J): $f(-3) = -f(3)$, because $-2 = -(2)$.

51. **B** Make a list of the integers from 299 through 1,000 which contain 1 as a digit. 301, 310, 311, 312 … 319 = 11 integers. 321, 331, 341, 351 … 391 = 8 integers. 11 + 8 = 19 integers from 299 through 399. Since this pattern will repeat 7 times from 299 to 999: 400 to 499, 500 to 599 … to 999, multiply $19 \times 7 = 133$. Finally, add 1 for the number 1,000 = 134 integers.

52. **G** You can immediately eliminate choices (J) and (K) because line $\overline{LM}$ increases as x increases, which means it has a positive slope. Because $\overline{NL}$ is parallel to the x-axis and ΔNLM is isosceles, the slope of $\overline{LM}$ is the negative of the slope of $\overline{MN}$. Find the slope of $\overline{MN}$ by rewriting the equation $y + \frac{2}{3}x = 2$ as $y = -\frac{2}{3}x + 2$, where the slope m is $-\frac{2}{3}$. The slope of $\overline{LM}$, therefore, is $\frac{2}{3}$.

53.   A   The notation $\sin^{-1}\left(\dfrac{x}{\sqrt{x^2+y^2}}\right)$ means find the angle that has a sine value of $\dfrac{x}{\sqrt{x^2+y^2}}$. Recall

that the sine of an angle is $\dfrac{opposite}{hypotenuse}$. The side marked x is opposite $\angle ACB$ so that's the angle in

question. Now, use SOHCAHTOA to find that $\tan(\angle ACB)=\dfrac{x}{y}$.

54.   H   The area of a circle is πr^2, which in this case is $\pi\,(12)^2$, or approximately 452. Choice (F) incorrectly calculates the circumference ($2\pi r$). Choice (G) creates a square by forgetting to multiply by π. Choice (J) calculates $2\pi r^2$, while (K) shows $\pi^2 r^2$.

55.   E   The general equation for a circle is $(y - h)^2 + (x - k)^2 = r^2$ (in which h and k are the x- and y-coordinates of the center of the circle, and r is the radius). You can eliminate choices (A), (B), and (C) because they are not in the correct equation form. Since the radius 12 must be squared, the correct answer is (E).

56.   F   If the 2 anchors are 30 feet apart, and Joy's dog is on a 20-foot leash, it can get within 10 feet of Melissa's anchor (30 − 20 = 10). Melissa's dog can run 12 feet from its anchor, so there is an overlap of 2 feet. Choice (G) is the difference of the two dog leashes. Choices (H) and (J) subtract each dog leash length from 30. Choice (K) is the sum of the two leashes.

57.   D   Look at the graph of the two equations. Find the range where the y-value of the equation $y=-(x+1)^2+4$ is greater than the y-value of the equation $y=(-x+1)$. According to the figure, the parabola has a higher y-value than the line between the x-values -2 and 1, making the best answer Choice (D).

58.   J   Test numbers to answer this question. Because you need two-digit integers, and you want the maximum value for $(y-x)$, y should be the larger value, and x the smaller. Say $t = 1$ and $u = 9$; that makes $y = 91$ and $x = 19$, and $(y-x) = 72$. The answer choice that yields the greatest value is (J).

59.   C   Use the formula for the area of a parallelogram *Area = base × height*. Find the length of the base by calculating the length of $\overline{AB}$: 8 − 2 = 6. Find the height by dropping an altitude perpendicular to the base from point D to point (4, −4), which has a length of 2. *Area* = 6 × 2 = 12. Choice (D) incorrectly uses side $\overline{AD}$ with length $2\sqrt{2}$ for the height.

60.   G   To determine the sixth term, you first need to find the common difference between consecutive terms in the sequence. Use the given formula to solve for x_1: $145=5\left(\dfrac{x_1+48}{2}\right)$, so

$x_1 = 10$. The common difference in an arithmetic sequence is basically the slope of a straight line: $difference=\dfrac{x_n-x_1}{n-1}=\dfrac{48-10}{5-1}=9.5$. The sixth term, therefore, is 48 + 9.5 = 57.5. Choice (F) calculates $n + 1$, rather than x_{n+1}. Choices (H) and (K) use averages, rather than a common difference. Choice (J) incorrectly adds the difference to the sum, rather than x_5.

TEST 3 READING EXPLANATIONS

1. **A** The narrator describes a volcano that lacks *air vents* as a potential outlet for the heat and pressure building internally, leading ever closer to an eruption. Choice (A) identifies the purpose of the figurative imagery as a way of depicting the friend's frustration toward the thoughts building up uncomfortably inside of him. Choices (B) and (D) are incorrect because the narrator is describing his friend's struggle, not attempting to offer consolation or advice concerning it. Choice (C) is incorrect because the metaphor does nothing to explain the physical impairment of the friend's speech but rather it describes the psychological effects of the impairment.

2. **H** The passage is consistently focused on the ongoing process of the narrator attempting to help his friend deal with a speech impairment. Choice (H) captures that and correctly identifies the exchange of letters between the narrator and his friend as a main source of ideas the passage discussed. The passage tells us nothing about the narrator's friend other than his speech impairment, so the passage is not a *detailed character study* as choice (F) suggests. The overwhelming voice of the passage is that of the narrator, so it is inaccurate to say that the narrator and his friend *take equal turns* debating the issue as choice (G) states. The passage is not focused on the narrator's legal career, nor does it mention any struggles related to being a lawyer as stated in choice (J).

3. **D** The narrator compares his friend's speech to *an oceanic cloud of dust and debris* and his friend's writing to *an omni-directional lava flow*. Choice (D) correctly points to speech and writing as vocal and non-vocal expression. Choices (A) and (C) are almost synonymous pairs of nouns, making either one a very unlikely correct answer.

4. **H** The narrator's *sympathetic* and *encouraging* attitude is revealed via his ongoing concern for his friend's frustration and goal of giving him a positive outlook on it; the friend shows his *anxiety* and *despondence* by saying *I fear I will eventually choke on my own thoughts* and by watching the narrator's speech with a *mix of pride and pain in his eyes*. Because the narrator is chiefly concerned with making his friend feel better, choice (F) is not correct to call the narrator *jaded* or *indifferent*. Although the friend occasionally disagrees with the narrator on points of their discussion, there is nothing *scornful* about his tone, making choice (G) incorrect. The friend is physically unable to speak his mind, but that does not make him *shy* or *reclusive* as choice (J) states.

5. **C** Little detail is provided about Cyrano de Bergerac other than that he *enlisted the help of a friend to speak his thoughts aloud* to a woman he was trying to woo. Choice (C) is supported by that detail. Choice (A) involves knowing the woman is *the love of his life*, which we do not. Choice (B) involves knowing that Cyrano had a physical impairment, which we do not. Choice (D) involves knowing that Cyrano was unable to express his emotions, which we do not.

6. **H** The passage states that pirates *share a common destiny but no longer pledge allegiance to any sovereign entity*, providing support for choice (H). Choice (F) is not known; pirates may have stringent rules of conduct for each other. Choice (G) is misleading language, borrowing the word *confusion* from the next sentence but presenting an unsupported idea. Choice (J) ignores the specific purpose of the pirate simile and merely relates pirates to the main topic of the passage.

7. A   The details in the passage that indicate what the friend values in vocal speech come in the final paragraph. The friend *deeply misses* the *expressiveness that a human voice can add to the meaning of words* and he prevents the narrator from speaking *too mechanically*. Choice (A) identifies that an expressive tone is something the friend values. Choice (B) is contradicted by the friend's distaste for overly mechanical speech, and choices (C) and (D) are not ingredients of vocal speech that are ever discussed in the passage.

8. G   Choice (G) is correct because the friend says *I fear that I will eventually choke on my own thoughts.* This reflects an expectation of suffering due to his inability to speak his mind. A fear of embarrassment is never discussed, making choice (F) incorrect. A concern of interfering with the narrator's legal career is never mentioned, making choice (H) incorrect. The friend never questions his capacity for creating well-orchestrated thought, as choice (J) suggests; he only clarifies that both written and vocal speech are capable of expressing it.

9. D   The narrator's mention of a puppet is an expression of his desire to allow his own voice to be used by his friend. Choice (D) correctly identifies the usage of puppet as a surrogate voice. Choices (A) and (C) are trap language based on other associations with the word *puppet*, and choice (B) relates to the subject of speech but does not correctly identify that the narrator would be a passive vehicle for his friend's ideas.

10. F   The narrator describes a look of *pride and pain* in his friend's eyes, knowing that his friend is enjoying but wrestling with the fact that the narrator can express himself *more lucidly than* the friend *may ever be able to again*. This combination of delight and deprivation justifies choice (F). Nothing in this paragraph suggests confusion, as choice (G) suggests, or overbearing annoyance to the narrator, as in choice (H). While the friend experiences pain and longing for his lost abilities, to say that he is *bitter* or *resentful*, as choice (J) does, is too strong.

11. A   The passage states that no one before has been able to directly link human behavior to ice-shelf breakup. Choice (A) must be correct because the passage states that human behavior has been proven to be connected to the rise in temperature that causes the collapse. Therefore, human behavior is both a considerable factor and a previously unproven one. Choice (B) is incorrect because while glaciological influences do contribute, nowhere is there evidence that human behavior is insignificant. Choice (C) is incorrect because there was no discussion of prior evidence showing human activity to be a more influential factor than is suggested by current evidence. Choice (D) cannot be correct because it's reiterated many times in the article that there are many factors contributing to ice shelf collapse, not just one.

12. J   Choices (F), (G), and (H) reflect information presented in the concluding paragraph of the essay. Only choice (J) is NOT listed as an effect of sea level rise but rather as a cause of sea-level rise, thus making it the correct answer to this question.

13. **A**   Choice (A) is the best answer because paragraph three discusses Dr. Marshall's study and cites evidence that climate change was a major factor in the collapse. In the following paragraph, lines 66–67 in reference to Glasser and Scambos, the passage reads as follows: *they acknowledge that global warming had a major role in the collapse.* Choice (B) is incorrect because all of the scientists agree that climate change was a contributing factor. Choice (C) can't be correct because while the scientists didn't find the same things, both studies found evidence to explain the collapse. Choice (D) is incorrect because while structural evidence is cited as a factor in one of the studies, it's not a common factor, nor was it the cause of the collapse.

14. **H**   In the lines to consider, the author quotes the scientist's two observations: one, that this is the first time anyone has demonstrated a human process linked to the collapse of a shelf, and two, that climate change doesn't impact the planet evenly—*as evidenced by the significant increase in temperatures in certain geological areas.* This most clearly agrees with (H). Choice (F) is the opposite of the point being made in these lines. Choice (G) is incorrect because there is no evidence in the passage on which to base the conjecture that the observed local phenomena would extend to the entire earth. Choice (J) isn't correct because there is no connection made between sea level and human activity.

15. **C**   The last sentence of paragraph two says, *the collapse of the Larsen B ice shelf seemed to be one of the most obvious and stunning signs of worldwide climate change,* making (C) the correct answer. (A) hasn't yet happened, at least on the scale presented in the conclusion, (B) and (D) may happen as a result of climate change, but neither melt water nor increased temperature was called *a stunning sign.*

16. **J**   Lines (65–69) say *the shelf was already teetering on the brink of collapse before the final summer, and though…global warming had a major role in the collapse…it is only one of a number of atmospheric, oceanic and glaciological factors* and then goes on to give an example of location and spacing of crevasses and rifts, showing that Choice (J), a combination of factors is the best answer. Choice (F) is incorrect for two reasons: one, it talks about glaciers, not ice shelves, and two, the lines ask about the purpose of the findings; the findings say that global warming was not a cause, but a contributing factor. Choice (G) has no evidence to support it, and choice (H) is the opposite of the argument in the paragraph.

17. **D**   The third paragraph discusses how human activity contributed to the collapse, which makes choice (D) the best answer. Choice (C) is a phrase found in the paragraph, but it is not the main idea. Choice (A) contradicts the evidence in the passage, and choice (B) is a main argument in the fourth paragraph, not the third.

18. **J**   (F), (G), and (H) are all given as contributing factors to the ice shelf's collapse in the passage. Deep ocean currents are never mentioned at all.

19. **B**   Choice (B) is clearly stated in the sentence…*stronger westerly winds in the northern Antarctic Peninsula, driven principally by human-induced climate change, are responsible for the significant increase in summer temperatures…* Choice (A) is disproven in the paragraph, as it is stated that the winds contribute to the warming, which contributes to the collapse of ice shelves. Choice (C) is not stated in the passage, and choice (D) is a detail unrelated to winds. Sea level has to do with glaciers speeding up after the shelves collapse.

20. **H** The remark comes just after a statement about how weather changes don't affect the planet evenly. Therefore, the specific information about the increases in temperature in that particular region is an example of how weather changes are more extreme in certain places. Choice (F) is incorrect because there is no support in the passage for the idea that scientists are prone to exaggeration. Choice (G) might be tempting because the paragraph was about how human behavior causes warming patterns; however, the remark was not intended to make people change their behavior. It was an example of the point made prior to that sentence. Choice (J) is incorrect because there weren't any misconceptions being discussed.

21. **A** The first paragraph introduces Rushdie and gives a little bit of information about his writing. It mentions where some of his books take place (India, Pakistan, and England), the fact that magical events sometimes occur, and that he is a *virtuosic*, or talented, writer. It does not, however, state what his intentions are as a writer, making choice (A) the best answer.

22. **G** The second paragraph states when and where Rushdie was born and raised. It then goes on to mention that he draws on all of these experiences in his writing. Although the passage states that Rushdie's parents were Muslim, it does not discuss his *personal faith*, as in choice (F). The passage mentions that there was a struggle between the Hindi and Muslim populations but it does not give any details as to the reason for that, as in choice (H). Although the paragraph mentions that Rushdie does eventually immigrate to England, it does not state his reasons for doing so, making choice (J) incorrect.

23. **C** The passage begins by mentioning how well-known Rushdie's life story is and then proceeds to explain some of the events in his life that seem to have influenced his work. Therefore, the best answer is choice (C), as that is the only answer that directly connects Rushdie's life experiences with his writing. Choice (A) incorrectly refers to Rushdie's *personal failings,* which are not mentioned in this passage. Choice (B) incorrectly focuses on the partition of India rather than Rushdie himself. Choice (D) incorrectly focuses on one of Rushdie's books instead of Rushdie himself.

24. **H** The description of Bombay, as seen by Rushdie, is in the beginning of the third paragraph. The author explicitly refers to the smells, colors, and people, but nowhere is the weather mentioned, making choice (H) the correct answer.

25. **C** The fourth paragraph deals with the book *Midnight's Children* and how it mirrors Rushdie's life and exemplifies some of his feelings about life in India and Pakistan. His focus, according to this paragraph, is on the struggle that the two countries have in trying to exist together yet create individual identities after the partition. Nowhere does the passage state that Rushdie's writing has a sense of *futility* or *sadness,* as in choices (A) and (B). The passage does mention a sense of *longing* but in the third paragraph, not the fourth.

26. **J** Although the passage refers to Rushdie's work repeatedly, nowhere does it give a precise number and only one book is mentioned by name. Choice (F) is answered in the first paragraph, when the author refers to the places that Rushdie describes, and is also mentioned throughout the passage. Choice (G) is answered in the third paragraph. Choice (H) is answered in the first sentence of the second paragraph.

27. **B** The second paragraph gives Rushdie's basic history and it states that *he immigrated to England to attend school*. Although he may have attended school in India, where he was born, the passage does not specify, making choice (B) the better answer.

28. **H** Most of the descriptions of Bombay are in the third paragraph, where it is described as *a raucous place, filled with colors, scents that assault the nostrils, and people thronging the…teeming with life and all that life entails*. The best match for that is choice (H). Although some people might find Bombay *frustrating* or *chaotic,* nowhere does the passage imply that Rushdie feels that way. Choice (J) incorrectly identifies a word used to describe Pakistan's beauty (*stark*) with a city in India.

29. **A** The line being referenced (*As interesting as his subjects are, it is the way that his prose draws readers into his world that makes his work so enduring*) serves as a way for the author to transition from a discussion of Rushdie's subject matter to his actual skill as a writer. The passage does not imply that Rushdie is too dependent on historical fact; the author of the passage seems to enjoy the historical nature of Rushdie's writing. The paragraph also goes on to state that Rushdie is likely to remain well-known for many years, making choice (C) incorrect. Choice (D) goes too far, although the author does state that it is Rushdie's skill rather than his subject matter that makes him great; nowhere is the subject matter called *uninteresting*.

30. **H** The final paragraph states that *certainly the way his prose draws readers into his world has been the essential factor in making his work so enduring*. Choice (F) is incorrect because it is too specific to Pakistan. Choice (G) incorrectly focuses on the partition of India, which is mentioned but is not part of Rushdie's contribution to literature. Choice (J) is incorrect because the passage deals more with the writing's ability to speak to readers than its literal beauty.

31. **D** Hypnotic analgesia *re-evaluate* and *manage a painful stimulus*, which is best reflected in choice (D). Choice (A) is a literal misinterpretation of *essentially change their brains*. Choice (B) suggests that hypnotic analgesia can be used to treat those diseases, rather than managing the pain felt from those diseases. Choice (C) is not supported by any evidence in the passage.

32. **G** The question asks you about the detection of pain, which according to the passage follows four pathways. Choice (G) correctly summarizes the first three pathways: *sensory neurons* detect stimuli from *damaged tissues*, the signals are transmitted to the spinal cord, and then the *information is relayed to structures of the brain*. The sympathetic nervous system is not mentioned in this process, so eliminate choices (F), (H), and (J).

33. **B** The exercise routines mentioned in the first paragraph *involve more than cardiovascular activity* by focusing on the breath and mental imagery, which is said to *improve overall health,* but *nutritious diet* is not mentioned. Choices (A), (C), and (D) are supported in the discussions of mindful movement exercises.

34. **F** With the sentence *When the central nervous system perceives a threat, the sympathetic nervous system is engaged*, the nervous system is described as triggered, so choice (F) is the best answer. Choices (G), (H), and (J) do not fit the context of the passage.

35. **C** The limbic system is *the brain center for emotion, memory, and autonomic nervous system* as well as *central representation;* choices (A), (B), and (D) are all true. Muscle movement was never mentioned directly in the passage.

36. **H** The passage states that the researchers have begun to *delve deeper into mind-body therapy efficacy*, thus choice (H) is the supported answer. The passage states that biomedicine has been *slower to embrace* these therapies, but not that it has *rejected* them, so eliminate choice (G). The passage states that mind-body therapy is *increasingly popular*, but does not indicate it is being used *in place of biomedicine*, so eliminate choice (F). Although research has shown prolonged beneficial effects from mind-body therapy, there is no evidence cited in the passage to show that these therapies have been successful in *curing* many diseases and conditions, so eliminate choice (J).

37. **D** Mind-body therapies may *alter responses to stressors* so that the *parasympathetic nervous system* is engaged, rather than the *sympathetic nervous system*, which activates the so-called *fight or flight* response, choice (D). The passage states that mind-body therapies may provoke positive reactions, but they do not impede the actual biological responses of the nervous system, so choice (A) should be eliminated. Effective mind-body therapies engage the parasympathetic, not the sympathetic, nervous system, so eliminate (B), and because these therapies do not act on the stressors themselves, only on our responses to them, choice (C) should be eliminated.

38. **F** As stated in paragraph 4, fight-or-flight responses had adaptive functions in ancestral conditions. Such responses are *automatic* and would be expected to provoke the processes discussed in Paragraph 3: The sympathetic nervous system releases stress hormones, such as cortisol. Thus, choice (F) is the credited response. Threats are perceived by the *central nervous system*, not stress responses, so eliminate choice (H). *Prolonged* stress responses may result in *negative* health consequences, such as *suppressed immune activity*, but the passage does not suggest that they directly lead to suppressed activity, eliminating (G). Decreased muscle tension results when the parasympathetic nervous system is engaged, and is mentioned in the passage as a benefit of conscious mind-body responses to stressors.

39. **C** The final paragraph states that *more investigation is needed* to determine the influence of a number of possible outside factors. Thus it can be inferred that research into mind-body therapy could be *affected by external variables*. Because *more investigation* is needed to determine the influence of *outcome expectations*, these factors may not be presently controlled for. Therefore, choice (C) is the best answer. There is no evidence to support choice (A), which implies that researchers should manipulate their results to make their studies look good. Although the Western therapies have researched mind-body therapies, the passage does not state that research results are valid *only* for Western therapies, so eliminate choice (B). Mind-body therapies *alter* pain experience and stress responses, but they do not *eliminate pain* or *fight stress*, so eliminate choice (D).

40. **H** The fifth paragraph states that mind-body therapies help to regulate stress by engaging the parasympathetic nervous system, which counteracts the negative effects of the fight-or-flight response. If the therapies were ineffective, then the parasympathetic would not be engaged, eliminating choice (G). There is no evidence to support the increase or decrease in pain detection or spinal cord activity, eliminating choice (F) and (J). Choice (H) is the best answer because the fight-or-flight reaction is a stress response, the prolonged effects of which can result in negative health consequences.

TEST 3 SCIENCE EXPLANATIONS

1. **C** The moon blocks the transmission of the Sun's rays over a range of 0.52 degrees. The lunar orbiter at Point P is located within this range of 0.52 degrees, so he or she is able to view only the moon and the Earth. Therefore, choice (C) is the best answer.

2. **F** Figure 1 shows that during a solar eclipse, the moon does not allow the transmission of the Sun's rays to the Earth. Therefore, the Sun's rays stop transmitting forward and do not continue to the Earth's surface, so choice (F) is the best answer.

3. **B** The water level is highest on the first day at around $t = 4$ hours. The water level is highest on the next day at around $t = 28$ hours. The difference in time between these instances is 24 hours, so choice (B) is the best answer.

4. **G** According to Figure 2, during the 60-hour period, the ocean surface level had a maximum of 6 feet above mean sea level and a minimum of 1 foot below mean sea level (–1 feet). Of the choices provided, only the month of March shows this exact range, so choice (G) is the best answer.

5. **D** Figure 2 indicates a water level of 6 feet at $t = 0$. The water then falls until about $t = 8$ hours when it reaches about –1 feet. Then, the water level rises again, reaching about 2 feet at $t = 12$ hours. Thus, choice (D) is correct.

6. **G** Examine the shale layer in Figure 2 closely—given the choices in the answers, find which site or city has the thickest layer of shale. The shale layers at Middleton at Site 1 clearly go deeper than those at Site 3 and West Union, so you can eliminate choices (H) and (J). Between Middleton and Site 1, look closely to see that the highest and lowest extremes in Site 1 are farther apart—the best answer is choice (G).

7. **A** From Figure 2, the limestone layer appears to increase in thickness as you move from Site 2 toward Site 3. Therefore, answer choices (B), (C), and (D) may be eliminated.

8. **H** Examine Figure 2; the shale layer at Site 2 is slightly thicker than that of Site 3, eliminating answer choices (F) and (J). A comparison of the shale thickness at Sites 1 and 2 shows that the shale layer at Site 2 is slightly less thick than that of Site 1, eliminating answer choice (G).

9. **A** Based on Figure 3, at greater depths below the surface the number of counts of uranium decreases. Therefore, the greatest counts of uranium should be observed closest to the surface as seen in answer choice (A).

10. **G** Examine Figure 2, Site 2 exhibits 8 counts of Uranium in the deepest layer. Using the equation given in Figure 3, the age of the rock at Site 2 is most nearly 8 (64/8) times 700 million or 5600 million years. Of the answer choices, only answer choice (G) matches this age.

11. **C** There is no mention of distance shot in Experiment 3, therefore answer choices (A) and (B) can be eliminated. Choice (D) is irrelevant to the experiment's results. As described, the results of Experiment 3 center around the visibility of bubbles in the cola, so choice (C) is best.

12. **J** For this question, look at the *before shaking* column of the two tables. Trials 3 and 5 both have distances of 6.42 meters.

13. **D** Experiment 2 asks you to determine how shaking the water gun affects how far the water gun shoots the flat-tasting cola. Neither density nor bubbles are addressed. In Table 2, compare the columns labeled *before shaking* and *after shaking*. In both trials listed, shaking the water gun decreased the distance shot.

14. **H** If you're not sure whether to answer *Yes* or *No*, make sure you look at the reasons presented in each answer choice. In Trial 5, before the water gun was shaken, it had been 1 hour since the gun had last been shaken. Experiment 3 addresses how quickly the bubbles generated by shaking the water gun disappear. It suggests that 10 minutes after shaking, some bubbles are still present, but by 1 hour after shaking, the bubbles have all disappeared. Therefore, choice (H) is correct.

15. **D** In this hypothetical trial, the cola is shaken, let sit for ten minutes, shot, shaken, and shot again (Trial 4); then let sit for an hour, shot, shaken, and shot again (Trial 5); and finally let sit for another hour and shot with the distance of the shot measured (the hypothetical test in this question). By comparing Trial 5 before the gun has been shaken with Trial 4 after the gun has been shaken, you know that letting the flat-cola-filled water gun sit for an hour after shaking it eliminates the effects of any previous shaking. This is to say that in the hour between Trial 4 after shaking and Trial 5 before shaking, the distance shot goes from 5.49 meters to 6.42 meters—back to the same distance as never having been shaken at all (cf., Trial 3 before shaking). Therefore, after an additional shaking and hour sitting, you should expect the cola to travel 6.42 meters.

16. **G** From Experiment 3, bubbles are visible 10 minutes after shaking and not visible 1 hour after shaking. Similarly, from Trial 4, you know that 10 minutes after the gun has been shaken, the bubbles still reduce the distance of the shot. From Trial 5, you know that the bubbles do not reduce the distance of the shot 1 hour after the gun has been shaken. Therefore, the time necessary for the bubbles to stop having an effect on the distance shot must be between 10 minutes and 1 hour—answer choice (G).

17. **D** According to Figure 1, the greatest reflectance for blue-green algae occurs around 550 nm. According to Table 1, a wavelength of 550 nm is associated with the color green, making choice (D) correct.

18. **H** Photosynthesis is the chemical reaction that identifies autotrophic organisms, which make their own food, specifically sugar. Binary fission is the asexual reproduction of bacteria. Condensation is the transition of water from gas to liquid. Respiration is the opposite reaction of photosynthesis, breaking down glucose rather than making it.

19. **A** Choice (A), 400 nm, is the only choice where the green algae curve is higher than the diatoms curve. For all of the other choices, the diatoms curve is higher than the green algae curve, so the relative reflectance is higher for diatoms.

20. **J** Protists are organisms which cannot be classified as plants or animals. They can be one or many celled, but are always simple in construction. Choice (J) is correct because all algae are protists.

21. **B** The first paragraph of the passage tells you that as the amount of algae in a water sample increases, the water sample reflects light more like the algae so you know that all you need to do with this question is look for the algae that reflects light like the water sample. The best way to figure out this question is to quickly locate the high and low points on the water sample graph. The water sample has peaks at 550 nm and 0.08 reflectance and at 700 nm and 0.07 reflectance. The water sample has low points at 350 nm and 0.03 reflectance and at about 660 nm and 0.04 reflectance. Now, look at the algae graph. Once you match those points to the algae graph, it is easy to see the choice (B), diatoms, is the correct answer.

22. **H** To get through this question quickly, you can try to estimate. Because temperature is rising as you go down Table 1, and density is falling, the additional sample would be a new line under Sample V. Solution mass is falling in the table, so eliminate choice (J). To decide among the remaining choices, note that the falling solution mass, while not linear, declines in relatively small increments and never more than .5 g. Thus, a reasonable guess would be choice (H). To be certain of the answer, focus on the density, which we know by looking at Experiments 1 and 2 together is the more important factor (mass fell even when temperature was held constant). In Experiment 1, 150 mL of each solution is measured in the graduated cylinder. Multiplying this volume by the density of the solution will give the mass.

$$density = \frac{mass}{volume}$$

$mass$ = (density)(volume)
$mass$ = (1.018 g/mL)(150 mL)
Either solve by long multiplication, or eliminate choices (F) and (G) by expanding the above expression:
$mass$ = (1.018 g/mL)(150 mL)
$mass$ = (100 g/mL)(1.5 mL) + (1.8 g/mL)(1.5 mL)
The last product above works out to 2.7 g, so only choice (H) is possible.

23. **A** All samples in Table 2 are at 10°C according to the description of Experiment 2. Salinity of 2.50% is not directly listed, but it does fall between those of samples VI and VII. Given that all samples are at the same temperature, the density of the proposed solution will fall between that of samples VI and VII.

24. **H** According to Experiment 2, where all water samples have a temperature of 10°C, the given salinity of 2.35% matches up most closely with the salinity in Sample VII. Looking at the results of Experiment 3 for Sample VII, *U3* sank and X2 remained afloat. This eliminates choices (G) and (J). Since the claim in the question states that U3 will function well at the *surface* of the water, the data do NOT support this. *U3* will sink in this environment and therefore cannot operate at the surface, eliminating choice (F).

25. **D** According to Table 3, all prototypes show a pattern of floating in samples toward the top of the table, and sinking in samples toward the bottom of the table. *R5* has the same results as choice (A), *X1* and *X2* each have the same results as choice (B), and *U3* has the same results as choice (C). However, a similar pattern to choice (D) cannot be found. If the new prototype did not float in water samples IV and V, it cannot possibly float in samples VI and VII because these water samples are less dense.

26. **H** According to the description of Experiment 1, the graduated cylinder was used to *measure 150 mL of the solution*. A mL is a unit of volume. Graduated cylinders are primarily used for accurate and precise measurements of volume. Mass is best assessed with a balance, eliminating choice (F). Salinity is typically measured indirectly through electrical conductivity, eliminating choice (G). Thermometers are used to measure temperature, eliminating choice (J).

27. **A** In Table 3, prototype *U3* floated in Sample V but sank in Sample VI. The density of an object must be less than that of the liquid for the object to float. If the density of the object exceeds that of the surrounding liquid, it will sink. Therefore, the density of U3 must be between the densities of Samples V and VI. The density of Sample V is 1.022 g/mL according to Table 1, and the density of Sample VI is 1.020 g/mL according to Table 2. Only choice (A) lists a value between these limits.

28. **J** According to Table 1, only the haloarchaeal and bacterial cells show + signs for either acid or CO_2 presence under green light. Therefore, (J) is the best answer.

29. **B** A plant cell alone produces only CO_2 and absorbs most of the light (i.e., has low transmittance) in the presence of red light. A haloarchaeal cell alone produces only acid and absorbs most of the light (i.e., has low transmittance) in the presence of green light. Since these two cell types do not interfere with each other, they will most likely continue to have production of CO_2 and low transmittance in the presence of red light, as well as the production of acid and low transmittance in the presence of green light. Choice (B) summarizes this.

30. **G** Only the plant and bacterium produce CO_2 in the presence of red light, so you can immediately eliminate choices (F) and (H). Then, under the green light, the bacterium produces both acid and CO_2 and the plant produces neither, making choice (G) the best answer.

31. **C** According to Experiment 1, the production of acid is a sign of growth. According to Experiment 2, low transmittance indicates that light is being absorbed by pigments to generate energy. The evidence that haloarchaea use light to generate energy and grow must include production of acid and low transmittance. These are both seen only in the presence of green light, so choice (C) is the best answer.

32. **G** In red light, the plant cell *Rosa carolina* will produce CO_2 but not acid. When CO_2 is present, a gas bubble appears above the solution. If acid is not present, then the solution appears colored. The illustration in choice (G) best represents this.

33. **C** The results of Experiment 1 show that bacteria and haloarchaea produce different products in the presence of red and green light. The passage does not mention any other relationship between haloarchaea and bacteria. Therefore, the best answer is choice (C): The two types of cells show different growth patterns, so we cannot conclude that they are closely related.

34. **G** The second sentence of the last paragraph for the 3-Domain Hypothesis implies that the more different the genetic sequence of rRNA, the farther back in time two groups of organisms diverged or split on the evolutionary tree. Similar genetic sequences would imply more closely related species, eliminating choice (F). A relationship between ester or ether linkages and divergence is not discussed in the passage, eliminating choices (H) and (J).

35. **D** Phospholipids have membranes but are not organelles themselves, eliminating choice (A). Ribosomes are not described as membrane-bound organelles in the passage, and the introduction implies that the Archaea have ribosomes because they have rRNA, eliminating choices (B) and (C). Nuclei are membrane-bound organelles found only in eukaryotes.

36. **J** The last paragraph states that eukaryotes and prokaryotes have ester linkages in their cell membranes, eliminating choice (F). The introduction defines the difference between eukaryotes and prokaryotes as the presence or absence of membrane-bound organelles, eliminating choice (G). Prokaryotes reproduce asexually as mentioned in the 2-Domain Hypothesis, eliminating choice (H). All of the organisms described in the passage are composed of cells.

37. **C** The scientist supporting the 2-Domain Hypothesis opens the argument by defining the Archaea as prokaryotes. The introduction states the Archaea contain rRNA, eliminating choice (A). Although ether linkages are found in the Archaea, this is an argument proposed by the scientist supporting the 3-Domain Hypothesis, eliminating choice (B). Protein synthesis can occur in the cytoplasm of all living organisms, and is not mentioned as a defining characteristic of any of the domains in the passage, eliminating choice (D).

38. **F** The observation of cellular metabolism similar to that found in eukaryotes discredits the arguments mentioned in the 2-Domain Hypothesis, eliminating choices (H) and (J). Since the metabolic process is similar to eukaryotes, choice (G) is also eliminated.

39. **C** Neither scientist makes the claim that the Archaea have membrane-bound organelles, eliminating choice (A). Microscopes play a vital role in accurately describing organisms, and this is not mentioned one way or the other in the passage, eliminating choice (B). The distance in relationship between eukaryotes and the Archaea is not the primary argument of each scientist. They are arguing more about whether to break up prokaryotes into bacteria and the Archaea, eliminating choice (D). The fact that the Archaea have ether linkages instead of ester linkages is mentioned by the scientist arguing for the 3-Domain Hypothesis as a significantly distinguishing characteristic, which allows the Archaea to occupy harsh environments.

40. **G** Phospholipids are described in the passage as having a water-soluble subunit and a water-insoluble subunit. Therefore, it makes the most sense that the water-soluble subunits (circles) would arrange in a manner such that they were exposed to water while keeping the water-insoluble subunits (lines) away from the water.

WRITING TEST

Essay Checklist

1. The Introduction
   Did you
   o start with a topic sentence that paraphrases or restates the prompt?
   o clearly state your position on the issue?

2. Body Paragraph 1
   Did you
   o start with a transition/topic sentence that discusses the opposing side of the argument?
   o give an example of a reason that one might agree with the opposing side of the argument?
   o clearly state that the opposing side of the argument is wrong or flawed?
   o show what is wrong with the opposing side's example or position?

3. Body Paragraphs 2 and 3
   Did you
   o start with a transition/topic sentence that discusses your position on the prompt?
   o give one example or reason to support your position?
   o show the grader how your example supports your position?
   o end the paragraph by restating your thesis?

4. Conclusion
   Did you
   o restate your position on the issue?
   o end with a flourish?

5. Overall
   Did you
   o write neatly?
   o avoid multiple spelling and grammar mistakes?
   o try to vary your sentence structure?
   o use a few impressive-sounding words?

NOTES

NOTES

Navigate the Admissions Process with Guidance from the Experts

Getting In

11 Practice Tests for the SAT and PSAT, 2011 Edition
978-0-375-42986-6 • $22.99/$26.99 Can.

ACT or SAT?
978-0-375-42924-8 • $15.99/$19.99 Can.

The Anxious Test-Taker's Guide to Cracking Any Test
978-0-375-42935-4 • $14.99/$18.99 Can.

College Essays that Made a Difference, 4th Edition
978-0-375-42785-5 • $13.99/$15.99 Can.

Cracking the ACT, 2011 Edition
978-0-375-42798-5 • $19.99/$22.99 Can.

Cracking the ACT with DVD, 2011 Edition
978-0-375-42799-2 • $31.99/$36.99 Can.

Cracking the SAT, 2011 Edition
978-0-375-42982-8 • $21.99/$25.99 Can.

Cracking the SAT with DVD, 2011 Edition
978-0-375-42983-5 • $34.99/$41.99 Can.

English & Reading Workout for the ACT
978-0-375-42807-4 • $16.99/$18.99 Can.

Math & Science Workout for the ACT
978-0-375-42808-1 • $16.99/$18.99 Can.

Essential ACT (flashcards)
978-0-375-42806-7 • $17.99/$19.99 Can.

Essential SAT Vocabulary (flashcards)
978-0-375-42964-4 • $16.99/$21.99 Can.

Essential TOEFL Vocabulary (flashcards)
978-0-375-42966-8 • $17.99/$22.99 Can.

Finding the Best School for You

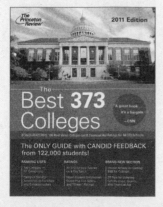

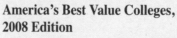

America's Best Value Colleges, 2008 Edition
978-0-375-76601-5 • $18.95/$24.95 Can.

The Best 373 Colleges, 2011 Edition
978-0-375-42987-3 • $22.99/$25.99 Can.

The Best Northeastern Colleges, 2011 Edition
978-0-375-42992-7 • $16.99/$18.99 Can.

Complete Book of Colleges, 2011 Edition
978-0-375-42805-0 • $26.99/$31.00 Can.